*Life Stress and Mental Health*

THOMAS A. C. RENNIE SERIES IN SOCIAL PSYCHIATRY

VOLUME II

*The Midtown Manhattan Study*

# Life Stress

# and

# Mental Health

THOMAS  S.  LANGNER

*and*

STANLEY  T.  MICHAEL

*THE FREE PRESS OF GLENCOE*
*Collier-Macmillan Limited, London*

# Foreword

ALEXANDER  H.  LEIGHTON

This second volume in the Thomas A. C. Rennie Series carries further the report on the findings of the Midtown Project. Since the creation of the project by Dr. Rennie and its subsequent development have already been outlined in Volume I, *Mental Health in the Metropolis: The Midtown Manhattan Study*, they need not be repeated here.

The present book takes its origin from certain broad questions raised by its predecessor and analyzes them in as great detail as the available information permits. Because the data are in fact numerous and the number of relevant theoretical questions enormous, the analysis is necessarily exceedingly complex. In addition to the Mental Health Rating (the indicator of psychiatric disorder employed in Volume I), symptom groups and estimates of diagnostic categories are now introduced, and considered in relation to these are 148 social variables. Yet obviously not everything is covered that might have been, and selection has had to be made repeatedly.

The primary responsibility for this has been taken by the senior author, Thomas S. Langner, a sociologist with training in both anthropology and clinical psychology. Except for Chapter 3 and Appendix A, he did all the actual writing of the book, directed the data processing and statistical analysis, and was assistant director of the survey that gathered the main body of information.

Stanley T. Michael, a psychiatrist with a background in physiological research, has contributed Chapter 3 and Appendix A. He has also made detailed comments on the several drafts that the book went through and gave particular attention to matters pertaining to psychiatric theory and practice. It was he who, together with Dr. Price Kirkpatrick, made all the psychiatric ratings for each respondent upon which the two volumes are based. The chapter and appendix he has written set down definitions of various psychiatric categories used in the course of the work and give some perceptions, interpretations, and reflections from the viewpoint of a clinical psychiatrist who participated in the ratings and in the analysis of the data.

Leo Srole, a sociologist with wide experience in anthropology and psychology, developed and was director of the Home Interview Survey that gathered the original data. He was the principal author of Volume I, *Mental Health in the Metropolis,* and the study's senior social scientist. To the present volume he has contributed numerous suggestions regarding the plan of analysis.

It is evident from the preceding that the present book is a collaborative effort involving a number of disciplines. Although it has its base in clinical psychiatry, the planning and analysis has been primarily under the influence of sociology. The choice of theoretical framework and the interpretations of the data are essentially those of the senior author.

As the reader approaches the volume, he should not expect easy reading. The delineation of complex relationships can rarely be so. He should also be aware that all the information is derived from a single source, responses to a questionnaire administered during one interview—that is, a particular point in time. Within these limits, however, he will find an extraordinarily ingenious analytic treatment of the data and a demonstration of how hidden relationships can be brought to light. Psychiatric epidemiology being a relatively new and untried field sets before the investigator a large number of problems for which there are no models of solution. This means that experiments in approach and the invention, adaptation, and trial of different analytic procedures have particular significance for the advance of the field.

The findings reported, together with their theoretical interpretation, will stimulate much discussion as to whether they are true. This will be particularly so where they run counter to a clinical viewpoint, or lean heavily on aspects of the questionnaire method that appear especially doubtful. Such discussion favors progress insofar as it sharpens issues, but it can be destructive if it results in dismissing a finding merely becaue there is room for doubt. At the present level of knowledge in psychiatric epidemiology there is room for doubt on almost all points and it is well to approach the topic with this realization. Advance depends on sifting the more and the less doubtful and the more and the less certain. Achievement will take many years of endeavor in which refinement of concepts, definitions, and methods will make it possible for different workers to check each other's findings by means of comparable studies. The history of science being what it is, it is a safe guess to say that when this point is reached, numbers of our currently most favored ideas will turn out wrong. It is also probable that currently unsuspected or lightly regarded relationships will emerge as genuine.

The volume is likely to be especially productive of new insights precisely because it approaches the problem of psychiatric disorder from an extra-clinical base. It brings to bear systematic information from a representative sample of adults, not patients only, and it subjects the data to a type of analysis never before attempted.

# Preface

Every author of a technical book would probably prefer to think that his readers will devour the contents from cover to cover. Unfortunately, few of us have either the necessary appetite or the stamina. Moreover, each reader has a different background and training which will make special parts of any work particularly interesting to him. For these reasons a short review of the contents is given here, as a guide for the selective and an appetizer for the omnivorous.

Those interested in theory will find in Chapter 1 a discussion of environmental stress and certain adaptations to it (strain). Appendix A gives a psychiatrist's view of the relationship between social and individual pathology. Chapter 16 reviews socioeconomic differences in life experience, and attempts to relate them to socioeconomic differences in the distribution of diagnostic types. Theories and hypotheses are brought briefly into the text at many points, but pp. 119–132 of Chapter 6, p. 383 of Chapter 14, and pp. 398–404, 410–422 of Chapter 15 concentrate on theoretical interpretation.

Psychiatric interpretations of the data and method are found in Chapters 3 and Appendix A. A description of the community is found in Chapter 4. For those who want summarized findings and would like to see the end product before they study the technical details, a summary of the major results of Volume I, *Mental Health in the Metropolis*, appears in Chapter 4 pp. 75–82. This is also an aid to those who have not read the first volume. Summaries will be found at the end of almost every chapter. Here the findings are verbalized with a minimum of statistics or interpretation. Chapter 7 also gives the "findings in a nutshell" with regard to stress and strain, covering all except the last two chapters. At the end of Chapter 16 there is a tabular summary of all socioeconomic differences in life experience and type of adaptation indicated by diagnosis, attitudes, and behavior, which gives our findings as well as hypotheses suggested in the literature.

The relationship of stress to psychiatric impairment is covered in Chapters 13, 14, and 15. Connections between stress and diagnostic type are explored in Chapters 15 and 16.

Readers interested primarily in socioeconomic differences may look into parts of Chapters 8 through 12, which deal with the 14 environmental stresses covered, in addition to the summary of Chapter 16. Pages 380–395 of Chapter 14 and Chapters 15 and 16 also discuss this topic.

Those who deal with patients or clients—the psychiatrist, social worker, or marriage counselor—may find particular topics of interest in Chapters 8 through 12. For example, those working in adoption agencies, divorce courts, and schools, as well as psychiatrists in private practice, might find Chapter 8, which deals with the relationship of psychiatric impairment to broken homes, remarriage, step-parents, and working mothers, germane to their daily tasks.

All persons appalled by statistics might skim Chapter 5, glance hastily at pp. 87–88, and could skip pp. 89–100 with complete impunity. The appendices are recommended for anyone planning to do epidemiological surveys of mental health. The Table of Contents and the Index will help in checking the validity of these suggestions.

T.S.L.
S.T.M.

# Acknowledgments

Activation of the Midtown Study became a reality with the allocation of grants by the National Institute of Mental Health, the Milbank Memorial Fund, the Grant Foundation, the Rockefeller Brothers Fund, and the Corporation Trust. Without the sustained confidence and support of these agencies, their several boards and executive officers, the Project and its embodiment in the memorial volumes to Thomas Rennie would not have reached fruition.

The Study was conducted under the auspices of the Department of Psychiatry, Cornell University Medical College, and the New York Hospital (Payne Whitney Psychiatric Clinic).

Two persons intimately connected with the planning and writing of the first volume are not represented as authors of this book. Their contributions, however, have been of the first magnitude. Dr. Thomas A. C. Rennie, who initiated the Study and guided it until his premature death in 1956, made the entire series possible, and the series is therefore dedicated to him.

Dr. Leo Srole was the senior social scientist of the Study. He directed the Home Interview Survey, and was the principal author of Volume I, *Mental Health in the Metropolis.* His major contributions to the content of the questionnaire, study design and methods, and to the initial analysis plan laid the foundation without which this book could not have been completed.

The total number of people who contributed in other ways to these volumes runs into the hundreds—including all interviewers, volunteers, advisers and staff—but a certain few played crucial roles.

First among these is Dr. Alexander H. Leighton, Director of the Cornell Program in Social Psychiatry and Director of the Midtown Study after Dr. Rennie's death. He has offered detailed comments on each draft of this volume. His suggestions, in addition to covering style and emphasis, have improved the theoretical framework and sharpened the interpretation of the data immeasurably. We wish to express warm thanks for his guidance.

Dr. Oskar Diethelm, former Chairman of the Department of Psychiatry of Cornell University Medical College, encouraged the pioneering work of Drs. Rennie and Leighton in the comparatively new field of social psychiatry, thus providing a positive atmosphere for the research.

Special acknowledgment is due Dr. Harry Alpert of the University of Oregon (then with the National Science Foundation) and to Dr. Irwin Bross of Roswell Park Memorial Institute (then with Cornell University Medical College), who at varying intervals served as technical consultants to the Midtown staff during the planning year of June 1952 to June 1953. From the latter date to 1959, Bross continued as adviser on methodological problems relating to sampling design and data analysis. His incisive role as critic and catalyst cannot be conveyed adequately in this note of indebtedness to him. In particular, his contribution of a new statistic, the ridit, made it possible for us to undertake the complex analysis demanded by this volume.

In the last two years Dr. Melvin S. Schwartz, Director, Division of Biometrics, Cornell University Medical College, has acted as a statistical adviser to the Cornell Program in Social Psychiatry, and in that capacity has made many valuable suggestions concerning the analysis of the Stress Scores to impairment and the diagnostic types.

Detailed comment covering statistics, general methodology, and theory has been given by Dr. John S. Harding of Cornell University. His written critique and stimulating discussions of the second and third drafts have been of great benefit to the final version.

During the years 1950–1951, prior to procurement of support for the Midtown Study, Dr. Rennie consulted a number of knowledgeable people who helped him to crystallize the focus of the Study. Among Cornell colleagues these included, in addition to Drs. Diethelm and Leighton, Drs. Allister M. Macmillan, Leo Simmons, Wilson Smillie and Emerson Day. Also important at this stage were Drs. Harry Alpert, Dorothy Bask, John Clausen, Ernest Gruenberg, Herbert Goldhamer, Molly Harrower, Marie Jahoda, Ann Kent, Seymour Klebanoff, Lawrence Frank, Raymond Mangus, Louis McQuitty, Melly Simon, and Livingston Welch.

In addition to those named above, others consulted in this period and later periods were Drs. Phillip McCarthy, Edward Suchman, Robin Williams, Frederick Mosteller, Albert Sherwin, and James Masterson.

Four categories of the Midtown Study staff personnel can be distinguished: (1) Senior Investigators, who, with some exceptions, participated in the planning phases and subsequently had major responsibility for one or another of the four field operations; (2) Research Aides, principally performing office functions of processing and tabulating field data; (3) Interviewers for the Home Survey operation; and (4) Volunteers, who carried out field, library, and office functions.

The Senior Investigators are listed in the order of their appointment to the Study staff. Immediately following each member's name is his self-defined professional identification, dates of inception and termination of services, and major research responsibility or assignment.

Thomas A. C. Rennie (psychiatrist), 1952–1956: Director of Midtown
   Study.
Leo Srole (research sociologist), 1952–1960: Director, Home Survey
   operation.
Marvin K. Opler (anthropologist), 1952–1958: Director, Ethnic Family
   operation (reported in Volume III of this Series).
Margaret Bailey (psychiatric social worker), 1952–1955: Treatment
   Census operation.
Frieda Taran (psychiatric social worker), 1952–1955: Treatment Census
   operation.
Arthur Weider (clinical psychologist), 1952–1955: Questionnaire Committee for the Home Survey operation.
Eleanor Leacock (anthropologist), 1952–1955: Assistant Director, Ethnic
   Family operation.
Price Kirkpatrick (psychiatrist), 1952–1955: Mental Health Evaluation
   of Home Survey Sample.
Guy LaRochelle (psychiatrist), 1952–1954: Home Survey operation.
Vera Rubin (anthropologist), 1953–1955: Assistant Director, Ethnic
   Family operation.
Thomas S. Langner (sociologist), 1953–1962: Assistant Director, Home
   Survey operation; Director, Data Processing and Statistical Analysis
   Department for Home Survey and Treatment Census operations.
Stanley T. Michael (psychiatrist), 1954–1962: Mental Health Evaluation
   of Home Survey Sample.
Alexander H. Leighton (psychiatrist), 1956–1962: Director, Midtown
   Study.

The Research Aides can be most easily divided into those who performed the statistical analysis, those who doubled in editing and secretarial work, and those who did chiefly secretarial or clerical tasks.

Several statistical assistants made noteworthy contributions to the project—far beyond the call of duty—to ridits, percentages, and correlations. Merton Hyman always came up with an insightful interpretation of the social variables in each statistical table. Elliott Camerman, during three years of incessant deadlines, managed to maintain the volume and accuracy of the work and to comment on theoretical problems. Irving Silverman organized and cross-referenced the hundreds of variables, scales, scores, and tabular "runs," and sharpened our thinking considerably. Jerold Heiss wrote a doctoral dissertation on interfaith marriage during his spare time. Other assistants, in order of their length of service, were Sally Pinkerton, Jan Snaauw, Michel DiLiscia, Uriel Hurwitz, Ira Greiff, Arnold Levine, Arnold Pollack, Milton Brawer, Harold Jarmon, and Mira Gess. India Hughley and Allyn Falls performed the major task of putting the questionnaire on punch cards. Thomas Rick took a major part in the sampling.

Those who helped in the mountainous task of editing as well as typing drafts of this volume were Malcolm Willison (who checked text and tables), and volunteers Isabel Bunker (who made valuable stylistic suggestions), Theresa Mullee (who checked quotations, references, and headings) and Diana Townsend. Alice Togo did extensive editing and research for Volume I. Amorita Suarez edited, proofread, and partially typed the final draft of this volume. Her help in the mechanical tasks of preparing the book was indispensable. She also gave constructive criticism of the manuscript. Beverly Givens typed the bulk of the final draft. She was assisted by Shirley Dee Taber and Shirley Elek. Secretarial staff who typed other drafts were Muriel Grant (who specialized in complex tables), Barbara Kennedy, and Anita Lowell. Those who worked primarily on the first volume were Frances Libby, who was for many years Dr. Rennie's secretary, Ann Jezer Avins, Dolores Kreisman, and Betty Bunes.

Shepard Wolman and Edwin Fancher were field supervisors of the interviewing staff. The following trained interviewers and social scientists completed twenty-five or more field interviews: Ruth Balter, Joseph Borello, Marjorie Cantor, Rosemary Dempsey, Helen Halley, John Kupyn, Claire Marck, Robert Marsh, Irene N. Norton, Jess Osterweil, Edmond Pollack, Florence Rothman, Edwin Seda, Esther Shaw, Sol Seigel, Elsie Siff, Ada Slawson, Robert M. Slawson, Janet Sperber, Isidore Weider, and Rosalind Zoglin.

A total of 99 voluntary workers were secured for the Study by Mrs.

Margaretta W. Treherne-Thomas, Director, Volunteer Department of the New York Hospital-Cornell Medical Center. The volunteers listed below met the criterion of contributing at least 500 working hours. These principal volunteers were Renee Apfelbaum, Maurice Bloch, Tillie Drucker, Lewis Faron, Warren Fox, Leila Freedberger, Mrs. Leonard Frutkin, Mrs. Howard Harris, Rene Hoguet, Percival Perkins, Kurt Porges, Eva Profeta, Samuel Reber, and Mrs. Mary J. Kempner Thorne. Special volunteers were Judith Bernays Heller and Philip C. Haydock.

All members of the principal author's family are thanked for their patience and support, especially Gerald B. Spiero, who helped in editing the proofs.

Many persons have contributed to the work that culminates in this volume. Other notes of appreciation appear at appropriate points in the following chapters. But we want to express, at this point, our warm gratitude to the 1660 persons in the Midtown community who opened their doors and their lives to us and whose bravery in meeting life's problems demands our respect and our admiration.

# Contents

xx

# Life Stress and Mental Health

# Stress and Strain

T H O M A S   S.   L A N G N E R

## The Midtown Project as Social Psychiatry

The Midtown Community Mental Health Research Project was initiated in 1952 by Dr. Thomas A. C. Rennie. The project was to investigate the relationship between mental disorder and the sociocultural
environment.

Mental disorder is roughly equivalent to the full range of disturbances
which the psychiatrist treats. This includes the neuroses and character disorders as well as the psychoses. It also includes a panoply of milder "subclinical" disturbances, some of which are unlikely to receive treatment.
*Mental illness* and *mental disease,* at one extreme, suggest only the
most severe impairment, and often imply some identifiable lesion caused
by a specific agent. *Mental health* connotes chiefly the absence of disease, and hence does not describe the broad range of possible human
adaptations. Therefore, the terms *mental disorder* and *mental disturbance* are best suited to describe our chief focus of investigation.

The Midtown Project was scheduled to produce several volumes. The
first of these volumes, *Mental Health in the Metropolis,* was published in
1961.[1] It related the demographic or "background" factors such as age,
sex, and socioeconomic status to mental disorder. The present volume, second in the series, examines the relationship of a large number of other
factors to mental disorder. These are stressful experiences or perceptions
of experiences in childhood, adolescence, and adult life, such as the
death of a parent, a lack of close friends, or marital worries.

The Midtown Project was an experiment in social psychiatry, a relatively new interdisciplinary field in the behavioral sciences. Dr. Rennie's
views on what constitutes the field of social psychiatry were set down in

1954, but they guided the development of the project before and after his tragic death in 1956.

He considered the determination of the total prevalence of mental disorder a part of the domain of social psychiatry. In fact, one of the major short-term goals of the project was to determine the total or true prevalence of mental disorder in Midtown. This included all persons with any degree of psychiatric impairment, whether or not they had ever had treatment. To measure the true prevalence of mental disorder a home interview survey was conducted with a random sample of the Midtown population, as well as a census of all out-patients and in-patients in private or public hospitals, and patients of private therapists. He did not, however, consider this the primary focus of social psychiatry.

It (social psychiatry) is not only the ascertaining of how many individuals in a given society are emotionally or mentally crippled, though such studies are worthy enough and are important for the mental health planning for a community or a nation.[2]

Dr. Rennie and his colleagues planned the Midtown Project in such a way that the sociocultural backgrounds of the mentally disturbed could be examined in great detail. He wanted to know specifically "who was mentally disturbed," and he relied on personnel in the fields of sociology and anthropology to utilize their skills in defining the "who" questions. He still did not feel, however, that this was the cardinal goal of social psychiatry.

Nor is social psychiatry limited to the study of the distribution of mental illness in particular groups of differing socioeconomic and cultural backgrounds, though this, too, is a worthy object of scientific inquiry having major importance for prevention and mental hygiene.[3]

People's attitudes toward mental disorder and their conceptions of what constitutes mental disorder entered only minimally into the Midtown research. The study of these attitudes and concepts was not considered the major focus of the field.

Again, social psychiatry is not merely the study of the attitudes of the individual and groups of persons toward mental illness, their misinformation and fears and taboos. Any or all of these facets of work might rightly be included in the domain of social psychiatry, but they are not the complete or main functions.[4]

Dr. Rennie felt that the *etiology* (the study of the sources) of mental disturbance was the primary goal of social psychiatry. The secondary foci of social psychiatry—such as total prevalence counts, demographic distributions of illness, attitudes toward or conceptions of mental disturbance, or even the analysis of therapeutic practices—might contribute to an understanding of the sources of mental disturbance. Insofar as they did this, they would properly belong in the domain of social psychiatry.

Social psychiatry, by our definition, seeks to determine the significant facts in family and society which affect adaptation (or which can be clearly defined as of etiological importance) as revealed through the studies of individuals or groups functioning in their natural setting. It concerns itself not only with the mentally ill but with the problems of adjustment of all persons in society toward a better understanding of how people adapt and what forces tend to damage or enhance their adaptive capacities.[5]

The great advantage of this definition is that it does not lose sight of the main goal of discovering the sources of mental disturbance, malfunctioning, and maladaptation. The use of terms with such different connotations as *mental illness, mental health, mental disturbance,* and *adaptation* will pose many problems for even the most casual reader. It is immediately obvious that the redefinition of mental health and illness must in itself be a continuous goal of social psychiatry. Such terms as *adaptation* and *adjustment* raise the question of "adaptation and adjustment to what?"

Another problem is that innovation may play a major role in adaptation. Innovation is an active rather than a passive form of adaptation. It is an attempt to change the means by which goals are usually attained. By what standards can we judge innovation and the deviation from societal norms which it implies? Since individual or social change is by definition a "disturbance," are most changes followed by *mental* disturbance? Further empirical research will doubtless help in providing better definitions and concepts in social psychiatry.

Social psychiatry, then, concerns itself primarily with forces in the social environment that affect the individual's ability to adapt, to adjust to, or to change himself and his environment. It seeks to redefine the concepts of mental health and disorder by relating these concepts to social pathology, social change, and to "normal" personality structure. In so doing, it initially attempts to learn *how many* are mentally disturbed, *who* they are, *what types* of disturbances they exhibit, *how they feel* about their own and others' disorders, and *what action* (if any) they take to prevent or to alleviate the symptoms of mental disorder.

Social psychiatry has stemmed primarily from the fields of medical epidemiology, psychiatry, and certain social sciences, particularly sociology, anthropology, and social psychology. Each of these fields brought different tools to bear on the problem of mental disorder, but they had one goal in common: uncovering the sources, origins, and causes of mental disorder. The epidemiologist may begin by asking "*Who* is mentally disturbed?" but he ends up by asking "Why do some groups have high rates of mental disturbance and not others?"

For example, he might ask "Why did I find such a high *rate* of mental disturbance among people who live in caves, as opposed to non-cave dwellers?" The psychiatrist may concentrate on HOW cave dwellers came to live in caves, and how this was related to their mental health. Perhaps they sought isolation, or perhaps the darkness in caves fostered the development of paranoid traits. The physical effects of cave-dwelling on respiration, diet, and vision would of course not be overlooked.

The sociologist might ask whether cave dwelling fostered the breakdown of community values and norms. The anthropologist could compare the mental health of cave dwellers in various parts of the world, and probably find that many groups of cave dwellers have stable personalities.

Regardless of their approach, all contributors to the field of social psychiatry eventually ask the questions "How did some cave dwellers get to be mentally disturbed?" "Why do cave dwellers generally exhibit worse mental health than other groups?" "Does it matter what *kind* of cave, apartment, tent, or igloo you live in?" In sum, "What particular facts or qualities of cave dwelling are associated with or conducive to mental disturbance?"

Certainly much can be done to stop the course of a disease before its origin or etiology is understood. Associated facts are noticed first. Closing the windows at night to keep out the bad air must have cut down the prevalence of *mal aria*, even though the mosquito was not suspected of being the vector that carried the parasite. How much more can be done to control the disease now that the etiology is certain: draining the swamps where mosquitos breed, the killing of the insect larvae with crude oil, spraying DDT to kill the fully developed insects, using repellents, and finally the prophylactic and therapeutic measure of taking quinine and its derivatives. Obviously one must do better than "close the windows" to keep out mental disturbance. A preventive program is needed, and this must eventually come out of research.

## The Conceptual Framework

A conceptual framework might seem unnecessary for a program in social psychiatry. Why not just say "The environment has an effect on mental health," and be done with it? In fact, why say it at all, since everyone knows what the implicit ideas are? There are, however, many who would say "The social environment has little or no effect on mental health. Heredity is the chief etiological factor in mental disturbance." Others might claim that the individual's physiological states are the chief determinants of his emotional states, and hence of his mental health. There is no arguing with these viewpoints, for there is no doubt that heredity and physiology have a great deal to do with mental disturbance.

The multiple causation of mental disorder in any individual case is always apparent to the clinician. Cases with deceptively simple etiology may turn out to be quite complex in origin.

A neurosis, for instance, may be based on predisposing factors that are hereditary, on malformation of personality due to infantile experience, and on precipitating strain in adult life. The same can be said for psychophysiological disorders such as ulcer and asthma, but here we must also add that there may be an organic element. A blow on the head that is followed by odd behavior might be considered a clear case of a single cause, yet even this is not a safe assumption. The patient's heredity, previous life experience, personality structure, and his perceptions regarding who gave the blow and why, may all enter into determining whether or not he will show symptoms, and if so, what kinds of symptoms.[6]

However, even the effects of constitutional differences and predispositions to mental disturbance may be exacerbated by social conditions. Rates of organic damage may be increased by cultural practices, such as the exclusive eating of polished rice by the wealthier classes in ancient China, or the habit of driving automobiles in the United States. The physiological state that accompanies fear or anger can become a crippling mechanism in societies permitting no immediate physical reaction to emergencies. In certain societies the police, legal procedures, and mass media melodramas substitute for individual physical expression.

When we say that the social environment has an effect on mental health, we are stating that of all the types of factors contributing to mental disorder, we are selecting *one* type to study, without denying the existence of the other kinds of factors. Therefore our framework should have a place in it for endowment and other factors.

Unfortunately, we are talking in rather static terms when we say environment affects mental health. Our conceptual framework should in itself give us some indication of *how* the social environment affects or is related to mental health. The social environment itself contains both pathogenic (noxious) and eugenic factors. It is unfortunate that to date we have made little progress in uncovering the more elusive eugenic factors that enable people to resist mental disorder. Our model, therefore, concerns itself mainly with the noxious factors.

In this conceptual scheme (which is by no means original, having been used in one form or another by thousands of clinicians, social scientists, and laymen over the centuries) the noxious, or *potentially* noxious[7] factors we shall call *stress*. The *reaction* to the stress we shall call *strain*.

We frequently use the words emotional stress, tension, strain, and pressure to describe *simultaneously* the forces we feel are working on us and our reactions to those forces. For scientific purposes the terms stress and strain are more useful if they are given clearly distinct meanings rather than used as synonyms. Our use of these terms will be similar to the engineering usage, particularly in testing the strength of materials.

In designing any structure or machine, the engineer must first determine the amount and kind of stress the various parts will be required to withstand; and he must know how the various materials will *react* when subjected to a known stress. . . .

Stresses which the parts of a structure or machine may be called upon to resist include tensions, compression, shearing stress and torsional stress. *Strain* is the *deformation*, or change of shape, produced by stress.

When a body is subjected to a longitudinal pull it is said to be under *tension* or tensile stress and the strain produced is a lengthening in the direction of the pull. . . . Any material is considered elastic in relation to the applied stress, if the strain disappears after the force is removed.[8]

The metaphor becomes all the more apt when we find strain defined as a *reaction* to stress, for we know that people react to the forces in their environment. So do molecules. The idea that strain is a deformation fits in well with our concepts of mental disorder. We know that personality, the sum of a person's relatively reliable ways of acting and reacting, can become deformed because of stress. That deformation, that strain, we may call mental disorder.

Our use of the word "stress" is to signify the environmental force pressing on the individual. We feel that the reaction to stress and the stress itself must be kept conceptually distinct, even if they tend to merge when we observe a human being. Our use of the word *strain,* on the other hand, corresponds to Wolff's or Selye's use of the word *stress,* and both are meant to connote a *reaction* to the external environment.[9]

The stress and strain conceptual model was adopted to explain the results of the study. It was not an explicit formulation when the study was initiated. The developments leading to its adoption will be described in great detail in later chapters. Briefly, a series of "factors" (perceptions or experiences) occurring in early or later life were found to be related to a psychiatric Mental Health Rating (our measure of mental disorder or impairment). The number of stress factors people reported was the best predictor of their Mental Health Rating. The more stresses they reported, the greater the probability of their exhibiting psychiatric impairment.

The physical analogy of stress and strain captures the essence of this relationship for us. As the number of environmental stresses increases, the average amount of strain (psychiatric impairment or disorder) also increases.

The analogy can be carried further, for the properties of the material being tested determine how much strain or distortion there will be for a given amount of stress. These properties in a human being are his personality organization: his resilience, his adaptability, his "ego-strength," his ability to resist life's wear and tear, his "inner resources." If these terms seem almost mystical, it is because we know so little about what makes for a mentally healthy person. If we knew more about the origins of mental health, we wouldn't have to ask ourselves how two people faced with the same apparent stress—such as military service, a concentration camp, or the death of a loved one—can react so differently, one with extreme strain, the other with relatively little.

Despite the attractive simplicity of the analogical stress and strain model, people are not wooden beams or iron bars; they differ from inanimate materials in many ways. To name a few: The properties of a material such as wood or iron are well known. If you put a $2 \times 12$ joist of long-leaf yellow pine of a given length under a given excessive floor load, it will *usually* break. A *person* put under a certain work, marital, or reproductive load is certainly less predictable. Perhaps our state of knowledge is such that our predictions are quite poor.

It is also a propensity of humans and higher animals to symbolize and to attach idiosyncratic meanings to objects, people, and events. This makes prediction of strain difficult, and it constitutes a major difference between the animate and inanimate. A human being can continue to react to the *idea* of stress even when the initial stress has disappeared. Even the anticipation of stress can be destructive and impairing.

Third, although the beam under pressure is in a state of physical equilibrium, a living organism exhibits a different sort of equilibrium, a *dynamic* equilibrium. An organism can shift its resources to compensate for depletion. A stress can initiate a chain of reactions. If more stress is applied, it may come at a time when the organism has regained its balance, its homeostasis, or it may hit a weak point and destroy the organism. A living system, then, is much more complex, and the stress-strain analogy can be only a superficial description of the intricate reactions to stress that probably take place.

Moreover, the stress and strain model is accurate only in describing the *average reactions of a large group of people* to all the stresses they have experienced. We found that the average impairment of those who reported two stresses is greater than the average impairment of those who reported one stress, and so forth. When we get down to individual cases, however, there is sometimes a great disparity between the number of stresses and the reaction to them.

In physics, a material will show a fixed number of units of strain for each unit of stress to which it is exposed. This relationship continues within a *range* of stress, but beyond the limits of this range the relationship breaks down. Once the elastic limits are exceeded, for instance, one unit of stress may produce one hundred or a thousand units of strain.

Individuals do not necessarily exhibit one unit of strain for each unit of stress to which they are exposed. People vary widely in their reaction to what is essentially the same stress. To take the example of a train wreck, some uninjured people will be calm, while some may become extremely agitated and later go into shock.

What factors can account for this difference in reaction, in strain? Endowment may account for some of it, for nervous systems may vary in their capacity to withstand stress. Previous experience may make a difference, for persons badly injured in a previous accident can be severely threatened, even though not physically injured by a second accident. The accident may stand for, or symbolize, some other type of loss or injury. Those who have lost a parent or sibling in a train wreck may be more threatened by the accident. To them a train wreck may mean a loss of love. Conversely, it may revive guilt feelings over the death of a competing parent or sibling whose removal was desired.

It is primarily this capacity of man to symbolize that turns a similar event into a catastrophe for one and a blessing for the other. If "one man's meat is another man's poison," how can we define stress in terms of the stimulus rather than the reaction? We can make some generalizations about what stress is because there are cultural and societal uniformities of "meat" and "poison" that are somewhat broader than the individual variations.

Within these limitations, the stress-strain model is best fitted to describe the findings of this volume. What then is stress, as the term is used in this book? A good definition is given by Dr. George Engel:

A stress may be any influence, whether it arises from the internal environment or the external environment, which interferes with the satisfaction of basic needs or which disturbs or threatens to disturb the stable equilibrium.[10]

Similar to others, Engel emphasizes the relativity of stress, which depends upon the strength of the organism, or its capacity to deal with a particular force at a particular time. He cites such examples as the different effects of separation from the mother at the age of one, six, and thirty years, or of a sexual approach at six, fifteen, and thirty years of age, or of smallpox virus before and after vaccination. When we say that stress is relative, we mean that there are certain factors that mediate between stress and strain. It is through them that stress is translated into strain. What are these factors?

First, there is the individual's *endowment*. By this we mean all constitutional factors, hereditary predispositions, physical, mental, and neurological "equipment." This in part determines how much strain will result from a stress. Chronological age is closely related to this factor, for aging is to some extent the unfolding of hereditary tendencies and patterns. The importance of endowment and the inheritance of complex behavior patterns (as opposed to the learning of such patterns) should not be underestimated. For example, the work of Lorenz with gulls and ducks has shown that "the differences in innate motor patterns which distinguish species from one another can be duplicated by hybridization. This suggests that motor patterns are dependent on comparatively simple constellations of genetic factors."[11]

Second is the individual's positive and stressful experience, both physical and emotional, up to the time of the particular stress in question. Poor diet, physical injuries, poisons, and parasites are examples of the former. Often overlooked is the critical role in adaptation of repeated blows to the head during childhood. These may be incurred during birth, falls, play, fighting, and parental punishment. The extreme example of the "punch-drunk" fighter may give some notion of how strain per unit of stress can be increased through this particular physical trauma. Whole occupational groups are exposed to noxious chemicals or minerals, which can result in skin reactions, systemic poisoning, silicosis, leukemia, and other toxic reactions. Whole cities and nations have been exposed to high doses of artificial radiation, either for destructive ends as in Hiroshima and Nagasaki or for therapeutic and diagnostic ends with X-rays and fluoroscopy.

The cumulative emotional experience up to the time of stress can be exemplified by the loss of a parent or any loved person, rejection by parents or peers, feelings of frustration or inadequacy due to minority group membership, or guilt induced by sexual taboos or by internalization of extremely competitive norms.

The cumulative physical, emotional, and social experience, combined with endowment, result in the formation of a personality; a usual way of behaving and reacting. It is the personality, then, that in the end mediates between stress and strain, for personality encompasses the total experience of the individual. A schematic representation of the theoretical model would look something like Figure 1-1.

The figure uses the horizontal dimension to show interaction occurring over time. This covers the life span from birth (A) to death (E). Intermediate points in time B, C, and D are also chosen to examine the relationship of the personality to the environment. The actual number of points at which one might examine this relationship approaches infinity. Therefore the decision to use three intermediate points in time in the figure is a purely practical one. The figure shows early stressful and supportive aspects of the environment interacting with genetic endowment starting at birth (A) or, more properly, at conception. These stressful and supportive physical, emotional, and social experiences combine with and shape the natural "equipment," eventually forming typical and enduring ways of reacting or adapting. In this fashion the child comes to develop what we call his personality (B). This interacts with the environment continuously during his lifetime (C, D, E). We have good reason to believe that his stresses tend to accumulate with advancing age. This is indicated by the increasing size of the figures representing stress. As a consequence, our data suggest, his impairment or strain tends to

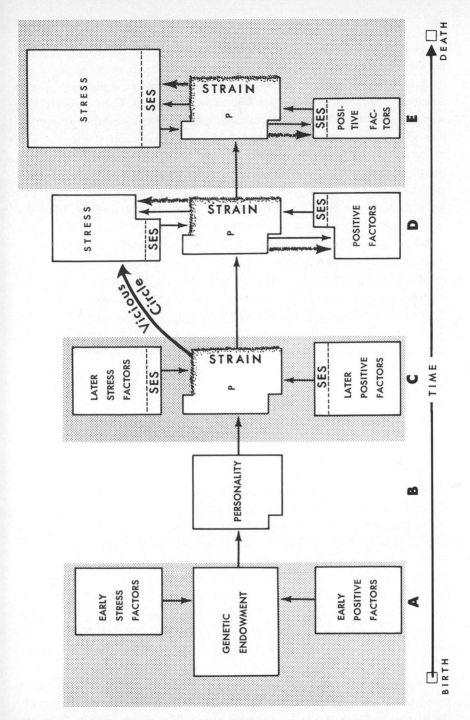

Figure 1-1. Interaction of Environmental Factors, Endowment, and Personality

increase with advancing age. Hence the strain or deformation of the personality is shown as increasing through the life span.

Might not experience, learning, or wisdom reduce the number of maladaptive responses to stress as the individual ages? This suggests that strain would be reduced with advancing age. On the contrary, our impression from the survey is that the decrease in maladaptive response due to learning is overshadowed by the greater increase in stress in later years, leaving a residuum of increasing impairment through time. Moreover, the gradual rigidification of personality through the years, which we call being "set in our ways," would tend to decrease the positive effect of learning new responses to new stresses.

At point D there is an attempt to illustrate graphically the relationship between stress and strain. The noxious or stressful aspects of the environment are represented above the personality, the positive or supportive aspects below. The stress factors are shown as "pressing" on the personality and producing a personality deformation, or strain, indicated by a wavy line. The strain is a reaction that attempts to cope with the stress. This reaction will never be wholly adaptive (straight arrow) or totally maladaptive (wavy arrow) but will result in some sort of compromise involving *some* strain or sacrifice in terms of personality functioning. This individual compromise, deformation, or strain we usually call a symptom. A specific collection of strains or symptoms we call a mental disturbance syndrome, or mental disorder.

The amount of impairment an individual exhibits at any point in time is a product of the interaction of his endowment, past and present environmental stresses and supports, and his personality which interprets the environment and fixes his modes of adaptation.

Socioeconomic status is part of the environmental stress and support system. We will find that SES mediates between other stresses and strain. SES will be seen to play a part in the type and severity of the reaction one has to stress. It is therefore represented graphically as a separate filter or sieve attached to the body of stresses and supports. Any interaction between the personality and the stressful or supportive environment must pass through, or be affected by, socioeconomic status. This will be the parents' status during the individual's childhood, and his own status in adult life.

Of course, this scheme is oversimplified, for it makes us think that stress produces strain, and that the causation is unidirectional. Actually, the strain is a reaction to an original stress. The strain may in turn increase the stress on the individual. For instance, a soldier may be under great stress from the personal attacks of his commanding officer. He evidences strain (sleeplessness, loss of appetite, and so on). As a strain-reducing adjustment he has elaborate reveries during which he plans to kill the officer. On confronting his commander he develops a glove-paralysis of the hand. This maladaptation to the strain results in a renewed source of stress, for now he cannot function as a soldier. This threatens his image of his own manhood, his friendship with fellow soldiers, and exacerbates his struggle with his commanding officer, who considers him a "goldbrick." Thus stress leads to strain, which in turn leads to new stress. This sequence is represented in Figure 1-1 by an arrow leading from strain (C) to increased stress at D.

Of course, this tendency to "snowball" or create a vicious circle is also present among supportive factors. There may be "benign circles" where a positive adaptation to a positive environment leads to an increase in environmental support. For example, a positive reaction to parental love may result in a personality that attracts much love and attention from friends, an eventual spouse, and later one's own children. Because our approach is usually through psychopathology, we are less likely to note "benign circles" than "vicious circles."

In the visual scheme and the example of the soldier's "vicious circle," the amount of stress grows as the maladaptive reactions to the stress accumulate and produce new stresses of their own. The scheme, of course, does not adequately represent the many successful stress-reducing reactions. Both fight and flight may be adaptive or maladaptive in relation to a stress. Since we used the term strain we have limited ourselves only to describing the principally maladaptive reactions to stress. The successful adaptations would be "mentally healthy." In some cases the stress might be met successfully by action (as in fighting, political action, working hard) or flight (running, changing jobs, leaving one's parents, getting a divorce, or fantasy). The adaptive reaction to stress through fantasy would be typified by the writer, painter, or poet. The penniless poet might reduce strain by his fantasy, but could thereby incur new external economic stresses.

A problem in causality is raised by this scheme. If stress causes strain, does the strain (symptom) stop when the stress is removed? We know that this is true in some instances and not in others. For example, Groen, a Dutch physician, had the opportunity of studying a group of his peptic-ulcer patients before, during, and after their internment in a concentration camp during World War II. They had been successful professionals and merchants with competitive careers. Many of them lost their ulcer during internment, only to regain it after release and return to their old way of life.[12] Remove the stress, such as a competitive subsociety, and the strain (ulcer) disappears. This is an example of simultaneous causation, but is not typical of the relationship between stress and strain. It is typical for strain to continue even after the original stress has been diminished or removed. For example, a war neurosis may continue to damage the subsequent relationship of the individual to his peacetime environment.

A more complex example is that of the Irish peasant immigrant to the United States.[13] His drinking (strain) was presumed to be due to the stress of living under the domination of a father whose farm would go to the favorite (not the eldest) son. The lack of primogeniture produced a stressful situation, for the son, aged forty or fifty, not knowing whether he or one of his brothers would inherit the farm, might still be working for his father. He would avoid sexual contact with women for fear of being unable to support a wife and child in marriage or of being an unwed father in a country where premarital intercourse was taboo. He would substitute male companionship and drinking for these other activities. On immigration to an American city the stressful farm constellation no longer exists, for there is no farm to inherit. The drinking (strain), at first a response to the original situation, still remains. Is it a culture pattern, operating long after its original cause has ceased to exist? Are other stresses now capable of producing the same strain? Have these children learned from their fathers to react to *any* stress with drinking? Certainly when stress is removed, strain continues in this case.

Stress may not necessarily be part of the groundwork that prepares the organism for future disorder. For example, maternal over-protection isn't an immediate stress during childhood (unless accompanied by covert rejection). Excessive sheltering may be supportive in a short-term view, but it makes the child vulnerable to stress in later life. This might be considered a positive emotional experience, and the young child does not necessarily develop symptoms or strain in relation to this experience. However, the lack of stress tolerance that shows up later seems to indicate a personality structure that has not developed adequate coping devices. Indeed, there has been little to cope *with* until the demands of higher education, earning a living, marriage, and parenthood arise with advancing age. This delayed or "sleeper" effect is another type of causal chain we may encounter in the etiology of mental disorder.

Briefly, then, we have noted simultaneous causation (the appearance and disappearance of ulcers with presence or absence of competitive striving) and chain or "historical" causation. Several types of historical sequences were cited: stress that precipitates an immediate and continuing strain (as in war neuroses), the "vicious circle" of stress, strain, increased stress, and the sleeper or delayed effect of absence of stress which may produce a weak personality incapable of coping with future stresses.

The idea of *cumulative strain* as the result of successive life stresses is a basic hypothesis in this research report. It is an idea that has been growing steadily in the last fifty years. If this seems like a self-evident postulate, it should be pointed out that the Freudian idea of a psychic trauma, deriving from the medical notion of a trauma or wound, is still widely accepted today. Whitehorn[14] points out that during World War I the concept of a single "trauma" was in wide use, and the term "shell-shock" exemplified this underlying conception of human nature. Human beings were considered to be like machines, which would continue to run unless hit by a sharp blow from outside. Shell shock was attributed to brain tissue damage caused by nearby explosions. In World War II the terms "effort syndrome" and "stress" replaced "shell shock." There was a recognition of the continuity of stress during the individual's lifetime. Battle experience came to be viewed as a possible precipitant of mental disorder.

The emphasis in this volume was originally intended to be on the differential accumulation of stress factors in the lives of lower and higher socioeconomic groups. The overwhelming impression on walking through Midtown was one of sharp socioeconomic contrasts. The importance of this impression was supported by the statistical evidence obtained once the data were gathered and analyzed. As detailed in the first volume of this series, the relationship between mental disorder and socioeconomic status[15] proved to be the strongest of eight demographic variables tested (age, sex, marital status, religion, ethnic background, generation, rural or urban childhood residence, and socioeconomic status). It was our feeling that stress factors were more abundant in the lives of adults of low socioeconomic status, and of children born into families of low socioeconomic status.

If it were true that people of low socioeconomic status (SES) are exposed to a greater number of life stresses, or the same stresses but in a more severe form, then the reason for their higher rate of mental disturbance would be self-evident. It was on the basis of this trend of thought that the term "component variable" was originally added to the analytic scheme of the project. Broken homes, poor health, and other stresses were assumed to be *component* of life at lower SES levels.

At this point it is necessary to distinguish between the theoretical framework (the concepts of stress and strain, personality, and endowment used in describing the relationship between mental disturbance and the environment) and the analytic framework (used in the analysis of survey data that designates the classificatory rubrics into which the various factors were placed). Although there inevitably is some overlap, the two frameworks are distinct in purpose.

## The Analytical Framework

The analytical framework uses the terms "independent variable," "intervening variable," "component variable," and "dependent variable." It does not concern itself with the role of endowment or of personality. It says "In our operation there is a group of factors or variables which seem to take place in time previous to the development of mental disturbance. These will be called the antecedent independent variables." The concern with the sequence of cause and effect is primary in this classification, and therefore the time element becomes most important. Our review and interpretation of this analytical framework is based upon Chapter 2 of Volume I of this series.

What is an independent variable? The most general use of the term is to indicate the variable *from* which you predict. Where knowledge of $x$ enables you to predict some variation in $y$, $x$ is the independent and $y$ the dependent variable. There is no suggestion that $x$ causes $y$ in this usage, nor is there any implication that $x$ precedes $y$ in time. In research involving an experimental design there is little problem of unraveling the causal time sequence. Group A is exposed to factor $x$, and group B is not. Differences in quality $y$ between the A's and B's can readily be attributed to factor $x$ if all other characteristics of A's and B's were controlled, matched, or equal.

In the analysis of questionnaire surveys or other nonexperimental research, such as the Midtown Study, the problem of time sequence becomes important. Most variables examined in a state of nature present this problem, for we do not know whether they are cause or effect, or merely associated (concomitant) variables not involved in the causal chain. Since this study, like most epidemiological research, employs a nonexperimental design, the choice of terms to designate and clarify time sequence and causality becomes extremely important.

It has been customary in survey research to designate the suspected causal factor (the factor that probably initiates the action, or acts upon it) as the independent variable. The factor acted upon (which changes, or which is a function of the independent variable) is called the dependent variable. Its value or variation depends on, or is a function of, the size, value, or action of the independent variable. In survey research the action of the variable designated independent is assumed to take place prior to the reaction or change in the dependent variable. If $x$ and $y$ are associated and $x$ always exists prior to $y$, then there is more reason to believe that $x$ causes $y$. The quality of antecedence, then, is of prime importance in attempting to establish the causal status of the presumed independent variable in nonlaboratory research.

As we shall see, these terms are only relative, for there are no absolutely clear-cut single causes that are unidirectional. It is quite difficult to find an effect that does not interact with the cause to bring about some changes in the cause, or to become subsequently a cause in its own right.

The dependent variable in this study was mental disorder. The various forms in which the dependent variable appeared will be discussed in Chapter 3, 4, and 15. They are the Mental Health Ratings, the Gross Typology, the Symptom Groups, and the Symptom Scores.

The independent variables fell into two main categories, somatic (including organic and constitutional) and sociocultural. Hereditary factors were recognized as important in the etiology of mental disease, but our study was not designed to gather such material. Somatic factors were gathered and given consideration when possible. Thus medical reports of brain damage were sometimes included in the data, but very little about diet, for instance. The reports of physical illness or injury, hospitalizations, and questions concerning general health gave some clues to the operation of somatic factors in mental disturbance.

The emphasis was, of course, on sociocultural factors. There is a virtually unlimited universe of sociocultural factors that might have an effect upon or interact with mental disorder. A first task, initiated in Volume I, Chapter 2, was to develop a taxonomy of factors to be a rough guide for ordering the analysis of the data. The first distinction was between the demographic variables and the component variables. The demographic variables are those generally used to locate the individual in the social system, such as his age, sex, and marital status. They are usually subsumed under the heading of social background on questionnaires, applications, and case records. The component variables, on the other hand, were those characteristics of the demographic variables that explained their association with mental disorder. In a previous example, the assumed greater prevalence of broken homes and poor health among persons of low socioeconomic status was thought to explain their higher rate of mental disorder. Therefore broken homes and poor health were tentatively labeled "components" of socioeconomic status. Similarly, poor health was labeled a component of age, since increasingly poorer health was considered as one explanation of the increase in rates of mental disorder with advancing age.

These demographic background variables were divided into the biosocial and the sociocultural. The first group included variables such as sex, age, and marital status. The second group included socioeconomic status, religion, generation (with respect to immigration to the United States), nationality or ethnic origin, and rural-urban origin (that is, the kind and size of community in which the individual grew up).

The demographic or background variables are also readily divided into two groups based upon their relationship to mental disturbance. The independent unidirectional demographic variables must be relatively uninfluenced by mental health or disorder itself. The death of a parent, for instance, is *usually* not caused by or influenced by the mental health of the child. The parent's death is presumed to influence the child's mental health, but the state of the child's mental health is presumed to have little or no part in causing the parent's death. The action between these factors which are antecedent to present mental status and the dependent variable is relatively unidirectional; that is, the independent variable acts upon the dependent variable, and not vice versa.

Sex and chronological age are typical independent demographic variables. It is virtually impossible for the individual to choose his age or change his sex. Again the relativity of independence should be pointed out, for it is not impossible that some changes in secondary and even primary sex characteristics can be effected through injections of testosterone or estrogens. In some exceptional cases in which persons seek to change their sex by surgical procedures, mental disorder may possibly *motivate* a change in sex.

The effect of the emotions on the production of the reproductive hormones is well known. The total cessation of menstruation among female prisoners in some of the German concentration camps is a case in point. If menstruation and childbearing are accepted as characteristics distinguishing women from men, then we might say that the strain induced by imprisonment and the threat of death had drastically affected the sex of these women.

We know, too, that although chronological age does not change under stress, physiological age does. The folk expression, "He lost ten years of his life in that minute" is based on common observation. Aging, if not age itself, is definitely a function of, or is influenced by, mental health.

By and large, however, age and sex determine one's mental health, and not vice versa. Let us estimate that 95 per cent of the action is unidirectional, that is, the independent is acting upon the dependent variable.

Now the reciprocal variables are in sharp contrast with the independent variables. The independent variables, as they are defined in Volume I, are unidirectional in relation to mental disorder. The reciprocal variables are two-directional in relation to mental disorder. Marital status, socioeconomic status, and religious affiliation are examples of reciprocal demographic variables. One's socioeconomic status certainly can affect one's mental health, as in the unidirectional variables. For example, the loss of a job might lead to depression, withdrawal or suspiciousness. Because socioeconomic status is reciprocal, it can also be a *result* of mental health or disorder. If a person is previously disturbed, he may lose his job or be unable to find one because of his irascibility, withdrawal, suspiciousness, or other symptomatic behavior. Thus a spiraling vicious circle is possible with a reciprocal variable. The hostile man may lose his job, but this loss in turn may make him more hostile.

A greater degree of choice or free will seems to be associated with reciprocal variables. For instance, an unmarried man may marry of his own free will. This may decrease his loneliness, satisfy his sexual and reproductive drives, and afford him the great pleasures of parenthood. It may also increase his responsibilities, threaten his sexual capacity, and burden him with parental duties. In any event, his marriage will influence the course of his mental health subsequent to the wedding. However, his mental health may in turn have been responsible for his marrying or remaining single in the first place. He may have been happy and outgoing, thus ready and willing to marry. He may also have been depressed and lonely, either seeking a companion or solitude. The state of his mental health prior to his marriage no doubt influenced his choice of marital status. It is clear that reciprocal variables involve the individual's choice of a marital, socioeconomic, or other status.

Somewhat more dramatic is the case of divorce, for the loneliness, rancor, and prolonged stress of a divorce may often lead to mental disturbance. On the other hand, some elements of mental disturbance enter into divorce. There is often the imputation that the mental disturbance of one or both parties brought about or led up to the divorce. Neither is cause nor effect alone. The two variables, mental disturbance and divorce, are in interaction with each other in a reciprocal relationship.

The relativity of this broad taxonomy of variables is again seen in the fact that *what we in the United States consider to be reciprocal variables* (within the power of the individual to change or influence) *may be unidirectional variables in other cultures.* For instance, marital status is more or less a matter of individual choice in the United States, and therefore subject to mental health influences. What of the child bride of India, or arranged marriages, or the harem bride? How much say does she have in the matter, and what little influence can her mental health have on her predestined marital state?

Socioeconomic status is certainly a reciprocal variable in our country, where a considerable amount of social mobility in an "open class" system allows the individual to rise or fall in status according to his will, ability, mental health, or the state of the labor market. How much choice of status has a member of the Untouchable caste in India, the slave laborer, or lifetime criminal prisoner? For that matter, how much was the American Negro's socioeconomic status a matter of free choice before his emancipation? Is the minority group member, even at this date, completely free to determine his status by his own efforts? Clearly, the reciprocal quality of the factor of socioeconomic status is only relative, and varies between cultures and subsocieties.

Religious affiliation is certainly reciprocal in a setting of religious freedom. It is thus a matter of choice to some extent. Yet in Nazi Germany being a Jew was not a matter of choice, for a Jew could not renounce his religious origins. This is also true in a theocracy, or in countries where one religious denomination holds absolute power. The religious affiliation of adults, then, may often be a unidirectional variable, and as such not open to the influence of mental health.

In the main, however, religion, marital status, and similar demographic variables are reciprocal with mental health in the population we are studying. For our purposes of classification, then, we can consider these factors as essentially reciprocal.

It was felt that the use of the parents' socioeconomic status[16] and the religious affiliation of the subject during his childhood would be relatively independent of his mental health. The mental health of the child can have little effect upon his parents' socioeconomic status (although some mentally disturbed children would have a devastating cumulative economic effect upon their parents). The religious affiliation of the child in his early years is not usually a matter of choice, therefore the child's mental health could have little part in determining it.

These independent unidirectional variables—parental socioeconomic status, generation with respect to immigration, ethnic background, childhood religion, and rural-urban upbringing—are indicators of different types of family atmospheres, different techniques of child rearing, differing philosophies of life. For example, low parental socioeconomic status might suggest that the offspring experienced certain types of food deprivation during childhood, or parental rejection or the absence of parents, such as a jailed father or a mother who had to work full time. Such characteristics of family life and atmosphere were called *component* variables. The absence or death of parents was assumed to be more frequent in low SES families, therefore the absence of parents was labeled a component of socioeconomic status.

It was hoped that the component factors would explain why low SES, for instance, was associated with poorer mental health. If more parents had died early or were absent in the low SES, if more parents had been domineering or rejecting in the low SES, then we would have had our answer. These component factors would have explained the relationship we found between low status and poor mental health. Our primary goal, however, *was to find other factors that were associated with mental health independently of the demographic factors.* For instance, the death of parents, to be considered a "live" factor, had to be associated with mental disorder within each socioeconomic level. If the death of parents was associated with mental disorder only in the low status group, but not among those of middle and high status, then *status* and not death of parents was probably related to the increase in mental disorder in the low SES group.

Our immediate task, then, was to search for variables that stood by themselves, that were related to mental health independently of (regardless of) socioeconomic status and similar demographic variables. A large number of these turned up. The details of the methods used to uncover these factors are given in Chapter 5. Suffice it to say that very few of these factors turned out to be "components" of either age or socioeconomic status. That is, *they did not vary proportionally with age or SES.*

As an example, the death of parents before the subject was sixteen occurred in about one-fourth of the low, middle, and high SES homes. Thus the death of parents during the individual's childhood was *not* a component of SES. One-third of those born into low, middle, or high SES families reported their parents were domineering or rejecting. Regardless of family socioeconomic status, then, one-third viewed their parents as rejecting or domineering. A negative view of one's parents is therefore *not* a component of SES. Almost without exception the childhood factors (the independent component factors) such as Childhood Poor Physical Health, Parents' Poor Mental Health, Parents' Poor Physical Health, Broken Homes, Parents' Quarrels, and Disagreements with Parents were *not* found to be components of SES. (They were obviously not components of the respondent's present age. Age and SES were the two demographic factors most closely related to mental health, as described in Chapter 4.) The only variable that showed up as a component of parental SES was Economic Deprivation. This might be called a redundant finding, since those with parents of low socioeconomic status would obviously have experienced some economic deprivation during childhood.

The independent (childhood) component factors, far from being components of demographic factors, proved to be entities in their own right that need further testing and placement in the social matrix. Our original emphasis on "components" shifted rapidly to an emphasis on "live" or "viable" variables. These variables were not necessarily related to the demographic variables, but were related to the Mental Health Ratings independent of SES and age. In the screening operation (further described in Chapter 5) all factors whose relationship to mental health could be "explained away" by age or socioeconomic status were dropped and not considered for further analysis. Only the "live" factors remained. These were the factors associated with mental disorder regardless of SES and age.

Another category of factors, the reciprocal component variables, were the *adult factors.* These will be described and derived in later chapters, but they dealt with Adult Poor Physical Health, Poor Interpersonal Affiliations, Parental Worries, Work Worries, Socioeconomic Status Worries, and Marital Worries. They were indeed found to be components of SES, since they varied proportionally with SES. Even though all these factors were associated with poorer mental health, some factors occurred with greater proportional frequency in the low SES, and some were more prevalent in the high SES. In other words, their over-all proportional distribution did not give us an easy and simple explanation of why the low SES group had worse Mental Health Ratings. In fact, the much more frequent Work Worries of the high SES, for instance, make us question why the high, instead of the low SES, did not have the worst Mental Health Ratings (see Chapter 12). The role of the component variables, whether independent or reciprocal, has been not to give us answers to *why* or *how* the demographic variables work. On the contrary, the components have turned out to be sociodynamic variables that give us clues to family and marital interaction and peer relations, but are not yet capable of being located in the larger (demographic) social system. They deserve and will receive treatment in their own right. However, emphasis will also be given to any data that help us to understand the psychodynamics of socioeconomic status and age.

The major variables discussed in these two volumes can be arranged as follows (this is an expansion of the typology of variables in Chapter 2 of Volume I):

1. Demographic Variables
    I. Independent (Unidirectional) Variables
        A. Biosocial Type
            1. Age
            2. Sex
        B. Sociocultural Type
            1. Parental socioeconomic status
            2. Parental generation level in U.S.
            3. Ethnic background of parents
            4. Parental religious affiliation
            5. Rural-urban residence during childhood
    II. Reciprocal (Two-Directional) Variables
        A. Biosocial Type
            1. Marital status
        B. Sociocultural Type
            1. Subject's present socioeconomic status
            2. Subject's present religious affiliation

2. Component or Explanatory Variables
  I. Independent (Unidirectional) Variables (Preadult or *Childhood Stress Factors*)
      A. Biosocial Type
          1. Parents' Poor Physical Health
          2. Parents' Poor Mental Health
          3. Childhood Poor Physical Health
          4. Broken Homes (due to death of parents)
      B. Sociocultural Type
          1. Broken Homes (due to divorce, separation, or desertion of parents)
          2. Parents' Quarrels
          3. Disagreements with Parents
          4. Childhood Economic Deprivation
          5. Parents' Character Negatively Perceived
  II. Reciprocal (Two-Directional) Variables (*Adult Stress Factors*)
      A. Biosocial Type
          1. Adult Poor Physical Health
      B. Sociocultural Type
          1. Work Worries
          2. Socioeconomic Worries
          3. Inadequate Interpersonal Affiliations
          4. Marital Worries (Applies to the Married Only)
          5. Parental Worries (Applies to Parents Only)
3. Dependent Variables
  I. Psychiatric Judgments
      A. Mental Health Rating I
      B. Mental Health Rating II
      C. The Gross Typology[17]
      D. Symptom Group Classification
  II. Psychometric Scores
      A. Symptom Scores
      B. Twenty-Two Item Symptom Score (A Screening Instrument)
  III. Antecedent-Dependent: The Childhood Mental Health Index

The last two reciprocal adult factors are contingent because they were applicable only to segments of the sample (persons who were married and those who were parents). Many variables covered by the study are not included in this list. All together, 148 items of information were tested to form the "component" variables that are the subject matter of this volume. Only the 31 items most closely related to the Mental Health Ratings (independent of SES) were combined into the childhood and adult stress factors mentioned above. The criteria for selecting these items and constructing the stress factors are detailed in Chapter 5, which deals specifically with the methods of this volume alone.

A type of factor difficult to classify is the *antecedent-dependent* variable, the Childhood Mental Health (CMH) Index. In the CMH Index the respondent's symptoms of mental disturbance during childhood and adolescence (preadult years) were combined. We assume that this index gives a crude indication of preadult mental health. Preadult mental health is a dependent variable in relation to the preadult factors, but is in itself an independent variable in relation to adult mental health. Because of this dual role it was treated separately, rather than as just another preadult factor. The CMH Index is considered at length in Appendix C. It was hypothesized that the level of mental health in childhood determines the impact of the adult factors on adult mental health. This hypothesis is tested later in this volume.

A schematic representation of the sequence of the types of variables through time is given in Figure 1-2.

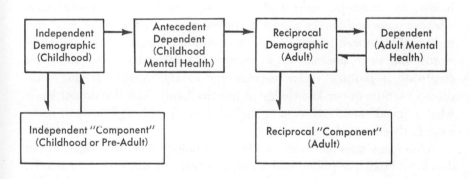

Figure 1-2. Schematic Representation of Types of Variables

This is an ideal scheme, and is meant primarily for classificatory purposes. The exact time sequence may not be correct for any specific factor that might be tested with the scheme. For instance, a boy of seven might be mentally disturbed. His father might become progressively more upset by his son's mental disorder. When the boy is ten years old his father might desert the family. This desertion (or broken home) could have been precipitated by the child's mental disorder. The boy's childhood mental health at this point in time can be seen as capable of causing or precipitating some of the "independent" demographic or component factors. For instance, the child's mental health may act as an agent in producing or exacerbating parents' mental disorders or physical illness, quarrels between parents, disagreements between child and parent, not to mention the effects it might have on the parents' socio-economic status. It might interfere with the father's education, reduce his income, reduce the family income by not allowing the mother to work, or use up income with high costs of psychiatric care and special schools. No one will deny that children, and in particular mentally disturbed children, have an effect on their parents and vice versa. The intervening variable, then, will often act in a reciprocal fashion and is not necessarily subsequent to all the independent variables.

## Some Preventive Implications

One philosophical note might be appended to this list. It is evident that the component factors are stated in negative terms. The broken homes, for example, are usually associated with mental disturbance, whereas unbroken homes would be linked to an absence of mental disturbance. Unbroken homes do not constitute a "eugenic" factor. In other words, *the mere absence of a presumed pathogenic factor does not constitute a positive factor making for mental health*. It just indicates a vacuum in our knowledge of healthy family life. We do not know what a "good" family is, or a "good" childhood, although we can make some fairly educated guesses.

As in many scientific fields, we learn pathology first. Medicine did not develop a branch of public health and preventive medicine until recently. We are learning slowly about the normal functioning of the human body. It is easier to find out "what went wrong," but when every organ is working perfectly, relatively little progress is made. It takes a man with an injury to his stomach to advance the knowledge of the digestive process. In the past it has usually taken a person with an "injury to his psyche" to advance our knowledge of family life and individual psychological processes.

This problem has often been considered in the literature. For example:

Most of our present-day knowledge of personality and our ideas of mental health are derived from clinical studies of individuals who do not have mental health. It is not a criticism to remind you that our interest and knowledge in this field comes largely from psychopathology. We have an etiology of mental disorders but we do not have an embryology or a physiology of personality. Also, we must realize that healthy personalities can develop only in a healthy society, and a healthy society can be developed and maintained only by healthy personalities.[18]

As a science ages, it turns its attention to the normal. Thus with the behavioral sciences, some of the attention given to the patient in treatment is now being given to the community and family setting, where most people are carrying on their daily functions. When we observe people in the home and community environment rather than the radically different social environment of a mental hospital, we can gain further clues to the origins of their illnesses. Just as with malaria, it is better to kill the mosquito than to close the window. The closer we are to the source of the disease, the better our theory, treatment, and prevention.

Even though the Midtown Project turned its attention to the community, and studied the mental health of a random sample of the population, it did not produce much evidence of eugenic factors or aids to mental health. Perhaps our dearth of knowledge is so great that we had best fill in the pathogenic or negative factors first. Maybe the qualities, events, or strengths that insulate people against the ravages of mental disorder are more elusive and subtle and require other methods of investigation than those we employed. Perhaps the self-esteem that comes with high socioeconomic status, with loving but not overindulgent parents, with acceptance by other racial, religious, and status groups is what helps to stave off mental disturbance even in the face of great stress. All our data point to a greater resiliency in the young and those of high status. The source of this resiliency, the source of this ability to "take" stress without much evidence of strain, remains for future investigation by longitudinal intensive research with various families, communities, and cultures.

In a causal chain or cycle, an action program can be introduced at any one point, or at several points in the system simultaneously. From the standpoint of preventive medicine, it is best to attack the system where it is weakest. This means that the point or points must be selected where the least amount of money, personnel, and effort will have to be expended to produce the greatest amount of change in the desired direction.

Efforts can be made, then, to change certain aspects of environmental stress, to change personality structure, and to alleviate or eradicate the symptoms of strain (mental disorder). For example, we can change the environmental stresses to some extent by: (1) educating parents, (2) educating teachers, (3) gradually integrating religious, racial, and national minorities, (4) eliminating some of the major inequities associated with social class differences, (5) resolving some of the political tensions on the local, national, and international level, (6) offering better health insurance programs and more widespread preventive medical care.

The personality structure of large groups of people probably can not be changed radically by present methods of therapy. However, the prolonged exposure of parents to more appropriate child-rearing practices and attitudes, particularly in lying-in hospitals and through mass media such as "pocket books" and television programs, might eventually have a salutary effect on the personality structures of new generations of Americans. The instillment of self-confidence, frustration tolerance, and other personality characteristics that might aid in resisting stress should be a positive goal. The isolation and study of these characteristics are, however, necessary prerequisites. Little is known about these positive personality characteristics, and the terminology describing them is much vaguer than the diagnostic and descriptive categories now in common use in psychiatry, psychology, and psychometrics.

The reduction of strain must go on, and will improve as new drugs and other treatment methods are uncovered by clinical psychiatry and its allied disciplines. From a public health standpoint, strain is the least likely point at which to attack the causal chain of mental disorder. By the time strain appears in a form severe enough to be socially unacceptable (recognizable and "worthy of treatment") much of the damage has been done. Repairs are expensive and take much time, training, and money. The dearth of facilities and the small number of persons willing to use psychiatric help, even when severely impaired by their symptoms, indicate that in the long run strain is not the most profitable point of attack from a public health standpoint. However, from the standpoint of the disturbed individual and his family who need help, reduction of strain rather than stress will always be the immediate goal.

The attack on strain through clinical practice will continue to supply personnel and ideas to the fields of preventive, industrial, military, and of course social psychiatry. Child psychiatry of necessity has already moved a step ahead by studying the family. The programmatic implications of the Midtown Study may not be clear now, but hopefully the influence of this and other research in social psychiatry will be felt in the community and the clinic.

What stands out most clearly is that there are a relatively large number of factors that can become focal points of change. Chronological age, for example, does not hold out as much hope of improvement as does socioeconomic status. Almost all of the "component" factors seem capable of influence: physical health, family frictions, divorce, parental behavior. The project, in its conception, choice of methods, and interpretations has been consistently antideterministic. The choice of the sociocultural variables for study in itself is probably related to an implicit faith that this part of the causal chain can be influenced and that it is to some degree subject to the will of human beings.

## Notes

1. Leo Srole, Thomas S. Langner, Stanley T. Michael, Marvin K. Opler, and Thomas A. C. Rennie, *Mental Health in the Metropolis,* Volume I, The Thomas A. C. Rennie Series in Social Psychiatry, McGraw-Hill, New York, 1961.
2. Thomas A. C. Rennie, "Social Psychiatry—A Definition," *International Journal of Social Psychiatry,* I: 1 (1955), 11–12.
3. *Ibid.,* p. 12.
4. *Ibid.,* p. 12.
5. *Ibid.,* p. 12.
6. Alexander H. Leighton, "Mental Illness and Acculturation," *Medicine and Anthropology,* International Universities Press, New York, 1959, pp. 121–122.
7. It has often been pointed out that no force or factor can automatically be labeled "noxious" until the consequences of that force are examined. For instance, Dr. G. Ronald Hargreaves asked, in a discussion of Dr. Harold Wolff's paper, "Was Roosevelt's polio noxious or did it 'make' Roosevelt?" See Harold G. Wolff, M.D., Discussion, in Conference on Mental Health and Mental Illness, Lincoln College, Oxford, England, July 1958, mimeographed.

The following reference is made to Dr. Hargreaves' comments in Harold G. Wolff, "Stressors as a Cause of Disease in Man," in Chapter 2, "Disorganization of Behavior in Man," J. M. Tanner (ed.), *Stress and Psychiatric Disorder,* The Proceedings of the Second Oxford Conference of the Mental Health Research Fund, Blackwell Scientific Publications, Oxford, England, 1960, p. 30, which is the published version of Dr. Wolff's mimeographed paper mentioned above.

"Professor Hargreaves objected to defining a stress in terms of a noxious stimulus because one could not say whether a stimulus was noxious or not until one knew its outcome in terms of psychological failure or success."
8. *The Columbia Encyclopedia,* "Strength of Materials," Columbia University Press, New York, 1944, ed. Clarke F. Ansley, p. 1697.
9. Doctor Selye tells us: "Stress is the state manifested by a specific syndrome which consists of all the nonspecifically induced changes within a biologic system." See Hans Selye, "Stress and Psychiatry," *American Journal of Psychiatry,* 113:5 (No-

vember 1956), 423. The syndrome to which he refers is the "stress-syndrome" or "general adaptation syndrome" (G.A.S.), which has a characteristic form.

Doctor Wolff carefully warns us that stress is an effect, not a cause, that it occurs in the individual, and is not part of his environment, ". . . that state within a living creature which results from the interaction of the organism with noxious stimuli or circumstances. Thus, it is a dynamic state within an organism; it is not stimulus, assault, load, symbol, burden, or any aspect of environment; internal, external, social or otherwise." Harold G. Wolff, "Stressors as a Cause of Disease in Man," *op. cit.,* p. 17.

In a fascinating discussion of Dr. Wolff's paper, Dr. Erich Lindemann questioned the idea that stress was always a feature of the organism (the *internal* environment).

"In the population which you studied did you distinguish between those individuals whose resources for problem solving were of such a nature that they were getting into a number of difficulties by virtue of their own techniques of dealing with social problems, and those individuals who, like prisoners of war or the train wreck victims, were exposed to an excessive effect of, let us say, at least a disorganized social situation, if you do not want to call it stress?" Harold G. Wolff, Discussion, in Conference on Mental Health and Mental Illness, *op. cit.*

10. George L. Engel, "Homeostasis, Behavorial Adjustment and the Concept of Health and Disease," *Mid-Century Psychiatry,* ed. Roy R. Grinker, Charles C Thomas, Springfield, Illinois, 1953, p. 51.

11. Konrad Z. Lorenz, "The Evolution of Behavior," *Scientific American,* 199: 6 (December 1958), 78.

12. John C. Whitehorn, M.D., "Stress and Emotional Health," *American Journal of Psychiatry,* 112:10 (April 1956), 781.

13. For a description of Irish peasant life before immigration, see Conrad M. Arensberg, *The Irish Countryman,* Macmillan, New York, 1937; and C. M. Arensberg and S. T. Kimball, *Family and Community in Ireland,* Harvard University Press, Cambridge, Massachusetts, 1940.

14. John C. Whitehorn, *op. cit.,* p. 781.

15. The index of the respondent's socioeconomic status was based on his income, education, occupation, and rent. These indices were combined, then divided into equally populated thirds to produce three SES groups: low, middle, and high.

16. The index of parental socioeconomic status was based upon the father's education and occupation.

17. The gross typology is an approximate diagnostic grouping. Since it was assigned to the individuals studied on the basis of written materials rather than a face-to-face clinical interview, the categories are labeled "Probable Psychotic Type," "Probable Neurotic Type," etc. The Gross Typology and the Symptom Group classification are described in Chapter 3.

18. John C. Whitehorn, *op. cit.,* p. 781.

# Research Methods: An Overview

### THOMAS S. LANGNER

## Introduction

The over-all goal of the project was described in the previous chapter; namely, the investigation of the relationship between stresses in the socio-cultural environment and strain, or mental disorder. More specifically, we wanted to know *how many* persons were psychiatrically impaired, to what degree they were impaired, what types of impairing disorders and symptoms they exhibited, *who* they were, and *how* they got that way. Obtaining clues to the last question, *how* or *why*, was our primary goal. The *how many*, *how much*, *what kind*, and *who* answers, while important in their own right, could be viewed primarily as grist for the etiological mill, the *how* and *why* of mental disorder.

In order to clarify these goals several conceptual and analytical frameworks had to be constructed. These were in effect extensions of the simple phrase "environment affects mental health." The conceptual framework pictured stress producing strain in the individual, mediated by his personality and endowment. The analytic framework divided the stress factors into independent and reciprocal, demographic and component, and thus defined the direction and priority of their relationship with mental health.

A further conceptual development was necessary in relation to the dependent variable, mental health. What was mental health, mental disorder, adjustment, functioning, normality? The conceptions of mental health and operational definitions finally adopted are described in Chapter 3 of this volume and in Volume I by the psychiatrists who made the individual evaluations.

The conceptual and analytic frameworks grew in detail and were considerably influenced by the research itself. Once the provisional concepts were constructed, the actual research operations were carried out to implement the project goals. The over-all operations are described in more detail in Volume I, Chapter 3; a more summary account is given here. Because this report deals with a large number of explanatory stress factors, the history of the development and application of the project methods has been minimized and more emphasis placed on the questionnaire content. Equal attention will also be given to the content of the strain, the symptoms of and reactions to stress, although the actual process of evaluating these symptoms will be described in Chapter 3.

The data contained in Volumes I and II come from three research procedures or operations. Of minor importance were the Community Sociography and the Treatment Census operations. The operation claiming the greatest expenditure of time, money, and effort was the Home Interview Survey, which will be treated at some length in this chapter.

## The Community Sociography Operation

Midtown is a residential area in Manhattan, a borough of New York City which is said to be the largest metropolis (in population if not area) in the world. If we are to understand the impact of the sociocultural environment on the individual's mental health, we must know the major sociographic characteristics of that environment. This would include the physical and structural aspects of the community, the formal affiliations and associations, and the informal social network. In other words, we would like to know about its *institutions:* the family, education, legal-military structure and police, and the economic, religious, and political structures. We would also want to know the general flavor or atmosphere of the community and its subdivisions.

The sociography operation utilized recorded vital statistics data from federal, state, and municipal sources. To a very small extent it also gathered interviews from key informants in the community and utilized participant observation of community life. As a substitute for extensive observation, the writings of commentators on life in Manhattan were culled from magazines and newspapers, and often complete autobiographies of Manhattanites were searched.

The respondents in the Home Interview Survey were also asked many questions about their housing, neighborhood, organization membership, and additional material with which we built a picture of the Midtown community.

The results of the sociography operation, supplemented with data from the interview, are given in Chapter 4.

## The Treatment Census Operation

The total number of people who have tuberculosis is the sum of those who are in treatment for tuberculosis *plus* an unknown number who have the disease but for various reasons have not recognized it or, having recognized it, have chosen to ignore or avoid treatment. The true total of individuals impaired by psychiatrically significant symptoms is the sum of those in treatment *plus* the much larger group of untreated ill. The Treatment Census was designed to give us an idea of how many Midtowners were receiving psychiatric treatment on an in-patient and out-patient basis.

Four types of psychiatric facilities were surveyed: (1) publicly supported mental hospitals at the municipal, state, and federal level within New York State; (2) private mental hospitals in New York and adjoining states, and a few large private mental hospitals in more distant states which often provide therapy for wealthier Midtown residents; (3) out-patient clinics, both public and private, in Manhattan; and (4) psychiatrists and psychologists in private practice with offices in Manhattan.

Dr. Margaret Bailey and Mrs. Freeda Taran were the project's psychiatric social workers. They carried out this complex operation by sending questionnaires to therapists in private practice and making visits to many of the private hospitals whose records were not available at Albany. (All public hospital cases were available on IBM cards from the State of New York.) A lengthy form giving diagnosis, date of onset, and many details of sociocultural background taken from the case records was filled out for each patient. The patient had to be a Midtown resident being carried as an "open-case." This included, of course, all patients in custodial care. Patients whose last address was in Midtown but had been in that particular mental hospital for five years or longer were not included in the survey. (This exception later proved unwise, for a considerable proportion of patients from Midtown had been continuous in-patients for more than five years. Thus our rates of the prevalence of treated mental disorder were considerably underestimated.)

Both prevalence and incidence rates were calculated for Midtown.

Prevalence refers to the total number of patients (usually per 100,000 population) who are open-case patients at any particular time, usually a particular day. It does not take account of how long these people have been in treatment. Incidence, on the other hand, is a measure of *new cases* during a time span (usually a year). Incidence rates are usually labeled "first admissions to Hospital *x* in Year *y*." Of course, incidence often does not take into account the fact that a patient has received treatment in another state or a private institution previous to his "first admission" to the reporting institution. Because of poor exchange of records or the patient's failure to report previous treatment, a "first admission" may often be an old case. At its best, however, incidence allows us to guess whether more people are *developing* treated mental disturbance in one year than in another. As the data in Volume I show, *treated* mental disorder is not a very good indicator of the extent, distribution, type, or duration of total mental disorder in the community.

The data on prevalence of treated mental disorder (as of May 1, 1953) assumed a more limited role as the study analysis progressed. Further details are given in Volume I, Chapter 3, and subsequent chapters.

## The Home Interview Survey

### A.   THE SAMPLE

The U.S. Census listed approximately 110,000 individuals aged twenty to fifty-nine in Midtown. This age range was chosen for study because psychiatric criteria for judging the mental health of individuals within these ages are somewhat clearer than they are for children, adolescents, or the aged. Since all these individuals could not possibly be surveyed, a random sample of 1911 were selected from the same number of dwelling units. These 1911 individuals are almost completely representative of the 110,000. No self-selection by the respondents or selection bias of interviewers was allowed to enter into the sampling process. The details of the sampling process are given in Volume I.

Only 13 per cent of the 1911 did not participate in the survey, a rate that compares favorably with other local and national samples. We actually interviewed 1660 individuals, or 87 per cent of the 1911 originally selected. We gathered data on approximately 1.5 per cent of the population. This is an acceptable proportion for a sample survey; many national samples contain only 2000 or 3000 cases.

The sample was closely representative of the population from which it was drawn. It was within one per cent of each age and sex category in Midtown as given in the 1950 census. This 1.5 per cent sample, at least with respect to age and sex, seems quite representative of the uninterviewed 98.5 per cent of the population. This similarity is a fair indication that the distribution of the uninterviewed on other characteristics, such as mental disorder, would be similar. The Treatment Census also covered people who had refused to be interviewed or could not be contacted. A careful check of the rate of psychiatric treatment of the 13 per cent who refused to participate or could not be reached showed that their rates of *previously treated* mental disorder and present "ambulatory" treatment were no higher than for the interviewed portion of the sample. Though this study suggests that treatment is not a good criterion for mental disorder, the treatment records of nonrespondents were used in the absence of better information.

### B.   THE INTERVIEW SITUATION

The interview had to be quite lengthy in order to cover the many aspects of each individual's history and background. These comprised the stress factors listed in Chapter 1. The other large body of material to be covered was composed of the signs and symptoms of mental and physical health.

Certain considerations entered into the choice of the home as the best physical location for the interview. Although it was not as private as a room in a psychiatric clinic, it had the advantage of being the "natural habitat" of the respondent, and might therefore make him more at ease. Coming to a clinic, particularly a psychiatric clinic, would have been a nuisance or a threat to a great many people, and might have doubled our nonparticipant rate.

Rather than running the risk of losing a respondent, a 65-page questionnaire that averaged two hours was administered in one interview. It was impossible to have psychiatrists make the 1660 home visits at the convenience of the respondents, particularly within the few months allotted to the field survey in our time schedule. The interviews were therefore conducted by persons trained to use interview schedules and questionnaires. Interviewers were recruited from the ranks of psychiatric social workers, clinical psychologists, anthropologists, and sociologists. These individuals also had skill in "depth interviewing," that is, in interviewing without a questionnaire or an interview guide.

The use of a questionnaire with predetermined answer categories minimized the individual differences in personality and training of the more than forty interviewers. It also increased the comparability of the data obtained on the 1660 individuals, making statistical analysis possible. In order to avoid turning the questionnaire into an uninteresting and completely de-individualized instrument, and to utilize more of his professional skills, the interviewer was asked to write down the respondent's comments and remarks verbatim. He was also asked to give a full description of the interviewee in his own words, approximately a page in length. As a third method of catching the flavor of the interview itself, a checklist was filled out giving the respondent's interest in and attitude toward the interview and interviewer, the distractions that occurred, and many other details of behavior and mien.

## C.  QUESTIONNAIRE CONTENT

*The Demographic Stress Factors.*    A full description of the history and development of the questionnaire is given in Volume I, Chapter 3. In sum, there were 10 drafts, and 145 individuals were interviewed during various "pre-tests." The final draft was precoded with answers numbered in such a way as to facilitate analysis by International Business Machines.

Essentially the questionnaire can be divided into items representing stress, and items representing strain. There were approximately 200 items of the total of 415 that might be considered as environmental variables possibly related to psychiatric impairment. Of course, each item included in the questionnaire represented a specific hypothesis with respect to mental health. These hypotheses were spelled out during the initial phases of the research. For instance, "low socioeconomic status is associated with poor mental health" was tested by the inclusion in the questionnaire of four socioeconomic status variables: occupation, education, income, and rent. It is unnecessary to list all these hypotheses, for they are, in effect, "stated" in the questionnaire.

The stress factors finally reported on were listed in Chapter 2. However, many more factors were examined in relation to the Mental Health Ratings. For various reasons, primarily because they were unrelated or weakly related to mental health, these factors were not reported at length. The principal factors deserve mention, and an attempt to list them will involve some crude and superficial groupings that should not be taken as a substantiation of an underlying relationship between the items thus grouped.

The demographic background variables which were reported deserve first mention. *Sex* and *age* were reported, the latter coded in five-year intervals, i.e., 20 to 24, 25 to 29, up to 59. *Marital status* was noted as follows: never married, presently married, presently divorced, presently separated, presently widowed. If an individual was previously divorced and remarried, he was considered married if still married at the time of the interview. *Generation* with respect to immigration was recorded in great detail. By and large, the first generation were immigrants to this country, the second generation were children born in this country of immigrants, the third generation were grandchildren of immigrants, and the fourth generation had all their grandparents born in this country.

*Religion* was recorded for the respondent and his parents. In general, Catholics, Jews, Protestants, and Eastern Orthodox were noted. The various Protestant denominations and Jewish groups were also recorded. The faith in which the respondent "grew up," his parents' faiths, and his present religious persuasion were set down.

The *size of the community* in which the subject was born, and in which he "grew up," was recorded as farm, village, town, small city, medium-sized city, big city, and New York City.

The nationality or *"ethnic" background* of the interviewee was often difficult to determine. His country of birth, as well as that of his parents and grandparents, was taken into consideration. If the parents were from different countries, and the maternal and paternal grandparents were evenly divided between two countries, then the respondent's own "ethnic identification" (for example, "I'm Irish," or "I'm Italian-American") had to suffice. The necessity for using this method of classification seldom arose, however. The various nationality groups represented were German-Austrian, Irish, Italian, Czech, Slovak, Hungarian, English-Scotch-Welsh, Russian-Polish-Lithuanian, Puerto Rican, and United States (fourth generation). Other nationality groups were not sufficiently populated to warrant separate codification, but were specified in each case by the interviewer.

The index of *socioeconomic status of the respondent's father* was based on the father's occupation and number of years of education. The father's income was not asked, since the child's knowledge in this area was likely to be inaccurate. The father's rent was not asked, since his past rent would not have been at all comparable with present rents.

The index of *socioeconomic status, or SES, of the respondent* was based upon his rent and income, as well as his occupation and education.

*Occupation* was elicited in detail. The level of the occupation was then classified on a six-point scale. White Collar workers (who in general do not change into work clothes when at work) were divided into high (professional and managerial), middle (semiprofessional), and low (sales and clerical). The Blue Collar workers (labor) were divided into high (skilled), middle (semiskilled), and low (unskilled or manual). The number of persons supervised and self-employment as opposed to employment by others were taken into account in assigning the occupational level.

*Education* was recorded in numbers of years of grade school, high school, college, and graduate school. Eight years of grade school, four of high school, and four of college were considered as "completion" of that level of schooling. The final six categories used in analysis of SES were the incompleted and completed levels of grade school, high school, and college.

Weekly "family" *income* was recorded in $25 intervals through most of the range from under $15 to over $300 per week.

Monthly *rent* (paid by the respondent or the head of the household) was noted in $10 intervals through most of the range from under $9 to over $300 per month.

These constitute the major demographic variables whose relationship to the Mental Health Ratings was reported in detail in Volume I. Among the many other characteristics of the population included in the questionnaire are the component variables.

*The Component Stress Factors.* The component or explanatory variables constitute the major focus of this volume. Because the grouping of these variables into the major stress factors is detailed in separate chapters, the content of the stress factors will be reviewed here only briefly. The answer to each question associated with greater mental disturbance is in bold type to aid the reader only where there are several alternative answers.

The *preadult* factors were considered to be independent variables in relation to mental health, and dealt with characteristics of the respondent's parents and his childhood and adolescent experiences.

Parents' Poor Physical Health was based on the respondent's positive answer to "When you were growing up (age six to eighteen) was either of your parents in poor health?"

Parents' Poor Mental Health was indicated by answers to several questions. Among these was a report of *psychosomatic* illnesses of the respondent's mother and father, the statement that one or both parents was "the worrying type," and that either or both parents had a "nervous breakdown." The way in which these answers were combined into stress factors will be explained in later chapters and appendices.

Childhood Economic Deprivation was indicated when the "chief problems of parents" were "unemployment" or "financial," when parents "often had a hard time making ends meet," and when the mother had to work full time outside the home for financial reasons.

Childhood Poor Physical Health was indicated by "As far as you can remember or have been told, was your health in early childhood good, fair, or **poor**?" and "As a child, did you catch cold fairly often?"

Childhood Broken Homes was initially indicated by answers to "Did you live together with both your real parents up to the time you were sixteen years old?" If both parents were not present till sixteen, because of separation, divorce, death, institutionalization, or other reasons, the interviewer asked the respondent's age at the time the home was "broken." **Homes broken before age seven,** those **broken from ages seven to sixteen,** and homes unbroken through age sixteen were considered progressively less stressful to the individual.

The stress factor of Parents' Character Negatively Perceived was based on answers to six items concerning how the respondent perceived his parents' behavior during childhood. The reasons for calling this factor a perception rather than a report are given in Chapter 6. The six items were "Father spends too little time with me" (**yes**), "Father wants to run his children's lives" (**yes**), "Mother doesn't understand me" (**yes**), "My parents are always proud of their children" (**no**), and "Parents don't practice what they preach" (**yes**). Whether a factual report or perception (a problem discussed at length in Chapter 6), this factor constituted a good predictor of adult mental health.

Parents' Quarrels was based on a single item: "Of course, all parents have their quarrels (arguments) with each other. In your home when you were growing up (age six to eighteen) did such quarrels occur **often,** occasionally, or rarely?"

Disagreements with Parents was again a single-item factor: "When you were a teenager (age thirteen to eighteen) did *you* have disagreements with your parents, **often,** occasionally, rarely, or never?"

The *adult* or reciprocal component factors bore a circular relationship to mental health, at once affecting mental health and being affected by it. Adult Poor Physical Health was based on the questions: "Would you say your health now is excellent, good, fair, or **poor?**" "How many times have you been a patient in a hospital (except for childbirth)?" and the number of physical ailments or complaints *not* included in the list of possible "psychosomatic" conditions.

Marital Worries was a factor based upon the question, "Would you say you worry about (your) marriage **often,** sometimes, or never?"

Parental Worries was a factor based upon, "Would you say you worry about (your) children **often,** sometimes, or never?" "Children give their parents more trouble than pleasure (**agree**)," and reports by the respondents that they had had problems with their children.

Work Worries was based upon reports of worrying about "my work" and "overwork" **often,** sometimes, or never.

Socioeconomic Worries was an index composed of worries about "my standard of living" and "getting ahead" **often,** sometimes, or never.

Poor Interpersonal Affiliations was an index based on answers to questions about the number of organizations to which one belonged, the number of neighbors with whom one was friendly, and the number of "close" friends one had (**none** or **few**).

A total of 148 component items or variables was tested altogether. Thirty-six items, constituting almost all of those that showed a strong relationship to mental health independently of socioeconomic status, were incorporated in the preadult and adult component stress factors reported in this volume. While a complete list of the original 148 items cannot be given, a few examples of the major types of items not reported in individual chapters can be outlined. Certain variables showed little or no relationship to mental disorder. Examples are birth order, number, and sex of the respondent's siblings. Other items essentially unrelated to mental health were crowdedness of childhood home and the size of the house, educational, religious, and ethnic homogeneity of the parents, father's social mobility and the parents' attitudes about "doing better than other children," the importance of religion to the parents and their church attendance, ethnic identification as noted by the languages spoken in the home and the number of traditional national practices in the childhood home, spatial mobility as assessed by the age at immigration or migration to New York City, and the number of communities inhabited before coming to New York.

Many adult items are not reported or detailed in this volume because they were generally unrelated to psychiatric impairment. These include intelligence estimates, comparison of occupational aspirations with present occupation, adult religiosity and church attendance, degree of ethnic identification as measured by participation in ethnic activities, crowdedness of the household and the building, satisfaction with the present residence, adult spatial mobility, satisfaction with Midtown as a neighborhood, and preferences for the city as opposed to the town or village. These are but a few of the variables unrelated to our mental health measures.

Scales measuring authoritarianism, racial prejudice, and *anomie* (feelings of futility and alienation) were also administered. The relation of these to mental disorder will be reported at length in other publications. All in all, the majority of items that showed a strong relationship to mental health *were* included in the preadult or adult stress factors, and are given full treatment in the text.

*Questionnaire Content That Assessed Strain.*    The dependent variable, as mentioned previously, took several forms; the most important were Mental Health Ratings I and II. Other forms of measuring or describing types of mental disorder were two additional psychiatric judgments (the Gross Typology and the Symptom Group classification), and the psychometric instruments, such as the Symptom Scores and the 22-Item Symptom Score.

The Mental Health Rating was based upon a global judgment of a six-page Psychiatric Summary of the 65-page interview of each respondent, and it was made independently by two psychiatrists. They were often heavily influenced in their judgments by verbatim elaborations or "spillover," the interviewer's observations and description of the respondent, attached reports of diagnosis and psychiatric treatment, and reports of service by any of the city's social agencies. However, *the major stimuli for the judgment were symptoms and signs of mental disturbance,* numbering 120. These appeared in standardized (mimeographed) format, and the individual's response to each item was circled in red pencil. (This Psychiatric Summary is reproduced in Volume I. It should be noted that blank spaces were left on the Summary form to indicate the age of onset and current status of various psychosomatic ailments.)

These signs and symptoms are quite heterogeneous in nature, and any attempt to classify them in terms of seriousness, source, or location would inevitably fail at this state of our knowledge. However, the description of these symptoms can be facilitated by lumping them into convenient categories that are not meant in any way to be etiologically meaningful.

The psychiatric raters were exposed to summarized data from various outside treatment facilities. The material from the Treatment Census and the Social Service Exchange records gave the raters some idea of previous and current treatment, agency contacts, and the like. Supplementing this was the respondent's own report of visits to a neurologist, psychiatrist, or psychologist, and his answer to the question about a "nervous breakdown" (a "nervous upset preventing your usual work or activities").

The respondent also indicated whether he had ever had or *now had* any of eleven conditions that have a high probability of being psychosomatic. Medical and lay terms were used to identify each disorder. These conditions were arthritis or rheumatism (stiff or painful joints), asthma (noisy and difficult breathing), bladder trouble (enuresis or bedwetting), colitis (or diarrhea with blood), diabetes (or sugar disease), hay fever (running nose and watery eyes not due to a cold), heart condition, high blood pressure, neuralgia or sciatica (pains in the muscles or nerves not due to injury), stomach ulcer (stomach pains *after* meals, relieved by eating), and skin conditions, like hives and rashes. The condition of epilepsy (fits or convulsions) was also noted, but not considered necessarily psychosomatic. The age of onset and the number of years the condition lasted were recorded in five- and ten-year intervals.

Somewhat related were a group of psychophysiological symptoms of mental disturbance. Most of these were asked with response alternatives of "often, sometimes, or never." Although the majority are signs of inner anxiety and tension translated into the musculature or linked directly to the autonomic "emergency" reaction, a few are more generalized, such as "nervousness." The quality of these items, which are the backbone of the Mental Health Rating, deserves full consideration at this point. They are, in the sequence of their appearance in the interview: "Would you say your appetitie is **poor, fair?**" "Would you say you have an upset stomach **pretty often, nearly all the time?**" "Are you ever troubled with headaches or pains in the head: **often, sometimes?**" "Do you ever have trouble in getting to sleep or staying asleep: **often, sometimes?**" "Are you ever troubled by your hands feeling damp: **often, sometimes?**" "Do your hands ever tremble enough to bother you: **often, sometimes?**" "Have you ever been bothered by your heart beating hard: **often, sometimes?**" "Have you ever been bothered by cold sweats: **often, sometimes?**" "Have you ever had spells of dizziness: **a few times or more than a few times?**" "Have you ever had any fainting spells: **a few times or more than a few times?**" "Are you ever bothered by nervousness (irritable, fidgety, tense): **often, sometimes?**" "I feel weak all over much of the time, **yes.**" "I have periods of such great restlessness that I cannot sit long in a chair, **yes.**" "I am bothered by acid (sour) stomach several times a week, **yes.**" "Every so often I suddenly feel hot all over, **yes.**" "There seems to be a fullness (clogging) in my head or nose much of the time, **yes.**"

Four questions relating to solid and liquid intake were asked: "Would you say you smoke (drink more coffee; drink more liquor, wine, or beer; eat) more than is good for you?"

Disagreement with the statement "My memory seems to be all right," together with the respondent's age and the interviewer's description of behavior and speech, gave the psychiatric judges some clues to organic brain damage. Diagnoses taken from agency records, however, constituted another source of this classification.

Some symptoms were interfering directly with the individual's role functioning, for example, on his job. These were, "I have had periods of days, weeks, or months when I couldn't take care of things because I couldn't get going, **yes.**" "I get pains in my back that interfere with my work, **yes.**" "I often have a hard time making up my mind about things I should do, **yes.**"

Other items were concerned with the social attitudes and interpersonal relations of the respondent. Some of these items were grouped in tentative categories because of surface similarity (though only a few categories were tested for unidimensionality).

These characteristics were given names that suggest clinical entities but include the whole range of the trait in question. For instance, *suspiciousness* included mild items ("Always be on guard with people") and items extremely paranoid in content ("I often worry about personal enemies"). The *extremeness* of each item, and the *number* of items of a particular type both contributed to the psychiatrists' eventual decision to classify a case as "suspicious."

The items are listed in Table 2-1 according to these tentative groupings. The proportion of the 1660 respondents giving the pathognomonic answer (in bold type) is included. The *Symptom Scores* (Immaturity, Rigidity, Suspiciousness, Withdrawal, Frustration-Depression, Neurasthenia, and Gastrointestinal Symptoms) are discussed in more detail in Chapter 15. The individual items are shown here so that the reader can form a better idea of the raw data on which the Mental Health Ratings and other classifications were based.

Often the meaning of these items varied with the age, sex, background, and other symptoms reported by the respondent. Some items were appro-

44

## Table 2-1
### Proportions of Respondents Giving Pathognomonic Responses to Symptom Questions, According to Symptom Scores

**Immaturity** | **Per Cent of Cases[a]**
---|---:
"I can't really enjoy myself when I am alone." **Agree** | 18.7
"I rarely make a mistake." **Yes** | 10.8
"Most of the time I don't care what others think of me." **Yes** | 42.7
"When I want something very much, I want it right away." **Yes** | 28.5
"I suppose I am a gambler at heart." **Yes** | 22.7
"As a rule, it's much better to do things on the spur of the moment than to think and plan ahead." **Agree** | 22.2
"Feelings of grief and sorrow are suitable (o.k.) for children but not for adults." **Agree** | 5.9
"A person does better for himself by keeping away from his family (close relatives)." **Agree** | 20.5

**Rigidity** |
"Whatever you do must be done perfectly. Would you give your child such advice?" **Yes** | 32.7
"One drink is one too many. Would you give your child such advice?" **Yes** | 27.8
"Never show your feelings to others. Would you give your child such advice?" **Yes** | 25.7
"Once your mind is made up, don't let anything change it. Would you give your child such advice?" **Yes** | 29.8
"Very often, the old ways of doing things are the best ways. Would you give your child advice?" **Yes** | 31.4
"If you want to keep your health, go to sleep at the same time every night." **Agree** | 30.2

**Suspiciousness** |
"Do 'personal enemies' worry you **often**, sometimes, or never?" | 1.0
"Always be on guard with people." **Yes** | 39.2
"Do you sometimes feel people are against you without any good reason?" **Yes** | 23.2
"Behind your back people say all kinds of things about you." **Agree** | 33.6

**Withdrawal** |
"When you go out do you usually prefer to go by yourself?" **Yes** | 11.0
"Do you feel somewhat apart even among friends?" **Yes** | 18.3
"A person has moments when he feels he is a stranger to himself." **Agree** | 36.7
"To avoid arguments, do you usually keep your opinions to yourself?" **Yes** | 47.6

**Frustration-Depression** |
"Do you feel you have had your share of good luck in life?" **No** | 17.7
"In general, would you say that most of the time you are in high spirits, good spirits, low spirits, or very low spirits?" **Low** | 6.0
**Very Low** | 0.7
"On the whole, life gives you a lot of pleasure." **Disagree** | 8.7
"Children give their parents more trouble than pleasure." **Agree** | 12.6
"You sometimes can't help wondering whether anything is worthwhile anymore." **Agree** | 26.7
"Nothing ever turns out for me the way I want it to." **Agree** | 11.3

| Neurasthenia (Immobilization) | Per Cent of Cases[a] |
|---|---|
| "I feel weak all over much of the time." **Yes** | 9.1 |
| "I have had periods of days, weeks, or months when I couldn't get going." **Yes** | 16.4 |
| "I often have a hard time making up my mind about things I should do." **Yes** | 22.8 |
| **Gastrointestinal Symptoms** | |
| "Now about such things as appetite, would you say your appetite is poor, fair, good, or too good?" **Poor** | 4.7 |
| "How often are you bothered by having an upset stomach? Would you say that you have an upset stomach: not very often, pretty often, nearly all the time?" **Nearly all the time** | 1.8 |
| "I am bothered by acid (sour) stomach several times a week." **Yes** | 10.1 |
| Total Number of Cases (N=100 per cent)    1660 | |

[a] Percentages do not total 100 per cent because of multiple answers.

priate to more than one category. Although the psychiatrists were exposed to the total "scores" each individual achieved on the several dimensions, they generally ignored these psychometric "scores" and relied on their cumulative impression of presenting problems and complaints, much as they would in their own clinical practice. The total impact of these symptoms can be derived only from a perusal of the Psychiatric Summary, which is reproduced in Volume I.

In all, there were 92 questions that might be considered current symptoms of impairment, disordered behavior, disrupted interpersonal relations, and internal malaise, tension, or conflict. Another 28 items dealt with signs of disturbance in childhood, and these are discussed in Appendix C.

## Problems of Estimation, Validity, and Reliability

The sources of these items, the construction of new items, and the roles played by various staff members[1] are elaborated in Volume I. The validation of most items by comparison of the responses of 139 hospitalized psychiatric patients and a group of 72 psychiatrically screened "wells" (also described in Volume I) insured that the questionnaire was sound material on which to base a psychiatric judgment.

Certainly we can make no claim that the questionnaire and the rating system described in Chapter 3 enabled us to estimate mental disturbance with complete accuracy in the community population. Even with face-to-face psychiatric interviews we could not make such a claim. There is published statistical evidence that psychiatrists, under the best of circumstances, and operating in the manner to which they are most accustomed, will not agree completely on the severity, diagnosis, etiology, or prognosis of a particular series of cases. This is no singular criticism, for it applies in many ways to all of medicine and the sciences. All judgments are made within certain limits of error, and sometimes agreement does not differ widely from pure chance.

A note of consolation can be sounded in this dirge because we can often tell in what areas or with what types of cases our estimates are poor. We think that psychopaths probably were not picked up by the questionnaire. Early alcoholics and drug addicts probably do not show up in our survey. People exhibiting some types of sociopathic behavior, such as criminals, or destructively "successful" individuals could not be identified with the types of questions we asked; many would appear as healthy and successful people. People of higher education were doubtless able to throw up a better defense against the interviewer's probing if they wanted to. The training of some of the professionals interviewed, such as doctors, teachers, and social workers, probably equipped them to recognize the more serious symptoms, and hence to deny having them.

Despite these shortcomings, among others, the survey method combined with psychiatric judgments has yielded valuable information.[2] There is some small comfort in the fact that our estimates of mental disorder, though inaccurate, are almost bound to be understatements. Intensive case studies generally bring to light more symptomatology. Additional data often *increase* the degree of impairment estimated, but seldom have mitigating effects.

The burden of symptoms carried by this sample of an American metropolis is certainly cause for alarm. On the other hand, we have found that the large majority of Midtowners are functioning, on the job, in their marriage, as parents, citizens, and friends. They do this *despite* the staggering burden of their symptoms, their complaints, their malaise and tension. If we have found one thing, it is that most people can carry on, even with a tremendous load of symptomatology.

Volume I, Chapter 3 deals in some detail with the orientation of the respondents. The introductory letters, the identification of the study as a Cornell Medical College Community Health Survey, the introductory format similar to the familiar medical history and the assurances of strict confidence were part of a carefully designed plan. The arrangement of the questionnaire with innocuous questions at first, and deeply personal questions only later, the dispersal of repetitive items to avoid boredom and "response set" (automatic admission to or denial of *all* symptoms), was a painstaking task.

Even though direct tests of validity and reliability were not made, other than on the symptom items, there is much evidence of the high quality of the data elicited. Most important is the cooperation that people gave to the study. Less than one per cent broke off the interview, even though these averaged 2 hours in duration. Only 3.5 per cent (compared to 8 per cent in the U.S. Census of 1950 in Midtown) refused to give their family income. Only 0.6 per cent refused to identify their religious faith (campared with 8 per cent) of the U.S. Census national sample). In general, a higher proportion of respondents were rated "relaxed" and "having high interest" at the end of the interview than at the beginning, indicating an increase in rapport as the interview progressed. Only 4 per cent "lacked interest" at the end of the visit.

## Summary

The study involved three operations: the Sociography Operation, describing the community; the Treatment Census, a collation of all records of psychiatric treatment of Midtowners; and the central operation, the Home Interview Survey. The Home Interview Survey, averaging two hours, was conducted with a random sample of 1660 adults aged twenty to fifty-nine. It was administered by professional interviewers using a 65-page questionnaire. The questionnaire contained 120 symptoms of mental disturbance and malfunctioning, and about 200 sociocultural background characteristics and explanatory environmental variables. A total of 148 environmental stress items were examined in relation to Mental Health Ratings. The ratings were assigned to each individual by two psychiatrists working separately. They also assigned a quasi-diagnostic Probable Gross Type and various Symptom Groups to each individual.

The rationale for judging mental health, and the methods used are described in Chapter 3.

## Notes

1. These were in particular Drs. Srole and Weider as the questionnaire committee, Drs. Rennie and Kirkpatrick in evaluating the importance of items suggested for inclusion, and Drs. Srole and Langner in the precoding and preparation of the tenth and final draft of the instrument.

2. A study that employed, among other methods, the community survey and psychiatric ratings was conducted by Dr. Alexander H. Leighton and his associates in

the Maritime Provinces of Canada. A careful reading of the "Stirling County" volumes and comparison with the methods described in the Midtown series is recommended for those planning to do similar research. The volumes are: Alexander H. Leighton, *My Name Is Legion*, Foundations for a Theory of Man in Relation to Culture. Volume I, Stirling County Study in Psychiatric Disorder and Sociocultural Environment. Basic Books, New York, 1959. Charles C. Hughes, Marc-Adelard Tremblay, Robert N. Rapoport, and Alexander H. Leighton, *People of Cove and Woodlot*, Communities from the Viewpoint of Social Psychiatry, Volume II, Stirling County Study. Basic Books, New York, 1960. Dorothea C. Leighton, John S. Harding, David B. Macklin, Allister M. Macmillan, and Alexander H. Leighton, *The Character of Danger: Psychiatric Symptoms in Selected Communities*. Basic Books, New York, in press.

# CHAPTER 3

# The Mental Health Ratings

STANLEY T. MICHAEL

In broadest outline the goals of this study were the estimate of the mental health of a community population, most of whom had never been psychiatric patients, and the study of the relatedness of mental health to a variety of demographic indices and to personal and social experience. Since mental health was the central theme, considerable effort was spent to achieve reasonable reliability and objectivity in the estimate of the mental health of each respondent. Information for the Mental Health Rating was obtained through a questionnaire-guided interview. The rationale for the questionnaire, its development and construction are described in Volume I, Chapters 3 and 4. The contents of the questionnaire are substantially enumerated in Chapter 2 of this volume and in Appendix F of Volume I. A series of items derived from previously developed questionnaires designed for preliminary screening of mental disorder, such as the Cornell Medical Index, the Army Neuro-Psychiatric Screening Adjunct, and the Minnesota Multiphasic Personality Inventory were selected as the "symptom core" of our questionnaire. Questions and probes used by psychiatrists in psychiatric examinations of clinical patients were also incorporated. Thus a broad cross section of information was assembled from which conclusions might be reached on the presence or absence of psychiatrically significant symptoms.

A number of questions dealt with such facts as age, sex, marital status, education, employment, income, religion, hospitalizations for somatic or mental illnesses, contacts with social agencies, and activities related to recreation and pleasure. Other items probed for perceptions and attitudes of the respondents. We could not be sure that the answers to the questions given by the respondents were always fact. Distortion of perception, projection, denial of experience, and lapse of memory contributed to the data submitted to the psychiatrist for the rating of mental health (this is more fully elaborated in Chapter 6). The rating psychiatrists constantly had to be aware of possible misrepresentations introduced by the mental mechanisms of the respondents and, when indicated, consider them in the evaluation of the Mental Health Rating.

The psychiatrists made essentially four psychiatric judgments on each respondent. Two described an over-all rating of mental health on a graded continuum from health to illness. A third classified the respondent's personality and his symptoms within a clinical framework of modified diagnostic concepts, and a fourth estimated some of the respondent's symptoms. It must be stressed here that these respondents were not clinical cases. Rather, we were dealing with an average non-patient population. It was necessary for us to maintain continuous awareness of a concept of "normal" mental health on the one hand and clinical psychopathology on the other. We faced this problem by acquainting ourselves with the various orientations about normal mental health and were particularly guided by the definitions provided by Rennie (see Chapter 4 and Appendix F of Volume I).

## Gradient Ratings of Mental and Social Functioning

The psychiatric ratings were not made directly from the questionnaire form. Rather, the data from the questionnaire were transferred to a Psychiatrist's Summary Form composed of two parts: Part I contained all data that could be safely conveyed to the psychiatrists without revealing the respondent's sociocultural functioning. Thus socioeconomic status, parental socioeconomic status, religion, parental religion, ethnic background, early childhood experience, and other items of social functioning were excluded from Part I. Responses in Section I related mostly to psychiatric symptoms and mental and emotional attitudes to society and health. Age and marital status were also revealed in this section. Although both age and marital status convey social functioning (especially in the negative aspects of marital status such as separation, divorce, or widowhood), these items were considered important, indeed essential, for the interpretation of the various psychiatric symptoms and attitudes. An independent rating was made on the "symptomatic" information contained in Part I of the Summary. This rating was called Mental Health Rating I

(MHR I). A second rating, Mental Health Rating II (MHR II), was formulated after review and study of that part of the respondent's Summary (Part II) that contained information pertaining to his or her social functioning. In a number of cases, additional objective information was obtained from social service files. Included here were records of hospitalization, court appearance, social service assistance, or application to welfare agencies.

MHR II differed from MHR I in approximately 25 per cent of the respondents. In 5 per cent, the second Mental Health Rating was better, in 20 per cent, worse. These two Mental Health Ratings consisted of graded estimates of severity of the psychiatric symptoms and of their effect on life functioning of the respondents.

Briefly reviewed, the seven steps in the Mental Health Rating scale were as follows:

0—No evidence of symptom formation (symptom free)
1—Mild symptom formation but functioning adequately
2—Moderate symptom formation with no apparent interference in life adjustment
3—Moderate symptom formation with some interference in life adjustment
4—Serious symptom formation, yet functioning with *some* difficulty
5—Serious symptom formation, yet functioning with *great* difficulty
6—Seriously incapacitated, unable to function.[1]

Two psychiatrists graded each respondent on this seven-point scale. The independent ratings of each psychiatrist were then combined or adjudicated and "collapsed" to form four gradations of mental health. The original ratings and the derivation of the final categories utilized in calculation of our mental health statistic, the ridit, are presented in Table 3-1.

The separation of the interview information into two independent divisions, each of which was given an independent Mental Health Rating, made it possible to test the items of social functioning and cultural experiences contained in the second part against a Mental Health Rating (MHR I) formulated independently of the items of social functioning (see Chapter 6).

It is important to stress here that these two Mental Health Ratings were derived not only from evaluation of the pathognomonic responses

## Table 3-1
### Key to Mental Health Categories

| Independent[a] Ordinal Ratings | Definitions | Combined[a] Ordinal Ratings | Final Category |
|---|---|---|---|
| 0 | No evidence of symptom formation (symptom free) | 0<br>1 | Well |
| 1 | Mild symptom formation but functioning adequately | 2<br>3 | Mild |
| 2 | Moderate symptom formation with no apparent interference in life adjustment | 4<br>5 | Moderate |
| 3 | Moderate symptom formation with some interference in life adjustment | 6 ⎫<br>7 ⎬ Marked | |
| 4 | Serious symptom formation, yet functioning with some difficulty | 8 ⎫<br>9 ⎬ Severe | Impaired |
| 5 | Serious symptom formation, and functioning with great difficulty | 10 ⎫ Nearly<br>11 ⎱ Incapacitated<br>⎰ or | |
| 6 | Seriously incapacitated, unable to function | 12 ⎭ Incapacitated | |

[a] Since the two raters independently assigned ordinal ratings from 0 to 6 to each respondent, the two independent ratings for each respondent were numerically joined to form combined ordinal values in a 0 to 12 range. One-step differences between the raters account for the odd numbered values in the combined ratings column. For example, if one judge rated a person 1 (Mild) and the other rated him 2 (Moderate), he received a combined rating of 3 (Mild). The combined rating therefore gave each individual the "benefit of the doubt" by placing cases of disagreement in the *healthier* category.

agreed to by the respondent but also from those pathognomonic questions that the respondent answered negatively either because they did not apply or because the respondent chose to deny their validity. The questionnaire instrument was a screening test for psychopathology. The passing of this test without revelation of psychopathology was also evidence to be evaluated in the Mental Health Rating.

No less important for the rating were the unsolicited, voluntary comments by the respondents. Some of these revealed additional psychopathology, others supplied evidence of positive zest for living.

At its original conception, the Midtown investigation was designed with the primary purpose of uncovering psychopathology in a predominantly nonpatient community population; the questionnaire was to probe for symptoms of psychopathology. No specific provision was made for the examination of personality assets, components of ego strength, moral and ethical principles, endurance of frustration, or persistence of effort and achievement. In part, the raters inferred such characteristics only secondarily from the absence of psychopathology. The deduction was made that the respondent who was able to sustain the stresses of normal living, maintain employment, and meet social and family obligations was possessed of reasonable strength of personality. The informal part of the questionnaire, the comments and asides of the respondents, supplied additional information to this point. Here the respondents talked about the means with which they met the impact of misfortune, how they coped with the pains of their symptoms (somatic and psychological), or how they assumed exceptionally constructive attitudes to social problems. These affirmations of the positive in life were interpreted by the psychiatrist as evidence of a compensatory drive even in the presence of psychopathology, and the Mental Health Rating was upgraded.

This upgrading undoubtedly influenced the calculations relating Mental Health Ratings to scores derived from questionnaire items. A linear correlation between the Mental Health Ratings (or their derivative, the ridits) and numbers of experience factors is not a necessary expectation. Discrepancies will be prevalent particularly in ratings derived substantially from free style comments and from such ancillary material as hospital, court, or social service records. Ratings at the morbid end of the scale were often based on revealing comments by the respondent. Certain diagnostic groupings, particularly the psychotic and organic types, were frequently based on clinic or hospital records. Personality pattern deviations were occasionally derived from court records or records of social agencies. In instances where scores derived from structured items of the questionnaire do not follow the arithmetically derived "rules," the extraneous information must be taken into consideration as a possible explanation of the discrepancies.

## Diagnostic and Symptomatic Ratings

The two gradient Mental Health Ratings provided an estimate of psychopathology—its presence or absence, its severity, and the degree of emotional distress or even interference in life adjustment. To the psychiatrist accustomed to a clinical diagnosis, a gradient mental health rating supplies only part of the information. In applied psychiatry, the clinical diagnosis is a primary consideration. It supplies important information bearing on treatment and prognosis. An unequivocal diagnosis, not always easily established, is founded on a clinical examination which by customary practice requires face-to-face confrontation, physical examination, and frequently laboratory procedures. The psychiatrists did not see the respondent and could not therefore subject him to the usual clinical examination to establish a diagnosis. It would even be doubtful practice to make a diagnosis on most of our "normal" respondents. But it was still felt desirable that the total configuration of the personality be evaluated in familiar concepts and designations usually related to the common clinical diagnoses. The rating psychiatrist was therefore directed to check from a list of a limited number of diagnostic groupings (see Tables 15-1 and 15-2) his estimate of the prevailing personality structure and the character of the symptoms in terms of a classical diagnostic framework. These descriptions were intended to convey not a diagnosis in the usual clinical meaning but rather the quality of the symptoms and of the personality setting in which the symptoms occurred. A precise diagnosis was not being made; therefore the check list was limited to broad general diagnostic groupings. To indicate the tentative nature of this judgment, the ratings were described as probable and further modified by the suffix *type* thus: Probable Neurotic Type. This judgment was intended to indicate only a gross classification and hence will be referred to as the Gross Diagnostic Types.

## Gross Diagnostic Types

Clinical experience of the psychiatric rater determined whether the information gained from the questionnaire was suggestive in the broadest interpretative sense of the clinical constellation implied in the diagnostic heading. The basis for assigning these types is given below.

### A.   PROBABLE ORGANIC TYPE

The evidence indicated that the disorder was probably caused by, or associated with, anatomical lesions of the brain. The respondents, who were frequently in our advanced age groups, suggested evidence of arteriosclerosis by a statement that a kidney or heart disease due to arteriosclerosis was present. If, in addition, this respondent agreed to the question that his "memory was not all right," and if there was further evidence either from the respondent's own statements or from observations by the interviewer that there was impairment of orientation, intellectual functioning and judgment, or lability of affect, the respondent was rated in this group. A history of childhood encephalitis, cerebral palsy, or other brain disease, associated with responses or symptoms that could be considered sequelae of the brain disease, also classified the respondent in this group. The remarkable clarity with which these symptoms were perceived from the questionnaire is attested by the fact that the two independent raters agreed in classification of these respondents with a probability exceeding 40 times chance.

## B.  PROBABLE PSYCHOTIC TYPE

With a few exceptions, psychotic responses were not easily perceived from answers to questions. Thus psychotic ideation could be interpreted from such responses as "I feel people are against me." "I often worry about personal enemies." "There are periods of days, weeks, months when I couldn't get going." However, any one of these responses alone was not sufficient to determine a psychotic type reaction. Rather, the total constellation of answers and, most frequently in this category, the quality of the free style statements of the respondent revealed the psychotic dissociation. The description of the respondent by the interviewer, the history given by the respondent of a previous hospitalization for a psychiatric disorder, a court record or record of hospitalization with established diagnosis, or a record of contact with a social agency with an objective report were likely to classify a respondent in this group.

## C.  PROBABLE NEUROTIC TYPE

Respondents whose anxiety was ascertained from agreement with statements concerning "nervousness" were classified in this category. These included agreement to "Such restlessness he can't sit long in a chair," that the respondent is "the worrying type," that "Personal worries get him down physically." In addition, such a respondent might agree to questions relating to psychophysiological reactions concerning "upset stomach," "trouble with sleep," "hands feel damp," "hands tremble often," and so on. The informal remarks of the respondents frequently added information about depression, conversion, displacement, or other neurotic reactions.

## D.  PROBABLE PSYCHOSOMATIC TYPE

In this category were classified patients who, by direct answers to questions concerning physical ailments, enumerated psychophysiological disorders such as cardiac neurosis, gastric neurosis, asthma, hay fever, peptic ulcer, hypertension, colitis, arthritis, neurotic "bladder disease," paroxysmal tachycardia, and other somatic reactions commonly associated with a psychogenic component. Also classified under this subheading were respondents whose main symptoms were of a psychophysiological type as ascertained from questions relating to "upset stomach," "heart beats hard," "hands feel damp," "feeling hot all over."

### E. PROBABLE TRANSIENT-SITUATIONAL PERSONALITY REACTION TYPE

This classification was used in instances of a more or less transient reaction to acute, severe situational stress in which an individual used psychiatric symptoms as immediate means of adjusting to an overwhelming emotional impact from his environment. An insignificant number of respondents was classified in this group and in later statistical elaborations this group was eliminated by adjudication into other groups, mainly the Probable Neurotic Type.

### F. PROBABLE PERSONALITY TRAIT TYPE

Here were classified respondents who seemed to indicate personality defects or pathological trends in their personality structure. These respondents were classified in part from their answers to questions relating to immaturity and rigidity such as: "One should do everything perfectly," "Never change your mind," "When I want something very much I want it right away." Evidence for this category was frequently derived from spontaneous statements, from observations by the interviewers, from court records and records of other social agencies.

This category lacked clear definition and consequently the respondents classified here cover a wide range of psychopathology incongruous in its mental mechanisms, etiology, or social significance. Many were obvious sociopaths, or persons who had difficulty in social adjustment because of personality deviations. More numerous were respondents with mild, vague symptoms that did not definitely fit any of the other diagnostic categories. These symptoms might be best described as mild character changes, or personality pattern deviations. As a consequence of the multiple characterization of this group, some of its members fall into categories of social and psychiatric impairment, while others are relatively free of morbid implication.

### G. ADJUDICATION OF DIFFERENCES IN RATINGS OF THE TWO PSYCHIATRISTS

Both rating psychiatrists did not always agree on the diagnostic category into which the respondent was classified. To resolve the differences in the most objective manner, it was decided that in all cases where one psychiatrist rated the respondent as organic or psychotic, this rating would prevail. Fortunately, the raters agreed with the greatest reliability in these two groups. The respondents in the Transient-Situational Personality Reaction Type, few in number, were adjudicated with the result that all but one were classified in the Probable Neurotic group. Those respondents classified Probable Neurotic Type by one rater and Probable Psychosomatic Type by the other were placed in a new group labeled Probable Neurotic Type with Prominent Psychosomatic Symptoms. Respondents labeled Probable Neurotic Type by one psychiatrist and Probable Personality Trait Type by the other were placed in a new group labeled Probable Neurotic Type with a Prominent Personality Trait Disorder.

## Symptom Groups

It is generally conceded that the average person has "neurotic symptoms" but these personality characteristics cannot be considered equivalent to symptoms found in a well-developed clinical case. Nevertheless, some description of these "normal neurotic symptoms" was desirable and a limited check list of symptoms and symptom complexes was provided for the psychiatrist who was expected to check those he thought applicable to the respondent (see Table 15-2). Unlike the probable diagnostic types (where each respondent was classified in one category only), in the symptom groups the psychiatrist was free to characterize the respondent by as many symptom descriptions as would fulfill his interpretation of the case record. It must be emphasized again that the respondents were not clinical patients and were not seen by the psychiatrist in a clinical setting. The symptoms checked were only inferred from certain responses in the questionnaire, and their meaning is in most instances quite different from that of the classical symptoms seen on clinical examination. This will be evident from the descriptions.

The list of symptoms was not intended to be a complete enumeration of all psychopathology. Rather, it is an array of descriptions and generalizations that could feasibly be extracted from the information contained in the questionnaire. It was formulated in part on interests of the several investigators involved in the study, and on a desire to check psychiatric ratings against scores derived from selected groups of questions. Suitability for statistical elaboration also imposed limitations on the selection.

In addition, there was initial doubt that the symptom ratings would yield useful information. As a consequence, the group of symptoms has little internal consistency; it spans several conceptual levels. Despite these shortcomings, the symptom ratings proved to be meaningfully associated with a number of findings. They are, therefore, presented here with notice of their limited application. The classification of the respondents into the various symptom groups was based on the broadest suggestions and interpretations from the questionnaire material with exceptions as indicated below.

### A. EPILEPTIC

This symptom was checked only if the respondent supplied this diagnosis on direct questioning, or if it was available from other objective records.

### B. INTELLECTUALLY RETARDED

This designation was most often derived from information obtained from records of social agencies. It was seldom possible to make this rating from the evidence of the questionnaire itself, except in instances when the interviewer indicated dull intelligence, or the school records, employment, or therapeutic measures supplied evidence of difficulty in this area.

### C. STRUCTURAL BRAIN DISEASE AND/OR SENILITY

This category was more or less identical with the diagnostic group Probable Organic Type, and its derivation was similar.

### D. ALCOHOLIC-PROBABLE ALCOHOLIC

This category was most often determined from the interviewer's description of the respondent, his home, his state of inebriation at an inappropriate time of the day, and on the respondent's own admission.

### E. SEXUAL DEVIANT

This category was checked only if the circumstances described by the interviewer were clearly indicative of a homosexual relationship, or if the respondent volunteered the information.

### F.   BEHAVIORAL PROBLEM-DYSSOCIAL

This category was checked usually on the basis of a record of contact with a social agency in which either the diagnosis was made on examination by the agency or behavior was described indicating conflict with usual social and moral codes.

### G.   MIXED ANXIETY

This category was checked by the rating psychiatrist in 70.8 per cent of the respondents. Because of the large number of respondents who were given this symptom, it proved to be of little significance in discriminating between demographic groups. A surprisingly large number of respondents agreed with the questions intended to elicit "nervousness," "worry," and "restlessness." In groping for an interpretation of the high frequency of responses indicating anxiety, an interpretation was reached consistent with the Freudian theory that anxiety is the basis of most symptoms. Consequently, the symptom "mixed anxiety" was also checked on that theoretical basis. With the benefit of hindsight, it is now recognized that it would have been to greater advantage had we defined a more rigid interpretation of anxiety and limited ourselves, for instance, only to manifest anxiety to the extent that it might have been recognized from the data. Such a definition might have proven more meaningful for correlations with other indices.

### H.   ANXIETY-FREE FLOATING

This reaction was implied if the symptoms and structure of the personality suggested the presence of diffuse anxiety not associated with definite situations or objects. It was assigned when no evidence could be found that the anxiety was evoked by, or attached to, specific psychological defense mechanisms. Anxiousness and expectation without direction or objective was the predominant emotional pattern.

### I.   ANXIETY-PHOBIAS

This symptom complex was assigned most frequently because the respondent affirmed the question: "High buildings, bridges, and tunnels make me tense, nervous." However, it was also checked if there was evidence of phobic behavior such as excessive worrying, fear of illness or dirt, or indication of other phobias. The information for this category was frequently derived from the spontaneous comments of the respondents.

## J. OBSESSIVE-COMPULSIVE TRENDS

This category was applied not only when there seemed to be good evidence of the classical reaction of anxiety with persistence of unwanted ideas or of repetitive compelling impulses to perform stereotyped acts, but also in instances when the respondent seemed to be unduly driven to perfectionism, punctuality, efficiency, or in other manner gave evidence of subclinical tendencies in the direction of the obsessive-compulsive syndrome. In interpreting this category, care must be exercised in distinguishing it from the classical, clinical obsessive-compulsive neurosis. In addition to the morbid individual of the ruminative, repetitive, rigidly stereotyped description whose symptoms are impairing, our group also includes a conscientious, effective, punctual type whose personality characteristics may be advantageous in social adjustment. Unfortunately, these two types were not differentiated into separate classifications at the time of the psychiatric rating. This symptom complex was thus deprived of an additional definition that might have contributed to our interpretations.

## K. SOMATIC PREOCCUPIED-HYPOCHONDRIASIS

Under this classification were considered respondents who agreed with many of the psychophysiological questions but, in addition, seemed to append comments to their answers which clearly indicated a distorted perception of their symptoms, or an unrealistic nature of their response. Not only were those with clearly indicated hypochondriasis classified into this category, but also a large number of respondents who seemed to have actual physical symptoms and illnesses, usually of a chronic nature, which were the subject of substantial preoccupation, either as a source of secondary gain in the psychoanalytic sense, or in terms of excessive, therapeutic ministrations or search for therapy. Here also were grouped the hypochondriacal delusions of the depressed and the preoccupations with health of the paranoid personalities. Excessive involvement with health fads and exercise also assigned the respondent this rating.

## L. NEURASTHENIA

This category was included to provide a listing of a syndrome of easy fatigability, feeling of physical and mental weakness, aches, pains, complaints of inadequate organic functioning, insomnia, and a general psychic and physical ineffectiveness. The designation was not intended to be specific for any particular syndrome and its significance as a category for a variety of grouped neurotic syndromes may be best estimated from the fact that 18.3 per cent of the respondents were given this designation. Key statements leading to this classification were: "I feel weak all over." "I have had periods of days, weeks, or months when I couldn't get going." "Pains in my back interfere with my work." When coupled with symptoms as enumerated above, they were evidence for inclusion in this category.

### M.   PASSIVE-DEPENDENT PERSONALITY

This category was checked frequently by the rating psychiatrists who found 27.2 per cent of the respondents fitting the description. Here again, the general constellation of the personality rather than individual responses ("I can't enjoy myself when alone") and information such as overconcern about marriage or dependence on a social agency were indications for inclusion. Evidence for this category was also derived from interviewers' notes depicting dependency relationships to members of the family or other significant individuals. Inability to make decisions, marked inclination to lean on others for advice, guidance, and support, a tendency to submit to the leadership of others as a dependent child to a supporting parent, or a plea of helplessness were all considered indications of passivity and dependency. Application for aid to social agencies and records of these agencies also supplied evidence for this classification.

### N.   DEPRESSION

This category was designated by the rating psychiatrists in 23.6 per cent of the respondents. Obviously it is not synonymous with the classical syndrome of depression seen in the manic-depressive psychosis or even in the reactive depression. Rather, it must be considered as a tendency of the respondent to assume a pessimistic viewpoint toward life situations, health problems, and interpersonal relationships. Persons who agreed with statements "I have had periods of days, weeks or months when I couldn't get going," "Most of the time I'm in low spirits, or very low spirits," "Nothing ever turns out for me the way I want it to," "You sometimes can't help wondering whether anything is worthwhile anymore," or who disagreed with the statement "On the whole, life gives you a lot of pleasure," or "I feel I have had my share of good luck in life," and respondents whom the interviewer classified as being noticeably depressed were included in this group. Answers to these questions obviously do not indicate the presence of a definite clinical syndrome of depression with profound motor retardation, stupor, suicidal ruminations, intractable insomnia, severe guilt feelings, somatic delusions, agitation, and the somatic symptoms that accompany the cyclic or endogenous depressions. Although subclinical forms of such psychotic depressions were found among the respondents and are included in this category, they form a small minority of this group.

## O.  RIGID PERSONALITY

Here were classified respondents who indicated excessive concern with adherence to standards of conscience or conformity or who were over-inhibited, overconscientious, and lacked a normal capacity for flexibility. Also included were persons intolerant of others, critical, and unbending. They agreed to such statements as "Whatever you do must be done perfectly," "One drink is one too many," "Never show your feelings to others," "Once your mind is made up, don't let anything change it," "To avoid arguments, I usually keep my opinions to myself," and others indicating unacceptance of emotional mobility.

## P.  SCHIZOID PERSONALITY-WITHDRAWN

Inherent traits in such personalities were (1) avoidance of close relationships with others. "When I go out I usually prefer to go by myself," "I feel somewhat apart even among friends," "Always be on guard with people," "Never show your feelings to others," "A person has moments when he feels he is a stranger to himself," "No one really understands me," "A person does better for himself by keeping away from his family"; (2) inability to express directly hostility or aggressive feelings; and (3) autistic thinking. Coldness, aloofness, emotional detachment, fearfulness, avoidance of competition, daydreams, shyness, sensitivity, and lack of sociability communicated through the questionnaire instrument and the responses led to the checking of 15.2 per cent of the respondents in this category.

## Q.  AGGRESSIVE PERSONALITY

Persons who showed consistent dominance over others were classified here. This dominance manifested itself by positive leadership or self-starting energies in the direction of creative work, or by irritability, temper tantrums, or hostile, acquisitive impulsiveness aimed at controlling or affecting other individuals.

### R.   SUSPICIOUS, HOSTILE PERSONALITY

In this category were classified respondents who exhibited overt sensitivity and touchiness in interpersonal relationships and a conspicuous tendency to utilize hostile projective mechanisms (suspiciousness, envy, extreme jealousy, and stubbornness). Affirmative answers to such questions as "hated school," "Always be on guard with people," "I sometimes feel people are against me without any good reason," "Behind your back people say all kinds of things about you," "No one really understands me," "I often worry about personal enemies" were signposts for inclusion. Of the total respondents, 28.4 per cent were checked into this group, and obviously not all these respondents had clinical paranoia. Rather, they must be viewed as tending to projection mechanisms and distrustfulness of social situations at a subclinical level.

### S.   SCHIZOPHRENIC

Respondents classified in this group were essentially similar to those of the Schizoid Personality-Withdrawn, but in addition to the schizoid pattern there was definite evidence of dissociation, affective and behavioral disturbance, emotional disharmony, unpredictability, regression, and unrealistic perception of the environment. The designations in this category were frequently based on spontaneous comments of the respondents usually of a bizarre nature, on definite knowledge of previous hospitalization for mental disorder, or on a record of a social agency or mental hospital.

### T.   CYCLOID-AFFECTIVE PSYCHOSIS

Only 0.3 per cent of the respondents were classified in this group, contrasting rather markedly with the 23.6 per cent respondents in the Depression category above, and thus supplementing it by an indication of probable psychotic intensity of the symptom. The designation into the category Cycloid-Affective Psychosis was usually based on a history of recurring severe mood swings with a tendency to remission and recurrence. Inclusion in this category was usually indicated by the respondent who supplied the diagnosis of manic-depressive psychosis or from hospital records.

Here were classified respondents who either were free of symptoms or had insignificant symptoms that did not fit into the limited number of designations supplied to the rating psychiatrists.

## Resolution of Symptom Group Ratings

As with the probable diagnostic types, the two psychiatrists did not always check the same symptoms on each respondent. On the rationale that the difference between the two psychiatrists was not due to the absence of symptoms but rather to the probability that the rater perceived these symptoms, but interpreted the same symptoms under a different symptom complex in the checklist, it was decided that each respondent would be credited with all symptoms checked by both psychiatrists, by simply adding the symptoms from both checklists. In this manner the judgments of both psychiatrists were preserved.

## Severity of Symptoms

The Gross Diagnostic Types and Symptom Complexes were checked on every respondent who was not rated "Mental Health Well—Symptom Free." All respondents who were given a gradient Mental Health Rating above "Symptom Free" in the two functional Mental Health Ratings were also credited with symptoms and one Probable Diagnostic Type. However, the symptoms themselves were not rated for severity, although they were checked only if they seemed significant and contributory to the Mental Health Rating. Consequently it is not possible to unravel from the checklist alone whether a symptom such as depression was mild or severe without referring to the functional Mental Health Rating in the same respondent. Even then the gradient Mental Health Rating indicated the degree of impact, the summary effect of all symptoms combined, and could not be referred to any one individual symptom. Thus, for instance, when the symptom "depression" was checked, it could be interpreted as indicating a degree of morbidity ranging from a mild pessimistic attitude toward life to full psychotic depression.

## Summary

We have presented in this chapter the methods and standards utilized by the two rating psychiatrists in the formulation of four psychiatric judgments made on each individual respondent:

1. Mental Health Rating I. This rating consisted of seven degrees of mental health functioning based on the presence and severity of symptoms alone, without the knowledge of the sociocultural background of the respondent.

2. Mental Health Rating II. This estimate of mental health was similar to the foregoing, but it was formulated after exposure to additional information on the respondent's social functioning and, where available, on evidence from records of such welfare institutions as courts, mental hospitals, and charitable agencies.

3. A Gross Diagnostic Type. This was an estimate of the prevailing personality structure and character of symptoms in terms of a summary diagnostic category.

4. Symptom Groups. This was an enumeration from a check list of limited symptoms and symptom groups of the respondent's principal psychopathology.

In the description of these judgments, we have pointed out the definitions and limitations that must be observed in the interpretation of those ratings. We particularly call attention to the fact that we were dealing not with clinical cases but rather with an essentially nonpatient population. Our judgments were based on a questionnaire interview, not on a clinical psychiatric examination. In explaining our procedure we conveyed the difficulties and complexities we encountered in the formulation of our rating judgments and the degree of objectivity we endeavored to achieve in a matter as controversial as the estimation of mental health.

## Note

1. The standards for these Mental Health Ratings and their derivation is described in detail in Appendix F, Volume I. This Appendix also contains examples of modified case records to illustrate the rating procedure.

# The Community
# Setting and Initial
# Demographic Findings

T H O M A S  S .  L A N G N E R

A separate sociographic operation,[1] mentioned before, was under-taken early in the project's history, in order to gather materials that would describe the community and its people. Historical data, newspaper clip-pings, and comments about Manhattan in novels and autobiographies were collected. These data, together with some field interviews and observations and the demographic statistics derived from the U.S. Census and our own Home Interview Survey, comprise what we know of Mid-town. The first four sections of this chapter constitute a summary of Chapters 5, 6, and 7 of Volume I, to which some statistical information has been added.

## The Place

Midtown is one small part of the "New York-Northeastern New Jersey Area," the largest urban complex in the United States, consisting of 13 million people in 4000 square miles. New York City covers only 315 square miles of this land, but contains 8 million people. Midtown is a residential area adjoining the central business section of the island of Manhattan, which in turn is one borough of New York City. Midtown is virtually the residential heart of the entire urban complex.

In addition to being a place of residence, Midtown lies in the center of a vast communications network. Commuters and produce pour into it by rail, highway, air, and water. It is a cosmopolitan area, for it has contact with the whole world.

Midtown's 175,000 residents live in relatively crowded conditions. The United States averages 50 people per square mile, the New York metropolitan area 3,300, New York City proper 25,000, and Manhattan about 90,000. Residential land is land occupied only by residential buildings. Manhattan has 380,000 people per square mile of *residential* land. This is over four times the population density figure that includes all land.

Midtowners tend to live in buildings with five or more dwellings. Most common are the four- or five-story "brownstones" that are "walk-ups," and the huge elevator apartment houses, from ten to thirty stories high. Many tenement or substandard dwellings (approximately 19 per cent of Midtown's 65,000 occupied dwellings) are still in existence. They lack running water, are run down, or were inadequately constructed. As of the 1950 Census, 26 per cent of all Midtown dwellings also lacked central heating. The greatest shortage is in middle-income housing, although there is an over-all shortage of dwellings. The continuation of rent control, a wartime emergency measure, has partially alleviated one of the problems of housing in Midtown.

Many changes have taken place since 1953, when the survey was conducted. The destruction of many of the substandard dwellings and the construction of new luxury apartments, with monthly rentals of $50 to $100 per room, has driven out some of the people interviewed in 1953.

## The People

Midtown is a typical "Gold Coast and Slum" area with high population density and a heterogeneous population. It is 99 per cent white; Manhattan is 79 per cent white. In the age range studied (twenty to fifty-nine) about one-third are immigrants, one-third are in-migrants from other cities or towns in the United States, and one-third were born in New York City. The national backgrounds of the Midtowners (traced back to the country of birth of their grandparents) are varied, but principally European. In order of their contribution to total population (in per cent) were those of German or Austrian background 20.3, Irish 14.8, Italian 8.6, Russian, Polish, and Lithuanian 8.4, Czech and Slovak 7.5, English, Scotch, and Welsh 6.0, Hungarian 4.5, and Puerto Rican 1.7. Persons of other nationality backgrounds constituted 12.2; 13.6 were fourth-generation Americans (all four grandparents born in the United States) and were not traced to their families' countries of origin. Only 2.4 per cent of the national backgrounds could not be determined from the Home

Interview Survey.[2] Of course, a considerable number of the second and third generation (about 33 per cent) had parents of different nationality backgrounds. These people were asked which national background they felt they "belonged" to, which languages they spoke, and which national holidays and customs they observed. Such considerations were the final determinants of their *ethnic identification*.

In round figures, 41 per cent of the Midtowners are foreign-born immigrants, 29 per cent the children of immigrants, 16 per cent the grandchildren of immigrants, and 14 per cent are the great-grandchildren of immigrants (fourth generation or more). The immigrants are older, poorer, and more predominantly female. As the number of generations in the United States increases, the average age decreases and the average socioeconomic level increases.

Midtown immigrants, in contrast to their predecessors, are not predominantly from rural areas of Europe. About one-fourth were from large cities of more than 500,000 people, two-fifths from smaller cities, and one-third from farms or villages. However, in-migrants to New York City were predominantly from towns and villages, particularly in the fourth generation. They comprise 30 per cent of the second, 47 per cent of the third, and 72 per cent of the fourth generation. In-migrants are therefore younger, wealthier, and more acculturated than immigrants.

The rapid assimilation of the third and even the second generation has reduced the evidences of cultural homogeneity within the several nationality or "ethnic" groups. Although the Irish, Germans, Czechs, and Italians are more concentrated in some clusters of blocks, in no area is any one group a numerical majority. Ethnic restaurants, bakeries, grocery stores, recreation and athletic halls, travel agencies, and newspapers reflect the "old" cultures, but these stores and restaurants also serve all members of the community.

In our interview sample we found that about half are of Catholic, one-third of Protestant, and one-sixth of Jewish parentage. The Catholics are predominantly of lower and middle economic status; the Protestants and Jews are of middle or upper economic status.

Children under fifteen years of age comprise 28 per cent of the American "urban" population (towns of 2500 or more), but only 15 per cent of the Midtown population. The proportion of people sixty-five and over is similar to that in the United States as a whole, about 10 per cent. The fact that there are 32 per cent unmarried over the age of fourteen in Midtown (compared with 22 per cent in the urban United States) may account in part for the lack of children, coupled with the relatively low birth rate in metropolitan areas. One-fourth of Midtowners live alone, more than twice the proportion in the urban United States. This is tied to in-migration and the low marriage rate.

Forty-three per cent of the resident-employed in Midtown are women, compared with 30 per cent nationally. Over half of Midtown wives are holding full-or part-time jobs, compared with 26 per cent of white married women in the urban United States. This may be associated with, if not causally related to, the low birth rate.

Women also outnumber men 125 to 100 in Midtown, and this imbalance holds true at all age levels above eighteen. The sex ratio is equal for children under fifteen, and for those born in New York City. For immigrants and in-migrants it is 160:100 and 175:100 respectively.

The socioeconomic diversity of Midtown can be clearly seen in the great range of income, rent, education, and occupation, the four factors on which the index of socioeconomic status was based. While 3 per cent paid less than $20 rent per month, about 5 per cent paid $300 or more per month, or 15 times as much. The modal rent category was from $30 to $39 a month. Over half the sample (51.4 per cent) had rents between $20 and $49 a month. Their dwellings are, of course, under New York City rent control, for $50 per month is not an unusual rental for a single room not under rent control.

The range of education is equally striking. Six respondents had no schooling whatsoever. Although 12.8 per cent did not complete grammar school, 17.4 per cent did; another 16.9 per cent had some high school, and 22.7 per cent completed high school. Again, 11.9 per cent did not complete college, whereas 18.3 per cent graduated from college and in many cases had further professional training. There are rather similar proportions of persons at the college and grammar school level, but an over-all predominance of those with a high school education. The typical Midtowner would have completed one year of high school.

Family income clearly reflects the "Gold Coast and Slum" character of Midtown. Whereas 11.7 per cent have a family income under $50 a week, another 9.8 per cent have an income of over $300 a week (over $15,600 a year). Forty-nine per cent have incomes between $50 and $99 a week, making the modal income around $75 a week. There is a "bi-modal" income distribution indicated by a hump at $75 and a hump at $300 a week, due to a larger proportion of people with these incomes. This shows us that the middle income people earning between $100 and $300 per week are rather less populous in Midtown.[3]

By far the largest occupational category[4] in Midtown is the Middle

White Collar—owners or managers of middle-sized businesses, semi-professionals, highly-paid sales personnel, and artists employed by others (26.9 per cent). The next largest group were High White Collar people, receiving income from investments as well as salary—owners, managers, and officials of large corporations, professionals and self-employed artists (18.4 per cent). The Low White Collar group—lesser sales and clerical personnel, and small owners, managers, and officials—comprised 14.9 per cent.

The Blue Collars usually change to work clothes on the job, and their work usually involves manual labor. The High Blue Collars, skilled labor, and upper status service workers, numbered 12.6 per cent. The Middle Blue Collars, or semiskilled, totaled 11.9 per cent. The Low Blue Collars, unskilled labor and low status service personnel, constituted 15.3 per cent of the sample. It is of interest that many of the Middle White Collar people with relatively high income and skills are living in low-rent apartments. Thus the modal rents are out of keeping with the modal occupational and income levels. Many families have been living in these same dwellings for twenty or thirty years, and they cannot move because of the dearth of true middle-income apartments. The middle and upper-middle occupational group is most likely to move voluntarily from New York City to the suburbs, for they feel the housing squeeze most directly. The poor cannot afford to move, and the wealthier do not need to. Moreover, the recent (1955–1963) increase in new buildings has made for involuntary moves of large numbers of low SES people from Midtown.

The wide range of these indices of social and economic status demonstrates the extreme heterogeneity of Midtown. Adding to this variegated picture is the fact that many Midtowners are in a state of *status disequilibration;* that is, some are educated and poor, some are rich but uneducated *arrivistes.* Many pay more rent or less rent than their incomes call for. "Proper" monthly rent is estimated by the Department of Welfare as one week's pay or 20 to 25 per cent of income. However, a substantial number of Midtowners are paying up to 50 per cent of their income for rent.

The SES, religious, and ethnic subdivisions of Midtown are too numerous and complex to recount in detail, but they all spell heterogeneity. Midtown is not really a "community" in the sociological sense; rather, it is a part of a "society," with many sets of values, languages, institutions, and organizations.

The study area is probably representative of other metropolitan areas on the Eastern seaboard. It is somewhat different in composition from the other boroughs of New York, but it is very close to the characteristics of the 1.6 million white population of Manhattan (of which it represents 11 per cent). Its similarity to other immigration centers is striking. Its unmarried adults, low fertility, working wives, predominance of women, crowdedness, ethnic, religious, and socioeconomic heterogeneity attest to this.

## Community Organization

Sociologists picture societies as composed of major areas of social organization. These major areas are called "institutions," and include the family, the military, educational, economic, legal, and other institutions. These institutions are in turn made up of organizations, both formal and informal. A school is an organization within the institution of education; a court is an organization within the legal institution. Teachers and pupils, judges, lawyers, jury, plaintiffs, and defendants all act more or less in accordance with a prescribed set of rules for behavior in school or court. These rules define *roles* for the members of an organization, and thus an organization is viewed as a set of interrelated roles.

The social structure of Midtown can be briefly described in terms of some of its institutions. Such a description will consist mainly of enumerating the actual organizations, for the most part formal, that comprise the institutions. The economic structure of Midtown is essentially that of a residential area. Although it borders on the main shopping section of Manhattan, Midtowners shop largely in local stores. There are a few chain stores, and many small dress shops, pet shops, bookstores and the like, catering to the entire socioeconomic range.

Most Midtowners work in the downtown office section of Manhattan; this is not true of the medical and allied professions, who practice by and large within the area. Although Midtown and Manhattan have equal proportions of dentists, chiropractors, and morticians, Midtown has four times the proportion of practicing physicians. Offices for private practice number about 250 per 100,000 population, compared with 18 for the rest of Manhattan and 3 for the United States.

Midtown has more than twice as many hospital beds per person as Manhattan or the United States; it also constitutes a medical center serving the metropolitan region and even areas beyond.

There are many religious organizations in Midtown. More than thirty Protestant churches, nearly twenty Catholic parishes, a number of synagogues, and several Eastern Orthodox churches were counted. The congregations vary greatly in size, from under 100 to over 2000 persons. The results of the survey show, however, that only 45 per cent attend church more than three times a year. These churchgoers are predominantly of the Catholic faith. The churches and synagogues have auxiliary organizations, such as nurseries, orphanages, residence clubs, adult education programs, and centers for the handicapped, the aged, and the young. These more or less secular appendages reach into the lives of as many or perhaps more people than the strictly religious church functions.

Higher status persons seem to belong to secular clubs exclusively, while those of middle and lower status often belong to both church and lay groups. The middle-class associations are less numerous and less powerful than in most American cities; they include a Chamber of Commerce, Lion's Club, businessmen's associations, veterans' groups, political clubs, the PTA's, League of Women Voters, and a chapter of Alcoholics Anonymous.

The working class individual, if he has membership in any formal organization, is most likely to belong to a church group, a union, or an "ethnic" social club, such as the "Sokol" and "Turn Verein," where eating, drinking, singing, and athletics are the chief activities. However, only 18 per cent of the first generation and 6 per cent of the second generation report attending meetings of these ethnic organizations.

The educational structure is best viewed in terms of the public, private, and parochial systems, each of which is independent (again indicating Midtown's diversity). There are twelve public, twenty private, and ten Catholic parochial schools. The private schools are almost exclusively attended by the children of wealthy families.

The institution of government is composed of two organizations: first the municipal government, which provides police, fire, sanitation, public education, and other services; second, the voluntary Citizens' Council, which guides health, housing, and family welfare. The Midtown Welfare and Health Council, composed chiefly of resident professionals, has attempted to improve housing and health services, and often includes city officials at its meetings. The rapid construction of new middle and high income housing and the consequent decrease in the lower socioeconomic population during the last five years has posed some difficult problems in planning services.

It is impossible at this point to cover in any detail the most basic institution of all, the family. Midtown families run the gamut in size, but seldom exceed six to a household. The number of children is well below average, and the number of unmarried adults and childless couples is high. A casual visitor would be struck by the large proportion of people living alone, in rooming houses, enjoying little contact with other human beings. The Midtown family is rather typical of the American family in general, consisting of parents and children, but not usually including the grandparents. A three-generation household is, of course, more common among lower status children of immigrants, who live in the parents' home and often derive the benefit of "built-in baby sitters." Typically, however, the later generations move toward the isolated nonextended family unit of parents and children. Even the practice of having godparents, such as the Puerto-Rican *comadre* and *compadre*, loses its meaning rapidly in the metropolitan environment. More details of the Midtown family structure will be found in chapters 7 to 12.

While reviewing aspects of community organization, it might be informative to look at statistics that are usually considered indices of social *dis*organization. Compared with the other boroughs of New York City, Midtown and the borough of Manhattan have an infant mortality rate one-fourth greater. This is in spite of the much greater "accessibility" of medical services in Midtown. Midtown has higher rates for deaths due to alcoholism and nonvehicular accidents. Midtown has twice the rate of active cases of tuberculosis. Its juvenile delinquency is half again as much as in most other comparable districts of the city. Taken together, these higher rates of death and disease in Midtown indicate a surprising degree of social pathology. In view of the better medical facilities in Midtown, the higher death and disease rates may indicate inadequate use of services, in itself another index of social disorganization.

## The Emotional Climate

Midtown and its parent borough, Manhattan, have been described as a place for the ambitious, the social climbers, and not a proper place to raise children. It seems that many other commentators have viewed it as the home of the poor, a slum environment more suited to breeding delinquency and poverty than to making a new generation of Horatio Algers. *Mental Health in the Metropolis* reviewed in detail what the novelists, biographers, poets, and historians have had to say about New York City. Their views seem to run the gamut, and it can be concluded only that the city is "all things to all people." They bring to it their own hopes and fears, their own values, their own way of perceiving the world.

Small wonder, then, that some found it a fearful, threatening town, while others thought it a heavenly haven from persecution, a city of opportunity welcoming the stranger.

Whether the immigrants and in-migrants were preselected in terms of personality or of mental health we do not know. It is only logical to think that not only the mentally disturbed, dissatisfied, and dyssocial people but also the more skilled, interpersonally gifted, and emotionally integrated people tend to migrate. If selective migration has operated to produce Midtown, it has brought both the mentally disordered and the well to our shores, and taken both the disturbed and the gifted from our farms and villages.

The tensions of city life, the physical crowdedness, the emotional isolation, the striving for financial improvement, the competition, the physical threat of automobiles, the lack of sunshine, to name but a few, have been cited in the literature on urbanism as factors that would make for worse mental health in the city. Although we tend to revere the farm and the village, as they are part of our historical development, similar objections can be raised to rural life. The physical crowdedness of many farmhouses and villages, the physical isolation from other families, the struggle for economic survival, the rigid conformity often associated with a homogeneous community (although homogeneity and absence of value conflicts are often cited as advantages of rural life), the low level of education and poor medical care are typical indictments.

Only longitudinal studies will tell us what influence selective migration has on the mental health of city populations. Assuming that some migrants come to New York because of poverty, others because of persecution, and still others because of ambition or other motives, such as leaving their families, avoiding emotional contact, seeking new social or marital ties, it is impossible to estimate what effect this combination of motives for migration will have on the total prevalence of mental disorder.

We know that younger people have better mental health, on the average. If younger people tend to migrate (particularly younger women, who are the chief in-migrants to Midtown), then the mental health of the area has been improved. On the other hand, we know that older, poorer women were the chief immigrants to Midtown, and their mental health was below average. The average mental health of the area has probably been improved by the in-migrants who come chiefly from villages and towns, and are predominantly younger women of middle socioeconomic status and of third and fourth generation "Yankee" stock.

Thus, although three out of four Midtowners are migrants in some sense of the word, we have no evidence implying that their mental health is better or worse. Nor, on the other hand, have we any evidence that "city life" has injured their psyches in any manner that would not have occurred had they been exposed only to "country life."

Regardless of where they spent their childhood, and regardless of migration, all these adults seem to have been affected by their parents' physical and mental health, the frequency with which their parents quarreled, the death or divorce of their parents before age six, and other factors to be enumerated below. The socioeconomic level of their parents (their father's occupation and education) also was predictive of their current mental health. The characteristics of the family unit probably have the greatest effect on the developing personality. A home can be quarrelsome in the country or the city. Farmers can be poor or rich, similar to city dwellers. Children may migrate because they have achieved independence and courage in a happy home or because they must flee family conflict in a last effort at self-preservation.

Our task will be to show what factors in the family and community during childhood and in adult life may be connected with mental disturbance. These *stress factors* associated with mental disturbance were isolated and analyzed after the relationship of the demographic factors to mental disturbance had been established. This initial phase, reported in Volume I, came up with one overriding finding among many; namely, *socioeconomic status is more closely associated with mental disturbance than any other demographic factor*. It was therefore necessary to demonstrate that the stress factors operated independently of socioeconomic status. Once this had been done, an attempt was made to explain the poorer mental health of the low status group in terms of what we know about their personality structure and their modes of adapting to life stress.

Before explaining the methods and findings of this second phase of the study, we will review the findings of the first phase.

## The Demographic Variables and Mental Health: Initial Findings Reported in Mental Health in the Metropolis

It is not easy to compress a highly technical book of several hundred pages into a few choice paragraphs. The reader desiring more information on method and some interpretation of the data can only be referred to the first volume, where all is spelled out. Our purpose here is to fill in the gap between the first and second phase of the analysis and to provide a base upon which to build interpretations of the stress factor material.

## A. THE MENTAL HEALTH RATING DISTRIBUTIONS

As described in Chapter 3, Kirkpatrick and Michael made independent psychiatric evaluations of each of the 1660 respondents on a seven-point scale of impairment. Because each psychiatrist assigned a rating from 0 to 6, each respondent had two ratings. These were combined to form a composite thirteen-point scale (0-12). This scale in turn was "collapsed," yielding final distributions of Ratings I and II (see Table 4-1).

### TABLE 4-1

### DISTRIBUTION OF 1660 RESPONDENTS ACCORDING TO SEVERITY OF SYMPTOMS AND ASSOCIATED IMPAIRMENT

| Category | Mental Health Ratings | Per Cent Rating I | | Per Cent Rating II | |
|---|---|---|---|---|---|
| Well | 0-1 | 18.8 | | 18.5 | |
| Mild Symptoms | 2-3 | 41.6 | | 36.3 | |
| Moderate Symptoms | 4-5 | 21.3 | | 21.8 | |
| Impaired | 6-12 | 18.3 | | 23.4 | |
| Marked Symptoms | 6-7 | | 10.7 | | 13.2 |
| Severe Symptoms | 8-9 | | 6.2 | | 7.5 |
| Incapacitated | 10-12 | | 1.4 | | 2.7 |
| Total Number of Cases (N = 100 per cent) | | 1660 | | 1660 | |

In terms of Mental Health Rating II, based upon the larger amount of data,[5] less than one-fifth of the population is well, about three-fifths exhibit subclinical forms of mental disorder, and one-fourth shows some impairment and constitutes the clinical or morbid range of the scale. We are fairly confident that at least 23.4 per cent exhibit some impairment in life functioning, for all the evidence indicates that our methods tended to *underestimate* the level of psychopathology. Dr. Rennie felt that the Impaired category of the Midtown sample corresponded roughly to the impairment range of patients he had seen in psychiatric clinics and hospitals.

Supporting evidence for the clinical validity of the study comes from the fact that the majority of the symptoms elicited by the questionnaire were validated on a hospitalized and screened well population. A large number of symptoms discriminated between the known sick and known well groups, thus indirectly validating the psychiatric judgments made on the basis of the questionnaires.

The Home Interview Survey, in addition to giving an estimate of psychiatric impairment in the community, also aimed at establishing relationships between major demographic variables or biosocial groups and mental disturbance. The findings are reported under the headings of the typical background or demographic categories.

### B. AGE

Mental disturbance increased with increasing age. In the twenties we found 15.3 per cent Impaired, in the thirties and forties 23.2 per cent, and in the fifties 30.8 per cent. There was a "plateau" between thirty and fifty, but the rate increased sharply after fifty to twice the rate of the twenties.

### C. SEX

No sex differences in impairment were found at the four age levels. However, women reported a greater number of psychoneurotic and psychophysiological symptoms.

### D. MARITAL STATUS

While age and sex are factors upon which mental health can have little influence, marital status can be directly affected by one's mental health. By this token it is a reciprocal variable, acting as *both* "cause and effect." Marital status groups were compared while holding both age and sex constant. No sex differences appeared among the married. Single men had much higher impairment rates than did single women when age was held constant. The divorced and separated of both sexes had even higher rates.

### E. FATHER'S SOCIOECONOMIC STATUS

Since the SES of the respondent's father could not have been greatly influenced by the respondent's mental health, it was considered an independent variable. The father's SES was based upon his education and occupation during the respondent's childhood. Respondents were divided into six groups of approximately equal size according to their father's SES. From high to low status, the proportions of Impaired (in per cent) were: 17.5, 16.4, 20.9, 24.5, 29.4, and 32.7. There was a definite increase in impairment as status decreased. The lowest third of the sample contained about twice the proportion of Impaired persons as the highest third.

This same trend appeared with even greater strength when the respondent's mental health was examined according to his present (adult) SES. In the Impaired category were 12.5 per cent of the highest of the six status groups and 47.3 per cent of the lowest status. Some of this increment, however, is due to the effect of mental disorder on socioeconomic status, as well as vice versa. No sex differences were observed in the SES trends. However, the age differences in impairment rates were maintained within each SES category. Within each age bracket, the relationship between impairment and SES origin was also maintained. Thus SES and age were both found to be related to the Mental Health Rating *independently of each other*.

## F.  OCCUPATIONAL MOBILITY

Male respondents were classified as upward, downward, or nonmobile according to whether they were higher, lower, or at the same occupational level as their fathers. The upwardly mobile were healthiest, the nonmobile less healthy, and the downwardly mobile the most impaired.

## G.  GENERATION

Immigrants were designated generation I, their children generation II, their grandchildren generation III, and their great-grandchildren or even more distant descendants generation IV. Functional impairment varied inversely with advancing generation position. Starting with generation I, the proportions of Impaired were 26.7, 22.9, 22.0, and 17.2 per cent. This relatively minor trend disappeared almost completely when age and parental SES were standardized (25.3, 23.0, 22.7, and 23.0 per cent). Thus the generation differences we have come to believe were a product of the rigors of acculturation in actual fact seem to be attributable to the more advanced age and lower socioeconomic status of immigrants. Had these immigrants been younger and wealthier when we interviewed them, it is doubtful that they would have been "worse off" than the rest of the population with respect to mental health.

### H.    RELIGIOUS ORIGIN

The parental religion was selected as the only proper antecedent variable, because mental health itself may effect a change in religious persuasion. When rates were standardized by age and SES origin, Protestants and Catholics appeared to be quite similar (24.7 per cent and 23.5 per cent). Jews had a somewhat lower rate (17.2 per cent), but they had a much higher proportion of Moderately disturbed. On any measure taking into account the entire range of pathology, no sharp religious differences would appear.

### I.    PARENTAL RELIGIOSITY

No relationship between parental religiosity and impairment was found among Jews. This was also true of high SES Protestants. On the other hand, Catholics and lower-status Protestants whose parents felt religion was "Not Important at All" were more likely to be Impaired. In this same religious and SES category, those whose parents felt religion was "Somewhat Important" were healthiest. Those from homes where religion was "Very Important" showed an intermediate proportion of Impaired.

### J.    RELIGIOUS MOBILITY

The present religious identification of the respondent was compared with his religious origins (parental religion). Interfaith changers showed less impairment than nonchangers no matter what their religious origins. On the other hand, those who changed from a childhood faith to "no religion" as adults had a higher Impaired rate.

### K.    RURAL-URBAN ORIGINS

In general, when age and SES origins are controlled, no difference in impairment is found between persons who spent their childhood in the Farm or Village, Town or Small City, Medium or Big City, and New York City. In the middle and high SES parental strata, there is some increase in impairment with progressively more urban origins. It may well be that minor socioeconomic variations *within* the parental SES categories are being caught or reflected by the rural-urban variable.

### L. NATIONAL ORIGIN

Some sharp differences in Impaired rates appeared between the various "ethnic" groups in Midtown, but these disappeared almost completely when parental socioeconomic status was standardized.

In the first generation 37.5 per cent of the Italians and 52.2 per cent of the Puerto Ricans were in the Impaired category. However, only 18.2 per cent of the first-generation Hungarians were Impaired. This seems due in part to the fact that both Puerto Rican and Italian immigrants were of low SES origins, whereas the Hungarians were predominantly from the middle stratum. Thus socioeconomic status again helps to account for the ethnic differences in mental health.

Within the second generation the socioeconomic background largely explains interethnic differences in mental health. The rural or urban background as well as the economic origins of an ethnic group will in part determine its average proportion of Impaired ratings.

Taken altogether, the most sizable, consistent, and independent relationship to impairment rates was exhibited by the factor of socioeconomic status (both parental and that of the adult respondent). Second in importance was age, which consistently showed a positive relationship to impairment rates. These factors form a foundation for the further investigation of the influence of sociocultural background on mental health.

In this volume we are attempting to investigate the relationship to mental health of broken homes, parental quarrels, parental mental health, parental physical health, the physical health of the respondent in childhood, and many other factors. Whether these stressful experiences or factors occurred more frequently in low status homes is always considered. The relationship between these factors and mental health is established within each socioeconomic category and each age category. In other words, a stress factor had to have a relationship with mental health independent of these two major demographic factors, SES and age. This did not mean, however, that a factor could not be *correlated* with SES. On the contrary, somewhat more homes among the low SES were "broken" before the respondent was age seven. Although there was some variation in the *proportion* of "early" broken homes, there was still a relationship between mental health and broken homes within each SES category.

After we examine the relationship of these factors to the Mental Health Ratings with only a secondary interest in their relationship to SES and age, we shall return to an analysis of socioeconomic status in the last third of the book.

### M.  THE GROSS TYPOLOGY AND THE SYMPTOM GROUP CLASSIFICATION

Drs. Michael and Kirkpatrick classified each respondent according to a Gross Typology that included the major diagnostic types. They also indicated the major areas of symptomatology evidenced by each respondent. These tasks were performed in addition to assigning the two Mental Health Ratings. Although little of this material could be reported in Volume I, it became of cardinal importance in the attempt to unravel the reasons for the disproportionate mental disturbance found in the low SES group.

The general finding that character disorders and psychoses are more common among those of low SES origin, while neuroses are more common in the high SES, will be elaborated in later chapters. The greater prevalence of suspiciousness, passive-dependency, and depressive symptoms among the low SES is also discussed. Such facts as the obsessive-compulsive tendencies of the upwardly mobile, and the alcoholism of the downwardly mobile will also help us to understand how certain personality types tend to accumulate at the extreme ends of the social ladder. This might be called the circulation of "emotional elites and non-elites."

### N.  THE PATIENT CENSUS

Careful examination of the records of all psychiatric hospitals, clinics, and private therapists having patients from Midtown resulted in a huge mass of data. This was analyzed in a fashion parallel to the Home Interview Survey data: by age, sex, SES, religion, and other variables. The many lacunae in the records, the difficulty of constructing comparable demographic categories, and countless other problems make these data anything but dependable. Although the results are of interest to those dealing primarily with studies of treated mental disorder, we feel that the space of this volume should be devoted entirely to the analysis of data on untreated mental disorder; namely, the Home Interview Survey. Many detailed analyses of prevalence rates according to age, sex, and socio-economic categories are available in Volume I. These are analyzed according to private and public patients and by in-patients and out-patients. Data on incidence (first admissions) are also available from the project files.

On the basis of these data one thing is certain: the treated ill are in many respects radically different from the untreated ill in Midtown. The treated ill are wealthier, of later generations, have more positive attitudes toward doctors and psychiatrists, are better educated, and are probably of very different diagnostic composition. The psychopaths, the dyssocial types, and the paranoid schizophrenics are less apt to get into treatment unless they come in conflict with the police. Some types of dissociation and withdrawal are socially acceptable in certain social strata. Thus different diagnostic types are drawn from different class levels in an elaborate selection process based in various parts upon the availability of therapy, attitudes toward such services, the subcultural definitions of what constitutes "illness," what is abnormal or socially unacceptable behavior, and the very recognition of and attitude toward mental disturbance by the potential patient, his family, and family doctor (if any). It is clearly paradoxical when the day laborer gets arrested and is sent to the emergency ward of a city hospital because he acted out his problems by punching his foreman in the nose, while his wealthier but not necessarily healthier counterpart is encouraged during his psychoanalysis to conquer his neurosis and understand or even express his repressed feelings toward the vice-president in charge of sales. One man's "character disorder" may be another man's therapeutic goal!

Thus the attempt to draw etiological conclusions from data on hospitalized, clinic, or private patients is seriously questioned. While individual dynamics and the progress of therapy and theory are constantly being fed by patient data, the current patient group—at least in Midtown —is grossly unrepresentative of mentally disturbed persons as a whole. Etiological generalizations should not be drawn from study of such groups alone. For example, "broken homes" has always loomed large as a factor in mental disturbance; many patients report they came from broken homes. We will see, however, that only 20 per cent of patients in Midtown came from broken homes, as compared with 36 per cent of nonpatients. *The products of broken homes, then, are overwhelmingly healthy adults!* Only in the perspective of data on the *total population* is the broken-home factor assigned its proper etiological emphasis.

## Summary

Midtown is an area of tremendous heterogeneity, in terms of socio-economic status, ethnic background, religious affiliation, immigrant status, and rural-urban origin. It is a metropolis that has meant all things to all people, reflecting their predispositions as well as preselecting certain types for migration. Both ill and well are attracted to the metropolis, and mental health rates are probably unaffected as a whole, since the two tendencies may balance each other. Midtown has fewer children, fewer married, and more childless couples. It also has more working women and working mothers.

It is not a community, but part of a metropolitan complex, being governed by state, municipal, and local bodies simultaneously. It has a disproportionate number of professionals, particularly doctors, and less of a middle class than other boroughs. There is only negligible participation in the "ethnic" organizations, and church attendance is moderate to infrequent except among Catholics. The family is typically the isolated unit of parents and children. Many people live alone.

The Mental Health Ratings assigned to each of the 1660 Home Interview Survey respondents were examined in relation to various demographic factors. Socioeconomic origin, present socioeconomic status, and age were highly related to the Mental Health Ratings, independently of all other factors examined, and of each other. These two factors, particularly socioeconomic status, constitute a demographic overlay, so to speak, through which we can view the interaction of environmental stresses and mental health more fruitfully.

Two further classifications, the Gross Typology and Symptom Groups, were made. The significance of these data for understanding the psychodynamics of our social class system will be pointed out in later chapters.

An elaborate patient census covering all forms of treated mental disorder led us to the conclusion that records on patients, particularly those of private therapists, are never completely available, and many of the available records are woefully inadequate, particularly where detailed demographic data are concerned. The comparison of treated and untreated psychopathology leaves no doubt that the preselection of persons for treatment makes them totally unrepresentative of the mentally disturbed as a whole. Patient data, therefore, should not be used alone in testing etiological hypotheses.

## Notes

1. The sociographic operation was performed by a team composed of Alice M. Togo, Ann Jezer, Samuel Reber, and Maurice Bloch, working under the direction of Dr. Srole.

2. Since the sample was found to be accurate for all age and sex categories according to the 1950 U.S. Census, proportions of other population characteristics are reported from the sample on the assumption that they will be good estimates of the true proportion in the population of Midtown as a whole.

3. The complete income distribution of the Midtown sample (in per cent) was as follows: under $15 (0.6), $15–24 (1.3), $25–49 (9.8), $50–74 (26.4), $75–99 (22.5), $100–124 (9.5), $125–149 (5.2), $150–174 (3.4), $175–199 (3.1), $200–299 (4.3), $300 and over (9.8).

4. For persons such as housewives or unmarried women who are not working outside the home, the husband's or father's occupation was taken as an indication of the occupational level of the respondent.

5. Rating II was unsuitable for correlational analysis against sociocultural variables without the methodological "insurance" of Rating I. The rationale of this elaborate rating method is discussed in Chapter 6, pages 132–135.

# Isolating the Stress Factors

THOMAS S. LANGNER

## Aims and Procedures

The analysis of data for this volume was undertaken in several stages. The first stage was finding the relative statistical contribution of each factor to the Mental Health Ratings[1] without any assumption of etiological significance. Here we were setting up a study of associations. Was factor A more closely associated with poor mental health than factor B? Or, putting it more accurately, "Was factor A better than factor B in separating the disturbed from the well?"

A second stage was the reduction of the number of factors involved, so as to clarify and simplify the process of analysis. A third stage involved examining combinations of factors in relation to the Mental Health Ratings. Were several factors more efficient than just one alone in separating the well and the impaired? Was the combination of factors A and B more closely associated with mental disturbance than the combination of B and C? Was B stronger when paired with A than when paired with C?

The three stages are described briefly on pages 85–86 and in more detail on pages 101–110.

## Stage One: The Screening Operation

In the short time allotted for analysis, we could not possibly treat all the 148 questionnaire items that looked most promising. A *screening operation* was instituted to separate the items into those with a strong or a weak relationship to the Mental Health Ratings. The screening had to find those items that showed a relationship to the respondent's mental health.

It also had to rank these relationships in order of strength and statistical confidence. If a particular item showed a relationship to mental health that was maintained within each socioeconomic group, it was considered an independently significant item, and was retained for further study.

The screening resulted, then, in a separation of the items into dead variables (unrelated to the ratings), live variables (independently significant, or related to the ratings within each SES group), and SES component variables (items whose relationship to the ratings disappeared within each SES group, showing them to be primarily a component of SES). Our interest here is primarily the live, not the dead or component variable.

## Stage Two: The Pyramiding of the Items into Factors

It was expected that about 40 items would survive the screening. It turned out that 120 of 148 items tested showed a relationship to mental health even when socioeconomic status was controlled, leaving us with more live items than we had expected. These remaining items and their interrelations could not possibly be treated in one volume. Therefore, the boiling-down process of screening had to be followed by a building up of the residue into larger and more easily handled stress factors.

Of the 120 live variables, we took 31 showing strong association with the Mental Health Ratings and combined them into clusters. This process was called pyramiding. A description of the pyramiding and the 14 stress factors constructed appears later in this chapter.[2]

## Stage Three: Combinations and Simple Scores of Factors

The pyramided factors were combined in pairs, triads, and larger groups to see if one combination was a better predictor than another. In general, we found that pair AB was no more predictive than pair BC or CD. However, ABC was always more predictive of mental health than AB, and similarly, ABCD was more powerful than ABC. Thus AB, BC, and CD were all given a score value of 2, ABC and BCD a score of 3, ABCD and BCDE a score of 4, and so on. The *number* of stress factors each individual had experienced was called his *stress score*. The development of these Stress Scores will be treated in Chapters 13 and 14.

## The Ridit

The measure of mental health used for the screening operation was Mental Health Rating II. This was the final rating of all respondents' mental health by the psychiatrists, who examined both the symptoms of the respondents and their sociocultural background. The rating process was described in Chapter 3. For the purposes of screening, this final Rating (II) was felt to be a more adequate approximation of a face-to-face psychiatric judgment than Rating I.

The statistical measure selected to describe the 13-point Mental Health Rating Scale was the "ridit."[3]

In Volume I the relation of eight major demographic variables to the proportion of respondents in the Impaired mental health category was investigated. In this volume, there were initially not eight but, as the reader will recall, 148 variables under consideration. The statistic describing the relation of the 148 variables to mental health also had to be a measure that could be expressed simply. In particular, it had to be a statistic that measured the entire distribution of ratings. The most obvious answer was an average mental health rating, or mean. There were serious objections to the use of such an average. It should be remembered that the psychiatrists individually assigned a mental health rating from 0 through 6 to each respondent. Since the ratings were ranked in order of severity of symptoms, this was an ordinal scale, meaning simply that a rating of 1 comes after a rating of 0, 2 comes after 1, and so on.[4] The subdivisions of an ordinal series are not necessarily equal in size. Therefore, these numbers could not be used as exact "weights" of mental health. They were intended to indicate only that a person with a rating of 2 was more disturbed than a person with a rating of 1. A person with a rating of 2 was *not* twice as disturbed as a person with a rating of 1. Similarly, the difference in severity between a rating of 2 and a rating of 3 might very well be less than the difference between a rating of 4 and a rating of 5. That equal increments in severity of symptoms and impairment were not denoted by the numbered ratings can be seen in the definitions attached to each rank number:[5]

### Mental Health Rating II

0   No evidence of symptom formation (symptom free).
1   Mild symptom formation *but* functioning adequately.

2   Moderate symptom formation with *no* apparent interference in life adjustment.

3   Moderate symptom formation with *some* interference in life adjustment.

4   Serious symptom formation, yet functioning with some difficulty.

5   Serious symptom formation, yet functioning with *great* difficulty.

6   Seriously incapacitated, unable to function.

The ridit indicates *how much* of a relationship exists (in terms of probability) and *how sure* we are that this relationship is not due to errors in the sampling.[6] It was chosen, then, in preference to other statistics[7] because it was particularly well suited to the measurement and presentation of data in this volume. The ridit has a range from 0.00 to 1.00. The ridits are applied to groups; they are similar to averages, although based not on arithmetical weights but on cumulative proportions. For the reader not interested in the exact meaning of the ridit, we can simply say that *the larger the ridit, the worse the mental health of the group. The smaller the ridit, the better the mental health of the group.*

The ridit has a simple interpretation in terms of probability, or chance. As a brief example, if the average mental health ridit of respondents with big feet is .40, and the average mental health ridit of respondents with small feet is .60, one can say that an individual selected at random from the "small-footed" group has a greater risk of having a worse mental health rating than an individual picked at random from the "large-footed" group. This does *not* tell us how *much* worse off the random *individual is*. It tells us only that he is about *twice as likely to be worse off*.[8] In other words, it measures the probability or "odds" that he will have a worse Mental Health Rating.

## Calculation of the Ridit\*

In this research, ridits were calculated first from the distribution of all the 1660 cases on MHR II.[9] This is the *identified distribution*. All

\* Those readers who are baffled by numbers will probably want to skip pages 89 to 100 which describe the calculation of the ridit, and give simple examples of its use. However, they should be forewarned that almost all the results of research discussed in this volume are in terms of the ridit. Without some familiarity with this measure, the reader's understanding of the findings will be considerably diminished.

other distributions of subclasses, such as men and women, high or low SES, will be "referred to" or compared with this identified distribution. The computation of the ridits of the reference (or *identified*) distribution is a very simple process. For example, let's take a hypothetical group of 1600 students who have been given intelligence ratings by their teacher. These nonnumerical ratings or judgments are "Excellent," "Good," "Fair," and "Poor."[10] After the ratings are made it is found that 400 students fall into each class. The ridits for the intelligence ratings are computed according to the instructions in Table 5-1.

## TABLE 5-1

## CALCULATION OF RIDITS FOR REFERENCE DISTRIBUTION IN A HYPOTHETICAL STUDY

| INTELLIGENCE RATING | COMPUTING FORM[a] | | | | | |
|---|---|---|---|---|---|---|
| | 1 | 2 | 3 | 4 | 5 | 6 |
| Excellent | 400 | 200 | 0 | 200 | .125 | 50.000 |
| Good | 400 | 200 | 400 | 600 | .375 | 150.000 |
| Fair | 400 | 200 | 800 | 1000 | .625 | 250.000 |
| Poor | 400 | 200 | 1200 | 1400 | .875 | 350.000 |
| Ridit Check | | | | | | 800.000 |
| Grand Total | 1600 | | | | | |

[a]1: The frequency distribution in the identified distribution (reference class).
2: One-half of the corresponding entry in Column 1.
3: The cumulate of Column 1 (displaced one category downward).
4: Column 2 plus Column 3.
5: The entries in Column 4 divided by grand total (1600).
6: Column 1 times Column 5 (the frequencies multiplied by the numbers are the ridits).

The average ridit for the total sample of 1600 students, the reference class, is by definition .50. An individual picked at random from the reference class has the same chance of being "worse off" or "better off" (less or more intelligent) as another individual selected at random from the reference class. Fifty per cent are less intelligent and 50 per cent are more intelligent than he is. The average ridit (.50) for the reference class is obtained by dividing the sum of column 6 by 1600, the number of cases.

Suppose we know that 900 students had a diet high in protein, while

700 had a low protein diet. Is the high protein class more intelligent than the low protein class?

Table 5-2 shows the frequency distribution of high and low protein consumers on the intelligence rating scale. Among high protein consumers the sum of the frequencies multiplied by the ridits for each rating (derived in Table 5-1) is 387.500. This is divided by the total number of cases in that class (900) which yields an average ridit of .43 (.431).[11] Similarly, the average ridit of the low protein class is .59 (.589).

## TABLE 5-2

### CALCULATION OF AVERAGE RIDITS FOR THE DISTRIBUTIONS OF TWO SUBCLASSES IN A HYPOTHETICAL STUDY

Subclass

| Intelligence Rating | LOW PROTEIN DIET | | | HIGH PROTEIN DIET | | |
|---|---|---|---|---|---|---|
| | Frequency | Ridit | Frequency x Ridit | Frequency | Ridit | Frequency x Ridit |
| Excellent | 100 | .125 | 12.500 | 300 | .125 | 37.500 |
| Good | 150 | .375 | 56.250 | 250 | .375 | 93.750 |
| Fair | 200 | .625 | 125.000 | 200 | .625 | 125.000 |
| Poor | 250 | .875 | 218.750 | 150 | .875 | 131.250 |
| Total | 700 | | 412.500 | 900 | | 387.500 |
| Average Ridit ($\bar{R}$) | | .589 | | | .431 | |

With respect to the total sample or reference class (.50), high protein consumers (.43) are "better off" in intelligence and low protein consumers "worse off" (.59). The higher the ridit, the worse the intelligence rating. The probability that a random individual in the low protein class will have a poorer intelligence rating than a random individual in the reference class is .59.

In terms of the percentile distribution of ridit scores in the entire sample, the *average* person in the high protein consumption group is surpassed in intelligence by 43 per cent of the total sample. The average person in the low protein consumption group is surpassed in intelligence by 59 per cent of the total sample.

Thus the ridit can be loosely translated by the reader into a statement of this type: "The average person in a group with a ridit of .60 is "worse off" (with respect to intelligence, mental health, or whatever the test variable may be) than 60 per cent of the entire sample.

Suppose we want to compare high and low protein consumers with each other, and not with the reference class as a whole. Bross says "An estimate of the corresponding relative probabilities for the two classes can be obtained very simply by adding .50 to the numerical difference."[12] The difference in this case is .16 (.59 minus .43). This difference added to .50 yields .66. In terms of odds this would mean that the chances are about 2 to 1 that the low protein consumer will get a worse intelligence rating than the high protein consumer.[13]

To give a more graphic illustration, suppose we have a deck of 1600 index cards. On each card is written the diet (low or high protein) and intelligence rating of a particular student. These cards are separated into *two* decks, the high and the low protein consumers. There are 900 cards in the high and 700 in the low protein deck. The high protein deck has 300 "Excellent," 250 "Good," 200 "Fair," and 150 "Poor" ratings. The low protein deck has 100 "Excellent," 150 "Good," 200 "Fair," and 250 "Poor" ratings. The high protein ridit is .43, the low protein ridit, .59. The odds (risks or chances) are 2 to 1 that the low protein consumer will get a worse intelligence rating than the high protein consumer. After shuffling the two decks, we take a random card (that is, an individual case) from each deck. Theoretically, if we do this three times, pulling *pairs* of cards from the two decks, *in two of the three pairs the intelligence rating of the low protein consumer will be worse than that of the corresponding high protein consumer.* This is what is meant by the "chance," the "risk," or the "odds" of being worse off.

In the Midtown Study, one is "worse off" or "better off" with respect to the Mental Health Rating, the major dependent variable. The non-numerical or judgmental scale is the Mental Health Rating. Its empirical or observed frequency distribution—the number of persons with a rating of 1, 2, 3, and so forth—is the *identified distribution,* or *reference distribution* for this study. The *reference class* is the total sample.

This reference distribution and its calculated ridits are presented in Table 5-3 for both Mental Health Rating I and II. It should be noted that the last two ratings, 11 and 12, were combined because of the small number of cases, making the final rating a 12-, rather than a 13-point scale. Actually, the last several ratings could have been collapsed into one group without doing much damage to the ridit values, since another property of the ridit is that it does not fluctuate much with reduction or expansion of the number of steps in the rating scale.

Another simple way of understanding (though not of computing) the mental health ridits is to treat them as a cumulative percentile distribution. An inspection of Table 5-3 under "Mental Health Rating I" shows there were 143 persons rated "0," 168 rated "1," and 441 rated "2," after the two psychiatrists' ratings were combined. These three figures divided by the total number of persons in the sample, 1660, amount to 8.6 per cent, 10.1 per cent, and 26.6 per cent of the sample respectively. If we want to find the average ridit of all persons having a mental health rating of "2," we can cumulate the percentages of rating "0" (8.6 per cent), rating "1," (10.1 per cent), and half of rating "2" (13.3 per cent). Why only half of rating "2"? Although 26.6 per cent were rated "2," the hypothetical *average man* in the "2" group stands in the middle of the group with respect to mental health. In other words, out of the 26.6 per cent, half (13.3 per cent) are healthier than he is, and half are less healthy (13.3 per cent). The *average* cumulated percentile for the "2" group then is 8.6 per cent (the "0s") plus 10.1 per cent (the "1s") plus 13.3 per cent (half of the "2s"). This makes a total cumulative percentage of 32.0 per cent. The corresponding ridit is .320. Looking at Table 5-3, we see that the average ridit for a final Mental Health Rating I of "2" is .320. Thus the average man among those with a mental health rating of "2" is exceeded in mental health by only 32 per cent of the sample. In other words, the "2" group has an average ridit of .32.

The ridits shown in Table 5-3 were utilized in the screening of the test variables, or items. As mentioned before, these variables were "controlled" by socioeconomic status. The tabular format for a typical screening table is shown in Table 5-4 (without the socioeconomic controls or subdivisions, and leaving out the Don't Knows and No Answers).

In this typical screening table the respondents' average mental health ridits are computed according to the physical health of the respondents' parents. In the first column appear the Mental Health Ratings, from 0 to 12. In the second column are the ridits corresponding to these ratings.

In columns 3, 5, 7, and 9 are the frequency distributions of the Mental Health Ratings according to Parents' Poor Physical Health. For example, in column 3 are the Mental Health Ratings of the 269 persons who reported that only their mother was in poor health. Of these 269 people, 20 received a rating of 0, 13 a rating of 1, and so forth.

The average ridit for the entire group of 269 (Only Mother's Health

## TABLE 5-3

# DISTRIBUTION AND RIDITS OF MENTAL HEALTH RATINGS I AND II
## (The Reference or Identified Ridit Distribution)

| Mental Health Score | MHR I Frequency | MHR I Ridit | MHR I Frequency x Ridit | MHR II Frequency | MHR II Ridit | MHR II Frequency x Ridit |
|---|---|---|---|---|---|---|
| 0 | 143 | .043 | 6.149 | 148 | .045 | 6.660 |
| 1 | 168 | .137 | 23.016 | 159 | .137 | 21.783 |
| 2 | 441 | .320 | 141.120 | 396 | .304 | 120.384 |
| 3 | 250 | .528 | 132.000 | 206 | .486 | 100.116 |
| 4 | 226 | .672 | 151.872 | 213 | .612 | 130.356 |
| 5 | 128 | .778 | 99.584 | 149 | .721 | 107.429 |
| 6 | 97 | .846 | 82.062 | 124 | .803 | 99.572 |
| 7 | 81 | .900 | 72.900 | 95 | .869 | 82.555 |
| 8 | 83 | .949 | 78.767 | 86 | .923 | 79.378 |
| 9 | 20 | .980 | 19.600 | 39 | .961 | 37.479 |
| 10 | 12 | .990 | 11.880 | 29 | .982 | 28.478 |
| 11 and 12 | 11 | .997 | 10.967 | 16 | .995 | 15.920 |
| Total | 1660 | | 829.917 | 1660 | | 830.110 |
| Average Ridit | | .500 | | | .500 | |

Poor) is obtained by multiplying each frequency (column 3) by the corresponding ridit (column 2). For example, 20 persons received a rating of 0 (column 3). When this is multiplied by the ridit for a rating of 0 (.045, which appears in column 2),[14] the result is .900, shown in column 4.

To continue the calculation, there were 13 cases with a rating of 1. The ridit for a rating of 1 is .137. Thirteen times .137 is 1.781, the product entered in column 4.

This procedure of multiplying the ridit by the number of cases (frequency) is continued until there are 12 products (as in column 4). These 12 products are then summed, yielding in this case a total of 149.842. This sum of the products is then divided by the total number reporting "Only Mother's Health Poor" (269 cases). This yields an average ridit of .557, or .56, for that particular class of people. We can now say that the average mental health ridit, or the mental health risk, of those who reported that only their mothers were in poor health, is .56.

## TABLE 5-4

## CALCULATION OF AVERAGE RIDITS FOR MENTAL HEALTH (MH II) ACCORDING TO PARENTS' PHYSICAL HEALTH

|  |  |  |  | Parents' Physical Health | | | | | |
|---|---|---|---|---|---|---|---|---|---|
|  |  | ONLY MOTHER'S HEALTH POOR | | ONLY FATHER'S HEALTH POOR | | BOTH PARENTS' HEALTH POOR | | NEITHER PARENT'S HEALTH POOR | |
| 1 | 2 | 3 | 4 | 5 | 6 | 7 | 8 | 9 | 10 |
| MH II Ratings | Ridits ($\bar{R}$) | Frequency ($f$) | Frequency times Ridit ($f \times \bar{R}$) | $f$ | $f \times \bar{R}$ | $f$ | $f \times \bar{R}$ | $f$ | $f \times \bar{R}$ |
| 0 | .045 | 20 | .900 | 14 | .630 | 1 | .045 | 113 | 5.085 |
| 1 | .137 | 13 | 1.781 | 22 | 3.014 | 3 | .411 | 119 | 16.303 |
| 2 | .304 | 59 | 17.936 | 49 | 14.896 | 3 | .912 | 282 | 85.728 |
| 3 | .486 | 30 | 14.580 | 25 | 12.150 | 7 | 3.402 | 140 | 68.040 |
| 4 | .612 | 36 | 22.032 | 21 | 12.852 | 3 | 1.836 | 151 | 92.412 |
| 5 | .721 | 33 | 23.793 | 22 | 15.862 | 6 | 4.326 | 85 | 61.285 |
| 6 | .803 | 25 | 20.075 | 19 | 15.257 | 5 | 4.015 | 75 | 60.225 |
| 7 | .869 | 19 | 16.511 | 11 | 9.559 | 7 | 6.083 | 54 | 46.926 |
| 8 | .923 | 18 | 16.614 | 9 | 8.307 | 3 | 2.769 | 55 | 50.765 |
| 9 | .961 | 5 | 4.805 | 6 | 5.766 | 4 | 3.844 | 22 | 21.142 |
| 10 | .982 | 10 | 9.820 | 3 | 2.946 | 1 | .982 | 15 | 14.730 |
| 11 and 12 | .995 | 1 | .995 | 1 | .995 | 1 | .995 | 12 | 11.940 |
| Total |  | 269 | 149.842 | 202 | 102.234 | 44 | 29.620 | 1123 | 534.581 |
| Average Ridits ($\bar{\bar{R}}$) |  |  | .557 |  | .506 |  | .673 |  | .476 |
| Average Ridits rounded off to nearest hundredth |  |  | .56 |  | .51 |  | .67 |  | .48 |

The same calculations are made for those answering "Only Father's Health Poor" (giving a ridit of .51), "Both Parents' Health Poor" (a ridit of .67) and "Neither Parents' Health Poor" (.48). We can now say that persons with both parents in poor health are worse off (.67) than persons whose parents were not in poor health (.48). We also know *how much* worse off they are. The odds of their being worse off are a little better than 2 to 1.[15]

The odds, or chances, are 2 to 1, then, that an individual selected at random from among the 44 cases of the "Both Parents' Health Poor" group will exhibit more mental disturbance (or have a higher or worse Mental Health Rating) than a corresponding individual picked from among the 1123 cases of the "Neither Parents' Health Poor" group.

Those who have gambled know that 2 to 1 odds are only moderate. However, there is no actual gamble involved in these statistics because one does not have a free choice of sick or well parents. Assuming, however, that a child could choose his parents, and that he knew the odds, he would be wise not to choose parents who were both in poor physical health.

On a completely different level from the absolute size of the odds, or the difference in the size of the two ridits, is the question of how confident we are that sampling error alone does not account for this difference. That is, the differences between the ridits should be an expression of the strength of the test item, and not a chance fluctuation due purely to sampling error. For this purpose a confidence interval, determining the limits of confidence, was calculated for each average ridit.[16] As Dr. Bross puts it, "The confidence interval on the average ridit involves the probability of a probability statement being true— hence a higher level probability."[17]

Table 5-5 was constructed from which the confidence limits at the 95 per cent level can be read. The table gives limits for ridits of different-sized samples from 2 to 13,333 cases. This is accomplished by adding and subtracting the confidence *semi-interval* from the average ridit.

The 95 per cent level of confidence indicates that in 95 out of 100 *samples* of the same size the true mean or average would fall inside the confidence limits. The confidence interval is applied here to the average ridit of a distribution, not to comparisons between the average ridits of two distributions.

When we want to use confidence intervals to test whether the average ridits of two groups are "significantly" different, the rationale is about like

## TABLE 5-5

### WIDTH OF 95 PER CENT[a] CONFIDENCE SEMI-INTERVALS[b] OF RIDITS FOR SAMPLE SIZES 2 THROUGH 13,333

| Number in Sample | Ridit Semi-Interval | Number in Sample | Ridit Semi-Interval |
|---|---|---|---|
| 2 | .41 | 19 to 21 | .13 |
| 3 | .33 | 22 to 25 | .12 |
| 4 | .29 | 26 to 30 | .11 |
| 5 | .26 | 31 to 36 | .10 |
| 6 | .24 | 37 to 46 | .09 |
| 7 | .22 | 47 to 59 | .08 |
| 8 | .20 | 60 to 78 | .07 |
| 9 | .19 | 79 to 110 | .06 |
| 10 | .18 | 111 to 164 | .05 |
| 11 to 12 | .17 | 165 to 272 | .04 |
| 13 | .16 | 273 to 533 | .03 |
| 14 to 15 | .15 | 534 to 1481 | .02 |
| 16 to 18 | .14 | 1482 to 13,333 | .01 |

[a] Commonly referred to as the "5 Per Cent Level" of Confidence (.05). In the text it is suggested that the one per cent level is approximated in the actual process of comparing the ridits of two groups.

[b] The length of the confidence interval is two semi-intervals. For example, in a group of 1000 respondents the average ridit turns out to be .60. The semi-interval (one-half the width of the interval) for 1000 cases is .02. If the semi-interval is added to the average ridit (.62), we have the upper limit of the interval. If it is subtracted (.58), we have the lower limit. The interval itself is .04.

this. We hypothesize that there is no difference between the "true" mean (average) ridit of Group A and Group B. We would expect the common true mean (common to both groups) to lie within the confidence interval of Group A and the confidence interval of Group B. However, if the intervals do not overlap, we have a pattern contradictory to this so-called "null" hypothesis. Then we say that the mean ridits are "significantly different." As the 95 per cent confidence intervals were used for each of the two means, we can say we are 95 per cent confident that our means are really different, and not due to sampling variation. The 95 per cent level of confidence is usually referred to as the "5 per cent level" or the ".05 level."

When using confidence intervals in this way, however, we actually attain much greater statistical significance. "As far as a comparison between just two series is concerned, the use of the 95 per cent confidence intervals and a nonoverlap rule gives a significance test that is closer to the one per cent than the 5 per cent level. Roughly speaking, for two equally large series the confidence intervals can overlap by about one-sixth and the chi-square test will still be significant."[18] Adding a 5 per cent interval to one mean, and a 5 per cent interval on another mean yields about a one per cent level when these intervals do not overlap. Since the one per cent level will not *always* be attained in cases of nonoverlap, these differences will be conservatively reported hereafter as being at the 5 per cent level.

The confidence interval overlap test is a way of showing that the differences between ridits of two groups are not due to sampling variation. Thus the larger the group, the less the error due to sampling variation. The size of the confidence interval varies inversely with the number of people in the particular group being ridited. If the 5 per cent confidence semi-intervals above and below the average ridit of one class do not overlap the 5 per cent confidence semi-intervals on either side of the average ridit of the other class, then sampling error alone does not account for the differences between two classes. The confidence limits of ridits for a typical screening item, "Were either of your parents in poor physical health?" are indicated in Table 5-6.

In Table 5-6 in the "Total" column the ridit of "Both Parents in Poor Physical Health" (.67) can again be compared with that of "Neither Parent in Poor Physical Health" (.48). There were 44 persons who reported "Both parents." Looking up sample size 44 in Table 5-5, we find a confidence semi-interval of .09 (sample sizes 37–46). To the mean or average ridit for the class "Both Parents in Poor Physical Health" (.67) we add the confidence semi-interval (.09), to get an upper confidence limit of .76. Similarly, we subtract the confidence semi-interval (.09) from the average ridit (.67), to get a lower confidence limit of .58.

The upper and lower limits of the average ridit of the class "Neither Parent in Poor Physical Health" are .50 and .46. The confidence semi-interval .02, based on 1123 cases, is much smaller, and is added to and subtracted from the average ridit for that class (.48).

In order to find out whether the difference between the two classes "Both Parents" and "Neither Parent" (.67 versus .48) is due to sampling error alone, the upper limit of the "Neither" group (.50) is compared

## TABLE 5-6

### CONFIDENCE LIMITS OF RESPONDENTS' AVERAGE MENTAL HEALTH RIDITS ACCORDING TO PARENTS' PHYSICAL HEALTH AND FATHERS' SOCIOECONOMIC STATUS

| PARENTS' PHYSICAL HEALTH | | FATHERS' SOCIOECONOMIC STATUS | | | |
|---|---|---|---|---|---|
| | | Low | Middle | High | Total |
| Only Mother's Health Poor | Upper Limit | .68 | .62 | .55 | .60 |
| | Average Ridit | .62 | $.56^*_x$ | .49 | $.56^*_x$ |
| | Lower Limit | .56 | .50 | .43 | .52 |
| | No. of Cases | (92) | (90) | (87) | (269) |
| Only Father's Health Poor | Upper Limit | .60 | .59 | .55 | .55 |
| | Average Ridit | $.52^*_z$ | .53 | .48 | $.51^*_w$ |
| | Lower Limit | .44 | .47 | .41 | .47 |
| | No. of Cases | (54) | (80) | (68) | (202) |
| Both Parents' Health Poor | Upper Limit | .93 | .78 | .76 | .76 |
| | Average Ridit | $.78^*_{z,y}$ | $.64^*_{x,w}$ | .60 | $.67^*_{w,u}$ |
| | Lower Limit | .63 | .50 | .44 | .58 |
| | No. of Cases | (14) | (17) | (13) | (44) |
| Neither Parent's Health Poor | Upper Limit | .57 | .49 | .46 | .50 |
| | Average Ridit | $.54^*_y$ | $.46^*_w$ | .43 | $.48^*_{x,u}$ |
| | Lower Limit | .51 | .43 | .40 | .46 |
| | No. of Cases | (318) | (468) | (337) | (1123) |
| Don't Know, No Answer | Average Ridit ‡ | – | – | – | – |
| | No. of Cases | (4) | (16) | (2) | (22) |
| Total Number of Cases | | | | | 1660 |

\* Differences in test variable at the 5 per cent level of confidence between ridits with same subscript.
‡ Ridits not computed.

with the lower limit of the "Both" group (.58). *The upper and lower limits do not overlap, indicating that the ridit difference between the two classes is not due to sampling error alone.* Thus our confidence that the differences between the two classes is not due to sampling error is assured.

In order to make sure that each test variable (e.g., Parents' Poor

## TABLE 5-7

## PROPORTIONS AND AVERAGE MENTAL HEALTH (MH II) OF RESPONDENTS ACCORDING TO PARENTS' POOR PHYSICAL HEALTH AND FATHERS' SOCIOECONOMIC STATUS

| Parents' Poor Physical Health | Fathers' Socioeconomic Status | | | | | | | |
|---|---|---|---|---|---|---|---|---|
| | LOW | | MIDDLE | | HIGH | | TOTAL | |
| | Per Cent | $\bar{R}$ | Per Cent | $\bar{R}$ | Per Cent | $\bar{R}$ | Per Cent | $\bar{R}$ |
| Mother | 19.1 | .62 | 13.4 | $.56^*_z$ | 17.2 | .49 | 16.2 | $.56^*_y$ |
| Father | 11.2 | .52* | 11.9 | .53 | 13.4 | .48 | 12.2 | .51* |
| Both | 2.9 | .78* | 2.5 | .64 | 2.6 | .60 | 2.7 | .67* |
| Neither | 66.0 | .54 | 69.8 | $.46^*_z$ | 66.4 | .43 | 67.6 | $.48^*_y$ |
| Don't Know, No Answer ‡ | .8 | — | 2.4 | — | .4 | — | 1.3 | — |
| Total Number of Cases (N=100 per cent) | 482 | | 671 | | 507 | | 1660 | |

\* Difference in test variable at the 5 per cent level of confidence between ridits with same subscript or adjacent to same asterisk.

‡ Ridits not computed.

Physical Health), and not SES, was accounting for the differences in the ridits, we had to control each test variable by SES. Table 5-6 shows the test variable Parents' Poor Physical Health divided into three groups according to socioeconomic level of the respondents' fathers. The difference between "Neither Parent" and "Both Parents" remains at the 5 per cent level of confidence *even though SES is controlled.*[19] The difference between "Mother in Poor Physical Health" and "Neither Parent in Poor Physical Health" is at the 5 per cent level in the middle SES. The tendency for differences to remain at the 5 per cent level of confidence, even within each SES level, shows that the poor health of parents accounts for some of the variation in respondents' Mental Health Ratings, independently of socioeconomic status. "Parents' Poor Physical Health," then, is a live variable that stands up under our screening technique.[20]

Without the SES controls during the screening process, the calculation of the confidence intervals would not have been meaningful. Controls were very crucial in the numerous instances where SES differences were as large as or larger than the differences due to the test variable. Confidence intervals were calculated for the subclasses with the test variable present and absent *within* each socioeconomic status category.

The tabular format of Table 5-6, which includes the confidence limits, would have been too complex if used in presenting the many test variables discussed in this volume. Table 5-7, a condensed version of Table 5-6, is shown directly after the original version. An asterisk between two adjacent ridits or appended asterisks with the same subscript are used to indicate that confidence limits do not overlap. For instance, in the Total column of Table 5-7, the difference between .67 and .48 is at the 5 per cent level of confidence. To signify this, an asterisk is placed between the adjacent ridits. The difference between .56 and .48 is also at the 5 per cent level of confidence. *The asterisks are placed to the right of the two adjacent ridits and are both labeled "y" to indicate that the difference between these ridits is at the 5 per cent confidence level.*

When two ridits (for example, .46 and .43) are both "significantly" different from but not adjacent to a third ridit (.69), the notation is as follows: .69\*$_{x,y}$, .53, .46\*$_{z}$, .43\*$_{y}$.

The use of the asterisk and the condensed table saves both time and space. The sight of the asterisks immediately conveys the message that "We are confident (95 per cent sure) that this test variable is related to the respondents' mental health."

The average ridits and their confidence intervals can be expressed graphically.

In Table 5-8 the average respondents' mental health ridit according to the Poor Physical Health of their parents are represented by solid bars. The confidence intervals are represented by the areas above and below the solid bar. The size of the areas depends, of course, on the total number of cases in each class. Note that the "Both parents" and "Neither parent" bars do not overlap. This is a visual representation of what is meant by two ridits being *significantly different:* that is, when the 5 per cent confidence intervals (which represent variations due to sample size alone) are added to the bar chart, the two bars still do not overlap.

Similarly the "Mother" and "Neither" bars do not overlap, nor do the "Father" and "Both" bars. The "Mother" and "Father," "Mother" and "Both," "Father" and "Neither" bars overlap, showing that their mean ridits are not significantly different.

The bars can also be compared to the average ridit of the total sample, .50, represented by a dotted line. The "Mother" and "Both" bars show a risk that is definitely higher than .50, the risk of the reference class (the

**Table 5-8**
**Confidence Limits of Average Mental Health Ridits, According
to Parents' Physical Health**

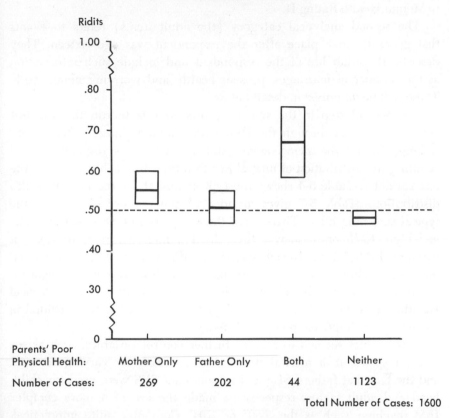

| Parents' Poor Physical Health: | Mother Only | Father Only | Both | Neither |
|---|---|---|---|---|
| Number of Cases: | 269 | 202 | 44 | 1123 |

Total Number of Cases: 1600

total sample). The bars for "Father" and "Neither" are on the border-
line, and so these answers are shown to be unrelated to mental health
risk in this sample.

## Details of the Screening Operation

The first step in the screening operation was to place the questionnaire
items[21] into two main categories, which according to the analytical framework were preadult or independent components and adult or concomitant
components.

The childhood items are most closely related in time to the Childhood
Mental Health Index which is based on preadult symptoms reported by
the now-adult respondents. In relation to these preadult items, the CMH

Index stands as the dependent variable. However, inasmuch as CMH precedes adult mental health, it is an independent variable. The preadult experiences were all screened in relation to the CMH Index as well as to Mental Health Rating II.

The second analytical category (the adult items) refers to events that generally took place after the respondent was age sixteen. They describe the adult life of the respondent and include such information as the number of marriages, present health, and worrying about work. These will be described in detail below.

The second step in the screening process was to run the 148 test variables or items through the IBM card-counting sorter, sorting (controlling, that is) the socioeconomic status of fathers or respondents and counting the distribution of mental health ratings for each subclass of the test variables. Table 5-4 shows the typical format for the mental health distributions. Table 5-7 gives an idea of the number of *cells* in the typical screening table. There were three divisions of SES: low, middle, and high. Each of these was then divided into categories of the test variable. Table 5-7 has 16 cells for which ridits were calculated, arranged into SES columns, and divided into four test variable categories: "Mother," "Father," "Both," and "Neither" of Parents in Poor Physical Health. (A "Total" column, normally part of the table, is not included in an attempt at simplification of Table 5-4.)

Often tables seemed to call for further control variables, such as sex of the respondent or marital status. This necessity for varying controls, and the fact that fathers' SES and respondents' SES were used for childhood and adult factors respectively, made the use of a more complex IBM machine, such as the "650" or "704" Computer quite impractical. The degree of control over each separate variable had to be maximal. The number of *contingent* variables related to sex, marital status, parental status, and job status made similar treatment of all test variables impossible. The use of the painstaking individual approach to each variable and the rather slow "075" Card-Counting Sorter were necessities rather than a choice between alternative methods.

We decided to give each variable a "screening rank" of 1, 2, or 3, depending upon a number of criteria set up in advance. Now that the reader is familiar with the ridit, and the tabular format, these criteria will be more easily understood.

The criteria for provisional rank order of test variables were as follows:

*Rank 1:* If a test item shows a difference between its mean ridits at the 5 per cent level of confidence and if such a difference occurs in one or more of the three socioeconomic groups, and if this difference is in the same direction in all three SES groups, the test item should be assigned to Rank 1.

*Rank 2:* A test item may not meet the 5 per cent level of confidence in any one of the three SES groups. If, however, there is a strong trend in a single direction, that is, the average mental health varies consistently in all three SES groups, then it may seem likely that upon collapsing the three SES groups (which would be legitimate where the trend is similar in all three SES groups) the 5 per cent level would be achieved merely by thus increasing the sample size for each of the test item subgroups. If this is indeed the case, the item is placed in Rank 2.

*Rank 3:* Those test items which show no consistent direction or trend, nor any difference at the 5 per cent level of confidence are assigned to Rank 3.

All Rank 1 and Rank 2 items were considered eligible for discussion in this volume. They are the "live" variables. We were statistically confident that they showed a relationship to mental health that was independent of socioeconomic status. Rank 3 variables were not live and were not used in pyramiding the factors or in any of the later sections of Volume II. Of the 148 items, 49 were in Rank 1, 71 in Rank 2, and 28 in Rank 3.

Only 31 of the Rank 1 and 2 items were finally utilized in building the 14 factors. A number of other Rank 1 and 2 items were examined as well but eventually eliminated or winnowed out in the pyramiding process. A fair number of Rank 1 and 2 items were not discussed at all in the analysis of the factors, since they did not enter into the construction of any of the factors. The items used in the factors and their rankings are given here.

## The Pyramiding

The factors selected for detailed treatment in this volume were chosen on the basis of several criteria: (1) they were to be composed if possible of items that were assigned to Rank 1 in the screening operation, (2) they were to be factors dealing with areas of generally accepted theoretical and clinical importance, (3) the factors were to be heterogeneous in nature, so that one factor would not be synonymous with another. Examination of the list of factors will show that a heavy preponderance of Rank 1 items went into their composition, and that they are of general

## Item Composition of Childhood and Adult Stress Factors in Mental Health[a]

### CHILDHOOD (PREADULT) FACTORS

| Stress Factor | Title | Screening Rank | Item |
|---|---|---|---|
| 1 | Parents' Poor Physical Health | 2 | "When you were growing up (age six to eighteen), were either of your parents in poor health?" |
| 2 | Parents' Poor Mental Health | | "Did any close relative ever have arthritis, asthma, bladder trouble, colitis, diabetes, hay fever, heart condition, high blood pressure, neuralgia or sciatica, nervous breakdown, epilepsy, stomach trouble, skin condition?" |
| | | 2 | "Father?" |
| | | 2 | "Mother?" |
| | | 1 | "Were either of your parents the worrying type?" |
| 3 | Childhood Economic Deprivation | 1 | "Looking back, what would you say were the chief problems or troubles that your parents had to face while you were growing up?" "Unemployment," "Financial." |
| | | 2 | "During the years you were growing up, did your parents ever have a hard time making ends meet?" "**Often,**" "Sometimes," 'Rarely.' |
| | | 2 | "From the time you were six till you were eighteen, about how many years would you say your mother worked?" "Why did she work outside the home?" To "**Earn Money,**" "Have a Career," or "Other" reasons? |
| 4 | Childhood Poor Physical Health | 2 | "How about your health in early childhood—that is, in the first six years of your life? As far as you can remember or have been told, was your health in early childhood good, fair, or **poor?**" |
| | | 1 | "As a child, did you catch cold **fairly often?**" |
| 5 | Childhood Broken Homes | 1 | "Did you always live together with both your real parents up to the time you were sixteen years old?" If "No," "What happened?" "How old were you when that happened?" |
| 6 | Parents' Character Negatively Perceived | | "During your school days children were often asked in school to write papers about their home life. I have here a few statements written by children some years ago. . . . Think back to when you were growing up and tell me whether you ever felt that way. . . . |
| | | 1 | Father spends too little time with me. |
| | | 1 | Mother wants to run her children's lives. |
| | | 1 | Mother does not understand me. |
| | | 1 | My parents are always proud of their children. (**No**) |
| | | 1 | My parents don't practice what they preach. |
| | | 1 | Father wants to run his children's lives." |
| 7 | Parents' Quarrels[b] | 1 | "Of course, all parents have their quarrels with each other. In your home, when you were growing up, did such arguments occur **often,** occasionally, or rarely?" |
| 8 | Disagreements with Parents | 2 | "When you were a teen-ager, did you have disagreements with your parents **often,** occasionally, rarely, or never?" |

[a] Where necessary, the pathognomic response has been set in bold type.
[b] The correlation of Respondents' Quarrels with Parents' Quarrels with each other is .61. Therefore the two items were combined into a common factor of Home Quarrels only in getting a Simple Score of factors.

104

## ADULT FACTORS

| Stress Factor | Title | Screening Rank | Item |
|---|---|---|---|
| 9 | Adult Poor Physical Health | 2 | "Part of every health history covers the time a person has spent in a hospital. Altogether, how many different times have you been a patient in a hospital either in New York or elsewhere, except to give birth?" |
| | | 1 | "About your health now, would you say it is excellent, good, fair, or **poor**?" |
| 10 | Work Worries | | "Recently there was an article in the papers by an authority on public opinion and problems in America. This authority found that almost everybody has personal worries these days. Here is a list of worries that people all over the country told him about. . . . Would you tell me whether it is something that worries you Often, Sometimes, or Never?" |
| | | 1 | "My work worries me: **Often**, Sometimes, or Never?" |
| | | 1 | "Overwork worries you: **Often**, Sometimes, or Never?" |
| 11 | Socio-economic Status Worries | 1 | "Getting ahead worries you: **Often**, Sometimes, or Never?" |
| | | 1 | "The cost of living worries you: **Often**, Sometimes, or Never?" |
| 12 | Poor Interpersonal Affiliations | 2 | "About how many neighbors around here do you know well enough to visit with?" (**None**) |
| | | 2 | "Altogether, about how many people are there whom you consider to be close friends—not counting relatives or neighbors?" (**None**) |
| | | 2 | "Altogether, how many organizations, societies, and clubs are you active in?" (**None**) |

### CONTINGENT ADULT FACTORS

| Stress Factor | Title | Screening Rank | Item |
|---|---|---|---|
| 13 | Marital Worries | 2 | "Marriage worries you: **Often**, Sometimes, or Never?" |
| 14 | Parental Worries | 1 | "Children worry you: **Often**, Sometimes, or Never?" |
| | | 1 | "Most parents have concerns or problems about their children. What are some of the problems you've had with yours?" (**Any problems**) |
| | | 1 | "Here are some ideas that people have expressed. Would you tell me whether you agree or disagree with each one?" "Children give their parents more trouble than pleasure." (**Agree**) |

theoretical interest. The relative independence of the factors is supported by Table 5-9, showing, with few exceptions, rather low correlations among the various childhood factors and among the adult factors.

In the actual construction of the factors, two methods were attempted.

At first, a simple additive score[22] was used in the factor construction. The Simple Score was "unweighted." That is, each pathognomonic answer to a questionnaire item was given an equal weight of 1. A person's total score was equivalent to the sum, or number of questions he answered pathognomonically.

The process of pyramiding involved the selection and addition of items in a "weighted' 'score. It is best understood by analyzing the construction of one of the major factors. A good example is Parents' Character Negatively Perceived. Originally there were nine items considered for inclusion. Two were discarded because they were different in content from the other items being considered. The first of these, "Were either of your parents the worrying type?" was considered to be an indicator of the mental health of the parents. The other question, "What one person do you take after the most in character?" was not a Rank 1 item, and seemed more useful as an explanatory variable, particularly where identification with one or the other parent might be an important item to control. One statement, "Parents are often way behind the times," was placed in Rank 3, and therefore not considered for inclusion in the final factor. This left six Rank 1 items.

At this point the screening information had been utilized, and we were ready to employ the pyramiding method. The pyramiding, in this particular case, did not eliminate any of the six items, but showed us only *how to group them most effectively.* "Mother wants to run her children's lives" and "Father wants to run his children's lives" were given the respective shorthand designations of "Mother dominating" and "Father dominating." "Mother does not understand me" and "Father spends too little time with me" were labeled respectively "Mother alienating" and "Father alienating." Let's see how these items were combined. The complete process of pyramiding this factor is shown in Appendix B, Section IV.[23]

The items referring to mother or father separately were crosstabulated. Since each item was split in a *"Yes"* group and a *"No, Don't Know, No Answer"* group, each pair constituted a fourfold table, with four cells. First we paired the "Mother dominating" and "Mother alienating" items. Where mothers neither alienated nor dominated (the No-No cell), the ridit was .47. In cases where mothers dominated but did not alienate (the Yes-No cell), the ridit was .52. Similarly, the No-Yes cell was .54. Where mothers were both dominating *and* alienating (.56) we expected a sharp increase in the ridit, but it did not occur. We therefore assigned a score weight of 0 to the No-No cell, and a weight of 1 to the

# TABLE 5-9
## THE INTERCORRELATIONS[a] OF CHILDHOOD AND OF ADULT FACTORS IN MENTAL HEALTH

### CHILDHOOD FACTORS

|  | Parents' Poor Physical Health | Parents' Poor Mental Health | Childhood Economic Deprivation | Childhood Poor Physical Health | Childhood Broken Homes | Parents' Character Negatively Perceived | Parents' Quarrels | Respondents' Quarrels with Parents |
|---|---|---|---|---|---|---|---|---|
| Parents' Poor Physical Health | — | .30 | .17 | .16 | .03 | .16 | .00 | .15 |
| Parents' Poor Mental Health | — | — | .14 | .23 | .13 | .25 | .24 | .26 |
| Childhood Economic Deprivation | — | — | — | .12 | .16 | .19 | .23 | .08 |
| Childhood Poor Physical Health | — | — | — | — | .03 | .21 | .17 | .13 |
| Childhood Broken Homes | — | — | — | — | — | .09 | .09 | .05 |
| Parents' Character Negatively Perceived | — | — | — | — | — | — | .39 | .38 |
| Parents' Quarrels | — | — | — | — | — | — | — | .46 |

### ADULT FACTORS

|  | Adult Poor Physical Health | Work Worries | Socioeconomic Status Worries | Poor Interpersonal Relations | Marital Worries | Parental Worries |
|---|---|---|---|---|---|---|
| Adult Poor Physical Health | — | .17 | .11 | .22 | .03 | .14 |
| Work Worries | — | — | .42 | .03 | .45 | .24 |
| Socioeconomic Status Worries | — | — | — | .11 | .25 | .26 |
| Poor Interpersonal Relations | — | — | — | — | .00 | .11 |
| Marital Worries | — | — | — | — | — | .55 |

[a] Tetrachoric correlations.

other three cells in the table, since their ridits were so similar (.52, .54, .56). (See Table B-2 in Appendix B.)

If the weights were assigned on the basis of a Simple (unweighted) Score, each "Yes" answer would receive a weight of 1. The scores would then be No-No 0, No-Yes 1, Yes-No 1, and Yes-Yes 2. The difference between the Simple Score and pyramided score, at this point, is that the Yes-Yes cell gets a score weight of 2 in the Simple and only 1 in this particular pyramided score.

A similar table for the two father items shows almost identical results. The No-No cell (.46) is assigned a 0, the other three cells a 1, since they are so similar in ridits (.55, .57, .56). Obviously, then, if one parent alone is pictured negatively, it does not make much difference in the respondents' mental health rating whether two items of information or only one are negative. In addition, we learn that risk associated with "alienating" parents is not noticeably different from the risk associated with "dominating" parents, since "Mother dominating" had a ridit of .52, "Mother alienating," .54, "Father dominating," .57, "Father alienating," .55.

A second step consisted of cross-tabulating one father item and one mother item. The results were quite similar in all combinations. For example, in pairing "Father alienating" and "Mother alienating" we found that the No-No cell ridit was .47, that of the cross cells (No-Yes and Yes-No) .52 and the Yes-Yes cell jumped to .61. The score weights now assigned were No-No 0, cross cells 1, and Yes-Yes 2 (see Table B-3 in Appendix B). The pyramiding of the Parents' Character factor is completed in the Appendix.

Pyramiding consists of analyzing combinations of items in relation to the Mental Health Rating (our major dependent variable). Many valuable facts were learned through this process, and these facts often had clinical implications. In the example given, we found that the *number* of negative perceptions of one parent did not seem to increase the mental health risk. However, if both parents were perceived negatively, the risk increased sharply. This suggests that when there is hostility in the relationship with both parents, both these potential sources of affection are cut off. Hostile relations between one parent and the individual may be balanced by the remaining parent, and the mental health risk of such individuals will probably remain about average (.52). The isolated conjugal unit composed of parents and children, the typical dwelling pattern of our society, sharply limits the parental surrogates available to the child. In societies where many adults live in the same household, hostile relations with both parents might not carry such a high mental health risk.

It is also possible that when both parents are perceived as rejecting, we are more likely to be dealing with the hostile projections of an adult paranoid. Such a person may perceive most people as hostile. This does not preclude the possibility that the individual's parents might actually have been rejecting.

The pyramiding of the Parents' Character factor, when completed, produced a weighted score ranging from 0 to 4. Each individual was assigned a score of 0, 1, 2, 3, or 4, depending upon the pattern of his answers to the questions concerning his parents. The higher the score, the greater the mental health risk involved (.45, .47, .56, .63, and .67).

By pyramiding this factor, we increased the number of people having a high mental health risk. For example, on the simple score for Parents' Character Negatively Perceived, the 143 persons receiving the highest scores, 4 to 6, had an average ridit of .63. On the pyramided scale for that factor, however, 195 persons with an average ridit of .63 were included in the highest scores (3 and 4 combined). Thus a pyramided scale which on its highest scores selects 195 persons with a ridit of .63 is a more efficient differentiator of the disturbed and the well than is the corresponding simple score which sorts out only 143 persons with the same ridit. Therefore the pyramiding of items was generally used in constructing the factors, since it is important that a factor be composed in such a way as to maximize both the size of the mental health ridit itself and the number of persons that are included in groups with such high average ridits.

What did we gain by pyramiding? We combined the items so as to maximize their "separating" power along the Mental Health Rating continuum. We also learned interesting facts about responses to these items that have clinical implications. Despite these advantages, the simple score ("unweighted") was often used when only a few items were available for constructing a factor, or the factor was composed of a single item. Moreover, in some trials a weighted score did not offer any real increase in discriminating power.

## Splitting the Scores (Dichotomization and Trichotomization)

After the resolution of a factor into a simple or pyramided score, it was necessary to dichotomize the factor, or split the score in two. We had to find a cutting point between what was to be considered pathological and nonpathological. Splitting the score range also enabled us to combine as many as seven factors simultaneously in a Simple Score of factors. When dichotomizing, we attempted to get about one-third of the sample into the "plus" group, the group with the higher ridit. The rationale behind these divisions is discussed in Chapter 6, pp. 136–140.

In the case of the factor of Parents' Character Negatively Perceived, we dichotomized the pyramided score range from 0 to 4 into a "minus" or healthier group with scores 0 to 1, and a "plus" or disturbed group composed of scores 2, 3, and 4. This placed 563 cases or 33.9 per cent of the sample in the "plus" group. It left 1097 persons (1660 less 563), or 66.1 per cent of the sample, in the "minus" group. The ridit (according to Mental Health Rating II[24]) for the "plus" group was .59, and for the "minus" group, .46 (see Table 5-10).

The dichotomized "plus" group could be used to compare the relative strength of the factors, since they usually included close to 33 per cent of the sample. However, the factors were also trichotomized, or split into three groups, for purposes of combining them into a score. This often proved more efficient than a dichotomized score. For example, the Parents' Character factor (see Table 5-10) was split three ways into: (1) a "plus" group of scores 3 and 4, with 195 cases, 11.7 per cent of the sample, and an average ridit of .63; (2) a "zero" or middle group scoring 2, with 368 cases, 22.2 per cent of the sample, and a ridit of .56; (3) a "minus" group of scores 0 to 1, with 1097 cases, 66.1 per cent of the sample, and a ridit of .46.

The chapters on the major factors include a table indicating both the dichotomized and trichotomized versions of the factor,[25] and the appropriate ridits.

Furthermore, the table for the factor of Parents' Character Negatively Perceived (Table 5-10) and all parallel tables give three sets of ridits for each category: ridits for the Childhood Mental Health Index, Adult Mental Health Rating I and Mental Health Rating II.

## The Organization of the Factor Chapters

The Childhood Mental Health Index was used as one of the measures of mental health in each chapter dealing with childhood factors. Therefore, it is necessary to understand the CMH Index as well as the development of the Adult Mental Health Ratings before proceeding to the factor chapters. The development and composition of the CMH Index is described in Chapter 6, pp. 135–136.

## TABLE 5-10
## DISTRIBUTION, PROPORTIONS, AND AVERAGE MENTAL HEALTH (CMH, MH I, MH II) ACCORDING TO PARENTS' CHARACTER NEGATIVELY PERCEIVED FACTOR, TRICHOTOMIZED AND DICHOTOMIZED

| PARENTS' CHARACTER NEGATIVELY PERCEIVED | | RESPONDENTS' AVERAGE MENTAL HEALTH | | | | |
|---|---|---|---|---|---|---|
| Scores | Trichotomy | CMH | MH I | MH II | No. of Cases | Per Cent of Cases |
| 3 to 4 | + | .66 | .63 | .63 | 195 | 11.7 |
|  |  | * |  |  |  |  |
| 2 | 0 | .58 | .56 | .56 | 368 | 22.2 |
|  |  | * | * | * |  |  |
| 0, 1 | − | .44 | .46 | .46 | 1097 | 66.1 |
|  | Dichotomy |  |  |  |  |  |
| 2 to 4 | + | .61 | .58 | .59 | 563 | 33.9 |
|  |  | * | * | * |  |  |
| 0, 1 | − | .44 | .46 | .46 | 1097 | 66.1 |
| Total Number of Cases (N=100 per cent) |  |  |  |  | 1660 |  |

* Differences in test variable at 5 per cent level of confidence between ridits adjacent to same asterisk.

Later chapters deal with the individual childhood and adult factors utilized in the Stress Scores. The factor chapters usually contain some of the following information:

1. *All items which were originally considered appropriate to that factor:* the items are discussed, and the more important items which actually were selected to compose the factor are represented by statistical tables.

2. *The screening of items related to that factor:* the screening rank of each related item will be discussed, and reasons for dropping items stated. An analysis of the relationship of each item to the respondents' Adult Mental Health Rating II is given, together with the statistical confidence levels of the average ridits of the various subclasses or divisions of the test variable. Each variable is also controlled by socioeconomic

status (fathers' SES for childhood items, respondents' SES for adult items).

3. *The pyramiding of the items into the factor:* the method of combining items into factors is discussed or else illustrated with a table. Particular attention is given to pyramiding which may illuminate relationships between items of clinical interest. Only items that came through the screening are considered for inclusion in the final factor.

4. *The weighting scheme:* a separate table may be included, illustrating the final combined weights of the items in the factor.

5. *The dichotomization and trichotomization of the factor:* a table is usually included which indicates the exact divisions of the final factor into two and three parts, and also gives the average mental health associated with each of these divisions. The "N" (total number of cases), the percentage, and the MH I, MH II, and CMH ridits are given for both the dichotomy and trichotomy. (Some factors, however, such as Parents' Poor Physical Health, could not be trichotomized.)

6. Toward the end of certain chapters the reader may find a detailed development of some of the items that made up the factors. For instance, one item in the Parents' Poor Mental Health factor was the simple score of mothers' and fathers' psychosomatic conditions. This score indicates only the number of conditions reported for each parent. It was felt, however, that it would be of great interest to the clinically oriented reader to know which particular parental conditions seemed to be most strongly associated with poor health in the respondents when they were children. The fact that mothers' ulcers are associated with an increase and fathers' ulcers with a decrease in the child's mental health risk is reported as information of great interest. Although this fact may not have much direct effect upon the Parents' Poor Mental Health factor, it may have important implications for future research and theory. Additional data that may clarify the meaning of an item or give us some clues to the dynamics of a factor are sometimes included.

Before turning to the factors themselves, a series of special problems of method and interpretation will be considered in Chapter 6.

## Summary

This volume had the major analytic goals of (1) relating 148 questionnaire items (the variables) to mental health, (2) comparing the relative strengths of the variables, (3) reducing the items in the prediction of the Mental Health Rating to 14 factors, and (4) relating combinations of factors to the Mental Health Rating.

A "screening operation" found that 120 of the 148 items were "live" (i.e., related to mental health). Using a pyramiding process, 14 factors were constructed from 31 of the 120 "live" items. The ridit was the statistic chosen to describe the 13-point Mental Health Rating Scale. The average ridit is a cumulative percentile rank, indicating the probability that one *group* is more disturbed or impaired than another *group*. The larger the ridit, the worse the mental health of the group. The smaller the ridit, the better the mental health of the group. The average mental health ridit of the entire population of Midtown is .50. Higher ridits than .50 indicate a worse-than-average group, lower ridits than .50, a better-than-average group.

When we are confident (more than 95 per cent sure) that the difference between two adjacent ridits is not due to sampling variation, an asterisk appears between them (asterisks with similar subscripts are placed beside nonadjacent ridits). In a bar chart, this level of confidence would be indicated by nonoverlapping bars.

This chapter described the ridit and its application in the screening operation and the pyramiding of factors. Later chapters deal with the 14 factors. They contain some of the following information: All items originally considered appropriate to the factor; The screening of items related to the factor; The pyramiding of the screened items into the factor; The weighting scheme used in pyramiding; The dichotomization and trichotomization of the factor; and a detailed development of those items composing the factor, and additional relevant data of clinical interest.

## Notes

1. It was decided to use MHR II for the screening operation and MHR I for pyramiding and later operations. This decision is discussed in Chapter 6.

2. Each of the factors was named after the negative or pathognomonic response. For instance, "Parents' *Poor* Physical Health," being associated with poor mental health in the respondent, was used rather than the generic title "Parents' Physical Health." This convention also follows the wording of the questionnaire items.

3. See Appendix B, Sections I and II for interpretation of the ridits as betting odds, and calculation of confidence limits. The term "ridit" derives from the phrase "*R*elative to an *I*dentified *D*istribution."

The ridit was developed by Dr. Irwin D. J. Bross. It was at his suggestion that the ridit was chosen for use in this volume, and with his guidance it was applied to the Midtown data.

Doctor Bross was the Head of the Statistical Service Section of Cornell University Medical College; Head of Research, Design and Analysis Service of the Sloan Kettering Foundation; and Statistical Consultant to Automotive Crash Injury Research. He is now Chief of the Statistical Services at Roswell Park Memorial Institute.

4. The difference between ordinal and other types of scales is clarified by the following schema, elaborated by S. E. Stevens in his article "On The Theory of Scales and Measurement" (*Science*, Volume 103, 1946, pp. 677–680, cited in Marie Jahoda, Morton Deutsch, and Stuart W. Cook, *Research Methods in Social Relations*, Holt, Rinehart & Winston, New York, 1951, pp. 119–127), in which four degrees of scale quantification are delineated—Nominal, Ordinal, Interval, and Ratio:

    a. *Nominal Scales* are scales only in the very loosest sense of the word. Such scales connote only differences in qualitative categories, with *no* assumptions at all of differences in degree or quantity. They are appropriate to typologies or classifications, not continua.

    b. *Ordinal Scales* define the relative position of items with regard to a characteristic, with no implications as to distance between positions on the scale.

    c. *Interval Scales* not only make possible the determination of greater, equal, or lesser rank, but by virtue of having equal units and intervals of measurement, they also make possible specification of distance between points. On an interval scale we may claim that the distance between one and two, two and three, three and four, and so forth, are all equal.

    d. *Ratio Scales* represent the highest development of mathematical precision in scale construction. On these scales we assume not only that the distances between consecutive points are equal, but also that the scale starts with an absolute point of zero. This means, for instance, that the ratios of four to two, six to three, eight to four, and so forth, are the same; that the ratios of three to two, six to four, nine to six are the same.

The Adult Mental Health Ratings (MH I, MH II) are individual psychiatric judgments. They are therefore ordinal scales. On the other hand, the Childhood Mental Health Index, based on a limited number of items that were equally weighted, might be considered an interval scale.

5. A lesser but related reason for not using averages is the problem of disagreement over the boundaries of the scale steps in an ordinal rating. It was expected that the two psychiatrists would not always assign identical ratings to a respondent. Most typical were "one-step differences," for example, where one rater assigned a 2, the other a 3. This was an entirely expected phenomenon, due to the inevitable fuzziness of the boundaries of scale steps. It occurred despite detailed specification added to the short definitions of the scale steps presented above.

Bross specifically warns that the assigning of exact weights necessary for computation of averages is misleading, and suggests that the ridit provides a good substitute for the average (or mean) when using subjective scales.

    . . . the scale for the factors, as interpreted by various individuals, tends to vary. Despite the fact that rigorous criteria have been established, there is a tendency towards "slippage" when a case falls near the boundary line between two categories. For this and various other reasons, if an attempt is made to assign a numerical value to a category in the scale, arithmetic means tend to be misleading. In general, the "weight" assigned to a category should involve the notion of probability. (Irwin D. J. Bross and Rivkah Feldman, *Ridit Analysis of Automotive Crash Injuries*, Division of Automotive Crash Injury Research, Department of Public Health and Preventive Medicine, Cornell University Medical College, New York, 1956, p. v.)

Of course the problem of "slippage" was solved to some extent by combining the two separate psychiatric ratings (from 0 through 6) into a final rating ranging from 0 to 12 (see Chapter 2). The distributions and calculated ridits of the Mental Health Ratings are presented later in this chapter (see Table 5-3). The table includes both Mental Health Rating I and Mental Health Rating II. The first rating is based principally on symptomatology, the second on symptomatology plus the sociocultural background of the respondent. Despite the attempt to control slippage by combining ratings, "slippage" was of course still one of the considerations leading to the choice of the ridit.

6. Bross says:

The analytical use of Ridits involves only simple computation and allows the "weights" to have an interpretation in terms of probability. In using Ridits, the "identified distribution" must first be chosen and Ridits calculated for each of the various categories (or cross categories), and confidence intervals are set up about these means. It is thus possible to give odds that one group is better off than the other with respect to a factor under study. (Irwin D. J. Bross and Rivkah Feldman, *ibid.*)

7. An acceptable statistic for the treatment of nonnumerical data is the "Chi-Square," $\chi^2$. While adequate, it only tells us that we are confident that a relationship exists between some variables. It does not tell us anything about how much of a relationship exists, although it can be converted to such a statistic, the coefficient of contingency.

8. See Appendix B, Section I, for calculation of "odds."

9. In this study, the "identified distribution" is the whole sample. However, when the whole sample consists of two or more different series (such as morphine, placebo, and test-agent groups), one of the subseries is picked as the standard (for example, morphine).

10. If for the sake of convenient notation "Poor" were assigned a rating of 0, "Fair" a 1, "Good" a 2, and "Excellent" a 3, this would in no way change the fact that these ratings form an ordinal, not an interval scale.

11. Throughout this volume, ridits are calculated to three decimal places, rounded off to the nearest hundredth and thereafter reported with two decimal places.

12. Bross and Feldman, *op. cit.*, p. 8.

13. See Appendix B, Section I, for calculation of "odds."

14. In the total sample, 148 persons were given a Mental Health II Rating of zero. This is about 9 per cent of the sample. These 148 are in the healthiest percentile of the sample. Actually, 4.5 per cent are healthier than the *average man* among this healthiest 9 per cent (and 4.5 per cent are sicker than this hypothetical man). Therefore the *average* ridit for this whole group with a Mental Health Rating of zero is .045, the midpoint of the group.

15. .67 — .48 is .19. Adding .19 to .50 we get .69, odds of a little better than 66.7 to 33.3, or 2 to 1.

16. For the calculation of confidence limits, see Appendix B, Section II.

17. Bross and Feldman, *op. cit.*, p. 6.

18. Bross, personal communication.

19. This is true in the low and middle, but not in the high SES.

20. Splitting the sample into almost equal thirds radically reduces the possibility of getting differences at the 5 per cent confidence level. The large confidence intervals for subclasses of 14 or even 54 cases, which appear in Table 5-6, under low SES, often make it difficult to obtain significant differences. If the trends are similar at all three SES levels (on criterion of a *live* variable), the lack of differences at the 5 per cent level may be partially discounted.

21. Excluding items which were considered part of the dependent variable, mental health, such as psychophysiological symptoms.

22. Pathological answers to the items on which the score was based were given a weight of 1.

23. Appendix B, Section IV, gives the details of steps II to V in the pyramiding of this factor.

24. In this context the MH II ridits are presented for both the preadult and the adult factors, since it was on the basis of Rating II that the pyramiding and the dichotomy were originally constructed. After the creation of the Childhood Mental Health (CMH) Index, the influence of childhood factors on CMH ridits and of adult factors on the MH I ridits was examined. It should be noted that there is virtually no difference between the Mental Health I and II ridits. For this reason, the decision to use the more inclusive Rating II in the screening could not possibly have kept some "dead" items in the screen nor have let some "live" items slip through the screen.

25. For more details of dichotomization versus trichotomization, see Chapter 6, pp. 136–140.

# Some Problems of Interpretation and Method

T  H  O  M  A  S      S  .      L  A  N  G  N  E  R

## Consequences of a Choice of Method

No research design is perfect, and the decision to adopt any particular method automatically involves the adoption of a number of inherent problems as well as advantages. For example, the choice of the case method has the advantage of understanding single individuals thoroughly, yet it usually involves small samples, and the data are often ungeneralizable. Mass survey methods are usually generalizable if careful sampling has been done, but the data are often superficial and may offer little understanding of the larger motivational or dynamic patterns of the subjects.

The decision to use an intensive interview on a large random sample grew out of one of the primary goals of the research. This goal was to make estimates of the level of mental health in the community. The questionnaire and the psychiatric ratings were designed to tell who and how much psychiatric impairment, and what type of disturbance accounted for this impairment. There was only a strong hope that out of the data would come some clues as to *why* such disturbances had arisen. We had of necessity sacrificed our understanding of the dynamics of individual cases in order to obtain estimates of mental disturbance in the community.

The attempts to understand the sources of mental disturbance, whether by the case or survey method, whether in a clinical or community setting, whether therapeutic or purely observational, have not been too successful. More and more the clinician and behavioral scientist tend to look on a particular mental disorder at a point in time as the product of the individual's hereditary endowment and all his previous experience or history. The importance of longitudinal research on influences in the development and course of mental disorder is now recognized. The examination of a patient in the clinic or a respondent in the community *at a point in time* cannot yield the developmental data necessary for an understanding of the genesis of the disorder.

Thus, in addition to the *extensive versus intensive* dimension of study, there is the dimension of time. Studies can be generally classified into longitudinal (those which follow the development of individuals) and cross-sectional (those which look at the individual at a point in time). The longitudinal method doubtless yields more complete information, but few therapists or investigators are able to spend a lifetime with a patient or respondent. At best, a few patients living outside hospitals are carried in long-term therapy of more than five years' duration, and only a few community studies are conducted over a similar period of time.

In order to compensate for the lack of firsthand knowledge concerning earlier development and experience, the therapist and behavioral scientist are forced to rely on the recall of the individual and close relatives. It is at just this point that the sacrifice involved in the choice of the cross-sectional (or short-term) approach is greatest.

It is well known that memory difficulties, retrospective falsification, impairment of reality-perception, and related symptoms are indicative of many types of mental disorder. It is not exaggerating greatly to say that the more disturbed the individual, the less accurate his recall of past events and his perception of present events. Similarly, the mentally disturbed person is less likely to recognize the way he interacts with other people, and is therefore more likely to give an untrue picture of his social relationships up to the time of treatment or interview. The obvious conclusion is that on the basis of recall we glean the least accurate picture of the lives of the most disturbed segment of the population, the very segment that interests us most.

There may, of course, be certain types of mental disturbance that involve a heightening of recall about early childhood experiences, or a greater concern with and more detailed memory for family relationships, in the past or present. Whether recall is heightened or distorted, the greatest difficulty arises in interpretation of the data gathered, for we are never entirely sure whether we are recording fact or fantasy. This problem comes up in many different contexts and parallel forms such as "fact versus fantasy," "report versus perception," "factor versus symptom," and "cause versus effect."

## Factual Report versus Distorted Perceptions and Fantasy

The concepts of fantasy and perception have different histories and origins and enough differences in meaning to make it worthwhile to distinguish between them. Fantasy in the sense of the projection of the content of the unconscious onto reality is somehow a more radical or basic concept than is perceptual distortion. It would seem artificial, however, to treat fantasy and perception as if they were unrelated. An example of a fantasy might be the seduction fantasy reported by Freud. An example of a perception might be the perception of the parents' character as dominating or alienating, as reported by the Midtown residents. One could just as easily say that a person "fantasied that his parents were dominating." The term fantasy, however, suggests somewhat wilder flights of imagination, somewhat greater distortion of reality.

One questionnaire item included in the factor Parent's Character Negatively Perceived was "Mother wants to run her children's lives. When you were growing up (age six to eighteen) did you feel that way too?" If the respondent answers "Yes," he is ostensibly expressing a feeling toward his mother which he had between ages six and eighteen. While his feelings toward his mother may be of primary importance from a therapeutic viewpoint, from the etiological viewpoint it is crucial to know whether his mother was *in fact* domineering, and to what degree.

Agreement with the statement "Mother wants to run her children's lives" can mean among other things: (1) The respondent's mother actually did want to run his life during his childhood. (2) The respondent's mother wanted to run his life in childhood and still does now (in the flesh or as an internalized image). His present relationship to his mother (or her image) may well determine whether he will agree with the statement. The more she dominates him now, the more likely he is to agree that she tried to run his life in childhood. (3) The respondent's mother didn't want to run his life during childhood, but she was resented for many reasons, and is now *perceived* as domineering during childhood. (4) The respondent has a strong desire to be dependent on his mother, and therefore merely perceives her as domineering, as complementary to his dependence.

Perhaps people who were or are still dominated by their parents are *least* likely to admit it, either because they have repressed the fact or they are utilizing the mechanism of denial. Some of the most disturbed neurotics and psychotics might not accuse their parents of any misbehavior. The fact that respondents who disagreed with all six negative statements concerning parents[1] had the low average mental health risk of .45 would seem to refute this hypothesis. However, even in this group there were 13 per cent with Mental Health I Ratings of 6 or more, indicating some impairment in life functioning. It is quite possible, then, to perceive the parents' character positively, and also have a high degree of psychiatric impairment. Within this 13 per cent there may be some persons whose mental disorders (such as brain injury cases, or epileptics) had very little to do with their parents' character. They would be giving an accurate report of their parents' good character. On the other hand, it is more likely that persons with Mental Health Ratings of 6 and over either *had* alienating and dominating parents or would *perceive* them negatively. Since the Impaired 13 per cent do not do the latter, the chances are that they may be denying or repressing their negative feelings against their parents, who were actually not excessively alienating or dominating. They may also be denying or repressing the actual *fact* that their parents were in reality alienating and dcminating.

The repression of excessively negative (or positive) feelings about parents, regardless of what the parents were actually like, is generally considered one of the central problems in a neurosis. The denial of the fact that parents were initially alienating or dominating (if such facts could be ascertained in the normal clinical setting) would also be considered evidence of psychopathology. The chances are strong, then, that among the ill who report their parents in a positive light, the positive report itself would be evidence of mental disturbance. Two "facts" would have to be determined to make a positive report into evidence of disturbance. There would have to be evidence that unconscious hostility to the parents actually existed, or that the parents actually were alienating and domineering during childhood. Obviously, such "facts" can be determined only by psychotherapeutic techniques combined with observational studies of child-parent relations, followed up by studies of the same individuals when adult. Such research is virtually nonexistent at present, although the near future will probably see a rapid development in this field.

Of similar concern is the problem of the mentally healthy persons reporting parents with negative characters. Are these perceptions or reports? Among the 29 persons who agreed with four negative statements about their parents, only one (3.4 per cent) had a Mental Health (I) Rating of 0 or 1 (Well). However, eleven (38 per cent) were in the Impaired category. The chances are very small that a person who perceives his parents extremely negatively will be "well." The haunting question is always "Which comes first, the chicken or the egg, rejecting parents or the child's mental disturbance?"[2]

Although the term "Parents' Character Negatively Perceived" is used throughout this book, we lean toward the hypothesis that these actually are rejecting parents, that children and adults can report rather objectively about their parents, and that rejection itself precedes and is causally related to mental disturbance in the child and adult.

Another equally tenable hypothesis is that mental disturbance in the child *produces* a distorted picture of the parents. It follows that *one of the goals of psychotherapy is the correction of this presumably distorted image of the parents*. Paranoid individuals in particular would be prone to project their hostility onto their parents, and then accuse their parents of being alienating. Similarly, dependent individuals may view their parents as domineering.

Where lies reality? Somewhere between these two extreme viewpoints? Certainly few investigators believe that all people answering questionnaires are reporting unadorned facts. Similarly, few clinicians would insist that parents are never evil, and that the parental wrongs reported by patients are *all* projections and figments of the imagination. (The child psychiatrist in particular gets a chance to see the behavior of his patients' parents.)

Perhaps our inability to reconcile these points of view comes from the different *sources* of information available to various disciplines in the behavioral sciences. Psychiatrists, and particularly the psychoanalysts, have produced the most detailed analyses of the psychodynamics of parent-child relations utilizing principally patients of higher socioeconomic status. The sociologist and applied anthropologist have historically been concerned with "problem areas" such as delinquency, divorce, drug addiction, racial and religious minorities, poverty and scarcity cultures. The case histories of child-parent relationships which they take, the observations they make, more usually than not involve people of low socioeconomic status. The clinician is probably correct in assuming that, on the average, the parents of his predominantly high status private patients are relatively mild in their child-rearing practices or at least are not physically violent with their children. When his high status patient tells him "My parents reject me," he is liable to discount it as fact, and *treat it more as a symptom than as a report*. This is because the clinician knows from personal experience about the normal range of parental behavior in families of higher social status. He was a child once himself in such a family.

Thus Freud eventually discounted the reports of parental seduction by his predominantly middle-class Viennese patients. These seductions were fantasy, not fact. However, a psychiatrist transplanted into some remote rural area in the United States or another country might find his patients frequently making factual reports of incest. It would be wrong to treat some of these facts as fantasy.

Examples of this type of distortion are occurring every day. Most important is the possibility that the rather specific experiences of the clinician and the sociologist are being *overgeneralized* to populations wherein they are no longer applicable. For us to insist that in general the respondents' statements are simply perceptions and not reports would be inaccurate. In particular, many respondents of low socioeconomic status may for all we know be reporting accurately the extreme physical and emotional punishment that their parents inflicted upon them. The questionnaire items may be severe understatements of the alienation and domination to which they were actually exposed. On the other hand, some high socioeconomic respondents may have had relatively mild parents, but reported them as alienating and dominating. Although we have no way of testing these hypotheses at present, *the negative reports of parents may perhaps be more factual in the low SES, and more projection and fantasy in the high SES.*

In materials dealing with the psychotherapy of higher status patients who are conscious of self, introspective, and communicative there is much evidence for the perception argument. Selective forgetting or selective retention of experience, the exaggeration of some events or characteristics and the minimization of others often become of cardinal importance in the therapeutic process. The projection of the patient's own undesirable characteristics onto the parents is also common. Selective forgetting and projection are well illustrated in the story of Lucy Freeman, who wrote of her psychoanalysis in *Fight Against Fears*. The patient or respondent initially recalling a rejecting mother and a loving father might well come up with the following statements after further probing:

My mother might storm at me for five minutes, then try to make me comfortable and happy the rest of the day, but I had remembered only those five minutes because they served my anger.

With my father I had remembered primarily the exciting, glorious moments, forgotten the times when he raged at me.[3]

Thus we tend to remember or forget in terms of the type of emotional problem we have. We see people essentially as it serves our personality needs to see them.

What if parents were clearly rejecting, unloving, and unlovable? Wouldn't it be pathological to perceive them neutrally or positively? Wouldn't this be just as much a distortion of reality? Perhaps for a child it would be an indication of mental disturbance, but among adults the ability to forgive or accept parents, regardless of how rejecting they actually were, is taken as a sign of maturity and mental health.

There is some evidence that we may be measuring not the actual experience of having rejecting parents but the ability or inability to accept the inevitably unfulfilled desire for affection and the inevitable discipline and domination that are part of the parent-child relationship. Data (not presented) show that the proportion of people reporting their parents negatively diminishes somewhat after age forty. Similarly, the proportion reporting that their parents quarreled frequently is reduced. The proportion of broken homes, of course, theoretically cannot vary with the age of the respondent, and *actually* does not. It shows the statistical stability that a factual item should have.[4]

If there is more of a tendency on the part of people over forty to "forgive and forget," the gradual acceptance of the parents may be part of the maturing process itself. Some tests of the *forgiving* hypothesis are possible using these data, and will be carried out in later analyses. For example, are people who have already become parents more tolerant of their own parents than those without children? If so, the sobering experience of raising children may have an influence on attitudes toward one's own parents. Another possibility is that as the problems of aging beset them, the problems of their early years may seem pale and insignificant and not worth reporting. Relative to their adult experiences, their childhood seems happy and content.

The problem of relativity is central to the problem of perception. We perceive and feel on a sliding scale, only in relation to what we or others about us have perceived or felt previously. For example, it was found that almost equal proportions of each socioeconomic group reported that their parents quarreled "often." This tells us nothing about the absolute number of times a week that parents quarreled (which might have been a better way to phrase this question). It tells us, for example, only that a particular low SES person's parents quarreled "often." His comparisons were probably made within his own SES group. The "often" of the low SES respondent might actually be once a day, and the "often" of the high SES respondent could be once a week. We have no way of knowing. The intensity of parents' quarrels is another matter, but we tend to assume that there is more physical violence between parents in the low

SES home. Whether this is more associated with poor mental health in the low SES offspring than the verbal battles or prolonged hostilities that probably occur more typically in the high status home is a matter of speculation. The association between frequency and intensity is also a matter for investigation.

In any event, the absolute frequency of quarrels is not crucial for the simple prediction of mental health risk. Regardless of the actual number of times parents quarreled, persons who *perceived* their parents as quarreling "often" run an increased mental health risk.

There are many factors influencing perception that have less to do with the personality structure of the individual who is perceiving, and more to do with his social and environmental position. It was somewhat surprising that the proportion of the respondents' *parents* reported in poor health did not vary by SES, while the poor health of the low SES *respondents* was strikingly greater in proportion. This same situation was found in reports of psychosomatic conditions. A smaller proportion of low SES parents were reported with psychosomatic conditions. It seems logical that the health of low status people, particularly twenty or thirty years ago, would be considerably worse than that of high status people. This "perception" is probably based on many factors, some of which we can guess at. For one, the low SES parents' ills probably didn't get diagnosed, so that their illnesses were not recognized and hence unreportable. The lack of medical care for the low stratum in past eras has been well documented. In addition, this stratum, particularly the European parents of immigrants, may have been trained to be stoical, fatalistic, and to accept all aches and pains as inevitable and not worth complaining about. Their lack of education enhanced the possibility that serious symptoms would pass unnoticed, or result in more rapid death. The lifetime morbidity rate may very well have been lower, for the mortality rate certainly was higher. You can't experience a lot of minor diseases if you die from an unrecognized major illness during early middle age. The children who lost a parent through early death would, of course, be much less able to report his or her illnesses. These early parental deaths are in fact slightly more prevalent among the low SES, and might help to account for the apparent good health of low SES parents.

While these external influences upon perception may be operating in many of the factors which were isolated, the internal influences (the personality needs and mental disturbance of the individual) may also be operating to produce perceptual distortion. In this instance it is not too much to assume that those adult respondents who are somatically pre-occupied will report their own *and* their parents diseases more readily, or perhaps excessively. Illness of all types will have a high salience for them, will occupy a central position in their thinking and influence their perception. They will notice illness with the eagle eye of those who have a need to notice illness in themselves and others. They will probably also remember illnesses better than most individuals, and cherish each episode of bedridden bliss. These internal factors may work in a similar, or in this case opposite, direction to the external influences on perception.

There is evidence, however, that the mental health of the respondent does not play a dominant role in his reports of the illnesses of family members. The validity of reports by one person about the symptomatology of immediate relatives is high, according to a study by Hoffer in rural Michigan.[5] Housewives were asked whether a list of symptoms pertained to themselves or any member of their family. The information was validated through actual physical examinations of one-sixth of the families. Complete agreement between the questionnaire reports and the physicians' examinations was found in 8 out of 10 cases.

To return to our own study, some checks of *internal validity* were made by using data from the Midtown questionnaire on the reporting of symptoms. For example, women might be expected to report a greater number of psychosomatic conditions for their mothers than for their fathers. This might have been the result of greater familiarity with their mothers' problems. We found that, on the contrary, women and men reported similar proportions of psychosomatic conditions for their fathers and mothers. The sex of the reporter did not influence the reporting, in this instance.

Another internal check which speaks well for the reportorial quality of some of the responses was the examination of the question "My parents often had hard times making ends meet." Those whose fathers died before the respondent had reached the age of sixteen were more likely to report "hard times" than those whose mothers died before the age of sixteen. It is logical to expect that the death of the family breadwinner is more likely to result in economic "hard times." If the death of the mother were more closely linked to the report of "hard times," we would tend toward the interpretation that the emotional deprivation of losing their mothers had colored the respondents' reports of the family financial situation and all other reports about their childhood.

The problem of report versus perception, or fact versus fantasy has been discussed in broad fashion. The reader must eventually judge for himself the degree to which each individual factor is reported accurately, or represents a perception or distortion on the part of the respondent. Among the preadult factors, Broken Homes (the death or divorce of parents) is probably the most factual in nature. Next in credibility come the Parents' Poor Physical Health, the respondent's Childhood Poor Physical Health, and the Parents' Poor Mental Health (based mostly on reports of "psychosomatic" conditions). Since the mental and physical health factors are based largely upon reports of what might appear to the respondent to be purely somatic illnesses (arthritis, diabetes, colds, and so on), the amount of actual concealment is probably small. However, the lack of recognition of their parents' symptoms and unfamiliarity with the parents must be considered. Many persons lost parents before they were old enough to talk or to recognize disease. What they remember depends very much on their *vocabulary* at the time the event occurred.

Reports of the frequency of Parents' Quarrels and Disagreements with Parents are somewhat lower on the list, because of the sheer relativity of the responses "Often, Sometimes, or Never." Parents' Character Negatively Perceived is labeled a perception, and is considered the least factual of the preadult factors.

If the factors were to be ranked in decreasing order of over-all credibility (based upon all the criteria suggested so far), the list would look something like this:

Rank                  Over-all Credibility of Factors

1    Broken Homes, Childhood Economic Deprivation
2    Childhood Poor Physical Health, Parents' Poor Physical Health, Parents' Poor Mental Health
3    Parents' Quarrels, Disagreements with Parents
4    Parents' Character Negatively Perceived


5    Adult Poor Physical Health, Poor Interpersonal Affiliations
6    Work Worries, Socioeconomic Status Worries, Marital Worries, Parental Worries

In this crude ranking of over-all credibility the adult factors are given lowest priority. Many seem to be more reportorial (for example, Adult

Poor Physical Health) than Parents' Character Negatively Perceived. The reason for their low placement is the inclusion of a second major criterion of credibility, "factor versus symptom."

## Cause versus Effect

The circularity of the adult factors has already been discussed in Chapter 1. It is obvious that these "factors" are simultaneously "cause and effect, and only the time dimension of the longitudinal study can tell us which comes first.

Clearly, the adult factors did not occur at a time prior to the existence of adult mental health. On the contrary, the adult factors, particularly the "worries" over family, status, and work, read like a second list of effects of mental disturbance. The difference is sharpened by comparing a preadult with an adult factor. For instance, we feel more or less certain that the Parents' Poor Mental Health was already present in some degree at the birth of the respondent. Although his birth and later behavior might to some degree influence his mother's or father's mental health, the preponderant direction of influence would be that of parent on child, not vice versa. The mental health of the parents is assumed in general to act upon the mental health of the child, although there is of course interaction between parent and child.

The adult factor Poor Interpersonal Affiliations (few friends or neighbors, and little membership in organizations) might just as well be the result of mental disturbance as a cause of mental disturbance. People who are withdrawn may not want or be able to make any friends. On the other hand, people who are rejected by others, perhaps because of their physical defects, religion, or some other characteristic beyond their power to control (i.e., not possibly related to mental health), may very well become mentally disturbed *because* of this rejection. They will have few friends, but not necessarily through any fault of their own. These two extreme types probably do not exist in reality, and most people lie somewhere in the middle, both rejecting others and being rejected.

Some researchers believed that people who were socially isolated, either sheltered from or ostracized by the prevailing culture, became ill because of this isolation, and developed schizophrenia. These were the denizens of the rooming houses in the high mobility or transient areas of large cities.[6]

Recently a study by Clausen and Kohn[7] has indicated that disturbed persons, particularly schizophrenics, tend to migrate to the transient areas of cities *in order to get away from the emotional demands of interpersonal relationships.* This research implies that persons who are *previously* disturbed tend to become socially isolated, and not vice versa.

Obviously, social isolation is a symptom of mental disturbance as well as a causal factor. Certainly it plays a great part in the development of disturbance in the child. The *feeling* of being alone, in spite of the presence of many friendly persons, is probably most indicative of mental disturbance. A study of over 400 grade school and high school students showed that, according to a group-administered Rorschach Test, children who were "popular" but thought they had no friends were severely disturbed. In contrast, children who were sociometrically "unpopular," those who received few choices as a friend, but thought they had many friends, were not severely disturbed. The number of outgoing choices, then, was more important than the number of incoming choices, from the standpoint of mental health.[8] According to these data (given the limitations of the facts that schoolchildren rather than adults were involved, and the use of the Rorschach Test), your attitude toward others rather than their attitude toward you is more closely indicative of your mental health.

Perhaps we are measuring this attitude of outgoingness, as well as "objective" facts of interpersonal affiliation, when we utilize the Midtown questionnaire items concerning friends, neighbors, and organizations. Some correlation between *outgoingness* in personality and the number of friends one makes must be present.

The problem for the etiologist is that the rejectors and the rejected are virtually inseparable, unless detailed observations of the individual in question are available over a long period of time. With our present data we cannot distinguish between those who were friendless against their will and those who were friendless by choice. This and other adult *component* variables are quite similar to the demographic *reciprocal* variables, such as marital status, adult socioeconomic status, and adult religious affiliation. We don't know whether divorced people are mentally disturbed prior to their divorces, or whether the divorce itself depresses them and thus is the cause of their disturbance. Both statements are partially true. Those who are somewhat more disturbed on the average are more likely to get divorced, and the divorce itself is a factor making for further disturbance (although it may involve only a short period of depression). The fact of the divorce may certainly create more anxiety in subsequent relationships, and enhance the possibility of further divorces.

In itself, divorce may be an adaptive mechanism, reducing the anxiety associated with a poor marriage.

Likewise, low status may depress or anger an individual, and this reaction may interfere with his promotion or even get him fired. Previous mental disturbance may cause him to lose status, or may prevent him from achieving higher status. Thus, his present socioeconomic status is reciprocal to his mental health, at once cause and effect, virtually inseparable. The adult component factors, having this same quality, might very well be called *reciprocal component factors* which places them clearly in the analytic framework of the entire study.[9]

In the last analysis, in the case of both the preadult and adult factors, we are unable to say that they show a causal relationship to mental disturbance in adult life. We can say only that they show an *association* with mental disturbance, as evidenced by an increase or decrease in the mental health risk. This should not be too disappointing, for contemporary research being conducted on a large scale in the epidemiology of coronary heart disease and lung cancer is no more conclusive. Although cigarette smoking is associated with increased incidence of lung cancer, a causal relationship has not been established. While a rise in blood cholesterol is associated with an increased risk of arteriosclerosis, a high cholesterol diet has not been established as the cause of coronary heart disease.

Association is a first step, but not the final step, in the establishment of a causal relationship. If we can establish an association between A and B, this does not mean that A causes B. It is only logical that responses which make the best predictors of mental disturbance are more likely to be *symptoms* of mental disturbance than causal or antecedent factors producing or predisposing to mental disturbance. Certainly, some of the more factual items have less predictive strength than the perceptions, such as Parents' Character Negatively Perceived.[10] Nevertheless, the greater the proportion of "factual" data we use in our search for the genesis of mental disurbance (as opposed to predictive schemes), the more reliable our results and interpretations will be, and the less circularity there will be in our future investigations.

A brief example will help to clarify this point. One way to *predict* whether a person will make a good business executive is to ask him the difference between Scotch, rye, bourbon, and Irish whiskey. Knowledge of whiskies is a superficial characteristic of executives and those on their way to becoming executives. They move in circles where social drinking is common, and a knowledge of whiskies is the natural result of their group membership. Yet drinking is far from being the cause or source of their executive ability. For an understanding of the dynamics of the executive type, we want to know about the executive personality, about ability to make decisions, to delegate authority, to organize work and family life, to lead and advise other people. For purely predictive purposes, the candidate's knowledge of the social graces, including when to consume what type of alcohol, will probably be adequate. For a true understanding of the *source* of his future executive success, we need facts about his behavior and life history. Though more costly, the latter method will tell us "why" as well as "who," and the "why" is really the final goal of prediction and the scientific method. "Who, what, and when" are questions partly answered in the initial stages of investigation. In this volume we can only make guarded guesses about the "why" of mental disturbance.

## Factor versus Symptom

Would it have improved the "purity" of the adult factors if we had not used questionnaire items that were also symptoms of mental disturbance? Could we have eliminated the factors concerned with worries about various roles the individual must play, such as breadwinner, parent, and spouse? If we asked the question "Does your marriage make you worry?" would it have been any different from asking the question we did ask, "Do you worry about your marriage?" Although the second version seems to imply that the worrying is primary, and the first that marriage is the cause of the symptom of worrying, there is obviously no real difference in the meaning of answers to the two questions. These worries can be relatively more realistic or unrealistic, but we have no way of finding out which is true in any single case.

The problem of what constitutes realistic and unrealistic worrying is not easily solved. For example, a study of attitudes based primarily on a sample of college students found that those who feared war within the next few years were more authoritarian in their attitudes. There was the implication that authoritarians were more emotionally disturbed, and their greater fear of war was interpreted as the projection of their unconscious hostile impulses onto world events. It was pointed out[11] that a simultaneous national survey found the *great majority* of the nation believing that we would soon be at war, and indeed, we were at war after the surveys were completed. Was the fear of war realistic or unrealistic? Does the ultimate reality of the war impugn the mental health of those who didn't fear war, or excuse the anxiety of those who feared war, prior to its advent?

The two adult factors that are not worries (Adult Poor Physical Health and Poor Interpersonal Affiliations) only *seem* to be more objective. The number of friends an individual reports seems more objective than the amount of worrying he does about his friendships. However the number of friends he reports is based on his subjective evaluation of. who his friends are. Thus we are faced with a problem of *relative objectivity*, since none of the factors is strictly objective. Even physical health is the respondent's own estimate of his health, not his physician's. The number of hospitalizations he has had might seem "objective," but it is principally a function of the amount of money he has for hospitalization, the attitudes he has toward doctors and preventive examinations, and the degree of his hypochondriasis (or to put it more positively, his concern with self-preservation). We shall find that the number of hospitalizations is much greater for persons of high SES, but the health of low SES persons is predominantly reported as "Poor." Are the sick people those who get treated, or the ones that don't? This applies to mental disturbance as well, and it is one of the thorniest problems in medical epidemiology.

There are indications that some worries are relatively objective. For example, persons of low SES worry more about the cost of living. This seems like a realistic worry. On the other hand, those of high SES worry considerably more about their work. It would seem more realistic from one standpoint if those in menial occupations with sporadic employment and low income worried more about their work. However, work may be a more central value in the ethic of the middle and upper SES groups, and it may therefore cause more worrying.

Although some direct questions can be asked in an interview, such as "How many close friends do you have?" or "How is your health?" it is more difficult to ask "Are you a good parent?" or "Do you have a good marriage?" We might actually want to ask "Has your marriage affected your health in any way? How?" Most people would not be able to tell us whether their marriage had caused or contributed to any of their symptoms. It would be difficult for the average person to report what is presumably unconscious material, particularly to an interviewer in a single home visit.

The stress of parenthood might better have been elicited by a question like "Has taking care of your children affected you in any way?" Such responses as "They make me worry," "I'm run down because of them," or "They make me irritable" would at least establish a conscious connection between the factor and the symptom. Even here, we would not have ascertained that children were the true cause or only cause of the parent's irritability, which might stem from the marriage, job, childhood experiences, physiological changes, or any number of combinations of other factors.

## Symptoms versus Sociocultural Background: MHR I and II

The separation of symptoms from sociocultural background on the case summaries has already been described. In a study of the relationship between a mental health rating and a series of environmental factors, it was necessary to keep the factors *out* of the rating system, for the time being. For example, we wanted to find out how socioeconomic status was related to the mental health ratings. Suppose the psychiatrists had considered low status as a *sign* of mental disturbance. Each time they saw low income, education, occupation, or rent, they would have given the respondent a worse mental health rating. Upon analysis of the data, we would have "discovered" a strong relationship between the mental health rating and socioeconomic status. The relationship might have been due solely to the influence of the respondent's status upon the psychiatrists' ratings. The relationship could be completely circular. Whether it was spurious or not could not be determined.

In order to circumvent this situation, we devised a system that made use of two Mental Health Ratings. Rating I was based chiefly upon psychophysiological symptoms and some worries and fears that did not have a large social component. Age, sex, and marital status were left in the first section of the summary, since these variables were felt to be essential even to the symptom rating. The meaning of the psychophysiological complaints, for example, could not be interpreted properly without knowing the age and sex of each individual. To this extent, then, these three variables are not methodologically "pure." We have no way of knowing whether bias (albeit a clinically sophisticated bias) on the part of the raters produced the relationship between these three variables and Mental Health Ratings I and II.

In the case of socioeconomic status, and all other demographic and stress variables, the symptom rating (Rating I), was assigned without any previous knowledge of the respondent's status, stresses, and so forth. The second Rating (II) was then made, based upon Rating I *and* the additional sociocultural background information (religion, generation, education, income, occupation, rent, nationality background, parents' background characteristics, worries about marriage, job, cost of living, work, overwork, and other worries linked to social background). In this case we found a relationship between Mental Health Rating II and socioeconomic status. Was it due to "bias," resulting from the inclusion of SES in the background data shown to the raters? A simple check showed that there was just as strong a relationship between SES and Mental Health Rating I, based purely upon symptoms. The relationship of SES and Rating II is therefore not artifactual. It is not due to any circularity in the methods we employed. This rather elaborate system of ratings, though it had certain flaws and could not include all the background variables, acted as our "methodological insurance."

Mental Health Rating II was certainly a more holistic rating. It more closely approximates what a psychiatrist usually does when he makes a judgment of impairment. The distinction between an impairment rating and a diagnosis is important. It is difficult for a psychiatrist to make a *diagnosis* without knowing the sociocultural background of the individual. All diagnoses in everyday practice are of necessity "contaminated" by some knowledge of the life circumstances of the patient. However, in our research, for purposes of establishing the relationships between these life circumstances and *impairment* (not diagnosis), we artificially "decontaminated" each case history, removing the social background material. This made it particularly difficult for the raters to judge impairment. They had to guess how much impairment due to psychiatric reasons was involved in, let us say, gastric ulcer, without knowing whether the man was employed, what type of work he did, his income, whether he had children, and many other facts that would indicate the degree to which the ulcer was impairing his functioning. At a more specific level, of course, the ulcer was impairing his digestive functions. When assigning Rating I the raters could only guess how much impairment of *role* functioning was associated with the ulcer. After seeing the sociocultural data, they might find the man greatly impaired: unemployed or sporadically employed, unmarried at forty-five, a college graduate who watched television but read no books, living with his widowed mother.

If the raters' first guess was correct, they repeated it. If the background data made the individual look more disturbed in functioning than he had in his symptoms alone, he was given a more severe rating. It is interesting that Rating II differed from Rating I in only 25 per cent of the sample. Five per cent of the sample received a better Rating II, while 20 per cent received a worse Rating II on the basis of their social functioning data. These ratings did not vary radically from the original ratings, and were usually no more than one step higher (or lower) on the original seven-point scale (0 to 6). In most instances, then, Rating I and Rating II are very close to each other, and the *relationship* of Rating I and II to any variable is almost identical. For example, the ridits for both ratings according to the respondent's perception of his parents' character (see Table 5-10) are identical (Mental Health Rating I: .63, .56, .46, Mental Health Rating II: .63, .56, .46).

It was decided that Mental Health Rating II would be used in the screening of the questionnaire stress items. The more holistic rating was felt to be preferable for this purpose. Rating II was also used during the pyramiding of items into factors. Once a factor was established, its Rating I and II ridits were calculated. When factors were combined into Stress Scores, however, it was felt that methodological purity was of utmost importance, for this was the crux of the analysis. Therefore Rating I ridits were calculated for each number of factors reported. The relationship between the number of stress factors and Mental Health Rating I is thus not open to the specific criticism of this type of methodological circularity.

The Gross Typology and the Symptom Groups are in the same category as Mental Health Rating II. They are not methodologically pure. The psychiatrists assigned a Gross Type and various Symptom Groups to each case *after* they had seen the sociocultural data. It was with some small hesitation that we included the Gross Typology and the Symptom Groups in this report, for we had no way of checking on their "purity."

In real life, nothing is methodologically pure. It should be remembered that no diagnosis or estimate of impairment is made of a patient without some knowledge of his background and functioning. The very fact of his arrival at an office, out-patient clinic, or state hospital indicates something about the extent to which he is functioning and his socioeconomic status. Moreover, his speech, language, and dress immediately signify much about his origins, education, and values. To sacrifice the stimulating and informative classifications of the *types* of mental disturbance because they were "socially contaminated" would be unrealistic, since clinical psychiatric diagnoses are always socially contaminated.

While impairment was found to be related to the *number* rather than to the pattern of stress factors and experiences, the *types* of mental disturbance showed definite relationships to particular patterns of experience. Much was gained, then, by analyzing the Gross Typology and Symptom Groups in relation to the stress factors and SES.

Again, if diminishing degrees of methodological purity were assigned to these various indices of mental health, their rank order would probably be Mental Health Rating I, Mental Health Rating II, the Gross Typology and, lastly, the Symptom Groups.

## Childhood Mental Health Index: Symptom or Factor?

The Childhood Mental Health Index is discussed in detail in Appendix C. In brief, it was a psychometric measure, based directly upon responses to questions concerning symptoms of childhood disturbance. The Index was made up of four subscores, the Childhood Neurotic Score, the Childhood Functioning Score, the Childhood Psychosomatic Score, and the Childhood Fear Score. The Childhood Mental Health Index (CMH) was an analytical afterthought, for it was found that a fair number of symptoms concerning childhood and adolescence were included in the questionnaire, enough to compose a general index of preadult impairment parallel to the Adult Mental Health Ratings. While some emphasis was placed upon the CMH Index in the analysis of the data, it was relegated to a minor role as the research progressed. Many reasons were involved, such as the complexity of the analysis of data using three separate independent variables (MHR I and II and the CMH Index). Moreover, several persons, acting as consultants to the project, felt that the childhood symptoms elicited did not cover behavior problems sufficiently, whereas the majority of presenting complaints in child psychiatric practice are behavior problems.

Nevertheless, the CMH ridits, as expected, bore a stronger relationship to the preadult factors than to the adult factors. They are presented, together with the ridits of Mental Health Ratings I and II, for each of the preadult factors. We also attempted to estimate the increment in risk due to individual adult factors over the average adult risk in three groups: those who had a poor, moderate, and good Childhood Mental Health Index. Logically, persons who were already severely disturbed in childhood did not show much increase in disturbance due to the advent of the adult factors.

The CMH Index was originally considered as an *intervening* factor, inasmuch as it seemed to intervene in time between the preadult and adult factors. However, the CMH Index includes symptoms from early childhood, preadolescence, and adolescence. The level of symptomatology at age nineteen might be considered *intervening*, but not the cumulative total of the symptoms covered from early childhood up to age twenty. The CMH Index, therefore, is better considered as another of the pre-adult factors, although it is not included in the Stress Score, because it is so heavily on the symptom side (strain). In relation to the preadult factors it is relatively more of a dependent variable, but in relation to the Mental Health Ratings it becomes merely another factor in the previous life experience, the symptoms themselves perhaps becoming a source of stress in later life.

## *Dividing the Factors into Two and Three Parts:*
### *A Problem in Measurement*

As indicated in Chapter 5, each factor was originally constructed in the form of a score. The entire range of each score was then divided into two and three parts, or dichotomized and trichotomized. Each person in the sample was assigned to a group depending on his answering pattern. For example, the respondents could be divided into the Often-Sometimes group versus the Never group. They could also be assigned to three groups: Often, Sometimes, and Never.

Why were the stress factors divided into three as well as two groups? The final goal of the screening and pyramiding stages was to construct a series of factors which in turn could be combined into an over-all Stress Score. When the Childhood Stress Score was initially devised, each factor was dichotomized. Each individual was scored as perceiving his parents negatively or positively, having poor or good health in childhood, and so forth. Each factor was either present or absent. This made interpretation of the total score very easy. A score of 5 would mean that the respondent had reported five out of the seven possible preadult factors utilized. A score of 2 would mean he had reported only two out of seven factors, and so forth.

At a later stage of analysis we increased the strength of the Childhood Stress Score by trichotomizing the factors. By dividing each factor into three parts rather than two, the number of people in the extreme stress group was decreased. At the same time, the intensity of the factor in this extreme group was increased. This usually meant a sharp increase in the Mental Health Rating risk of that group.

For purposes of *comparing the relative strengths* of the various factors, however, the dichotomy was most useful, since it was possible to obtain a *plus* or stressful group composed of about 33 per cent of the sample for each factor.

The trichotomies, however, cut off plus groups of various sizes, ranging from 183 to 258 cases. These groups are not directly comparable, and have a wider ridit range due in part to the differences in the size of the groups alone.[12] The trichotomies, as will be shown later, were most useful when combined into Stress Scores. Stress Scores based on seven trichotomized childhood factors were much more predictive of the Mental Health Ratings than similar dichotomized scores. Both the dichotomy and the trichotomy of each factor are presented, since they serve different purposes.[13]

The accuracy of the division of these factors may seem exaggerated because of the elaborate methods employed. Actually our methods might be likened to measuring cordwood with a micrometer. There is no assurance that the category "parents quarreled **often**" is in any way equivalent in intensity or frequency to the category "I had disagreements with my parents **often**." Ideally, each factor should be measured in units of duration and intensity. We might do better to equate one hour of a screaming quarrel between parents with one hour of a screaming disagreement between child and parent. We could then compare directly the Mental Health Rating risk *per unit of quarreling*. As it was impossible to gather adequate data on the intensity and duration of each event or factor, the stress factors can only be compared with each other roughly. The great similarity in risk involved (with the exception of two factors, Parents' Character Negatively Perceived and Adult Poor Physical Health) leads us to believe that the "measurement" of the factors has been rather similar in each case. The improvement in ridit range (predictive power) gained by pyramiding some factors was not great and would not account for their differential strength. Similarly, the number of items involved in each factor was not crucial, for many factors consist of only one item and have predictive power as great as the pyramided (weighted) factors.

These details of factor construction become most relevant when the Stress Scores are considered in later chapters. A large number of factors of apparently equal power (ridit range), when placed in a simple (unweighted) score, predict the Mental Health Rating risk quite well. On the other hand, the *patterns* of these factors in various combinations tell us nothing more than the total *number* of these factors have already told us. An obvious question arises, "*If* the factors had been more unequal in strength, wouldn't the patterns or combinations, such as a weak with a strong factor, two weak factors, or two strong factors, have produced much more variation in risk?"

We can only point to the fact that the dichotomization of all the factors included about a third of the sample in the more stressful group. Our relativistic (rather than absolute) definitions of mental health and disorder have made us rely on the statistical distribution of a symptom for an interpretation of its severity. If hallucinations are rare, we tend to regard them as a serious symptom. In a culture where they are common, we tend to discount their severity in making diagnoses. Similarly, though without actual proof, we tend to rank stress factors on the basis of their prevalence. We feel that poverty is a stress *relative* to the poverty of one's reference group. If a whole society is poor, we tend to discount the importance of this factor in the *differential* mental health of the individuals within the society. If people are physically ill with tuberculosis but don't recognize it, does it constitute less of a stress factor for them? To a limited degree this may be so, but tuberculosis still severely limits their functioning.

We have no evidence at this time of the degree to which a child's reference group can mitigate the impact of his stressful experiences. For example, in an ethnic or SES group where all parents quarrel, is the amount of stress on the child due to parental quarrels reduced?

A woman, asked whether she had teen-age disagreements with her parents, said "Sure, occasionally with my mother about going out. But all my girl-friends had the same thing." She also said her parents had a hard time making ends meet, "but it was during the depression. We weren't the only ones. I had a good childhood." Many respondents verbalized the mitigating effects of the wide prevalence of a stress factor.

Just how much stress can be alleviated by a consciousness that others are also exposed to it? Is the death of a parent before age six less threatening to a child of low socioeconomic status simply because there are many similar low SES children who have lost or are losing their parents early in life? The fallacy in this statement lies mainly in the fact that the preschool child is not conscious of the statistics and does not have a well-developed reference group outside the immediate family. An older child, exposed to poverty, ill health, and parents' quarrels may find some solace in the fact that his friends are in a similar situation. At any rate, he is not stigmatized or socially isolated by these experiences. In order for stress to be reduced, there must be communication of the wide prevalence of that stress factor in the social group. The stress factor may even become highly valued where the factor is endemic, as reflected in many religious beatitudes. (Blessed are the poor, for theirs is the kingdom of heaven. Blessed are the meek, for they shall inherit the earth.) The mitigating power of being "one among many" can be seen in wartime, for the isolated individual faced with the stress of bombing or hand-to-hand combat will fight rather than run (which is his most sensible and natural instinct) if others are in the same situation. It is well known that the stress of concentration camps produced much strain in Jews and assorted nationals of conquered countries, but somewhat less strain among political prisoners who banded together.

Perhaps a major function of therapy is to convey to the patient that he is not alone in his guilt, his apparent transgressions, and his emotional problems. While the therapist does not condone these feelings or behavior, he makes them seem less idiosyncratic, more widespread.[14] Simply by pointing out the universality of emotional problems, the therapist becomes less judgmental, more charitable. Conscious realization of the relativity of the individual's feelings, behavior, and stressful experience is an aid in therapy; it is also a major dilemma for etiological research in mental disturbance. Since the amount of strain experienced varies with conscious realization of the relative prevalence of a stress, it makes prediction quite difficult.

We have pointed out that absolute units of quarreling and other stresses, measured in terms of duration and intensity, would have been helpful in making objective comparisons between various stress factors. Even if we had been able to equate the stresses with some precision, there would still remain the relativity of the factor to its occurrence in the individual's reference group. This relativity is also linked to the dominant values within each subculture or group. For example, school failure would be more stressful to children whose families and social groups placed great emphasis on schooling.

The use of a standard cutting point of approximately 33 per cent in dichotomizing the factors has to some extent made them more comparable. If the relativistic point of view is acceptable, then the number of people sharing in a factor partially determines its potential stress. Using a cutting point of 33 per cent for all factors, we have by this token allowed an equal number of people to be exposed to each stress. The amount of strain (or Mental Health risk) associated with each stress factor should now be independent of the prevalence of that factor. We have, in effect, given each factor equal prevalence in the community, a 33 per cent prevalence. Broken Homes occur at about the same rate as Parents' Quarrels or Parents' Poor Physical Health. Since these factors were also constructed in such a way as to have minimum intercorrelations and maximum independence from each other, the similar rates are not a result of two factors simply being identical (for example, Parents' Quarrels didn't have a strong tendency to occur only in Broken Homes).

It was not possible to obtain exact cutting points at 33 per cent for all the factors. Obviously in the case of factors based on one item, the only available groups were "Often, Sometimes, and Never" in the proportions yielded by the respondents' answers. This was particularly true of the adult "worry" factors. The size of the dichotomized plus group ranges from 12.1 per cent to 18.7 per cent for the adult, and from 26.9 per cent to 43.2 per cent for the preadult factors. This difference does not account for the greater predictive power of the adult factors, however. That power lies rather in the reciprocal quality they have, partaking of symptom as well as factor.

## Physical versus Mental Health

Although we recognize the philosophical objections to the mind-body dichotomy, physical health and mental health are necessary operational distinctions. There is no doubt that physical and mental health are intertwined. That we have not been able to separate them into neat compartments is no more due to the use of the questionnaire technique than it is to the state of conceptualization in the mental health field. If making the distinction between physical and mental illness is difficult for a trained diagnostician face-to-face with a single patient, it is virtually impossible to establish on a mass sample using a questionnaire survey. Though our measures of physical and mental health are not completely distinct from each other, we feel that the attempt to make such a distinction is necessary to the analysis of the data.

Two factors deal with "physical health": Childhood Poor Physical Health and Adult Poor Physical Health. At best, we can say that these factors are somewhat more on the physical than on the mental side. Poor health in childhood is based on a report of health at that time as "good, fair, or poor," and the frequency of catching cold. Both items are obviously open to the influence of the state of mind of the adult respondent. "Catching cold frequently" may also be interpreted as a symptom of mental disturbance in childhood. It may involve acting out certain passive wishes, the avoidance of school, peer activities, and other childhood responsibilities.

Adult Poor Physical Health was based upon the respondent's report of his present health as "excellent, good, fair, or poor," and the number of hospitalizations (excluding pregnancies). Again the emotional state of the respondent could influence his report of health, while it might also have influenced his seeking medical attention.

Certainly the amount of treatment an individual receives is often as good an index of mental disturbance as it is of physical illness. This is particularly true when a series of minor ills such as colds, backaches, stomach upsets, and similar conditions predominate. But are hospitalized patients with *serious* physical illness any less prone to be mentally disturbed? A study at Mount Sinai Hospital in New York City showed that 66.8 per cent of a sample of nonpsychiatric medical ward patients were found to exhibit "some diagnosable psychiatric disorder."[15] Only a longitudinal study could tell us whether these symtoms were present before the illness or were the result of the stress of the physical illness and the hospital environment. This study is a good example of the difficulty of distinguishing between physical and mental illness. The difficulties are compounded by the self-selection of patients. Only by longitudinal study of large random samples in the community can we get away from the preselection bias involved in treatment.

The most obvious case in which mental disturbance precedes a physical disturbance (and its treatment) is among *polysurgicals,* who are constantly seeking major operations because of their underlying masochism.[16] Guilt and the desire for punishment or even destruction may aid in the development of a great many diseases. We know that there is a "TB personality" as well as an "ulcer personality." An increasing number of diseases are found that have a tendency to develop in certain types of people with particular predisposing mental disturbance or conflicts.

The use of the respondent's health estimate and his hospitalizations is not meant to be a substitute for a physical examination. Although it does not measure physical health as distinct from mental health, in this shortcoming our index merely reflects a general problem in medicine.

The mental disturbance component in the physical health factors has been examined, but what of the physical illness component in the Mental Health Ratings? Ratings I and II relied heavily on psychophysiological symptoms such as headaches, back pains, sweaty palms, sour stomach, dizziness, and fainting. What proportion of these items is physical and what proportion psychological in any given case? Even careful differential diagnosis often fails to give us answers in such ubiquitous complaints as lower back pain. The heavy use of psychophysiological symptoms as indices of mental health is a necessity, when little is known of the adult's functioning in the various roles assigned him by society. For that matter, we know next to nothing of the actual role demands made by our various subcultures for different ages and sexes. The physiological symptoms can be viewed as adaptive mechanisms, or first attempts at self-preservation. As such, they are temporary substitute measures of mental disturbance while we look for better ways of defining and measuring mental health. When a correlation between physical health and mental heatlh is found, we must question it for these very reasons.

Moreover, items referring to childhood physical health were not kept from the psychiatrists while they made their first Mental Health Rating (MH I). They were to base their rating on present symptomatology, but were exposed to both present and past symptoms. While present symptoms were given the heaviest weight, some indication of general childhood health had to be included to help them in making their judgments of adult mental health. Thus the relationship between Adult Mental Health Rating I and Childhood Poor Physical Health is not methodologically "clean," as are the other childhood factors. It is possible that childhood physical symptoms influenced the psychiatrist in giving the adult a better or worse mental health rating. If it had been a biasing factor, however, we would expect it to be more closely related to adult mental health than it is.

The reader must excuse the *caveat* that "physical" and "mental" are just temporary labels. Many may question the wisdom of trying to separate these factors at all, when "mind and body are one." The hope is that greater specificity, if temporarily inaccurate, will bring to light more stimulating data than will sweeping generalizations.

## Father's and Respondent's Socioeconomic Status

In Volume I great pains were taken to distinguish between the independent demographic factor of father's socioeconomic status and the reciprocal variable of the respondent's socioeconomic status. Presumably the SES of one's father is antecedent to one's independent status upon working, leaving home, or marrying (in the case of women). The relationships of father's and respondent's SES to Mental Health Rating II were similar in direction (although the respondent's own SES bore a much stronger relationship to Rating II).

Our purpose in this volume, while describing the screening operation, is to control SES, to eliminate it temporarily, and see how other variables act independently of SES in relation to the Mental Health Rating. We decided to use the father's SES as a control for all variables related to the preadult period, and the respondent's present SES for all variables related to his adult life. For example, Childhood Poor Physical Health would be controlled by the father's SES, and Adult Poor Physical Health would be controlled by the respondent's SES. Where both preadult and adult factors were combined, as in a Stress Score, the respondent's present SES would be used. This decision, like many others made during the course of the research, was arbitrary, for there is little or no precedent for research of this nature.

The use of past and present SES as controls in the same study stems from the fact that present SES is reciprocal; it may be a result of the mental health of the individual as well as a cause. The past SES, however, is more independent, less apt to be influenced by the respondent's own mental health. It is therefore the "purer" of the two measures of SES, from the standpoint of method.

The father's SES index was composed of the father's education and occupation. The respondent's SES index was composed of his education, occupation, income, and rent. The details of the construction of the indices of socioeconomic status are given in Appendix C, Section II.

## Summary

The choice of the questionnaire survey at a point in time makes it difficult to answer questions concerning the causes or origins of mental disturbance.

The present data limit us to a study of associations between various factors and Mental Health Ratings. We can predict the Ratings by means of the factors, to a limited extent. We cannot say, however, that the factors "cause" mental disturbance or its absence. Contemporary studies of lung cancer and coronary heart disease have also failed to establish causal relationships.

Two criteria determine our confidence in a factor. First, is it a fact or a fantasy, a report or a perception? How open is it to distortion due to the personality needs of the respondent? Second, is it a real factor, a symptom, or both? Is it reciprocal in nature, similar to adult socio-economic status, which might be both a cause and a symptom of mental disturbance?

On the basis of these two criteria, the factors appear to have a rough rank order of over-all credibility: (1) Broken Homes, Childhood Economic Deprivation, (2) Childhood Poor Physical Health, Parents' Poor Physical Health, Parents' Poor Mental Health, (3) Parents' Quarrels, Disagreements with Parents, (4) Parents' Character Negatively Perceived, (5) Adult Poor Physical Health, Poor Interpersonal Affiliations, (6) Work Worries, Socioeconomic Status Worries, Marital Worries, Parental Worries.

Two Mental Health Ratings were employed: Rating I was based on symptoms, Rating II on symptoms *and* sociocultural background data that often concerned the individual's role functioning (job, marriage, parenthood). The quasi-diagnostic categories of the Gross Typology and the Symptom Groups were also utilized in the analysis. Ratings I and II differ only slightly from one another, and their average risks for any factor are almost identical. Rating II was used in screening the stress items, Rating I in the analysis of the Stress Scores, to assure methodological purity. The various aspects of the dependent variable acquired different degrees of confidence, in the following order of diminishing confidence: Mental Health Rating I, Mental Health Rating II, the Gross Typology, the Symptom Groups.

The Childhood Mental Health Index was a psychometric measure based directly upon responses to questions concerning symptoms of childhood disturbance. It assumed a secondary importance in the analysis. It showed a stronger relationship to the preadult factors than did the Adult Mental Health Ratings.

Respondents were grouped according to their answers to certain questions. Each question or group of questions, which we called a factor, was divided into two and three parts (dichotomized and trichotomized) to yield scoring categories for the Stress Scores. The dichotomies were usually split so that 33 per cent of the sample would fall into the "plus" or more stressful group. The trichotomy involved a splitting of the dichotomous plus group into an extreme plus and a moderate category. The dichotomized factors could be roughly compared in strength, since approximately the same number of people appeared in their plus or stressful group. The trichotomized factors were not directly comparable due to variations in the size of the plus group. However, the trichotomies were more useful in composing Stress Scores with greater power to predict mental disturbance. The measurement of the various factors has not been equally efficient, but we feel they have been measured as well as they could be, given the methods and their limitations. The equality of the measurement of the factors is crucial, for this could have influenced the apparent similarity of predictive strength of the factors.

Physical and mental health are hopelessly intertwined in the data, although an attempt has been made to separate the two in analysis. This problem is not only one of method. It is also a basic philosophical question of body and mind. It becomes a practical medical problem in differential diagnosis. The stress factors of adult and childhood physical health are contaminated with mental health. Reports of poor health, frequent colds, and hospitalizations may be due to the state of mental health of the reporter. Similarly, the *Mental* Health Ratings are already "contaminated" because they rely heavily upon reports of psycho*physiological* symptoms. Any correlation between physical and mental health in the data may be spurious.

The *father's* socioeconomic status is used as a control for the preadult experiences, stresses, and attitudes. The respondent's *adult* socioeconomic status is reciprocal, in that it stems from his mental health as well as being a factor influencing mental health. It is used as a controlling variable for the respondent's adult experience, stresses, and attitudes.

## Notes

1. See list of items in preadult factors, Chapter 5.
2. It is clear that each parent *reacts* initially to the child's endowment—its size, irritability, coloring, appetite, and so forth. The child in turn reacts to this reaction. To call this *interaction* is correct, but to say that the concept of interaction obviates the necessity for causal analysis seems incorrect.
3. Lucy Freeman, *Fight Against Fears*, Pocket Books, New York, 1953, p. 272.
4. The possibility that parents were less dominating or rejecting from about 1900 to 1930, when the older respondents were children, is slim, but should be considered. That they quarreled less frequently, at least in front of the children, is not only possible but also probable. It is important to keep historical trends in mind when interpreting such data. A recent study by Urie Bronfenbrenner, "Socialization and Social Class Through Time and Space," in Eleanor E. Maccoby, T. M. Newcomb, and E. L.

Hartley, *Readings in Social Psychology*, Holt, New York, 1958, pp. 400–425, covering shifts in the severity of child training practices, unfortunately treats only changes in the United States from the 1930s on, which were all in the direction of milder training. This may have been true of European training, which·would apply to the immigrants in the sample. Our older respondents report less dominating parents, which seems a contradiction if Bronfenbrenner's trend also holds true from 1900 on.

5. Charles R. Hoffer, "Medical Needs of the Rural Population in Michigan," *Rural Sociology*, Volume 12, 1947.

6. See R. Faris and H. W. Dunham, *Mental Disorders in Urban Areas*, University of Chicago Press, Chicago, 1939.

7. John Clausen and Melvin Kohn, "Social Isolation and Schizophrenia," *American Sociological Review*, 20:3 (June, 1955).

8. Thomas S. Langner, "Normative Behavior and Emotional Adjustment," Ph.D. Dissertation, Department of Sociology, Columbia University, New York, 1954.

9. See Chapter 1.

10. The rank order of the over-all credibility of the factors does not correspond to the rank order of mental health risk. For example, the highest ranking (most credible or factual) factors, Broken Homes and Childhood Economic Deprivation, have low and high Mental Health Rating risks, respectively.

11. Herbert Hyman and P. B. Sheatsley, "The Authoritarian Personality—A Methodological Critique," in R. Christie and M. Jahoda (eds.), *Studies in the Scope and Method of "The Authoritarian Personality,"* The Free Press of Glencoe, New York, 1954.

12. The upper and lower values of the ridit decrease steadily to .50, as the size of the subclasses involved approaches 1660.

13. The Childhood Mental Health Index had already been constructed when the decision to trichotomize was made. The childhood factors were therefore trichotomized on the basis of the CMH ridits, rather than on the basis of the Mental Health Rating I ridits. The actual division of these factors might have been slightly different had we used the Adult Mental Health Ratings throughout. The preadult factors exhibited a much wider range of CMH ridits than of Mental Health Ratings I ridits. The trichotomous divisions of the preadult factors, then, are the most predictive divisions we can make on the basis of all our data.

14. A paper by Dr. Hans Syz of the Lifwynn Foundation and Payne Whitney Psychiatric Clinic discusses this function of therapy with great insight and detail. See Hans Syz, "An Experiment in Inclusive Psychotherapy," in *Experimental Psychopathology*, Grune & Stratton, New York, 1957, pp. 150–151.

15. M. Ralph Kaufman, Samuel Lehrman, Abraham N. Franzblau, Samuel Tabbat, Leonard Weinroth, and Stanley Friedman, "Psychiatric Findings in Admissions to a Medical Service in a General Hospital," *Journal of the Mount Sinai Hospital*, 26:2 (March–April, 1959).

16. Karl Menninger, *Man Against Himself*, Harcourt, New York, 1938.

# Stress and Strain: The Findings in a Nutshell

### T H O M A S   S .   L A N G N E R

It's easier to find the road if you know your destination. The reader of technical volumes can "follow the road" with greater ease if he knows what the research is "driving at." If he knows his destination, the questions that he asks of the data will be more pertinent, similar to requests for directions on the road. Although the element of suspense is lost when we name the villains at the beginning, we are not writing a detective story or mystery novel. In view of the difficulty of communicating one simple message in the midst of complex methods and multiple findings, this summary is offered as a guide through the following chapters.

The composition of the 14 stress factors was given in detail in Chapter 5. The exact Mental Health Rating risks associated with each of these factors and each of the items involved in their construction will be given in subsequent chapters. The frequency with which each factor was reported in the three socioeconomic groups will also be discussed, because a major research goal is a better description of the stresses, attitudes, and types of mental disturbance associated with life in each of the SES groups.

## The Factors

A brief review of the content of the factors will suffice here. The preadult factors were based upon the respondent's reports of his childhood and his description of his parents at that time. The first childhood factor was Parents' Poor Mental Health. It was based upon reports of

147

the parents' psychosomatic conditions, whether they were the "worrying type," and whether they had ever had a "nervous breakdown." Parents' Poor Physical Health consisted of reports that father or mother was in poor health during the respondent's childhood. Childhood Economic Deprivation was composed of reports of parents' "unemployment and financial problems," the fact that the mother worked to earn money, and that "parents had a hard time making ends meet." Childhood Poor Physical Health was based upon the report of poor general health in childhood, and frequent catching of colds. Childhood Broken Homes was defined as not having lived with both biological parents until age sixteen. Parents' Character Negatively Perceived was based on the respondent's report about how he felt toward his parents when he was in school. Typical items included "Father spends too little time with me," "Mother (or father) wants to run her (his) children's lives," "Mother does not understand me," and "My parents don't practice what they preach." Parents' Quarrels was simply a report of the frequency of quarrels between the parents. Disagreements with Parents was a report of the frequency of the respondent's disagreements with his parents during adolescence.

The adult stress factors pertained to the respondent's present life experiences. First was his report of his present health status as poor rather than fair, good, or excellent, and his mentioning a large number of nonpsychiatric hospitalizations. This was called Adult Poor Physical Health. Work Worries consisted of worrying about "work" or "overwork." Socioeconomic Worries comprised worrying about "getting ahead" and the "cost of living." Poor Interpersonal Affiliation was based upon having no neighbors, no close friends, and no organizational memberships. Two factors applied to only part of the sample. Marital Worries was based on a report by married persons that they frequently worried about their marriage. Parental Worries consisted of the reports by parents that they often worried about their children, as well as their agreement that "Children give more trouble than pleasure," and that they had problems with their children.

The 14 childhood and adult factors incorporated almost all the items of information that were closely associated with the Mental Health Ratings. The degree of this association was called the mental health risk, and was measured by the ridit. In brief, the ridit transforms the mental health classification into a number ranging from zero to one. This allows a direct interpretation in terms of probability. The average Midtowner had a ridit of .50, because 50 per cent of the population was better off with respect to mental health than he was, and 50 per cent was worse off. The larger the ridit, then, the worse the average mental health risk of the subgroup involved. For example, persons reporting Childhood Economic Deprivation had a risk of .57. Thus 57 per cent of the population is healthier than the average person reporting economic deprivation in childhood.

## A Stress Score of Ten Factors Used to Predict Mental Health Risk

In general, the risk involved in any one factor was small. However, Childhood Broken Homes involved relatively little risk, while Parents' Character Negatively Perceived and Adult Poor Physical Health involved a much greater mental health risk. After examining the relative strengths of the factors, ten were selected for combination in a score. For various reasons, four factors were not utilized in the Stress Score: Parents' Poor Physical Health, Disagreements with Parents, Marital and Parental Worries.

For scoring purposes, each factor was divided into three parts according to mental health risk. For instance, the frequency of Parents' Quarrels was divided into "Often," "Sometimes," and "Rarely or Never" categories, with risks of .58, .51, and .48 respectively. These categories were given weights of 2, 1, and 0. A person reporting only that his parents quarreled "often" would get a total score of 2. He might also have reported a Broken Home. If he reported that a parent died before he was seven, *and* his parents or step-parents quarreled often, he got a total score of 4. If one of his parents died while he was between seven and sixteen years old, and his parents quarreled often, he was assigned a total score of 3.

It was found that the sheer number of factors reported is the most efficient method of predicting mental health risk. The group reporting none of the ten factors had an average risk of .24, while those who had a Stress Score of 13 had an average risk of .91, which is almost four times as great. Those with a score of 1 had a risk of .35, those with a score of 2 had a risk of .38. The higher the Stress Score, the greater was the mental health risk ( see Table 14-3, Figure 14-1 ).

Most important is the fact that the *number* rather than the pattern of the negative factors is what predicts the mental health risk. Suppose the ten factors are called A, B, C, D, up to J. People reporting both A and B fell into pattern AB. We found that the mental health risk of the ABs hardly differed from that of the ACs, ADs, BCs, BDs, CDs, and so on. These people all experienced two factors or received a score of 2. However, the ABCs, ABDs, ACDs, and BCDs who experienced *three* factors all had a higher mental health risk than any of the pattern groups with a score of 2. The mere *number* of factors tells us as much about mental health risk as an examination of the particular combination or pattern of factors the group has experienced.

It is important to emphasize that the number of factors predicts the *average* mental health risk of a group of persons. If the clinician knows the number of these factors reported by his patient, he can then say, for instance, that a patient chosen at random from the group with a Stress Score of 10 will be in poorer mental health than a random patient from the group with a Stress Score of 1, approximately nine out of ten times. Yet it is possible that a particular individual is the one exception out of ten who is healthier. Any prediction scheme, then, deals with averages and groups, and should not be rigidly applied to individuals in a therapeutic situation.

The statistical materials lend support to the hypothesis that two stress factors will generally involve greater psychiatric impairment than one stress factor. Similarly, any three stresses will involve greater impairment risk than any two. These stresses seem more or less additive in their effects. There is no pair of stresses that seem to "spark" each other, none that produce a synergistic effect greater than the sum of their individual effects. There is no single stress factor which when reported in the life history automatically places all individuals in the Impaired category.

If this is true, then the importance of the single traumatic experience in producing psychiatric impairment may be questioned. Certainly the death of one or both parents during a person's childhood is a stressful experience and is frequently considered to be traumatic. We should expect to find that most of those who lost their parents before age six were in the Impaired category, no matter how good a life they led after this point. On the contrary, we do not find that this presumed "trauma" is associated with a great impairment risk in the adult. The experience of a large number of stressful events surely seems linked to adult impairment; however, there is no *one* stress or event that by itself dooms all those subjected to it to severe psychiatric impairment.

Again, the risk of impairment seems to bear a linear, or straight line, relationship to the number of stresses. There is no point, no particular number of stresses, at which the slope of the line suddenly becomes very steep. This suggests that there is no "breaking point" in the number of stresses, beyond which virtually all persons are bound to be totally impaired by their symptoms. There is no number, such as five stresses, or fourteen, which is the environmental straw that breaks the back of *every* camel. This doesn't mean that each *individual* does not have a breaking point, for indeed he must. It is only that within the limits of the ordinary life stresses we've examined there is a fairly wide range of impairment at each stress level for the community population as a whole. On the average, we can say the greater the life stress, the greater the deformation or disturbance of the human material being put to the test. Later on we'll use the phrase "The more, the unmerrier" to describe this relationship.

Our first reaction to this finding was that we had found the answer to why the low SES had poorer mental health. Our preoccupation with socioeconomic status, as mentioned before, stemmed directly from the fact that of all the common demographic factors, it alone showed a strong and independent relationship to mental health. The mental health risk of the low socioeconomic status group was .59, and considerably greater than that of the middle SES risk of .50, or the high SES risk of .41.[1] If being of low socioeconomic status simply meant that you suffered proportionately *more* of the slings and arrows of outrageous fortune, this would very neatly explain why the low status group had worse mental health.

We tested this hypothesis by examining the average Stress Score of each SES group. To our amazement, the difference between the averages was very small. The score range was 0 to 18, yet the average scores of the Lows, Middles, and Highs were 5.7, 5.3, and 4.7 respectively. Although the Lows had a slightly harder life according to these averages, the difference was not enough to account for our finding of a mental health risk ranging from .41 among the Highs to .59 among the Lows. Looking back at the individual factors, we found that the Lows did not report a more stressful childhood than the Highs. About one-third of each of the three status groups came from broken homes, and equal socioeconomic proportions of poor health in childhood, mentally disturbed parents, physically ill parents, parents' quarrels, and so forth were reported. Only one childhood factor, economic deprivation, varied sharply with socioeconomic status, involving 30 per cent of the Lows and only 15 per cent of the Highs.

The Lows did report a somewhat more stressful adult life than the Highs or Middles. For instance, 34 per cent of the Lows and 11 per cent of the Highs said they were now in poor or fair health. Again, 13 per cent of the Lows and 2 per cent of the Highs said they had no close friends in whom they could confide. Similarly, "Children give more trouble than pleasure" to 21 per cent of the Low and only 4 per cent of the High parents. These are the *only* major proportional differences in the life-experience of the socioeconomic groups that favor the High status group; many favor the Lows. The fact that the average number of stresses on the status groups is rather similar is confirmed by examining the separate factors.

## Stress Scores and Mental Health Risk of Three SES Groups

Because the number of stress factors did not vary radically with SES, the SES differences in mental health risk were still largely unexplained. In an attempt at clarification we examined the score of ten factors in relation to mental health risk *within* each SES group. The three groups of persons reporting none of the ten factors (one group from each SES level) had virtually identical risks. These were .26, .25, and .24 in the low, middle, and high SES groups respectively. Regardless of their status, their risks were similar. This seemed to contradict our general finding that low status people had worse mental health.

It might appear that the stress factors had "explained away" the differences in the mental health of the three SES groups, and that our troubles were over. When we removed most of the stresses, the SES groups seemed to have identical mental health. However, quite the opposite was true. With the exception of the group that experienced none of the factors, those of low status consistently exhibited greater mental health risk, regardless of the number of factors they experienced. Holding life experiences "constant," the Lows still run more risk. For instance, if we consider only persons with a Stress Score of 6, the risks are .57, .52, and .46 in the low, middle, and high SES, respectively. Taking people who have been exposed to a more difficult life, those with Stress Scores of 10 to 18, we find the risks are .83, .67, and .68 for low, middle, and high SES. The Lows are now considerably "worse off" than the Middles or Highs. Those with Stress Scores of 14 to 18 have certainly been exposed to very heavy life stress. Their mental health risk is .93 among the Lows, and .79 and .76 among the Middles and Highs. No matter what the number of stress factors reported (with the exception of "none"), the low SES group consistently runs a higher risk (see Table 14-4).

There is a residual mental health variation between the socioeconomic groups which cannot be accounted for by the stress factors alone. Generally, this variation, or difference, increases as the Stress Score increases.

Thus, while the three socioeconomic levels start out with almost identically low risks in the group reporting no stresses, the risk of the low SES increases more rapidly than that of the Middles and Highs as the stress score increases. If one were to plot this relationship, with the Stress Score on the *x* axis and mental health risk on the *y* axis, the three lines representing the three status levels would start fairly close to the same point (.25) and fan out. The pitch or slope of the Lows' line would be the steepest, while the pitch of the Middles' and Highs' would be somewhat closer to the horizontal (see Table 14-4 and Figure 14-2).

Several hypotheses can be invoked to explain why the low SES risks are larger, even when the number of factors is controlled. Suppose we liken the environmental stresses to hammer blows. The low status group may have *poor resistance* to the stress of the blow, less ego strength, or weaker average personality structure. A corollary hypothesis is that the high status group has a more *resilient personality*.

The blow on the high SES, although of equal force originally, may also be *cushioned* by various advantages that accrue to this stratum.

In addition, *the meaning and interpretation of the factors* may vary among the socioeconomic groups. For instance, what the low status person reports as good health the high status person may report as poor health, for we tend to compare or refer our health to friends of similar age, sex, religion, and social class.

## Strain as an Adaptation to Stress

Our data show that, generally, strain is directly proportional to stress. As environmental stress factors increase in number, the reaction to or attempted adaptation to stress increases. This reaction or attempt at adaptation which we have called strain is evidenced in the development of various symptoms. These can be viewed as a hierarchy of regulatory devices that enable the individual to maintain homeostasis, as suggested by Menninger.[2] These levels of strain can be briefly categorized as Well, Nervousness (mild discomfort and increase in tension), Neurotic phenomena, Episodic and explosive discharges, and Persistent and severe disorganization.

These levels seem to lie on a general continuum of progressive deterioration or disorganization. We found an impairment risk of .82 for Probable Psychotics, .57 for Probable Neurotics, and .11 for Wells, which supports this ranking of adaptive mechanisms. As each device fails to alleviate the stresses, more drastic devices are probably utilized.

New stresses may disturb a previous balance achieved by one of the minor devices. On the other hand, the alleviation of some stresses (such as the death of a dominating parent, a good marriage after a lonesome celibacy, a bettering of one's economic situation after severe poverty) may allow the individual to drop some of the devices he has previously used.

These levels correspond roughly to the Gross Typology diagnostic classifications of Well, Personality Trait Types, Neurotic Type, Psychotic Type, and Organic Type. The average impairment found for each of these classifications indicates that they do lie on a continuum of associated impairment.

## Socioeconomic Differences in the Use of Adaptive Devices

The differential utilization of various kinds of adaptive devices may then partially account for the socioeconomic differences in impairment under similar stress. In the hierarchy of devices, the low SES individual is more likely to use the "acting out" devices and to exhibit explosive discharges more typical of psychotics. The high SES person is more prone to use milder "nervous" and neurotic devices.

For example, a much larger proportion of the Lows were classified as Probable Psychotic Types, 13 per cent of the Lows and only 3.6 per cent of the Highs. In contrast, more Highs than Lows were Probable Neurotic Types, 42.5 per cent of the Highs and only 24.5 per cent of the Lows. We know that the average impairment of the Psychotics is much greater than of the Neurotics. Clearly, then, more of the Highs exhibit a reaction that is less impairing, while more of the Lows behave in a way that is more impairing.

Other evidence indicates the Psychotic Reaction is more typical of the Lows. The proportion of Probable Psychotics increases uniformly as the Stress Score increases in the low SES. At the greatest stress level, almost 27 per cent of the Lows utilize this device. Among the Highs, however, the proportion of Psychotics never exceeds 6.4 per cent, no matter how great the stress. The exact opposite is true of the proportion of Probable Neurotic Types, which never exceeds 32 per cent among the Lows, but climbs rapidly to 61.7 per cent among the Highs exposed to greater stress.

Other findings suggest that the Highs exhibit more obsessional symptoms, such as obsessional worrying. These symptoms, however, can be adaptive or maladaptive, depending on the appropriateness of the subject worried over. As we'll see, this high SES person worries more about his work, so that it is the focus of his obsession which is different from the low SES person. His adaptive worrying insures his staying in the high income brackets.

To say, then, that the low SES group has less "ego strength" or a "weaker personality structure" is somewhat misleading. This was a first impression, drawn only from the relationship of stress factors to the impairment ratings (Mental Health Ratings). An examination of the type of disturbance (rather than the level of impairment) shows the use of different adaptive devices at different social levels. There also appear to be specific relationships between certain groups of stress factors and particular adaptive devices. *The sheer number of factors is no longer as meaningful as the pattern of factors when examining types of adaptation.* This is expectable, for when we ask what types of adaptation and symptoms are exhibited by various social levels, we must know *to what they are adapting, to what they are adjusting.* Then the differential life experience of the three SES groups becomes crucial for understanding these different adaptive devices.

A further question is raised by our findings: How do the different SES groups become predisposed to utilize a particular mode of reaction? The third portion of this volume is devoted to an analysis of the types of reactions or adaptive devices utilized by the three SES levels. The differences in their ways of life and life experiences, and the variations in stress factors to which they are exposed, are given detailed consideration. An attempt is made to show how their differential adaptive patterns might be determined in part by emotional experiences in the family and other aspects of their environment. Section II, then, is devoted to stress and strain as measured by impairment in functioning, the Mental Health Rating. Section III examines the relation of stress and strain as indicated by different symptom and diagnostic classifications. Section II finds the low SES showing greater impairment regardless of stress. Section III shows that the adaptive devices used by low SES persons tend to be the less effective types, often producing much impairment on their own. The "acting out" mechanisms and paranoid projections of the low SES, then, are less socially approved by our society as a whole, and are more likely to get the user into trouble on the job and with the law. The inhibition of the high and middle SES may cut down on emotional satisfaction and expression, but it preserves the jobholder rather effectively, particularly when combined with mild compulsivity in work habits.

The impairment rating and the diagnostic classifications are both necessary for a better understanding of the mental health of the socio-economic groups. Because socioeconomic status is a reciprocal variable, we know that it must be a result of one's mental disturbance as well as a cause. The third section discusses the *recruitment* of the SES levels according to symptoms and adaptive devices. Social mobility between the parents' and children's status indicates who is moving into what class. The upwardly mobile tend to be obsessive, utilizing the mechanism of inhibition or repression. The downwardly mobile tend to be alcoholics and to have character disorders, particularly the suspicious and passive-dependent varieties. These involve both acting out and more severe withdrawal devices, alcoholism in particular being associated with self-destructive tendencies. The low SES stratum, then, tends to accumulate people who have used these relatively maladaptive or impairing devices in an unsuccessful attempt to solve or relieve their stress situations. As people move up and down in our social system they make for an accumulation of different psychological types at various levels. The elites of our society are those who are also emotionally elite in a broad sense. They are not necessarily in better mental health, but they have used the particular adaptive devices that are socially approved by our society and are most effective in achieving and maintaining high social position.

## Childhood Stress and Adult Behavior

The sequence and content of the individual stresses experienced seems to have little bearing on degree of impairment in the adult, as measured by the Mental Health Rating. The individual stresses, however, do exhibit quite specific relationships to the adaptive devices employed, as measured by the Gross Typology and the Symptom Groups. Two types of adult reaction (the Probable Personality Trait Type and the Probable Psychosomatic Type) are significantly associated with one childhood stress, Parents' Poor Physical Health.

The Probable Organics, Neurotics with Personality Traits, and Neurotics with Psychosomatic Features are linked to a background of two stresses; namely, Parents' Poor Physical Health and early Broken Homes. Since most of the early Broken Homes were due to the death of one or both parents before the child was seven, this pattern seems to be a stronger statement of Parents' Poor Health, poor health that often ended in death.

In addition to poor parental health and a broken home, the Probable Psychotics' typical stress experience included a negative perception of their parents' character. Thus a report of domineering or rejecting parents adds an important new dimension to a family history of poor health.

Finally, the Probable Neurotics shared in the widest variety of early stresses. In addition to their parents' poor health they also reported their own poor health in childhood. They also perceived their parents negatively. In addition, Probable Neurotics tended to have parents who quarreled frequently. As a group they were more prone to disagree with their parents during adolescence. The new stress dimension among Neurotics, as opposed to other types, is their apparently quarrelsome pre-adult family life.

Viewed from another angle, each stress or combination of stresses seems to favor particular adaptive devices. The most striking associations are found between quarrelsome homes and neurosis, and between the early death of parents and psychosis. A negative perception of one's parents seems associated with both neurosis and psychosis.

Although more details of the relationship between adult behavioral adaptation and early experiences were found, they seem to throw little light on why the low and high SES groups should adapt so differently. The early death of parents occurs slightly more often among the Lows, but not significantly so. A somewhat greater proportion of Highs report that they quarreled with their parents, but similar proportions of each SES group perceived their parents negatively, and said their parents quarreled often. The differential occurrence of the stress factors, then, does not seem to account for the SES differences in adaptation. We can only speculate in the final chapters as to what aspects of socialization, what variations in values and goals, and what external circumstances combine to produce these striking socioeconomic group differences in adaptation to their environment.

## Notes

1. Mental Health Rating I, based on symptoms.
2. See Karl Menninger "Regulatory Devices of the Ego Under Major Stress," in A Psychiatrist's World, The Viking Press, New York, 1959, pp. 497–515.

# Childhood Broken Homes

T H O M A S   S .   L A N G N E R

## Defining Broken Homes

Almost all the social ills to which man is heir have been placed at the door of the broken home. Juvenile delinquency, drug addiction, and mental disease are only a few of the evils that have in the past been blamed directly on broken homes.

Psychiatric opinion on the importance of a continuous parent-child relationship was re-emphasized a few years ago by the collision of the ocean liner *Andrea Doria*. Drs. Paul Friedman and Louis Linn, both present at the disaster, came to the conclusion that,

> The application of the "women and children first" principle on the *Andrea Doria* resulted in some poignant, and in at least one case, tragic separations and isolations . . . with possibly disastrous psychological consequences. . . . The authors are convinced that a modification of the "women and children first" rule by insistence that a parent accompany the child, even if the only parent available be the father, would represent a sound application of modern psychiatric insights.[1]

They point out the similar conclusions in the Freud-Burlingham report, on the effect of the wartime blitz bombing on the children of London, that "such disasters as war have comparatively little significance for children so long as they only threaten their lives or material comforts, but become enormously important the moment they break up family life and uproot the first emotional attachments of the child within the family group."[2]

The Midtown data suggest that the Childhood Broken Homes factor is related to mental health only under certain conditions. The purpose of this chapter is to specify these conditions.

Childhood Broken Homes were defined by the question, "Did you also live together with *both* your *real* parents up to the time you were sixteen years old?" Those who answered "No" were considered to come from broken homes. Strikingly enough, 35.2 per cent or 585 of the sample respondents were no longer living with both their biological parents by the age of sixteeen. This fact by itself should be of great interest to the clinician. While he may encounter in his practice what appears to be a very large proportion of patients from homes broken in childhood, this proportion may be no larger in the patient population than in the metropolitan population as a whole. As a matter of fact, the proportion of Midtown expatients from homes broken in childhood is not much different from the proportion among nonpatients in the Midtown area as a whole (see Table 8-1). About 38 per cent of the expatients and 35 per cent of the nonpatients come from broken homes, compared with an even smaller proportion of current outpatients (20 per cent). So, the private therapist is *less likely* to see the products of broken homes than if he were to select his patients from the general population by a statistically random procedure (see Table 8-1).

### TABLE 8-1

### PROPORTIONS OF RESPONDENTS ACCORDING TO THEIR TREATMENT FOR MENTAL HEALTH, AND BROKEN HOMES

| Childhood Broken Homes[a] | RESPONDENTS' MENTAL HEALTH TREATMENT | | |
|---|---|---|---|
| | Outpatients Per Cent | Expatients Per Cent | Nonpatients Per Cent |
| Broken | 20.0 | 38.4 | 35.0 |
| Unbroken | 80.0 | 61.6 | 65.0 |
| Number of Cases (N=100 per cent) | 40 | 182 | 1434 |
| Total Number of Cases | | | 1656[b] |

[a]"Did you always live together with *both* your *real* parents up to the time you were sixteen years old?"

[b]Four respondents did not know or gave no answer.

What broke up the childhood homes of these Midtown residents? Those who said they did not live with their real parents through the age of fifteen were asked, "What happened?" The various reasons given for the breakup of the home were distributed as follows:

|  | Number of Cases | Per Cent of Sample |
|---|---|---|
| Death of father | 262 | 15.8 |
| Death of mother | 145 | 8.7 |
| Divorce | 60 | 3.6 |
| Separation | 44 | 2.7 |
| Desertion by father | 17 | 1.0 |
| Desertion by mother | 3 | 0.2 |
| Father in hospital or other institution | 2 | 0.1 |
| Mother in hospital or other institution | 10 | 0.6 |
| Respondent lived away from living parents | 82 | 4.9 |
| Other reasons | 55 | 3.3 |
| No answer | 1 | 0.1 |
| Total Number of Reasons for Broken Homes | 681 | 41.0 per cent of 1600 |

Since a childhood home could be broken for a combination of reasons, there are 681 reasons given by 585 persons. The percentages add up to 41 per cent of 1660, while in reality only 35.2 per cent of these 1660 persons came from broken homes. If these combinations of reasons for broken homes are sorted out, as in Table 8-2, a clearer picture is obtained.

The most immediate impression given by Table 8-2 is that the death of parents is the primary cause of broken homes. The "Total" column shows 64.8 per cent of homes unbroken, leaving the 35.2 per cent of broken homes to be divided among the various causes of broken homes. If these proportions are converted back to the number of cases involved, we can calculate what proportions of all broken homes are caused by death. About three-fifths of broken homes (58.0 per cent) were due to the death of one or both parents. Less than one-fifth (17.8 per cent) were due to divorce, separation, or desertion by the parents. Various combinations of causes of broken homes accounted for the other fifth, but it should be noted that the combination of death *and* divorce, desertion, or separation was *not* included in this category. There were only five cases of death combined with divorce, desertion, or separation, and they comprised less than one per cent of all cases of childhood broken homes.

One-fifth of the sample (20.8 per cent) lost one or both parents through death before age sixteen. It is interesting to compare this finding with that of Hilgard, Newman, and Fisk.[3] Among 3579 patients in a state mental hospital they found 27 per cent who had lost parents through

## TABLE 8-2

### PROPORTIONS AND AVERAGE MENTAL HEALTH (MH II) OF RESPONDENTS ACCORDING TO SINGLE AND MULTIPLE CAUSES OF CHILDHOOD BROKEN HOMES AND FATHERS' SOCIOECONOMIC STATUS

| Causes of Childhood Broken Homes | Fathers' Socioeconomic Status | | | | | | | | |
|---|---|---|---|---|---|---|---|---|---|
| | LOW | | MIDDLE | | HIGH | | TOTAL | | |
| | Per Cent | $\bar{R}$ | Per Cent | $\bar{R}$ | Per Cent | $\bar{R}$ | No. of Cases | Per Cent | $\bar{R}$ |
| Both Parents' Death Only | 2.3 | .56 | 2.7 | .56 | 0.4 | (.92)*y* | 31 | 1.9 | .58 |
| Fathers' Death Only | 15.1 | .53* | 10.0 | .53 | 12.6 | .39 | 204 | 12.3 | .48 |
| Mothers' Death Only | 7.9 | .70*z | 6.4 | .49 | 4.5 | .47 | 104 | 6.3 | .56 |
| Divorce, Separation, or Desertion Only | 4.1 | .54 | 6.3 | .58 | 8.3 | .44 | 104 | 6.3 | .52 |
| Both Death and Divorce, Separation or Desertion Only | .2 | (.49) | .3 | (.59) | .4 | (.55) | 5 | .3 | (.55) |
| Parents Only Institutionalized ‡ | .8 | — | .4 | — | .6 | — | 10 | .6 | — |
| Other Multiple and Single Causes ‡ | 8.5 | — | 7.2 | — | 7.5 | — | 127 | 7.7 | — |
| Unbroken Homes | 61.1 | .54*z | 66.9 | .46 | 65.7 | .46*y | 1075 | 64.8 | .48 |
| Total Number of Cases (N = 100 per cent) | 482 | | 671 | | 507 | | 1660 | | |

* Difference in test variable at the 5 per cent level of confidence between ridits with same subscript or adjacent to same asterisk.

‡ Ridits not computed.

Parentheses ( ) enclose ridits based on less than ten cases.

death. This compared with 21 per cent of the general population in the same age range. While our figure for the community sample is almost identical, the Midtown proportions of broken homes among expatients (38.4 per cent) and current outpatients (20 per cent) need some explanation. Private psychiatric patients are less likely to come from broken homes due to death or other causes. The Midtown expatient group, many of whom were once mental inpatients, are therefore more similar in proportion of broken homes to the state mental hospital patients. These differences will be shown to be a function of low SES, since members of this stratum are more typically public inpatients rather than private outpatients, and also tend to lose their parents earlier in life.

In the sample as a whole (see Table 8-2), respondents were about twice as likely to lose their fathers (12.3 per cent) as they were to lose their mothers (6.3 per cent). This is doubtless due in part to the earlier death of males in general, combined with the fact that the man is usually the older spouse in a marriage.

A question of great interest is whether the death of the father or the death of the mother involves a greater mental health risk. Those respondents with both parents dead or only their mother dead before they were sixteen had an average mental health risk of .58 and .56. They are worse off than those whose fathers alone died (.48). (See Table 8-2.) Ignoring SES differences, those whose fathers died before they were sixteen (.48) were no worse off than those who came from unbroken homes (.48). Thus, while fathers died twice as frequently as mothers, their death shows less association with the mental health of their children.

It is not enough to generalize about which parent is "more important," since the degree of impact associated with the death of a parent varies by socioeconomic status. In the *low SES, the death of the mother alone is much worse* than death of the father or of both parents. In the *middle SES, the death of the father is slightly worse* than the death of the mother, and the death of both somewhat worse than the death of either one. Respondents whose high SES fathers died before the respondents were sixteen seem to be somewhat *better off* than those from *unbroken* high SES homes. The death of high SES mothers is no better or worse than an unbroken home.[4]

One might expect that the death of a father would be more destructive in the low SES since there is no economic cushion once the father dies. This would probably mean that the mother has to work as the sole remaining provider for the family. On the contrary, however, the father's death does not seem strongly related to impairment at any of the three SES levels. Any attempt to interpret these results must await examination of data concerning the remaining parent's remarriage, for with remarriage the mental health risk of the children seems to *increase*.

A respondent born in a low SES family is more likely to lose a parent before he is sixteen than one born in the middle or high SES (see Table 8-2). Low SES respondents are twice as likely to have lost their mothers before they were sixteen (7.9 per cent) as high SES respondents (4.5 per cent). Not only are there twice as many deaths of mothers in the low SES but the mental health risk associated with the death of the mother is also much greater in the low SES (.70) compared with unbroken homes in the low SES (.54). In the high SES, those whose mothers died (.47) and those from unbroken homes (.46) show almost no difference in mental health risk.

The proportion of those whose childhood home was broken by divorce, separation, or desertion is twice as great in the high SES (8.3 per cent) as in the low (4.1 per cent). Although the individual contributions of divorce, separation, and desertion to these totals cannot be examined, it is probable that a greater divorce rate exists in the high SES due to the attitudes toward marriage in this group and the availability of money to obtain a divorce. On the other hand, separation and desertion may be more common at lower SES levels. A large proportion of the low SES parents are Catholic, and this would reduce the probability of their obtaining a divorce.

More important than these variations in the causes of broken homes is the fact that 35 to 40 per cent of each of the three SES groups came from broken homes. Broken homes, then, are not necessarily the product of slum areas and poverty. In Midtown, they occur with similar frequency among rich and poor alike, and they are predominantly due to death, not to parental incompatibility.

The way in which the respondent's home was broken in childhood is clearly associated with some of his behavior patterns in adulthood. Since the relationship between childhood and adult factors will be treated later, only two examples dealing with broken homes will be given here. First, the divorce rate among respondents whose childhood home was broken by divorce, separation, or desertion is much higher than among those who suffered broken homes due to the death of one or both of their parents or those who came from unbroken homes. Persons who have ever been married but not widowed constitute the total population on which we base the divorce rate. Only 10.1 per cent of those who were ever married (but not widowed) who came from unbroken homes are divorced or separated[5] (see Table 8-3). A slightly larger proportion, 13.8 per cent, of this group (the ever-married and nonwidowed) who experienced a childhood broken home due to the *death* of one or both parents are divorced or separated. Even more striking are the 23.9 *per cent* divorced and separated found among those (ever-married and nonwidowed) who experienced a childhood home broken by divorce, separation, and desertion of the parents.

### TABLE 8-3

### PROPORTIONS AND AVERAGE MENTAL HEALTH (MH I) OF EVER-MARRIED, NONWIDOWED RESPONDENTS ACCORDING TO PRESENT STATUS OF MARRIAGE AND SINGLE CAUSE OF CHILDHOOD BROKEN HOMES

| | Childhood Broken Homes | | | | | |
|---|---|---|---|---|---|---|
| Present Marital Status | BROKEN BY DEATH ONLY | | BROKEN BY DIVORCE, SEPARATION, OR DESERTION ONLY | | UNBROKEN | |
| | Per Cent | $\bar{R}$ | Per Cent | $\bar{R}$ | Per Cent | $\bar{R}$ |
| Divorced or Separated | 13.8 | .60 | 23.9 | .63 | 10.1 | .62 |
| Still Married | 86.2 | .50 | 76.1 | .46 | 89.9 | .46 |
| Total Number of Cases[a] (N = 100 per cent) | 232 | | 67 | | 738 | 1037 |

[a]The total excludes widowed and never-married respondents, and those who did not know or gave no answer.

*Divorce, separation, and desertion by the parents more than doubles the probability that the children will also become divorced or separated. Note, however, that those who are presently divorced or separated seem to have a quite similar mental health risk, regardless of whether they came from unbroken homes (.62), homes broken by death (.60), or homes broken by divorce (.63).*

The person whose childhood home was broken by divorce, separation, or desertion is not only more likely to get divorced or separated as an adult, but also, if married, more apt to worry about his present marriage. Only 2.7 per cent of married persons from unbroken childhood homes and 3.8 per cent from homes broken by death worry often about their marriage, whereas 7.4 per cent from homes broken by divorce, desertion, or separation often worry about their own marriage (see Table 8-4).

### TABLE 8-4

### PROPORTIONS AND AVERAGE MENTAL HEALTH (MH I) OF MARRIED RESPONDENTS ACCORDING TO THEIR WORRYING ABOUT MARRIAGE AND CERTAIN CAUSES OF CHILDHOOD BROKEN HOMES

|  | Childhood Broken Homes | | | | | |
|  | BROKEN BY DEATH ONLY | | BROKEN BY DIVORCE, DESERTION, OR SEPARATION ONLY | | UNBROKEN | |
| Marital Worries | Per Cent | $\bar{R}$ | Per Cent | $\bar{R}$ | Per Cent | $\bar{R}$ |
| Often | 3.8 | (.92) | 7.4 | (.79) | 2.7 | .72 |
| Sometimes | 14.5 | .57 | 22.2 | .45 | 13.9 | .54 |
| Never, Don't Know, No Answer[a] | 81.7 | .47 | 70.4 | .45 | 83.4 | .45 |
| Total Number of Cases [b] (N = 100 per cent) | 213 | | 54 | | 717 | 984 |

[a] A small percentage of persons who did not know whether they worried about marriage or did not answer were included with the persons answering "Never."

[b] Of the 1660 respondents, 676 were not married at the time of their interview.

Parentheses ( ) enclose ridits based on less than ten cases.

Persons who come from a childhood background of divorce are almost three times as likely to worry often about their marriage as persons whose childhood home was unbroken. Those adults who worry often about their marriage also exhibit extremely poor mental health, on the average, *regardless* of their childhood background of unbroken or broken homes (unbroken, .72; broken by death, .92; broken by divorce, .79).

These data give strong support to the hypothesis that divorce of parents, much more than death of parents, involves incorporation of poor marital-role models. Such identification may lead to worry about the possible failure of one's own marriage because the parents' marriage failed. Of course, it may also lead to avoidance of marriage as well as to divorce or fear of marriage failure. While the death of parents may be somewhat associated with later divorce and marital worries, the divorce of parents shows an even greater association. One possible inference is that divorce of parents sets the pattern for later marital problems and is a specific precursor of these problems rather than a general "trigger" for all types of behavioral pathology. The effect of parental divorce is illustrated in the story of Bill R.*

Bill R.'s present marriage is going on the rocks. He has been in various kinds of trouble since his father "drank himself to death." His parents separated about a year before that, having quarreled frequently. He was in his early teens at the time, and can't remember feeling anything about his father.

Now Bill's own marriage is going on the rocks. He and Jane had never been very sociable people. They only went out visiting seven times during eleven years of marriage. He was often given to crying spells of depression during which Jane comforted him. This behavior would alternate with periods when he would humiliate her verbally, and occasionally hit her. After he took up with another woman, Jane walked out on him. Now he is worried over the results of this separation on his child, and fears that it will all end in divorce. "My daughter is on her way to becoming neurotic—she'll develop problems just like mine if I'm not straightened out." His work is suffering. He feels he is going downhill, and that it's irreversible.

Bill senses that his fear of rejection has prompted him to withdraw from his wife and his child before they withdraw from him. This is the same defense he used when his parents separated, and when his father died. His bitter early experience with a broken home seems to have laid the groundwork for his own marital difficulties. He has had no model of stable family life as a guide. In fact, he has in part modeled his own marriage on his parents' marriage, which foundered when he was only a little older than his daughter now is.

An examination of the age of the respondent at the time his home was broken showed that early broken homes, those broken before the

---

* In order to give reality and dimension to the various statistical abstractions which we have called stresses, illustrative material has been used throughout this volume. Many of these illustrations are based on clinical material drawn from facilities in the Midtown area. Background characteristics such as age or occupation have been changed to protect privacy. Material in quotations has also been altered. The vignettes, then, are not scientifically accurate data, but syntheses of life experiences designed only as illustrations. No single illustration resembles exactly the life or characteristics of any person.

respondent was seven years old (.57), involved the greatest risk (see Table 8-5). Respondents whose homes were broken between the ages of seven to fifteen (.50) were not very much worse off than those who came from unbroken homes (.48).

### TABLE 8-5

### PROPORTIONS AND AVERAGE MENTAL HEALTH (MH I) OF RESPONDENTS ACCORDING TO FATHERS' SOCIOECONOMIC STATUS AND RESPONDENTS' AGE WHEN HOME BROKEN

| Age When Home Broken | *Fathers' Socioeconomic Status* | | | | | | | |
|---|---|---|---|---|---|---|---|---|
| | LOW | | MIDDLE | | HIGH | | TOTAL | |
| | Per Cent | $\bar{R}$ | Per Cent | $\bar{R}$ | Per Cent | $\bar{R}$ | Per Cent | $\bar{R}$ |
| Through Age Six | 19.9 | .64 | 14.0 | .58 | 13.8 | .46 | 15.6 | .57 |
| Ages Seven to Fifteen | 19.1 | .54 | 19.2 | .55 | 20.5 | .42 | 19.6 | .50 |
| Unbroken Before Age Sixteen | 61.0 | .54 | 66.8 | .46 | 65.7 | .46 | 64.8 | .48 |
| Total Number of Cases (N = 100 per cent) | 482 | | 671 | | 507 | | 1660 | |

At first glance this finding would seem to corroborate the view that the first six years are the "formative years." During this period any trauma to which the child is exposed is assumed to leave its mark. This may be true by and large, but the thesis of infantile determinism in the specific area of the broken home must be called into question. Although homes broken before age seven seem to involve a poor mental health risk for the sample as a whole, any generic statement about early broken homes is quite misleading. It is true that respondents from low SES homes broken early are indeed much worse off (.64) than those from unbroken low SES homes (.54). This is also the case in the middle SES. In the high SES, however, homes broken early (.46) or late (.42) show no increase in mental health risk over unbroken homes (.46).

This finding also has theoretical implications bearing on the hypothesis that there is more "personality absorption" or "smother-love" in the middle and upper SES than in the low SES. Arnold Green found that among low SES Polish-Americans "while lack of identification with the parents virtually obviates demonstrations of affection, it also saves the children from feelings of guilt and repressed hostility."[6] Green's "middle class"[7] child tends to suffer from personality absorption, ". . . the physical and emotional blanketing of the child, bringing about a slavish dependence upon the parents."[8] These differences in child-parent relationships are claimed to be responsible for the higher rate of neurosis in the middle SES. According to this theory, upper-middle SES parents become more emotionally involved with their children and make more emotional demands on them than do low SES parents. The low SES children are assumed by this theory to be less emotionally dependent upon their parents, to gain early independence and responsibility, and to be less exposed to "conditional love" which is given only upon compliance with the parents' wishes.

If upper and middle SES children were more absorbed by or emotionally involved with their parents, the death of their parents might be expected to be more destructive of mental health than the death of a relatively uninvolved low SES parent. The reverse, however, is indicated in our study. The mental health risk due to death of parents is greatest in the low SES, and disappears in the high SES. The Midtown data, then, while not directly refuting the hypothesis, seem to call it into question. In our sample, the hypothetically "unabsorbed" low SES children seem to have worse mental health if their parents die than the hypothetically more "absorbed" and "slavishly dependent" high SES children.[9]

It is probable that there is actually more, not less, absorption or dependency in low SES broken homes. We know that regardless of broken homes, more Lows were classified as "passive-dependent," along with their other symptoms.

Rhoda A. (see footnote, page 166) came from a low SES home. Her father died when she was five. "I remember him being carried to the hospital. I was holding the chocolate cookie he used to give me every morning." Her mother never remarried. "She was so good to me. She never said 'You can't have that. Since your father's death we can't afford it.' So, when it came to marriage, my mother always came first." Her mother died at the age of seventy-five. Rhoda married three years later, but her husband died shortly after. She went on for a while, but suddenly developed a choking feeling. She couldn't swallow. "They had to give me baby food. Then everybody babied me." For a period of ten years she has had fits of great rage which she can't remember clearly. She often sees her mother's face in front of her and remembers how she bought her mother a new coat with her own last thirty dollars, just because her mother said her children didn't love her any more. Now she cleans the house many times a day, and eats chocolate cookies when she can't get to sleep, which is often.

How important is the cause of the broken home? Homes broken by parents' divorce, desertion, or separation seem to involve about the same mental health risk as homes broken by the death of the parents. In our attempt to trichotomize the broken home factor, we were looking for some aspect of broken homes which would divide the sample legitimately into three groups and maximize the mental health differences among these groups. The only other aspect of broken homes available to us which seemed applicable to all broken homes was the criterion of the age at which the break occurred. The data (see Table 8-4) showed that, particularly in the low SES, it is the early broken homes as opposed to all others that are associated with poor mental health. Although the separating power of this factor was not very great, we nevertheless considered it important enough to have a place as one of the childhood factors. The proportions and ridits of the factor are given in Table 8-6.

## Remarriage of the Remaining Parent

We used the term "remaining parent" to describe the surviving parent who has been widowed or the parent who remains with the child after separation, divorce, or desertion. It was hypothesized that the "repair" of the broken home by the remarriage of the remaining parent would be a eugenic factor associated with better mental health in the respondent. The data, however, proved otherwise.

People whose remaining parent[10] remarried were worse off (.59) than those whose remaining parent did not remarry (.49). (See Table 8-7.)

The latter had a risk close to those who came from unbroken homes (.48). Particularly in the low SES, the remarriage of the remaining parent is linked to the offspring's poor mental health (.70). At all three SES levels the remarriage of the remaining parent increases the mental health risk of respondents. In the high SES, those who stayed with the remaining parent alone are better off (.40) than those from unbroken homes (.46) or from broken homes where the remaining parent remarried (.47). Remarriage therefore cannot accurately be described as the "repair" of a broken home but rather as an *attempt* to repair a broken

## TABLE 8-6

### DISTRIBUTION, PROPORTIONS, AND AVERAGE MENTAL HEALTH (CMH, MH I, MH II) ACCORDING TO CHILDHOOD BROKEN HOMES, TRICHOTOMIZED AND DICHOTOMIZED

| Childhood Broken Homes | | CMH | MH I | MH II | No. of Cases | Per Cent |
|---|---|---|---|---|---|---|
| | | | Respondents' Mental Health | | | |
| *Trichotomy* | | | | | | |
| Broken Through Age Six | + | .52 | .56$_z^*$ | .57$_y^*$ | 258 | 15.5 |
| Broken, Ages Seven to Fifteen | 0 | .50 | .49 | .51 | 327 | 19.7 |
| Not Broken Before Age Sixteen | − | .50 | .49$_z^*$ | .48$_y^*$ | 1075 | 64.8 |
| *Dichotomy* | | | | | | |
| Broken Before Age Sixteen | + | .51 | .52 | .53 | 585 | 35.2 |
| | | | | * | | |
| Not Broken Before Age Sixteen | − | .50 | .49 | .48 | 1075 | 64.8 |
| Total Number of Cases (N = 100 per cent) | | | | | 1660 | |

*Difference in test variable at the 5 per cent level of confidence between ridits with same subscript or adjacent to same asterisk.

home which more often fails as far as the mental health of the step-children is concerned.

In the sample as a whole, 38.8 per cent of the remaining divorced or widowed parents remarried, and there is little SES variation (35.9, 42.2, and 39.6 per cent respectively, of low, middle, and high SES remaining parents remarried). (See Table 8-7.) The significance of the remarriage comes to light when we ask the question, "How well did you get along with your substitute parent?" Almost one-fourth (24.5 per cent) of those whose remaining parent remarried got along "Not so well" or "Not at all" with their step-parents (see Table 8-8).

Those who did not get along with the step-parent were considerably worse off (.64) than those who did get along (.54). This was not true at all three SES levels, but only in the low and high SES. Of course, those who did not have any substitute parents because they came from

## TABLE 8-7

### DISTRIBUTIONS, PROPORTIONS, AND AVERAGE MENTAL HEALTH (MH II) OF RESPONDENTS ACCORDING TO THEIR REMAINING PARENT'S REMARRIAGE AND FATHERS' SOCIOECONOMIC STATUS

*Fathers' Socioeconomic Status*

| Remaining Parent's[a] Remarriage | LOW | | | MIDDLE | | | HIGH | | | TOTAL | | |
|---|---|---|---|---|---|---|---|---|---|---|---|---|
| | No. of Cases | Per Cent[b] | $\bar{R}$ | No. of Cases | Per Cent[b] | $\bar{R}$ | No. of Cases | Per Cent[b] | $\bar{R}$ | No. of Cases | Per Cent[b] | $\bar{R}$ |
| No | 97 | 64.1 | .53*$_z$ | 95 | 57.8 | .54 | 85 | 60.4 | .40 | 277 | 61.2 | .49 |
| Yes | 56 | 35.9 100.0 | .70*$_{z,y}$ | 73 | 42.2 100.0 | .56 | 57 | 39.6 100.0 | .47 | 186 | 38.8 100.0 | .59 |
| Other Broken Homes | 32 | | .57 | 50 | | .62*$_x$ | 30 | | .49 | 112 | | .57 |
| Don't Know, No Answer‡ | 3 | | – | 5 | | – | 2 | | – | 10 | | – |
| Unbroken Homes | 294 | | .54*$_y$ | 448 | | .46*$_x$ | 333 | | .46 | 1075 | | .48 |
| Total Number of Cases (N = 100 per cent) | 482 | | | 671 | | | 507 | | | 1660 | | |

a "Remaining Parents" include those who brought up respondents after divorce as well as death of the other parent.

b Percentages of the total number answering "No" or "Yes."

* Difference at 5 per cent level of statistical significance between ridits with same subscript.

‡ Ridits not computed.

## TABLE 8-8

### PROPORTION AND AVERAGE MENTAL HEALTH (MH I) OF RESPONDENTS ACCORDING TO FATHERS' SOCIOECONOMIC STATUS AND HOW WELL THEY GOT ALONG WITH SUBSTITUTE PARENTS

|  | Fathers' Socioeconomic Status | | | | | | | |
|---|---|---|---|---|---|---|---|---|
|  | LOW | | MIDDLE | | HIGH | | TOTAL | |
| Relations with Substitute Parents[a] | Per Cent | $\bar{R}$ | Per Cent | $\bar{R}$ | Per Cent | $\bar{R}$ | Per Cent | $\bar{R}$ |
| Got Along Well | 52.9 | .60 | 59.2 | .56 | 62.5 | .44 | 57.9 | .54 |
| Got Along Not So Well | 16.7 | .77 | 12.5 | .54 | 12.5 | .51 | 13.9 | .63 |
| Got Along Not At All | 14.7 | .74 | 9.2 | .54 | 7.5 | (.57) | 10.6 | .64 |
| Don't Know, No Answer[c] | 15.7 | .59 | 19.1 | .57 | 17.5 | .53 | 17.6 | .56 |
| Total Number of Cases (N = 100 per cent) | 102 | | 121 | | 80 | | 303[b] | |

[a] Substitute Parents includes all persons "Who brought you up" — grandparents, aunts or uncles, foster parents, and institutions as well as step-parents.

[b] There were 1357 cases to whom these questions did not apply, 1075 of whom lived with both their parents up to the age of sixteen, 246 who lost one parent, but were brought up by the remaining parent alone, and 36 who for various reasons were not brought up by both parents, remaining parent alone, or substitute parents, such as the 11 who were brought up by institutions.

[c] Ridits were calculated because of the large proportion who did not know how to answer.

Parentheses ( ) enclose ridits based on less than ten cases.

unbroken homes were better off (.48) than the average respondent who had substitute parents (see Table 8-7). There is always the question of whether children who are already disturbed over the loss of one parent are consequently unable to adjust to the step-parent. This would mean that those children whose mental health was already impaired would be more hostile to the parent substitute, rather than that the advent of the parent substitute caused the mental disturbance. Unfortunately, we are unable to differentiate between these two hypotheses.

In general, the older the respondent at the time the remaining parent remarried, the worse off is the respondent with respect to mental health.

### TABLE 8-9

### PROPORTIONS AND AVERAGE MENTAL HEALTH (MH II) OF RESPONDENTS WHOSE REMAINING PARENT REMARRIED, ACCORDING TO THEIR AGE AT PARENT'S REMARRIAGE AND FATHERS' SOCIOECONOMIC STATUS

| | *Fathers' Socioeconomic Status* | | | | | | | |
|---|---|---|---|---|---|---|---|---|
| *Respondents' Age at Parent's Remarriage* | *LOW* | | *MIDDLE* | | *HIGH* | | *TOTAL* | |
| | *Per Cent* | *R̄* | *Per Cent* | *R̄* | *Per Cent* | *R̄* | *Per Cent* | *R̄* |
| Through Age Six | 31.9 | .69 | 29.5 | .52 | 18.0 | .42 | 26.6 | .56 |
| Ages Seven to Fifteen | 46.8 | .68 | 34.4 | .56 | 46.0 | .45 | 41.8 | .56 |
| Age Sixteen and Over | 21.3 | .68 | 36.1 | .62 | 36.0 | .50 | 31.6 | .59 |
| Total Number of Cases (N = 100 per cent) | 47 | | 61 | | 50 | | 158[a] | |

[a]This total did not include 12 cases who did not know or gave no answer and 16 cases of those who did have a step-parent, but who were not asked this question. The total is 186 cases.

These relationships hold true in the middle and high but not in the low SES. There is no difference between parents' remarriage when their children are aged one to six and aged seven to fifteen with respect to the mental health of these children (both .56). (See Table 8-9.) However, those whose remaining parent remarried after they were sixteen years of age show a slight tendency to be worse off (.59).

If respondents whose remaining parents did not remarry are better off, then we would expect late remarriages to involve less risk than early remarriages (before sixteen). The data show the opposite effect, with late remarriages involving more risk. Perhaps the relationship between the remaining parent and the child becomes much more intense through the years, so that the parent's decision to remarry after the child is sixteen comes as more of a blow to the child. On the other hand, the intensity of the relationship has been great enough to bind parent and child, excluding possible remarriage partners. The extremely dependent child will attempt to prevent the parent from remarrying. The dependent parent will hold on to the children until they leave home or marry. Pre-existing mental disturbance on the part of the child may in part account for the increase in risk. This disturbance may be linked to the remaining parent's late remarriage. It may even have been one of the factors delaying the remarriage, particularly if the child's disturbance was severe.

An association between mental health risk and late remarriage of the remaining parent was found only in the middle and high SES. It is in these two groups that a greater proportion of late remarriages occurs. Thirty-six per cent of middle and high SES remarriages of the respondent's remaining parent occurred after the respondent was sixteen. Only 21.3 per cent of low SES remarriages occurred after the step-child was sixteen. The proportion of early remarriages, before the respondent was seven, is correspondingly greater in the low and middle SES (31.9 and 29.5 per cent, respectively) than in the high SES (18.0 per cent).

There are some logical reasons that might account for these differences. Some of our data show the low SES parents marry at a younger age. They probably have children more rapidly after marriage, and we know they remarry at a younger age when their children are younger. Late remarriage is one variable that seems to occur more frequently and to show more association with mental disturbance at high rather than low SES levels. This association, however, is not very strong.

A larger proportion of low SES respondents (31.4 per cent) than of middle and high respondents (21.7 and 20.0 per cent) did not get along with their step-parents (see Table 8-8). What can account for this? Could it be that there are actually more early remarriages (before the step-children are seven years old) in the low SES than in the high SES?[11] (See Table 8-9.) Is it possible that those children whose parents remarried when the respondent was very young were less able to "get along" with their step-parents? Table 8-10 gives some support to this hypothesis, since more than 70 per cent of those who were sixteen or more and only about 58 per cent of those who were under sixteen at the time their parent remarried "got along well" with their step-parent.

It should be noted, however, that in a remarriage taking place long after

## TABLE 8-10

## PROPORTIONS AND AVERAGE MENTAL HEALTH (MH II) OF RESPONDENTS FROM BROKEN HOMES WHOSE REMAINING PARENT REMARRIED, ACCORDING TO RESPONDENTS' RELATIONS WITH THEIR STEP-PARENTS

| | *Respondents' Age At Remaining Parent's Remarriage* | | | | | |
|---|---|---|---|---|---|---|
| | THROUGH AGE 6 | | AGES 7 TO 15 | | AGES 16 AND OVER | |
| *Relations with Step-parents*[a] | *Per Cent of cases* | $\bar{R}$ | *Per Cent of cases* | $\bar{R}$ | *Per Cent of cases* | $\bar{R}$ |
| Got Along Well | 58.5 | .48 | 57.6 | .54 | 71.5 | .54 |
| Got Along Not So Well | 24.4 | .69 | 21.2 | .66 | 17.1 | (.51) |
| Got Along Not At All | 17.1 | (.67) | 21.2 | .51 | 11.4 | (.81) |
| Total Number of Cases (N=100 per cent) | 41 | | 52 | | 35 | 128[b] |

[a]"How well did you get along with your (substitute parent)? Would you say you got along well, not so well, not at all?" This table includes only those respondents whose parents remarried.

[b]Twenty-nine cases did not give their age at remaining parent's remarriage and 29 did not answer the question on how well they got along with their step-parent. The total is 186 cases.

Parentheses ( ) enclose ridits based on less than ten cases.

age sixteen, the respondent might have moved out of the home and would not be forced to "get along" at all with the step-parent.

It is possible only to guess at some of the factors that make it more difficult for low SES children to get along with their step-parent. Another hypothesis is that low SES children are already somewhat more mentally disturbed prior to the arrival of the step-parent on the scene. The adjustment to a new step-parent would therefore be more difficult. Perhaps discipline and authority are more irrational in the low SES, in the sense that parents derive their authority just by virtue of being the biological parents. In the upper SES levels, parents are more often expected to earn and maintain their position of authority by virtue of their kind, just, and rational behavior.[12] The low SES step-parent, by this token, may be less able to command the respect and admiration of the children, since authority is something that is vested in the "real" or biological father, but not in the step-father. The low SES step-child, therefore, may have more difficulty in accepting the authority of the nonbiological parent (the step-parent) than the upper SES step-child.

Resentment of their step-children may actually be greater among low SES step-parents who will have a harder time feeding, clothing, and supporting them than an upper SES step-parent would. Another possibility is that the low SES child is more dependent on the new step-father for financial support. The wealthier widow in the high SES can provide for the wants of her children from her own bank account rather than the step-father's. This may make for less friction between high SES step-children and their step-fathers.

The Mental Health Ratings are available, of course, only for respondents, not for their parents. From these ratings we know that widows have somewhat poorer mental health (.54) than married women (.49) and women who never married (.47), but better mental health than presently divorced and separated women (.62). Widowers, on the other hand, are in poorer mental health (.51) than married males (.46), but are in better mental health than males never married (.57) or presently divorced and separated males (.63). There were only 11 widowers and 82 widows in the adult sample of 1660 persons aged twenty to fifty-nine. These persons are obviously atypical, particularly the widowers, since women live longer than men, and it is comparatively rare for a man under sixty to become a widower. (In the age group over sixty in the Midtown community, there are five widows to one widower,[13] but among those aged twenty to fifty-nine the ratio is about 7.5 to 1.)

Although widowers are atypical, they seem slightly better off (.51) than widows (.54). Given the error in the ridits based on such a small group as eleven cases, there is no significant difference in the mental health of widows and widowers under sixty.

## Remarriage of Widowed Parents, and Conflict with Step-parents

In our attempt to gain some clues about what happens to the child in a broken home, it might be profitable to focus on the widowed parent who is virtually the sole source of the child's emotional security.

What happens to the widowed parent after the spouse dies? Dickinson and Beam[14] found evidence of severe sexual tension among widows. This tension might also be found among widowers, but perhaps less frequently, since males usually have more socially approved extramarital sexual outlets. Is it possible, then, that the mental health of both widows and widowers declines unless they remarry, due to the tension created by sexual frustration and the severe "relative deprivation" suffered by those who have known these and other comforts of marriage?

What little evidence we have indicates that the sexual frustration of widows and widowers is not very different. While 66, 70, and 74 per cent of married, never-married, and widowed-divorced-and-separated males, respectively, agreed that: "Most people think a lot about sex matters," only 46, 50, and 53 per cent respectively, of corresponding females agreed. The major differences in answering this question are sex differences. Relatively minor proportional differences appear according to marital status. It is assumed that the majority of persons answering "Yes, most people think a lot about sex" are projecting their own sexual preoccupation. By this token, widows are not significantly more preoccupied with sex matters than are married or unmarried women. Similarly, widowers are not significantly more preoccupied with sex than other males.

A parallel attempt to assess mental health differences between those respondents' *parents* who were widows and those respondents' parents who were widowers, used the item, "Were either of your parents the worrying type?" No difference in the proportions of worrying widows and widowers appeared in the parent generation.[15] Although again inconclusive (due to the use of one questionnaire item alone to assess parents' mental health), this is additional evidence that widows and widowers are similar in having little more than average mental disturbance.

We know from examining the widowed respondents that the mental health of the widowed who have remarried is not really different from that of the widowed who are still unremarried.[16] However, the *children whose widowed parent remarried run a greater mental health risk than those whose remaining widowed parent did not remarry.*

In Table 8-11, we find that the average mental health of the 193 persons whose widowed parent did not remarry is .47, slightly healthier than the average of .50 for the population as a whole. On the other hand, the 109 persons whose widowed parent remarried are in considerably poorer mental health (.58).

The fact that remarriage of the widowed is associated with poorer mental health of the children seems to run counter to common sense. We might have expected that raising their children while remaining unmarried would have placed an extra burden on the widowed. This burden

## TABLE 8-11

### DISTRIBUTION AND AVERAGE MENTAL HEALTH (MH I) OF MALE AND FEMALE RESPONDENTS WHO LOST ONE PARENT BY DEATH, ACCORDING TO THE SEX AND REMARRIAGE OF THEIR REMAINING PARENT

| Sex of Remaining Parent Compared with Respondents' | RESPONDENT MALE | | | RESPONDENT FEMALE | | TOTAL | |
|---|---|---|---|---|---|---|---|
| | No. of Cases | $\bar{R}$ | | No. of Cases | $\bar{R}$ | No. of Cases | $\bar{R}$ |

*Remaining Parent Not Remarried*

| | | | | | | | |
|---|---|---|---|---|---|---|---|
| Father Not Remarried | 15 | .42 | Mother Not Remarried | 90 | $.44^{*}_{z}$ | | |
| Mother Not Remarried | 58 | .48 | Father Not Remarried | 30 | .58 | | |
| Number of Cases | 73 | | | 49 | | $193^{a}$ | .47 |

*Remaining Parent Remarried*

| | | | | | | | |
|---|---|---|---|---|---|---|---|
| Mother Remarried | 17 | .55 | Father Remarried | 30 | .55 | | |
| Father Remarried | 24 | .58 | Mother Remarried | 38 | $.61^{*}_{z}$ | | |
| Number of Cases | | | | | | $109^{a}$ | .58 |
| Total Number of Cases | | | | | | 302 | |

*Difference at 5 per cent level of statistical significance between ridits with same subscript.

[a] The sex of the remaining parent was known in the case of the death of a parent, but was not asked in the cases of a divorce of a parent, thus reducing the number of cases available for this table.

might have caused resentment and fatigue in the lone parent, and thus negatively affected the mental health of the children. The data indicate just the opposite.[17]

What was the remarriage rate of the widowed? Ony 28 per cent of the widowed mothers of respondents remarried. However, of the widowed fathers, 53 per cent remarried. It might well be expected that widowers with growing children would be more likely than widows to remarry. Unless they are wealthy, they are unable to take care of the children and simultaneously provide for them financially. Furthermore, the mother traditionally plays a more important role in the training and upbringing of the children, so that she is better equipped by virtue of training, values, and expectations to raise the children. Therefore, it is quite surprising that approximately half the widowers raised their children without remarrying.

It was possible to determine the sex of the remaining parent only in cases where the respondent told us of the "death of mother" or "death of father." Due to an error in directions to interviewers, the question, "Did your (remaining parent) remarry?" was asked of respondents whose parents had divorced as well as of respondents who had suffered the death of one parent. Therefore, in cases of divorced parents, we were not able to determine the sex of the "remaining" parent, that is, the parent with whom the respondent stayed after the divorce. In divorces in this country, the children are usually awarded to the mother, but practices may differ in the various countries of origin of respondents' parents. Therefore, the data pertaining to the sex of the "remaining parent" always involves only cases of widowed, not divorced, parents of respondents.[18]

If remarriage of the widowed parent increases the mental health risk of the children, the next question is, which is worse, the remarriage of a widow or a widower? We found this varied by the sex of the child.

Sons are worse off (.58) when they acquire a step-mother by their father's remarriage. Daughters are worse off (.61) when they acquire a step-father (see Table 8-11).

In keeping with the classical Oedipus Complex, one might expect that sons whose mothers married step-fathers would exhibit the poorest mental health. The fulfillment of the Oedipal wish (the death of the father *and* having the mother for oneself), followed by a return of a biologically unlegitimated father in the person of the step-father, should create a situation of potential conflict, hence poor mental health. On the contrary, however, the sons are not in the poorest mental health (.55) if their widowed mothers remarry. They *are* worse off than if their widowed mothers did not remarry (.48) or widowed father did not remarry (.42), but they are not as badly off as sons whose widowed father remarried (.58). Similarly, daughters are not as badly off if their fathers remarried (.55), as if their mothers remarried (.61). However, daughters differ from sons in that nonremarriage of their fathers is associated with poorer mental health (.58) and nonremarriage of mother with better mental health (.44).

In general, we can see that it is best for sons if fathers do not remarry (.42), worse if they do (.58). Likewise, it is best for daughters if their mothers do not remarry (.44), and worse if they do (.61). These findings indicate that the *like-sex* widowed parent is more closely linked to the mental health of the child. The fact that sons with unremarried fathers and daughters with unremarried mothers are healthier (.44) than the sample as a whole would suggest that children's identification with their parent of the same sex is supported by living with the like-sex parent alone. This identification may be threatened when and if the like-sex parent remarries (.58, .61).

Of course, another possible interpretation is that a step-mother accentuates the normal Oedipal rivalry between father and son, since she is a societally sanctioned sex object for the son as well as the father, not being the biological mother. The possibility of the father's remarriage to a considerably younger woman (as in Eugene O'Neill's *Desire Under the Elms*) would exacerbate the rivalry. (This would not usually be true for widows, however, since they would tend to marry older men.)

The Oedipal interpretation looks doubtful in view of the fact that not getting along well with the step-parent was associated with poorer mental health (see Table 8-8). The Oedipal interpretation would hinge on the son's "getting along" much too well with the step-mother, or the daughter's overattachment to the step-father. Since "getting along" with the step-parent is linked to good mental health, the hypothesis of identification with the like-sex parent is more plausible.

The relations of the remaining parent, the step-parent, and the step-child are important in their own right, since such a large proportion of the population comes from broken families into which step-parents may be introduced. In addition, the structure of the unbroken home may possibly be more clearly seen by observing what happens when that structure is broken.

Here is a fertile field for future observation. We have relied too long on elaborate analyses of folk culture and ideal patterns. How different are these results from what a foreign social scientist might predict on the basis of analyzing our European heritage of folk tales. He might be struck by the cruel step-mother who appears in our classic (European) fairy tales, such as *Cinderella*. He would be inclined to fear for the mental health of a girl with a step-mother in our culture.

How diametrically opposed to our data his conclusions would be. The mental health of girls with step-mothers is considerably better (.55) than of girls with step-fathers (.61). Moreover, step-mothers seem no harder to get along with than step-fathers. Thirty-four per cent of respondent step-children did not get along with their step-fathers, while 36 per cent did not get along with their step-mothers.

There are indications that the remarriage of the widowed parent involves increased resentment on the part of the children *toward the widowed parent* as well as toward the step-parent. A larger proportion of those whose widowed parents remarried perceived the widowed parent negatively. For instance, 30 per cent of the sample as a whole said that as children they would have agreed with the statement, "Mother does not understand me." While a similar 30 per cent of those whose widowed mothers did not remarry agreed, 35 per cent of those whose widowed mothers did remarry agreed. In other words, there is a slight increase in the proportion of those who perceive the widowed mother negatively if she remarries. Although this increase is not reliable statistically, it is partially supported by other findings. In answer to another question, "Mother wants to run her children's lives," 24 per cent with widowed unremarried mothers agreed, in contrast to 27 per cent with widowed remarried mothers.

A similar but more definite increase can be seen in the negative perception of remarried widowed fathers. One-fourth of the entire sample felt that "Father spends too little time with me." Thirty-two per cent whose widowed fathers did not remarry, as opposed to 41 per cent of those whose widowed fathers remarried, agreed with the statement. Again, 19 per cent of the entire sample and 22 per cent of those with unremarried widowed fathers felt that "Father wants to run his children's lives," compared with 32 per cent of those with remarried widowed fathers.

Thus, there may be some increase in the child's feelings of domination or rejection by the remaining parent if this remaining widowed parent remarries. These feelings are certainly not as specific as the content of the questions might suggest. They probably indicate there has been some increase in hostility toward the widowed parent which may be connected with his remarriage. While the loss of one parent due to death may have some impact, the "loss" (due to remarriage) of the *second* parent, the chief remaining love object, deserves further attention by therapists and researchers. The practical problem of how to make remarriage into an emotional gain for the step-children rather than have them feel it as a loss deserves our full consideration.

## Working Mothers

Both experts and laymen have at times considered the working mother to be for a child the equivalent of living in a "semibroken home." A report of the Mid-Century White House Conference on Children and Youth comments:

It may well be questioned whether most mothers can, without undue strain, carry a full-time job and still give responsive and attentive care to the physical and emotional needs of small children. The first six years have been shown to be crucial years for the child, who would seem to need a substantial share of the mother's time and attention during this period.[19]

While this is the traditional attitude toward the working mother, there are certainly arguments for the opposite point of view.[20]

Do our data corroborate the notion that working mothers are more likely to have disturbed children? Respondents whose mothers worked full time have a greater mental health risk (.55) than those whose mothers worked part time (.49) or not at all (.49). (See Table 8-12.)

In the low SES, however, respondents whose mothers worked part time have less risk (.51) than those whose mothers did not work at all (.56). In the middle SES, those with nonworking mothers run less risk (.47) than those with mothers working part time (.50). In the high SES, those with mothers working part time are again better off with respect to mental health (.41) than those whose mothers did not work at all (.45). At all three SES levels, the mental health risk is greater if the mother works full time. *However, in both the low and the high SES one is best off with respect to mental health if one's mother works part time rather than full time or not at all.*

It may be that the part-time working mother in the low SES was helping to provide for her children and alleviating some of the economic pressure on the family. One-third of low and only one-fifth of high SES mothers were working. On the other hand, the part-time working mother in the high SES may have been a well-integrated individual who was able to satify the demands of both family and career. It is also possible that part-time working mothers in the low and high SES obtain most of the gratifications from the job which the full-time working mother obtains, but in addition are able to spend longer periods of time with their children. While the differences in mental health risk are not great, there is some indication that the mother who works part time is probably effecting a good compromise between her own needs and those of her children.

## TABLE 8-12

## PROPORTIONS AND AVERAGE MENTAL HEALTH (MH II) OF RESPONDENTS ACCORDING TO THEIR FULL-TIME, PART-TIME AND NONWORKING MOTHERS' AND FATHERS' SOCIOECONOMIC STATUS

| Respondents' Mothers Worked | Fathers' Socioeconomic Status | | | | | | | |
|---|---|---|---|---|---|---|---|---|
| | LOW | | MIDDLE | | HIGH | | TOTAL | |
| | Per Cent | $\bar{R}$ | Per Cent | $\bar{R}$ | Per Cent | $\bar{R}$ | Per Cent | $\bar{R}$ |
| Full Time | 23.7 | .59 | 17.9 | .55 | 13.6 | .46 | 18.2 | .55$_{\bar{z}}^{*}$ |
| Part Time | 15.6 | .51 | 15.8 | .50 | 6.5 | .41 | 12.9 | .49 |
| Not at All | 58.9 | .56 | 64.6 | .47 | 79.7 | .45 | 67.6 | .49$_{\bar{z}}^{*}$ |
| Others, Don't Know, No Answer ‡ | 1.8 | – | 1.7 | – | 0.2 | – | 1.3 | – |
| | | | | | | | | |
| Total Number of Cases (N=100 per cent) | 482 | | 671 | | 507 | | 1660 | |

* Difference at 5 per cent level of statistical significance between ridits with same subscript.

‡ Ridits not computed.

The suggestion that children of part-time working mothers are healthier has already been made. Are part-time mothers *themselves* any healthier than full-time and nonworking mothers? Adequate information on the mental health of working mothers of respondents is not available.[21] However, an examination of the mental health of the mothers who are respondents (see Table 8-13) shows that in the low and middle SES part-time working mothers of children under eighteen are indeed in better mental health than full-time working or nonworking mothers. In the high SES, however, nonworking mothers exhibit the best mental health. Nonworking mothers, all of whose children are over eighteen, are still worse off than comparable part-time working mothers in the low and middle SES. With the exception of the high SES, mothers of both older or younger children are themselves likely to be in better mental health if they work part time.

As expected, the proportion of part- and full-time working mothers increases as their children pass the age of eighteen. In the middle SES,

## TABLE 8-13

### PROPORTION AND AVERAGE MENTAL HEALTH (MH II) OF WORKING RESPONDENT MOTHERS ACCORDING TO THE AGE OF THEIR CHILDREN AND THEIR SOCIOECONOMIC STATUS

*Respondents' Socioeconomic Status*

| Respondent Mothers Working | LOW | | | | MIDDLE | | | | HIGH | | | | TOTAL | | | |
|---|---|---|---|---|---|---|---|---|---|---|---|---|---|---|---|---|
| | Under 18 | | Over 18 | | Under 18 | | Over 18 | | Under 18 | | Over 18 | | Under 18 | | Over 18 | |
| | Per Cent | R̄ | Per Cent | R̄ | Per Cent | R̄ | Per Cent | R̄ | Per Cent | R̄ | Per Cent | R̄ | Per Cent | R̄ | Per Cent | R̄ |
| Full Time | 15.1 | .59 | 23.3 | .53 | 14.2 | .51 | 34.8 | .61 | 10.9 | .45 | 15.2 | .48 | 13.6 | .53 | 23.9 | .55 |
| Part Time | 13.7 | .49 | 17.2 | .53 | 5.3 | .43 | 13.0 | .30 | 7.3 | .57 | 5.1 | .71 | 9.0 | .45 | 12.5 | .49 |
| Not At All | 71.2 | .58 | 59.5 | .62 | 80.5 | .48 | 52.2 | .53 | 81.8 | .39 | 79.7 | .42 | 77.4 | .48 | 63.6 | .52 |
| Total Number of Cases (N=100 per cent) | 212 | | 116 | | 190 | | 69 | | 165 | | 79 | | 567 | | 264 | |

for instance, about 20 per cent work when they have young children, 48 per cent work when their children are over eighteen. This contrasts with about 29 per cent and 41 per cent in the low SES, 18 per cent and 20 per cent in the high SES. Little change takes place in the woman's work role in the high SES as the children grow older. This may be partly accounted for by the fact that the high SES mother does not stay out of work primarily because of her children (since she presumably has maids and nurses available), but chiefly because she is expected not to work to earn money.

In the population as a whole, 18.2 per cent of respondents had mothers who worked full time, 12.9 per cent had mothers who worked part time, and 67.6 per cent had mothers who did not work outside the home while the respondent was aged six to eighteen.[22] (See Table 8-12.) The higher the socioeconomic level, the larger the proportion of mothers of respondents who did not work outside the home (58.9 per cent of the low, 64.6 per cent of the middle, and 79.7 per cent of the high SES). About 15 per cent of the low and middle SES had mothers who worked part time, compared with only 6.5 per cent of the high SES. The higher the SES level, the smaller the proportion whose mothers worked full time (23.7 per cent of the low, 17.9 per cent of the middle, and 13.6 per cent of the high SES). The proportion of working mothers at various socioeconomic levels seems to bear little relationship to the mental health of the children of these mothers.

The number of years the mothers worked while the respondent was between ages six and eighteen does not seem to bear any consistent relationship to the respondents' mental health. In particular, for those whose mothers worked less than ten years, there is no consistent increase in mental health risk the greater the number of years they worked (.42, .49, .54, .49, .50). (See Table 8-14.) Only those whose mothers worked ten to twelve years out of the twelve year period have a much higher than average mental health risk (.57).

As mentioned previously, it was found that about 41 per cent of the low, 35 per cent of the middle, and 20 per cent of the high SES respondents had working mothers. If we calculate the average number of years these three groups of mothers worked, only small SES differences appear. The average number of years the mother worked (while the respondent was between six and eighteen) is 7.7 years in the low, 7.5 years in the middle, and 7.2 years in the high SES. Looking at the actual distribution, we find that close to half of the *working* mothers at all three SES levels worked steadily, that is, ten to twelve years during the time that their

## TABLE 8-14

## PROPORTIONS AND AVERAGE MENTAL HEALTH (MH II) OF RESPONDENTS BY NUMBER OF YEARS MOTHER WORKED AND FATHERS' SOCIOECONOMIC STATUS

| Number of Years Mother Worked | Fathers' Socioeconomic Status | | | | | | | |
|---|---|---|---|---|---|---|---|---|
| | LOW | | MIDDLE | | HIGH | | TOTAL | |
| | Per Cent | $\bar{R}$ | Per Cent | $\bar{R}$ | Per Cent | $\bar{R}$ | Per Cent | $\bar{R}$ |
| 1 | 2.3 | .45 | 1.5 | .48 | 2.6 | .34 | 2.1 | .42 |
| 2 | 3.1 | .53 | 2.3 | .44 | 1.8 | (.49) | 2.4 | .49 |
| 3 | 2.5 | .53 | 2.8 | .56 | 1.2 | (.51) | 2.2 | .54 |
| 4–6 | 6.6 | .58 | 7.3 | .46 | 3.4 | .39 | 5.9 | .49 |
| 7–9 | 4.8 | .55 | 6.6 | .51 | 2.4 | .37 | 4.8 | .50 |
| 10–12 | 19.1 | .58 | 14.0 | .58 | 8.9 | .50 | 13.9 | .57 |
| Mother Did Not Work | 58.9 | .56 | 64.6 | .47 | 79.7 | .45 | 67.6 | .49 |
| Don't Know, No Answer ⌐ | 2.7 | – | 0.9 | – | 0.0 | – | 1.1 | – |
| Total Number of Cases (N= 100 per cent) | 482 | | 671 | | 507 | | 1660 | |

⌐ Ridits not computed.

Parentheses ( ) enclose ridits based on less than ten cases.

respondent offspring were aged six to eighteen. While almost equal proportions of mothers at the three status levels worked full or part time during those twelve years, a much larger proportion of high SES *working* mothers worked only one year (12.7 per cent), compared with low and middle SES *working* mothers (5.0 per cent). The only striking difference in the length of time that the mothers of the three status groups worked was that high SES *working* mothers tended to take jobs for one year, more than twice as frequently as low and middle SES *working* mothers. With this exception, we can say that once the mothers of our present respondents decided to work, the number of years they worked was not a function of their SES. Their *decision* to work, however, is a function of their SES. They are twice as likely to decide to work outside the home if they are of low SES. The number of years they work does not bear a strong relationship to the mental health of their children.

## Summary

Just over one-third of the sample respondents declared that they did not "always live together with both their real parents" up to the time they were sixteen years old. This was our definition of a Childhood Broken Home. However, a psychiatrist in private practice is actually less likely to see the product of broken homes. *Only one-fifth of private psychiatric patients come from broken homes in the Midtown area, as opposed to one-third of the general population.*

About three-fifths of these broken homes were due to the death of one or both parents. Slightly less than one-fifth were due to the parents' divorce, separation, or desertion. Respondents were twice as likely to lose their fathers as they were to lose their mothers before reaching age sixteen. Those who lost both parents or mothers by death before they were sixteen are worse off than those whose fathers only had died by that time. Those whose fathers died are no worse off than those who came from unbroken homes. In the low socioeconomic group, those whose mothers died are markedly worse off in terms of mental health.

There are twice as many deaths of mothers before the child was sixteen years old in the low as in the high SES. The mental health risk associated with the death of the mother is also greater in the low SES. In the high SES, however, the death of fathers and mothers seems to bear little relationship to mental health risk.

The proportion of respondents whose childhood home was broken by divorce, separation, or desertion was twice as great in the high as in the low SES. However, about one-third of all three SES groups came from broken homes, showing that the broken home is not necessarily the product of poverty alone.

Divorce, separation, and desertion of the parents more than doubles the probability that the children will also become divorced or separated. Persons who came from a childhood background of divorce are almost three times as likely to worry often about their marriage as persons whose childhood home was unbroken.

Homes broken before the respondent was seven years old are associated with poor mental health in the sample as a whole. Homes broken from ages seven to sixteen were no worse than unbroken homes. However, this did not hold true in the high SES.

Those respondents whose divorced or widowed parent later remarried are worse off than those whose remaining parent did not remarry. Remarriage therefore cannot accurately be described as the "repair" of a broken home, but rather as an *attempt* to repair a broken home which more often fails as far as the mental health of the step-children is concerned.

A larger proportion of low SES respondents did not get along with their step-parents. Those who got along poorly show considerably greater impairment as adults than those who got along well. An increase in mental health risk occurs if the parent remarried after the child was sixteen.

The mental health of the children whose widowed parent remarried is much worse than the mental health of those whose remaining widowed parent did not remarry.

The mental health of sons is best if their fathers did not remarry, and worse if they did. Likewise, the mental health of daughters is best if their mothers did not remarry, and worse if they did. Therefore, the *like-sex* widowed parent seems more closely linked to the mental health of the child. Contrary to expectations, the mental health of girls with step-mothers is only slightly worse than that of the female population as a whole. Step-mothers are not harder to "get along with" than step-fathers. The remarriage of the widowed parent involves greater resentment on the part of the children toward the widowed parent as well as toward the step-parent. A larger proportion of those whose widowed parents remarried perceived the widowed parent negatively.

Working mothers are sometimes considered to be the equivalent of a "semibroken home" for the child. In both the low and high SES, children exhibit the best mental health if their mother worked part time rather than full time or not at all. Far from creating a "semibroken home," the part-time working mother seems to have healthier children. In the low and middle SES, part-time working mothers of children under eighteen are themselves in better mental health than mothers who work full time or not at all.

## Notes

1. P. Friedman and L. Linn, "Some Psychiatric Notes on the *Andrea Doria* Disaster," *American Journal of Psychiatry*, Volume 114, No. 5, November 1957, pp. 428–429.

2. P. Friedman and L. Linn, *ibid.*, p. 429. They are referring to A. Freud and D. T. Burlingham, *War and Children*, New York, Medical War Books, 1945.

3. Josephine R. Hilgard, Martha F. Newman, and Fern Fisk, "Strength of Adult Ego Following Childhood Bereavement," *American Journal of Orthopsychiatry*, Volume 30, No. 4, October 1960, pp. 788–798.

4. The two high SES respondents who lost both parents were extremely disturbed, however, with an average ridit of .92.

5. The divorced or separated respondents include only those who were divorced or separated from their spouses at the time of the interview, and not those formerly divorced and now remarried, or those separated and later reunited.

6. Arnold W. Green, "The Middle-Class Male Child and Neurosis," *American Sociological Review*, Volume 11, February 1946, pp. 31–41, reprinted in *Mental Health and Mental Disorder*, Arnold M. Rose (ed.), W. W. Norton & Company, New York, 1955, p. 345.

7. Green's "middle class" includes both the middle and most of the upper class, since he defines middle class as "that class whose members have welded their attitudes and values into a life-long striving toward an improvement of personal socio-economic position within the class structure" (Arnold W. Green, *ibid.*, p. 346). Therefore, his middle class corresponds roughly to the upper part of the Midtown middle SES and most of the high SES.

8. Arnold W. Green, *ibid.*, p. 346.

9. Our fathers of high socioeconomic status are roughly equivalent to Green's middle class. Our low SES is roughly equivalent to the Polish immigrant families he observed in Massachusetts.

10. This includes all divorced parents, in *addition* to widowed parents previously described.

11. Of low, middle, and high SES remarried remaining parents, 31.9, 29.5 and 18.0 per cent remarried before the respondent was seven years old (see Table 8-9).

12. Erich Fromm, "Individual and Social Origins of Neurosis," *American Sociological Review*, Volume 9, August 1944, pp. 380–384.

13. Bernard Kutner, David Fanshel, Alice M. Togo, and Thomas S. Langner, *Five Hundred Over Sixty*, New York, Russell Sage Foundation, 1956, p. 62.

14. Robert Latou Dickinson and Lura Beam, *A Thousand Marriages. A Medical Study of Sex Adjustment*, Williams and Wilkins, 1931, pp. 270–287.

15. Widows and widowers in the parent generation should not be compared with widowed persons in general, since the mental health of the former group is probably better than that of the latter. This arises from the fact that only couples who had children (now respondents) would be *parent* widows and widowers. Persons with children seem to have better mental health than those without. In particular, the remaining parent may derive emotional support from his children. Unmarried widows and widowers, while not left with the burden of raising and supporting their children alone, at the same time are less likely to have the emotional support of a family group.

16. We did not examine the respondent widows according to whether or not they had children. It is surprising that widows run the same risk whether they remarry or not. One would think that the loneliness of widowhood would be impairing to mental health. However, the responsibility for and emotional attachment to her children would be a strong factor in maintaining the homeostasis of the widow, even in the face of her great loss, and even without remarriage. If such analysis is possible in the future, we would expect that the unremarried widows without children would run a much greater mental health risk than those with children.

17. Perhaps the widow or widower who does not remarry has had a very strong and positive relationship with the deceased spouse, and because of the idealization of the first mate does not desire remarriage. This possibility is suggested by Willard Waller in *The Family: A Dynamic Interpretation*, Holt, Rinehart & Winston, New York, revised edition, 1951, p. 496.

18. Only 56 respondents had step-fathers and 58 respondents had step-mothers out of 397 persons who had a widowed parent. The sex of the remaining parent could be definitely determined only in those cases where the father or the mother had died and the remaining parent had remarried, a total of 114 cases.

19. Quoted in Stella B. Applebaum, *Working Wives and Mothers*, Public Affairs Pamphlet No. 188, New York, November 1952, p. 20.

20. For instance, Applebaum discusses the negative aspects of the full-time household wife and mother,

> Actually we all know the stay at home wife who sacrifices her life to her home and family. One psychiatrist calls her the passive martyr. . . . But, let's be fair. Not every working wife is destroying her husband's ego, disparaging his abilities, or perpetuating the battle of the sexes. (See Stella B. Applebaum, *ibid.*, p. 13.)

Dr. Benjamin Spock suggests that the increase in the number of working mothers may be due to a desire not only to help the husband financially and to join the more companionable and exciting environment of the office but also to avoid tension and irritation that arises in caring for children.

It is possible that children are better off when their mothers are doing some work outside the home. The few hours the mother does spend with the children may be less tense and more emotionally rewarding to the child.

Margaret Mead has warned against the increasing exaggeration of the mother's importance as the sole biological and emotional support of the infant.

> At present, the specific biological situation of the continuing relationship of the child to its biological mother and its need for care by human beings are being hopelessly confused in the growing insistence that child and biological mother, or mother surrogate, must never be separated, that all separation even for a few days is inevitably damaging, and that if long enough it does irreversible damage. This, as Hilde Bruch has cogently pointed out, is a new and subtle form of antifeminism in which men—under the guise of exalting the importance of maternity—are tying women more tightly to their children than has been thought necessary since the invention of bottle feeding and baby carriages. Actually, anthropological evidence gives no support at present to the value of such an accentuation of the tie between mother and child. On the contrary, cross-cultural studies suggest that adjustment is most facilitated if the child is cared for by many warm friendly people. (Margaret Mead, "Some Theoretical Considerations on the Problem of Mother-Child Separation," *American Journal of Orthopsychiatry*, Volume XXIV, July 1954, p. 477.)

21. To assess differences in the mental health of full-time, part-time, and non-working mothers of respondents, we need a more sensitive measure than the Mother's Psychosomatic Score or the item "Mother was the worrying type." The mental health of respondent mothers is intended only as a substitute for the mental health of mothers of respondents. Most closely comparable are the mothers among the respondent generation (*respondent mothers*) with children under eighteen years of age. Only 13.6 per cent of respondent mothers themselves work full time, compared with 18.3 per cent of mothers of respondents. Only 9.0 per cent of respondent mothers work part time, compared with 12.9 per cent of mothers of respondents. The proportion of respondent mothers not working is 77.4 per cent, compared to 67.5 per cent of mothers of respondents. It should be remembered that working outside the home is reported for mothers of respondents while the respondent was aged six to eighteen. Respondent mothers therefore probably have proportionally more children *under* the age of six, and consequently are less likely to be working outside the home. The differences between mothers of respondents and respondent mothers are not greater than what we might expect, due to the discrepancy in the ages of the children (six to eighteen versus birth to eighteen). For this population, then, the proportion of working mothers has changed very little compared with their parents' generation, a rather unexpected finding in view of the literature describing the increase in the proportion of working mothers. (See, for example, Stella B. Applebaum, *op. cit.*, pp. 8, 10.) The large immigrant population of the area (about one-third)

and the large proportion of second-generation respondents whose parents were immigrants may explain the high proportion of working mothers of respondents; that is, mothers of low socioeconomic status as in our sample, are most likely to work outside the home.

The picture is confused by the fact that respondent mothers were asked "Are you working now?" which would yield a smaller number of working mothers, since some of them may work sporadically. The mothers of respondents were reported as "ever having worked" during the time the respondent was six to eighteen. Therefore a larger proportion of mothers of respondents are reported than if a one-day prevalence question had been asked for them also. For example, "Was your mother working at the time of your tenth birthday?" The respondent generation, then, probably has a much greater proportion of working mothers over the years, but this is not indicated by our question, which measures the proportion working at a point in time (the day of the interview).

22. The question was, "During those years you were growing up (age six to eighteen), did your mother (or mother substitute) ever do work outside the home?"

# Parents' Poor Mental and Physical Health, and Childhood Poor Physical Health

### T H O M A S   S .   L A N G N E R

## Parents' Poor Mental Health

### A.   "PSYCHOSOMATIC" AND "WORRYING" PARENTS

It is easy to say that disturbed parents have disturbed children, but quite difficult to substantiate. Only limited materials were available for a rough indication of the mental health of the respondents' parents. The major source of data was the respondent's report of certain conditions of his mother and father which might be psychosomatic: arthritis, asthma, "bladder trouble," colitis, diabetes, hay fever, high blood pressure, neuralgia, stomach ulcer, and "skin condition."[1] These ten conditions were combined into a simple score (each condition receiving a weight of one) for the respondent's mother and the respondent's father separately.

The number of psychosomatic conditions the respondent reports for his mother bears only a moderate relationship to his Adult Mental Health Rating. It is only when the mother has had four or more psychosomatic conditions that the respondent's mental health risk increases sharply to .70 (see Table 9-1).

This is true for persons of middle socioeconomic status. In the low SES, however, the mental health risk increases sharply if the mother had as few as *two* psychosomatic conditions. Forty-six per cent of all respondents had mothers with one or more psychosomatic conditions. High SES mothers tend to have more psychosomatic conditions than those of middle and low SES. Approximately 59, 55, and 48 per cent of the low, middle, and high SES mothers of respondents, respectively, had no psychosomatic conditions.

### TABLE 9-1

### PROPORTIONS AND AVERAGE MENTAL HEALTH (MH II) OF RESPONDENTS ACCORDING TO THEIR MOTHERS' PSYCHOSOMATIC SIMPLE SCORES AND FATHERS' SOCIOECONOMIC STATUS

| Mothers' Psychosomatic Simple Score | Fathers' Socioeconomic Status | | | | | | | |
|---|---|---|---|---|---|---|---|---|
| | LOW | | MIDDLE | | HIGH | | TOTAL | |
| | Per Cent | R̄ | Per Cent | R̄ | Per Cent | R̄ | Per Cent | R̄ |
| 0 | 59.2 | .55 | 54.6 | .47 | 48.1 | .44 | 54.0 | .49 |
| 1 | 23.9 | .53 | 27.4 | .51 | 30.0 | .45 | 27.0 | .49 |
| 2 | 12.2 | .62 | 10.9 | .53 | 13.6 | .44 | 12.1 | .52 |
| 3 | 4.1 | .65 | 6.0 | .51 | 5.5 | .50 | 5.3 | .54 |
| 4 | .6 | (.88) | 1.0 | (.68) | 2.0 | .65 | 1.2 | .70 |
| 5 | – | – | – | – | .2 | (.80) | .1 | (.80) |
| 6 | – | – | – | – | .2 | (.61) | .1 | (.61) |
| 7 | – | – | .1 | (.87) | .4 | (.72) | .2 | (.77) |
| Total Number of Cases (N=100 per cent) | 482 | | 671 | | 507 | | 1660 | |

Parentheses ( ) enclose ridits based on less than ten cases.

In contrast to the mothers' psychosomatic conditions, the number of psychosomatic conditions of the respondents' fathers seem to be unrelated to the respondents' adult impairment risk (see Table 9-2).

In the high SES particularly, there seems to be no relationship. Even though slight increases in risk occur where fathers had three or more conditions, these statistics are unreliable because of the small number of cases. With some exceptions, facts about the father seem to have less bearing on the mental health of the respondents than facts about the mother.

Similar to the high SES mothers, there is some tendency for high SES fathers to have more reported psychosomatic conditions. About 70, 64, and 57 per cent of low, middle, and high SES fathers, respectively, had no psychosomatic conditions. This might be attributed to lack of knowledge on the part of low SES respondents, who would be less able to recognize and therefore to report their fathers' or mothers' conditions.

## TABLE 9-2

### PROPORTIONS AND AVERAGE MENTAL HEALTH (MH II) OF RESPONDENTS ACCORDING TO THEIR FATHERS' PSYCHOSOMATIC SIMPLE SCORES AND SOCIOECONOMIC STATUS

| Fathers' Psychosomatic Simple Score | Fathers' Socioeconomic Status | | | | | | | |
|---|---|---|---|---|---|---|---|---|
| | LOW | | MIDDLE | | HIGH | | TOTAL | |
| | Per Cent | $\bar{R}$ | Per Cent | $\bar{R}$ | Per Cent | $\bar{R}$ | Per Cent | $\bar{R}$ |
| 0 | 70.3 | .56 | 63.8 | .49 | 57.4 | .45 | 63.5 | .50 |
| 1 | 21.2 | .55 | 23.4 | .50 | 27.0 | .43 | 23.9 | .49 |
| 2 | 6.8 | .55 | 9.7 | .47 | 12.0 | .51 | 9.6 | .50 |
| 3 | 1.7 | .64 | 2.4 | (.58) | 2.4 | .37 | 2.2 | .52 |
| 4 | – | – | .6 | (.67) | .8 | (.37) | .5 | (.52) |
| 5 | – | – | .1 | (.14) | .2 | (.30) | .2 | (.22) |
| 6 | – | – | – | – | .2 | (.72) | .1 | (.72) |
| Total Number of Cases (N=100 per cent) | 482 | | 671 | | 507 | | 1660 | |

Parentheses ( ) enclose ridits based on less than ten cases.

The fact that the mothers' psychosomatic conditions (as an index of their mental health) appear to be more relevant to the respondents' mental health than the fathers' conditions raises an interesting problem. Presumably the child inherits an equal proportion of genetic characteristics from both its parents. If tendencies to develop poor mental health were hereditary, why shouldn't they be inherited equally from the father and the mother? The greater importance of the mother as an environmental influence would seem to be the better hypothesis in this case than the hyp' thesis of heredity.

It was felt that the sex of the child might have something to do with the determination of these tendencies or conditions. We therefore analyzed male and female respondents' Mental Health Ratings according to fathers' and mothers' psychosomatic conditions (see Table 9-3). For the sake of classification we considered parents with two or more psychosomatic conditions as "psychosomatic." The data show that it is the sex of the psychosomatic parent, and not the sex of the child, that is predictive of mental disturbance.

### TABLE 9-3

### PROPORTIONS AND AVERAGE MENTAL HEALTH (MH I) OF MALE AND FEMALE RESPONDENTS ACCORDING TO THE PSYCHOSOMATIC CONDITIONS OF THEIR PARENTS

| | Sex of Respondents | | | | |
|---|---|---|---|---|---|
| | MALE | | FEMALE | | TOTAL |
| Parents Psychosomatic[a] | Per Cent | $\bar{R}$ | Per Cent | $\bar{R}$ | Per Cent |
| Mother | 13.6 | .54 | 16.8 | .55 | 15.5 |
| Father | 10.1 | .50 | 8.1 | .50 | 9.0 |
| Both | 2.5 | .55 | 4.1 | .55 | 3.4 |
| Neither | 73.8 | .49 | 71.0 | .49 | 72.1 |
| Total Number of Cases (N=100 per cent) | 690 | | 970 | | 1660 |

[a] Parents with two or more conditions were considered to be "psychosomatic."

Persons with psychosomatic mothers are worse off (.54 and .55) than those with psychosomatic fathers (.50), regardless of sex. Those with both parents psychosomatic are no worse off than those with psychosomatic mothers, indicating that the mother is probably the chief contributor to mental health risk when both parents are involved. When neither parent is psychosomatic, the risk (.49) is reduced below the risk associated with psychosomatic mothers, but it is approximately equal to the risk associated with psychosomatic fathers.

The fact that the mothers' psychosomatic conditions are more important than the fathers' regardless of the sex of the child has again at least two possible interpretations: first, that predispositions toward poor mental health are carried by the mothers' chromosomes alone (a doubtful supposition), or second (a more plausible interpretation), that the mother's central role in training her children, and her prolonged contact with them, make any defect in her personality more dangerous to the mental health of the children than a similar defect in the father.

Another datum on the mental health of parents was the respondent's answer to the question, "Were either of your parents the worrying type?" Those who reported that one or both of their parents were the worrying type have an increased mental health risk (.55) over those who didn't report a worrying parent (.44). Similar to the psychosomatic conditions, the mothers' worrying in general seems slightly more related to the respondents' mental health (.55) than the fathers' worrying (.52). (See Table 9-4.)

## TABLE 9-4

### PROPORTIONS AND AVERAGE MENTAL HEALTH (MH II) OF RESPONDENTS ACCORDING TO PARENTS' WORRYING TYPE AND FATHERS' SOCIOECONOMIC STATUS

| Parents The Worrying Type | Fathers' Socioeconomic Status | | | | | | | |
|---|---|---|---|---|---|---|---|---|
| | LOW | | MIDDLE | | HIGH | | TOTAL | |
| | Per Cent | $\bar{R}$ | Per Cent | $\bar{R}$ | Per Cent | $\bar{R}$ | Per Cent | $\bar{R}$ |
| Mother | 34.4 | $.60^*_z$ | 35.9 | $.55^*_x$ | 31.8 | $.50^*_w$ | 34.2 | $.55^*_v$ |
| Father | 8.7 | $.66^*_y$ | 10.1 | .48 | 9.3 | .48 | 9.5 | $.52^*_u$ |
| Both | 8.9 | .61 | 8.9 | .55 | 9.9 | .54 | 9.2 | .56 |
| | | | | * | | * | | * |
| Neither | 45.3 | $.50^*_{z,y}$ | 42.4 | $.43^*_x$ | 47.0 | $.38^*_w$ | 44.6 | $.44^*_{v,u}$ |
| Don't Know, No Answer ‖ | 2.7 | — | 2.7 | — | 2.0 | — | 2.5 | — |
| Total Number of Cases (N=100 per cent) | 482 | | 671 | | 507 | | 1660 | |

* Difference in test variable at the 5 per cent level of confidence between ridits with same subscripts or adjacent to same asterisk.
‖ Ridits not computed.

There is one exception to this trend: in the low SES group a worrying father is less favorable (.66) than a worrying mother (.60).[2] Nevertheless, the proportion of persons at each SES level reporting worrying mothers and fathers is almost identical. About 34 per cent report their mothers were worriers, while only 10 per cent report worrying fathers.

The psychosomatic scores of the mother and father, and the item "Were either of your parents the worrying type?" were combined into a single index of Parents' Poor Mental Health. The resulting risks of the factor are shown in Table 9-5.

As customary, the CMH Index and Mental Health Ratings I and II ridits are shown. The dichotomy shows significant differences for all three measures of impairment. The differences between the trichotomized plus and zero (moderate) group are not significant, however. The trichotomization was completely ineffectual in selecting a more disturbed group of people as far as the Adult Mental Health Ratings were concerned, but it was effective with respect to the CMH Index.[3]

### B.    "PSYCHOSOMATIC" PARENTS AND THEIR CHILDREN

The respondent's psychosomatic conditions were incorporated in his Mental Health Rating. It is therefore not surprising that the average number of psychosomatic conditions, an aspect of adult mental health, was related to the parents' psychosomatic scores. However, the female respondents' average psychosomatic scores are somewhat more related to their parents' psychosomatic scores than the average scores of males. Men with neither parent "psychosomatic"[4] have an average score of 0.9 conditions themselves. Males with one "psychosomatic" parent average 1.2 conditions, and where both parents are "psychosomatic" the men average 2.2 conditions. Similar averages for females are 1.0, 1.4, and 2.5 conditions, respectively. This finding is also related to the over-all greater number of psychosomatic conditions among females.

Whether we consider sons or daughters, the mothers' psychosomatic scores are more predictive of the respondents' psychosomatic scores. "Psychosomatic" mothers have sons with an average psychosomatic score of 1.29. "Psychosomatic" fathers have sons with a lower average score of 1.13. On the other hand, if we consider daughters, psychosomatic mothers have daughters with an average score of 1.52. This is greater than that of psychosomatic fathers, whose daughters have an average score of 1.39. While the increment of the mothers over the fathers is not great, it is nevertheless consistent, and remains regardless of the sex of the respondent. The mother's involvement in her children's mental health is probably greater than the father's although it is not as great as some writers would have us believe.[5] The impact of two "psychosomatic"

## TABLE 9-5

## DISTRIBUTION, PROPORTIONS, AND AVERAGE MENTAL HEALTH (CMH, MH I, MH II) ACCORDING TO PARENTS' POOR MENTAL HEALTH, TRICHOTOMIZED AND DICHOTOMIZED

| Parents' Poor Mental Health | Respondents' Mental Health | | | | |
| --- | --- | --- | --- | --- | --- |
| | CMH | MH I | MH II | No. of Cases | Per Cent |
| Trichotomy | | | | | |
| + | $.62^*_z$ | $.56^*_y$ | $.56^*_x$ | 185 | 11.1 |
| 0 | .54 | .57 | .57 | 262 | 15.8 |
| | * | * | * | | |
| − | $.46^*_z$ | $.48^*_y$ | $.48^*_x$ | 1213 | 73.1 |
| Dichotomy | | | | | |
| + | .60 | .57 | .57 | 447 | 26.9 |
| | * | * | * | | |
| − | .46 | .48 | .48 | 1213 | 73.1 |
| Total Number of Cases (N = 100 per cent) | | | | 1660 | |

*Difference in test variable at the 5 per cent level of confidence between ridits with same subscript or adjacent to same asterisk.

parents (linked to an average of 2.42 conditions in the child) is much greater than the impact of a psychosomatic mother alone (1.44 conditions), indicating that the father still has some importance in child development.

The tetrachoric correlation between the two parents' psychosomatic scores is somewhat greater when reported by females (.20) rather than males (.11). However, in view of the general low degree of correlation, it would seem that "psychosomatic" individuals (parents) did not tend to marry each other. Only 3.4 per cent of the respondents reported parents who *both* had two or more psychosomatic conditions (see Table 9-3). While this may be partially the result of errors in respondents' reporting, the low correlations are a stimulus to further research along these lines. Are those who "somatize" as a method of adapting to stress a group of people fairly distinct from those who try to adapt by "acting out?" Is it possible that somatizers tend to avoid marrying other somatizers? The data would seem to suggest this. It would be interesting to test the hypothesis that somatizers tend to marry those who act out. The attraction and interaction between various adaptive types is not a new topic, but it is one seldom approached on a statistical and clinical basis simultaneously.

### C.   THE IMPAIRMENT RISK OF SPECIFIC PSYCHOSOMATIC CONDITIONS

The specific psychosomatic conditions of their mothers and fathers, with a few exceptions, are only moderately related to the adult mental health (MH I) of the respondents (see Table 9-6). These exceptions are as follows: if the respondents' mothers had asthma (.60), neuralgia (.60), or stomach ulcers (.59), their own adult mental health risk is considerably increased over the sample as a whole. If their fathers had colitis, their risk is also high (.65).

However, if the respondents' fathers had hay fever (.39) or an ulcer (.34), their own mental health risk is actually reduced. This may very well be the effect of the high socioeconomic status associated with both hay fever and ulcers in the father's generation. Despite their ailments, perhaps because of them, these fathers with hay fever and ulcers may have been good providers. There is no way of separating interpersonal security from economic security on the basis of these data. However, it may well be that economic security is as important as interpersonal (or emotional) security in the case of *high* SES fathers, whose death (as shown in Chapter 8) seems unrelated to the mental health of their children.[6]

### D.   RESPONDENTS' TYPES OF DISTURBANCE AND PARENTAL PSYCHOSOMATIC CONDITIONS

No one condition of either parent is more strongly associated with the total number of the respondents' conditions than any other. Those whose mothers had psychosomatic conditions have an average of about one-and-a-half conditions themselves. Those whose fathers had psychosomatic conditions average about the same.

Asthma and ulcers in the mother seem associated with higher rates of "Probable Psychosis"[7] in the respondent. Ulcers in mothers also showed a particularly high rate of "Probable Neurosis" in their children as respondents.

## TABLE 9-6

### DISTRIBUTION AND AVERAGE MENTAL HEALTH (MH I) OF RESPONDENTS ACCORDING TO THEIR MOTHERS' AND FATHERS' PSYCHOSOMATIC CONDITIONS

| | Respondents' Parents | | | |
| | MOTHERS' | | FATHERS' | |
| Psychosomatic Conditions[a] | No. of Cases | $\bar{R}$ | No. of Cases | $\bar{R}$ |
|---|---|---|---|---|
| Asthma[b] | 59 | .60 | 59 | .48 |
| Neuralgia | 116 | .60 | 52 | .54 |
| Stomach Ulcer | 31 | .59 | 72 | .34 |
| Bladder Trouble | 70 | .55 | 49 | .56 |
| Diabetes | 71 | .54 | 49 | .55 |
| Skin Condition | 47 | .54 | 23 | .49 |
| High Blood Pressure | 255 | .52 | 141 | .48 |
| Hay Fever | 36 | .51 | 35 | .39 |
| Arthritis | 239 | .50 | 98 | .50 |
| Colitis | 27 | .48 | 18 | .65 |

[a] Certain conditions were included in the original list of "psychosomatic conditions" but later were deemed not fit for such a list. Too frequently a heart condition might be simply somatic and not psychogenic in origin. This would be particularly true of congenital malformations or of rheumatic heart damage. Epilepsy was placed on the somatic side of the ledger, and "nervous breakdown" was considered too general for inclusion in the psychosomatic symptoms.

[b] Listed in rank order of risk according to mothers' conditions.

Jim R. (see footnote, page 166) has annoying pains in his arm. They sometimes interfere with his job as an elevator man. They usually get worse when he gets excited or angry. He has fought a great deal with his wife, and wishes he had never married. "My wife claims I always tried to win my mother's affection, to be her favorite. They never got along. My mother went to a fortune teller who told her that my wife's children weren't really mine. I dream that I'm flying away from my mother, even though she's dead now. I'd like to be alone and rid of my wife too. When Dad died I was three years old. My mother took up with another man. Well, when I was fourteen, he beat me up. Then later mother put me out. I told her to housebreak the dog, 'cause he was messing the whole house. She said, 'I can't train you, and I can't train the dog. It's you or the dog.' So then I left home."

Jim came from a slum background, and in his teens got in trouble with the police. However, "nothing bothers him" . . . even when his wife is "oversexed," or when his mother died. Only his arm bothers him.

His mother suffered from asthma, arthritis, and high blood pressure. Her common-law husband left her when she was forty-seven, and from then on "she'd be lonely, cling to me, and just sit and look. I didn't have the freedom my friends had. She didn't want me to marry. It made me mad the way she used my money to buy my sisters new clothes, while I wore hand-me-downs."

Jim's story seems to illustrate the high risk of children of asthmatic mothers. The frequent rages, alternating with overprotection, to which he was exposed, seem to have incapacitated him. He is unhappy with his wife. He is dissatisfied with his job, and the pains are starting to interfere with operating the elevator. The impressive number of his mother's psychosomatic conditions also reflects the increasing risk as the number of mother's conditions increases.

The respondents whose mothers had psychosomatic conditions showed a remarkably low rate of Probable Personality Trait Types. These types were characterized by the rating psychiatrists according to the respondents' symptoms of rigidity, hostility, suspiciousness, and dependency. Fourteen per cent of those whose mothers and fathers had *no* psychosomatic ailments were "Trait Types." However, only 5 per cent of those whose mothers had one or more of these conditions were classified as Trait Types.

This is so striking that it deserves some comment, especially since it is to some extent true of the fathers' conditions as well. One of many possible hypotheses is that "psychosomatic" parents typically somatize rather than act out. Their children may learn to react to stress in a similar manner. The proportion of acting out children raised by psychosomatic parents would then be quite small. Since mothers are very important in setting the early patterns for handling rage and fear, their psychosomatic symptoms would be more predictive of the children's ways of handling these same emotions.

Diabetes and high blood pressure in the father, on the other hand, seem most related to "Probable Neurosis" in the respondent offspring.

The parents' psychosomatic conditions were examined to see whether they showed a relationship to the various "personality scores" of the respondents (based on the categories of Immaturity, Rigidity, Frustration-Depression, Intake, Tension-Anxiety, Neurasthenia, Appetite-Stomach, Headaches Vaso-Lability, Suspiciousness, Withdrawal). These scores were based on the items in the questionnaire (see Chapter 2). The only score that showed a consistently marked relationship to psychosomatic conditions of mother or father was the Tension-Anxiety Score. This consisted of five questions, to which the more disturbed response is in bold face type below.

Do you ever have any trouble in getting to sleep or staying asleep? Would you say: **often,** sometimes, or never?

Are you ever bothered by nervousness (irritable, fidgety, tense)? Would you say: **often,** sometimes, or never?

I have periods of such great restlessness that I cannot sit long in a chair. **Yes,** No.

Are you the worrying type? **Yes,** No.

I have personal worries that get me down physically. **Agree,** Disagree.

Those whose mothers had neuralgia, ulcers, and "bladder trouble" were most likely to be tense and anxious (nervous, restless, sleepless, worrisome). Those whose fathers had "bladder trouble," arthritis, colitis, and diabetes were most apt to be tense and anxious. With the exception of parents' hay fever and fathers' "skin condition," those respondents whose parents had psychosomatic ailments show higher average Tension-Anxiety Scores than those whose parents did not.

Additional data indicate that mothers' asthma is associated with a high Frustration-Depression Score in the respondent.

In sum, the parents' particular psychosomatic conditions seem to have no specific connections with eleven psychological scores of the respondent offspring. One important exception is the association of tension and anxiety in the respondent with most of his parents' psychosomatic conditions.

### E. RESPONDENTS' TYPES OF PSYCHOSOMATIC CONDITIONS IN RELATION TO THOSE OF THEIR PARENTS

Although the number of parents' psychosomatic conditions seems to bear only a moderate relationship to adult impairment, there are some interesting connections between the parents' psychosomatic conditions and their children's psychosomatic conditions. For example, the child is more likely to have a particular condition, such as arthritis, if his parents had arthritis. To show this relationship, a statistical technique is employed. The actual number of cases is compared with the number of cases expected on the basis of chance alone.

Table 9-7 shows the "expected" number of cases that would have been found had chance alone been operating. For example, on the basis of pure chance we should have expected to find 41.9 cases of respondents with arthritis among those whose mothers had arthritis. There were actually 68 cases, which is well above chance, in fact, 1.6 times as great

## TABLE 9-7

### ACTUAL AND EXPECTED FREQUENCIES OF RESPONDENTS' PSYCHOSOMATIC CONDITIONS CONTROLLED BY PARENTS' CONDITIONS

| PSYCHOSOMATIC CONDITIONS | MOTHERS' CONDITIONS | | | FATHERS' CONDITIONS | | |
|---|---|---|---|---|---|---|
| | Actual Cases | Expected Cases | Ratio of Actual to Expected Cases | Actual Cases | Expected Cases | Ratio of Actual to Expected Cases |
| Arthritis | 68 | 41.9 | 1.6 | 32 | 12.0 | 2.7 |
| Asthma | 6 | 2.4 | 2.5 | 5 | 1.4 | 3.6 |
| Bladder Trouble | 15 | 5.8 | 2.6 | 3 | 2.3 | 1.3 |
| Colitis | 3 | 1.5 | 2.0 | 4 | .7 | 5.7 |
| Diabetes | 3 | .5 | 6.0 | – | – | – |
| Hay Fever | 9 | 3.3 | 2.7 | 11 | 1.8 | 6.1 |
| High Blood Pressure | 31 | 28.4 | 1.1 | 20 | 9.7 | 2.1 |
| Neuralgia | 31 | 12.5 | 2.5 | 15 | 3.9 | 3.8 |
| Stomach Ulcer | 2 | 1.1 | 1.8 | 2 | 1.7 | 1.2 |
| Skin Trouble | 19 | 11.0 | 1.7 | 13 | 3.5 | 3.7 |

as chance. In other words, those with arthritic mothers have an increased chance of having arthritis themselves.

The ratios of actual over expected frequencies show that the mothers' conditions of arthritis, asthma, "bladder trouble," hay fever, neuralgia, and "skin condition" are likely to be shared by her children. The father's conditions of arthritis, asthma, colitis, hay fever, high blood pressure, neuralgia, and "skin condition" are more apt than chance to appear in their children.

## F.  WORRYING PARENTS

Worrying by itself cannot be considered as a symptom of mental disturbance. The circumstances under which a person worries determine to a large degree whether mental disturbance of psychiatric significance is present. Worrying is sometimes a realistic apprehension of present and probable future events. Unrealistic worry is often termed anxiety. Anxiety is usually present when a person worries over something that probably won't happen, or worries without being able to say what worries him. (The terms normal or existential anxiety as opposed to

neurotic anxiety are also employed to describe legitimate and pathological worrying.)

The distinction between realistic worrying and anxiety is not always
easy to make in a clinical interview. It is doubly difficult in a questionnaire interview. We used worrying as one measure of the mental health
of parents, even though it might not necessarily indicate psychopathology in any one case. We knew, for instance, that many respondents
were children during the economic depression of the 1930s. If their
unemployed fathers had *not* worried under such circumstances their
mental health might have been called into question.

The content or object of worrying might be an aid in determining the
reality orientation of worrying, were it not for the fact that parents
of different social status worry about different things. If financial problems are uppermost in the eyes of low SES parents, interpersonal problems may loom large in the eyes of the high SES parent. Respondents
were asked to report what were the "chief problems or troubles" of their
parents. Large proportions of low SES parents had "unemployment,"
"work,"[8] and "financial" problems. High SES parents were more often
reported as having such problems as "father-mother conflict," "myself,"
"siblings," or "no problems at all." Equal proportions of low, middle, and
high SES parents were reported to have had problems of "illness." If the
respondents' reports of parents' problems are accurate, then we may
assume that worrying parents at each SES level actually worried about
the problems most prevalent at that level.

The problem of what type of worrying is a sign of mental disturbance
in the worrier cannot be solved here. However, the data indicate that
the *children* of a worrying parent probably have an increased mental
health risk, no matter what the content and circumstance of the worries.
The low SES father may have very realistic or legitimate worries about
money and unemployment, but the legitimacy of these worries does not
decrease the mental health risk of his children.

If the parents worry but are reported as not having any "problems,"
will their children have an increased mental health risk? What is the
mental health of offspring of parents who are possibly "neurotic
worriers," that is, parents who worry but don't have many problems?
*Vis-à-vis* their children's mental health, how do these parents compare
with the parents who have lots of problems, but are not worriers?

Table 9-8 shows that worrying parents with no problems are somewhat more likely to have offspring with poorer adult mental health

(.49) than the offspring of nonworrying parents with problems (.44). While the difference is not great, it is at the 5 per cent level of statistical confidence. This indicates that it may be a little better to have parents who do not worry about the problems they have, rather than parents who worry but don't have many problems. Best of all, from a mental health standpoint, are parents who have neither problems nor worries (.40), and worst of all are worriers with problems (.56). In general, parental worries and problems are additive, and each has its independent effect on the offsprings' mental health.

### TABLE 9-8

### PROPORTIONS AND AVERAGE MENTAL HEALTH (MH II) OF RESPONDENTS WHOSE PARENTS WERE THE WORRYING TYPE BY PARENTS' PROBLEMS

|  | PARENTS HAD PROBLEMS | | PARENTS HAD NO PROBLEMS | | TOTAL | |
|---|---|---|---|---|---|---|
|  | Per Cent | $\bar{R}$ | Per Cent | $\bar{R}$ | Per Cent | $\bar{R}$ |
| Mother, Father, or Both Were the Worrying Type | 57.7 | .56 | 39.3 | .49 | 54.3 | .55 |
| Neither Was the Worrying Type | 42.3 | .44 | 60.7 | .40 | 45.7 | .43 |
| Total Number of Cases (N = 100 per cent) | 1320 | | 298 | | 1618[a] | |

[a] 42 cases did not know whether their parents were the worrying type or gave no answer.

Worrying parents definitely tend to have worrying children. On the average, three-fifths (60.7 per cent) of worrying parents have worrying children (see Table 9-9). However, only about 31 per cent of nonworrying parents have worrying children.

Only 56.3 per cent of respondents with worrying mothers describe themselves as worriers. However, 68.6 per cent of respondents with worrying fathers are worriers themselves. Therefore worrying fathers are somewhat more likely to have worrying children than are worrying mothers. However, the average mental health risk of those with worry-

## TABLE 9-9

### PROPORTIONS AND AVERAGE MENTAL HEALTH (MH I) OF RESPONDENTS WHO WERE THE WORRYING TYPE BY PARENTS WHO WERE THE WORRYING TYPE

| | Worrying Parents | | | | | | | Nonworrying Parents | |
|---|---|---|---|---|---|---|---|---|---|
| | MOTHER | | FATHER | | BOTH | | TOTAL | NEITHER | |
| *Respondent Worrying Type* | *Per Cent* | $\bar{R}$ | *Per Cent* | $\bar{R}$ | *Per Cent* | $\bar{R}$ | *Per Cent* | *Per Cent* | $\bar{R}$ |
| No | 43.7 | .43 | 31.4 | .40 | 31.1 | .44 | 39.3 | 68.8 | .36 |
| Yes | 56.3 | .65 | 68.6 | .58 | 68.9 | .62 | 60.7 | 31.2 | .59 |
| Total Number of Cases (N = 100 per cent) | 554 | | 153 | | 151 | | 858 | 727 | 1585[a] |

[a]The total number of cases is 1585. Seventy-five respondents reported Don't Know, No Answer to one or both of the questions.

ing fathers is less (.58) than those with worrying mothers (.65). While respondents' worrying is somewhat more associated with worrying fathers, *worrying mothers pose a greater mental health risk.* It should not be forgotten that, in the total sample, 34 per cent reported worrying mothers, while only 9 per cent reported worrying fathers. *One is not only "worse off" with a worrying mother, but mothers are also four times more likely to be reported "the worrying type" than are fathers.*

Joyce R. (see footnote, page 166) has a background of parental psychosomatic disease and mental disorder. Her mother was a worrier, had hypertension, and was in a mental hospital.

Joyce teaches modern dance and painting at a local high school. Lately she's been drinking each night till she passes out, and she eats only a few nibbles a day. Her job suffers. Light drinking helped her for a while in enjoying her relationship with her boyfriend, but she got to feel more and more like a prostitute. Her mother often said, "Joyce, never have anything to do with a man who isn't nice to you outside as well as inside a bed."

Her mother claimed that her husband tried to rape her. Following years of quarreling, her mother moved permanently from her husband's room into Joyce's bed. Joyce was fourteen then. Joyce's greatest fear was that her mother would wake up. She didn't know why. To avoid this she'd lie stiff as a board, holding her breath. At college she had an affair with another girl, but has resisted this urge since then. She still has trouble sleeping, which is why she usually drinks till she passes out.

Joyce's mother focused all her affection and hostility on her daughter. She showed this by excessive worrying and domination. At forty-three her mother became unmanageable after a minor illness, and had to have shock therapy. She has partially recovered, but still tries to wheedle her daughter into coming back home. "My life is so empty. Your father was so cruel. Can't you just be my little girl again?" At fifty-two, her mother has developed very high blood pressure.

Her father was always withdrawn. He had some engineering training, but never got a degree. He made sly critical remarks about everybody. After his wife left his bed, he developed a stomach ulcer. In return for financial support, he always demanded affection and obedience from his wife and daughter. Joyce's boyfriend seems to resemble him in this respect, and in his lack of spontaneous affection.

Joyce's life with her disturbed mother has left its mark. She no longer has to pull her mother off window ledges or head her off as she sleepwalks toward the lake. Nevertheless, her mother is constantly with her.

It seems that her father's passive or covertly aggressive behavior was never directed toward saving her from her mother. For this purpose he was useless, "without spirit, not much of a man." His inability to express fully either positive or negative feelings may also have led to his ulcer.

Although we found that children whose fathers had ulcers ran less risk, this doesn't seem to fit Joyce's particular case. Her father was a moderately good provider, so that she had economic security. However, he demanded love and obedience as a condition of support. "He was always proud of me, as long as I did what he wanted. He'd say, 'I gave you money, now love me.' My mother would say 'I brought you into this world, so you must love me.'" The economic security didn't really compensate for the lack of emotional security.

Respondents tend to identify with ("take after the most in character, personality, temperament") the worrying rather than the nonworrying parent. When the mother is a worrier but the father is not, approximately 44 per cent "take after" her,[9] and only about 29 per cent "take after" him.[10] When the mother is not a worrier, but the father is, only 32 per cent "take after" her,[11] while 44 per cent "take after" him[12] (see Table 9-10). There seems to be a pronounced tendency to identify with whichever parent worries, regardless of the sex of the respondent or the parent.

When *both* parents were worriers, their respondent offspring took after them in equal proportions (about 31 per cent of the children took

## TABLE 9-10

### PROPORTIONS AND AVERAGE MENTAL HEALTH (MH II) OF MALE AND FEMALE RESPONDENTS ACCORDING TO WHICH PARENT RESPONDENTS TAKE AFTER AND WHICH PARENT WAS THE WORRYING TYPE

Parent Worrying[b]

| Parent Taken After[a] | MOTHER | | | | FATHER | | | |
|---|---|---|---|---|---|---|---|---|
| | MALE | | FEMALE | | MALE | | FEMALE | |
| | Per Cent | R̄ | Per Cent | R̄ | Per Cent | R̄ | Per Cent | R̄ |
| Mother | 42.4 | .57 | 45.5 | .58 | 32.8 | .50 | 31.5 | .53 |
| Father | 29.3 | .50 | 28.9 | .52 | 48.4 | .44 | 41.6 | .57 |
| Both | 14.3 | .51 | 13.2 | .55 | 10.9 | .34 | 23.6 | .48 |
| Neither[c] | 14.0 | .63 | 12.4 | .56 | 7.9 | .62 | 3.3 | .58 |
| Number of Cases | 229 | | 325 | | 64 | | 89 | |

| | BOTH | | | | NEITHER | | | |
|---|---|---|---|---|---|---|---|---|
| Mother | 32.3 | .59 | 30.3 | .52 | 36.9 | .47 | 34.0 | .41 |
| Father | 32.3 | .61 | 36.0 | .58 | 36.2 | .40 | 39.2 | .45 |
| Both | 12.9 | .54 | 23.6 | .52 | 14.9 | .38 | 16.5 | .43 |
| Neither | 22.5 | .67 | 10.1 | .45 | 12.0 | .45 | 10.3 | .48 |
| Number of Cases | 62 | | 89 | | 309 | | 418 | |
| Total Number of Cases (N = 100 per cent) | | | | | | | 1585[d] | |

[a]"What person do you take after the most in character (personality, temperament)?"

[b]"Were either of your parents the worrying type?"

[c]Identification with "Other" person than parents.

[d]75 respondents did not answer.

after the mother only and about 34 per cent took after the father only, when both parents were worriers). This contrasts with the fact that when one parent worried and the other did not, approximately 44 per cent of the respondents took after the worrying parent and only about 30 per cent took after the nonworrying parent. Apparently, when both parents are worriers, there is an equal chance of identifying with the father or mother.[13]

"Taking after" a worrying mother involves an equally high mental health risk for males and females (.57, .58). This is a greater risk than "taking after" the nonworrying father (mother worries, .50, .52). Taking after a worrying father has a high risk for females (.57) but a lowered risk for males (.44). Taking after a nonworrying mother (father worries) has an equally moderate risk for both men and women (.50, .53).

Taking after one's mother seems to be associated with poor mental health. However, when the mother is *not* a worrier, but the children take after her, the mental health risk of both son and daughter seems to decrease (from .57 and .58 to .50 and .53). In sum, *identification with a worrying mother, but not with mothers in general, involves a higher mental health risk.*

Male respondents who take after worrying fathers have a remarkably low mental health risk (.44). There is a possibility that taking after a father who worries may be a sign of good mental health in a male. The basis for this is perhaps clarified by our data showing that respondents who are fathers are more apt to "worry often" about "getting ahead," "my work," and "overwork," than are respondents who are mothers. Yet the mental health risk of these worrying respondent fathers is much lower than that of worrying respondent mothers, who typically worry often about "children" and "loneliness."

There is evidence that the high SES father who worries about "work" or other problems in the economic sphere is healthier; identification with him by his sons may possibly be conducive to their better mental health. The large proportion of respondent mothers who tend to worry about "children" and "loneliness" exhibit worse mental health than mothers who worry about "work," physical health, or other problems not *primarily* interpersonal in nature. Identification with the "interpersonal worrying" mother may lay the foundations for poorer mental health in the respondent offspring. (See later chapters for a detailed analysis of Work Worries and Poor Interpersonal Affiliations.)

When both parents worry, the over-all risk is greater and particularly so for males (.59, .61). When neither parent worries the risk is greatly reduced (.44), and is even lower (.40, .41) when children take after the parent of the same sex. If the respondent says he takes after a worrying parent, he is very likely to report that he himself is a worrier. Of those who take after a worrying father, mother, or both worrying parents, 73.4 per cent are worriers themselves (see Table 9-11). Conversely, only 30.3 per cent of those who say they take after nonworrying parents (mother, father, or both) are worriers themselves.

Worriers who identify with worrying parents show worse mental health (.62) than nonworriers who identify with worrying parents (.41). Worriers who identify with nonworrying parents also exhibit worse mental health (.58) than corresponding nonworriers (.36). The *adult* worries of the worrying respondents account for a ridit increase of about .20 over the presently nonworrying respondents (.41 to .62, .36 to .58).

What is the effect of the childhood factor "Identification with a worrying parent?" For example, among nonworriers, those who identified with worrying parents were only a little worse off (.41) than those who identified with nonworrying parents (.36). The difference of .05 is only one-fourth as great as .20.

### TABLE 9-11

### PROPORTIONS AND AVERAGE MENTAL HEALTH (MH I) OF RESPONDENTS IDENTIFYING WITH PARENT(S) ACCORDING TO RESPONDENTS' AND PARENTS' WORRYING

| | Respondent Takes After | | | |
|---|---|---|---|---|
| | WORRYING PARENT(S) | | NONWORRYING PARENT(S) | |
| Respondent Worriers | Per Cent | $\bar{R}$ | Per Cent | $\bar{R}$ |
| No | 26.6 | .41 | 69.7 | .36 |
| Yes | 73.4 | .62 | 30.3 | .58 |
| Total Number of Cases (N = 100 per cent) | 755 | | 647 | |
| | | | | 1402[a] |

[a]258 respondents did not identify with parents or did not answer.

Actually, while children of worrying parents seem to identify with the worrying parent, and themselves tend to be worriers, it is their *present adult worrying that is directly related to their present mental health*. Since proportionally more adult worriers have identified with a worrying parent, this childhood variable, "Identification with a worrying (hence possibly disturbed) parent," may indirectly set the scene for the development of poor adult mental health.

## Parents' Poor Physical Health

If we had asked the respondents to distinguish between their parents' physical and mental health, they would obviously have been unable to do so. We asked, instead, whether their parents had been in poor health. We decided to call this "Parents' Poor Physical Health" principally to distinguish it from the dependent variable, mental health, used throughout the book. The background for this decision is discussed in Chapter 6, since the distinction between physical and mental health is a general methodological problem in this type of research.

There were only two questionnaire items related to the physical health of the respondents' parents. The first item was worded as follows:

Looking back, what would you say were the chief problems or troubles that your parents (or parent substitutes) had to face while you were growing up (age six to eighteen)?

Since the interviewer did not read any choice of answers to the respondents, this question was "open ended." Among the answers entered by the interviewers[14] 11 per cent in the sample as a whole reported that "illness" had been one of the chief problems of their parents. These 11 per cent were only slightly worse off in mental health risk (.52) than the rest of the population (.50). This was one reason why the item was not used in the final factor of Parents' Poor Physical Health. Incidentally, almost equal proportions of respondents at the three socioeconomic status levels reported parents' illness as a chief problem, a somewhat unexpected result.

The respondents also reported on the general health of their parents.

When you were growing up (age six to eighteen), were either of your parents (or parent substitutes) in poor health? No, **Yes.**

(If Yes) Was it your mother (or mother substitute) or father (or father substitute)? Mother, Father, Both.

Poor health reported for both parents carried a high mental health risk for their respondent offspring (.67). Poor health of mother (.56) or father (.51) alone brought appreciably less risk, although still high, when compared with the remainder of the sample which did not report either parent in poor health (with an average mental health ridit of .48). The differences between both parents and neither parent in poor health and between both parents and father alone in poor health are statistically significant. Table 9-12 illustrates these significant differences that occur when 5 per cent confidence intervals do not overlap.

The fathers' poor health is not strongly associated with poor mental health in their respondent progeny. A similar finding is reported in Chapter 8, where the death of the father generally seems less important than the death of the mother.

## TABLE 9-12

### PROPORTIONS AND AVERAGE MENTAL HEALTH (MH II) OF RESPONDENTS ACCORDING TO PARENTS' POOR PHYSICAL HEALTH AND FATHERS' SOCIOECONOMIC STATUS

| | Fathers' Socioeconomic Status | | | | | | | |
|---|---|---|---|---|---|---|---|---|
| Parents' Poor Physical Health | LOW | | MIDDLE | | HIGH | | TOTAL | |
| | Per Cent | $\bar{R}$ | Per Cent | $\bar{R}$ | Per Cent | $\bar{R}$ | Per Cent | $\bar{R}$ |
| Mother | 19.1 | .62 | 13.4 | $.56^*_z$ | 17.2 | .49 | 16.2 | $.56^*_y$ |
| Father | 11.2 | .52 | 11.9 | .53 | 13.4 | .48 | 12.2 | .51 |
| | | * | | | | | | * |
| Both | 2.9 | .78 | 2.5 | .64 | 2.6 | .60 | 2.7 | .67 |
| | | * | | * | | | | * |
| Neither | 66.0 | .54 | 69.8 | $.46^*_z$ | 66.4 | .43 | 67.6 | $.48^*_y$ |
| Don't Know, No Answer ǂ | .8 | – | 2.4 | – | .4 | – | 1.3 | – |
| Total Number of Cases (N = 100 per cent) | 482 | | 671 | | 507 | | 1660 | |

\* Difference in test variable at the 5 per cent level of confidence between ridits with same subscripts or adjacent to same asterisk.

ǂ Ridits not computed.

Of the sample, about 16 per cent report poor health of mother while only about 12 per cent report poor health of father (about 3 per cent reported both parents in poor health). This difference is only slight, but may well be due to the fact that a larger proportion of fathers die early in the child's life. This death is not reported as "poor health." A recent study has shown that women tend to have a larger number of minor illnesses, whereas men tend to have fewer but more serious illnesses, which often end in death.[15] Moreover, the mother, who lives longer on the average, is perhaps more likely to have her illnesses noticed. She is also in closer contact with the child, which makes her physical ailments more "visible."

The proportions of parents reported in poor health was strikingly similar in the three socioeconomic groups. This is somewhat contrary to expectations, since the physical health of lower socioeconomic levels is well known to be poorer. However, many severe medical problems may tend to be accepted rather fatalistically by lower status persons. In fact, because of lack of education, much disease at this level tends to go unrecognized. In addition, low SES persons, particularly under immigrant conditions (who in all probability have poorer physical health than higher SES persons), may let their ailments continue undiagnosed because of the lack of medical care. Furthermore, their attitudes toward health, similar to those of the aged, may involve acceptance of many curable aches and pains as their lot. Therefore, the similarity in the reported physical health of parents in the three SES levels is probably due to the underreporting of poor health among the low SES parents of respondents.

A final dichotomization of the Parents' Poor Physical Health factor resulted in the frequencies and risks shown in Table 9-13: poor health of one or both parents reported by 515 respondents (31 per cent), with a mental health risk (MH II) of .55 in the "plus" group, and a "minus" group consisting of 1145 cases (69 per cent), with a ridit of .48. It was not possible to trichotomize the Parents' Poor Physical Health factor, since only 3 per cent reported the extreme situation in which both parents were in poor health.

If the "mother alone in poor health" category were included to enlarge the plus group, this would leave only the fathers in the middle group. The effect of such a trichotomization would have been to change the name of the factor to "Mothers' Poor Physical Health." Throughout the analysis we attempted to avoid trichotomizing the factors along "mother-versus-father" lines. For this reason, and because poor physical health of parents proved to be a relatively weak factor, it was not included in the final Stress Score.

Although Parents' Poor Physical Health does not show a very strong relationship to the adult respondents' mental health, even this moderate relationship calls for some explanatory hypotheses. The most obvious explanation would be a hereditary one. If persons inherit tendencies toward

## TABLE 9-13

### DISTRIBUTION, PROPORTIONS, AND AVERAGE MENTAL HEALTH (CMH, MH I, MH II) OF RESPONDENTS ACCORDING TO THEIR PARENTS' POOR PHYSICAL HEALTH DICHOTOMIZED

| Parents' Poor Physical Health[a] | Respondents' Mental Health | | | | |
|---|---|---|---|---|---|
| | CMH | MH I | MH II | No. of Cases | Per Cent |
| Dichotomy | | | | | |
| + | .54 | .54 | .55 | 515 | 31.0 |
| | * | * | * | | |
| − | .48 | .48 | .48 | 1145 | 69.0 |
| Total Number of Cases (N = 100 per cent) | | | | 1660 | |

*Difference in test variable at the 5 per cent level of confidence between ridits adjacent to same asterisk.

[a] Parents' Poor Physical Health is the only factor that has not been trichotomized because of the small number of people (80 persons, or less than 5 per cent of the sample) who say both parents were in poor physical health. The "plus" group consists of those reporting Mother, Father, or Both in poor health. The "minus" group comprises those who reported Neither Parent in poor health.

the physical illness of their parents, perhaps they also inherit tendencies to develop mental disorder. Our data show that persons whose parents were reported in poor physical health are quite likely to report their own physical health as poor. There is also a strong association between Adult Poor Physical Health and the Adult Mental Health Rating of respondents; this is, in fact, the strongest relationship between any one factor and mental health. Thus, if Parents' Poor Physical Health is moderately related to the respondents' Adult Poor Physical Health, and in turn Adult Poor Physical Health is strongly related to poor adult mental health, a genetic relationship may be involved.

On the other hand, there are some indications that being physically ill may put more of a strain on parents, and lead to a subtle rejection of the children. Only 10 per cent of respondents, themselves parents in "excellent" or "good" health, agreed with the statement "Children give their parents more trouble than pleasure." In contrast, 22 per cent of respondent parents in "fair" or "poor" health agree that children give more trouble than pleasure. However, physically ill parents did not worry more frequently about their children, nor report more problems with their children than did physically well parents.

It would seem that the limited data available to us at this point would not support either a biological or a social explanation of the rather moderate relationship between poor physical health in parents and poor mental health in their children.

## Childhood Poor Physical Health

Several questionnaire items relating to the respondent's health during childhood exhibited differences in mental health risk. These items are difficult to classify as purely physical health, for each has an obvious psychological component. For instance, "frequent colds" may in some cases be partly psychogenic.

In order to distinguish these items from the Childhood Mental Health Index we have used the term "Childhood Poor Physical Health" to describe the final factor that evolved. By comparison with the Childhood Mental Health Index, which is composed of rather obvious childhood psychiatric symptoms, the Childhood Poor Physical Health factor is well over on the "physical" side.[16]

One item of related information was not utilized in the final factor. Each respondent was asked "As far as you know, were you born with any physical condition that later needed correction?" Regardless of socioeconomic status, those who had childhood conditions or defects ran a greater mental health risk than those who did not have defects. However, the differences were not statistically significant (see Table 9-14). This is chiefly due to the fact that only 110 persons, or 6.6 per cent, said they had physical defects in childhood.

There is no significant difference between the proportions of each socioeconomic group reporting physical defects that needed correction (5.8 per cent of the Lows, 5.7 per cent of the Middles, and 8.7 per cent of the Highs). The slight increase in the proportion among the high SES may be due to the interpretation by parents of various classes as to just what type of defect calls for corrective measures. It is more likely that high SES families would consider minor eye trouble or dental deformity as something that was "worth correcting." The very same defects in a child from a low socioeconomic family might not be considered as defects, or might not warrant a large medical expenditure in view of

## TABLE 9-14

### PROPORTIONS AND AVERAGE MENTAL HEALTH (MH II) OF RESPONDENTS ACCORDING TO CHILDHOOD DEFECTS NEEDING CORRECTION AND FATHERS' SOCIOECONOMIC STATUS

| Childhood Defects Needing Correction | Fathers' Socioeconomic Status | | | | | | | |
|---|---|---|---|---|---|---|---|---|
| | LOW | | MIDDLE | | HIGH | | TOTAL | |
| | Per Cent | $\bar{R}$ | Per Cent | $\bar{R}$ | Per Cent | $\bar{R}$ | Per Cent | $\bar{R}$ |
| No | 93.8 | .55 | 94.0 | .49 | 90.1 | .44 | 92.8 | .50 |
| Yes | 5.8 | .66 | 5.7 | .52 | 8.7 | .52 | 6.6 | .55 |
| Don't Know, No Answer ‡ | .4 | – | .3 | – | 1.2 | – | .6 | – |
| Total Number of Cases (N = 100 per cent) | 482 | | 671 | | 507 | | 1660 | |

‡ Ridits not computed.

more pressing needs. Since the number of persons involved was very small, the item "congenital defects" was not used in the final factor.

One question concerning the general health of the respondent in childhood yielded significant differences in mental health risk in the middle SES group and the sample as a whole. The respondents were asked, "Now, about your health in early childhood—that is, in the first six years of life? As far as you can remember or have been told, was your health in *early* childhood good, fair, or **poor**?" In the sample as a whole, 9.3 per cent reported poor health and 14.6 per cent fair health (see Table 9-15). Furthermore, people with poor health in early childhood were consistently worse off with respect to mental health than those with fair or good childhood health.[17]

Strikingly, there is no socioeconomic variation in the proportions reporting poor health in childhood. It may well be that this item taps the respondent's *assessment* of his early childhood health, which is psychologically indicative even though not medically exact. The chances are very strong that the children of low socioeconomic parentage actually had poorer health, even though as adults they don't report it (see discussion in Chapter 6).

## TABLE 9-15

### PROPORTIONS AND AVERAGE MENTAL HEALTH (MH II) OF RESPONDENTS ACCORDING TO THEIR GENERAL CHILDHOOD HEALTH AND FATHERS' SOCIOECONOMIC STATUS

| | Fathers' Socioeconomic Status | | | | | | | |
|---|---|---|---|---|---|---|---|---|
| Childhood Health | LOW | | MIDDLE | | HIGH | | TOTAL | |
| | Per Cent | $\bar{R}$ | Per Cent | $\bar{R}$ | Per Cent | $\bar{R}$ | Per Cent | $\bar{R}$ |
| Good | 75.1 | .55 | 74.6 | $.47^*_{z,y}$ | 75.1 | .44 | 75.0 | $.48^*_x$ |
| Fair | 13.9 | .59 | 15.5 | $.57^*_z$ | 14.2 | .45 | 14.6 | .54 |
| Poor | 10.0 | .62 | 9.2 | $.58^*_y$ | 8.9 | .53 | 9.3 | $.58^*_x$ |
| Don't Know, No Answer ‡ | 1.0 | – | .7 | – | 1.8 | – | 1.1 | – |
| Total Number of Cases (N=100 per cent) | 482 | | 671 | | 507 | | 1660 | |

\* Difference in test variable at the 5 per cent level of confidence between ridits with same subscript.

‡ Ridits not computed.

Another question included in the final factor was: "As a child did you catch cold fairly often?" Those who said "Yes" were consistently worse off with regard to mental health. (Differences were statistically significant for the low SES and the sample as a whole.) Somewhat less risk was attached to having frequent colds as a child in the high SES, in which group a somewhat larger proportion reported frequent colds (28.2 per cent) than in the sample as a whole (23.9 per cent). (See Table 9-16.)

The childhood physical health factor in its dichotomized form was composed of persons who had "colds often," or "fair and poor childhood health," or both (the "plus" group) as opposed to persons reporting they had good health and did not catch cold fairly often (the minus group). The trichotomized factor involved those with both colds and poor health (the plus group), those with either colds or poor health (the zero or middle group), and those with neither colds nor poor health (the minus group).

The results show that the trichotomy has no more separating power than the dichotomy (see Table 9-17) when examined in terms of adult

## TABLE 9-16

## PROPORTIONS AND AVERAGE MENTAL HEALTH (MH II) OF RESPONDENTS ACCORDING TO PREVALENCE OF CHILDHOOD COLDS AND FATHERS' SOCIOECONOMIC STATUS

| Childhood Colds Often | Fathers' Socioeconomic Status | | | | | | | |
|---|---|---|---|---|---|---|---|---|
| | LOW | | MIDDLE | | HIGH | | TOTAL | |
| | Per Cent | $\bar{R}$ | Per Cent | $\bar{R}$ | Per Cent | $\bar{R}$ | Per Cent | $\bar{R}$ |
| Yes | 23.9 | .64 | 20.7 | .55 | 28.2 | .47 | 23.9 | .55 |
| | | * | | | | | | * |
| No | 74.0 | .54 | 76.8 | .48 | 69.2 | .44 | 73.7 | .48 |
| Don't Know, No Answer ⨍ | 2.1 | – | 2.5 | – | 2.6 | – | 2.4 | – |
| Total Number of Cases (N=100 per cent) | 482 | | 671 | | 507 | | 1660 | |

\* Difference in test variable at the 5 per cent level of confidence between ridits adjacent to same asterisk.
⨍ Ridits not computed.

mental health. However, it is considerably more effective when childhood mental health is considered.

The Childhood Poor Physical Health factor is fraught with problems. First, have we measured physical health, or a combination of physical and mental health in childhood, with an emphasis that is perhaps physical? Second, how accurate is the recall of adults for their health before age six? How much is this a reflection of their own feelings about health as adults? How is the child's health related to the parents' health?

The latter question was tested by examining simultaneously the health of parents and child (as reported by the adult offspring). There was a tetrachoric correlation of .16 between Parents' Poor Physical Health and respondents' Childhood Poor Physical Health (see frequencies, Table 9-18). The relationship of the two factors is not very strong.

Interestingly, those who reported poor health for themselves *and* parents ran a much higher risk (.61) than those who said they had poor

## TABLE 9-17

### DISTRIBUTION, PROPORTIONS, AND AVERAGE MENTAL HEALTH (CMH, MH I, MH II) ACCORDING TO CHILDHOOD POOR PHYSICAL HEALTH, TRICHOTOMIZED AND DICHOTOMIZED

| Childhood Poor Physical Health | Respondents' Mental Health | | | No. of Cases | Per Cent |
|---|---|---|---|---|---|
| | CMH | MH I | MH II | | |
| Trichotomy | | | | | |
| + | $.64^*_z$ | $.57^*_y$ | $.56^*_w$ | 247 | 14.9 |
| 0 | $.55^*_z$ | $.54^*_x$ | $.55^*_v$ | 377 | 22.7 |
| − | $.45^*_z$ | $.47^*_{y,x}$ | $.47^*_{w,v}$ | 1036 | 62.4 |
| Dichotomy | | | | | |
| + , | .59 | .55 | .55 | 624 | 37.6 |
| | * | * | * | | |
| − | .45 | .47 | .47 | 1036 | 62.4 |
| Total Number of Cases (N=100 per cent) | | | | 1660 | |

* Difference in test variable at the 5 per cent level of confidence between ridits with same subscript or adjacent to same asterisk.

childhood health but whose parents were healthy (.52). The general additivity of the factors accounts for most of this increase.

It is interesting to speculate that poor health may be concentrated in these 227 families where parent and child have poor health. Tendencies to poor health may be transmitted genetically from one generation to another. In that event, we would expect a higher correlation than .16 between parents' and child's health. Perhaps some hereditary factors may be involved along with the social "transmission" of a tendency to be of low SES.[18] This in itself would increase the probability of poor physical and mental health.

The manner in which serious physical illness interacts with other stress factors in the history of mentally disturbed individuals shows great variation. When the illness leaves a person handicapped, there may often be overprotection on the part of the family, particularly

## TABLE 9-18

### DISTRIBUTION, PROPORTIONS, AND AVERAGE MENTAL HEALTH (MH I) OF RESPONDENTS' CHILDHOOD PHYSICAL HEALTH DICHOTOMY ACCORDING TO PARENTS' POOR PHYSICAL HEALTH DICHOTOMY

| Childhood Poor Physical Health | | Parents' Poor Physical Health | | | | | |
|---|---|---|---|---|---|---|---|
| | | MOTHER, FATHER, OR BOTH IN POOR PHYSICAL HEALTH + | | | NEITHER PARENT IN POOR PHYSICAL HEALTH − | | |
| | | N | Per Cent | R̄ | N | Per Cent | R̄ |
| Child's Health Fair or Poor | + | 227 | 44.1 | .61 | 397 | 34.7 | .52 |
| Child's Health Good (Not Fair or Poor) | − | 288 | 55.9 | .49 | 748 | 65.3 | .46 |
| Total Number of Cases (N=100 per cent) | | 515 | | | 1145 | | 1660 |

parents. This is experienced as domination, and results in hostile feelings and a desire for independence.

Ambivalence about dependence and independence is evident in the story of Roger C. (see footnote, page 166). His physical illness, later handicap, his rejecting weak father who finally deserted the family, and his self-sacrificing but dominating mother posed a series of stresses which he was unable to withstand.

Although his health was good in early childhood, Roger was slight of build. It bothered him that his father, because of back trouble, didn't fight in World War II. "He thought he was a big guy, but he just threw the bull. My mother kept him out of the Army. He was always knocking everybody, but was he so hot?" His parents fought a good deal. There was one thing they agreed on. After Roger got muscular dystrophy at twelve, they thought he should go to a special boarding school. He tried to run away, but was caught and brought back. His rehabilitation went very slowly. His sister, on a visit, told him that his parents were fighting a lot. This interfered with his progress, particularly at age thirteen, when his father finally left the family.

Sports often proved impossible, particularly football. History, however, was a favorite subject. "I read about Hannibal—what a master mind! He was a real fighter for freedom. Today we democracies have to take care of ourselves, build ourselves up. We're getting physically . . . well, lazy. If it weren't for my leg, I'd like to box, or learn judo or karate, so that when guys jump on me, I'll . . . you know. I thought my tough environment toughened me up, but it didn't. I'd really like to learn wood carving, or maybe I should be a pilot. But you see, my leg is missing, so I can't."

Although Roger has both legs, one leg is as good as missing to him, because of the muscular dystrophy. He can walk quite well, but visualizes himself as an amputee. Freedom from his mother and restoration of physical prowess are the main themes of his fantasy life. His physical illness is the key to his dependency and his resentment, for if he had not been weakened by the muscular dystrophy, he might have left home as his older sister did.

## Summary

*Parents' Poor Mental Health.*    Respondents were asked to report the psychosomatic conditions of their mothers and fathers separately. These conditions were considered to be possibly psychosomatic: arthritis, asthma, "bladder trouble," colitis, diabetes, hay fever, high blood pressure, neuralgia, stomach ulcer, and "skin condition." Respondents whose mothers had four or more of these conditions showed a sharp increase in mental health risk. The number of the fathers' conditions did not show a relationship to the respondents' mental health. The sex of the child was not a factor in determining which parents' conditions were related to mental health. Both men and women with "psychosomatic" mothers are worse off than those with "psychosomatic" fathers.

Persons whose parents were "the worrying type" have poorer mental health. A worrying mother seems slightly worse with respect to the offspring's mental health than a worrying father. A third of the mothers were worriers, but only a tenth of the fathers.

The psychosomatic scores of mother and father, and responses to the question, "Were either of your parents the worrying type?" were combined into a single factor called "Parents' Poor Mental Health." Adult respondents whose parents had poor mental health had considerably greater mental health risk than those whose parents had relatively good mental health.

The mother's asthma, neuralgia, and stomach ulcers were linked to increased mental health risk in her children. The father's colitis was associated with increased mental health risk in his children, while his hay fever and ulcers were linked to reduced risk.

Asthma and ulcers in the mother were associated with high rates of Probable Psychosis in the respondent. Mothers' ulcers were also related to a high rate of Probable Neurosis in their progeny. In general, however, "psychosomatic" mothers had offspring with surprisingly low proportions of Probable Personality Trait Types (e.g., rigid, suspicious, and dependent types). The fathers' diabetes and high blood pressure were related to high rates of Probable Neurosis in the offspring.

Offspring of "psychosomatic" parents responded markedly to questions indicating tension and anxiety. Those whose mothers had neuralgia, stomach ulcers, and "bladder trouble," or whose fathers had arthritis, "bladder trouble," colitis, or diabetes, were most apt to report more symptoms of tension and anxiety. Mother's asthma was related to greater "Frustration-Depression" in the progeny.

If the parent has certain conditions, the child is more likely than chance to have these same conditions. The mother's arthritis, asthma, "bladder trouble," hay fever, neuralgia, and "skin trouble" are apt to be shared by her children. The father's arthritis, asthma, colitis, hay fever, high blood pressure, neuralgia, and "skin trouble" are likely to be shared by his children.

"Worrying" among parents was examined with respect to whether they actually had "problems" to worry about. Offspring of worrying but problemless parents had slightly poorer mental health than offspring of nonworrying parents with problems. Those with parents who worried *and* had problems are even worse off in regard to mental health.

About three-fifths of worrying parents have worrying children, while less than one-third of nonworrying parents have worrying children. A worrying father involves less mental health risk than a worrying mother. Moreover, mothers are four times more likely to be reported as a worrier.

If a parent worries, respondents are more likely to "take after them in character and temperament," regardless of the sex of the respondent or of the parent.

Identification with ("taking after") a worrying mother, involves a higher mental health risk for the offspring. Identification with a worrying father involves a high risk for females, but a very reduced risk for males. Respondents who are fathers worry more about "getting ahead," "my work," and "overwork," and their mental health is better than that of respondent fathers who do not worry about the work role. Perhaps fathers who worry about their work are more reality-oriented. In their case, worry is less apt to indicate anxiety. Identification with such fathers may be conducive to better mental health in their sons.

Of those who identify themselves with a worrying parent, three out of four are themselves worriers. Of those who identify with nonworrying parents, only one in three are worriers. In general, it is present adult worrying that involves a high mental health risk. Identification with worrying parents has an indirect relationship to the respondents' mental health, since it seems to set the scene for adult worrying.

*Parents' Poor Physical Health.*    One questionnaire item, "Were either of your parents in poor health?" was used as the factor, "Parents' Poor Physical Health." Those with both parents in poor health, although few in number, showed considerably greater mental health risk than the rest of the sample. Respondents whose mothers were in poor health showed some increase in mental health risk. Fathers' poor health showed virtually no relationship to the mental health of the respondent-offspring.

About one-third of each socioeconomic level reported one or both parents in poor health.

The Parents' Poor Physical Health factor was dichotomized, but could not be trichotomized. It proved to be a relatively weak factor compared to most other childhood factors.

*Childhood Poor Physical Health.*    This factor was composed of the respondent's report of his health in early childhood, and his answer to the question, "As a child did you catch cold fairly often?" The worse the Childhood Physical Health, the greater the mental health risk involved.

Parents' and children's poor physical health were not highly correlated (.16). When both parent and child had poor health, the risk increased sharply.

### Notes

1. Each respondent had already been asked whether he himself ever had any of these conditions.

2. The "work" worries of high SES male respondents involve less risk, and they worry proportionally more about work. The worries of the low SES fathers may not have been of this "adaptive" type, which may explain the higher risk involved.

3. For the rationale behind dichotomization and trichotomization, see Chapter 6.

4. A parent with two or more psychosomatic conditions was arbitrarily considered as "psychosomatic."

5. See Margaret Mead's discussion of Hilde Bruch's point that the insistence that the child and mother never be separated is a subtle form of antifeminism by which men, under the guise of exalting maternity, are tying women more tightly than ever to their children. M. Mead, "Some Theoretical Considerations on the Problem of Mother-Child Separation," *American Journal of Orthopsychiatry*, Volume XXIV, July 1954, p. 477, quoted in note 20, Chapter 8.

6. Ulcers seem to have been a distinctly middle and high SES disease in the parents' generation. Of middle and high SES fathers, 4.9 per cent and 5.1 per cent, respectively, were reported to have had ulcers, as compared to 2.7 per cent in the low SES. Likewise, mothers in the middle and high SES groups, where 2.2 per cent and 2.4 per cent respectively, were reported to have had ulcers, contrasted with only 0.8 per cent among low SES mothers. However, proportionally more high SES fathers had two other conditions, high blood pressure and neuralgia. These two conditions both involved an average mental health risk close to that of the total sample, .50 (high blood pressure, .48, neuralgia, .54). The other two conditions more prevalent among high SES fathers involved even lower mental health risk (hay fever, .39, ulcers, .34). Since three of these fathers' conditions that are associated with better than average mental health (.34, .39, .48) in the offspring are more prevalent in the high SES, an explanatory hypothesis can be formulated. The lower mental health risk involved in the conditions of fathers' ulcers, hay fever, and high blood pressure may well be due not to the diseases themselves, but to the fact that these diseases are associated with an explanatory factor, socioeconomic status. We already know that high socioeconomic status in the fathers is associated with better than average mental health in the respondent offspring.

7. The Gross Typology classification made by the psychiatrists is explained in detail in Chapter 3.

8. It should be remembered that work worries seem to be part of a good adjustment in the high SES, involving a decrease in risk.

9. 42.4 per cent of 229 males and 45.5 per cent of 325 females.

10. 29.3 per cent of males, 28.9 per cent of females.

11. 32.8 per cent of males, 31.5 per cent of females.

12. 48.4 per cent of males, 41.6 per cent of females.

13. The fact that these questions were on the same page of the questionnaire may have led some of the respondents to make their answers internally consistent. However, it is doubtful that this alone could account for the findings.

14. Under the headings "None, Unemployment, Work, Financial, Father-Mother Conflict, Illness, Myself, Sibling(s), Other kin, Father inadequate, Mother inadequate, Housing, Neighborhood influences, Other."

15. See Lawrence E. Hinkle, Jr., Ruth Redmont, Norman Plummer, and Harold G. Wolff, "An Examination of the Relation Between Symptoms, Disability, and Serious Illness, in Two Homogeneous Groups of Men and Women," *American Journal of Public Health*, Volume 50, No. 9, September 1960, p. 1327.

16. The final factor, as it evolved, was composed of the respondent's report of his "health" in early childhood (good, fair, poor) and "As a child did you catch cold fairly often?" Both of these items could catch a sizable proportion of psychosomatic illness in childhood, but it would not be as large as the proportion screened by the Childhood Mental Health Index.

17. In the middle SES, the difference appears between *good* as opposed to *fair* and *poor* health. In the sample as a whole, the difference is between *good* and *poor* health.

18. This would be more true of a society of fixed social strata, or a caste system, than of our "open class" society.

# Childhood Economic Deprivation and Family Atmosphere

(PARENTS' QUARRELS, PARENTS' CHARACTER NEGATIVELY PERCEIVED, AND DISAGREEMENTS WITH PARENTS)

THOMAS S. LANGNER

## Childhood Economic Deprivation

### A. UNEMPLOYMENT AND FINANCIAL PROBLEMS

An index of the socioeconomic status of the respondent in early childhood was constructed for the Midtown respondent, because we felt that their present SES could easily be a result of their previous mental disturbance as well as a contributing factor. The status of the respondent in childhood was assumed to be that of his father or father-substitute. Consequently, the father's occupation and education were utilized in an Index of Fathers' Socioeconomic Status (see discussion, Chapter 6).

The father's education and occupation told us very little directly about the deprivation suffered by the child as a consequence of the father's economic plight. Only three items of information were obtained which indicated that the respondent had suffered economic deprivation as a child. The first of these was a question concerning the problems of the respondent's parents:

Looking back, what would you say were the chief problems or troubles that your parents (parent substitutes) had to face while you were growing up (age six to eighteen)?

The interviewer allowed the respondent to answer freely, and coded the answer under one or more of the following categories: None, unemployment, work, financial, father-mother conflict, myself, siblings, other kin, father inadequate, mother inadequate, housing, and neighborhood influences.

If the respondent reported that his parents had had unemployment or financial problems it was considered a sign of economic deprivation in childhood. Four per cent of the sample reported that their parents had suffered "unemployment" and 56 per cent reported "financial" problems. Having parents with financial problems hardly increased the mental health risk of the respondent at all (.51). However, parents' unemployment did increase the risk (.55).

Table 10-1 shows that the risk associated with these problems is not very high with the exception of unemployment of high SES fathers, represented by five cases (.66). The ineffectiveness of these items in predict-

## TABLE 10-1

### PROPORTIONS AND AVERAGE MENTAL HEALTH (MH II) OF RESPONDENTS WHOSE PARENTS' CHIEF PROBLEMS WERE UNEMPLOYMENT OR FINANCIAL TROUBLES ACCORDING TO FATHERS' SOCIOECONOMIC STATUS

| | Fathers' Socioeconomic Status | | | | | | |
|---|---|---|---|---|---|---|---|
| | LOW | | MIDDLE | | HIGH | | TOTAL | |
| Parents' Chief Problems | Per Cent | $\bar{R}$ | Per Cent | $\bar{R}$ | Per Cent | $\bar{R}$ | Per Cent | $\bar{R}$ |
| Unemployment | 7.9 | .59 | 3.4 | .46 | 1.0 | .66 | 4.0 | .55 |
| Financial Troubles | 66.0 | .56 | 58.4 | .51 | 42.0 | .45 | 55.6 | .51 |
| Total Number of Cases (N = 100 per cent)[a] | 482 | | 671 | | 507 | | 1660 | |

[a]Since each person mentioned several chief parental problems, the total proportions of all problems adds to over 100 per cent. This table refers to only two out of twelve problems.

ing mental health and their low statistical reliability led us to exclude them from the final economic deprivation factor.

The socioeconomic variation in the proportion of unemployed parents was in accordance with expectations; 7.9 per cent of the low, 3.4 per cent of the middle, and 1.0 per cent of the high SES parents were reported to have "unemployment problems." Similarly, the proportion of parents with "financial problems" decreases from 66 per cent among parents of low SES to 42 per cent among parents of high SES. It is noteworthy that as much as 42 per cent of those with fathers in a high socioeconomic status reported that their parents had financial problems. This may be due to several factors. The depression of the 1930s posed temporary financial problems for a great many families, including those of high status. Also, wealthy parents, as well as poor ones, may feel that they don't have enough money to live in the style to which they would like to accustom themselves. "Financial problems," as reported by the children of these parents, must have included many types of problems that could be considered not true economic deprivation but only a feeling of deprivation relative to the financial aspirations of the parents or child. Perhaps this accounts for the weakness of "financial problems" in predicting the mental health of the respondent.

Children often feel deprived when they compare their father's income or occupation with the occupations of their friends' fathers. There is apparently nothing rare about dissatisfaction with one's father's occupation. Mangus[1] found in his study of 1638 fourth- to sixth-grade school children in Ohio that a rather large proportion of children (46 per cent of the boys and 34 per cent of the girls) wished that their father had a better job. Perhaps in a general atmosphere of economic striving, dissatisfaction with one's father's occupation is not pathognomonic. The adult's recall of Childhood Economic Deprivation is no doubt a mixture of subjective perception (relative deprivation) and objective reporting.

### B.   A HARD TIME MAKING ENDS MEET

Each respondent was asked about "hard times" during childhood:

During the years you were growing up (age six to eighteen), did your parents (those who brought you up) ever have a hard time making ends meet (making a living, buying what the family needed)?

(If Yes): Did they have such a hard time: often, sometimes, or rarely?

People whose parents *often* had "a hard time making ends meet" show a substantial increase in mental health risk (.57). However, if parents had a "hard time" *sometimes* or *rarely,* the risk is just slightly greater (.48 and .49) than if their parents *never* had a hard time (.46). (See Table 10-2.)

## TABLE 10-2

### PROPORTIONS AND AVERAGE MENTAL HEALTH (MH II) OF RESPONDENTS ACCORDING TO "PARENTS HAD HARD TIMES IN MAKING ENDS MEET" AND TO FATHERS' SOCIOECONOMIC STATUS

| Parents Had Hard Times Making Ends Meet | Fathers' Socioeconomic Status | | | | | | | |
|---|---|---|---|---|---|---|---|---|
| | LOW | | MIDDLE | | HIGH | | TOTAL | |
| | Per Cent | $\bar{R}$ | Per Cent | $\bar{R}$ | Per Cent | $\bar{R}$ | Per Cent | $\bar{R}$ |
| Often | 38.0 | .59 | 29.7 | $.58\frac{*}{2}$ | 15.0 | $.52^*_y$ | 27.6 | $.57^*_x$ |
| Sometimes | 28.0 | .53 | 26.8 | .48 | 15.0 | .41 | 23.6 | .48 |
| Rarely | 3.9 | .61 | 5.5 | .48 | 6.7 | .44 | 5.4 | .49 |
| Never | 28.4 | .54 | 37.0 | $.44^*_z$ | 62.5 | $.44^*_y$ | 42.3 | $.46^*_x$ |
| Don't Know, No Answer ‖ | 1.7 | – | 1.0 | – | .8 | – | 1.1 | – |
| Total Number of Cases (N = 100 per cent) | 482 | | 671 | | 507 | | 1660 | |

*Difference in test variable at the 5 per cent level of confidence between ridits with same subscript or adjacent to same asterisk.

‖ Ridits not computed.

About one-fourth of the population reported "hard times" *often.* These comprised 38 per cent of the low, compared to only 15 per cent of those whose fathers were of high socioeconomic status. This indicates a good deal of objectivity in the respondents' reports. Correspondingly, about 28 per cent of the parents with low and about 63 per cent of the parents with high SES *never* had a hard time. "Hard times" are highly correlated with parental SES. The association of "hard times" with the respondents' mental health, however, does not vary greatly between socioeconomic groups.

### C.    MOTHER WORKED

While the dichotomization of the Childhood Economic Deprivation factor was fairly simple, the trichotomization involved some difficulty. In brief, it was found that "hard times" involved a substantial risk, while "unemployment and financial problems" did not make for any additional risk. These were dropped, but the item, "Mother worked outside the home while you were aged six to eighteen," was added.

The logic of this scheme was supported by the data. The proportion of working mothers increases steadily as the parents' hard times become more frequent. Only 19.4 per cent of the mothers worked in families which "never" had hard times; 44.8 per cent of the mothers worked in families which had hard times "often."

It must be remembered that these are working mothers with school-age children, and 25 per cent of mothers of preschool children (one to six) worked at some time during the year in the United States.[2]

Among adult respondents in Midtown who were mothers with children under eighteen, 22.6 per cent were working in 1953 at the time of the interview.

Around 1925, when our average respondent was about twelve years old (midway between the school ages of six and eighteen), the proportion of working mothers reported by respondents was 31.1 per cent.[3] The higher proportion (44.8 per cent) of working mothers in families which had hard times "often" indicates that this group was somewhat deviant from the majority of the population at that time. Today they would not be considered unusual, since 40 per cent of mothers with school-age children are working[4] (14 per cent of women workers in the United States have children under six years, and about 24 per cent have children between six and eighteen years[5]).

The final division of the Childhood Economic Deprivation factor, based on "Parents had a hard time making ends meet" and "Mother worked," yielded three groups with distinctly different mental health risks (see Table 10-3).

The plus or extreme group, containing 204 cases, had a Mental Health II ridit of .58, the zero or moderate group of 393 cases a ridit of .54, and the minimal deprivation group of 1063 cases a ridit of .47. The Mental Health I ridits are identical, indicating no bias in ratings.

The actual degree of risk involved in economic deprivation is about the same as for most of the other childhood factors. The odds are about

## TABLE 10-3

### DISTRIBUTION, PROPORTIONS, AND AVERAGE MENTAL HEALTH (CMH, MH I, MH II) OF RESPONDENTS ACCORDING TO CHILDHOOD ECONOMIC DEPRIVATION TRICHOTOMIZED AND DICHOTOMIZED

| Childhood Economic Deprivation | Respondents' Mental Health | | | | |
|---|---|---|---|---|---|
| | CMH | MH I | MH II | No. of Cases | Per Cent of Cases |
| *Trichotomy* | | | | | |
| + | $.58_z^*$ | $.58_y^*$ | $.58_x^*$ | 204 | 12.3 |
| 0 | .56 | .54 | .54 | 393 | 23.7 |
| | * | * | | | |
| − | $.46_z^*$ | $.47_y^*$ | $.47_x^*$ | 1063 | 64.0 |
| *Dichotomy* | | | | | |
| + | .58 | .57 | .57 | 496 | 29.9 |
| | * | * | * | | |
| − | .47 | .47 | .47 | 1164 | 70.1 |
| Total Number of Cases (N = 100 per cent) | | | | 1660 | |

*Difference in test variable at the 5 per cent level of confidence between ridits with same subscript or adjacent to same asterisk.

3 to 2 that a person reporting economic deprivation in childhood will show greater impairment than one not so reporting.

The interpretation of the data on economic deprivation poses a more difficult problem than the selection of "economic" items which show an independent relationship to mental health. However, the selection of the items in itself determines what the interpretation will be. For instance, 55.6 per cent of the sample reported their parents had "financial problems," while only 27.6 per cent reported their parents "often had a hard time making ends meet." The word "often" apparently has been able to select people whose families were in more severe economic straits, simply by selecting a smaller proportion of the sample. This is certainly true of the "unemployment" category, constituting only 4 per cent of the total sample. Perhaps the words "often had a hard time making ends meet" imply a worrisome and harried home atmosphere.

In an attempt to get at the meaning of the response "My parents often had a hard time making ends meet," we can test various hypotheses through the analysis of other items of information related to the economic sphere. A most interesting, and at first sight a most tenable hypothesis, is that the impact of "hard times" comes principally from the loss of affection, rather than from any direct financial deprivation. In families where parents had "hard times often," 44.8 per cent of the mothers worked, while only 19.4 per cent of the mothers in families which "never had hard times" worked outside the home. Doesn't this mean that hard times deprive you of your mother's love, which in turn leads to poor mental health? On the contrary, the inclusion of the item "Mother worked" in the economic deprivation trichotomy *did not increase the mental health risk.* It was simply used as a logical item to separate the "hard times" dichotomy into three categories. Having a working mother does not automatically increase one's mental health risk, and a mother who works part time may be a mental health asset to her children and herself (see Chapter 8). Therefore, the hypothesis that "hard times" involves emotional deprivation due to separation from the mother does not seem tenable.

## D.   HARD TIMES, OCCUPATION, AND EDUCATION

What of the father's role? Can various aspects of his status tell us more about the meaning of "hard times"? If we examine the proportion of respondents reporting parents' hard times by their fathers' occupation and education simultaneously, it becomes clear that their fathers' occupational level is more closely related to hard times than fathers' education.[6] In our opinion, if the father's education were more important, this would be an indication that "hard times" was measuring something closer to the father's personality structure and attitude system. The greater his education, for example, the more likely he might be to have acquired a conscious philosophy of child-rearing. The fact that the "hard times" response varies more with the father's occupation than his education tends to argue for the objectivity of the "economic deprivation" label. The adult's economic situation would be expected to vary more with the job than with education.

There are indications that we are measuring something more than the economic situation *per se*, perhaps the financial security associated with the job is beneficial over and above the income that it brings. We know that in the entire sample, 27.6 per cent reported their parents had "hard times often." What particular types of occupations are associated with "hard times often?" Table 10-4 shows the proportions of parents who had "hard times often" according to the father's occupation.

In the white collar group, the small proprietors and the lower clerical and sales positions seem to have a higher proportion of hard times compared with other white collar occupations.

We know these occupations, particularly the small proprietors, are constantly exposed to the threat of extinction. There is a more sporadic quality to their labor market. While close to the manual laborer in income they are typically nonunionized.

### Table 10-4
### Proportions of Parents Who Had "Hard Times Often" According to Father's Occupation

| | OCCUPATION | PER CENT |
|---|---|---|
| **White Collar High** | High Status Owners and Proprietors | 4.9 |
| | High Status Managers and Officials | 17.9 |
| | Self-Employed Professionals | 18.7 |
| | Self-Employed Artists | 40.0 |
| | Professionals Employed by Others | 18.5 |
| **White Collar Middle** | Artists Employed by Others | 28.6 |
| | Middle Owners and Proprietors | 12.7 |
| | High and Middle Farmers (Owners) | 22.9 |
| | Middle Managers and Officials | 10.6 |
| | Semiprofessionals | 25.0 |
| | High Sales and Clerical Personnel | 25.2 |
| **White Collar Low** | Low Owners and Proprietors | 35.6 |
| | Low Managers and Officials | 23.8 |
| | Low Sales and Clerical | 35.4 |
| **Blue Collar High** | High Service | 32.6 |
| | Skilled Manual Self-Employed | 29.2 |
| | Low Farmers (Owners and Managers) | 27.9 |
| | Skilled Manual Employed by Others | 30.9 |
| **Blue Collar Middle** | Semiskilled Self-Employed | 36.4 |
| | Semiskilled Employed by Others | 43.0 |
| **Blue Collar Low** | Tenant Farmers | 40.9 |
| | Low Service | 25.9 |
| | Unskilled Labor | 44.8 |

Skilled labor does not seem to have a higher proportion of "hard times" than the sample as a whole. Although they are lower in the scale of occupational prestige, skilled manual workers, high service workers, and farmers who own small farms are somewhat less likely to have hard times than small proprietors and low sales and clerical workers. Noticeably higher proportions of hard times were found among tenant farmers

(40.9 per cent) and unskilled labor (44.8 per cent). Although this might have been expected, because they are at the bottom of the scale, some occupations, even though of high status, showed similar high proportions.

Artists whether self-employed (40.0 per cent, or two out of five cases) or employed by others (28.6 per cent, or two out of seven cases) had a typically high proportion of hard times. They should, of course, be compared to other high-status occupations. Again, the unsteadiness of the labor market over and above the level of skill or status, seems to be operating as a factor associated with the reporting of "hard times often."

### E.   HARD TIMES AND MOBILITY

Another indication that "hard times" reflects instability in the father's work situation (as well as the actual level of deprivation) is found in the proportion reporting "hard times often" according to their fathers' occupational mobility between the time the respondent was eight and eighteen years old.[7] The father's mobility was measured on a six-step scale based on the categories of high white collar (professional and managerial), middle white collar (semiprofessional and lower managerial), low white collar (sales and clerical), high blue collar (skilled labor), middle blue collar (semiskilled labor), and low blue collar (unskilled labor). If a father moved from a high blue collar to a low white collar occupation during the ten years under consideration, he was considered to be "one step" upwardly mobile. If he moved from low blue collar to high blue collar he was considered "two steps" upwardly mobile. The same system applied to downwardly mobile individuals. More occupationally mobile parents (fathers) had "hard times often" than did nonmobile parents. (This table is not included.)

The more mobile the father, whether upward or downward, the greater was the proportion of "hard times often" reported. Only 23.4 per cent of the nonmobile fathers had "hard times often," compared to 37.5 per cent of the one-step and 40.9 per cent of the two-step upward mobiles. Similarly, 30.6 per cent of the one step and 43.3 per cent of the two-step downward mobiles had "hard times often." While these mobility groups range in size from 30 to 44 cases, the somewhat U-shaped curve of "hard times" which they yield should not be overlooked. The occupational movement of the father (rather than the direction of movement) is apparently related to reporting of "hard times often." Perhaps among those whose fathers moved upward, the "bad old days" when the family was poorer stood out by contrast. Likewise, the downwardly mobile families may have compared their present low status (at age eighteen) with their high status in the "good old days" (at age eight). The *change* in status, then, may render the "hard times" perceptible, for they stand out against the background of the "good times."

This poses another question. Does the relationship of "hard times" to mental health derive its impact from the instability of the family economy? If economic deprivation alone were involved, a smaller proportion of the upwardly mobile would report that their parents had "hard times." As their fathers' occupational level rose, their real economic deprivation would in all probability decrease. (This would hold true unless the number of children or general cost of living increased faster than the salary increases associated with the rise in occupation. This would be possible, but unlikely, during the space of ten years when the respondents were aged eight to eighteen.) Perhaps, then, the Childhood Economic Deprivation factor, based primarily upon "parents had a hard time making ends meet," is to some extent also a measure of family instability.

The "family instability" hypothesis, however, is seriously questioned or perhaps refuted by our data on father's mobility and respondent's mental health. The father's occupational mobility shows no consistent relationship to the respondent's mental health. Persons with downwardly mobile blue collar fathers show a marked increase in risk. However, in the white collar fathers' group, those with upwardly mobile fathers show a slight increase, and those with downwardly mobile fathers, a slight decrease in risk. We do not find that the father's mobility itself, whether up or down, increases the offspring's mental health risk. It is, however, associated with a greater proportion reporting "parents had hard times often" and thus acts indirectly to screen out families which have actually experienced "hard times" at some period.

"Hard times" stands for a series of events often found together in the history of the low SES individual.

Laura K.'s (see footnote, page 166) parents were on relief when she was a child. Her mother had nephritis; her father had silicosis. They both had tuberculosis, and her own health was poor. She contracted diphtheria and influenza as well as the usual array of childhood diseases. Her parents constantly quarreled, often about money. She disagreed with her mother about the boys she was dating. "If I was old enough to work full time at seventeen, I was old enough to date too. I was an honor student in school, and I liked school. I wanted to continue, but I couldn't. I had to work. It always seemed that father favored the boys." Now Laura has terrible pressure in her stomach, and feels very weak.

She only feels comfortable when lying down, and her job as a telephone operator is suffering.

In Laura's family poor health seems related to poverty. Family quarrels and her own fights with her mother often involved money, particularly arguments about giving up school, and working. She still seems to resent the workaday world which has few compensations for her. She would like to be taken care of, to be protected from economic stress, but she has never been. The first time she has been able to lie down and let others (her husband) struggle has been since she developed her symptoms.

### F.   HARD TIMES AND DEATH

Further evidence of the objectivity of the reporting of "hard times," which points away from interpretations about instability or considering these reports as simply adult projections,[8] is found in data concerning the death of the parents. We hypothesized that the father's death would have a worse effect on the family economy than the mother's death. If this did not hold true, a great deal of adult projection might be involved in the reports of deprivation. Among those from low status families whose mothers died before they were sixteen, 34.1 per cent reported "hard times often," compared to 51.2 per cent of those whose fathers died before sixteen. Among persons from middle status families, 20 per cent whose mothers died and 36.7 per cent whose fathers died reported "hard times often." In the high SES, 7.1 per cent whose mothers died and 14.3 per cent whose fathers died reported "hard times often." At each socioeconomic level, then, the death of the father rather than the mother was associated with a higher proportion reporting "hard times." This confirms our faith in the relative objectivity of the reports of economic deprivation.

## Parents' Quarrels

The atmosphere of the economically deprived home showed a tendency to be associated with increased mental health risk in later life. Perhaps there were other family characteristics related to the emotional atmosphere of the childhood home which also were associated with increased disturbance in the adult. Several items of this nature were found during the screening process, and were converted into indices.

### A.   PARENTAL HETEROGENEITY

Conflict between parents is generally considered to be a factor in the development of mental disturbance in children. We assumed that traces of this mental disturbance would still be discernible in the adult respondent. Several items included in the questionnaire seemed to offer an indirect measure of conflict or disagreement between parents. It was our hypothesis that differences between the background characteristics of the parents, such as education, religion, or nationality, would be closely tied to differences in values and life goals. These differences in values in turn might have two effects: first, they might cause open arguments between the parents which might disturb the child, and second, they might expose the child to extreme value conflicts and contradictory demands made by his parents, which in turn could lead to mental disturbance.

Persons whose fathers and mothers were educationally heterogeneous turned out to be better off (not worse off, as expected) with respect to mental health risk than those whose parents were educationally homogeneous. Respondent's whose fathers had a higher education than their mothers had an average Mental Health II risk of .45. This was significantly less than those with parents of the same educational level (.51). (See Table 10-5.) This result might have been expected, for it is fairly typical in higher status families for the father to have more education than the mother. This is particularly true of families with professional and semiprofessional fathers. The proportions of fathers with higher education than their wives (0.2 per cent of the low, 10.1 per cent of the middle, and 49.0 per cent of the high SES) in the three status groups explains, rather strikingly, why heterogeneity of parental education does not increase mental health risk when the father is of higher education. It is simply the fact that most of the educationally "heterogeneous" parents are in high status families with highly trained fathers. When SES is controlled, these differences immediately disappear. For instance, there is no significant difference in the high SES between persons whose fathers had more education than their mothers (.44), and those with parents of the same education (.42). This is also true in the middle SES (.50 vs. .49). Thus the socioeconomic factor "explains away" the relationship of "educational heterogeneity" to mental health.[9]

Less explicable is the fact that respondents whose fathers' education was lower than their mothers' *also* had a reduced mental health risk (.43). This relationship is significant in the middle SES (.41 vs. .49) and shows a similar trend in the low SES (.48 vs. .56). On the contrary, in the high SES, the respondent is not any healthier if his father's education was lower than his mother's. In low and particularly in middle

## TABLE 10-5

## PROPORTIONS AND AVERAGE MENTAL HEALTH (MH II) OF RESPONDENTS WHOSE PARENTS HAD HOMOGENEOUS OR HETEROGENEOUS EDUCATION, BY FATHERS' SOCIOECONOMIC STATUS

*Fathers' Socioeconomic Status*

| Parents' Education | LOW | | MIDDLE | | HIGH | | TOTAL | |
|---|---|---|---|---|---|---|---|---|
| | Per Cent | $\bar{R}$ | Per Cent | $\bar{R}$ | Per Cent | $\bar{R}$ | Per Cent | $\bar{R}$ |
| Father's Education Higher Than Mother's | .2 | (.14) | 10.1 | .50 | 49.0 | .44 | 19.1 | .45$^{*}_{y}$ |
| | | | | | | | | * |
| Same | 68.7 | .56 | 59.5 | .49 | 25.8 | .42$^{*}_{z}$ | 51.9 | .51 |
| | | | | * | | | | * |
| Father's Education Lower Than Mother's | 5.2 | .48 | 13.4 | .41 | 6.5 | .42 | 8.9 | .43 |
| | | | | * | | * | | * |
| Don't Know, No Answer | 25.9 | .57 | 17.0 | .57 | 18.7 | .54$^{*}_{z}$ | 20.1 | .56$^{*}_{y}$ |
| Total Number of Cases (N = 100 per cent) | 482 | | 671 | | 507 | | 1660 | |

*Difference in test variable at the 5 per cent level of confidence between ridits with same subscript or adjacent to same asterisk.

Parentheses ( ) enclose ridit based on less than ten cases.

SES families, the better educated mother may have used milder child-rearing practices, or she may have paid more attention to her child in her attempts to train him to achieve higher social status. It is quite atypical at all social levels for the mother to have a better education, and without the data we might tend to think of such a situation as conducive to or predictive of poor mental health in the children. However, for reasons as yet unknown, the products of such situations have better mental health, on the average. Parents' educational heterogeneity, for various reasons, is associated with lower mental health risk, contrary to our expectations.

Religious heterogeneity of the parents shows virtually no association with mental health risk (see Table 10-6). Persons with parents of the

## TABLE 10-6

## PROPORTION AND AVERAGE MENTAL HEALTH (MH II) OF RESPONDENTS WHOSE PARENTS WERE OF SAME OR DIFFERENT RELIGION, BY FATHERS' SOCIOECONOMIC STATUS

| | Fathers' Socioeconomic Status | | | | | | | |
| | LOW | | MIDDLE | | HIGH | | TOTAL | |
| Religion | Per Cent | $\bar{R}$ | Per Cent | $\bar{R}$ | Per Cent | $\bar{R}$ | Per Cent | $\bar{R}$ |
|---|---|---|---|---|---|---|---|---|
| Same | 88.0 | .55 | 87.7 | .49 | 81.6 | .45 | 85.9 | .50 |
| Different | 10.8 | .65 | 10.7 | .48 | 17.0 | .45 | 12.7 | .51 |
| Don't Know, No Answer ‖ | 1.2 | – | 1.6 | – | 1.4 | – | 1.4 | – |
| Total Number of Cases (N = 100 per cent) | 482 | | 671 | | 507 | | 1660 | |

‖ Ridits not computed.

same religion (.50) were similar in mental health to persons whose parents were of different religions (.51). It is of great interest that only 12.7 per cent came from mixed religious backgrounds. The fact that such families are relatively rare has no mental health implications. Only in the low SES (where the ridit differences are just below statistical significance) does religious intermarriage seem to show an increase in the offspring's mental health risk. Perhaps the fact that these are predominantly inter-marriages of Catholics (who comprise the majority of the fathers' low socioeconomic group) with people of other religions is a clue. The Catholic respondents attend church much more frequently and feel religion is more important to them than Protestants or Jews. (See Volume I, Chapter 15.) It is probable that the parents of Catholic respondents were in turn more devout than parents of Protestants and Jews. This intensity of religious feeling and practice would be more likely to cause conflict with the non-Catholic spouse than marriages between Protestants of two different denominations, or between a Protestant and a Jew.

The tendency for secularization to increase at higher socioeconomic levels is seen in the larger proportion of high SES parental intermarriages (17.0 per cent) as opposed to the middle and low SES (10.7 per cent and 10.8 per cent). The decreasing importance of religion in the lives of higher status parents (and respondents) may be one reason why we find parental religious heterogeneity essentially unrelated to mental health.

It was only reasonable to expect that persons whose parents came from different national backgrounds, or whose parents were from two different generations with respect to immigration (one an immigrant, the other U.S. born), would be exposed to more value conflicts and more parental disagreements, and therefore would exhibit poorer mental health. On the contrary, we found no significant differences in the mental health risk of respondents whose parents were of similar and dissimilar national background (see Table 10-7).

Persons with 'no foreign-born grandparents were considered fourth generation and were not further identified as to nationality background.

## TABLE 10-7

### PROPORTIONS AND AVERAGE MENTAL HEALTH (MH II) OF RESPONDENTS WHOSE PARENTS WERE ETHNICALLY HOMOGENEOUS OR HETEROGENEOUS, BY FATHERS' SOCIOECONOMIC STATUS

| | Fathers' Socioeconomic Status | | | | | | | |
| | LOW | | MIDDLE | | HIGH | | TOTAL | |
| Parents | Per Cent | $\bar{R}$ | Per Cent | $\bar{R}$ | Per Cent | $\bar{R}$ | Per Cent | $\bar{R}$ |
|---|---|---|---|---|---|---|---|---|
| Homogeneous | 74.5 | .55 | 68.3 | .51 | 40.8 | .48 | 61.7 | .52* |
| Heterogeneous: U.S. vs. Foreign | 12.2 | .59 | 18.6 | .45 | 21.3 | .45 | 17.6 | .48 |
| Heterogeneous: Foreign vs. Foreign | 7.3 | .55 | 6.7 | .51 | 6.9 | .50 | 6.9 | .52 |
| No Foreign-born Grandparents | 5.6 | .60 | 6.3 | .47 | 30.8 | .41 | 13.6 | .45* |
| Don't Know, No Answer ∤ | .4 | – | .1 | – | .2 | – | .2 | – |
| Total Number of Cases (N = 100 per cent) | 482 | | 671 | | 507 | | 1660 | |

*Difference in test variable at the 5 per cent level of confidence between ridits with same subscript.

∤ Ridits not computed.

This group alone was significantly healthier than the 61.7 per cent of the sample with nationally homogeneous foreign-born, first- or second-generation parents. Again, this is due to the fact that the fourth-generation group is almost totally of high socioeconomic status, and it is by this token that they have a decreased mental health risk (.45) compared with the homogeneous category (.52). It is of interest to note that the category with the highest risk (.60) is comprised of fourth-generation respondents who are in the low SES. If these are principally static individuals, socioeconomically speaking, certain hypotheses suggest themselves. Whether these are downwardly mobile individuals, from middle and high status families, or socially static people who were born into low status third-generation families would be an interesting problem to investigate. Perhaps those families which do not rise in the social system simply by virtue of having been in America longer than the more recent immigrants are psychiatrically suspect to begin with. Perhaps there are pockets of physically and mentally derelict families who stay at, or migrate to, the bottom of the social ladder, despite any advantages they may have (such as being from "old families"). Perhaps in this 1.6 per cent of the total population (there were 27 low status fourth-generation respondents) hereditary factors might play a more important role in the development or perpetuation of psychopathology. On the other hand, if these are downwardly mobile individuals, the argument of the "drift theory," though still applicable, is not so plausible.

Educational, religious, and national heterogeneity of the parents were combined into a Parental Heterogeneity Score. Respondents whose parents were heterogeneous on none of the three items received a score of "0," while those whose parents were heterogeneous on only one item received a score of "1," and so forth. The lower and upper ends of the score range were significantly different. However, the great variability of the factors taken individually, and the many contradictions which have been enumerated, militated against using the Parental Heterogeneity Score as a major childhood factor. In particular, socioeconomic status was responsible for many of the differences found, and we did not want factors which were not somewhat independent of SES in their relation to mental health.

### B. PARENTS' QUARRELS

Perhaps an even better reason for not utilizing the heterogeneity material was that it purported to measure parental conflict indirectly, and this conflict might take the form of arguments or simply the transmission of conflicting values to the child. However, a single question about parents' quarrels seemed to be a much more direct measure of parental conflict, and perhaps also of conflicting parental value systems:

Of course, all parents have their quarrels (arguments) with each other. In your home, when you were growing up (age six to eighteen) did such quarrels occur often, occasionally, or rarely?

There was a significant difference between the mental health of persons whose parents quarreled "often" (.58) and persons whose parents quarreled "rarely" (.46). (See Table 10-8.)

There was a slight, though not statistically significant, tendency for low and middle SES persons who reported their parents "never" quarreled to have worse mental health ratings. A large proportion of the sample, 14.5 per cent, said "Never" despite the fact that the interviewer read out loud only "Often, Occasionally, or Rarely." This increase in mental health risk among respondents who say "never" is reminiscent of

## TABLE 10-8

### PROPORTIONS AND AVERAGE MENTAL HEALTH (MH II) OF RESPONDENTS WHOSE PARENTS QUARRELED OFTEN, OCCASIONALLY, RARELY OR NOT AT ALL, BY FATHERS' SOCIOECONOMIC STATUS

| | *Fathers' Socioeconomic Status* | | | | | | |
|---|---|---|---|---|---|---|---|
| | LOW | | MIDDLE | | HIGH | | TOTAL |
| *Parents Quarreled* | *Per Cent* | $\bar{R}$ | *Per Cent* | $\bar{R}$ | *Per Cent* | $\bar{R}$ | *Per Cent* $\bar{R}$ |
| Often | 14.3 | .65$_z^*$ | 16.1 | .55$_y^*$ | 14.8 | .55 | 15.2   .58$_{x,w}^*$ |
| Occasionally | 29.3 | .55 | 28.9 | .52 | 23.1 | .44 | 27.2   .51 |
| Rarely | 34.9 | .52$_z^*$ | 34.9 | .44$_y^*$ | 40.0 | .44 | 36.4   .46$_x^*$ |
| Never | 12.0 | .55 | 15.8 | .46 | 15.0 | .41 | 14.5   .47$_w^*$ |
| Don't Know, No Answer ‡ | 9.5 | – | 4.3 | – | 7.1 | – | 6.7   – |
| Total Number of Cases (N=100 per cent) | 482 | | 671 | | 507 | | 1660 |

* Difference in test variable at the 5 per cent level of confidence between ridits with same subscript.
‡ Ridits not computed.

Captain Corcoran in Gilbert and Sullivan's "H.M.S. Pinafore." He sings that he is "Never, never sick at sea." The chorus asks "What, Never?" The Captain replies, "Well, hardly ever." There is always the suspicion that everyone has a little bout of seasickness at some time, and those who deny it are probably liars, for they protest too much. Greater sophistication in item construction is called for as our knowledge increases, and the problem of the meaning of answers to questions, particularly those probing mental health, is a question for the social psychiatrist as well as the public opinion methodologist.

Again it is surprising that almost equal proportions of each SES group reported their parents quarreled "often" (15.2 per cent of the total sample). Once more there is the problem of the relativity of the term "often." Low status parents might quarrel "rarely" by comparison with other low status families, but "often" by comparison with high status families.

The Parents' Quarrels factor was dichotomized with a plus group of "Often" and "Occasionally," and trichotomized with a plus group of "Often" (see Table 10-9). In terms of adult mental health risk, Parents' Quarrels is a factor of moderate strength.

As is so often the case, the dynamics behind the facts are rather obscure. If Parents' Quarrels are associated with poorer mental health in children and adult offspring, how does it come about? Are children traumatized by observation of their parents' conflicts? Do they feel that their parents' arguments are an implicit rejection of them, "My parents don't love each other, therefore they can't love me"?

Many of Ellen B.'s (see footnote, page 166) friends in school have divorced parents. Sometimes Ellen comes home and finds her parents arguing. It worries her, and she often asks her father, "You're not going to divorce Mommy, are you?" At ten Ellen still sucks her thumb and has nightmares. She recounts the gory accidents reported in the newspapers, and worries about her parents dying. She has asked if she's an adopted child. Her anxiety has interfered somewhat with her school grades and her concentration on homework. Before bedtime her mother has to reassure her, "I'll see you tomorrow morning," or she won't go to sleep. One of her greatest fears seems to be of waking to find herself abandoned. Her parents' quarrels, which she thinks might result in divorce, appear to exacerbate her fear of being left alone.

Does the sight of parents engaged in physical or verbal combat arouse the unconscious wishes of a child to kill and replace the like-sex parent? (Certainly a boy's "protection" of his mother from the onslaught of a drunken father is a socially acceptable excuse for fulfilling such

## TABLE 10-9

### DISTRIBUTION, PROPORTIONS, AND AVERAGE MENTAL HEALTH (CMH, MH I, MH II) ACCORDING TO PREVALENCE OF PARENTS' QUARRELS, TRICHOTOMIZED AND DICHOTOMIZED

| Parents' Quarrels | | CMH | MH I | MH II | No. of Cases | Per Cent of Cases |
|---|---|---|---|---|---|---|
| *Trichotomy* | | | | | | |
| Often | + | .63 | .58$^*_z$ | .58$^*_y$ | 252 | 15.2 |
| | | * | | | | |
| Occasionally | 0 | .54 | .51 | .51 | 452 | 27.2 |
| | | * | | | | |
| Rarely, Never, Don't Know, No Answer | − | .45 | .48$^*_z$ | .48$^*_y$ | 956 | 57.6 |
| *Dichotomy* | | | | | | |
| Often, Occasionally | + | .57 | .53 | .53 | 704 | 42.4 |
| | | * | * | * | | |
| Rarely, Never, Don't Know, No Answer | − | .45 | .48 | .48 | 956 | 57.6 |
| Total Number of Cases (N=100 per cent) | | | | | 1660 | |

Respondents' Mental Health

* Difference in test variable at the 5 per cent level of confidence between ridits with same subscript or adjacent to same asterisk.

wishes.) Is the impact the same for both sexes? Are quarrels involving the child more destructive than quarrels that are the parents' "own business"?

An example of the involvement of the child in the parents' struggle seems to show greater destructive impact.

Edgar P. (see footnote, page 166) is convinced that somebody is trying to bash his head in. He can feel the wounds on the back of his head, and is constantly looking behind him. He can't seem to settle down to a job, or marriage, and feels guilty still living with his parents at the age of forty. When he feels these wounds, he sometimes has an irresistible impulse to take a knife and cut up his attackers.

"My mother and father just didn't get along. I guess I hated my father. Mother always said she was just putting up with him because of her children. 'If it wasn't for you, I'd leave him,' she always told me. She claimed he never showed her enough affection. I know he was hard to talk to, and sort of a cold intellectual. He was always bossing everybody. I guess I was too attached to my mother."

Are open quarrels less threatening to a child than quarrels in which the parents "hold a grudge" against each other, or refuse to talk? Very little is known about the effects on mental health of these aspects of parents' quarrels. One expert feels that divorces which are heralded by frequent and violent quarrels are less of a shock to the child than divorces which come about abruptly (where the parents have presumably concealed their differences from the child, and argued in private).[10]

If the marriage does not end in divorce, is it better for the child's mental health that the conflict be open? Current theory would probably recommend that the child learn the expression of emotions, hostility as well as love. Thus parents who scream at each other and at their child are possibly less destructive in the long run than parents who grit their teeth and say nothing, but communicate their hostility anyhow.[11]

We'll see later that Parents' Quarrels seem to involve more risk increment[12] for males (.14) than for females (.08). This increment of .14 among the males is greater than that of any other childhood factor except Parents' Character Negatively Perceived. Perhaps this experience has less lasting repercussions for girls than for boys.

Parents' Quarrels show some correlation with Parents' Poor Mental Health (tetrachoric coefficient = .24) and Childhood Economic Deprivation ($r_{tet}$ = .23, see Table 5-9). However, Parents' Quarrels' highest correlation ($r_{tet}$ = .39) is with Parents' Character Negatively Perceived. This is the second highest intercorrelation between two childhood factors. Considering that the factors were specifically chosen so as not to be overlapping or intercorrelated, this is a rather high correlation in an absolute as well as a relative sense. It is rather logical that quarrelsome parents also tend to be alienating and dominating parents. This might also be stated differently. For instance, "Respondents who perceive their parents as quarrelsome also tend to view them as alienating and dominating." Perhaps there is an underlying theme hidden in these correlations. Certain people may in their over-all answering patterns be saying "*My parents were no good:* they were in poor mental health (had psychosomatic symptoms, were worriers), they were poor providers (unemployed, had a hard time making ends meet), they were alienating and dominating and they were quarrelsome." It is not the selection of items used in the questionnaire that made for such a predominance of factors having to do with parents. The items which were "live," which showed a strong relationship to adult mental health, were retained for use in constructing the factors. There is no doubt that parents' behavior and the perception of their behavior is a primary factor in mental health. This study would only be a very extravagant way of bolstering this widely accepted viewpoint unless it could add some nuances and specify "where" and "how much." There are specific conditions under which risk increases. For example, we found that broken homes (one aspect of parents' behavior) are of little significance for mental health risk by themselves. However, remarriage of the like-sex parent involves increased risk, particularly in the low SES. There are also differences in the strengths of the various factors (within the accuracy of our crude measurements). The manner in which people perceive their parents' character is a relatively strong factor.

## Parents' Character Negatively Perceived

Several items concerning the behavior of the respondent's parents were incorporated in the questionnaire. These reports about parents' behavior may be factual, or they may be mere fantasy. We prefer to be on the safe side by calling the factor based on such items a perception of the parents' character.

The reasons for selection of the items, the tabular material, and the details of the pyramiding of these items into a factor were given in Chapter 5. This section will review the pyramiding process briefly, and concentrate on an interpretation of the results. (Interpretation of perceptions is treated in Chapter 6.)

Of nine items originally considered for this factor, three were eliminated as irrelevant or because they weren't associated with increased mental health risk. The six remaining items were given shorthand designations as follows:

Father spends too little time with me. When you were growing up did you feel that way too? (**Yes**)

Father alienating

| | |
|---|---|
| Father wants to run his children's lives. (**Yes**) | Father dominating |
| Mother wants to run her children's lives. (**Yes**) | Mother dominating |
| Mother does not understand me. (**Yes**) | Mother alienating |
| My parents are always proud of their children. (**No**) | Parents not proud |
| My parents often don't practice what they preach. (**Yes**) | Parents don't practice |

We found that if the mother was alienating or dominating, the respondent's risk increased, compared with those whose mothers were neither alienating nor dominating. However, the risk of persons reporting mother was *both* alienating and dominating was no worse than the risk of those reporting mother was *either* alienating or dominating. Once the mother is viewed negatively, the *number* of negative views (two as opposed to one) the respondent holds of her does not increase his mental health risk. Similarly, once the father is seen as dominating *or* alienating, seeing him as *both* dominating and alienating doesn't increase the risk.

The generality of the items is interesting. The risk of alienating parents is similar to that of dominating parents. The risk of mother dominating ($.57$) is close to that of mother alienating ($.54$). Likewise, the risk of father dominating ($.57$) is similar to the risk of father alienating ($.55$). There is, however, a tendency for the risk associated with negative perception of father to be higher (though not significantly so). This is unexpected, because the mother seems to be more closely related to the respondent's mental health (e.g., death of mother, see Chapter 8).

We also found that if the respondent perceived *both* parents negatively, his risk increased sharply. For instance, take the paired item father alienating–mother alienating. If a person answered yes to one item his risk increased to $.52$. If he answered yes to both items, thus perceiving both parents as alienating, his risk rose sharply to $.61$. The same results occurred when both parents were viewed as dominating. Thus, when both parents are perceived negatively, the risk is much greater than when only one is so perceived.

The finding that "if you feel rejected by one parent, you're better off than if you feel rejected by both parents" may seem to be an elaborate statement of the obvious. Some alternative hypotheses are just as obvious.

For instance, one often hears the statement, "It's the mother who counts. The father is just a vague and shadowy figure and doesn't influence the child very much." An alternative hypothesis is, "It's better for a child to feel rejected by both parents. Those who feel rejected by only one parent are in a state of conflict, and therefore don't develop any independence. Instead they develop overdependence on the parent who is not rejecting. Efforts to break away from the rejecting parent would always be negated by similar efforts to stay close to the nonrejecting parent." Neither of these hypotheses seems supported by the data, even though they also appear self-evident at first glance.

Since either one or two negative perceptions of the character of one parent had an equal effect on the respondent's mental health risk, we cross-tabulated Mother's Character Negatively Perceived with Father's Character Negatively Perceived. Both parents negatively perceived yielded a risk of .60, one parent approximately .50, and neither .46.

The items dealing with both parents were found to be additive. Giving the disturbed response to both items involves a greater mental health risk (.62) than responding in that manner to only one item (.56) or the other (.58). The Father-Mother Scale and the Parent Scale were combined to produce a pyramided score from 0 to 4 (see Appendix B, Table B-4). A score level of 0 indicates that the respondent disagreed with all six items, while those with a score of 4 agreed with both "parent" items, and with at least one "mother" and one "father" item.

The Parents' Character Negatively Perceived factor was dichotomized by dividing the pyramided score between 0 to 1 and 2 to 4 (MH I ridits of .46 and .58). The factor was also trichotomized into 0 to 1 (.46), 2 (.56), and 3 to 4 (.63). Table 5-10 shows the final factor and its ridits. It is the "strongest" of the childhood factors in relation to childhood and adult mental health.

The dichotomies (having "plus" groups more equal in size) can be compared directly with one another. In Table 13-1, columns 3 and 4 from the left, the differences between the Mental Health I ridits of the plus and minus categories ("ridit increments") of each childhood factor are .06, .09, .10, .08, .03, .12, .05, and .00. The largest difference, .12, is found between the risk of those who did and did not perceive their parents negatively. The Parents' Character factor is apparently the strongest childhood factor.

One of the most remarkable "negative findings" is that the proportion of persons perceiving their parents negatively is quite similar at all three socioeconomic levels: 13.7 per cent of those from low socioeconomic families, 10.7 per cent of the Middles, and 11.1 per cent of the Highs fell into the trichotomized "plus" category. If there were any major differences, we would expect to find them in this extreme "plus" group. A perusal of the items considered in making up the factor uncovers little SES variation. About 35 per cent of each SES group said: "My parents always wanted me to do better than other children" (see Table 10-10).

### TABLE 10-10

### PROPORTIONS AND AVERAGE MENTAL HEALTH (MH II) OF RESPONDENTS WHOSE PARENTS WANTED THEM TO DO BETTER, CONTROLLED BY FATHERS' SOCIOECONOMIC STATUS

| My Parents Always Wanted Me To Do Better Than Other Children | Fathers' Socioeconomic Status | | | | | | |
|---|---|---|---|---|---|---|---|
| | LOW | | MIDDLE | | HIGH | | TOTAL |
| | Per Cent $\bar{R}$ | | Per Cent $\bar{R}$ | | Per Cent $\bar{R}$ | | Per Cent $\bar{R}$ |
| Yes | 33.6 | .60 | 35.0 | .54 | 35.1 | .47 | 34.6 .53 * |
| No | 64.3 | .54 | 63.7 | .47 | 63.9 | .44 | 64.0 .48 |
| Don't Know, No Answer ‡ | 2.1 | – | 1.3 | – | 1.0 | – | 1.4 – |
| Total Number of Cases (N=100 per cent) | 482 | | 671 | | 507 | | 1660 |

* Difference in test variable at the 5 per cent level of confidence between ridits adjacent to same asterisk.
‡ Ridits not computed.

About 25 per cent of all three levels thought: "Father spends too little time with me" (see Table 10-11).

Again, about 28 per cent of all three levels agreed that "Mother wants to run her children's lives" (see Table 10-12).

Slightly more people from high SES families disagreed with the statement: "My parents are always proud of their children" (see Table 10-13) and agreed that "Mother doesn't understand me" (see Table 10-14).

On the other hand, a somewhat greater proportion of low SES persons said that, "My parents often don't practice what they preach" (see Table

## TABLE 10-11

### PROPORTIONS AND AVERAGE MENTAL HEALTH (MH II) OF RESPONDENTS WHOSE FATHERS SPENT TOO LITTLE TIME WITH THEM, CONTROLLED BY FATHERS' SOCIOECONOMIC STATUS

|  | Fathers' Socioeconomic Status | | | |
|---|---|---|---|---|
| Father Spends Too Little Time With Me | LOW | MIDDLE | HIGH | TOTAL |
|  | Per Cent  $\bar{R}$ | Per Cent  $\bar{R}$ | Per Cent  $\bar{R}$ | Per Cent  $\bar{R}$ |
| Yes | 24.9  .61 | 27.0  .56 | 23.1  .50 | 25.2  .56 |
|  |  | * |  | * |
| No | 66.8  .54 | 69.3  .46 | 72.2  .44 | 69.5  .47 |
| Don't Know, No Answer ‡ | 8.3  – | 3.7  – | 4.7  – | 5.3  – |
| Total Number of Cases (N=100 per cent) | 482 | 671 | 507 | 1660 |

* Difference in test variable at the 5 per cent level of confidence between ridits adjacent to same asterisk.

‡ Ridits not computed.

10-15) and "Father wants to run his children's lives" (see Table 10-16).

These differences are not very large, and tend to cancel each other out. The fact that the mother was reported as more rejecting or alienating in the high SES families and the father as more dominating in the low SES families might easily be due to random statistical variation. All in all, the similarities in the proportions are astonishing, considering that so many other variables in the study show distinct socioeconomic differences.

If lower status parents are indeed more negative in their behavior toward their children, there is little evidence of it in these proportions. Again, if persons who are mentally disturbed are more likely to project their hostility onto their parents (and the low SES level *is* on the average more mentally disturbed), there is no evidence for it in the similar proportion of these responses found at each SES level.

A negative perception of parents is significantly associated with signs of both psychosis and neurosis. How does this perception fit in with the rest of the person's life history and symptoms? One of the most common

## TABLE 10-12

### PROPORTIONS AND AVERAGE MENTAL HEALTH (MH II) OF RESPONDENTS WHOSE MOTHERS WANT TO RUN CHILDREN'S LIVES, CONTROLLED BY FATHERS' SOCIOECONOMIC STATUS

| Mother Wants To Run Her Children's Lives | Fathers' Socioeconomic Status | | | | | | | |
|---|---|---|---|---|---|---|---|---|
| | LOW | | MIDDLE | | HIGH | | TOTAL | |
| | Per Cent | $\bar{R}$ | Per Cent | $\bar{R}$ | Per Cent | $\bar{R}$ | Per Cent | $\bar{R}$ |
| Yes | 27.5 | .59 | 27.7 | .55 | 29.6 | .47 | 28.3 | .54 |
| | | | | * | | | | * |
| No | 69.2 | .55 | 70.0 | .47 | 68.4 | .44 | 69.1 | .48 |
| Don't Know, No Answer ‖ | 3.3 | – | 2.3 | – | 2.0 | – | 2.6 | – |
| Total Number of Cases (N=100 per cent) | 482 | | 671 | | 507 | | 1660 | |

* Difference in test variable at the 5 per cent level of confidence between ridits adjacent to same asterisk.
‖ Ridits not computed.

pictures is of domination or rejection by one parent, with an absence or weakness on the part of the other.

Virginia R. (see footnote, page 166) has been in and out of mental hospitals for the last ten years. She is thirty-eight now, unmarried, and incapable of holding a job or a man for over a few weeks. She says "They just heap up one responsibility on you after another. I get panic-stricken. The boss told me my steno was 'crummy' so I went in the bathroom and threw up!"

Her mother tries to run her life, even now. "She never understood me. I used to beg for understanding, but she's incapable. She's domineering, and my father's been weak all his life.

"My mother is a quarrelsome woman. She'd pick a fight with my father any time. He would resist by maintaining a stony silence. That would infuriate me. He would never stand up and be the man of the family. All men seem weak, bland, and stupid to me. I guess that's why I'm a virgin still. While my mother angers me beyond words, I merely despise my father."

With anger toward her mother and no support from her father, Virginia felt abandoned. This feeling, coupled with her implacable anger, has been behind her several suicide attempts.

## TABLE 10-13

### PROPORTIONS AND AVERAGE MENTAL HEALTH (MH II) OF RESPONDENTS WHOSE PARENTS ARE PROUD OF THEIR CHILDREN, BY FATHERS' SOCIOECONOMIC STATUS

| My Parents Are Always Proud Of Their Children | Fathers' Socioeconomic Status | | | | | | |
|---|---|---|---|---|---|---|---|
| | LOW | | MIDDLE | | HIGH | | TOTAL |
| | Per Cent | $\bar{R}$ | Per Cent | $\bar{R}$ | Per Cent | $\bar{R}$ | Per Cent $\bar{R}$ |
| Yes | 83.6 | .54 | 84.8 | .48 | 80.3 | .43 | 83.1  .48 |
| | | * | | * | | * | * |
| No | 14.5 | .67 | 12.4 | .57 | 17.9 | .54 | 14.7  .59 |
| Don't Know, No Answer ∤ | 1.9 | – | 2.8 | – | 1.8 | – | 2.2  – |
| Total Number of Cases (N=100 per cent) | 482 | | 671 | | 507 | | |
| | | | | | | | 1660 |

* Difference in test variable at the 5 per cent level of confidence between ridits adjacent to same asterisk.
∤ Ridits not computed.

## Disagreements with Parents

### A.   FREQUENCY OF DISAGREEMENTS

Perhaps those who have experienced stricter upbringing (in the physical sense) have a greater fear of parental reprisals. Later we will find that low status respondents who disagreed with their parents "often" are much worse off than similar high status respondents. Perhaps it is anormative for low status children to disagree with their parents. Perhaps such disagreements are met with more tolerance at higher status levels. It is important to remember the predominantly European upbringing of the low SES, which is relatively authoritarian compared to the native American methods of the third and fourth generation.

It was assumed that conflict between parent and child would certainly be associated with increased mental disturbance. In order to test this assumption, a series of items about disagreements between parent and child was included in the questionnaire. The initial question was,

## TABLE 10-14

### PROPORTIONS AND AVERAGE MENTAL HEALTH (MH II) OF RESPONDENTS WHOSE MOTHERS DID NOT UNDERSTAND THEM, CONTROLLED BY FATHERS' SOCIOECONOMIC STATUS

| Mother Does Not Understand Me | Fathers' Socioeconomic Status | | | | | | | |
|---|---|---|---|---|---|---|---|---|
| | LOW | | MIDDLE | | HIGH | | TOTAL | |
| | Per Cent | $\overline{R}$ | Per Cent | $\overline{R}$ | Per Cent | $\overline{R}$ | Per Cent | $\overline{R}$ |
| Yes | 27.6 | .60 | 28.6 | .56 * | 33.1 | .49 | 29.7 | .55 * |
| No | 69.5 | .55 | 68.7 | .46 | 65.7 | .43 | 68.0 | .48 |
| Don't Know, No Answer ‡ | 2.9 | – | 2.7 | – | 1.2 | – | 2.3 | – |
| Total Number of Cases (N=100 per cent) | 482 | | 671 | | 507 | | 1660 | |

*Difference in test variable at the 5 per cent level of confidence between ridits adjacent to same asterisk.
‡ Ridits not computed.

When you were a teen-ager (age thirteen to eighteen), did *you* have disagreements with your parents (parent substitutes): often, occasionally, rarely, or never?

Respondents who said they disagreed with their parents "Often" had an average Mental Health (II) risk of .55, which was significantly different from those who reported disagreements "Rarely" (.45). (See Table 10-17.) However, midway between these two responses was the risk of those who "never" had disagreements with their parents (.51), involving a large proportion of the sample (29.3 per cent). Although the "Never" category has a risk similar to the entire sample (.50) and the "Occasionally" category (.49), it is worse off than the "Rarely" group.

Again we are faced with the problem of fact and fancy. In this case, as with such factors as Parents' Character Negatively Perceived or Parents' Quarrels, the interpretation remains somewhat ambiguous. It is possible that people who say their parents "Never" had quarrels or never alienated or dominated them are distorting the truth. It is also possible, and perhaps more plausible, that this fairly large proportion (29.3 per cent) of respondents in reality never had any disagreements with their parents. Some credence is given to this position by the fact that only

## TABLE 10-15

PROPORTIONS AND AVERAGE MENTAL HEALTH (MH II) OF
RESPONDENTS WHOSE PARENTS DID NOT PRACTICE WHAT THEY
PREACHED, CONTROLLED BY FATHERS' SOCIOECONOMIC STATUS

| My Parents Often Don't Practice What They Preach | Fathers' Socioeconomic Status | | | | | | | |
|---|---|---|---|---|---|---|---|---|
| | LOW | | MIDDLE | | HIGH | | TOTAL | |
| | Per Cent | $\bar{R}$ | Per Cent | $\bar{R}$ | Per Cent | $\bar{R}$ | Per Cent | $\bar{R}$ |
| Yes | 22.4 | .63 | 20.6 | .59 * | 15.2 | .51 | 19.5 | .58 * |
| No | 76.0 | .54 | 77.2 | .46 | 83.8 | .44 | 78.8 | .48 |
| Don't Know, No Answer ǀ | 1.6 | – | 2.2 | – | 1.0 | – | 1.7 | – |
| Total Number of Cases (N=100 per cent) | 482 | | 671 | | 507 | | 1660 | |

*Difference in test variable at the 5 per cent level of confidence between ridits adjacent to same asterisk.
ǀ Ridits not computed.

one-fifth of the high SES as opposed to one-third of the low and middle SES "Never" had disagreements. This fits in with what we know about the predominantly authoritarian attitudes of the lower status groups. The concluding chapter shows about one-third of the high SES and three-quarters of the low SES agreeing with items from the "Authoritarian Scale." Adults who are authoritarian are more likely to *report* that they never disagreed with their parents, and in all likelihood they actually never did disagree openly with their parents.

Again, the definitions of a "disagreement" may vary widely between the status groups, which is the same problem we faced with "Parents' Quarrels." It is interesting that the greatest ridit difference occurs between the "Rarely" and "Never" categories in the middle SES. At this status level, those who "Never disagreed with their parents" were even worse off with respect to mental health (though not significantly) than those who disagreed "Often."

If normative behavior were the only criterion for mental health, then persons who never disagreed with their parents should be healthier in a group such as the low SES, where more people, "Never disagree." Such is not the case, however. By the same token, the "Never disagrees"

## TABLE 10-16

### PROPORTIONS AND AVERAGE MENTAL HEALTH (MH II) OF RESPONDENTS WHOSE FATHERS WANT TO RUN CHILDREN'S LIVES, CONTROLLED BY FATHERS' SOCIOECONOMIC STATUS

| *Father Wants To Run His Children's Lives* | *Fathers' Socioeconomic Status* | | | | | | | |
|---|---|---|---|---|---|---|---|---|
| | *LOW* | | *MIDDLE* | | *HIGH* | | *TOTAL* | |
| | Per Cent | R̄ | Per Cent | R̄ | Per Cent | R̄ | Per Cent | R̄ |
| Yes | 21.4 | .64 | 19.4 | .54 | 16.8 | .53 | 19.2 | .57 |
| | | * | | | | | | * |
| No | 70.3 | .53 | 76.3 | .48 | 78.3 | .44 | 75.1 | .48 |
| Don't Know, No Answer Ɨ | 8.3 | — | 4.3 | — | 4.9 | — | 5.7 | — |
| Total Number of Cases (N=100 per cent) | 482 | | 671 | | 507 | | 1660 | |

*Difference in test variable at the 5 per cent level of confidence between ridits adjacent to same asterisk
Ɨ Ridits not computed.

should be somewhat worse off among the high SES, for at that level such authoritarian behavior is somewhat more anormative. There is, however, no sharp rise in the risk of the "Nevers" in the high SES.

Using a less relativistic approach than the concept of "normative behavior," we might suspect that children who are *incapable* of quarreling with their parents are more emotionally disturbed than those who can express some of their negative feelings. This, of course, rests on the assumption that all children have some negative feelings toward their parents from time to time, but the reader will probably accept the validity of this assumption.

Both extremes, those who disagreed "Often" and those who "Never" disagreed, are somewhat worse off with respect to mental health than the moderate group who disagreed "Occasionally" and "Rarely." It is possible, then, that there is a curvilinear rather than a linear relationship between impairment and Disagreements with Parents.

### B. AREAS OF DISAGREEMENT

All respondents who said they disagreed to some extent were asked the following question:

## TABLE 10-17

## PROPORTIONS AND AVERAGE MENTAL HEALTH (MH II) OF RESPONDENTS WHO HAD TEEN-AGE DISAGREEMENTS WITH PARENTS, BY FATHERS' SOCIOECONOMIC STATUS

| Frequency of Teen-Age Disagreements With Parents | Fathers' Socioeconomic Status | | | | | | | |
|---|---|---|---|---|---|---|---|---|
| | LOW | | MIDDLE | | HIGH | | TOTAL | |
| | Per Cent | R̄ | Per Cent | R̄ | Per Cent | R̄ | Per Cent | R̄ |
| Often | 10.2 | .62 | 12.7 | .53 | 14.8 | .54 * | 12.6 | .55* |
| Occasionally | 30.3 | .54 | 28.0 | .50 | 34.3 | .42 | 30.6 | .49 |
| Rarely | 23.7 | .54 | 25.2 | .43 * | 26.8 | .42 | 25.2 | .45* |
| Never | 33.9 | .57 | 31.6 | .56 | 21.7 | .45 | 29.3 | .51 |
| Don't Know, No Answer ǀ | 1.9 | – | 2.5 | – | 2.4 | – | 2.3 | – |
| Total Number of Cases (N=100 per cent) | 482 | | 671 | | 507 | | 1660 | |

* Difference in test variable at the 5 per cent level of confidence between ridits adjacent to same asterisk.
ǀ Ridits not computed.

"Were the disagreements ever about such things as these: (1) About how you spent your free time? (2) About religious matters? (3) About the foods you liked? (4) About money matters (allowances, earnings)? (5a) (Males only) About going out with girls? (5b) (Females only) About going out with boys? (6) About your school work? (7) About what to do when you were sick? (8) About deciding things for yourself? (9) Anything else?"

With one exception, there were no striking socioeconomic differences in the proportion of disagreements with parents about various matters (see Table 10-18). More friction over religious matters might have been expected in the low SES, yet about 5 per cent of all three levels reported disagreement. Similarly, money matters might easily have been a focus of conflict in poorer families, yet about one-fifth of each SES level reported disagreements over money.

We tend to assume that school work is heavily emphasized by the higher status parents, but the disagreements in this area are not signifi-

## TABLE 10-18

### PROPORTIONS AND AVERAGE MENTAL HEALTH (MH II) OF RESPONDENTS WHO HAD PARTICULAR TEEN-AGE DISAGREEMENTS WITH PARENTS, BY FATHERS' SOCIOECONOMIC STATUS

| Disagreement About | Fathers' Socioeconomic Status | | | | | | | |
|---|---|---|---|---|---|---|---|---|
| | LOW | | MIDDLE | | HIGH | | TOTAL | |
| | Per Cent | $\bar{R}$ | Per Cent | $\bar{R}$ | Per Cent | $\bar{R}$ | Per Cent | $\bar{R}$ |
| How They Spent Their Free Time | 32.0 | .54 | 27.1 | .49 | 28.8 | .44 | 29.0 | .49 |
| Religious Matters | 3.9 | .53 | 5.7 | .49 | 6.3 | .54 | 5.4 | .52 |
| Foods They Liked | 16.8 | .55 | 14.3 | .52 | 14.0 | .46 | 14.9 | .51 |
| Money Matters | 22.2 | .56 | 20.9 | .49 | 17.2 | .50 | 20.1 | .51 |
| Going Out With Boys And Girls | 19.1 | .59 | 18.8 | .51 | 24.1 | .45 | 20.5 | .51 |
| School Work | 19.5 | .54 | 20.9 | .50 | 26.0 | .47 | 22.0 | .50 |
| What To Do When They Were Sick | 8.1 | .61 | 6.9 | .51 | 8.5 | .49 | 7.7 | .53 |
| Deciding Things For Themselves | 22.0 | .53 | 21.5 | .50 | 33.4 | .42 | 25.4 | .48 |
| Total Number of Cases[a] (N=100 per cent) | 482 | | 671 | | 507 | | 1660 | |

[a]Including those who had no disagreements.

*Note:* Percentages only of respondents who answered "yes" to each item. Percentages total more than 100 per cent.

cantly more frequent in the high SES (about 22 per cent of all levels). One study has found that lower status parents urge their children to do well in grade or high school but do not urge them to attempt higher levels of education. Fewer middle class mothers (35 per cent) than working class mothers (50 per cent) stressed the importance of the child's doing well at school. However, 70 per cent of the middle class mothers, as opposed to only 24 per cent of the working class mothers, expected their child to go to college.[13]

In Midtown, conflict over spending free time (29 per cent), food (14.9 per cent), dating (20.5 per cent), and what to do when sick (7.7 per cent) showed only minor socioeconomic differences. The only major SES difference was that high SES respondents reported more disagreements over "deciding things for themselves" (33.4 per cent) than the Lows or Middles (about 22 per cent). This one item among eight dealing with disagreements does not argue for a predominance of parental control in the high SES. All together, there is a surprising lack of socioeconomic difference in the proportions reporting conflict over these areas of behavior. As with "school work," the words probably mean different things to members of different status groups, and cannot really be equated too closely, except as general indicators of conflict with parents.

The mental health risk associated with each of these areas of disagreement does not vary perceptibly from that of the sample as a whole. However, high SES respondents who report they disagreed with their parents over religious matters run a considerably higher risk (.54) than the high SES as a whole (.45). Their parents may be somewhat atypical to begin with, for we know that in our respondent population (present rather than parent generation) religiosity decreases as the average socioeconomic status increases.

## C. DISAGREEMENT WITH FATHER OR MOTHER

If the respondent indicated disagreement with his parents over one or more of the areas mentioned, or over some additional area, he was asked the following question, "During those years, with whom did you mostly have this (these) kind(s) of disagreements: your father (substitute) or mother (substitute)?"

There were no statistically significant differences in mental health risk between persons who answered father, mother, or both father and mother, or mentioned some other person with whom they disagreed (see Table 10-19). It is interesting, however, to note the tendency for disagreements with father to involve a somewhat elevated mental health risk in both the high and low SES, but not in the middle SES. While just a suggestion of a trend, it could be an indication that disagreeing with father is more pathognomonic at the extremes of social status, and not as indicative in the middle SES. However, the proportions of persons disagreeing with the father alone do not vary between SES groups (about 19.2 per cent, as in the total sample). The mental health risk of respondents who disagreed with "Both" father and mother (.47) is somewhat better than the mental health of persons who disagreed with "Father"

## TABLE 10-19

### PROPORTIONS AND AVERAGE MENTAL HEALTH (MH II) OF RESPONDENTS WHO HAD DISAGREEMENTS WITH PARENTS, ACCORDING TO FATHERS' SOCIOECONOMIC STATUS

| | *Father's Socioeconomic Status* | | | | | | | |
|---|---|---|---|---|---|---|---|---|
| | LOW | | MIDDLE | | HIGH | | TOTAL | |
| *Disagreements* | Per Cent | R̄ | Per Cent | R̄ | Per Cent | R̄ | Per Cent | R̄ |
| Father | 18.9 | .62 | 18.6 | .47 | 20.3 | .49 | 19.2 | .52 |
| Mother | 30.3 | .52 | 33.1 | .49 | 36.2 | .42 | 33.3 | .47 |
| Both | 7.7 | .51 | 8.6 | .50 | 13.8 | .42 | 9.9 | .47 |
| Other | 4.6 | .58 | 2.4 | .46 | 3.6 | .56 | 3.4 | .54 |
| Did Not Disagree | 36.9 | .57 | 35.2 | .51 | 23.5 | .46 | 32.1 | .52 |
| Don't Know, No Answer ‡ | 1.7 | – | 2.1 | – | 2.6 | – | 2.1 | – |
| Total Number of Cases (N=100 per cent) | 482 | | 671 | | 507 | | 1660 | |

‡ Ridits not computed.

only (.52). Persons who disagreed with both parents are also more prevalent in the high SES (13.8 per cent).

Disagreeing with one's mother involves considerably less risk than disagreement with father in both high and low SES, but about equal risk in the middle SES. Again there is some hint that mothers are equal in authority to the father in the middle socioeconomic group, and that fathers wield greater authority than mothers in the high and low status groups. (The assumption here is that disagreement with a parent who is accorded authority is associated with poorer mental health, while disagreement with parents who are not accorded much authority would involve less of a mental health risk.)

In sum, the overwhelming fact is that there are no significant differences in the mental health of those who disagreed with mother, father, or both, or did not disagree at all.

It was just possible that the sex of the respondent was the factor that determined whether disagreements with father or mother were linked to poor mental health. Consequently, we examined teen-age disagreements according to the sex of the respondent, mother and father, and the father's socioeconomic status (split into a Low and High group only, so as to provide more cases in each cell). The results (see Table 10-20) show that cross-sex and like-sex disagreements are about equally associated with mental health. This is true even when socioeconomic status is held constant.

### TABLE 10-20

## PROPORTIONS AND AVERAGE MENTAL HEALTH (MH II) OF RESPONDENTS WHO HAD TEEN-AGE DISAGREEMENTS WITH MOTHER, FATHER, BOTH, AND NEITHER, ACCORDING TO SEX AND FATHERS' SOCIOECONOMIC STATUS

| | | Fathers' Socioeconomic Status | | | | | |
|---|---|---|---|---|---|---|---|
| | | LOW | | HIGH | | TOTAL | |
| Teen-age Disagreements | | Per Cent[a] | $\overline{R}$ | Per Cent | $\overline{R}$ | Per Cent | $\overline{R}$ |
| Mother | Male | 30.2 | .53 | 28.4 | .45 | 29.4 | .49 |
| | Female | 33.5 | .51 | 38.6 | .43 | 36.0 | .46 |
| Father | Male | 20.0 | .56 | 28.1 | .48 | 23.8 | .51 |
| | Female | 16.5 | .56 | 15.4 | .49 | 16.0 | .52 |
| Both | Male | 9.2 | .54 | 15.0 | .44 | 11.9 | .48 |
| | Female | 5.8 | .48 | 11.4 | .44 | 8.6 | .45 |
| Neither | Male | 36.9 | .56 | 24.1 | .46 | 30.9 | .52 |
| | Female | 37.5 | .53 | 28.3 | .50 | 29.9 | .52 |
| Don't Know, | Male ǂ | 3.8 | — | 4.4 | — | 4.0 | — |
| No Answer | Female ǂ | 6.7 | — | 6.3 | — | 6.5 | — |
| Total Males = 100 per cent | | 370 | | 320 | | 690 | |
| Total Females = 100 per cent | | 496 | | 474 | | 970 | |
| Total Number of Cases (N = 100 per cent) | | | | | | 1660 | |

[a]30.2 per cent of all 370 low SES males disagreed with mother. 33.5 per cent of all 496 low SES females disagreed with mother.

ǂ Ridits not computed.

It is of interest, however, that a somewhat larger proportion of the higher status males (28.1 per cent) than of lower status males (20.0 per cent) have disagreements with their fathers. This is rather expectable, from what we know about authority patterns in the low socioeconomic group. High status females have a slight tendency to disagree more with their mothers than do low status females. Moreover, a much larger proportion of the Highs disagree with both parents. Among those who disagreed with only one parent, there is more SES variation in like-sex disagreements.

The teen-ager is apparently more apt to have disagreements with the like-sex parent; 36 per cent of females and only 29.4 per cent of males reported disagreements with their mothers. Again, more males (23.8 per cent) disagreed with their fathers than did females (16.0 per cent). It is probable that the father does more of the disciplining of boys, particularly during the teens, when the mother no longer has control over her sons.

The greater proportion of like-sex disagreements in the high SES (cross-sex disagreements do not vary with SES) may be linked to the problem of authority. If like-sex parents typically do the disciplining, the increasing' proportion of disagreements may indicate a partial breakdown of like-sex parental authority in the higher SES levels. It is also likely that adolescent rebellion takes different forms at different SES levels. The low SES youth may express his rebellion against the larger society rather than against his parents directly. He does this by virtue of being in a gang, which often contravenes parental values as well. The middle or high SES youth may join political groups which symbolize protest against parental and societal values. The chief forms of expression, however, will be in faulty school work and sexual activity. Disagreements with their parents over school and dating do not occur exclusively in the high SES. However, the parental concern over these activities is greater. The high status youth may argue with his parents, because his parents are concerned. The low status adolescent comes into open conflict with the police, and is less likely to have disagreements with or cautious control by his parents.

The Highs have more like-sex disagreements with their parents. Is it possible, then, that the Oedipus Complex is enhanced by the high status parents' attachment to, concern for, and control over their children? The Lows, in contrast, may by their lack of supervision—and in some cases lack of involvement or affection—encourage the development of dyssocial behavior. We know that much earlier heterosexual expression is prevalent among the Lows, perhaps as a result of less supervision. This lack of sexual suppression and repression may minimize oedipal struggles among the Lows. This might help to explain why we found the Highs tending toward neurosis, which is linked in theory with unresolved oedipal conflicts. At the same time, it might aid in understanding the large proportion of Probable Psychotics and Probable Personality Trait Types found among the Lows.

### D. RISKS OF THE FACTOR

Since neither the sex of the parent nor the area of disagreement was related to mental health, the mere frequency of disagreements with parents (often, occasionally, and rarely-never) was utilized as a factor by itself. However, the somewhat increased mental health risk of the "Never" category, as mentioned previously, tended to weaken the power of this factor. The trichotomized ridits (MH I) are .55 in the plus, .49 in the moderate, and .50 in the minus category (see Table 10-21).

Neither the area of disagreement nor the sex of the parent seemed crucial in disagreements. However, the flavor and intensity of the feeling associated with responses to this question are the key to its importance. This is more clearly seen in the statements of individuals in the impaired category.

Women often quarreled with their mothers or both parents over dating and sex matters.

I occasionally disagreed with my mother about going out. All my girl friends had the same thing. Nobody gets out of that house till they're married. "Who is he? He got a job? You can only go with one feller." They were strict. I know, cause I tried to go with two or three at a time. But even though they were strict, I enjoyed living. I told my mother, "Whatever can happen at night can happen in the afternoon too."

Sometimes the arguments were over clothing. "She had her own ideas about my short dumpy figure. How I was to dress. It was always 'Mother knows best.'"

The men, too, seem concerned with asserting their independence. Their disagreements repeat the theme of struggle against a feeling of domination and dependence.

"I always wanted more freedom than my very permissive parents were willing to give." There is no feeling of resolution of this struggle.

An unimpaired girl however says, "At twelve I argued a lot, but by fourteen I didn't bother. It wasn't worth it." This calm resolution of the problem is in sharp contrast to the intense conflict still present in many of the impaired adults.

The weakness of Disagreements with Parents as a factor lies in the fact that lack of any rebellion may be just as indicative of psychopathol-

## TABLE 10-21

### DISTRIBUTION, PROPORTIONS, AND AVERAGE MENTAL HEALTH (CMH, MH I, MH II) ACCORDING TO RESPONDENTS' DISAGREEMENTS WITH PARENTS, TRICHOTOMIZED AND DICHOTOMIZED

| Respondents' Disagreements With Parents | Respondents' Mental Health | | | | |
|---|---|---|---|---|---|
| | CMH | MH I | MH II | No. of Cases | Per Cent of Cases |
| *Trichotomy* | | | | | |
| + | .59 | .55 | .55 | 209 | 12.6 |
| 0 | .52 | .49 | .49 | 508 | 30.6 |
| − | .47 | .50 | .49 | 943 | 56.8 |
| *Dichotomy* | | | | | |
| + | .55 | .50 | .51 | 717 | 43.2 |
| − | .47 | .50 | .49 | 943 | 56.8 |
| Total Number of Cases (N = 100 per cent) | | | | 1660 | |

ogy. For example, a middle-aged man reports that he rarely disagreed with his parents.

I wasn't allowed to express myself. Maybe I became a homosexual as a rebellion, just to punish them deliberately. My mother treated me like a doll, not like a person.

Even though this man had come from a low SES home, where few argue with their parents, his lack of self-assertion is outstanding. An occasional disagreement with one or both parents is probably one element of mental health, and too much or too little disagreement may both be pathognomonic.

## Summary

*Childhood Economic Deprivation.* The final factor was based upon "Parents had a hard time making ends meet" and "Mother worked outside the home to earn money." This yielded Mental Health I risks of .58, .54, and .47, indicating a factor of moderate strength.

The report that "Parents had a hard time making ends meet" seems to be more on the factual side. The death of fathers rather than mothers is associated with this response, coinciding with the greater economic deprivation expected in the event of the father's death. The fact that the mother worked did not increase the mental health risk of the respondents.

Persons whose fathers were in unstable occupations, regardless of the prestige attached to them (artists, for example) were more likely to report "hard times" for their parents. Those with occupationally mobile fathers (whether upward or downward) tended to report more "hard times" for parents. It is possible that children in such families suffer more *relative* deprivation.

*Parents' Quarrels.*    People wth parents of different backgrounds were expected to show increased mental health risk. In part, this was due to an assumption that they would have been exposed to greater value conflicts and more frequent parental quarrels.

On the contrary, persons whose parents had different levels of education were somewhat better off with respect to mental health than those who came from educationally homogeneous backgrounds. It is typical of the high status family for the father to have more education than the mother. This occurred in half of the high SES families, and almost none of the Lows. Since high SES respondents have less risk in general, not heterogeneity, but SES accounts for the lowered risk. However, a respondent whose father's education was *less* than his mother's also had less risk (.43) than a respondent whose parents had similar education, particularly in the middle and low SES.

Religious heterogeneity of the parents showed no association with mental health risk. Only 12.7 per cent came from mixed religious background, and they showed no differences from the general population. More high SES intermarriages were found. The increase in secularity with increasing social status may account for the fact that high SES people make interfaith marriages more frequently. This may also account for the fact that their risk is not increased.

Parental differences in ethnic background were not related to mental health risk. Cultural differences, often cited as a source of conflict and stress for the child, do not seem to have been a factor in the mental health of Midtowners. Persons with one immigrant and one native-born parent also showed no ridit increment, which questions the role of acculturation in mental disturbance.

Those who said their parents quarreled often showed a significant increase in impairment risk. The item was used by itself as a factor, and yielded risks of .58, .51, and .48.

*Parents' Character Negatively Perceived.* Agreement with the following six statements was the basis for a weighted score which constituted the factor:

Father spends too little time with me, Father wants to run his children's lives, Mother wants to run her children's lives, Mother does not understand me, My parents are (not) always proud of their children, My parents often don't practice what they preach.

If a parent was viewed negatively, the associated risk did not vary, whether one or two items were involved. However, if both parents were viewed negatively, a substantial increase in risk occurred. No difference in risk between "alienating" and "dominating" parents was found.

Apparently, if you are rejected by (or reject) one parent, you're better off than if rejected by (or rejecting) both parents. The final factor yielded risks of .63, .56, and .46, making it the most powerful of all the childhood factors.

Although we are told that lower status parents exhibit more negative behavior toward their children, the equal proportions of each SES level reporting parents negatively does not seem to support this assertion.

*Disagreements with Parents.* Those who disagreed often with their parents had an increased mental health risk. This item was utilized as a factor, yielding risks of .55 (often), .49 (occasionally), and .50 (rarely or never). It was one of the weaker factors, particularly since the minus category in which the noxious factor was presumably absent ("Never") showed a very slight increase instead of a sharp decrease in risk.

The risk associated with having disagreements over any particular area of behavior did not increase significantly over the risk of the whole sample.

Disagreements with father, mother, or both parents showed no statistically significant differences in risk. However, disagreements with father in both high and low SES involved some increase in risk.

The teen-ager is more likely to have disagreements with the like-sex parent. High status respondents had more of a tendency to disagree with their like-sex parents, or with both parents. This does not constitute an argument for permissiveness, but merely indicates that permissiveness and lower impairment risks are both found in the high SES. Such association, however, does not indicate they are causally related.

## Notes

1. A. R. Mangus and R. H. Woodward, *An Analysis of the Mental Health of Elementary School Children,* The Division of Mental Hygiene of the Ohio State Department of Public Welfare, The Ohio State University, The Ohio Agricultural Experiment Station in cooperation with The Butler County Mental Hygiene Association, Hamilton, Ohio, July, 1949, p. 6.

2. Stella B. Applebaum, "Working Wives and Mothers," Public Affairs Pamphlet No. 188, New York, November 1952, p. 20.

3. The average age of the Midtown sample is forty. Since the interviews were conducted in 1953, the average respondent was therefore in the middle of the school-age range, or twelve, in 1925. The report covers all mothers who worked *at any time* during the twelve years between age six and eighteen, and the proportion (31.1 per cent) is therefore somewhat inflated, when compared with the proportion working *at a point in time.*

4. See Chapter 8 for further statistics on working mothers.

5. S. Applebaum, *op. cit.,* p. 10. These figures in turn are no longer accurate.

6. Among fathers with elementary schooling, only 23.2 per cent in high occupations (high and middle white collar), 32.3 per cent in middle occupations, 8 per cent in lower-middle occupations (low white collar and high blue collar, or skilled labor) and 39.8 per cent in low occupations (low and middle blue collar, or semiskilled and unskilled labor) had "hard times often." Among fathers with high-school education and high, middle, and low occupations, 15.7, 20.3, and 42.9 per cent respectively had "hard times often." Among college level fathers in similar occupational strata, 13.2, 34.5, and 27.3 per cent had "hard times often." Comparing educational levels *within* occupational level (e.g., within middle occupations the three educational levels show 32.3, 20.3, and 34.5 per cent), we find less variation, and where there is variation, it is more erratic.

7. Only 1175 respondents were able to report their fathers' occupation when the respondents were both eight and eighteen years old. Several hundred lost their fathers through death before they were eighteen. A much smaller number did not know their fathers' earlier occupation.

8. For example, the depressed adult might say his parents had hard times.

9. It is also possible that in heterogeneous families the high status parent dominates, thus making the child-rearing atmosphere more consistent.

10. Judson T. Landis, "The Trauma of Children When Parents Divorce," *Marriage and Family Living,* Volume 22, No. 1, February 1960, pp. 7–13.

11. Milton R. Sapirstein and Alis De Sola, *Paradoxes of Everyday Life: A Psychoanalyst's Interpretations,* Random House, New York, 1955.

12. *Risk increment* is the difference between the ridits of the healthiest and most disturbed category of the factor.

13. See R. Sears, E. Maccoby, and H. Levin, *Patterns of Child Rearing,* Row, Peterson & Co., Evanston, Ill., 1957, p. 426.

# Adult Poor Physical Health and Poor Interpersonal Affiliations

T H O M A S   S .   L A N G N E R

## Antecedent and Reciprocal (Adult) Component Factors

Chapters 9 and 10 described the construction of the preadult factors and their relationship to mental health risk. Chapters 11 and 12 deal with the adult factors. They are generally composed of information about the present life stresses of the adult individual at the time he was interviewed.

The childhood component factors did not really tell us much about *why* the major demographic factor, socioeconomic status, bears a relatively strong relationship to mental health. They do, however, offer us a series of life experiences and perceptions that bear an independent relationship to mental health. They are important because they are independently related to mental health, not because they are part of larger demographic rubrics. For instance, Parents' Quarrels is not important because it explains why the low status family setting is more likely to be associated with mental disturbance. On the contrary, Parents' Quarrels are reported just as frequently in the low as in the high SES. Regardless of the social stratum under consideration, the mental health risk of those exposed to frequent parental quarrels is greater than that of persons seldom exposed. While we are primarily interested in the role of social factors in producing mental disturbance, we have for the time being *laid aside,* or controlled, the broad socioeconomic factor to see what *additional* social factors play a role in mental health and disturbance.

The adult component variables differ greatly from the childhood component variables. They are not clearly antecedent to the adult mental health of the individual. They are reciprocal component variables, and can be considered symptoms of mental disturbance as well as sources of stress. For example, one can be socially rejected, which could lead to mental disturbance. On the other hand, the original mental disturbance could lead to social rejection by others, or it could also have as one of its symptoms the rejection by the individual of others. The problems of the reciprocal character of the adult factors have been discussed in some detail in Chapter 6 and need not concern us further at this point. With these words of caution we turn to the factor of Adult Poor Physical Health.

## Adult Poor Physical Health

Many questions concerning the respondent's physical health were included in the questionnaire. One reason for this was that the interview was introduced as a health survey, and height, weight, and other questions evocative of the familiar medical history were used to "warm up" the respondent. Also, physical illness is inextricably intertwined with mental disturbance. The psychophysiological symptoms that predominate in the questionnaire are indicative of both physical and mental disturbance. The following questions labeled "physical health" are only so called because they lie a little more on the physical than on the psychological side. Moreover, as is the case with all the adult factors, "Adult Poor Physical Health" is as much a symptom as it is a cause of mental disorder.

The most important questions concerning health were the respondent's health self-estimate, "About your health now, would you say it is excellent, good, fair, or poor?" and his report of the number of times he was hospitalized. These items, when combined, showed the closest relationship to the Mental Health Ratings of all the health items.

### A. HEALTH SELF-ESTIMATE

The respondent's estimate of his own present health was virtually a predictor of mental health risk by itself. Those who said their health was excellent were much better off with respect to mental health risk (.38) than those who said their health was poor (.86). The differences are statistically significant in all three SES groups. It is interesting to note that 51.8 per cent of the high SES and only 20.6 per cent of the low SES said they were in excellent health (see Table 11-1).

## TABLE 11-1

### PROPORTIONS AND AVERAGE MENTAL HEALTH (MH II) OF RESPONDENTS ACCORDING TO PRESENT GENERAL HEALTH BY RESPONDENTS' SOCIOECONOMIC STATUS

| Respondents' General Health Now | Respondents' Socioeconomic Status | | | | | | | |
|---|---|---|---|---|---|---|---|---|
| | LOW | | MIDDLE | | HIGH | | TOTAL | |
| | Per Cent | $\bar{R}$ | Per Cent | $\bar{R}$ | Per Cent | $\bar{R}$ | Per Cent | $\bar{R}$ |
| Excellent | 20.6 | $.48^{*}_{z,y}$ | 31.8 | $.40^{*}_{x}$ | 51.8 | $.33^{*}_{w,v}$ | 34.9 | $.38^{*}_{u}$ |
| Good | 44.6 | $.52^{*}$ | 46.4 | $.50^{*}_{x}$ | 36.6 | $.48^{*}_{v}$ | 42.5 | $.50^{*}_{u}$ |
| Fair | 25.7 | $.71^{*}_{z}$ | 18.7 | $.62^{*}_{x}$ | 10.4 | $.57^{*}_{w}$ | 18.2 | $.65^{*}_{u}$ |
| Poor | 8.5 | $.87^{*}_{y}$ | 2.9 | $.84^{*}_{x}$ | .7 | $(.88)^{*}_{v}$ | 4.0 | $.86^{*}_{u}$ |
| Don't Know, No Answer ‖ | .6 | – | .2 | – | .5 | – | .4 | – |
| Total Number of Cases (N=100 per cent) | 544 | | 556 | | 560 | | 1660 | |

\* Difference in test variable at the 5 per cent level of confidence between ridits adjacent to same asterisk.
‖ Ridits not computed.
Parentheses () enclose ridits based on less than ten cases.

The health self-estimate was available to the psychiatrists making the first Mental Health Rating (I), and it is therefore not methodologically "clean" (see discussion in Chapter 6). It is probable that a statement of "poor health," taken with other statements of health preoccupation and hypochondriasis, contributed to a worse Mental Health Rating. The health estimate is the only item of information to which the psychiatrists were exposed during the first rating that was also included among the "factors."

No methods used to avoid bias of mental health ratings by data on physical illness could possibly produce a clear separation of these subjects, for there is no separation of mind and body. The psychophysiological complaints were given most credence during the rating process. Such symptoms are found in most case histories. This welding of the physical and mental is clearly seen in a woman who was alternately in general and mental hospitals.

Rachel W. (see footnote, p. 166) says her health is poor, and so it has been, from birth on. She was the only daughter of a butcher in a delicatessen shop. At three months, she came down with whooping cough and soon after her recovery developed rickets. She remembers having many colds and always being allergic. Her father also was sickly and her mother had to take over his job. When Rachel was very young he died of tuberculosis, leaving the family in serious financial difficulties. Fortunately, her mother managed carefully, and life continued in a relatively normal pattern until Rachel was thirteen, when her mother had a nervous breakdown. Rachel was forced to leave school, where she was very happy. After eight years of grammar school she went to work as a package wrapper in a department store. Thin and frail, she developed slowly and did not begin menstruation until her late teens. Unimpressed by boys and sex during adolescence and early adulthood, Rachel focused all her love and interest on her mother and sister. When she finally married in her late thirties, it was only for companionship after the death of her mother and the marriage of her sister.

After her marriage Rachel's health grew worse. She developed high blood pressure, suffered from sciatica, and had severe headaches. After a few years of marriage, her husband died of hepatitis. Completely alone, her poor health prevented her from going out and making friends or developing new resources. Her doctor told her that she would never be able to work. The shock of the death of her husband was followed by a hysterectomy, which brought on a breakdown. After that Rachel felt incapable of even going to a movie. Restricted by her physical illness to the company of her poodle dog and potted geraniums, she retreated into the life of her memories. Periodically she would take all of her mother's clothes and jewelry out of the trunk where she kept them. She would count them and if any were missing, she became frantic. When her sister or former friends visited her, she was irritable and hypersensitive. Her headaches became more severe and she was again hospitalized for a nervous breakdown. After that she had another internal operation and was on the critical list for five days.

Despite all the treatment that she has received, Rachel's health is still poor. She suffers from nosebleeds and headaches. Her legs get numb, and she walks poorly. She had a light stroke recently which increases her irritability and irrational behavior. Rachel's original poor health has been made more unbearable by her obsessive-compulsive traits which in turn are intensified by the organic illness. She remarked woefully, "My whole life I've lived with sickness."

## B.  NUMBER OF HOSPITALIZATIONS

The number of hospitalizations was not by itself a powerful discriminator of mental health. In the sample as a whole (see Table 11-2) only those persons who had been hospitalized eight or more times showed significantly poorer mental health than those who were hospitalized once, twice, or never.

Yet this item, combined with the "health self-estimate," enabled us to

## TABLE 11-2

### PROPORTIONS AND AVERAGE MENTAL HEALTH (MH II) OF RESPONDENTS ACCORDING TO NUMBER OF HOSPITALIZATIONS BY RESPONDENTS' SOCIOECONOMIC STATUS

Respondents' Socioeconomic Status

| Number of Hospitalizations | Per Cent | $\bar{R}$ | Per Cent | $\bar{R}$ | Per Cent | $\bar{R}$ | Per Cent | $\bar{R}$ |
|---|---|---|---|---|---|---|---|---|
| None | 32.5 | $.51^*_{z,y}$ | 28.1 | $.45^*_x$ | 18.0 | .35 | 26.1 | $.45^*_v$ |
| 1 – 2 | 47.4 | .60 | 50.1 | $.50^*_w$ | 44.8 | .41 | 47.5 | $.50^*_u$ |
| 3 – 4 | 12.5 | $.73^*_z$ | 14.4 | .53 | 22.7 | .46 | 16.6 | .54 |
| 5 – 7 | 3.3 | .68 | 5.4 | .58 | 9.6 | .40 | 6.1 | .50 |
| 8 or more | 2.5 | $.79^*_y$ | 1.1 | $(.79)^*_{x,w}$ | 3.6 | .50 | 2.4 | $.64^*_{v,u}$ |
| Don't Know, No Answer ǂ | 1.8 | – | .9 | – | 1.3 | – | 1.3 | – |
| Total Number of Cases (N=100 per cent) | 544 | | 556 | | 560 | | 1660 | |

*Difference in test variable at the 5 per cent level of confidence between ridits with same subscript.
ǂ Ridits not computed.
Parentheses ( ) enclose ridits based on less than ten cases.

divide the sample into three groups. The mental health risks associated with these levels of adult physical health are .70, .51, and .38, as shown in Table 11-3.

Actually the addition of the number of hospitalizations has not greatly improved the separating power of the health estimate question. As seen in Table 11-1, persons reporting fair health (.65) or poor health (.86) if combined into one category would yield a risk of approximately .70. For future predictive studies of a gross nature, the health estimate would be more than adequate by itself. A further objection to the inclusion of the number of hospitalizations is that low SES people who report poor health clearly have fewer hospitalizations than high SES people who report poor health. It is apparent that low SES persons with health at least as poor as that of comparable high SES persons get less hospitalization.

Incidentally, the Childhood Mental Health Index bears a very weak relationship to Adult Poor Physical Health (when compared with Adult

## TABLE 11-3

### DISTRIBUTION, PROPORTIONS, AND AVERAGE MENTAL HEALTH (CMH, MH I, MH II) ACCORDING TO ADULT POOR PHYSICAL HEALTH TRICHOTOMIZED AND DICHOTOMIZED

| Adult Poor Physical Health | Respondents' Mental Health | | | | |
|---|---|---|---|---|---|
| | CMH | MH I | MH II | No. of Cases | Per Cent of Cases |
| **Trichotomy** | | | | | |
| + | .55$^*_z$ | .70$^*_y$ | .70$^*_x$ | 310 | 18.7 |
| 0 | .51 | .51$^*_x$ | .51$^*_x$ | 772 | 46.5 |
| − | .47$^*_z$ | .38$^*_y$ | .38$^*_x$ | 578 | 34.8 |
| **Dichotomy** | | | | | |
| + | .55 | .70 | .70 | 310 | 18.7 |
| | * | * | * | | |
| − | .49 | .45 | .45 | 1350 | 81.3 |
| Total Number of Cases (N = 100 per cent) | | | | 1660 | |

*Difference in test variable at the 5 per cent level of confidence between ridits with same subscript or adjacent to same asterisk.

Mental Health). This finding is repeated throughout the adult factors. It is of course only logical that adult experiences will be more closely related to an Adult Mental Health Rating. Similarly, as we indicated in previous chapters, childhood experiences generally are more closely related to the CMH Index. That these findings appear despite the differences in construction between the childhood and adult measures of mental health (the first being psychometric, the second a judgment) offers some support for their validity.

Although the final Adult Poor Physical Health factor was composed of the health estimate and the number of hospitalizations, several other items were under consideration; for various reasons they were not utilized.

### C. OTHER AILMENTS

The number of nonpsychosomatic ailments reported by the respondent showed a strong relationship to the Mental Health Ratings. Following a list of symptoms such as fainting spells and "nervousness," each respondent was asked, "Do you now have any *other* ailments or health problems that keep you from feeling your best?" The number of ailments *exclusive* of the list of psychosomatic conditions was then recorded by the interviewer.

Persons who reported no disorders other than those included in the list ran a low mental health risk of .47 (see Table 11-4). They were significantly better off than those reporting two, or three to six conditions (.68, .72).

### TABLE 11-4

### PROPORTIONS AND AVERAGE MENTAL HEALTH (MH II) OF RESPONDENTS ACCORDING TO NONPSYCHOSOMATIC DISORDERS BY RESPONDENTS' SOCIOECONOMIC STATUS

| Respondents' Nonpsychosomatic Disorders | Respondents' Socioeconomic Status | | | | | | | |
|---|---|---|---|---|---|---|---|---|
| | LOW | | MIDDLE | | HIGH | | TOTAL | |
| | Per Cent | $\bar{R}$ | Per Cent | $\bar{R}$ | Per Cent | $\bar{R}$ | Per Cent | $\bar{R}$ |
| None | 65.9 | $.55^*_{z,y}$ | 69.8 | $.48^*_x$ | 60.6 | $.37^*_{w,v}$ | 65.5 | $.47^*_{u,t}$ |
| One | 25.4 | .62 * | 24.5 | .53 | 30.2 | .46 * | 26.7 | .53 * |
| Two | 6.4 | $.82^*_z$ | 3.8 | $.69^*_x$ | 6.1 | $.54^*_w$ | 5.4 | $.68^*_u$ |
| Three to Six | 1.9 | $.84^*_y$ | 1.5 | (.70) | 2.4 | $.63^*_v$ | 1.9 | $.72^*_t$ |
| Don't Know, No Answer ‖ | .4 | – | .4 | – | .7 | – | .5 | – |
| Total Number of Cases (N=100 per cent) | 544 | | 556 | | 560 | | 1660 | |

* Difference in test variable at the 5 per cent level of confidence between ridits with same subscript or adjacent to same asterisk.
‖ Ridits not computed.
Parentheses ( ) enclose ridits based on less than ten cases.

It is interesting that a slightly larger proportion of the high SES group reported these other disorders. This is the reverse of the question, "About your health now, would you say it is excellent, good, fair, or poor?" In that instance the low SES reported much worse health. Several interpretations of this finding are possible. Perhaps it is due to the fact that high SES persons, with more treatment and more communication with their doctors (who treat them as social and intellectual equals), tend to know the diagnoses of their various conditions. Low SES individuals may feel they are in poor health, but may not be able to give the names of actual disease entities which the interviewer could "count." A less likely explanation is that the health of the various SES groups is almost identical, and that the low SES just complains more. This alternative is rather untenable in view of what is known about the socioeconomic distribution of most diseases. First of all, despite the combined efforts of government, management, labor, and the medical profession itself, there is unequal access to medical care which favors the wealthier segment of the population. Second, even when there is a clearcut case of equal access to medical care, such as the Salk poliomyelitis vaccine, persons of low education do not take advantage of the free vaccine at the public health stations. This was demonstrated in New York City, where many thousands of children under the age of five failed to receive polio shots. The Health Commissioner appealed to low-income parents to use the facilities of the health stations so that their children might be immunized before the polio season started. Education and attitudes toward health, medicine, and the medical profession are important factors in the use of available facilities and also in the recognition of symptoms. Thus income and education are two crucial factors affecting the reporting of specific physical ailments.

### D.  HEALTH TODAY COMPARED WITH FIVE YEARS AGO

A larger proportion of the low SES group feel their health is not as good today as it was five years ago (see Table 11-5).

While 20.2 per cent of the Lows said their health was not so good as five years earlier, only 12.5 per cent of the Highs felt the same way. On questions where health is estimated, then, we find the low SES reporting poorer health. Where somewhat more "objective" disease entities are counted, the low SES seems as healthy as, or even healthier than, the high SES. It is our feeling that the more subjective measures of general health, while reflecting in part the greater mental disturbance of the low SES, give a better picture of the actual socioeconomic differences in physical health.

It should be noted that persons who feel their health is worse than it was five years earlier are consistently in poorer mental health than persons who feel their health is the same. However, those who say their health is better than it was five years ago are in poorer mental health

## TABLE 11-5

### PROPORTIONS AND AVERAGE MENTAL HEALTH (MH II) OF RESPONDENTS ACCORDING TO THEIR HEALTH FIVE YEARS AGO COMPARED WITH THEIR PRESENT HEALTH BY RESPONDENTS' SOCIOECONOMIC STATUS

| Respondents' Health | Respondents' Socioeconomic Status | | | | | | | |
|---|---|---|---|---|---|---|---|---|
| | LOW | | MIDDLE | | HIGH | | TOTAL | |
| | Per Cent | $\bar{R}$ | Per Cent | $\bar{R}$ | Per Cent | $\bar{R}$ | Per Cent | $\bar{R}$ |
| Same | 59.9 | .54* | 68.5 | .45* | 69.1 | .37*<br>* | 66.0 | .45*<br>* |
| Better | 19.3 | .60<br>* | 16.7 | .53 | 18.4 | .47 | 18.1 | .54<br>* |
| Not So Good | 20.2 | .73* | 14.6 | .66* | 12.5 | .56* | 15.7 | .66* |
| Don't Know, No Answer ‖ | .6 | – | .2 | – | 0.0 | – | .2 | – |
| Total Number of Cases (N=100 per cent) | 544 | | 556 | | 560 | | 1660 | |

* Difference in test variable at the 5 per cent level of confidence between ridits adjacent to same asterisk.
‖ Ridits not computed.

than those who report their health has stayed the same. This is true in all three SES groups, and is statistically significant in the high SES and the sample as a whole. If this were a rare response, it might be suspect just because of its rarity. However, about 18 per cent feel their health is better now; almost one-fifth of the sample. Perhaps we start out with the wrong assumption; namely, that people who say their health is better are optimistic, and therefore should exhibit better mental health. Perhaps this 18 per cent had experienced a major illness or operation during the last five years. They are "better" now in the sense that they have recovered from the particular illness. However, the particular illness or operation may have left psychological scars as well as physical ones. Perhaps these people who are now "better" had to feel "worse" at some time during the previous five years. They may, therefore, be a selected group who have worse mental health now because they have recently been through a physical ordeal which has left its mark on their psychological makeup. The fact that the seemingly "optimistic" response is associated with somewhat worse mental health risk may very well indicate that this report of health is more objective than subjective.

### E.   HEALTH WORRIES

A much more subjective item was "Health is something that worries me: often, sometimes, or never." Those who often worried about their health ran a very high mental health risk of .75, as opposed to those who worried sometimes (.55), or never (.42). (See Table 11-6.) A much larger proportion of Lows (13.6 per cent) than of Highs (3.9 per cent) worried often about their physical health. Since we had other items of health information available, we did not use "health worries" in the final physical health factor.

The large proportion who reported that they "never" worried about their health (53.7 per cent) is quite striking. The denial of health prob-

### TABLE 11-6

### PROPORTIONS AND AVERAGE MENTAL HEALTH (MH II) OF RESPONDENTS WHO WORRY ABOUT HEALTH BY RESPONDENTS' SOCIOECONOMIC STATUS

| "Health Is Something That Worries Me" | Respondents' Socioeconomic Status | | | | | | | |
|---|---|---|---|---|---|---|---|---|
| | LOW | | MIDDLE | | HIGH | | TOTAL | |
| | Per Cent | $\bar{R}$ | Per Cent | $\bar{R}$ | Per Cent | $\bar{R}$ | Per Cent | $\bar{R}$ |
| Often | 13.6 | .79* | 7.9 | .72* | 3.9 | .66* | 8.4 | .75* |
| | | * | | * | | * | | * |
| Sometimes | 37.3 | .63 | 35.6 | .55 | 38.4 | .48 | 37.1 | .55 |
| | | * | | * | | * | | * |
| Never | 47.6 | .49* | 55.8 | .43* | 57.5 | .35* | 53.7 | .42* |
| Don't Know, No Answer ⟩ | 1.5 | — | .7 | — | .2 | — | .8 | — |
| Total Number of Cases (N=100 per cent) | 544 | | 556 | | 560 | | 1660 | |

* Difference in test variable at the 5 per cent level of confidence between ridits adjacent to same asterisk.
⟩ Ridits not computed.

lems might in itself be considered a symptom of mental disturbance. People who "never" worried about their health might not get yearly physical examinations or take out health insurance. A fair amount of "socialized anxiety" is probably necessary for survival. Certainly a person with no concern about walking in front of cars would be considered mentally disturbed.

Where fear or concern is justified, it should be associated with positive mental health or constructive adaptation (as for example, the fear experienced when crossing a crowded street or highway). Again, where fear is justified, but is absent (the inveterate jay-walker), mental disturbance is suspected. Similarly, where fear is not justified, it can be considered anxiety, and a sign of mental disturbance (for example, severe anxiety experienced when crossing a little-traveled country road with a clear view and no car in sight). It was possible to check the appropriateness of the respondent's health worries by cross-tabulating them with his health estimate. This can be represented by the following paradigm:

HEALTH ESTIMATE

|  | | EXCELLENT | POOR |
|---|---|---|---|
| WORRIES ABOUT HEALTH | OFTEN | The Hypochondriac <br> Ⓐ <br> .60 <br><br> He has anxiety about his health *(unjustified worries and fears).* | Ⓑ <br> .92 |
|  | NEVER | Ⓒ <br> .35 | The Denier <br> Ⓓ <br> (.85) <br><br> *(He denies or ignores his health problems.)* |

Figure 11-1. Justified and Unjustified Health Worries

People whose health is excellent (or so report it) but who often worry about their health (Group A) show anxiety over their health which seems unjustified. They are likely to be considered hypochondriacs. We expected them to exhibit worse mental health than the legitimate worriers, whose health is poor and who worry about it often (Group B). This is not the case, however, since the Bs have a risk of .92, and the As a risk of only .60. We see that the poor health estimate and worrying about health are roughly additive, and reporting both is worse than reporting only one.

What about Group D which denies that it worries about its poor health? The Ds (.85) do not have worse mental health than the Bs (.92), although they should, according to our hypothesis. Those in poor health who never worry about it should be more disturbed than those in poor health who do worry about it. In general, however, people who "never worry" have a risk of .42, so that the Ds risk of .85 is extremely high. Also, if we examine Table 11-7 carefully we see that among those in poor health, those who "never worry" (.85) are worse off than those who "sometimes" worry about their health (.77).

Even though this difference is not statistically reliable, there is enough evidence here to support the hypothesis that persons who never worry about serious physical health problems tend to be mentally disturbed. No parallel support for the hypothesis about hypochondriasis is found in the data. Perhaps this is a less severe symptom than the denial of health problems. It is certainly more socially acceptable behavior in the "Aspirin Age" of pills, patent remedies, and self-administered pep and tranquilizing drugs.

In such a study we are always faced with the problem that inconsistency in answering questions is in itself a sign of mental disturbance. If in one part of an interview a person says that his health is poor, and in another part he says that he never worries about his health, he is in a way being inconsistent. Only 8 people out of 1660 (12.3 per cent of 65, see Table 11-6) answered in this fashion. We have no way of knowing whether only these *responses* to a questionnaire are inconsistent or whether these responses reflect a real inconsistency between the respondent's health and his concern about his health. At any rate, inconsistency, whether in questionnaire responses or in actual behavior, is probably a good indicator of mental disturbance.

How do multiple hospitalizations and health worries combine with low SES in the mentally disturbed person? Often very serious illness in a spouse can markedly affect the economic status of a fairly stable wage earner. The low status of those in poor health, both physical and mental, may often be a *result* of their illness.

Martha F. (see footnote, p. 166) has poor physical health and worries about it to the point of being preoccupied with death. She was born in a small city

## TABLE 11-7

## PROPORTIONS AND AVERAGE MENTAL HEALTH (MH II) OF RESPONDENTS WHO WORRY ABOUT HEALTH, BY RESPONDENTS' PRESENT HEALTH

*Respondents' Present Health*

| "Health Is Something That Worries Me" | EXCELLENT | | GOOD | | FAIR | | POOR | | TOTAL | |
|---|---|---|---|---|---|---|---|---|---|---|
| | Per Cent | R̄ | Per Cent | R̄ | Per Cent | R̄ | Per Cent | R̄ | Per Cent | R̄ |
| Often | 3.1 | .60* | 5.4 | .63* | 15.7 | .78* * | 56.9 | .92 | 8.5 | .75 |
| Sometimes | 26.7 | .42 | 40.5 | .56 * | 52.3 | .63 | 30.7 | .77 | 37.4 | .55 |
| Never | 70.2 | .35* | 54.1 | .44* | 32.0 | .61* | 12.3 | (.85) | 54.1 | .42 |
| Total Number of Cases (N = 100 per cent) | 577 | | 699 | | 300 | | 65 | | 1641ᵃ | |

[a] There were 19 cases who replied "Don't Know or No Answer" to one or both questions.

*Difference in test variable at the 5 per cent level of confidence between ridits adjacent to same asterisk.

Parentheses ( ) enclose ridits based on less than ten cases.

near Midtown, the daughter of a paper hanger with a grammar school education. One of several children, she remembers her childhood as "carefree," except for poor physical health. Plagued by the semiannual bouts with bronchitis, in addition to more than her share of the routine childhood diseases, she envied the good health of others. She contrasted herself with her mother: "I'd like to have her health." Suddenly, in her early teens, her father had a "melancholy nervous breakdown." Martha reacted violently to his illness. A feeling of oddness came over her. For quite a while she thought that she was going to die. Her father recovered in the hospital, but Martha's life began a tempestuous spiral.

She married before finishing secondary school and her husband shortly ran away. Martha, now in her early forties, remarried and had three children. This time poor health returned to upset the marriage. Her life became a succession of intervals in the hospital. Five years ago she had a tumor removed. Her husband took her to California to recover where she was hospitalized for gall bladder trouble. The next year she had a hysterectomy. She thought she would die. When she slept she was afraid that she wouldn't wake up and begged for help. After the hysterectomy, she threw up continually and lost 15 pounds in a month. Two years ago she had a nervous breakdown and a serious chest operation, after which her death fears returned. "I feel something icy cold come over me and then I can't catch my breath. I lose my strength, my knees buckle, I just fall to pieces." These physical symptoms were accompanied by an extreme fear of death and a propensity for contemplating graves and ghosts.

Martha's ill health disrupted all other aspects of her life and of her family. Her husband lost his job over her sickness. He had to stay with her because she became so frightened. Unable to cope with the responsibility of a home, they moved in with her brother. The expected friction resulting from a large number of people living together in a small house was aggravated by her ill health and subsequent touchiness and irritability. She feels that her husband no longer understands her. She argues continuously with her brother and sister-in-law over trifles. They feel that she has changed somehow, that she is different from what she used to be. Unable to stand the "chatter of crowds" Martha is becoming increasingly ingrown, preoccupied with health worries and death fears which in turn worsen her condition by interfering with eating and sleeping, and delaying her recovery from her physical illnesses. Her husband's inability to provide a separate home has increased her problems. Yet her need for constant supervision has continually lost him good jobs. Only her hospitalization can break this vicious circle and restore economic and emotional stability to the father and children.

## F.   HEIGHT

Tangentially related to physical health is the respondent's height. All respondents were asked their height in four-inch intervals. Surprisingly enough, taller persons, on the average, had better mental health (see Table 11-8).

## TABLE 11-8

## PROPORTIONS AND AVERAGE MENTAL HEALTH (MH II) BY RESPONDENTS' HEIGHT AND FATHERS' SOCIOECONOMIC STATUS

Fathers' Socioeconomic Status

| Respondents' Height | LOW | | MIDDLE | | HIGH | | TOTAL | |
|---|---|---|---|---|---|---|---|---|
| | Per Cent | R̄ | Per Cent | R̄ | Per Cent | R̄ | Per Cent | R̄ |
| *MALE* | | | | | | | | |
| 5'1'' - 5'4'' | 3.7 | (.66) | 7.8 | .55 | 1.6 | (.50) | 4.9 | .57 |
| 5'5'' - 5'8'' | 44.5 | .57 | 36.8 | .51 | 30.7 | .48 | 37.3 | .53 |
| 5'9'' - 6' | 45.0 | .53 | 48.2 | .50 | 47.4 | .45 | 47.1 | .49 |
| 6'1'' - and more | 5.8 | .59 | 7.2 | .46 | 20.3 | .44 | 10.4 | .46 |
| Don't Know, No Answer ‡ | 1.0 | – | 0.0 | – | 0.0 | – | .3 | – |
| Total Number of Cases (N = 100 per cent) | 191 | | 307 | | 192 | | 690 | |
| *FEMALE* | | | | | | | | |
| 4' or less - 4'8'' | 1.0 | (.86) | 2.2 | (.58) | .6 | (.55) | 1.3 | .64 |
| 4'9'' - 5' | 10.6 | .56 | 7.7 | .58 | 2.2 | .34 | 6.8 | .54 |
| 5'1'' - 5'4'' | 55.7 | .57 | 56.9 | .48 | 40.0 | .46 | 51.1 | .51 |
| 5'5'' - 5'8'' | 31.3 | .52 | 31.3 | .46 | 52.1 | .44 | 38.0 | .47 |
| 5'9'' - 6' | 1.4 | (.77) | 1.9 | (.45) | 5.1 | .38 | 2.8 | .45 |
| Total Number of Cases (N = 100 per cent) | 291 | | 364 | | 315 | | 970 1660 | |

‡ Ridits not computed.

Parentheses ( ) enclose ridits based on less than ten cases.

While the differences between taller and shorter persons are not all statistically significant, the trend between taller and shorter persons is strong enough for us to consider the results seriously. Since the height range of men and women is quite different, the respondent's sex was controlled. Again, since we suspected that diet and other factors tend to keep persons of lower socioeconomic status from attaining their full growth, the socioeconomic status of the respondent's father was also controlled. The relationship between mental health and height still remains, despite sex and SES controls. The importance of these controls is evident if we examine Table 11-8 more closely.

If we look at the males who are 6'1" or more, we find that they constitute only 5.8 per cent of the low and 7.2 per cent of the middle SES males. However, 20.3 per cent of the high SES males are 6'1" or over. Since height is so closely correlated with socioeconomic status (for both men and women, as our table shows), it was necessary to show that height is related to mental health *within* each socioeconomic level. One exception to this trend is found among the tallest males and females in the low SES, who show a tendency to run a slightly higher mental health risk than those of moderate height.

There is a stereotype of the tall woman as ungainly and encountering difficulty in finding suitable male companionship. This is probably a false stereotype, for women in the 5'9" to 6' category show extremely good mental health ratings in the middle to high SES. If they were very isolated from male companionship it is doubtful that they would exhibit such a low mental health risk. The fulfillment of such goals as dating, marriage, and childbearing is therefore probably not frustrated among tall women, since their impairment risk drops rather than rises.

If height showed a clear relationship to mental health, would it continue to do so if weight were controlled? After all, our judgments of obesity, which have often been considered a concomitant of mental disturbance, are based on a combination of height and weight. An index was therefore constructed which took account of height and weight simultaneously. The sample was divided into thirds by weight, and then examined by height (short, low medium, high medium, and tall). In general, taller people still exhibited better mental health. However, among the "underweight" third, the "high medium" group was significantly more disturbed (.63) than the average for "underweights" in general (.56). (This table is not included because of its complexity.) Some SES variation was noticeable. For example, tall thin persons of high SES had an extremely low mental health risk, as opposed to similar middle and low SES persons who had very high risks. Moreover, all low SES underweights, no matter what height, ran risks above .67. There is a general tendency for tall *thin* people to have somewhat worse mental health, while other categories of tall persons (particularly those in the middle range of weight and of high SES) tend to have excellent mental health.

The myriad interpretations suggested by these findings can be treated only sketchily here. Although we know that the upper limit or range of height is genetically determined, we also suspect that diet, climate, and many other factors can encourage or discourage growth within those limits. No man is fifteen feet tall, nor one foot high. Yet we know that the second generation in the United States is, on the average, taller than the immigrant generation. Suppose we partially control such factors as diet, by examining only those *born into* high SES families. We still find that taller people are mentally healthier. This is true even if they are a little thin or "underweight." Perhaps their height is an advantage in their social relationships. Perhaps both men and women who are tall command the respect and attention of their peers. This may bolster their mental health. It is also possible that physical and athletic prowess are associated with height as well as with general physical vigor. These are certainly considered assets in our society and might be important in the development of a positive self-image.

On the other hand, we know that anxiety, depression, and elation are emotional states associated with the production of chemical substances. These may be related to the production of pituitary hormones. Much research is needed before we can say how growth is related to emotions and mental health.

There is strong evidence in the data that height is associated with the health estimate. Tall people are most likely to report excellent health. This is true of both men and women. Similarly, a larger proportion of short people report that they are in fair or poor health. Among men 5′1″ to 5′4″ only 11.8 per cent say they are in excellent health, compared with 50 per cent of those 6′1″ or over. As height increases, the proportion of those in "excellent health" increases steadily. Again, women show the same trend. Although all three women under 4′4″ report excellent health, the trend holds for all women 4′5″ or above. In the 4′5″ category, only 10 per cent of the women say their health is excellent, compared with 51.9 per cent of the women 5′9″ to 6′ tall.

Why do taller people report better health? Is it because they actually are in better physical condition? Is it because they *feel* better about everything in general, including their health, or is it a combination of many factors? Some clues can be derived from data that have not yet been introduced. In Chapter 13, we will find that the proportion of adults in Poor Physical Health increases sharply with age. While only 9 per cent report poor health in the twenties, 26.8 per cent report it in the fifties. It is only reasonable to expect that the deteriorative diseases, part of the natural process of aging, will begin to take their toll in the later decades. This increasing proportion of persons reporting poor health as age increases lends credence to the relative objectivity of the report.

However, many factors are interwoven in the relationship between height and mental health. Tall people may very well be in better physical health, but tall people are also nonimmigrant. They are also younger, for immigrants in Midtown are mostly in their forties and fifties. We know that younger people have better mental health. In Volume I, age was the one factor which, along with SES, showed a clear and independent relationship to mental health.

Does this mean that older people have poorer mental health simply because they are in poorer physical health? When age and physical health are simultaneously related to mental health, we find that age and physical health differences are independent of each other. Within each physical health category, there are increasing risks with each advancing age decade. The differences between risk of the twenties and the fifties average .07. Similarly, within each age decade, the differences between the risks of those in good and poor physical health averages .30.

This shows us that although the mental health risks of aging and of poor physical health are to some extent independent, the risk variation of Poor Physical Health is about four times greater. Therefore, even though there are proportionally more older people reporting poor health, chronological age itself is nowhere as important to mental health as is physical health (at least up to age sixty).

In view of this, it is probably because height is related to physical health rather than to age that it shows a relationship to mental health. Similarly, the fact that immigrants have a greater mental health risk than the native born may be linked more to their height and physical health rather than to the assumed stresses of immigration and acculturation. In fact, in Volume I we found that immigration's relationship to mental health virtually disappeared when socioeconomic status was controlled.

Although time has not permitted a more thorough analysis of these complex relationships, an obvious first step in secondary analysis would consist of establishing the relationship between age, mental health, parental socioeconomic status, and height simultaneously. There is reason to believe that older people of low status are shorter. (We know they are in poorer physical health, and height is related to physical health.) It would be of interest to know whether controlling SES and age explains away the differences in mental health found between tall and short people, or whether these are equally important factors in mental health risk.

## Poor Interpersonal Affiliations

It is quite unnecessary to document the fact that most students of human behavior consider interpersonal relationships to be intimately associated with mental health and disturbance. Poor interpersonal relationships may be both the result and the cause of mental disturbance. This does not mean that attempts to specify the conditions under which poor relationships are causal or not have been abandoned. A recent study of schizophrenic patients showed that they had sought isolation in transient accomodations in large cities, rather than having been isolated or rejected by society. This study and others are cited in Chapter 6 in a discussion of social isolation as a symptom or a cause of mental disturbance.

An attempt was made to choose items for the Interpersonal Affiliations factor that were more, rather than less, objective. Questions were chosen so that the units the respondent reported could be counted. Thus the number of his close friends, the number of organizations to which he belonged, and the number of neighbors with whom he was friendly were combined into an index of Interpersonal Affiliations for each respondent. The exact wording of the items is reported here, to allow the reader to judge the meaning of the responses.

Altogether about how many people are there whom you consider to be *close* friends—not counting relatives or neighbors? (*If necessary, add:*) Just give a rough estimate. (*Definition of a "close friend"*: A person to whom you can tell what's on your mind.)

Do you attend meetings or affairs of any organization, societies, or clubs? (*If Yes*) How many altogether?

About how many neighbors around here do you know well enough to visit with?

## TABLE 11-9

### PROPORTIONS AND AVERAGE MENTAL HEALTH (MH II) OF RESPONDENTS ACCORDING TO NUMBER OF CLOSE FRIENDS AND RESPONDENTS' SOCIOECONOMIC STATUS

| Number of Close Friends | Respondents' Socioeconomic Status | | | | | | | |
| | LOW | | MIDDLE | | HIGH | | TOTAL | |
| | Per Cent | R̄ | Per Cent | R̄ | Per Cent | R̄ | Per Cent | R̄ |
|---|---|---|---|---|---|---|---|---|
| None | 12.7 | .74 | 5.9 | .69 | 1.8 | .55 | 6.7 | .71*$_{zyxwvu}$ |
| 1 | 10.8 | .67 | 4.5 | .63 | 0.5 | (.33) | 5.2 | .65* |
| | | | | | | | | * |
| 2 to 3 | 24.2 | .59 | 27.6 | .53 | 17.7 | .47 | 23.1 | .53*$_z$ |
| 4 to 5 | 19.3 | .52 | 19.5 | .46 | 21.4 | .39 | 20.1 | .45*$_y$ |
| 6 to 9 | 10.8 | .58 | 14.7 | .44 | 18.6 | .40 | 14.8 | .46*$_x$ |
| 10 to 14 | 10.1 | .53 | 14.7 | .47 | 20.7 | .42 | 15.2 | .46*$_w$ |
| 15 or more | 8.5 | .52 | 10.4 | .43 | 16.1 | .36 | 11.7 | .42*$_v$ |
| Other | 1.8 | .58 | 1.8 | .42 | 2.1 | .46 | 1.9 | .48*$_u$ |
| Don't Know, No Answer Ɨ | 1.8 | – | 0.9 | – | 1.1 | – | 1.3 | – |
| Total Number of Cases (N=100 per cent) | 544 | | 556 | | 560 | | 1660 | |

* Difference in test variable at the 5 per cent level of confidence between ridits with same subscript or adjacent to same asterisk.
Ɨ Ridits not computed.
Parentheses ( ) enclose ridit based on less than ten cases.

### A.   NUMBER OF CLOSE FRIENDS

The number of the respondent's close friends was very highly associated with mental health risk. Table 11-9 shows that having no friends (.71) involved considerably greater risk than having two to fifteen or more friends.

Two to three friends were reported by the largest number of persons (23.1 per cent) and their risk of .53 is just a little bit above par (.50). The decrease in risk above four friends is not significant or striking. In general, however, the more friends one reports, the less one's mental health risk. This is true at all three SES levels.

The proportion of persons with no close friends is amazingly different in the three SES groups: 1.8 per cent of the Highs, 5.9 per cent of the Middles, and 12.7 per cent of the Lows. The increase in risk (over the average for their SES group) for the friendless is about the same: .15 among the High friendless (.55 compared to the group average of .40), .19 among the Middles, and .14 among the Lows. On this basis we can say that being friendless is of approximately equal significance for those of each SES level.

Almost twice as many Highs as Lows have six or more friends. In addition, 16.1 per cent of the Highs and only 8.5 per cent of the Lows have 15 or more friends. This ratio is also reflected in other categories.

Obviously we cannot say that the Lows are more disturbed and therefore make fewer friends, nor can we prove that Lows are more isolated and therefore develop poorer mental health. Such questions cannot be answered by this study. The very concept of "close friendship" may vary greatly between the social levels, despite the printed definition offered each respondent. We find almost no SES variation in the number of neighbors with whom the respondents are friendly. Friendship patterns vary with SES, while the degree of neighboring does not. All we can claim is that close friendship (whatever that may mean to people of various social levels) is strongly associated with mental health risk.

The circular interplay of social rejection and the isolating effects of mental disturbance are shown in the story of Horace Bronson. His nervous symptoms make him appear strange and unattractive to potential friends. His own preoccupation with his symptoms aggravates people's initial distaste by making him dull and imperceptive, incapable of successfully relating to others. The social isolation inflicted on him only causes him to withdraw further.

Horace (see footnote, page 166) was born in a small town in the northeast. His family was of low SES, and he has remained a Low, despite a chance at a college education which he couldn't complete. His father was an auto mechanic with a grade school education. His mother had always had a hard life, just wanting her boys to grow up and do well. Horace himself matured slowly. He was over three before he began talking the way children usually do a year earlier. His mother impressed this on him by constantly recalling that he wasn't a talker. When he finally began to talk it became apparent that Horace suffered from stuttering. He remembers being unable to pronounce "train" and "pussy cat." The other kids would tease him. After this initial rejection Horace showed progressive withdrawal, becoming obsessively concerned with his body, doing odd things as pulling out hairs and continually scratching his temples.

At college Horace avoided his contemporaries and often roamed the streets trying to remember each street name. He spent hours studying elaborate maps.

He couldn't remember the names of his fraternity brothers or his professors even though he took a memory course. He would confuse people who didn't even look alike. He also had trouble remembering words and was afraid to ask for a job or express an opinion. Horace's painful awareness of his inability to communicate is symbolized by his hobby, collecting "valuable" words. "I'm studying vocabulary till my eyes burn. I've bought vocabulary books and two dictionaries and write them in longhand on cards . . . collecting words."

Horace also seeks solace in his wildly fantastic dreams. In reality he is a mail clerk. In his fantasies, however, he becomes an expert in communication, a "popular public relations man or a writer for a big corporation." He realizes that he is not attractive to girls. He feels that sex is never what he has built it up to be, yet he dreams of being "the world's biggest playboy." Even in his daydreams Horace does not seem to conceive of warm human companionship but only of superficial commercialized images: the public relations man and the playboy.

### B. NUMBER OF ORGANIZATIONS

The number of organizations whose meetings the respondents attended was only moderately related to mental health. The greatest significant difference was observed between those who mentioned no organizational activity (.54) and those who were involved with one or more organizations (about .45; see Table 11-10).

There was also a slight decrease in risk from those who belonged to one or two organizations (.47) to those who belonged to three, four, or five, or more organizations (.41, .38, and .39).

This item merely helped in culling a few persons who were very integrated in their society, belonged to many organizations, and were anything but social isolates. They constitute about 20 per cent of the sample. Again, they are predominantly high SES in composition (comprising about 10 per cent of the Lows and about 38 per cent of the Highs). We tend to think of the middle stratum as the "joiners," the Babbitts who need to belong and therefore join everything and anything. At least in Midtown, principally individuals at the upper end of the middle and the upper stratum belong to two or more organizations.

About 44 per cent of the Highs belong to no organizations, compared with about 64 per cent of the Lows. However, the low status nonjoiners are much "worse off" (.62) than the low status joiners. The high status nonjoiners (.43) are no better or worse off than high status joiners. Being a member of a club or association may be a more frequent phenomenon among the Highs, but (perhaps just because of its frequency) joining has almost no implications for mental health among the Highs.

## TABLE 11-10

### PROPORTIONS AND AVERAGE MENTAL HEALTH (MH II) OF RESPONDENTS ACCORDING TO NUMBER OF ORGANIZATIONS IN WHICH ACTIVE, AND RESPONDENTS' SOCIOECONOMIC STATUS

| Number of Organizations | Respondents' Socioeconomic Status | | | | | | | |
|---|---|---|---|---|---|---|---|---|
| | LOW | | MIDDLE | | HIGH | | TOTAL | |
| | Per Cent | $\bar{R}$ | Per Cent | $\bar{R}$ | Per Cent | $\bar{R}$ | Per Cent | $\bar{R}$ |
| 1 | 23.3 | .55 | 24.8 | .44 | 18.9 | .40 | 22.3 | $.47^*_y$ |
| 2 | 6.8 | $.49^*_z$ | 5.4 | .50 | 11.3 | .44 | 7.8 | .47 |
| 3 | 2.4 | .46 | 4.7 | .48 | 10.2 | .36 | 5.8 | $.41^*_x$ |
| 4 | 0.4 | (.22) | 2.5 | .34 | 5.9 | .40 | 3.0 | $.38^*_w$ |
| 5 or more | 0.6 | (.57) | 1.6 | (.36) | 10.2 | .39 | 4.2 | .39* |
| No Organizational Activity Mentioned | 63.6 | $.62^*_z$ | 57.9 | .53 | 43.5 | .43 | 54.9 | $.54^*_{y,x,w}$ |
| Don't Know, No Answer ‡ | 2.9 | – | 3.1 | – | 0.0 | – | 2.0 | – |
| Total Number of Cases (N=100 per cent) | 544 | | 556 | | 560 | | 1660 | |

* Difference in test variable at the 5 per cent level of confidence between ridits with same subscript.
‡ Ridits not computed.
Parentheses ( ) enclose ridits based on less than ten cases.

### C. NUMBER OF NEIGHBORS

The number of neighbors with whom the respondent was friendly also showed only a moderate relationship to mental health. Persons friendly with no neighbors, or one, or two, or three, were close to the average on mental health risk (.52, .54, and .50; see Table 11-11). Only persons friendly with ten or more neighbors (.44) were significantly healthier than the rest of the sample.

Almost one-third of the sample reported they were friendly with no neighbors. This is a rather interesting commentary on the structure of friendships in a metropolis such as Midtown. Perhaps this figure would be much reduced in a rural area where physical proximity is more of a factor in social relationships. The availability of public transportation in the city is also a factor to be considered, for one can have friends widely distributed and yet within easy traveling distance and need not depend as much on geographically close neighbors.

We felt that neighboring would be more of a low SES pattern and that close friends would be more numerous in the high SES. Close friends did abound among the Highs, but neighbors were equally distributed between the social levels. Almost identical proportions of the three SES levels reported being friendly with one, two to three neighbors, and so on. Although neighboring was an item of only moderate strength, it enabled us to divide the sample with ease into three groups when combined with "friends" and "organizations."

These three items were fused into a final factor by considering persons with less than four friends, less than two neighbors, and with membership

## TABLE 11-11

### PROPORTIONS AND AVERAGE MENTAL HEALTH (MH II) OF RESPONDENTS ACCORDING TO NUMBER OF NEIGHBORS WITH WHOM FRIENDLY AND RESPONDENTS' SOCIOECONOMIC STATUS

*Respondents' Socioeconomic Status*

| Number of Neighbors | LOW Per Cent | $\bar{R}$ | MIDDLE Per Cent | $\bar{R}$ | HIGH Per Cent | $\bar{R}$ | TOTAL Per Cent | $\bar{R}$ |
|---|---|---|---|---|---|---|---|---|
| None | 31.8 | .63 | 32.7 | .53 | 33.3 | .43 | 32.7 | $.52^*_z$ |
| 1 | 11.1 | .66 | 11.9 | .54 | 8.6 | .41 | 10.1 | $.54^*_y$ |
| 2 to 3 | 19.7 | .57 | 17.1 | .52 | 18.8 | .42 | 18.5 | $.50^*_x$ |
| 4 to 5 | 12.1 | .54 | 11.5 | .49 | 11.6 | .38 | 11.7 | .47 |
| 6 to 9 | 7.2 | .52 | 6.8 | .44 | 7.7 | .44 | 7.2 | .47 |
| 10 or more | 14.3 | .56 | 17.1 | .41 | 18.6 | .39 | 16.7 | $.44^*_{z,y,x}$ |
| Don't Know, No Answer ‡ | 3.5 | – | 2.9 | – | 1.4 | – | 2.6 | – |
| Total Number of Cases (N=100 per cent) | 544 | | 556 | | 560 | | 1660 | |

* Difference in test variable at the 5 per cent level of confidence between ridits with same subscript.
‡ Ridits not computed.

## TABLE 11-12

### DISTRIBUTION, PROPORTIONS, AND AVERAGE MENTAL HEALTH (CMH, MH I, MH II) ACCORDING TO POOR INTERPERSONAL AFFILIATIONS TRICHOTOMIZED AND DICHOTOMIZED

| Poor Interpersonal Affiliations | *Respondents' Mental Health* | | | | |
|---|---|---|---|---|---|
| | CMH | MH I | MH II | No. of Cases | Per Cent of Cases |
| Trichotomy | | | | | |
| + | $.55^*_z$ | $.64^*_y$ | $.65^*_x$ | 209 | 12.6 |
| 0 | .53 * | $.52^*_y$ | $.53^*_x$ | 597 | 36.0 |
| − | $.47^*_z$ | $.45^*_y$ | $.45^*_x$ | 854 | 51.4 |
| Dichotomy | | | | | |
| + | .55 | .64 * | .65 * | 209 | 12.6 |
| − | .49 | .48 | .48 | 1451 | 87.4 |
| Total Number of Cases (N = 100 per cent) | | | | 1660 | |

*Difference in test variable at the 5 per cent level of confidence between ridits with same subscript or adjacent to same asterisk.

in no organizations as poor risks with regard to the Mental Health Rating. The Mental Health I risks, given in Table 11-12, are .64, .52, and .45. Since a wide ridit range is also achieved in the dichotomy, the factor can be considered one of the strongest isolated.

Several items in the questionnaire were available for the construction of the Interpersonal Affiliations factor, other than the three utilized. They are nevertheless of interest to both the clinician and the student of community organization. Tabular presentation of these items is not made.

### D. RELATIVES' FAMILIES

Only 8.9 per cent said "None" to the question "How many families do you see fairly often (about 5 to 6 times a year) of your relatives in and around New York City?" Those who said "None" (.58) were significantly worse off with respect to mental health than those who said "two or three"

(.48) or "ten or more" (.41). They were somewhat worse off than persons answering one, four or five, and six, seven, eight, or nine (.52, .50, .52). No significant differences appeared within the SES groups, although persons reporting "no families visited fairly often" show increased risk at each SES level.

There are no proportional differences between the SES groups greater than 4 per cent. This is noteworthy, for we are often inclined to believe that persons of low status (and particularly immigrants, who by and large are of low status in this sample) have an extended familial structure, and tend to rely on cousins and uncles as well as siblings' families. The distribution for the total sample is as follows: none 8.9 per cent, one 16.7 per cent, two to three 23.7 per cent, four to five 12.8 per cent, six to nine 6.7 per cent, ten or more 5.1 per cent, no relatives in New York City 24.8 per cent. At least in the metropolis, immigrants as well as the native born seem to visit more with neighbors and friends than with extended family who live outside the household.

Jean O. demonstrates the importance for the immigrant of having an extended family. She is isolated from both friends and siblings by her depression and irritability. Immigration has been a trigger for her depression. In turn, the irritability that often accompanies a depression has cut her off from her few relatives, potential friends, and even her jobs. The friendlessness of some Lows may be to some degree associated with their immigration.

Jean O. (see footnote, page 166) was born in a rural county, one of several children in a low SES family. When she was in her teens her mother died of a stroke. Her father, an unskilled laborer, was hospitalized for a nervous breakdown. Then Jean was offered passage to New York. This seemed a fortuitous escape from the domination of a mentally disturbed father who had undergone shock treatment. He had been very strict and disapproved of going steady with one boy. The change unfortunately did not prove idyllic. Shortly after her arrival in New York she began arguing with her sister-in-law Sally and her brother Donald. They seemed to Jean to have set up a conspiracy against her. Sally wore her clothes when she was out. That didn't seem fair, even though Jean in turn borrowed Sally's clothes. She felt that Donald argued continually and voiced opinions on things like washing machines when he didn't actually know anything about them.

Her sister didn't want her in their apartment. All she had left of her family was Sally and Donald, and they both irritated her.

Jean began to develop various complaints. She was unable to sleep and had to be treated by a doctor for her nerves. She was given tranquilizing pills but people at home, on the street, and in the office continued to annoy her. In the process of rushing to work they seemed to be making a special effort to push against her in the subway. "Men follow me and make passes." Noise and excitement, and people in crowds upset her. Jean felt that she was extremely sensitive and resented an imaginary hostility or criticism on the part of others. Her growing irritability and distaste for criticism cost her several jobs.

Jean's irritability and boredom were not confined to the office and home, but rather molded all her interpersonal relationships. Though she claims a few close friends, this seems unlikely considering her volatile temperament. She complained, "I'm slow to make friends . . . I don't understand them, and they don't understand me. They have a different sense of humor from people back home. I happen to be funny. I joke and kid." She insinuated that these potential friends are less interesting than she is, especially the boys who don't interest her at all. They only bore her when they keep calling her ·up. Jean says she would like to marry a rich man, but when she finally met one, she wasn't interested. She is bored, even when she does something she should be enjoying.

### E.  RECREATION

The amount and type of recreation an individual reported was considered to give clues to his interpersonal relations. Each person was asked, "Outside of spending time with your family, friends, and work, what are the main things you do in your spare time?" The sheer number of activities mentioned showed a moderate relationship to mental health (significant in the total sample, but not within the SES groups). Persons reporting none, one, two, three to four, and five or more spare-time activities had risks of .60, .54, .52, .49, and .42 respectively, the last risk being significantly less than the first three.

The high SES, as might be expected, engaged much more in spare-time activities, since 23.9 per cent reported five or more activities compared with 4.8 per cent of the Lows. The distribution of activities in the whole sample was none, 2.5 per cent, one, 10.0 per cent, two, 25.9 per cent, three to four, 47.7 per cent, five or more, 13.9 per cent. A large proportion of these activities involved attendance of mass media, such as radio, television, and movies.

Although no attempt has yet been made to calculate the average mental health risk of each spare-time activity, the distribution of these activities in itself is of interest. Over three-fifths of the sample (62.5 per cent) utilized mass media (radio, TV, and movies); another 48.5 per cent engaged in reading; about a third (34.9 per cent) participated in outdoor activities, sports or walking. Less popular were arts or handicrafts, such as painting or sewing (25.1 per cent), music, such as playing instruments, records, attending concerts or operas (24.1 per cent), other hobbies (14.6 per cent), and spectator sports (12.7 per cent). The least common spare-time activities were volunteer work for charities or other organizations (9.3 per cent) and "self-improvement" through school or on the job (9.0 per cent). Only 2.5 per cent reported no spare-time activities, while 42.4 per cent had one or more activities which could not be classified in these categories. Since almost half the sample engaged in three or four activities, we can say that Midtowners seem to be active, although they are not necessarily "industrious" (turning more to mass media and reading than to handicrafts and "self-improvement"). It is easy to see that not all these activities fall into the category of creative activity. Yet, creative or not, activity seems to be associated with decreased mental health risk.

We felt that those activities which involved positive action or effort on the part of the respondent would probably be associated with good mental health. On the other hand, we guessed that passive or spectator participation, such as watching television or listening to the radio, would be linked to poorer mental health. The data seemed to support this guess: in the sample as a whole, people whose spare time was taken up with what we classified as "active participation" (hobbies, sports, reading) were somewhat better off (.48) than those who "passively" ingested the mass media (.53).

If one were to find through clinical experience that people with active interests and hobbies were in better mental health, it would not be surprising. Only 48.0 per cent of the Lows are "active," compared to 59.6 per cent of the Middles, and 73.9 per cent of the Highs. Their respective risks are .57, .49, and .41, very close to the risks of .60, .49, and .40 for the three SES levels as a whole. What one would be observing, then, is the relationship between "active participation" and social status, which partly explains the slight relationship between active participation and mental health.

The degree of social contact involved in these spare-time activities was suspected of being related to mental health. All activities were classified into *solitary, small group,* and *large group.* Each person was then assigned to one of these three categories, depending on the type of activity predominant in his present life. The hypothesis proved tenable, for the more solitary had a risk of .52, those in small groups .48, and those in large groups had a risk of only .41. These categories are significantly different from each other in the total sample.

In the whole sample, 69.2 per cent, a strong majority, carried on predominantly solitary activities outside the job and family. This figure alone would call into question the cohesion of the society in which we live, particularly the cohesion of the cities which encompass the greatest part of our national population. Yet lack of cohesion (at least in the sense of face-to-face contact during leisure activity) is certainly not synonymous with mental disturbance. Far from it, for the "solitary" majority only have a risk of .52.[1]

The Lows and Middles have slightly more "solitary" types than the Highs (72.7, 70.7, and 64.3 per cent). Correspondingly, the proportion participating in small groups increases from low to high SES (19.5, 23.2, and 25.9 per cent). This same trend is even more pronounced for those with activities in large groups (national and professional associations, etc.). Here we find only 1.7 per cent of the Lows, 3.2 per cent of the Middles, and 6.8 per cent of the Highs.

These data show us that engaging in group activity is not just another index of social status; it may also have positive mental health implications at all three SES levels. Certainly participation, membership in, or interaction with a group lends a sense of strength to the individual, and brings the emotional support that many people crave. On the other hand, joining in certain types of group activity indicates a *pre-existent* capacity for interpersonal relationships and an absence of preoccupation with self. This makes it possible to relate to others and see the other person's point of view. It presupposes a minimal level of anxiety and hostility which might interfere with communication between oneself and others. To recapitulate, one must have some of the characteristics we already consider to be signs of mental health in order to participate in groups. The circular relationship of mental health and interpersonal affiliations cannot be doubted, for each enhances the other.

There is some reason to suspect that participation in large groups, as well as solitary activity, requires less emotional energy or output. Simmel, for instance, points out the superficial level of conversation at a "party" of four or five people, as contrasted with the intensity sometimes found in conversations of two or three people.[2] The larger the group, the more "socializing" there is, and the greater is the pressure to avoid all topics of conversation which might lead to argument or disharmony. The superficiality of cocktail party conversation is an obvious example. If this is so, why do people in large group activity have even less risk than those in small group activity? Perhaps small groups are more emotionally demanding and hence disturbing. Perhaps large groups, particularly professional or fraternal groups, offer a certain subtle anonymity and protect the individual from disturbing emotional involvement and demands. At the same time they make him feel part of a large and important group or body. This package of status and "belongingness" without the demand for individual emotional output is perhaps what makes large group activity most conducive to mental health (if not most conducive to creativity).

The superficiality and status aspects of interpersonal relationships are not of course confined to cocktail parties or large groups. Often an individual accumulates friends like a rare coin collector with the intention of displaying them rather than achieving close interpersonal relationships. Such friendships stem not only from social and economic rapacity but also from a sense of personal inferiority and inner emptiness. An attempt is made to allay this sense of insufficiency by associating with prestigeful people, the socially secure.

Byron T. (see footnote, page 166) was born in Midtown into a socially prominent and wealthy family. His earliest memories were of "doing things together" with his parents and brother. The idyllic scene faded rapidly during Byron's adolescence. The family had financial problems. His father began drinking. His home became an unsavory environment both emotionally and socially. Byron was embarrassed by his father's drinking when he had a friend home from college. This embarrassment was accentuated by the emphasis which his parents had previously placed on social rather than intellectual standards: "The prime objective for my parents was to have us get along with people." He was under constant pressure to "get along," yet he had neither the emotional preparation for friendship nor a suitable home in which to entertain. *Making* rather than *being* friends came to assume primary importance for him. "I wanted to make friends with people and would go out of my way to make them like me. I tried to be a good pal, especially to people who were important at school. I took the big guy's part against the little guy's or I would just tell the big guy to beat up the little guy. One boy was a real hell-raiser and I didn't want to seem a sissy to him, so I played along by taking part in escapades."

This kind of parasitic friendship was based on a fear of being alone, rather than any positive desire to communicate with people. Now in his fifties, Byron is no longer motivated as much by the prestige involved in "getting along" as by an overwhelming fear of loneliness. "I've gotten scared of being alone, especially during the summer when my wife takes the kids to the shore. I'm not the club-man type and I hate being alone at home."

The degree of active participation is measured rather well by the respondents' occupancy of leadership roles as officers of organizations. It turns out that officers of clubs or organizations are somewhat (.46) (but not significantly) better off than all others (.50). Only 23.5 per cent hold such offices. However, this breaks down to 12.3 per cent of the Lows, 20.1 per cent of the Middles, and 37.7 per cent of the Highs. In the low SES, these "leaders" are slightly worse off (.61) than the rest of the Lows (.58). In the middle and high SES, the leaders are not very different from the rest of the group (.49 vs. .50, .41 vs. .41). The only reason officers of organizations in general are healthier is that they are primarily of high rather than low SES (in a ratio of 3 to 1). Actually the low SES officers are somewhat worse off than their fellow Lows. Perhaps this is associated with the deviance of the low SES officer or leader, whose personality has developed in this fashion despite a predominantly "follower" atmosphere in his subculture.

The hypothesis that a "neurotic pattern of power" is found among those achieving leadership in voluntary organizations does not seem to be borne out by these data, particularly in the middle and high SES. That neuroses would be more frequent among such leaders (rather than character disorders or psychoses) might be connected with their SES (see Chapters 15 and 16). The fact that the officers exhibit a low mental health risk argues against a high proportion of neurotics in their ranks.

## F.  SOME INTERPERSONAL SYMPTOMS

Several items in the questionnaire dealt with interpersonal relations, but they were so subjective in nature that they were considered to be symptoms of mental disturbance, effects rather than causes of mental disturbance. For instance, people who "can't enjoy themselves when alone" run a higher risk (.58) than those who can (.48). More Lows (31.1 per cent) than Highs (7.5 per cent) say they can't enjoy themselves when alone. Yet a greater proportion of the Lows are virtual isolates. Perhaps their dependence on others, coupled with their social isolation, makes for greater stress.

Satisfaction with the number of one's friends does not seem related to mental health. The question was phrased, "Do you feel you have as many friends as you want, or would you like to have more friends?" Those who said "As many as I want" were not significantly healthier (.49) than those who said they wanted more friends (.51). The desire for more friends might at first seem to indicate dissatisfaction with one's present relationships. However, it may in many instances be an indication of a general outgoingness, a desire to communicate with others, which is usually associated with positive mental health. Interestingly enough, 45.2 per cent of the Highs and only 25.0 per cent of the Lows say they want more friends. This fact is an additional reason why those who want more friends are as healthy as those who have as many as they want; they are predominantly of high SES.

In the case of Interpersonal Affiliations, we were fortunate in being able to ask direct questions which would give some idea of the interpersonal environment. Although the questions "How many close friends do you have?" or "How is you health?" can be asked directly, it would be somewhat difficult to ask "Are you a good parent?" or "Do you have a good marriage?" Thus "worries" about one's marriage or children have to be taken as a second-best substitute for an index of the stress induced by marriage and parenthood. This also applies to the pressures of work and the struggle for status and a higher standard of living. These factors were also assessed by the respondent's "worries" about them. It would be difficult, though not impossible, to gather more objective data about the pressures of the job on the individual.

In the case of Poor Interpersonal Affiliations, the item "Do you worry about loneliness?" (often, sometimes, or never) was not utilized as part of the final factor, for less subjective items were available, such as the number of friends. Very often the more subjective item will have a stronger relationship to mental health. For example, those who often worry about loneliness have a risk of .77, while those who never worry about it have a low risk of only .44.

The connections between mental disturbance and loneliness, wanting more friends, and being excluded from childhood gangs and adult organizations are seen in the case of Nigel. (See footnote, page 166).

Nigel is a moderately wealthy "socially acceptable" bachelor in his early thirties. His mother was an alcoholic and during his childhood his parents always quarreled. At an exclusive prep school, no one liked him. "I was little and skinny and all the other boys beat me up." He was very lonely and "even the beatings were better than being ignored." In college he discovered a certain flair for telling comic stories. He was determined to become a character, a suitable mixture of Max Beerbohm and Beau Brummell. Nigel bought immaculately-tailored suits which artfully concealed his slender frame, and smoked expensive Havanas. He developed an elaborate routine for clipping off the end of his cigar and preparing it for smoking which always accompanied his anecdotes. After the last of his clubmates married, Nigel was still unable to reconcile himself to being alone. He began a round of bars and taverns seeking anyone who would listen to him. His need for alcohol grows out of, and is part of, his search for ease in social relations.

## Summary

*Antecedent and Reciprocal Component Factors.*    The preadult factors were originally labeled as antecedent component factors, because it was felt that Parents' Quarrels, Broken Homes, and so forth would be the components of the low socioeconomic family setting. The components of SES would be those factors which made low SES a noxious environment and high SES a eugenic environment. It was soon discovered that almost none of these factors showed any proportional variation with socioeconomic status.

The analysis design for this volume called for the establishment of factors independent of SES in their relationship to the Mental Health Ratings. The preadult factors, then, were related to psychiatric impairment but were *not* components of socioeconomic status, age, or sex.

The adult factors were not clearly antecedent to the present mental health of the individual. They were labeled "reciprocal" to indicate that they could be considered symptoms as well as sources of mental disturbance.

*Adult Poor Physical Health.*    This factor was composed of the respondent's self-estimate of his present state of health (as excellent, good, fair, or poor), and the number of reported hospitalizations (excluding pregnancies and mental hospitals). The worse the health estimate, the greater the mental health risk. It was apparent that a low SES person with the same level of health estimate as a high SES person is less likely to have been hospitalized. This may be a function of reporting, differential utilization of medical facilities, or many other variables.

Mental health risk varied directly with the number of "nonpsychosomatic ailments." Those reporting no additional disorders had a risk of .47; those with three or more disorders had a risk of .72.

People who feel that their health is worse or better than it was five years ago run an increased mental health risk over those whose health stayed "the same." More people of low SES said their health was worse.

People who often worry about their health had a risk of .75, compared to those who never worried about it (.42). Over half the sample said they never worried about their health. The hypochondriacs (who say their health is excellent but often worry about it) are not as badly off (.60) as those in poor health who worry about their health (.92). Both these types worry, but it is their report of their health that is most strongly related to the impairment rating.

Height was inversely related to the Mental Health Ratings. Both men and women within all (fathers') SES groups show less impairment if they are taller. A height-weight index showed that underweight persons generally exhibited a greater mental health risk. Tall, thin people seemed to have a greater risk, while tall middleweights of high SES exhibited the lowest risks.

The taller a person is, the more likely he is to say he is in excellent health. About 10 per cent of short men and women report excellent health, compared with some 50 per cent of tall men and women (over 6 feet and 5'9" respectively).

Persons who report excellent health, regardless of age, have less impairment risk. Age (up to sixty) is not as good a predictor of impairment risk as the health estimate.

Despite the excellent predictive power of the health factor, the reader is warned that it is methodologically "impure" because it is part of the original Mental Health Rating (I) and hopelessly intertwined with the psychophysiological symptoms given a great deal of weight in the psychiatrists' rating procedure.

*Poor Interpersonal Affiliations.* This factor was composed of a weighted score based upon the number of a person's close friends, the number of organizations to which he belonged, and the number of neighbors with whom he was friendly. Having no friends (.71) involves much greater risk than having two or three (.53). About 2 per cent of the Highs and about 13 per cent of the Lows were friendless.

Those friendly with ten or more neighbors ran less than the average risk. One-third of the sample had no friendships with neighbors. Although belonging to an organization was generally linked with less risk, this was most true of the low SES group. More Highs belonged to organizations. The final factor yielded risks of .64, .52, and .45, a wide variation indicating a strong factor.

Other items of related information were considered. Persons who visited few relatives' families were "worse off" than those who visited several.

The greater the number of spare-time activities reported, the less the mental health risk involved. The high SES reported more activities. Over three-fifths of the sample utilized mass media (radio, TV, and movies), one-half engaged in reading, and one-third had outdoor activities. About one-fourth engaged in painting, sewing, and music.

Those actively involved had a slightly lower risk (not statistically significant) than those who were spectators or passive in participation. The Highs had more active interests.

Persons in solitary activities had an average risk, while those in large groups showed a greatly decreased risk. Two-thirds had only solitary activities outside family and job.

Officers of organizations run less risk in the high and more risk in the low SES. One-eighth of the Lows and one-third of the Highs are officers in organizations.

People who "can't enjoy themselves when alone" show increased risk. This is interesting, in view of the fact that two-thirds of the sample engage in solitary spare-time activities. Solitary activity is widespread, and the ability to engage in it comfortably may well be one minor criterion of mental health in our society.

Persons who wanted more friends had the same risk as those who were satisfied with their present number of friends. A greater proportion of Highs than Lows wanted more friends.

## Notes

1. Note, however, that as the number of persons in a subgroup approaches 1660, their maximum ridit (risk) also approaches .50.
2. See *The Sociology of Georg Simmel*, Translated and Edited by Kurt H. Wolff, The Free Press of Glencoe, New York, 1950; Chapter 3, on Sociability, pp. 52–53.

# Worries: Work, Socioeconomic, Marital, and Parental

### T H O M A S  S .  L A N G N E R

It was difficult to obtain good "measuring rods" for many of the stresses of adult life. In their roles as providers, spouses, and parents, adults find many gratifications. However, these roles are also a source of stress and often make tremendous demands on the individual which he is ill equipped to meet. The size of the demand and the personality equipment with which it is met will determine the degree of resulting impairment. Since we cannot measure the stress of a marriage, for example, except in terms of the reaction to that stress, indices of stress often sound more like strain itself. The stress factor often sounds like a symptom of mental disorder.

Worrying about a particular role was taken as an index of the stress associated with that role. Worrying in itself is a symptom of mental disturbance, but specific worries about job, status, marriage, and children were not included in Mental Health Rating I. To this extent they are methodologically "clean." In the broader sense, however, these factors should always be interpreted as having a reciprocal relationship with mental disturbance. The difficulties of constructing an "objective" index of marital stress or occupational stress without including the patient's or respondent's subjective evaluation of his situation are obvious (see Chapter 6).

## Work Worries

In the minds of the psychiatrists who made the Mental Health Ratings, the work role assumed the most importance. We know this for a fact because of the highly intricate system of mental health ratings which they were asked to follow. To recapitulate, the psychiatric judges were asked to make an initial rating of each respondent's mental health based upon a three-page summary of his symptoms. Only after this were they allowed to see the respondent's social background, such as socioeconomic status, religion, nationality origins, education, occupation, job satisfaction, and his worries about work, overwork, and status. On the basis of the additional sociocultural background information the psychiatrists made a second Mental Health Rating.

In general, both ratings remained identical. In roughly one-fourth of the cases Rating II was different from Rating I. Within this fourth, one person was given a better rating to every four who were given worse ratings. This confirmed the finding of much previous research that the more information one has about a person, the more likely one is to discover clinically significant symptomatology. The raters were asked to note the reason or reasons why they made a change (for better or worse) in Mental Health Rating I. In three-fourths of the rating changes the reason given was "occupation." Many people, particularly males, were working in occupations far below their educational level.

## A.  THE  WORK  ETHIC

The importance of the occupational role is one of the characteristics always noted by visitors to the United States. The centrality of work in our culture and in the *Protestant ethic* is widely recognized. Thus it cannot help but be taken into account in making mental health ratings. "Doing one's work well" and, for that matter, just "working" are primary values in our culture. The clinician must take account of the values and sentiments of the society whose members he is evaluating. When he rates members of his own society, he makes use of the value system which he himself has incorporated. Perhaps his ratings of functional impairment are less accurate as he rates members of subgroups distinct from his own segment of society (such as persons of low SES). These comments apply principally to Mental Health Rating II, however, for SES was not known when the "symptom" rating was made (MHR I).

In addition to the importance of the work ethic in our culture, there was another reason for the close connection we found between occupational performance and MHR I. This was simply the differential amount of information in the questionnaire concerning the various roles that individuals perform. Some questions were asked about the marital role, but we felt that many questions could not be asked in this area, for fear of creating resentment in the respondents. As it later turned out, people were generally quite willing to talk about their sex life, but they were very defensive about their politics and income. The areas of privacy have obviously changed since the Victorian period, with the advent of the cold war and high income taxes. Because we felt it was less risky to ask questions about occupation than about sexual behavior, proportionally more questions about occupation were included in the questionnaire. It is a virtual certainty that if had we asked questions concerning adult sexual behavior and marital relationships, these would have emerged as strong factors in relation to Mental Health Rating I. Thus for practical reasons (in addition to the theoretical importance of the work ethic in our clinical and cultural tradition) the occupational sphere was given strong emphasis in this study.

It is always desirable to isolate relatively objective factors. Unfortunately, the only item approaching objectivity was unemployment. This meant that we could classify only a small proportion of the men in the sample. We could say nothing about housewives, for they would never be clearly "unemployed." Similarly, unemployment might not mean the same thing for a working female as for a working male. With this objective factor eliminated, because it classified the sample in an "either-or" fashion and placed only a small fraction in the pathognomonic group, we turned to other items dealing with work. Satisfaction with one's work was certainly not objective in the sense that it could be equally a symptom and a source of mental disturbance. Interruptions in work because of health problems certainly indicate an impairment in functioning, but we could hardly say that poor health due to certain predominantly somatic diseases, diseases due to occupational hazards such as silicosis, or accidents caused by poor working conditions were all psychogenic.

Since truly objective "work" items could not be found, we decided to select those items that correlated most highly with mental health. These turned out to be worrying about "work" and "overwork." These two items were in a series of worries, each of which was asked separately of the respondent. Answers of "Often, Sometimes, or Never" were suggested.

One great advantage of these items lay in the fact that they applied equally to both men and women and to people in various marital states. Housewives, for instance, could and did report that they worried about their work and about overwork.

## TABLE 12-1

### PROPORTIONS AND AVERAGE MENTAL HEALTH (MH II) OF MALE AND FEMALE RESPONDENTS ACCORDING TO WORRYING ABOUT WORK, FEMALES' MARITAL STATUS, AND RESPONDENTS' SOCIOECONOMIC STATUS

| Sex | Worrying About Work | Respondents' Socioeconomic Status | | | | | | | |
| --- | --- | --- | --- | --- | --- | --- | --- | --- | --- |
| | | LOW | | MIDDLE | | HIGH | | TOTAL | |
| | | Per Cent | $\bar{R}$ | Per Cent | $\bar{R}$ | Per Cent | $\bar{R}$ | Per Cent | $\bar{R}$ |
| Males | Often or Sometimes | 40.9 | .65 | 46.3* | .58 | 65.5 | .44 | 51.2 | .54 |
| | Never | 57.2 | .54 | 52.9 | .46 | 33.6 | .35 | 47.6 | .47 |
| | Don't Know, No Answer } | 1.9 | – | .8 | – | .9 | – | 1.2 | – |
| | Average Ridit | | .60 | | .52 | | .41 | | .51 |
| | Number of Cases (N=100 per cent) | 215 | | 240 | | 235 | | 690 | |
| | Per Cent Males by SES | 39.5 | | 43.1 | | 42.0 | | 41.6 | |
| Never-Married Females | Often or Sometimes | 31.1 | .64 | 49.0 | .46 | 57.6 | .45 | 48.0 | .48 |
| | Never | 65.6 | .58 | 51.0 | .42 | 41.4 | .31 | 50.8 | .44 |
| | Don't Know, No Answer } | 3.3 | – | 0.0 | – | 1.0 | – | 1.2 | – |
| | Average Ridit | | .61 | | .44 | | .39 | | .46 |
| | Number of Cases (N = 100 per cent) | 61 | | 96 | | 99 | | 256 | |
| | Per Cent N. M. Females by SES | 11.2 | | 17.3 | | 17.7 | | 15.4 | |
| Ever-Married Females | Often or Sometimes | 29.9 | .68 | 25.5 | .60 | 35.8 | .46 | 30.4 | .58 |
| | Never | 67.9 | .53 | 72.7 | .47 | 62.4 | .41 | 67.6 | .47 |
| | Don't Know, No Answer } | 2.2 | – | 1.8 | – | 1.8 | – | 2.0 | – |
| | Average Ridit | | .58 | | .49 | | .42 | | .51 |
| | Number of Cases (N = 100 per cent) | 268 | | 220 | | 226 | | 714 | |
| | Per Cent E. M. Females by SES | 49.3 | | 39.6 | | 40.3 | | 43.0 | |
| | Total Number of Cases (N = 100 per cent) | 544 | | 556 | | 560 | | 1660 | |

## B.   WORRYING ABOUT WORK

Strangely enough, people of high socioeconomic status tended to worry more about their work. For instance (see Table 12-1), proportionally more people in the high SES worry about their work often or sometimes.

Among males, only 40.9 per cent of the Lows contrasted with 65.5 per cent of the Highs worry about their work. Similar differences are found among never-married females, and ever-married females (the presently married, and the divorced, separated, and widowed). Because the high SES tend to worry about work, the over-all mental health risk of those who have work (and overwork) worries is *less* than for those who don't worry. This result is artifactual, however. If we examine the data according to SES, sex, and marital status, we find that in every pair of cells the worriers are "worse off" than the nonworriers. (It is just that the relatively numerous and unimpaired high SES work worriers pull down the risk of work worriers in general.) This is true for all three sex-and-marital-status categories, and it is particularly pronounced among ever-married females (mostly housewives). It is the consistency with which the worriers are worse off than the nonworriers that is impressive, though the differences do not usually reach statistical significance.

## C.   WORRYING ABOUT OVERWORK

Worries about overwork (see Table 12-2) are not more frequent in the high SES except among never-married females. However, those who worry about overwork are consistently worse off with respect to the Mental Health Ratings than the nonworriers.

Fewer people worry about overwork than worry about work. This is particularly true of males. Moreover, high SES males, and women who have never married are much more prone to worry about their work but not about overwork. The data indicate that work worries among the high SES may be normative.

The prevalence of work worries in the high SES may be evidence of channeled anxiety which aids in the achievement of socially-approved goals. While it is associated with a greater mental health risk, it occurs most typically among people (high SES) who are relatively healthy and can afford an increased risk. This still leaves them better off than the average man in the population as a whole. For that matter, if 65 per cent

## TABLE 12-2

## PROPORTIONS AND AVERAGE MENTAL HEALTH (MH II) OF MALE AND FEMALE RESPONDENTS ACCORDING TO WORRYING ABOUT OVERWORK, FEMALES' MARITAL STATUS, AND RESPONDENTS' SOCIOECONOMIC STATUS

| | | Respondents' Socioeconomic Status | | | | | | | |
|---|---|---|---|---|---|---|---|---|---|
| | | LOW | | MIDDLE | | HIGH | | TOTAL | |
| Sex | Worrying About Overwork | Per Cent | R̄ | Per Cent | R̄ | Per Cent | R̄ | Per Cent | R̄ |
| Males | Often or Sometimes | 25.1 | .68 | 23.3 | .60 | 29.8 | .46 | 26.1 | .57* |
| | Never | 73.0 | .56 | 75.4 | .49 | 68.9 | .39 | 72.5 | .48 |
| | Don't Know, No Answer | 1.9 | – | 1.3 | – | 1.3 | – | 1.4 | – |
| | Average Ridit | | .60 | | .52 | | .41 | | .51 |
| | Number of Cases (N = 100 per cent) | 215 | | 240 | | 235 | | 690 | |
| | Per Cent Males by SES | 39.5 | | 43.1 | | 42.0 | | 41.6 | |
| Never-Married Females | Often or Sometimes | 23.0 | .68 | 24.0 | .51 | 36.4 | .48 | 28.5 | .53 |
| | Never | 73.7 | .58 | 76.0 | .42 | 63.6 | .33 | 70.8 | .43 |
| | Don't Know, No Answer | 3.3 | – | 0.0 | – | 0.0 | – | 0.7 | – |
| | Average Ridit | | .61 | | .44 | | .39 | | .46 |
| | Number of Cases (N = 100 per cent) | 61 | | 96 | | 99 | | 256 | |
| | Per Cent N.M. Females by SES | 11.2 | | 17.3 | | 17.7 | | 15.4 | |
| Ever-Married Females | Often or Sometimes | 20.9 | .70* | 21.8 | .61* | 19.9 | .47 | 20.8 | .60* |
| | Never | 76.9 | .54 | 75.9 | .47 | 79.2 | .41 | 77.4 | .48 |
| | Don't Know, No Answer | 2.2 | – | 2.3 | – | 0.9 | – | 1.8 | – |
| | Average Ridit | | .58 | | .49 | | .42 | | .51 |
| | Number of Cases (N = 100 per cent) | 268 | | 220 | | 226 | | 714 | |
| | Per Cent E.M. Females by SES | 49.3 | | 39.6 | | 40.3 | | 43.0 | |
| | Total Number of Cases (N = 100 per cent) | 544 | | 556 | | 560 | | 1660 | |

## TABLE 12-3

### DISTRIBUTION, PROPORTIONS AND AVERAGE MENTAL HEALTH (CMH, MH I, MH II) ACCORDING TO WORK WORRIES FACTOR, TRICHOTOMIZED AND DICHOTOMIZED

| Work Worries Factor | Respondents' Average Mental Health | | | No. of Cases | Per Cent of Cases |
|---|---|---|---|---|---|
| | CMH | MH I | MH II | | |
| Trichotomy | | | | | |
| + | $.55^*_z$ | $.64^*_y$ | $.70^*_x$ | 225 | 13.6 |
| 0 | .51 | $.54^*_y$ | $.51^*_x$ | 274 | 16.5 |
| − | $.47^*_z$ | $.46^*_y$ | $.38^*_x$ | 1161 | 69.9 |
| Dichotomy | | | | | |
| + | .52 | .59 | .56 | 499 | 30.1 |
| | * | * | * | | |
| − | .47 | .46 | .38 | 1161 | 69.9 |
| Total Number of Cases (N = 100 per cent) | | | | 1660 | |

*Difference in test variable at the 5 per cent level of confidence between ridits with same subscript or adjacent to same asterisk.

of a subgroup (high SES males) worry about their work, their worrying has practically become a way of life. This suggests the stereotype of the Wall Street stockbroker or the Madison Avenue advertising account executive. They may be work worriers, but they have less impairment of functioning than the majority of the population.

The two worries, "work" and "overwork" were combined in the work worries factor. The strong association between the Work Worries factor and mental health risk is shown in Table 12-3. The Mental Health I ridits are .46, .54, and .64 for those who don't worry about work, worry moderately, and worry frequently. The Mental Health II ridits show a considerably wider range, or closer association, with work worries (.38, .51, and .70). This is probably due to the psychiatrists' knowledge of the respondents' work role and behavior when making Rating II. We have therefore only considered Mental Health Rating I in this analysis.

### D.  JOB SATISFACTION

The Work Worries factor was finally established on the basis of two items of information, but several other items relating to the work area were also considered. One was job satisfaction, as measured by the question "How much do you like the work you are now doing?" For married women who were working, the question was changed to "How much do you like the outside work you are now doing? Would you say Very Much, Fairly Much, Not so Much, or Not at All?" Dissatisfaction with one's job can, of course, be a symptom of mental disturbance if one has a "suitable" job. If circumstances do not permit one to find a suitable job (for instance, among Puerto Rican males this is a common problem) then job dissatisfaction can become a cause of mental disturbance. As with all the adult data, much circularity is involved.

The job satisfaction of the regular work force, which includes men and never-married women, is shown in Table 12-4. ("Ever-married women," that is, housewives and women who are divorced, separated, or widowed, are treated separately, in Table 12-5).) It is immediately clear that proportionally more persons of high SES like their work "very much." More low SES persons like their work "fairly much" or "not at all." In the sample as a whole, and in the middle SES, there are significant differences in the mental health of people at different levels of job satisfaction. Those who are more dissatisfied have a higher mental health risk.

Women who work outside the home and who are now or have been married (this category is composed predominantly of working wives) in general like their work as well as the men and never-married women. About 62 per cent of the wives who do outside work and 57.5 per cent of the working men and never-married women liked their work. Apparently, housewives, too, like a chance to get out of the house and be independent. Low SES housewives who like their work very much are better off, from a mental health standpoint, than their husbands or never-married low SES women. Moreover, those married women who did not like their outside work at all were still somewhat better off (.61) than corresponding men and never-married women (see Table 12-5). The working housewife, then, has a somewhat decreased mental health risk.

She can have her cake and eat it, as it were, for she has two roles which can complement each other. This finding has cropped up before when the mental health of part-time working mothers (as opposed to full-time or nonworking mothers) was found to be somewhat better.

## TABLE 12-4

## PROPORTIONS AND AVERAGE MENTAL HEALTH (MH II) OF RESPONDENTS (MEN AND NEVER-MARRIED WOMEN) WHO DID OR DID NOT EXPRESS SATISFACTION WITH THEIR OCCUPATION

| Satisfaction With Occupation | Respondent's Socioeconomic Status | | | | | | | |
|---|---|---|---|---|---|---|---|---|
| | LOW | | MIDDLE | | HIGH | | TOTAL | |
| | Per Cent | $\bar{R}$ | Per Cent | $\bar{R}$ | Per Cent | $\bar{R}$ | Per Cent | $\bar{R}$ |
| Very Much | 43.0 | .58 | 51.6 | .46$^*_z$ | 75.6 | .39 | 57.5 | .45$^*_{y,x}$ |
| Fairly Much | 36.0 | .57 | 32.9 | .50 | 15.9 | .49 | 27.9 | .59$^*_y$ |
| Not so Much | 12.5 | .63 | 8.4 | .58 | 4.1 | .52 | 8.1 | .52$^*_w$ |
| Not at All | 4.1 | .68 | 5.9 | .65$^*_z$ | 1.9 | (.71) | 3.9 | .67$^*_{x,w}$ |
| Don't Know, No Answer ∤ | 4.4 | – | 1.2 | – | 2.5 | – | 2.6 | – |
| Total Number of Cases (N = 100 per cent) | 272 | | 322 | | 320 | | 914 | |

*Difference in the test variable at the 5 per cent level of confidence between ridits with same subscript or adjacent to same asterisk.

∤ Ridits not computed.

Parentheses ( ) enclose ridit based on less than ten cases.

(Even though small groups make for an absence of significant differences in this table, the trends are consistent.)

### E.  HUSBANDS WITH WORKING WIVES

It was hypothesized that husbands whose wives were working (particularly full time) would have a greater mental health risk. This was based upon several hunches. Perhaps these men were not playing the role of provider as fully as they might, so that their wives had to work. This would imply poor role functioning on the part of the husband, hence greater psychiatric impairment. Again, a wife's insistence upon working outside the home might provoke anger or anxiety in some husbands, which in turn would impair their functioning. The reverse hypothesis, that a healthy permissive husband would allow his wife to do outside work, because of his own self-confidence and his confidence in his wife

## TABLE 12-5

## PROPORTIONS AND AVERAGE MENTAL HEALTH (MH II) OF EVER-MARRIED FEMALE RESPONDENTS WHO DID OR DID NOT EXPRESS SATISFACTION WITH THEIR OCCUPATION

| Satisfaction With Outside Job | LOW | | MIDDLE | | HIGH | | TOTAL | |
|---|---|---|---|---|---|---|---|---|
| | Per Cent | $\bar{R}$ | Per Cent | $\bar{R}$ | Per Cent | $\bar{R}$ | Per Cent | $\bar{R}$ |
| Very Much | 54.5 | .52 | 61.7 | .45 | 71.7 | .41 | 61.9 | .46 |
| Fairly Much | 26.2 | .50 | 29.2 | .56 | 22.1 | .45 | 25.9 | .51 |
| Not So Much | 11.0 | .67 | 4.2 | (.44) | 3.5 | .65 | 6.6 | .62 |
| Not at All | 6.2 | (.61) | 1.6 | (.90) | .9 | (.05) | 3.2 | .61 |
| Don't Know, No Answer‡ | 2.1 | – | 3.3 | – | 1.8 | – | 2.4 | – |
| Total Number of Cases (N = 100 per cent) | 145 | | 120 | | 113 | | 378 | |

‡ Ridits not computed.

Parentheses ( ) enclose ridits based on less than ten cases.

and in their relationship, was not considered. Such a husband would not be threatened by his wife's earnings or successes. In the low SES, he might be quite gratified by the financial aid given him by his wife. (That is, provided she didn't have a *better job* than he did, which turns out to be a situation relatively common in the low SES.)

Among the Lows, husbands whose wives work part time are somewhat better off (.51) than husbands whose wives don't work (.59) or work full time (.61). (See Table 12-6.)

Apparently the part-time working housewife arrangement is best for the mental health of the low SES husband (.51). Additional revenue is provided, together with child care, cooking, and housecleaning. Perhaps when the housewife functions drop out completely (and the wife works full time) the stress on the low SES husband is greater.

In the high SES, on the other hand, husbands whose wives do not work at all are best off (.37), and comprise a larger proportion of the group (71.1 per cent) than in the low and middle SES (61.8 per cent and

## TABLE 12-6

### PROPORTIONS AND AVERAGE MENTAL HEALTH (MH II) OF MARRIED AND EVER-MARRIED MALE RESPONDENTS WHOSE WIVES WORK FULL TIME, PART TIME, OR NOT AT ALL, CONTROLLED BY RESPONDENTS' SOCIOECONOMIC STATUS

| | Respondents' Socioeconomic Status | | | | | | | |
| | LOW | | MIDDLE | | HIGH | | TOTAL | |
| Wife Working | Per Cent | R̄ | Per Cent | R̄ | Per Cent | R̄ | Per Cent | R̄ |
|---|---|---|---|---|---|---|---|---|
| Part time | 3.8 | .51 | 13.1 | .46 | 7.2 | .53 | 11.2 | .49 |
| Full time | 23.1 | .61 | 26.8 | .50 | 20.6 | .47 | 23.4 | .52 |
| Does not Work | 61.8 | .59 | 57.7 | .45 | 71.1 | .37 | 63.8 | .46 |
| Don't Know, No Answer ‡ | 1.3 | – | 2.4 | – | 1.1 | – | 1.6 | – |
| Total Number of Cases (N = 100 per cent) | 160 | | 168 | | 180 | | 508 | |

‡ Ridits not computed.

57.7 per cent. High SES women tend to work full time or not at all. At this SES level, the husbands of these women run less mental health risk than the husbands of the part-time workers (.53). The matter of custom or normative behavior does enter the picture here. The career woman and full-time mother are normative figures in the high SES. Their husbands are somewhat better off in terms of mental health risk. In the low SES, the part-time working wife, while not more numerous than full-time or nonworkers, is likely to have a healthier husband. When she doesn't work, her husband's risk does not drop sharply (.59) as in the high SES (.37).

### F.  STOPPED WORK BECAUSE OF HEALTH

All working men and never-married women were asked, "Did you ever stop working for any long periods because of health reasons?" Those who said they did stop working for health reasons are consistently worse off with respect to the Mental Health Rating than persons who said they did not stop[1] (see Table 12-7).

A considerably larger proportion of low SES workers (30.9 per cent)

## TABLE 12-7

### PROPORTIONS AND AVERAGE MENTAL HEALTH (MH II) OF MEN AND NEVER-MARRIED WOMEN WHO STOPPED WORKING FOR A LONG PERIOD OF TIME BECAUSE OF HEALTH REASONS[a]

| Stopped Working | Respondents' Socioeconomic Status | | | | | | | |
|---|---|---|---|---|---|---|---|---|
| | LOW | | MIDDLE | | HIGH | | TOTAL | |
| | Per Cent | $\bar{R}$ | Per Cent | $\bar{R}$ | Per Cent | $\bar{R}$ | Per Cent | $\bar{R}$ |
| No | 66.5 | .56 | 76.1 | .47 | 80.0 | .40 | 74.6 | .47 |
| | | * | | * | | | | * |
| Yes | 30.9 | .70 | 22.4 | .60 | 8.4 | .47 | 23.6 | .60 |
| Don't Know, No Answer ‖ | 2.6 | – | 1.5 | – | 1.6 | – | 1.9 | – |
| Total Number of Cases (N=100 per cent) | 272 | | 322 | | 320 | | 914 | |

[a] Not included are married females, students, and the retired. Included in the 914 cases are working men and working never-married women.

* Difference in test variable at the 5 per cent level of confidence between ridits adjacent to same asterisk.

‖ Ridits not computed.

"stopped working because of health," compared with 8.4 per cent of the Highs (see Table 12-7). This fits in with what was found about the poorer physical health of the low SES in general.

The Midtown questionnaire had many excellent indicators of poor role functioning for men and women who do work outside the home. Unemployment, or any break in the work patterns, such as absenteeism or illnesses interfering with work, are signs to the clinician that all is probably not well with the individual's mental health.

A parallel measure of the housewife's functioning was not easily assessed by the questionnaire. She can accomplish her work without sharp breaks even when somewhat ill. She cannot be counted as an absentee, for she is always "on the job." Unless she is bedridden, she appears to be working, watching the house, attending to her functions, at least to the superficial observer, and certainly to the unseeing reader of a questionnaire. The difficulty of assessing the mother's and the housewife's functions by means of a questionnaire interview must be apparent. Thus, MHR II is more accurate for males and for female jobholders. Since more role functioning information is available on jobholders, they may turn up with a worse mental health rating than they deserve in comparison with housewives. This is on the assumption that the more information you have about a person, the more disturbed he looks, since the statistical chances of a symptom showing up are increased.

## G.  WORK UPSET HEALTH

Men and never-married women were asked "Has your work ever affected your digestion, sleep, or upset your health in any other way?" If the respondent said "Yes," he was asked, "Why was that?"[2] During the pretesting of the questionnaire we found that the responses fell into rather definite categories. Uncongenial work, long hours, physical conditions, and heavy responsibilities were associated with a high risk in the low SES (averaging about .70). Uncongenial work and physical conditions were associated with poorer mental health in the middle SES (about .65). In the high SES group these reasons (about .58) together with "poor management" and "co-workers" (.66 and .56) are also linked to a higher risk.

One clue to the meaning of work in the various social status levels is found in the variation in the mental health risk according to SES. For instance, "long hours" involves a risk of .70 in the low SES (which is greater than the risk of the low SES men and never-married women as a whole). The same reason is given by mentally-healthier-than-average people in the middle (.47) and high SES (.40). The respondents may feel that long hours affect their digestion or sleep or their health in general. However, high SES people who report this are better off than the average of their group, and the low SES are worse off. This is despite the fact that almost equal proportions of each SES level report "long hours" (Low, 7.4, Middle, 8.1, and High, 10.4).

Although none of the ridit differences between the various reasons why work upset health is statistically significant, there is a significant difference between those people who said their work upset their health (.59) and those who said it did not (.50). The differences are also significant within each SES level.

Of some interest is the proportional distribution of reasons why work upset health according to socioeconomic status. More Lows than Highs (10.7 per cent vs. 2.1 per cent) said that the physical conditions under which they worked had affected their health. It will be remembered that this complaint was accompanied by a high mental health risk at all three SES levels.

Another insight into socioeconomic differences in work attitudes is afforded by the fact that only 4.5 per cent of the Lows and 24.3 per cent of the Highs said that "heavy responsibilities" had affected their health. While this response is associated with increased risk among the Lows (.69) and the Middles (.60), it is just about par for the high SES group (.47). One interpretation is that high status people in general worry about their work and the responsibility it entails. While this acceptance of responsibility may have some effect on their general health, it in itself is a sign of mental health among those of high status. It is in a way normative behavior for a professional or executive (male or female) to complain about the burden of work and responsibility. The job, however, may be the very thing that is preserving these individuals. In a way they derive their identity from their jobs; they "are" their jobs. The concept of the job as a "social corset" holding the personality together is quite apt here. "Long hours" involve a decreased risk in the high and middle SES but an increased risk in the low SES. If there is emotional involvement in a job, as among the Highs, then longer hours are perhaps only an indicator of greater identification with one's work. Long hours for the unskilled laborer, on the other hand, probably mean that he isn't earning enough at his hourly rate to support his family and is forced to work longer hours.

Often the same fact or experience will have different connotations and mental health risks in different socioeconomic groups. Such materials were avoided when possible in the construction of the stress factors, but they add much to our knowledge of the dynamic structure of our society. So far we find the Highs worry about their jobs but like them better. Though they complain more of heavy responsibility it does not seem to increase their impairment. The Lows more often stop work because of their health. Their impairment risk is increased by long hours, while the Highs' risk is decreased. The High likes his job, worries about it and thrives on increasing responsibility and involvement with his work. In contrast, the Low dislikes his work, worries (concerns himself) less about it, and suffers impairment from long hours.

It is no accident that the Highs are mostly Protestants. They exhibit the responses one might expect of persons raised in the Protestant work ethic. To work is to win salvation. Work is not a distasteful task necessary for survival. It is a way of life, an end in itself. If salvation in this world can be partially equated with freedom from severe mental disorder, then the hardworking among the Highs seem to have achieved it.

## Socioeconomic Status Worries

Though related to the work area, concern with status and one's standard of living seemed to be a separate entity. It was felt that attitudes toward occupational level, income, and money itself might have an effect on one's mental health (and might also constitute symptoms of mental disturbance). In any event, these attitudes would certainly be associated with increased mental health risk.

### A.   GETTING AHEAD

Two items were selected as a measure of socioeconomic status worries because they bore the closest relationship to the Mental Health Rating. The first of these was worded, "Is getting ahead something that worries you: often, sometimes, or never?" In all three SES groups those who answered "often" showed considerably greater impairment than those who "never" worried about getting ahead (see Table 12-8). Those who worried "often" had a risk of .62; those who worried "sometimes" or "never" ran risks of .49 and .47.

### TABLE 12-8

### PROPORTIONS AND AVERAGE MENTAL HEALTH (MH II) OF RESPONDENTS WHO WORRY ABOUT GETTING AHEAD, BY RESPONDENTS' SOCIOECONOMIC STATUS

*Respondents' Socioeconomic Status*

| Worry About Getting Ahead | LOW Per Cent | $\bar{R}$ | MIDDLE Per Cent | $\bar{R}$ | HIGH Per Cent | $\bar{R}$ | TOTAL Per Cent | $\bar{R}$ |
|---|---|---|---|---|---|---|---|---|
| Often | 14.3 | $.70^*_z$ | 15.1 | $.63^*_y$ | 11.4 | $.52^*_x$ | 13.6 | $.62^*_w$ |
|  |  | * |  | * |  |  |  | * |
| Sometimes | 38.1 | .57 | 39.9 | .47 | 36.8 | .42 | 38.3 | .49 |
| Never | 46.1 | $.57^*_z$ | 44.1 | $.47^*_y$ | 51.3 | $.38^*_x$ | 47.1 | $.47^*_w$ |
| Don't Know, No Answer ‡ | 1.5 | — | .9 | — | .5 | — | 1.0 | — |
| Total Number of Cases (N=100 per cent) | 544 |  | 556 |  | 560 |  | 1660 |  |

* Difference in the test variable at the 5 per cent level of confidence between ridits with same subscript or adjacent to same asterisk.
‡ Ridits not computed.

About half of each status group worries about getting ahead. It might seem that low SES people, who are certainly farther "behind," should be most anxious to "get ahead." Perhaps they are, but a direct question such as this does not elicit the fact. Moreover, low SES individuals are more likely to "act out" this problem than to admit they are frustrated in "getting ahead." They may utilize socially disapproved means of becoming successful.

Dick B. (see footnote, p. 166) worked at a job that paid too little to provide the luxuries he felt were his due. He charged what he couldn't pay for, and clashed with the law. Jobs that followed invariably put him under pressures he could not sustain, yet making big money and achieving prestige was a drive that he could not deny. "I see myself as an industrial magnate, charitable, solving the world's problems, people coming to me for advice." His deep-rooted desire for radios, cars, and TV sets, and his financial inability to attain them, depressed him to the point of tears. He remembered that his mother always wanted him "*to do well.*"

His two sisters and brother have good jobs and keep them, in contrast to his frequent work changes. This he does not resent perhaps because their jobs are not of the "caliber" to which he aspires.

The Lows may also set up a rigid defense system by denying that they care about success, by "blaming the system," or by invoking fate or luck. Thus they are no more likely to worry about getting ahead than the Highs despite their low position. We find that 11.4 per cent of the Highs, 15.1 per cent of the Middles, and 14.3 per cent of the Lows worry about getting ahead often. These proportions are not significantly different. It might have been expected that a great majority of status worriers were persons of low status. Quite the contrary, the results tend to argue for the resignation of the low SES.

It has often been suggested that the poor and less educated person may not have internalized the high success goals of the middle and upper status American. He often does not hold values, such as a high esteem for advanced education, which might prepare him for success. He is less likely to possess the slightly compulsive personality structure which might help him "get ahead." It is also possible that those of low status, even in early adolescence, learn to set their sights much lower. This lowering of aspiration has been viewed by some as a form of mental disturbance. It can, however, also be seen as an attempt to preserve self-esteem in an intolerable situation.

Little evidence was found that more of the people who are farthest behind want to get ahead. Perhaps it is a question of our point of reference. If the Lows compare their status only with that of their peers, they may remain quite content. If they look beyond their own circle of friends and acquaintances (as Dick B. does), they may feel more dissatisfaction, *relative* to those of higher status, and hence more desire to "get ahead." Such concepts as Merton's "relative deprivation"[3] help to explain why there is not more dissatisfaction among the Lows.

### B.    COST OF LIVING

The second question utilized in the SES Worries factor asks, "Is the cost of living something that worries you; would you say often, sometimes, or never?" Since the question asked directly about the cost of living, the respondent's weekly (family) income was taken into account. Table 12-9 shows that at all income levels (except $300 per week or over) those who worried often about the cost of living ran a higher mental health risk than those who never worried.

It is noteworthy that only after an income of $15,000 a year does worry over the cost of living  become unrelated to mental health. In the sample as a whole, those who worried often had a risk of .60, while persons who worried sometimes or never had a risk of only .46.

The proportion of persons who "never" worry about the cost of living varies surprisingly little with income; it remains around 28 per cent. However, the proportion of those who worry "often" ranges from 31.4 per cent among those with an income under $50 a week to 13.4 per cent of those with $300 or more a week. The sharpest increase in worrying is seen among those in the lowest income bracket.

Worries about the "cost of living" and "getting ahead" were combined into one factor labeled Socioeconomic Status Worries, or simply SES Worries.

The Mental Health Rating I and II risks associated with frequent SES Worries is .63; less frequent SES Worries bear a risk of .57, while absence of SES worrying bears a risk of only .46. (See Table 12-10.)

### C.    MONEY IS MOST IMPORTANT

Two additional items and an index were originally considered for inclusion in the SES Worries factor. One of the attitude items in the questionnaire attempted to assess the salience or importance of money in the individual's value hierarchy. It was found that those who agreed with the statement "Next to health, money is the most important thing in life"

# TABLE 12-9

## PROPORTIONS AND AVERAGE MENTAL HEALTH (MH II) OF RESPONDENTS ACCORDING TO WORRYING ABOUT COST OF LIVING AND RESPONDENTS' INCOME LEVELS

| Worrying About Cost of Living | Respondents' Weekly Income | | | | | | | | | | | | | |
| --- | --- | --- | --- | --- | --- | --- | --- | --- | --- | --- | --- | --- | --- | --- |
| | Up to $49 | | $50 to $74 | | $75 to $99 | | $100 to $149 | | $150 to $299 | | $300 & Over | | TOTAL[a] | |
| | Per Cent | $\bar{R}$ | Per Cent | $\bar{R}$ | Per Cent | $\bar{R}$ | Per Cent | $\bar{R}$ | Per Cent | $\bar{R}$ | Per Cent | $\bar{R}$ | Per Cent | $\bar{R}$ |
| Often | 31.4 | .71 | 23.3 | .62*$_z$ | 21.2 | .60*$_y$ | 19.2 | .58 | 18.9 | .48 | 13.4 | .40 | 20.8 | .60*$_x$ |
| Sometimes | 35.1 | .61 | 48.2 | .51 | 50.8 | .46 | 47.3 | .38 | 53.3 | .41 | 52.5 | .42 | 46.2 | .46 |
| Never | 32.5 | .52 | 27.4 | .50*$_z$ | 28.0 | .45*$_y$ | 33.1 | .46 | 27.2 | .37 | 33.5 | .41 | 28.4 | .46*$_x$ |
| Don't Know, No Answer‡ | 1.0 | — | 1.1 | — | 0.0 | — | 0.4 | — | 0.6 | — | 0.6 | — | 0.6 | — |
| Total Number of Cases (N = 100 per cent) | 194 | | 438 | | 372 | | 245 | | 180 | | 164 | | 1593 | |

[a] Not including 67 cases, 4.0 per cent, who did not know or gave no answer as to their weekly income.

* Differences in test variable at the 5 per cent level of confidence between ridits with same subscript or adjacent to same asterisk.

‡ Ridits not computed.

## TABLE 12-10

## DISTRIBUTION, PROPORTIONS, AND AVERAGE MENTAL HEALTH (CMH, MH I & MH II) ACCORDING TO SOCIOECONOMIC STATUS WORRIES TRICHOTOMIZED AND DICHOTOMIZED

| | Respondents' Mental Health | | | | |
|---|---|---|---|---|---|
| *SES Worries* | *CMH* | *MH I* | *MH II* | *No. of Cases* | *Per Cent of Cases* |
| *Trichotomy* | | | | | |
| + | $.61^*_z$ | $.63^*_y$ | $.63^*_x$ | 200 | 12.0 |
| 0 | .57 | .57 | .57 | 274 | 16.5 |
| | * | * | * | | |
| − | $.47^*_z$ | $.46^*_y$ | $.46^*_x$ | 1186 | 71.4 |
| *Dichotomy* | | | | | |
| + | .59 | .60 | .60 | 474 | 28.6 |
| | * | * | * | | |
| − | .47 | .46 | .46 | 1186 | 71.4 |
| Total Number of Cases (N = 100 per cent) | | | | 1660 | |

*Differences in test variable at the 5 per cent level of confidence between ridits with same subscript or adjacent to same asterisk.

ran a consistently greater risk (.57) than those who disagreed (.46). (Tabular material is not included.) When these responses were examined with income controlled, only persons in the $300-a-week bracket had similar risks, whether they agreed or not. This finding is consistent with the lack of correlation of mental health risk and worrying about the cost of living in this same high income bracket. Apparently after one reaches the $15,000-a-year level, emphasizing money or worrying about it is no longer related to mental health risk.

One might think that just the opposite would be true and that relatively wealthy people who worry about money despite their wealth would be unrealistic and mentally disturbed. On the contrary, these wealthy worriers run a low risk. The poor, however, who worry about the cost of living and place money on a pedestal, show a greater risk than their income-peers who do not worry about the cost of living or say money is most important. This argues against the subjective interpretation of the SES Worries factor, and supports it as a relatively objective factor. At least in this population, people's mental disturbance and SES Worries increase as their objective financial standing decreases. Worrying about the cost of living and placing a high value on money are by this token more apt to be measuring *real* financial deprivation. Such worries are more possibly indications of an external environmental situation which is conducive to the development of mental disturbance in the individual. These objective worries by the same token are less likely to be merely additional symptoms of mental disturbance.

Although the "importance of money" showed a significant difference in risk for the sample as a whole, it did not increase the range of mental health risk when added to the two items making up the SES Worries factor. For this reason, it was not included as part of the final factor.

### D.   OCCUPATIONAL AMBITIONS

Also available was further information about present status that might possibly affect the individual's mental health. Each working male was asked, "When you left school, what particular kind of occupation or life work was it your ambition to reach some day?" Working females were asked "When you left school, what were your ambitions for the future?" These answers were classified on a six-point occupational scale of Low, Middle, and High Blue Collar, corresponding roughly to unskilled, semi-skilled, and skilled labor, and Low, Middle, and High White Collar corresponding roughly to sales and clerical, semiprofessional, and professional-top managerial (see Table 10-4). These occupational aspirations were compared with the present occupational level of each individual, also on the same six-point scale. A person could move from one to five steps up or down, depending on his aspiration level, or he could remain at the same level as his original aspiration.

In general, a person whose present occupation is at the same level as his original aspiration runs the least mental health risk (.47). On the other hand, those in one level higher occupation (.57) or two to four level higher occupations (.54), or in lower level jobs (.54) than their aspirations are somewhat worse off (see Table 12-11). This holds true in general in all three SES groups. However, low SES persons who have risen two or more levels above their aspirations have an equal or even slightly decreased risk (.56) when compared to that of other Lows who are at the same level as their aspirations (.57).

## TABLE 12-11

## PROPORTIONS AND AVERAGE MENTAL HEALTH (MH II) OF OCCUPATIONAL ASPIRATIONS OF MEN AND NEVER-MARRIED WOMEN COMPARED WITH PRESENT OCCUPATION, BY RESPONDENTS' SOCIOECONOMIC STATUS

| Occupational Aspirations | Respondents' Socioeconomic Status | | | | | | | |
|---|---|---|---|---|---|---|---|---|
| | LOW | | MIDDLE | | HIGH | | TOTAL | |
| | Per Cent | $\bar{R}$ | Per Cent | $\bar{R}$ | Per Cent | $\bar{R}$ | Per Cent | $\bar{R}$ |
| Up 2 to 4 | 8.5 | .56 | 6.5 | .54 | 0.3 | (.05) | 4.9 | .54 |
| Up 1 | 4.8 | .69 | 7.8 | .55 | 4.1 | .50 | 5.6 | .57 |
| Same | 59.2 | .57 | 60.2 | .48 | 74.7 | .40 | 65.0 | .47 |
| Down 1 to 3 | 2.9 | (.71) | 4.0 | .56 | 4.7 | .44 | 3.9 | .54 |
| Not Employed | 2.9 | (.70) | 1.6 | (.63) | 0.6 | (.55) | 1.7 | .65 |
| Don't Know, No Answer ‡ | 21.7 | – | 19.9 | – | 15.6 | – | 18.9 | – |
| Total Number of Cases (N = 100 per cent) | 272 | | 322 | | 320 | | 914 | |

‡ Ridits not computed.

Parentheses ( ) ridits based on less than ten cases.

These findings may seem unexpected, but they turn out to be quite explicable. Persons who have jobs higher than their aspirations are somewhat worse off. A person who achieves more than he set out to achieve might be subject to conflict or ambivalence concerning his goals. Certainly those who achieved approximately what they report they set out to achieve are in the majority and show less impairment risk. It is also interesting that proportionally more of the high SES (74.7 per cent) knew what they wanted and got it. This portion of the Highs also had less risk. The high SES always seems to have a larger proportion of people with these healthy or low-risk characteristics. The ability to "know where you're going" and what your capacities are comes under the heading of a mental health *asset* which is so hard to find. In research which of necessity is still oriented toward pathology, the mental health asset is rarely found. The ability to assess one's skills, pick out an appropriate goal, and attain it involves a great deal of self-knowledge. It is also an excellent test of reality orientation.

The discrepancy between occupational ambitions and achievement did not prove, however, to be a very powerful tool for discriminating between the impaired and the well. For one thing, the great majority of people had jobs that matched their ambitions. Moreover, none of the differences between those who achieved their aspirations and those who did not were statistically significant (see Table 12-11). In part, this may be due to the fact that preadolescent fantasies concerning ambitions are repressed quite early in life. By the time an individual is twenty years old or more, his recall for his innermost ambitions has probably been lost. It has also been noted that the majority of low status high-school seniors change their adolescent "ambitions" during the very last part of their senior year, as they come face to face with reality. They give up their hopes of becoming professionals and begin to content themselves with sales, clerical, and mechanics' jobs. Just what level of fantasy the questionnaire elicits, or the age at which this occupational aspiration was really determined, we cannot tell. Its importance for mental health seems to be rather negligible, however. In addition, the applicability of the index is limited to those in the labor force.

## E. RENT PROPORTIONAL TO INCOME

Extreme concern with status is often assumed to lead to mental disturbance. Certainly it is indicative of social pressure to compete and conform to certain behavioral norms. Do people who utilize "conspicuous consumption" exhibit poorer mental health? We felt that one index of this high status concern would be the proportion of one's income spent on rent. The emphasis on one's dwelling to the exclusion of other needs was assumed to be indicative of high status concern. Most people in Midtown (47.8 per cent) spend 15 per cent of their income for rent; they run a risk of .49 (MH II). Those who spend from 30 per cent to 34 per cent (.56) and 40 per cent to 45 per cent (.58) show some increase in risk. However, this is not indicative of a trend, for the 3 per cent of the population who spend 45 per cent or more of their income on rent (.49) have the same low risk as those who spend 15 per cent. The proportion of income one spends on rent appears to be generally unrelated to mental health.[4]

This index, of course, is particularly unsuited to Midtown, where rent control is still in effect in some dwellings, and not in others. Luxury apartments with rentals over $400 a month have been decontrolled. All new or renovated apartments are also not controlled. The rental paid by the Midtowner is very much a function of the vicissitudes of the rent control laws. Furthermore, low SES families, which tend to be large families, must of necessity pay proportionately more of their income for rental of larger apartments. Many other sound motives for paying higher rent in relation to income may be operating (along with unsound motives related to status), which reduce the correlation with mental disturbance.

In sum, the Highs are more likely to know where they're going and to get there. They seem to have more of such assets than the Lows. The Lows worry more about the cost of living. This seems realistic but carries with it increased impairment risk. SES Worries add to our picture of the Highs' work ethic. A set of positive values concerning work enables them to choose an appropriate occupational goal and achieve it. Once they achieve it they are more likely to be highly involved with it, and apparently benefit from long hours of work. In the original sense of the phrase "worldly asceticism," hard work keeps them out of emotional mischief, reduces their symptomatology. They don't *act out* their conflicts, they *work* them out. This may not be the optimal goal, for obsessive concern with work is itself a symptom. However, it's socially acceptable, usually well rewarded, and it maintains the Highs in their social position.

## Marital Worries

### A.   WORRYING ABOUT MARRIAGE

In Chapter 10 of Volume I we found that single men and the divorced of both sexes have on increased mental health risk. Marital status was included in the first volume because it is generally considered one of the common demographic factors, along with age and sex. It is, however, a *reciprocal* variable similar to all the adult factors. It is not clearly antecedent to adult mental health status, nor is mental health status clearly a result of marital status.

It was felt, however, that marital pressures, being such an important part of the adult environment, should be considered here as well. Rather than examine marital status again, we decided to test marital worries as an indicator of marital stress. Furthermore, we decided to focus principally upon those people who were being influenced directly by their marriage, rather than by their lack of marriage or former marriage. Thus we concentrated upon the married people in the sample.

One item was chosen from among several which dealt tangentially with marriage: "Is marriage something that worries you: often, sometimes, or never?" (Marital worries did increase the mental health risk of the never-married and those formerly married, though not significantly.) Since we felt that marriage places rather different pressures on men and women, the sexes were kept separate within each SES level. Table 12-12 shows that when sex is controlled, marital worries are always associated with an increase in mental health risk. (This is statistically significant only among married men and women of low SES.)

## TABLE 12-12

### PROPORTIONS AND AVERAGE MENTAL HEALTH (MH II) OF MARRIED RESPONDENTS WHO REPORTED MARRIAGE IS SOMETHING THAT WORRIES THEM BY RESPONDENTS' SOCIOECONOMIC STATUS AND SEX

| | Respondents' Socioeconomic Status | | | | | | | |
|---|---|---|---|---|---|---|---|---|
| Worrying About Marriage | LOW | | MIDDLE | | HIGH | | TOTAL | |
| | Per Cent | $\bar{R}$ | Per Cent | $\bar{R}$ | Per Cent | $\bar{R}$ | Per Cent | $\bar{R}$ |
| *Married Males* | | | | | | | | |
| Often, Sometimes | 9.4 | .79 | 15.1 | .50 | 26.4 | .46 | 17.5 | .53 |
| | | * | | | | | | |
| Never | 90.6 | .54 | 84.9 | .44 | 73.6 | .35 | 82.5 | .45 |
| Number of Cases (N = 100 per cent) | 138 | | 146 | | 163 | | 447 | |
| *Married Females* | | | | | | | | |
| Often, Sometimes | 19.7 | .76 | 13.2 | .56 | 20.9 | .50 | 18.2 | .62 |
| | | * | | | | | | * |
| Never | 80.3 | .51 | 86.8 | .46 | 79.1 | .36 | 81.8 | .49 |
| Number of Cases (N = 100 per cent) | 188 | | 159 | | 182 | | 529 | |

*Difference in test variable at the 5 per cent level of confidence between ridits adjacent to same asterisk.

Of course, persons who are married run a lower risk to begin with, so that any differences we find within the married group are that much more unexpected. The risk of men with marital worries is not much less than that of women with marital worries, although somewhat diminished in the low and middle SES. The proportion of males who worry about marriage increases directly with SES (Lows, 9.4 per cent, Middles, 15.1 per cent, and Highs, 26.4 per cent). However, no such trend is apparent among women.

When the total group of married is examined, disregarding sex, the differences between marital worriers and nonworriers is significant (see Table 12-13).

The marital worry item (considered a factor by itself) showed a risk of .78 for those who often worried about marriage, .54 for those who worried sometimes, and .45 for those who never worried. However, only 3.1 per cent of the 987 married people worried often about marriage (31 cases). Since a contingent factor (one which applied to part of the sample only) could not readily be combined into a score of factors, the small number of cases in the plus group was of no consequence.

Persons who worry about their marriages can adapt in a variety of ways. A common reaction is the development of a psychophysiological symptom.

Mildred W.'s (see footnote, page 166) worries about marriage were constant although she saw them as sporadic. Physical symptoms (in this case a recurring tightness in the throat) appeared primarily when she was undergoing extreme tenseness, as when her father died and she separated from her husband. She had "broken up" with her husband when he lost his job—"too much fighting" —and she couldn't take "the things he said about my mother." The feeling in her throat was compounded by difficulty in sleeping, loss of appetite, and lack of interest in sexual relations whenever the totality of her life was threatened either by her husband's drinking, or his insults to her family. "I don't like him when he drinks—thinks he knows everything—talks about how they'll get to the moon or boxing, and I want to talk about buying clothes and what the kids are doing."

Although still loving her husband, she is taking no steps toward a resumption of their stormy relationship. Her psychosomatic symptoms and her general lassitude reappear whenever her feelings of separation are reactivated.

An even more common reaction to marital stress is depression. In this instance it was quite severe.

Mindy C. (see footnote, page 166) was also separated from her husband not long ago. She has found another man whom she is on the verge of losing if

## TABLE 12-13

### DISTRIBUTION, PROPORTIONS, AND AVERAGE MENTAL HEALTH (CMH, MH I, MH II) OF RESPONDENTS ACCORDING TO MARITAL WORRIES TRICHOTOMIZED AND DICHOTOMIZED

| Worry About Marriage | Respondents' Mental Health | | | | |
|---|---|---|---|---|---|
| | CMH | MH I | MH II | No. of Cases | Per Cent of Cases |
| *Trichotomy* | | | | | |
| + | $.62^*_z$ | $.78^*_y$ | $.78^*_x$ | 31 | 3.1 |
| 0 | .55 * | $.54^*_y$ | $.53^*_x$ | 143 | 14.5 |
| – | $.46^*_z$ | $.45^*_y$ | $.45^*_x$ | 813 | 82.4 |
| *Dichotomy* | | | | | |
| + | .56 * | .58 * | .58 * | 174 | 17.6 |
| – | .46 | .45 | .45 | 813 | 82.4 |
| Total Number of Cases (N = 100 per cent) | | | | 987 | |

*Difference in test variable at the 5 per cent level of confidence between ridits with same subscript or adjacent to same asterisk.

she hasn't already lost him. Mindy married an alcoholic who consistently abused her during their eight years together. He provided insufficient support and even stole the children's money from her purse. She is subconsciously fearful of trusting another man-woman relationship, although she yearns deeply for it. Recently, she has resorted to several suicide attempts. Fearful that she is losing her mind largely because her lover has criticized and rejected her, she seems to have lost the capacity to enjoy anything.

Even her responsibility to her two children no longer deters her from attempts at self-destruction. However, marital stress is only one trigger for her depression. A deeply ingrained fear of death has been with her since childhood. There has scarcely been a time in her life when she has been panic-free.

### B. EXCLUSION OF MARITAL STATUS

It should be re-emphasized that the married were healthier to begin with. The (MH I) risk of the married is .48, the never-married, .51, the widowed, .53, and the divorced or separated, .62. Age has something to do with the differences, but when age is controlled differences still remain. The married and never-married are significantly healthier than the divorced or separated group.

Marital status was of course known to the psychiatric raters at the time they made their first Mental Health Rating. It was felt that even though religion, ethnic background, SES, education, generation, and all other social background variables were unknown to them until they made Rating II, they still had to have age, sex, and marital status to make any intelligent evaluation of the symptoms with which they were being presented. The symptom rating (MH I) is therefore slightly contaminated with respect to marital status. For instance, if the psychiatrists gave the respondent a more impaired rating every time the word "divorce" appeared in the record, then there would be of necessity a correlation between divorce and the Mental Health Rating. For this additional reason the marital worries item was utilized since it was unknown to the psychiatrist at the time he made his first rating. Our findings actually tend to corroborate and strengthen those found in the examination of marital status described in Volume I.

## C.   RELIGIOUS INTERMARRIAGE

Other more "objective" items were examined for their relationship to mental health risk. The religious heterogeneity of the marital partners was considered a potential source of marital stress which in turn might lead to strain (mental disturbance). However, persons who married a partner of a different major faith (Protestant, Catholic, or Jewish) in general showed no greater risk (.51) than those with a spouse of the same faith. Only in the middle SES was there some increment (spouse of same religion, .46, different religion, .55), but this was not statistically significant (tabular material not included).

Perhaps greater importance may be attached to the fact that 28 per cent of the sample had married persons of another religion. Interestingly, 34.9 per cent of the Highs had religious out-marriages, while this was true of only 26.1 per cent of the Middles, and 23.2 per cent of the Lows. There is some evidence here that as the socioeconomic status of the immigrant increases, he is more inclined to marry out of his religious group. However, the high SES is practically synonymous with the fourth generation "Old American" group, principally of Yankee Protestant background. If in four generations only one-third show religious intermarriage, one can surmise that any breakdown in the religious barriers to intermarriage will proceed at a relatively slow rate. It is in the high SES, where most inter-faith marriages occur, that the least mental health risk is involved (inter-faith, .42, intrafaith, .41). This seems reasonable in view of the loss of ethnic, religious, and other values in the high SES and their replacement by other aspects of the American ethos. A high SES interfaith marriage probably does not contravene group values and mores as much as a similar marriage in the low SES.

## D.   ETHNIC INTERMARRIAGE

The ethnic heterogeneity of marriages in turn showed no significant relationship to mental health risk. Those with a spouse from another national background (Irish, Italian, German, Czech, Slovak, and others) were not significantly "worse off" (.52) than those who married a person of the same national background (.49). A similar small difference of .02 ridits was found at each SES level. The proportion of ethnic out-marriages tended to decrease as socioeconomic status increased. Among all those ever married, 23.8 per cent had ethnic out-marriages. This is similar to the proportion who had religious out-marriages. Neither is related to mental health status (tabular material not included).

While 30.4 per cent of the married Lows chose mates of a different nationality background than their own, this was true of 24.0 per cent of the Middles, and only 20.3 per cent of the Highs. Of course, an artifact is at work here, in that persons who were the great-grandchildren of immi-grants (or whose families had been in the United States for four genera-tions or more) were considered to be "Old American." They were no longer considered as belonging to an "ethnic group." These fourth generation individuals predominated in the high SES, which may account for the apparent ethnic homogeneity of marriages among the Highs. De-tailed information on national origins was gathered only as far back as the respondent's four grandparents.

## E.   EDUCATIONAL DIFFERENCES
## BETWEEN SPOUSES

Educational differences between the spouses also showed no con-sistent relationship to the Mental Health Rating. The six levels of educa-tion were "no schooling or incomplete grade school, completed grade school, some high school, completed high school, some college, and completed college or higher."

In the low SES, those who had had the same amount of education as their marital partners had a risk of .57. Those who were one, or two-or-more levels *above* their spouse showed a slight but not significant increase in risk ( .60, .59), as did those who were one or two-or-more levels *below* their spouses' education ( .59, .58). Among the Lows, educational homogeneity showed a slight tendency to be associated with a lower mental health risk.

In the middle SES, spouses of the same education ( .51) were slightly worse off than those above their partners ( .46, .48) or those below their partners ( .47, .51). These differences, due to the small number of cases in each category, are not statistically significant. Among the Highs there is no relation between the spouses' two educational levels and mental health risk ( tabular material not included ).

The proportion of educational heterogeneity increases as SES increases. Thus 60.3 per cent of the Highs, 58.3 per cent of the Middles, and only 41.2 per cent of the Lows are married to persons of a different educational level. Only 11.9 per cent of the Lows report they have a better education than their spouses, compared to about 26 per cent of the Middles and Highs. No analysis by the sex of the respondent was attempted, but it might have been illuminating, particularly since it has been noted that upper-class males have a tendency to marry women beneath them socially, while this is not true of upper-class females. (Perhaps because of the resulting shortage of eligible high SES males, high status women have a sharply decreased rate of marriage.)

F.  OCCUPATIONAL DIFFERENCES
    BETWEEN SPOUSES

Of all the attempts to relate heterogeneity in the background of marital partners to mental disturbance, only one showed a positive relationship. It was actually a corroboration of one of the central theses of this book when we found that occupational heterogeneity of husband and wife *was* indeed related to mental health risk.

This fact appeared only when the sex of the spouse was taken into account. It was of course expected that husbands whose wives were in high occupations would have a greater mental health risk (see Table 10-4, ranking of occupations). This would be expected in a society where

## TABLE 12-14

## PROPORTIONS AND AVERAGE MENTAL HEALTH (MH II) OF MARRIED RESPONDENTS WHO ARE BOTH WORKING OUTSIDE THE HOME, ACCORDING TO SEX AND OCCUPATIONAL LEVEL OF THE MARITAL PARTNERS

| | *Respondents' Socioeconomic Status* | | | | | | | |
|---|---|---|---|---|---|---|---|---|
| *Respondent* | *LOW* | | *MIDDLE* | | *HIGH* | | *TOTAL* | |
| *Is Husband* | *Per Cent* | *R̄* | *Per Cent* | *R̄* | *Per Cent* | *R̄* | *Per Cent* | *R̄* |
| Husband Higher Than Wife | 22.0 | .54 | 43.3 | .60 | 49.0 | .42 | 37.9 | .52 |
| Same | 44.1 | .53 | 23.9 | .41 | 35.4 | .50 | 33.9 | .49 |
| Lower ＇ | 33.9 | .65 | 32.8 | .41 | 15.6 | .63 | 28.2 | .54 |
| Total Number of Cases (N = 100 per cent)[a] | 59 | | 67 | | 51 | | 177 | |
| *Respondent Is Wife* | | | | | | | | |
| Husband Higher Than Wife | 43.9 | .52 | 43.8 | .52 | 39.0 | .36 | 42.4 | .47 |
| Same | 28.8 | .55 | 19.6 | .45 | 42.9 | .49 | 30.1 | .50 |
| Lower | 27.3 | .54 | 36.6 | .47 | 18.1 | .39 | 27.5 | .48 |
| Total Number of Cases (N = 100 per cent)[a] | 132 | | 112 | | 105 | | 349 | |

[a]Totals are small, since only the married are involved, and among them only persons with a working spouse.

the male derives his status chiefly from his occupational role, rather than his role as parent, husband, son, or citizen.

Table 12-14 shows that husbands in the low and high SES whose wives are in higher occupations do indeed show a pronounced increase in mental health risk. (These differences are not statistically significant, due to the small number of working marital pairs involved.) Among the

Lows, if the respondent-husband is at the same level or a higher occupational level than his wife (.53, .54), his risk is considerably less than if he is in a lower level occupation than his wife (.65). Even more strikingly, among the Highs, husbands who are above their wives in occupational status have the low risk generally associated with this social group (.42). Husbands of high SES at the same job level as their wives (.50) run a greater risk than Highs in general (.41), while those who are in jobs at lower levels than their wives run a risk of .63.

Strangely enough, in the middle SES the picture is reversed. The risk of husbands who are at higher occupational levels is greater (.60) than husbands with wives at the same or lower occupational levels (.41, .41). This may be artifactual and simply due to random fluctuations in the ridit, since the groups are small in size. The size of the disparity in risk and the reversal of the expected trend in the middle SES are good reasons to consider the data further. Could it be that the middle SES husband is more egalitarian, and thus finds unbearable the stress of holding a more prestigeful job than his wife? This is extremely doubtful, since when he is at a lower job level than his wife, also a nonegalitarian situation, he is likely to run even less risk than Middles in general. It is also possible that middle SES families generally feel more strongly than Lows or High that the woman should not work to earn money, and do not emphasize a career for the woman. The middle SES wife would be likely to work only if her husband were an inadequate earner (a source of stress). The High wife, however, might work for a career more than money, thus posing less of a threat to her husband's ego.

Again, the structure of the middle SES family may be quite different, and the working wife, rather than the husband, might more often be the decision maker, child trainer, and bill payer. On the other hand, the low and high SES families may both call for a stronger father and husband, and a somewhat more submissive wife and mother. If these requirements are not met, as, for instance, in the Puerto Rican immigrant family or the Negro family, where the wife often has better job opportunities than her husband, there may be divorce, separation, and perhaps much mental disturbance may ensue. While our data are only suggestive, they raise problems well worth investigating. The way in which our social and economic system affects the power relationship, interpersonal dynamics, self-images, and sexual relations of the marital pair is only just beginning to be understood. Notable contributions have been made by Kardiner and Ovesey,[5] and Komarovsky.[6]

It is interesting and expectable that the level of their husband's occupation relative to their own seems almost unrelated to the mental health risk of wives. In only one instance is there a noteworthy increase in risk; among the high SES women whose husbands are at the same occupational level. Possibly these women need to work because their husbands are not earning enough, despite their professional status. Thus some impairment on the husband's part might increase his wife's risk too.

One inference can be drawn from this difference between the sexes in their reaction to disparity between their job and that of their spouses. It is probably not the disparity itself that is crucial, otherwise it would be crucial for both sexes. If, let us say, some emotion or motivation such as competition, jealousy, or simply squabbles over how to spend the money were involved, then women would be equally affected with men. Since men alone are affected by job disparity, it is plausible that they are being threatened by their wives' high occupational status. Perhaps if their subculture (Highs and Lows) calls for their husbands to be in a higher occupation and they are not, they show signs of strain or increased risk. If their subculture (Middles) calls for the husband to subordinate himself to children and wife, and he is in fact subordinate to his wife in occupation, then he shows a marked decrease in risk. Possibly longitudinal studies will be able to test some of these hypotheses by studying families at various social levels.

### G. NUMBER OF MARRIAGES

Some other aspects of marriage were also considered for inclusion. Among these were the number of marriages in which the respondent had been involved. While no significant differences appeared, this was mainly because very few people married more than once. In the low and middle SES, those who had only one marriage are better off (Lows, .57, Middles, .48) than those never-married (.62, .52) or those with two or more marriages (.68, .57). In the high SES, however, the never-married, once-married, and often-married share virtually the identical risk (.41) (tabular material not included).

A much larger proportion of the married high SES are in their second marriage, this despite the fact that they are a younger group and have had less time to devote to the hobby of multiple marriages. A surprising 17.3 per cent of the ever-married high SES[7] had more than one marriage, compared to 6.6 per cent of the married Middles, and 10.0 per cent of the married Lows. The last proportion, while relatively small, is larger than expected in view of the fact that the low SES group is predominantly Catholic, and by this token divorce and remarriage should be less frequent among the Lows.

If remarriage is more frequent and less stressful among the Highs, so is remaining single. This may be because a large group of high SES never-married women (154 cases) are probably supported by wealthy fathers, are relatively young, and are not exposed to the stresses of the economic system. They might not get as much mental health "benefit" from marriage, since it does not necessarily enhance their economic position, and may in fact damage it somewhat. The primary deterrent to their marriage is the paucity of males of equal status, since men can acceptably marry women of equal or lower status than themselves, while women ordinarily are expected to marry men of equal or higher status than their own fathers.

There is little difference in the mental health risk of men and women who have remarried. Presently remarried men (.44) run a risk which is not significantly different from that of presently married men in their first marriage (.47). Among neither men nor women is remarriage associated with a great increase in mental health risk. As we found before, this is to some extent a function of the fact that a larger proportion of high SES persons marry more than once, and the Highs as a group have a lower risk.

## H. AGE AT FIRST MARRIAGE

The respondent's age at the time of his or her first marriage is generally unrelated to mental health. This is true at all SES levels. It was felt that early marriages (between age fifteen and nineteen) might be associated with poorer mental health ratings. There is a slight, though not significant, tendency in this direction. Those who married from fifteen to nineteen have a somewhat higher risk than those who married from twenty to twenty-four. After the early twenties there is again an increase in risk among the twenty-five to twenty-nines. This pattern is true of the Middles and Highs, but not the Lows, who show a decrease in risk from twenty to twenty-nine.

The modal age of marriage in all three SES groups is twenty to twenty-four; that is, the largest number of people get married between those ages. The fact that many people engage in a certain activity at a certain time does not automatically insure that they are in good mental health. A numerical majority by itself does not constitute a causal factor. As a matter of fact, among the Highs the respondents whose first marriages were between ages thirty to forty-four have even a slightly lower risk (.37) than those married from twenty to twenty-four (.41). All in all, the age at which persons first get married does not seem consistently related to their mental health.

How does marital stress fit into our developing picture of socioeconomic differences in behavior? Not only are the Highs more work oriented, benefiting from occupational involvement and long hours, but the men in particular seem more worried about their marriages. Again this worry does not entail increased risk of psychiatric impairment for the Highs. They make more religious out-marriages, but show the least risk in these unions, while the Lows show substantial risk. Again, the Highs exhibit greater educational heterogeneity in their marriages, but this involves no risk at any SES level. The more frequent remarriages of the Highs again showed no increase in impairment risk, while the opposite was true for the Lows.

The advantages seem to accrue to the Highs in each instance. There is a sharp increase in risk among both Highs and Lows if the husband is in a lower occupation than his working wife. However, there is a greater number of such couples among the Lows. There are two ways in which the Highs maintain a low risk. First, a smaller proportion of them usually report experiencing the stress factors. Second, if we interpret these results correctly, they seem to exhibit less impairment than Lows, no matter what the stress involved. They almost seem to "benefit" from what would normally be considered stressful circumstances, such as remarriage or long hours. Their freedom to remarry and their reported satisfaction with their work of course help in understanding why their risk is not increased.

## Parental Worries

### A. PROBLEMS WITH CHILDREN

Just as Marital Worries applied only to the married, Parental Worries were pertinent only to parents. Parents who reported they had "problems with their children" ran a higher risk (.54) than parents who reported no problems with their children (.42). This trend appeared in all three SES groups; it was significant among the Lows and Highs (see Table 12-15).

# TABLE 12-15

## PROPORTIONS AND AVERAGE MENTAL HEALTH (MH II) OF RESPONDENTS ACCORDING TO PROBLEMS WITH THEIR CHILDREN AND RESPONDENTS' SOCIOECONOMIC STATUS

| Problems With Children | Respondents' Socioeconomic Status | | | | | | | |
|---|---|---|---|---|---|---|---|---|
| | LOW | | MIDDLE | | HIGH | | TOTAL | |
| | Per Cent | R̄ | Per Cent | R̄ | Per Cent | R̄ | Per Cent | R̄ |
| Problems | 73.5 | .62 | 70.0 | .52 | 70.7 | .46 | 71.6 | .54 |
| | | * | | | | * | | * |
| No Problems | 24.4 | .52 | 28.5 | .46 | 26.9 | .26 | 26.4 | .42 |
| Don't Know, No Answer ‡ | 2.1 | – | 1.5 | – | 2.4 | – | 2.0 | – |
| Total 'Number of Cases— Parents With Children (N=100 per cent) | 328 | | 260 | | 249 | | | |
| | | | | | | | 837 | |

\* Difference in test variable at the 5 per cent level of confidence between ridits with same subscript or adjacent to same asterisk.
‡ Ridits not computed.

That a child can be a source of severe stress on a parent, and vice versa, is common knowledge. Parental problems were often the focus of the whole family's psychopathology.

Louisa F. (see footnote, page 166) has a deteriorating relationship with her oldest son Andrew. Her problem as a parent was closely connected with her own emotional struggles with her husband. Currently given to outbursts during which she beat the boy with her hairbrush, she was sometimes fearful of losing control completely and inflicting more serious damage on the child. His recent evaluation of her was expressed by "You are not a good mother. I want to grow up to be a decent human being, not a juvenile delinquent, and who can with your yelling and beating me?"

Among all parents, 71.6 per cent reported they had some problems with their children, and this proportion did not vary between the SES levels. About three-quarters of all parents feel that they have at least one problem with their child. This is not surprising in view of the wording of the question, "Most parents have concerns or problems about their children. What are (were) some of the problems you've had with yours?" This positive statement was meant to elicit and probably did encourage the reporting of "problems."

While the meaning of the terms "delinquent behavior" or "bad companions" may vary considerably between socioeconomic groups, these alternatives were *not* read out loud to the respondent by the interviewer. They were simply used as categories for coding or classifying the responses given. An essentially middle or high SES judgment by the interviewers was involved in the interpretation of the respondent's verbalizations about these problems. However biased these interpretations may have been, they were probably consistent because of the homogeneously high educational background of the interviewers. It is therefore worth examining the relative differences between the socioeconomic groups in reporting problems with children.

As with their own reports of physical health, the parents of various SES levels did not report different proportions of children with physical health problems.

Also, as expected, a greater proportion of the low SES parents (who reported problems) mentioned "bad companions" and "delinquent behavior." Among the Lows, Middles, and Highs, 13.7, 9.9, and 5.1 per cent respectively, mentioned "bad companions" as a problem with their children. Similarly, 5.4, 2.7, and 2.3 per cent mentioned "delinquent behavior."

On the other hand, somewhat more Highs mentioned "child-parent conflict" (17.4, 15.9, and 19.3 per cent), "sibling conflict" (3.7, 6.0, and 8.5 per cent), and "peer adjustment" problems such as withdrawn behavior in the play group (6.2, 7.1, and 13.6 per cent). The greater concern of the Highs with interpersonal relations, in their own life as well as that of their children, is evident in these proportions. The "other-directedness" of the higher status groups has been noted by Riesman.[8] These statistics, particularly the proportions of "peer adjustment problems," show us how the higher status child gets pushed in the direction of caring about what the other fellow thinks; of caring so much about others' opinions that he has his "radar" working constantly, picking up signals from other people.

*Habit disturbances* (thumbsucking, bedwetting, and others) were reported more frequently by the middle SES parents. This also seems to corroborate the general belief that those of middle status are more concerned with "good" behavior such as punctuality, cleanliness, and manners, which will enable them to move up in the social system and prepare them for the socioeconomic struggle, since these qualities are highly prized, particularly in the middle bureaucratic echelons. Conversely, those in the lowest status don't care about "good" behavior, which won't gain them any prestige or material goods and is viewed as essentially ineffectual behavior.

Persons of the highest status don't care quite as much what others think, for they already have achieved or have inherited their prestige. For instance, the more flamboyant sexual behavior and dress of both the very lowest and highest strata have been pointed out many times before. The middle class, by and large, has never been noted for its excesses, but rather for the lid that it puts on extremes of emotional, sexual, or other types of expression and behavior. Thus 12.9 per cent of the Lows and 13.6 per cent of the Highs report "habit disturbances" in their children, while almost twice as many Middles (23.6 per cent) are concerned with such behavior.

The Highs and the Lows also express more generalized concern over their children (39.2 per cent and 30.3 per cent) while the Middles express less (18.1 per cent). Perhaps the generalized anxiety of the Middles tends to be reduced, since it is fixed on particular habit disturbances. This may have the function of reducing some of the parental anxiety among the Middles, for it focuses attention on a mechanical problem such as thumbsucking, while drawing attention away from the possible interpersonal origins of such behavior on the part of the child. The Highs are, of course, more concerned with the quality of interpersonal relationships than with the seemingly mechanical problems of enuresis, thumbsucking, or feeding difficulties.

### B.   CHILDREN GIVE MORE TROUBLE THAN PLEASURE

One attitude item seemed to be a very good indicator of parental stress: "Children give their parents more trouble than pleasure." Parents who agreed with this statement ran a considerably higher mental health risk (.67) than those who disagreed (.47). This was true in all three SES groups, but particularly pronounced among low SES parents (see Table 12-16).

The assumption is that we are dealing with responses to a projective question. Parents who agree are presumably saying in effect, "*My* children

## TABLE 12-16

### PROPORTIONS AND AVERAGE MENTAL HEALTH (MH II) OF RESPONDENTS ACCORDING TO CHILDREN GIVING MORE TROUBLE THAN PLEASURE, MARITAL AND PARENTAL STATUS, AND RESPONDENTS' SOCIOECONOMIC STATUS

| Children Give More Trouble Than Pleasure EVER−MARRIED PARENTS | Respondents' Socioeconomic Status | | | | | | | |
|---|---|---|---|---|---|---|---|---|
| | LOW | | MIDDLE | | HIGH | | TOTAL | |
| | Per Cent | $\bar{R}$ | Per Cent | $\bar{R}$ | Per Cent | $\bar{R}$ | Per Cent | $\bar{R}$ |
| Agree | 21.3 | .72 * | 10.7 | .59 | 3.6 | (.50) | 12.8 | .67 * |
| Disagree | 76.6 | .52 | 85.5 | .47 | 95.6 | .40 | 84.9 | .47 |
| Don't Know, No Answer ‖ | 2.1 | − | 3.8 | − | .8 | − | 2.3 | − |
| Total Number of Cases (N=100 per cent) | 328 | | 260 | | 249 | | 837 | |

* Difference in test variable at the 5 per cent level of confidence between ridits adjacent to same asterisk.
‖ Ridits not computed.
Parentheses ( ) enclose ridits based on less than ten cases.

give *me* more trouble than pleasure." This inability to derive gratification from the parental role is indicative of serious malfunction, and can, of course, be considered a symptom of disturbance as well as a source of environmental pressure.

It is possible that the conditions under which families live may influence the amount of pleasure that parents can derive from their children. It is interesting that only 3.6 per cent of the High parents agreed that children given more trouble, compared to 10.7 per cent of the Middles, and 21.3 per cent of the Lows. Perhaps the problems of supporting children tend to outweigh the gratifications of parenthood in this one-fifth of the low SES families. Further examination may reveal these parents to be in the very lowest portion of the low SES. Certainly the children in such families will receive less affection from their harassed parents. Whether the parents' harassment is purely financial or is partially the result of previous mental disturbance, this fifth of the low SES children seem likely candidates for mental disturbance themselves. Longitudinal studies of poor families with mentally healthy parents may give us clues as to whether childhood financial deprivation alone can act as a causal agent in mental disturbance.

While we are not directly concerned with married nonparents, it is noteworthy that a consistently larger proportion of them agree that children give more trouble than pleasure. Among the Lows, for instance, 34.0 per cent of married nonparents agreed, compared with only 21.3 per cent of the parents. Is it possible that their attitudes have kept these married people from having children? Is it simply a case of "sour grapes," a denial that children are pleasurable by people who want to have children but so far have failed to produce any?

Perhaps negative attitudes toward children decrease with age, and those who are negative are primarily young married couples. By this token they are closer to their own childhood. Many of the Lows and Middles may have been responsible for the care of younger siblings when they were in their teens. At this time children, particularly younger brothers and sisters, without doubt give more trouble than pleasure. This interpretation is not supported by additional data. The proportion reporting severe Parental Worries increases from 3.9 per cent in the twenties to 19.3 per cent among those in their fifties. Negative attitudes toward children (at least among parents) increase with age, so other explanations of the negativity of nonparents to children, such as "sour grapes," seem more plausible.

## C.   WORRYING ABOUT CHILDREN

Parents who worry "often" about their children consistently run a greater risk (.65) than parents who worry "sometimes" (.52) or "never" (.44). The trend is similar and significantly so at all three SES levels (see Table 12-17). This item is close in content to the "problems" parents had with their children. (The tetrachoric correlation between the two items is .56.) If one has a "problem" with one's children, one is also likely to worry about the children. It seems safe to say that if one takes successful action concerning some area of the child's behavior, one no longer considers this area a "problem," nor worries about it.

About half the parents worried to some extent about their children, regardless of SES. (Similarly, three-fourths report problems with children, regardless of SES.) What is striking is that a *large majority of*

## TABLE 12-17

### PROPORTIONS AND AVERAGE MENTAL HEALTH (MH II) OF RESPONDENT PARENTS WHO WORRY ABOUT CHILDREN, BY RESPONDENTS' SOCIOECONOMIC STATUS

| Worry About Children | Respondents' Socioeconomic Status | | | | | | | |
|---|---|---|---|---|---|---|---|---|
| | LOW | | MIDDLE | | HIGH | | TOTAL | |
| | Per Cent | $\bar{R}$ | Per Cent | $\bar{R}$ | Per Cent | $\bar{R}$ | Per Cent | $\bar{R}$ |
| Often | 17.1 | $.71^*_z$ | 14.2 | $.63^*_y$ | 13.4 | $.56^*_x$ | 15.1 | $.65^*_w$ |
| Sometimes | 29.6 | .60 | 31.8 | .51 | 42.5 | .45* | 34.1 | .52* |
| Never | 52.1 | $.51^*_z$ | 52.9 | $.44^*_y$ | 43.7 | $.32^*_x$ | 49.9 | $.44^*_w$ |
| Don't Know, No Answer ⌶ | 1.2 | — | 1.1 | — | .4 | — | .9 | — |
| Total Number of Cases (N=100 per cent) | 328 | | 260 | | 249 | | 837 | |

* Difference in test variable at the 5 per cent level of confidence between ridits with same subscript or adjacent to same asterisk.

⌶ Ridits not computed.

*parents have problems with and worry about their children,* and that an increase in mental health risk is definitely involved, despite the majority of parents involved. The implication is that parenthood is indeed a stressful role, which may very well be conducive to strain.

These items: problems with children, worries about children, and "children give more trouble than pleasure" were combined into the Parental Worries factor. This yielded risks of .66, .53, and .42 (MH I). Parental worriers, then, exhibit a distinct increase in risk (see Table 12-18). About 13 per cent of parents seem to fall into the extreme category, but more than half of all parents are involved in some parental stress.

The moral in these data might run, "It is better to worry about your children and your problems with them than not to derive any pleasure from them." Parents who presumably did derive pleasure from their children (those who disagreed with the statement) usually had a sharply lowered mental health risk, regardless of parental worries or problems.

## TABLE 12-18

### DISTRIBUTION, PROPORTIONS, AND AVERAGE MENTAL HEALTH (CMH, MH I, MH II) OF RESPONDENTS ACCORDING TO PARENTAL WORRIES TRICHOTOMIZED AND DICHOTOMIZED

| PARENTAL WORRIES | RESPONDENTS' MENTAL HEALTH | | | | |
|---|---|---|---|---|---|
| | CMH | MH I | MH II | No. of Cases | Per Cent of Cases |
| *Trichotomy* | | | | | |
| + | .53 | .66$^*_z$ | .67$^*_y$ | 107 | 12.8 |
| 0 | .52 | .53$^*_z$ | .54$^*_y$ | 352 | 42.1 |
| | $^*$ | | | | |
| − | .44 | .42$^*_z$ | .42$^*_y$ | 378 | 45.1 |
| *Dichotomy* | | | | | |
| + | .53 | .66 | .67 | 107 | 12.8 |
| | | $^*$ | $^*$ | | |
| − | .48 | .48 | .48 | 730 | 87.2 |
| Total Number of Cases (N=100 per cent) | | | | 837 | |

* Difference in test variable at the 5 per cent level of confidence between ridits with same subscript or adjacent to same asterisk.

The ability to derive pleasure from one's children seems to decrease risk, despite other parental worries, and may be one of the *eugenic* factors which social psychiatry is looking for.

We've seen that the Lows get less pleasure from their work. They also appear to get less pleasure from their children. About one-fifth of the Low parents say children give more trouble than pleasure, or five times the rate among the Highs. This is associated with a sharp increase in risk. It also seems a direct contradiction of the popular statement that the pleasure of the poor is in their children, that this is their form of "wealth." We've found that the Lows are disadvantaged or suffer greater impairment in conjunction with their friendships and interpersonal relations, their health, their work, marriage, and parenthood. Later chapters will attempt to explain this socioeconomic disparity in impairment, even in situations where the stress seems comparable.

Surely the ability to enjoy one's children, marriage, or job is not a *solely* external eugenic factor. It may also be partly a function of the personality structure and mental health of the individual. In the final analysis, as with all the adult factors, we are forced to recognize the existence of this circular relationship (see Chapter 6). As it is, we have learned many details and conditions of this relationship on the way to constructing the stress factors, which may serve in understanding the burden of mental disturbance in our society.

## Summary

*Work Worries.* The work sphere is extremely important in judging the mental health of the individual. "Work worries" and "overwork worries" were the best predictors of mental disturbance, and were therefore combined into a single "work worries" factor. The factor risks in increasing frequency of work worries were .47, .51, and .64 (MH I).

People who are satisfied with their jobs show less impairment than those who don't like their work. About three-fifths of men and unmarried women and of working wives like their work. However, working wives who don't like their work don't run a very high risk. Their investment in the occupational role is apparently not quite as great.

Husbands whose wives work part time are best off in the low SES. Among the Highs, nonworking wives are commoner, and their husbands show the least risk. People who had to stop work for health reasons ran higher risks, and were typically of low SES.

Those who said their work upset their health also showed greater impairment. None of the various reasons they gave for the upset showed significant differences. Uncongenial work, long hours, physical conditions, and heavy responsibilities were linked to increased risk in the low SES. Long hours involved an increase in risk for the Lows, but a decrease for the Highs. The close identification of the high SES individual with his job, which is more congenial even though more taxing, seems to act as a eugenic factor.

*Socioeconomic Status Worries.* The "cost of living" and "getting ahead" are areas of great concern to about one-eighth of the population, and moderate concern to about another sixth. This combined group of about one-fourth of the population who have socioeconomic status worries runs an increased mental health risk. There is some indication that those of low status who are "resigned" to their position are in better mental health than those who worry about their status. With the exception of persons with a weekly income of $300 or more, those who thought "money is the most important thing in life" ran an increased risk.

Those who reported early occupational aspirations on the same level as their present job showed somewhat less impairment than those who exceeded or fell short of their goals. Persons who pick out an appropriate goal and attain it are reality oriented and this may be reflected in the better mental health ratings of the Highs.

*Marital Worries.*    Those who worried about their marriage "often" or "sometimes" showed increased impairment risk, regardless of sex. More high SES men worried about marriage.

Those with frequent marital worries exhibited a sharp rise in impairment risk. Religious intermarriage was unrelated to impairment. Religious out-marriage was more common among the high SES. Ethnic intermarriage (spouses of different nationality backgrounds) showed an increase in risk. Spouses of differing educational level were no more or less impaired than marriage partners who completed the same number of years of schooling.

Husbands whose wives were in higher level occupations than their own exhibited a sharp increase in risk. This was reversed in the middle SES. The relative level of their husbands' occupations bore no relation to the impairment risk of wives.

The number of marriages was directly related to risk (but not significantly so). In the high SES, however, the once-married and the often-married have the identical risk. More high SES people had multiple marriages. They also contributed more than their share of unmarried, particularly unmarried women. The paucity of men of equal status may account for this low marriage rate in the high SES. The low impairment rates originally found for unmarried women, as contrasted with unmarried men, may in part be due to their concentration in the generally healthier high SES.

*Parental Worries.*    Parents who reported they had "problems with their children" ran a higher risk. A large majority of parents (71.6 per cent) reported one or more problems with their children. More Lows mentioned "delinquent behavior" and "bad companions." High SES parents were more prone to mention interpersonal problems such as "child-parent conflict," "sibling conflict," and "peer-adjustment." The middle SES group reported "habit disturbances" more frequently, in keeping with its concern over control of behavior and emotional expression.

Parents who said that children gave "more trouble than pleasure" had greatly increased impairment risk, particularly in the low SES. Only 3.6 per cent of the Highs, in contrast to 21.3 per cent of the Lows found children "more trouble." Parents who worry about their children often show greater risk than those who worry sometimes or never. Parents who worry about their children also report "problems with children" (tetrachoric correlation = .56). About half of all parents worried about their children.

Three items, "problems with children," "worries about children," and "children give more trouble than pleasure," were combined into a single factor of Parental Worries, with risks of .66, .52, and .42 (MH I). About 13 per cent of parents fall in the severe Parental Worries category (.66), but more than half of all parents report some parental stress.

Deriving pleasure from one's children seems to eliminate the risk associated with parental worries and problems. The ability to derive pleasure from children is probably a sign of good mental health as well as an indication of lack of stress.

## Notes

1. We can safely assume, therefore, that *items* screened only against Mental Health Rating II would indeed still show a relationship to mental health if Rating I were employed. It should be noted that MHR II is involved here, as it is in all other tables run during the screening operation. For this reason the findings are somewhat circular. The psychiatrists were greatly influenced by this particular questionnaire item. However, as we have seen with the factor tables, which present MHR I as well as II, the symptom rating (I) is somewhat less closely related to the factors than the rating based on both background and symptoms (II). The association between these factors and mental health does *not* disappear when we examine MHR I. Though showing slightly less of a ridit with Rating I than with Rating II, the factor nevertheless still maintains a strong association with Rating I.

2. Tabular material on reasons why "work upset health" is not included.

3. See Robert K. Merton and Alice S. Kitt, "Contributions to the Theory of Reference Group Behavior," in R. K. Merton and P. F. Lazarsfeld (eds.), *Continuities in Social Research: Studies in the Scope and Method of the American Soldier,* The Free Press of Glencoe, New York, 1950.

4. The risks associated with each proportion of income paid for rent are as follows: less than 15%, .49; 15% to 19%, .51; 20% to 24%, .51; 25% to 29%, .52; 30% to 34%, .56; 35% to 39%, .50; 40% to 44%, .58; 45% or more, .49.

5. Abram Kardiner and Lionel Ovesey, *The Mark of Oppression: A Psychosexual Study of the American Negro,* W. W. Norton, New York, 1951.

6. Mirra Komarovsky, *The Unemployed Man and His Family,* Holt, Rinehart & Winston, New York, 1940.

7. Those who are now married, or were married and are now widowed, divorced, or separated.

8. David Riesman, *The Lonely Crowd,* Yale University Press, New Haven, 1950.

# The Relationship of the Childhood and Adult Factors to the Mental Health Ratings

## THOMAS S. LANGNER

We have previously seen how the screening process turned up a large number of "live" questionnaire items that were related to the Mental Health Ratings independently of socioeconomic status. These items in turn were gathered into factors by a pyramiding process. Our first task in this chapter is to show that the *stress factors* made up of these items also bear a relationship to mental health which is independent of SES.

## The Factors Are Associated with Mental Health Risk

Let us review what we have learned in Chapters 8 to 12, which examined the factors separately. Table 13-1 shows the Childhood Mental Health Index and Adult Mental Health I ridits of the dichotomized and trichotomized childhood factors. Several generalizations of interest can be drawn from these data.

On the whole, persons reporting each factor (represented by a +) had a greater mental health risk than those who didn't. This is true of both the dichotomized and the trichotomized versions of the childhood and adult factors, and for the CMH Index and MH I.

In general, the childhood factors show a stronger relationship to the Childhood Mental Health ridits than to the Adult Mental Health ridits, and this is just what we would expect. The adult factors, on the other hand, bear a closer relationship to the Adult Mental Health ridits than to the Childhood Mental Health ridits (see Table 13-2).[1]

## TABLE 13-1

## AVERAGE MENTAL HEALTH (CMH, MH I) OF RESPONDENTS ACCORDING TO DICHOTOMIZED AND TRICHOTOMIZED CHILDHOOD FACTORS

| Childhood Factors | Respondents' Mental Health | | | | | |
|---|---|---|---|---|---|---|
| | CMH | | MH I | | No. of Cases | |
| Dichotomy | + | − | + | − | + | − |
| | $\bar{R}$ | $\bar{R}$ | $\bar{R}$ | $\bar{R}$ | | |
| Parents' Poor Physical Health[a] | .54 | .48 | .54 | .48 | 515 | 1145 |
| Parents' Poor Mental Health | .60 | .46 | .57 | .48 | 447 | 1213 |
| Childhood Economic Deprivation | .58 | .47 | .57 | .47 | 496 | 1164 |
| Childhood Poor Physical Health | .59 | .45 | .55 | .47 | 624 | 1036 |
| Childhood Broken Homes | .51 | .50 | .52 | .49 | 585 | 1075 |
| Parents' Character Negatively Perceived | .61 | .44 | .58 | .46 | 563 | 1097 |
| Parents' Quarrels | .57 | .45 | .53 | .48 | 704 | 956 |
| Disagreements with Parents | .55 | .47 | .50 | .50 | 717 | 943 |
| Trichotomy | + | 0 | − | + | 0 | − | + | 0 | − |
| Parents' Poor Mental Health | .62 | .54 | .46 | .56 | .57 | .48 | 185 | 262 | 1213 |
| Childhood Economic Deprivation | .58 | .56 | .46 | .58 | .54 | .47 | 204 | 393 | 1063 |
| Childhood Poor Physical Health | .64 | .55 | .45 | .57 | .54 | .47 | 247 | 377 | 1036 |
| Childhood Broken Homes | .52 | .50 | .50 | .56 | .49 | .49 | 258 | 327 | 1075 |
| Parents' Character Negatively Perceived | .66 | .58 | .44 | .63 | .56 | .46 | 195 | 368 | 1097 |
| Parents' Quarrels | .63 | .54 | .45 | .58 | .51 | .48 | 252 | 452 | 956 |
| Disagreements with Parents | .59 | .52 | .47 | .55 | .49 | .50 | 209 | 508 | 943 |

Total Number of Cases      1660
(N=100 per cent)

[a] This factor was only dichotomized because there were too few cases in the trichotomized "plus" group.

## TABLE 13-2

## AVERAGE MENTAL HEALTH (MH I) OF RESPONDENTS ACCORDING TO DICHOTOMIZED AND TRICHOTOMIZED ADULT FACTORS

| Adult Factors | Respondents' MH I | | | No. of Cases | | |
|---|---|---|---|---|---|---|
| *Dichotomy* | + | − | | + | − | |
| | $\bar{R}$ | $\bar{R}$ | | | | |
| Adult Poor Physical Health | .70 | .45 | | 310 | 1350 | |
| Work Worries | .64 | .48 | | 225 | 1435 | |
| Socioeconomic Status Worries | .63 | .48 | | 200 | 1460 | |
| Poor Interpersonal Affiliations | .64 | .48 | | 209 | 1451 | |
| *Contingent Factors* | | | | | | |
| Marital Worries | .58 | .45 | | 174 | 813 | |
| Parental Worries | .66 | .48 | | 107 | 730 | |
| *Trichotomy* | + | 0 | − | + | 0 | − |
| Adult Poor Physical Health | .70 | .51 | .38 | 310 | 772 | 578 |
| Work Worries | .64 | .54 | .46 | 225 | 274 | 1161 |
| Socioeconomic Status Worries | .63 | .57 | .46 | 200 | 274 | 1186 |
| Poor Interpersonal Affiliations | .64 | .52 | .45 | 209 | 597 | 854 |
| *Contingent Factors* | | | | | | |
| Marital Worries | .78 | .54 | .45 | 31 | 143 | 813 |
| Parental Worries | .66 | .53 | .42 | 107 | 352 | 378 |
| Total Number of Cases | | | | | 1660 | |

## The Factors Are Related to Mental Health Risk Independent of SES

The previous chapters dealing with the individual factors have shown that the items and the factors themselves exhibited mental health variation independent of the fathers' or the respondents' socioecenomic status. Tables 13-3 and 13-4 illustrate this point and summarize the results for all the childhood and adult factors. For instance (see Table 13-3), a

# TABLE 13-3

## AVERAGE MENTAL HEALTH (CMH, MH I) OF RESPONDENTS ACCORDING TO TRICHOTOMIZED CHILDHOOD FACTORS AND FATHERS' SOCIOECONOMIC STATUS

| | | Fathers' Socioeconomic Status | | | | | |
| | | LOW | | MIDDLE | | HIGH | |
| Childhood Factors | | CMH $\bar{R}$ | MH I $\bar{R}$ | CMH $\bar{R}$ | MH I $\bar{R}$ | CMH $\bar{R}$ | MH I $\bar{R}$ |
|---|---|---|---|---|---|---|---|
| Parents' Poor Physical Health[a] | + | .57 | .59 | .56 | .55 | .50 | .49 |
| | – | .52 | .54 | .47 | .48 | .45 | .43 |
| Parents' Poor Mental Health | + | .72 | .64 | .64 | .54 | .59 | .54 |
| | 0 | .66 | .66 | .62 | .57 | .51 | .52 |
| | – | .50 | .53 | .46 | .48 | .44 | .42 |
| Childhood Economic Deprivation | + | .56 | .56 | .58 | .60 | .68 | .56 |
| | 0 | .58 | .57 | .56 | .54 | .51 | .48 |
| | – | .50 | .55 | .45 | .46 | .45 | .44 |
| Childhood Poor Physical Health | + | .66 | .62 | .63 | .59 | .63 | .50 |
| | 0 | .63 | .61 | .54 | .55 | .50 | .48 |
| | – | .48 | .62 | .46 | .46 | .41 | .42 |
| Childhood Broken Homes | + | .55 | .64 | .51 | .58 | .51 | .45 |
| | 0 | .57 | .54 | .50 | .53 | .43 | .41 |
| | – | .53 | .54 | .50 | .47 | .47 | .46 |
| Parents' Character Negatively Perceived | + | .70 | .67 | .67 | .68 | .61 | .53 |
| | 0 | .61 | .63 | .59 | .54 | .56 | .51 |
| | – | .48 | .51 | .44 | .45 | .42 | .42 |
| Parents' Quarrels | + | .71 | .65 | .61 | .55 | .58 | .55 |
| | 0 | .57 | .56 | .52 | .51 | .53 | .44 |
| | – | .48 | .53 | .45 | .47 | .42 | .43 |
| Disagreements With Parents | + | .64 | .61 | .57 | .52 | .59 | .53 |
| | 0 | .56 | .54 | .54 | .50 | .47 | .43 |
| | – | .51 | .56 | .47 | .49 | .43 | .44 |
| Average Ridit of Total SES Group | | | .55 | | .50 | | .45 |

[a] This factor was not trichotomized.

typical childhood factor, Parents' Poor Mental Health, exhibits MH I variation (reading from the "minus" to the "plus" category) of .53 to .64 in the low, .48 to .54 in the middle, and .42 to .54 in the high SES. That is, within each SES group, Parents' Poor Mental Health is independently associated with adult mental health risk. Ridit differences of .11, .06, and .12 attest to this independent variation.

The same is true of Adult Mental Health Rating I in relation to the

## TABLE 13-4

### AVERAGE MENTAL HEALTH (MH I) OF RESPONDENTS ACCORDING TO TRICHOTOMIZED ADULT FACTORS AND RESPONDENTS' SOCIOECONOMIC STATUS

| Adult Factors | Trichotomy | Respondents' Socioeconomic Status | | |
|---|---|---|---|---|
| | | LOW $\bar{R}$ | MIDDLE $\bar{R}$ | HIGH $\bar{R}$ |
| Adult Poor | + | .78 | .64 | .58 |
| Physical | 0 | .53 | .51 | .48 |
| Health | − | .47 | .40 | .33 |
| Work Worries | + | .81 | .60 | .55 |
| | 0 | .64 | .58 | .43 |
| | − | .55 | .46 | .38 |
| Socioeconomic | + | .74 | .62 | .52 |
| Status Worries | 0 | .66 | .57 | .46 |
| | − | .54 | .46 | .39 |
| Poor | + | .69 | .61 | .53 |
| Interpersonal | 0 | .59 | .53 | .43 |
| Affiliations | − | .54 | .44 | .40 |
| *Contingent Factors* | | | | |
| Marital Worries[a] | + | .77 | .55 | .47 |
| | − | .54 | .46 | .36 |
| Parental Worries | + | .71 | .62 | .44 |
| | 0 | .61 | .53 | .47 |
| | − | .48 | .43 | .32 |
| Average Ridit of Total SES Group | | .59 | .50 | .41 |

[a] This factor was dichotomized because there were only 30 cases in the trichotomized "plus" group, to be divided among three SES groups.

adult factors (see Table 13-4). For example, Adult Poor Physical Health shows variation in the low SES from .47 to .78, in the middle SES from .40 to .64, and in the high SES from .33 to .58 (differences of .31, .24, and .25 respectively). With the exception of Childhood Broken Homes (Table 13-3) where variation within SES groups is negligible, all childhood and adult factors show mental health variation that is independent of SES.

Contrary to expectations, the difference or "effect" on Adult Mental Health ridits is not consistently greater in the low SES (fathers') when childhood factors are considered. For example, Childhood Economic Deprivation seems to involve more risk in the high and middle SES than in the low SES. There is no ridit increment (over the average ridit of .56 for the low fathers' SES) among those who suffered Childhood Economic Deprivation. In the high and middle SES, there is an increment of .10 and .11. It is quite possible that the emotional consequences of economic deprivation are strongest when the deprivation is relative to a wealthier reference group, or former wealthy position. Stated another way, those who are inured to hardship and expect little more are not as likely to suffer from it as those who are used to the silver spoon.

A special case where a childhood factor seems to have no effect on the Adult Mental Health I ridits in the high, but some effect in the low and middle SES, is that of Childhood Broken Homes. This may be due to the division of this factor into "early broken," "late broken," and unbroken homes. The early broken homes are somewhat more frequent in the low SES.

In contrast, when the adult factors are considered, the low SES usually seems to show a much greater ridit effect than the middle and high SES. Thus the Lows show more impairment associated with the same adult experience. The low SES appears particularly affected by work, marital, and parental worries.[2] In the following chapters, it will be seen that the low SES shows more evidence of strain (poor Mental Health Ratings) per "unit" of stress (number of factors) than does the high SES.

Regardless of these socioeconomic differences, we must not lose sight of our immediate point, that these differences in mental health are due to the factors themselves, not to SES. This hypothesis is substantiated by Tables 13-3 and 13-4. The factors exhibit mental health variation even when SES is controlled. That is, the factors show ridit variation within each SES group in the expected direction, and are therefore related to mental health independently of SES.

## The Factors Are Related to Mental Health Risk
## Independent of Age

While the screening phase of the project controlled socioeconomic status, it did not control age, one of the demographic variables shown to be responsible for mental health variation independently of SES. For this reason, we had to control age. All the childhood and adult factors show mental health variation which is independent of the respondent's age (see Tables 13-5 and 13-6). This is encouraging, since it again increases our confidence that we have isolated live stress factors that cannot be explained away by demographic factors.

Two subsidiary facts are worth mentioning. First, the CMH ridits decrease slightly as the age of the respondent increases. This is more marked, for instance, in the case of Parents' Poor Mental Health. We know that one's childhood mental health could not very well be affected by one's present age. This would mean that the older one is, the better one's childhood mental health, an anomalous finding. Several hypotheses occur. Perhaps the increase in physical infirmity associated with aging tends to obscure the minor psychological symptoms that occurred in childhood. The older person may fail to consider childhood symptoms worth reporting. A second possibility is that some of the details of childhood symptoms are forgotten by age fifty. This is unlikely, however, since we know that particularly in later years, the sixties and seventies, childhood memories are sharpened, and immediate recall becomes weaker.

Another even more doubtful possibility is that people whose early childhood was in the 1900s actually were in better mental health and were exposed to less familial stress. Still another explanation is that persons who have lived for forty or fifty years without either dying or becoming invalids or ending up as permanent inpatients in a mental hospital must have been physically and mentally healthier to start with. This might be a partial explanation, if we did not already know that older persons tend to come from low SES families of origin and are primarily first-generation immigrants.

A second subsidiary finding is that there are definite (though moderate) increases in Adult Mental Health ridits as age increases. These age increases are expected, but they do not vitiate the finding that the factors show ridit variation which is independent of age. In fact, the ridit

## TABLE 13-5

### AVERAGE MENTAL HEALTH (CMH, MH I) OF RESPONDENTS ACCORDING TO TRICHOTOMIZED CHILDHOOD FACTORS AND RESPONDENTS' AGE

| Childhood Factors | | 20 to 29 CMH $\bar{R}$ | 20 to 29 MH I $\bar{R}$ | 30 to 39 CMH $\bar{R}$ | 30 to 39 MH I $\bar{R}$ | 40 to 49 CMH $\bar{R}$ | 40 to 49 MH I $\bar{R}$ | 50 to 59 CMH $\bar{R}$ | 50 to 59 MH I $\bar{R}$ |
|---|---|---|---|---|---|---|---|---|---|
| Parents' Poor Physical Health[a] | + | .58 | .52 | .59 | .54 | .52 | .53 | .49 | .59 |
| | – | .51 | .40 | .48 | .48 | .46 | .48 | .48 | .55 |
| Parents' Poor Mental Health | + | .71 | .51 | .61 | .52 | .69 | .63 | .54 | .58 |
| | 0 | .63 | .51 | .58 | .55 | .57 | .60 | .58 | .66 |
| | – | .49 | .41 | .48 | .48 | .44 | .46 | .46 | .54 |
| Childhood Economic Deprivation | + | .64 | .54 | .63 | .55 | .50 | .57 | .56 | .64 |
| | 0 | .55 | .47 | .56 | .54 | .55 | .54 | .57 | .59 |
| | – | .50 | .41 | .47 | .47 | .45 | .47 | .44 | .53 |
| Childhood Poor Physical Health | + | .67 | .53 | .66 | .54 | .63 | .59 | .58 | .61 |
| | 0 | .56 | .49 | .55 | .54 | .55 | .54 | .56 | .61 |
| | – | .47 | .39 | .47 | .47 | .42 | .45 | .44 | .53 |
| Childhood Broken Homes | + | .56 | .52 | .58 | .55 | .49 | .57 | .49 | .61 |
| | 0 | .55 | .46 | .51 | .47 | .44 | .48 | .51 | .56 |
| | – | .52 | .41 | .51 | .50 | .49 | .48 | .48 | .55 |
| Parents' Character Negatively Perceived | + | .62 | .52 | .66 | .67 | .71 | .69 | .65 | .66 |
| | 0 | .60 | .54 | .60 | .54 | .60 | .53 | .54 | .62 |
| | – | .49 | .39 | .45 | .45 | .41 | .45 | .45 | .53 |
| Parents' Quarrels | + | .62 | .54 | .67 | .56 | .63 | .60 | .58 | .61 |
| | 0 | .54 | .41 | .54 | .55 | .53 | .50 | .54 | .58 |
| | – | .50 | .43 | .45 | .45 | .42 | .47 | .44 | .54 |
| Disagreements With Parents | + | .59 | .50 | .61 | .57 | .58 | .63 | .57 | .49 |
| | 0 | .50 | .43 | .57 | .54 | .51 | .43 | .50 | .57 |
| | – | .53 | .43 | .45 | .45 | .45 | .50 | .47 | .56 |
| Average Ridit of Total Age Group | | | .44 | | .50 | | .49 | | .56 |

[a]This factor was not trichotomized.

## TABLE 13-6

### AVERAGE MENTAL HEALTH (MH I) OF RESPONDENTS ACCORDING TO TRICHOTOMIZED ADULT FACTORS AND RESPONDENTS' AGE

|  |  | Respondents' Age | | | |
|---|---|---|---|---|---|
|  |  | 20 to 29 | 30 to 39 | 40 to 49 | 50 to 59 |
| Adult Factors |  | $\bar{R}$ | $\bar{R}$ | $\bar{R}$ | $\bar{R}$ |
| Adult Poor Physical | + | .63 | .69 | .70 | .72 |
| Health | 0 | .49 | .52 | .49 | .54 |
|  | – | .35 | .39 | .38 | .41 |
| Work Worries | + | .59 | .63 | .66 | .69 |
|  | 0 | .47 | .56 | .50 | .63 |
|  | – | .40 | .46 | .46 | .52 |
| Socioeconomic Status | + | .61 | .61 | .62 | .70 |
| Worries | 0 | .48 | .59 | .59 | .60 |
|  | – | .40 | .45 | .45 | .53 |
| Poor Interpersonal | + | .55 | .63 | .66 | .68 |
| Affiliations | 0 | .50 | .52 | .51 | .56 |
|  | – | .38 | .46 | .45 | .51 |
| *Contingent Factors* |  |  |  |  |  |
| Marital Worries[a] | + | .49 | .57 | .60 | .68 |
|  | – | .39 | .45 | .43 | .52 |
| Parental Worries | + | .27 | .67 | .69 | .67 |
|  | 0 | .54 | .55 | .46 | .60 |
|  | – | .36 | .41 | .42 | .46 |
| Average Ridit of Total Age Group |  | .44 | .50 | .49 | .56 |

[a]This factor was not trichotomized.

variation due to age does not approach in magnitude the ridit variation due to the adult factors.

Although it might have been expected, there are no definite trends in MHR I differences or "effects" as age increases. It might be logical to think that worries, poor health, and lack of friends might have a more deleterious "effect" on the mental health of a fifty-year-old person than on a twenty-year-old. However, not only are the ridit differences similar in each age decade, but the ridit increment over the average mental health of each age group also indicates no age trend. Regardless of age, then, the factors seem to involve the same mental health risk.

What does this mean to the clinician? For one thing, poor health in an older person is no more and no less significant to the psychiatrist than poor health in a younger person. There is no reason to discount aches and pains of aging, for they have just as much importance for mental disturbance as the aches and pains of the young. In addition, the wisdom and experience of the older person does not make his burdens any easier to bear. Even his negative childhood experiences seem to have as much "impact" on him as they do on young adults. Time apparently does not heal all wounds.

Two exceptions to these generalizations must be noted. First, worrisome parents in their twenties have less mental health risk (.27) than those who have no Parental Worries (.36) or those who are moderately worrisome (.54). This result may be an artifact due to the very small number of cases involved. A second exception, this time to the general finding that the impact of the factors is similar in all age decades, is found in the fact that Marital Worries among persons forty or over are associated with a slightly increased mental health risk (comparing the plus and minus groups). With this exception, the factors show no age changes in impact or statistical "effect" between ages twenty to fifty-nine.

## The Factors Are Related to Mental Health Risk
### Independent of Sex

The third demographic factor to be controlled was the sex of the respondent. Although there were no sex differences evident in the whole sample, it was just possible that sex differences in mental health might appear when the stress factors were introduced. For instance, it might turn out that Parental Worries involved mental health risk for women but not for men, or that Work Worries seemed to increase the ridits of males but not females. Happily these possibilities did not eventuate. Tables 13-7 and 13-8 illustrate that the CMH and MHR I vary with the factors regardless of sex. The factors, then, are independent of the sex variable, just as they are independent of SES and age, in their relation to mental health.

To turn to the minor sex differences that do appear, the Adult Mental Health ridits are quite similar for males and females within each factor

# TABLE 13-7

## AVERAGE MENTAL HEALTH (CMH, MHI) OF MALE AND FEMALE RESPONDENTS ACCORDING TO TRICHOTOMIZED CHILDHOOD FACTORS

| | | | | | |
|---|---|---|---|---|---|
| | | *Respondents' Mental Health* | | | |
| | | *MALE* | | *FEMALE* | |
| *Childhood Factors* | | CMH $\bar{R}$ | MHI $\bar{R}$ | CMH $\bar{R}$ | MHI $\bar{R}$ |
| Parents' Poor | + | .51 | .53 | .56 | .55 |
| Physical Health[a] | − | .46 | .48 | .50 | .48 |
| Parents' Poor | + | .64 | .59 | .61 | .56 |
| Mental | 0 | .56 | .58 | .60 | .57 |
| Health | − | .43 | .47 | .48 | .48 |
| Childhood | + | .56 | .58 | .60 | .58 |
| Economic | 0 | .53 | .52 | .58 | .55 |
| Deprivation | − | .43 | .47 | .48 | .47 |
| Childhood Poor | + | .60 | .59 | .66 | .56 |
| Physical | 0 | .51 | .53 | .59 | .56 |
| Health | − | .43 | .46 | .46 | .47 |
| Childhood | + | .49 | .56 | .55 | .57 |
| Broken | 0 | .45 | .46 | .53 | .51 |
| Homes | − | .48 | .49 | .51 | .48 |
| Parents' Character | + | .63 | .64 | .68 | .63 |
| Negatively | 0 | .56 | .58 | .60 | .54 |
| Perceived | − | .42 | .45 | .46 | .47 |
| Parents' | + | .60 | .60 | .64 | .57 |
| Quarrels | 0 | .51 | .52 | .56 | .50 |
| | − | .42 | .46 | .47 | .49 |
| Disagreements | + | .57 | .57 | .60 | .53 |
| with Parents | 0 | .51 | .49 | .53 | .48 |
| | − | .44 | .49 | .49 | .51 |
| Average Ridit of Total Sex Group | | .50 | .50 | .50 | .50 |

[a]This factor was not trichotomized.

## TABLE 13-8

### AVERAGE MENTAL HEALTH (MH I) OF MALE AND FEMALE RESPONDENTS ACCORDING TO TRICHOTOMIZED ADULT FACTORS

| | | Respondents' Mental Health | |
| | | MALE | FEMALE |
| Adult Factors | | $\bar{R}$ | $\bar{R}$ |
|---|---|---|---|
| Adult Poor | + | .67 | .72 |
| Physical | 0 | .52 | .51 |
| Health | − | .39 | .37 |
| Work Worries | + | .60 | .70 |
| | 0 | .55 | .54 |
| | − | .46 | .46 |
| Socioeconomic | + | .57 | .69 |
| Status Worries | 0 | .54 | .59 |
| | − | .47 | .45 |
| Poor Interpersonal | + | .66 | .63 |
| Affiliations | 0 | .53 | .52 |
| | − | .45 | .45 |
| Marital Worries[a] | + | .53 | .62 |
| | − | .44 | .46 |
| Parental Worries | + | .64 | .68 |
| | 0 | .47 | .57 |
| | − | .43 | .42 |
| Average Ridit of Total Sex Group | | .50 | .50 |

[a]This factor was not trichotomized.

category. When the Childhood Mental Health Index is considered, however, the females have consistently higher risks in the plus group of each factor, with the exception of Parents' Poor Mental Health. It may well be that the CMH Index is subject to some sex bias in reporting. Then again, it may be that girls actually have more symptoms of psychiatric significance than boys, although these differences tend to disappear in adulthood.

It must be remembered that the CMH Index is psychometric in nature and does not involve psychiatrists' judgments. A similar psychometric measure of symptomatology, a score composed of 22 major symptoms, showed that the adult females in the sample have a larger *number* of symptoms than the adult males.[3] It is possible that some of their symptoms, such as dizziness and feeling "hot all over" may be discounted by the experienced clinician as merely menopausal symptoms of little psychiatric significance. This would account for the larger number of *symptoms* among adult women, but equal proportions of Impaired *ratings* in both sexes.

There is no difference in the average mental health risk of men and women (.50). Women do seem to have a larger risk increment than the males if they have experienced the adult factors. This is especially true of the SES, Work, and Marital Worries factors. Worries about SES (getting ahead, and the cost of living) are associated with a ridit increase of .24 among females and only .10 among males. Worries about work ("my work" and "overwork") show a ridit increase of .24 among females and only .14 among males. Women, then, seem to be more impaired by worries that might on the surface seem to be exclusively male. The direct and daily concern of women with the cost of living, and their strong sense of status is apparent in these results.

Regardless of the fact that women seem to show more of a ridit increment due to the adult factors, the fact remains that both childhood and adult factors show mental health variation independent of the sex of the respondent. The degree of the variation is not as important as the fact of its independent existence. The finding that Marital Worries seem to involve more risk for women than men is of interest, but peripheral to our main concern, which is to make sure that the factors we have isolated are not just demographic variables in other clothing.

## The Factors Are Related to Mental Health Risk Independent of Age and SES Controlled Simultaneously

As a final check on the viability of the factors, two were selected which had a very high positive correlation with age and a very high negative correlation with SES. (The age and SES variables were the most powerful demographic factors isolated in the first phase of the research.) Adult Poor Physical Health was chosen since it shows a strong inverse variation with SES and a strong direct variation with age. Parental Worries was chosen for the same reason. Both factors were related to mental health risk independent of simultaneous age and SES controls.[4]

Our confidence about the independence of the factors is surely increased by the fact that the control of closely correlated demographic variables in no way reduces the statistical effect of these factors (their relationship to the mental health ridits). The mental health risk associated with the childhood and adult factors which have been isolated are by no means "spurious" in the sense that they are really the result of socio-economic position, age, or sex. Even when the respondent's socioeconomic status and his age—the two background variables most highly correlated with mental health and with the factors themselves—are controlled, the factors exhibit a residual relationship with mental health which is almost equally strong.

## The Original Rationale for Pattern Analysis of Factors

After finding out the relationship of each single factor to mental health it was only natural that we should want to know how combinations of these factors were related to mental health. The first question to be answered was whether "the whole is greater than the sum of the parts." Are two factors taken together associated with greater impairment risk than when taken separately?

We can measure the statistical effect of each factor on mental health risk by subtracting .50 (the average mental health ridit for the whole sample) from the ridit (or average mental health) of those who answered positively and are in its "plus" cell. Suppose factor A has a plus group with a ridit of .55, and so do factors B and C. The increments or "effects" due to each factor separately are all .05. If the whole is equal merely to the sum of the parts, then those persons who share in all three factors, or pattern ABC, should have an average ridit of .65 (.05 plus .05 plus .05; that is, an increment of .15, added to .50, the average for the entire population). If having all three factors is worse than the sum of the effect of each of the three factors, then the average ridit of the group with pattern ABC should be greater than .65. If pattern ABC actually shows a ridit of .65, the factors are merely additive. However, if ABC has an average ridit of .70 or .60, the factors are interactive; that is, taken together, they are *synergistic*, each increasing (or decreasing) the strength of the other. Later in this chapter, data are presented which show rather conclusively that the factors we selected were essentially additive rather than interactive in their relation to mental health.

A corollary question arises from the problem of additive and interactive factors: Is there a "straw that breaks the camel's back"? After people have experienced a certain number of factors, do they all suddenly "break down"? Our findings indicate that, quite to the contrary, the larger the number of factors, the worse the average mental health of the group, with no "breaking point" at any particular number of factors.

Another reason for investigating patterns of factors was to see whether any particular pair of factors, say, A and B, involved more mental health risk than another pair, A and C. For instance, pattern AB might only have an average ridit of .55, while pattern AC had one of .60. This could mean that the "effect" of A was heightened by C, but not by B. It could also mean that C was stronger than B in its own effect, and the additive effect of AC was therefore greater. The latter explanation now seems most tenable, in the light of our data.

Purely from the historical viewpoint it is important to relate another reason why the patterns of factors were closely studied. (This reason was later found to be unjustified.) It was felt that the factors, particularly those related to childhood, could be arranged in temporal sequence. This was called "chain analysis," since each link or factor was presumed to follow another in time. The rationale for the chain analysis was based on several propositions: (1) the pathogenic process can begin at any point in the life history; (2) the earlier it begins the more serious the ultimate pathology is likely to be; (3) once the process is initiated, each factor tends to have psychological consequences which in turn precipitate other factors with their own consequences, creating a cumulative spiraling or snowballing effect; (4) theoretically, the snowballing can be stopped or its momentum reduced by the subsequent intrusion of an important eugenic factor. The hypothesized temporal sequence of childhood factors was as follows: Parents' Poor Physical Health, Parents' Poor Mental Health, Childhood Poor Physical Health, Childhood Broken Homes, Parents' Quarrels, and Respondents' Disagreements with Parents. (Childhood Economic Deprivation could be given only a tentative temporal position after Parents' Poor Mental Health.) For instance, the parents' physical and mental health was presumed to have been in existence before the respondents' physical health, that is, before the birth of the respondent. This temporal sequence, therefore, was assumed to be at least somewhat parallel to a causal sequence. For example, the physical health of the parents would more likely affect the physical health of the child, even though in some cases a sick child could very well cause his parents' physical health to deteriorate. If this temporal sequence was in fact a true "chain of events," A would usually be followed by BCDEF, B would usually be followed by CDEF, C by DEF, D by EF, and E by F. These *pure chain patterns,* then, would be more numerous than nonchain patterns if the chain hypothesis were correct. It was soon evident that this was not the case, and the temporal or chain hypothesis was not substantiated.

Another hypothesized effect not substantiated by subsequent analysis of the data was a clearly "eugenic effect" of particular factors. Let us suppose that an individual had experienced four stress factors, A, B, C, D, but that, on the other hand, he had not experienced the stressful aspect of factor E, for example, parental rejection. This means that his parents loved him rather than rejected him. His pattern would read + + + + −. The minus, or eugenic factor of parental love, might very well protect him against the effects of the four stress factors. The interpretation of a low mental health risk for the pattern + + + + − would be "No matter what happens to him he will be mentally healthy as long as his parents love him." On the other hand, a pattern of − − − − + with a high ridit would indicate that factor E, no matter what other social or emotional advantages persons with this pattern had in life, would increase his chances of being mentally disturbed. However, the "eugenic" effects of the absence of *one* stress factor ( − ), and the "pathogenic" effects of the presence of *one* stress factor ( + ) were not found in the data, over and above their original additive effects.

Although it will not be necessary to discuss again the unsubstantiated chain hypothesis, snowballing effect, or effect of single "eugenic" factors, the development of the patterns of factors (without reference to their temporal sequence) will make up the rest of this chapter. The essentially negative findings of the pattern analysis have theoretical and methodological importance for the understanding and analysis of life history materials. As will be shown later, these results call into question any elaborate sequential analysis of events in the life history purely for purposes of predicting *gross impairment ratings.*

## Patterns of Childhood Factors: Paired Factors

One of the most important questions answered by the pattern analysis was that of "additivity versus interaction," discussed previously. The additive situation is present when the paired factors (or pattern) AB have about the same "effect" on the respondents' average mental health ridits as the sum of the individual effects of factor A and factor B operating separately. Almost all pairs of factors show this additivity. Furthermore, generally speaking pattern AB has about the same average mental health ridit as patterns BC, CD, DE, or AC, ED, and so forth. In other words, with a few exceptions, any *pair* of factors is about as powerful as the next pair. Similarly, patterns ABC, BCD, CDE, and so forth are equally powerful, and because of the general additivity of the factors all of them are more powerful than any of the pairs. In the same way, tetrads are more powerful than triads.

Most of the actual ridits are slightly below the additive or expected ridits. In the case of two pairs of factors, however, Parents' Poor Physical Health—Parents' Character Negatively Perceived, and Childhood Economic Deprivation—Childhood Poor Physical Health, the actual ridit is as high as the expected ridit, indicating true additivity.

Three pairs are of particular interest, for they show some signs of a weak positive interaction rather than being merely additive; that is, the actual ridits are slightly higher than the expected ridits. The first of these is the pair of Parents' Poor Physical Health and Childhood Poor Physical Health. The actual ridit for this pair, .65, is slightly greater than the expected, .63. While this is not a large increment in mental health risk over the sum of the separate effects of each factor, it is worth noting because of its rarity in these data. The physical health of both parents, the childhood physical health, and the present physical health of an adult patient assume additional importance in the psychiatric case history, for these factors increase mental health risk when they occur together.

The factor pair of Parents' Poor Mental Health and Childhood Broken Homes also shows some slight interaction. Note, however, that Childhood Broken Homes is quite weak when dichotomized (an increment above .50 of only + .01), while Parents' Poor Mental Health is relatively strong (+ .10). These disproportionate strengths may have something to do with the interaction, since the stronger factor may bolster the weaker one. For instance, it is just possible that selecting persons whose mentally disturbed parents had a broken home may cull more parents who separated violently, as opposed to those (less mentally disturbed) parents who were separated by death alone. Thus the parents' mental disturbance would add a new dimension to the Broken Homes factor, and enhance its power to predict mental health. Certainly if one takes the time to explore more deeply, it is possible to isolate broken home situations, such as the remarriage of the like-sex widowed parent, which seem to be associated with a much greater risk than broken homes in general. However, simple pairing with these particular six factors does not greatly enhance the power of the Broken Homes factor.

Another slightly interactive pair is that of Parents' Poor Physical Health and Parents' Quarrels, with an expected ridit of .61, but an actual ridit of .63. One can only assume from this that quarrels between parents, one or both of whom is physically ill, may have more serious consequences or concomitants than, let us say, quarrels associated with some of the other childhood factors, such as Economic Deprivation, Parents' Poor Mental Health, or Parents' Quarrels that end in a broken home.

The fact that there are few instances of interaction between the childhood factors, regardless of the factors involved or their numbers, indicates that these factors (at least as measured by responses to questionnaire items) do not "spark" each other.

If the childhood factors are trichotomized, only one interactive pair emerges: Parents' Poor Mental Health—Childhood Broken Homes. The expected ridit of .64 is greatly exceeded by the actual ridit of .77. This pair already showed slight interaction when dichotomized, and when trichotomized shows a much greater risk than combining the ridits would suggest. This finding calls for research, since the effect of Broken Homes alone is only + .02, that of Parents in Poor Mental Health + .12, a total of + .14. Yet when combined, the actual effect is + .27 (.50 subtracted from a ridit of .77), twice that expected. Future research should look for the special impact on children of divorces and separations which arise from the parents' mental disorder. The loss of a mentally disturbed parent through institutionalization or suicide would be yet another experience pattern worthy of investigation. What happens to the children of mental patients? What is the effect of a mentally disturbed spouse on the remaining parent? Does the child remain with the more disturbed parent? What pattern of divorce is more closely associated with mental disorder in the partners, the divorce following a prolonged series of quarrels, or the sudden divorce? Do these patterns have different effects on the child's mental health?

The dichotomized pairs of adult factors show much the same additive situation as the childhood factors. However, perhaps because the adult experiences have occurred closer to the time of the interview, and particularly because the Adult Mental Health Rating was based on present impairment and present symptoms, the adult factors show more of an increment in MHR I ridits.[5]

## An Example of Patterns of Four Dichotomized Childhood Factors and Their Stress Score

Having examined the patterns of paired childhood and adult factors and found them roughly additive, it would not be surprising if we found the same to be true of combinations of three factors, four factors, five factors, and so forth. The combinations of four arbitrarily selected childhood factors will be analyzed in detail at this point, to illustrate the techniques involved and to substantiate the major finding of additivity illustrated in the paired factors. While combinations of up to seven factors were analyzed, the reader will more readily grasp this example of tetrads. Four factors are adequate to illustrate the principle involved in a score of stresses. It is less complex than a score of seven factors, for example, which would involve 128 patterns.

The first pattern, A (four minus scores), was found in 445 cases, or 27.4 per cent of the sample. The four minuses tell us that these respondents' parents were not in poor physical or mental health, and that as children the respondents did not suffer economic deprivation and were not themselves in poor physical health. They have an average CMH ridit of .39, well below .50, the average for the population as a whole. (The CMH Index ridits are used in this example with the patterns of childhood factors, while the AMH I ridits were used with patterns of adult factors.) While the absence of poor health does not necessarily mean excellent health, the absence is associated with a reduction in mental health risk.

How much worse off are those who reported one of the four factors (a single plus)? There are, of course, four such patterns (B, C, D, and E). The first, Pattern B, is a plus on Parents' Poor Physical Health alone, a minus on the other three factors. The pattern is therefore $+ - - -$; 8 per cent showed this pattern, and they had an average ridit of .40, just slightly higher than the .39 of those with four minuses. Having the Parents' Poor Physical Health factor has not added much to the respondents' mental health risk. The second pattern, C (with one plus for Parents' Poor Mental Health), has a ridit of .53, a much sharper increase over .39. The third pattern, D, indicates that these persons have experienced only Economic Deprivation as children. They have a ridit of .51. Pattern E describes those who had only Childhood Poor Physical Health. Their average mental health ridit is .49. With the exception of Parents' Poor Physical Health (Pattern B), the patterns of a single plus

## TABLE 13-9

### PROPORTIONS AND AVERAGE MENTAL HEALTH (CMH) OF RESPONDENTS ACCORDING TO PATTERNS OF STRESS SCORES ON FOUR DICHOTOMIZED CHILDHOOD FACTORS

| | Childhood Factors | | | | Respondents' Mental Health | | | |
| | Parents' Poor Physical Health | Parents' Poor Mental Health | Childhood Economic Deprivation | Childhood Poor Physical Health | Per Cent of Cases | $\bar{R}$ | Stress Score | $\bar{R}$ |
|---|---|---|---|---|---|---|---|---|
| A | − | − | − | − | 27.4 | .39 | 0 | .39 |
| B | + | − | − | − | 8.0 | .40 | | |
| C | − | + | − | − | 6.2 | .53 | | |
| D | − | − | + | − | 9.3 | .51 | 1 | .48 |
| E | − | − | − | + | 12.7 | .49 | | |
| F | + | + | − | − | 3.7 | .53 | | |
| G | + | − | + | − | 3.7 | .47 | | |
| H | − | + | + | − | 2.1 | .58 | 2 | .56 |
| I | + | − | − | + | 4.7 | .58 | | |
| J | − | + | − | + | 4.2 | .60 | | |
| K | − | − | + | + | 4.5 | .61 | | |
| L | + | + | + | − | 1.9 | .56 | | |
| M | + | + | − | + | 3.3 | .64 | | |
| N | + | − | + | + | 2.8 | .64 | 3 | .64 |
| O | − | + | + | + | 2.6 | .68 | | |
| P | + | + | + | + | 2.9 | .77 | 4 | .77 |
| Total Number of Cases (N = 100 per cent) | | | | | 1660 | | | |

seem to have ridits around .50. Indeed, the average ridit of all persons having any of the four patterns of one plus (or what we shall call a Stress Score of 1) is .48. (See the ridits under "Stress Score" in the last column of Table 13-9.)

In Chapter 5, the number of stress factors each individual had experienced was called his "Simple Score." This is a technical term indicating an unweighted score. Rather than use the technical term, we have substituted "Stress Score."

There are six patterns of two plusses (Patterns F, G, H, I, J, and K). Their ridits range from .47 (Pattern G) to .61 (Pattern K), but four of the six range from .58 to .61 (Patterns H, I, J, and K). Only one of these patterns of two plusses has a ridit lower (.47) than the average for the patterns of one plus (.48). There is little overlap, therefore, between the ridits of a Stress Score of one and a Stress Score of two factors. The weakest patterns of two plusses are Pattern F (.53) and Pattern G (.47). Both involve plus scores on Parents' Poor Physical Health, which by itself is quite weak, since a plus in that factor alone gives an average ridit of only .40 (Pattern B). However, when the Parents' Poor Physical Health plus combines with the Childhood Poor Physical Health in Pattern I, we get a fairly high ridit, .58; this very pair was previously found to show some interaction. The average ridit of all the patterns comprising the Stress Score of 2 is .56.

The four patterns which make up a Stress Score of three plusses (Patterns L, M, N, and O) have ridits of .56, .64, .64, and .68. All together, they average .64. It is clear that they are all as high as or higher than the average ridit for a Stress Score of 2 (.56).

The group with a pattern of four plusses, that is, those who have experienced all four of these childhood factors (Pattern P), has a ridit of .77. This means that 77 per cent of the population is healthier than they are. It also mean that the chances are 4 to 1 that a random individual with Pattern P is worse off than a random individual in the Pattern A group.[6] These are considerable odds.

What do these data tell us? They indicate that there is some minor variation between patterns with the same Stress Score. For instance, the patterns of one plus range from .40 to .53, two plusses from .47 to .61, three plusses, from .56 to .68. Although these ranges do overlap, the overlap is not great, and usually is due to patterns numerically smaller and of wider variability than the other patterns within the same Stress Score.

The graphic representation of the ridits of all 16 patterns (see Figure 13-1) shows that most of the ridits fall along a straight line and do not overlap. The strongest impression one gets from Figure 13-1 is the steady increase in mental impairment as the number of factors, or Stress Score, increases. This impression seems to override any of the smaller variations in ridits of patterns within each Stress Score level.

This impression is confirmed if the Stress Score alone is examined (see Table 13-9 and Figure 13-1). As the number of stress factors experienced by the respondents increases (indicated by the rising Stress Scores of 0, 1, 2, 3, 4), the average mental health risk increases steadily: .39, .48, .56, .64, .77.

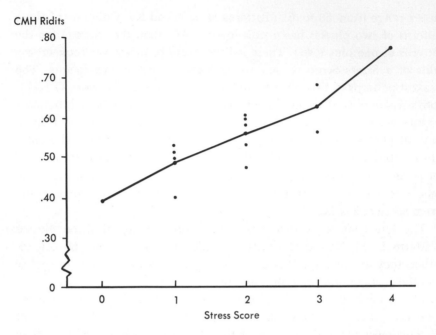

**Figure 13-1. Average Mental Health Risk (CMH) of Respondents, According to Patterns and Stress Scores Based on Four Dichotomized Childhood Factors**

Not only these four factors in combination but any of approximately 25 sets of patterns involving both childhood and adult factors showed this same strong relationship between the Stress Scores and the mental health ridits. In almost all cases, the ridit variation of patterns within Stress Scores was comparatively negligible. The implications of these data are far-reaching. They tell us that it is not so much *what* happened to the individual as it is *how many things* happened to him that seems related to his mental health impairment ratings.

When this part of the research was planned, we expected that striking interactive effects would come to light. Some patterns would involve tremendous risks, some would hardly have any effect at all. The data, in one statistical table after another, showed that, to the contrary, the particular patterns were relatively unimportant. Everything pointed instead to the additive importance of the number of factors involved, that is, to the Stress Score. From the standpoint of further research we must ask ourselves whether the detailed life history, with its careful specification of the sequence and interrelation of factors, is necessary for the crude predictions of impairment sometimes required in social psychiatry. If, twenty years from now, we are no longer working from case to case but identifying whole segments of the population which may be in need of preventive psychiatry, a simple index composed of the number of stress factors in the life history may be quite adequate to the task. It will be within the group with the highest number of factors, the highest Stress Score, that we will find the greatest number of disturbed people with a minimum per capita screening cost.

Although there is no substitute for careful sequential case histories for an adequate understanding of the etiology of mental disturbance in one individual, a rough count of the number of stress factors may well turn out to be the datum of choice in a screening program. Certainly one fruitful task would be the improvement of the stress factors as a screening instrument. We should have a better understanding of their dynamics: why are they related to mental health; are they causally and directly related; if not, are they indirectly related? Are they just concomitant or correlated variables which only have an actuarial relationship to mental health?

When we constructed a graph with the mental health ridits on the $y$ axis and the number of stress factors (Stress Score) on the $x$ axis (see Figure 13-1), we found that the points formed an approximately straight line. This means that the greater the number of plusses, the worse was the mental health risk.

Regardless of their relationship to mental health, how frequent are the various patterns? Are there any particular patterns which are so common that they deserve being called "experience syndromes"[7] rather than "experience patterns"? Are there certain factors which are always found in each other's company, so that if an individual reports Factor A, he will always report Factor B? We have found that there are rather low intercorrelations between the factors themselves, averaging around .20 (see Table 5-9). Since the correlation squared is an approximation of the proportion of variation in Factor B which is explained by Factor A, our average factor only accounts for about 4 per cent of the variation in any other factor. In view of these low correlations between factors, it is only logical to expect that there will be few patterns, if any, which occur so frequently that we could call them an "experience syndrome."

A simple statistical procedure can tell us whether any patterns are occurring more than we might expect on the basis of pure chance. Only one pattern, P, a Stress Score of four out of the four factors, clearly occurs more than expected on the basis of chance alone. Approximately three times the expected number of people exhibit this pattern. There is a tendency for all four factors to occur together, but only at the upper end of the Stress Score, and only among a small group of people.

It may very well be that there exists a segment of the population which has all the trouble, all the stressful experiences, and all the negative perceptions and worries that accompany these experiences. Such groups have been found in studies of the distribution of welfare cases and arrests for juvenile delinquency. Such problems tend to be concentrated in a relatively small segment of the population.

However, the Childhood Stress Score of four is not exclusively a low socioeconomic phenomenon. In Table 13-10 we see that about 3.5 per cent of those in the low and middle SES and 1.6 per cent of those of high SES had a Stress Score of four. Of the 48 persons with this score, 31, or 65 per cent, came from families of middle and high SES. This means that

## TABLE 13-10

### PROPORTIONS AND AVERAGE MENTAL HEALTH (CMH) OF RESPONDENTS ACCORDING TO STRESS SCORES ON FOUR DICHOTOMIZED CHILDHOOD FACTORS AND FATHERS' SOCIOECONOMIC STATUS

| | *Fathers' Socioeconomic Status* | | | | | | | |
|---|---|---|---|---|---|---|---|---|
| | LOW | | MIDDLE | | HIGH | | TOTAL | |
| *Childhood Stress Scores* | Per Cent | $\bar{R}$ | Per Cent | $\bar{R}$ | Per Cent | $\bar{R}$ | Per Cent | $\bar{R}$ |
| 0 | 24.3 | .42 | 28.3 | .39 | 29.2 | .37 | 27.4 | .39 |
| 1 | 34.5 | .50 | 37.2 | .47 | 36.4 | .47 | 36.2 | .48 |
| 2 | 25.7 | .61 | 21.3 | .57 | 22.5 | .51 | 22.9 | .56 |
| 3 | 12.0 | .65 | 9.8 | .66 | 10.3 | .59 | 10.6 | .64 |
| 4 | 3.5 | .83 | 3.4 | .73 | 1.6 | (.76) | 2.9 | .77 |
| Total Number of Cases (N = 100 per cent) | 482 | | 671 | | 507 | | 1660 | |
| Average Ridit of Total SES Group | | .54 | | .50 | | .47 | | .50 |

Parentheses ( ) enclose ridits based on less than ten cases.

the Lows have no monopoly on extreme stress, at least as measured by these factors.

Due to the small number of persons usually involved, the group of people reporting all the factors in a Stress Score does not have any effect on the intercorrelations of the factors in 97 per cent of the population. For an estimated 97 per cent of the population, the correlations between the factors are quite low. For some 3 per cent, a highly selected group, all the factors "go together": "everything happens to them," "it never rains but it pours."

This group, it should be repeated, is not necessarily synonymous with the very low SES group. If it were, we would have a simple explanation of why socioeconomic status was the one demographic factor (aside from age) which was strongly and consistently related to the Mental Health Ratings. In brief, we could say, "everything happens to the low SES— poor health of parents, broken homes, all the ills to which man is heir —ergo, more of the Lows are mentally disturbed." However, the low SES does *not* report a greater proportion of broken homes or childhood illness. In general they are no more likely to have these varieties of hard luck than the persons of middle or high SES.

Given the same number of stresses, however, the Lows show greater impairment risk than comparable individuals of high SES. For instance, Lows with a Stress Score of four (see Table 13-10) have a ridit of .83; Highs with the same number of stresses have a smaller ridit, .76.

## Patterns of Adult Factors

The patterns of the adult factors tell us little more than the patterns of the childhood factors. A Stress Score based upon four adult factors seems adequate to reflect the generally additive effects found in the patterns.

## Summary

We have found that the stress factors, when combined, seem to have an additive rather than a synergistic statistical effect on mental health risk. In short, the summed effect of these stresses occurring together is seldom greater (or smaller) than their individual effects. This finding makes it only logical to combine the factors into scores in order to increase their actuarial or predictive power in relation to mental health risk. Both Childhod Stress Scores and Adult Stress Scores were constructed. Impairment risk was found to be clearly related to the number of stresses reported.

*Notes*

1. For example, the physical health of the child and the adult are somewhat comparable factors. The childhood health trichotomy yields a CMH ridit range of .45 to .64, or a difference of .19. Its Adult Mental Health ridit range is .47 to .57, or a much smaller difference of .10. In extreme contrast, the Adult Physical Health factor yields an Adult Mental Health ridit range of .38 to .70, or a ridit difference of .32. Given a comparable factor, then, the childhood factor has an "effect" of .19 on Childhood Mental Health ridits, and of only .10 on Adult Mental Health ridits. The adult factor has three times the "effect" on Adult Mental Health ridits (.32) that the childhood factor has (.10).

In general, the CMH differences average .14 for the childhood factors, while the Adult Mental Health I differences average only .10. However, the Adult Mental Health ridit differences average .24 for the adult factors and only .10 for the childhood factors. The childhood factors are more related to the CMH Index than to MH I. The adult factors, in turn, are much more closely related to adult mental health than are the childhood factors.

Among the adult factors, those which bear a particularly strong relationship to adult mental health are Adult Poor Physical Health (.32 difference), Marital Worries (.33), and Parental Worries (.24).

2. The differences (from − to +) are more than twice as large in the low as in the high SES. The Work Worries difference is .22 among the Lows, .14 among the Highs; and the Parental Worries difference is .12 among the Lows, but only .03 among the Highs.

3. Separate publications will deal with the relationship of the 22-item Screening Score and the psychiatric Mental Health Ratings. See Thomas S. Langner, "A Twenty-Two Item Screening Score of Psychiatric Symptoms Indicating Impairment," *Journal of Health and Human Behavior*, Vol. 3, Winter 1962, pp. 269–276.

4. Adult Poor Physical Health varies inversely with SES, since 28.7, 17.3, and 10.4 per cent of the low, middle, and high SES respectively were in poor health. It varies directly with age, since 9.0, 16.0, 20.8, and 26.8 per cent of respondents in their twenties, thirties, forties, and fifties were in poor health. If the "effects" on mental health ridits associated with any factor could be eliminated by controlling the demographic variables of SES and age, the ridit "effects" of Adult Poor Physical Health certainly could be eliminated. Since poor health is so intertwined with aging and with low status, controlling the latter two variables might very well eliminate the "effects" of poor health. An examination of the ridit differences (from − to +) within the four decades of the three respondents' SES groups (12 cells) shows that the average "effect" is .26, and the only "effect" below .22 occurs in the middle SES twenty-year-olds who comprise only 12 persons. Thus, when age and SES are controlled, Adult Poor Physical Health is just about as powerful a factor in relation to mental health as when age and SES are not controlled. (No tables are included to illustrate simultaneous SES and age controls.)

Another factor, Parental Worries, showed a strong inverse relationship to SES and a strong direct relationship to age. Since this was a factor contingent upon being a parent, the entire sample was not involved. This made for very small frequencies in the plus, or worrying group. This in turn made for some inversions in the ridits, or cases where the average mental health of the parental worriers was better (a lower ridit) than that of the nonworriers. This occurred in five cells containing six or less cases. If the 0, or moderate group, is included with the plus group, there is not one of the 12 age-and-SES categories within which there is not a substantial mental health difference according to Parental Worries. The average ridit difference associated with Parental Worries is approximately .18, despite the demographic controls so closely tied to the factor itself.

5. The MHR I increments range from .13 to .20 for the adult trichotomized factors. The CMH Index increments range from .02 to .16 for the childhood trichotomized factors.

6. Using a rule of thumb to calculate the "odds," .77 minus .39 is .38, added to .50 is .88; 88:22 is 4:1.

7. The use of the phrase "stress syndrome" was studiously avoided because of its wide use to describe the physiological reactions to stress.

# The Stress Score, Impairment Risk, and Socioeconomic Status

THOMAS   S.   LANGNER

## Improving the Stress Score

A great. deal of effort went into the construction of various Stress Scores. Then, each score was examined in relation to various ratings of impairment. During this process several important facts were learned. A Stress Score composed of seven dichotomized childhood factors increased the ridit range considerably over that of the four factors. Again the low SES group seemed to run more risk at greater stress levels. The Lows, however, did not experience a more stressful childhood than the Middles or Highs, according to their reports. The average Childhood Stress Scores were similar in the three SES groups.

The trichotomization of the factors substantially increased the predictive power of the various Stress Scores, compared to the dichotomized scores. A five-factor score was found to be most closely related to the Childhood Mental Health Index.

Again the SES differences in risk were found. A low SES person reporting a certain number of stresses in childhood is likely to report more symptoms of emotional disturbance in childhood (as measured by the CMH Index) than a high SES person reporting the same number of stresses. Regardless of the measure, the Lows almost always run more risk per unit of stress.

## The Childhood Stress Score Is Related to the Adult Mental Health Ratings

The impact of six trichotomized childhood factors on the AMH I Ratings (see Table 14-1) is somewhat similar to their impact on the CMH

## TABLE 14-1

## AVERAGE MENTAL HEALTH (MH I) OF RESPONDENTS ACCORDING TO SIX-FACTOR TRICHOTOMIZED CHILDHOOD STRESS SCORES AND FATHERS' SOCIOECONOMIC STATUS

| Six-Factor Scores | Fathers' Socioeconomic Status | | | |
|---|---|---|---|---|
| | LOW | MIDDLE | HIGH | TOTAL |
| | $\bar{R}$ | $\bar{R}$ | $\bar{R}$ | $\bar{R}$ |
| 0 | .39 | .39 | .38 | .38 |
| 1 | .51 | .45 | .40 | .44 |
| 2 | .54 | .41 | .47 | .47 |
| 3 | .57 | .49 | .42 | .49 |
| 4 | .59 | .58 | .49 | .56 |
| 5 | .57 | .56 | .50 | .55 |
| 6 | .72 | .57 | .53 | .62 |
| 7 | .63 | .70 | .60 | .65 |
| 8 to 10 | .68 | .77 | .64 | .70 |
| Total Number of Cases (N = 100 per cent) | 482 | 671 | 507 | 1660 |
| Average Stress Score | 3.13 | 2.94 | 2.65 | 2.93 |

Index. However, the range of the ridits is decreased and there are more inversions (reversals of sequence) as the Stress Score increases. This indicates, as expected, a weaker relationship between childhood factors and adult mental health. Nevertheless, a ridit range of .32 (.38 to .70) for the entire sample indicates that there is a definite and strong connection between childhood experiences and adult mental health which is not to be discounted. The primary focus of our study is, after all, on the mental health of the adult at a point in time, and on what factors, past or present, are associated with the mental health of adults from ages twenty to fifty-nine. In general, the impairment risk of Midtown adults increases as their Childhood Stress Score increases.

## The Adult Stress Score Is Related to the Adult Mental Health Ratings

The range of the Adult Mental Health ridits for a Stress Score of four trichotomized adult factors[1] (see Table 14-2) was .60 (from .31 at a

## TABLE 14-2

### PROPORTIONS AND AVERAGE MENTAL HEALTH (MH I) OF RESPONDENTS ACCORDING TO FOUR-FACTOR TRICHOTOMIZED ADULT STRESS SCORES AND RESPONDENTS' SOCIOECONOMIC STATUS

| | Respondents' Socioeconomic Status | | | | | | | |
| Four-Factor Scores | LOW | | MIDDLE | | HIGH | | TOTAL | |
| | Per Cent | $\bar{R}$ | Per Cent | $\bar{R}$ | Per Cent | $\bar{R}$ | Per Cent | $\bar{R}$ |
|---|---|---|---|---|---|---|---|---|
| 0 | 7.0 | .36 | 12.2 | .34 | 20.5 | .28 | 13.3 | .31 |
| 1 | 17.6 | .45 | 23.6 | .41 | 29.7 | .38 | 23.7 | .41 |
| 2 | 25.0 | .52 | 23.4 | .46 | 22.7 | .44 | 23.7 | .47 |
| 3 | 22.1 | .65 | 17.1 | .56 | 11.6 | .48 | 16.8 | .58 |
| 4 | 15.0 | .70 | 11.5 | .62 | 7.3 | .52 | 11.3 | .63 |
| 5 | 7.2 | .78 | 7.0 | .68 | 6.0 | .65 | 6.7 | .71 |
| 6 | 3.3 | .80 | 4.5 | .71 | 1.4 | (.48) | 3.1 | .70 |
| 7 | 1.3 | (.93) | 0.5 | (.73) | 0.4 | (.71) | 0.7 | .85 |
| 8 | 1.5 | (.92) | 0.2 | (.90) | 0.4 | (.90) | 0.7 | .91 |
| Total Number of Cases (N = 100 per cent) | 544 | | 556 | | 560 | | 1660 | |
| Average Stress Score | 2.75 | | 2.40 | | 1.88 | | 2.29 | |

Parentheses ( ) enclose ridits based on less than ten cases.

score of 0 to .91 at a score of 8). This range is considerably greater than the range of MH I ridits found for the Childhood Stress Score.

The Lows have an average Adult Stress Score of 2.75, compared with 1.88 among the Highs. The Lows, therefore, tend to report substantially more adult stresses than the Highs. This tendency was much less pronounced with the childhood stresses. The disadvantages of the Lows seem to be more pronounced in adult life than in childhood. Another indication of this SES difference is that only 7 per cent of the Lows, compared with about 20 per cent of the Highs, reported none of the four adult factors.

The score of four adult factors is fairly good at predicting adult mental health. If Adult Stress Score levels four to eight are considered, 374 cases can be selected with an average mental health risk of .68. This score alone, then, is a moderately efficient screening device, since it culls a fairly large number of people with a fairly high average mental health risk.

## The Relationship of Childhood and Adult Factors

An obvious way to improve the predictive power of the stress factors was to combine the childhood and adult factors. Before this could be accomplished, however, the relationship between these factors had to be explored.

There was a slight tendency for the childhood factors to increase the probability of one's experiencing the adult factors. Reporting any one of the childhood factors also increased the chance that one would report a larger number of adult factors. This was most true, however, of Parents' Character Negatively Perceived. The Pearson correlation between the Childhood and Adult Stress Scores is only .19, indicating that these stresses are relatively independent.

The MH I Rating was more closely related to the Adult Stress Score; the CMH Index showed a closer relationship to the Childhood Stress Score. In addition, persons having a worse CMH Index were more likely to report the adult stresses.

Despite these findings, the low correlation between childhood and adult stresses does not support a deterministic view of the individual's "life chances." One can have a stressful childhood and a relatively un-stressful adulthood. In view of the relative independence of the Child-hood and Adult Stress Scores, it was deemed feasible to combine them in one single Stress Score. Had they been highly correlated, the creation of a combined score might have been redundant.

## The Combined Stress Score of Six Childhood
## and Four Adult Factors

Six trichotomized childhood factors and four trichotomized adult factors were utilized in the final combined Stress Score, with a range of 0 to 18. The childhood factors were Parents' Poor Mental Health, Childhood Economic Deprivation, Childhood Poor Physical Health, Childhood Broken Homes, Parents' Character Negatively Perceived, and Parents' Quarrels. The adult factors were Adult Poor Physical Health, Poor Interpersonal Affiliations, Work Worries, and Socioeconomic Status Worries.

Persons who reported none of the ten stress factors had a risk of .24, while those who had Stress Scores of 13 to 18 had average risks ranging from .72 to .94. The higher the Stress Score, the greater was the mental health risk, generally (see Table 14-3).

This combined Childhood and Adult Stress Score does to a degree increase the range of MH I variation shown by the Adult Stress Score. It also shows one large and three smaller inversions (points at which the ridits decrease rather than increase as the Stress Score increases).

However, the range of the ridits is not as crucial as the number of people

## TABLE 14-3

## AVERAGE MENTAL HEALTH (MH I) OF RESPONDENTS ACCORDING TO CHILDHOOD-ADULT COMBINED STRESS SCORE

| Stress Score | No. of Cases | $\bar{R}$ |
|---|---|---|
| 0 | 42 | .24 |
| 1 | 132 | .35 |
| 2 | 153 | .38 |
| 3 | 215 | .39 |
| 4 | 216 | .47 |
| 5 | 203 | .52 |
| 6 | 177 | .51 |
| 7 | 159 | .60 |
| 8 | 103 | .63 |
| 9 | 96 | .62 |
| 10 | 66 | .68 |
| 11 | 45 | .69 |
| 12 | 27 | .79 |
| 13 | 14 | .91 |
| 14 | 3 | .72 |
| 15 | 5 | .94 |
| 16 | 2 | .93 |
| 17 | 1 | .90 |
| 18 | 1 | .85 |
| Total Number of Cases | 1660 | |
| Average Ridit | | .50 |

with high risk. For example, the combined Stress Scores between 9 and 18 yield a large number of persons (260), with the high average MH I risk of .69. Of this group of 260 people, 40.8 per cent are in the Impaired category.

If we want to consider a higher cutting point on the Stress Score, the screening becomes more efficient. For example, 88 per cent of persons with a Stress Score of 13 or more fall into the Impaired category. The Impaired ratings indicated that the individual could be considered in need of help of some kind, such as therapy, employment, or a change of environment.

The combined Stress Score of 13 or more identifies 1.5 per cent of the sample of adults in the Midtown area as Impaired. However, a total of 18.3 per cent of the sample were rated as Impaired (MHR I). Since a Stress Score of 13 or more selected only 1.5 per cent, it has found only one-twelfth of all the Impaired people. The Stress Score, then, can hardly be considered at this time as a screening instrument for mental disturbance, although it shows a consistent relationship to the Mental Health Ratings. (For this purpose a Screening Score of 22 psychophysiological and psychoneurotic symptoms has been assembled which is highly correlated with the Mental Health Ratings and distinguishes between mental patients and screened "wells." The 22-Item Screening Score is reported elsewhere.)[2]

More important than the question of screening efficiency is the fact that the number rather than the pattern of the negative factors is apparently sufficient to specify mental health risk. The group of people who experienced three stress factors will have a higher average mental health risk than the group which experienced two factors. The mere *number* of factors seems to tell us as much about the average mental health risk as an examination of the particular combination or pattern of factors the group has experienced. This is illustrated graphically by Figure 14-1.

The Stress Score is represented on the $x$ axis, the MHR I ridits on the $y$ axis. The relationship can be described by a straight line. As the Stress Score increases, the average impairment also increases. This linear relationship suggests the pertinence of the stress-strain model, when dealing wih psychiatric impairment ratings. While this model is grossly oversimplified as a description of the etiology of mental disturbance—allowing neither for types of stress, types of strain, nor interaction between them through time—it is an aid in describing the data obtained at this point.

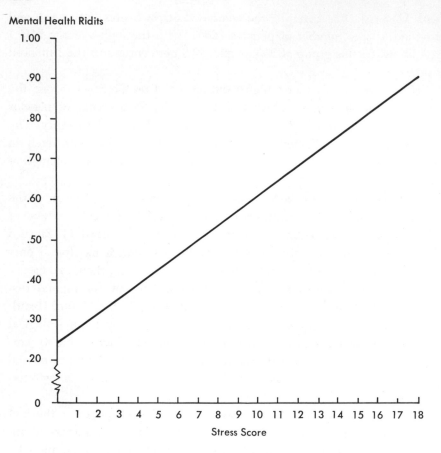

Figure 14-1. Average Mental Health (MH I) of Respondents, According to Childhood-Adult Combined Stress Score

## Some Implications of the Finding that Mental Health Risk (Strain) Increases as the Stress Score Increases

What are some of the implications of these findings? First, and perhaps most important, is the strong suggestion that the factors associated with mental disturbance (and perhaps influencing it) are purely additive in their effects. If it is true that the more negative experiences people have, the greater their mental health risk, then the concept of a single "traumatic experience" is called into question. If single traumatic events, such as the death of a parent or a severe childhood illness, could be the *sole* cause of mental disturbance, then we would find that certain factors are associated with great mental health risk, no matter what other factors enter the picture. This "all or none" principle is given little support by our data. Events in the life history seem to "pile up" increasing impairment, but there is no one event which by itself automatically spells mental disaster for all who experience it.

Nor, on the other hand, is there any suggestion of the principle of "the straw that broke the camel's back." That is to say, stressful events do not accumulate to a certain point beyond which all persons are bound to collapse. There is no "breaking point" in the number of factors beyond which there is a sudden marked increase in mental health risk. The linear principle governing the relationship of environmental stress factors to mental health risk seems to be "the more, the *un*merrier."

A second finding is that childhood experiences, at least as we have measured them, are not as closely correlated with adult mental health as are adult experiences. The childhood experiences are more highly correlated with childhood mental health (as measured by a score of childhood symptoms). For purposes of etiology, there can be no doubt that the investigator must both observe and understand the childhood experiences of his subjects. However, the data seem to indicate that for the broad purposes of mental health screening and categorizing, the present adult life situation is far more efficient. Childhood experiences certainly lay the groundwork for the development of mental health or disorder, but the life situation of the adult as he functions in the here and now seems most closely related to his present mental health. In essence, of course, his adult life situation *is* his mental health. We were able to make only an artificial methodological separation of the sociocultural situation of the individual and our estimate of his mental health.

Of major interest is the fact that the low SES group does not report a more deprived childhood, generally speaking. This may be only their perception, while in truth they may have been much more deprived than the high SES. However it is often one's perception of the world that seems to be related to mental disturbance. (An obvious exception would be dietary deficiency, unknown to the individual, which might predispose him to nervous disorder.) The low SES, on the other hand, reports considerably more stresses in adult life. Again it is the present adult life situation which is tied in with the poorer mental health of the Lows. These data do not suggest that we ignore the early life experiences of the low SES, but rather that we try to find out by what means some of them are able to live with or adapt to stress, and whether these styles of adaptation have implications for their adult mental health.

## Persons of Low SES Have a Greater Mental Health Risk than Persons of High SES, Even When the Number of Their Life Stresses Is Similar

The average scores of childhood stresses reported by the SES strata are similar (Lows 3.13, Middles 2.94, Highs 2.65). (See Table 14-1.) However, the low SES reports somewhat more adult stress than the High SES, on the average (Lows 2.75, Middles, 2.40, Highs 1.88). (See Table 14-2.) Wouldn't this explain the fact that the Lows have a greater over-all impairment risk than the Middles or Highs? The MHR I risks, according to the respondents' SES, are .59 for the Lows, .50 for the Middles, and .41 for the Highs. If the low SES group experienced more adult stresses, why indeed shouldn't it exhibit greater impairment risk?

If being of low socioeconomic status simply meant that you suffered proportionately more of the "slings and arrows of outrageous fortune," this would very neatly explain why the Lows had worse mental health. We tested this hypothesis again by examining the average combined Childhood and Adult Stress Score of each SES group. The difference between the averages was not very large. The average Stress Scores of the low, middle, and high SES groups were 5.7, 5.3, and 4.7 (see Table 14-4). The combined Stress Score did vary somewhat with SES, but not enough to account for the sizable status group differences in impairment risk.

If the frequency of exposure to stress could by itself explain the increased impairment of the low SES group, then for a given level of stress the impairment risk of the three SES groups should be almost identical. Accordingly, the impairment risk (MHR I) of each SES group was examined at each level of the Stress Score (see Table 14-4). We found that people reporting none of the ten factors did have almost identical risks, regardless of their socioeconomic position. Their risks were .26, .25, and .24 in the low, middle, and high SES respectively. It might appear that the stress factors had explained away or accounted for the differences in the mental health of the three SES groups.

On the contrary, with the exception of the group that reported none of the ten stress factors (or a score of zero), the Lows continue to exhibit greater mental health risk, regardless of the number of factors experi-

## TABLE 14-4

### AVERAGE MENTAL HEALTH (MH I) OF RESPONDENTS ACCORDING TO CHILDHOOD-ADULT COMBINED STRESS SCORE AND RESPONDENTS' SOCIOECONOMIC STATUS

| | Respondents' Socioeconomic Status | | |
| Combined Stress Score | LOW $\bar{R}$ | MIDDLE $\bar{R}$ | HIGH $\bar{R}$ |
|---|---|---|---|
| 0 | .26 | .25 | .24 |
| 1 | .42 | .36 | .29 |
| 2 | .41 | .36 | .33 |
| 3 | .46 | .37 | .35 |
| 4 | .53 | .46 | .40 |
| 5 | .56 | .56 | .42 |
| 6 | .57 | .52 | .46 |
| 7 | .67 | .60 | .47 |
| 8 | .78 | .55 | .53 |
| 9 | .73 | .58 | .54 |
| 10 | .77 | .59 | .69 |
| 11 | .79 | .68 | .56 |
| 12 | .86 | .76 | .73 |
| 13 | .93 | .89 | .88 |
| 14 | .95 | .53 | .67 |
| 15 | .94 | .93 | — |
| 16 | .93 | — | — |
| 17 | .90 | — | — |
| 18 | — | — | .85 |
| 10-18 | .83 | .67 | .68 |
| 14-18 | .93 | .79 | .76 |
| Total Number of Cases (N=100 per cent) | 544 | 556 | 560 |
| | | | 1660 |
| Average Stress Score | 5.7 | 5.3 | 4.7 |

enced. Holding life stresses "constant," the Lows still run more risk. For example, persons with a Stress Score level of 6 had risks of .57, .52, and .46 in the low, middle, and high SES. Again, if we consider only those with a Stress Score level of 14 or more, the average mental health of the Lows is .93, compared with .79 and .76 of the Middles and Highs, a considerable difference. There is a residual mental health variation between the socioeconomic groups which seems to be independent of the stress factors; it cannot be accounted for by the number of stress factors alone.

These results are shown graphically in Figure 14-2. The actual regression line expressing the relationship between the Stress Score and the MHR I ridits was calculated for each SES group separately. The slope of the three lines differs considerably.[3] Impairment risk increases more sharply with stress among the Lows than among the Highs. The residual SES variation in risk is shown by the fanning out of the lines. From the vertical bars we see that the Lows start off with a greater average risk at lesser stress levels (about .10) than the Highs. This difference in risk becomes greater as the Stress Score increases. The vertical bar at the upper end of the Stress Score shows that the SES difference in risk has

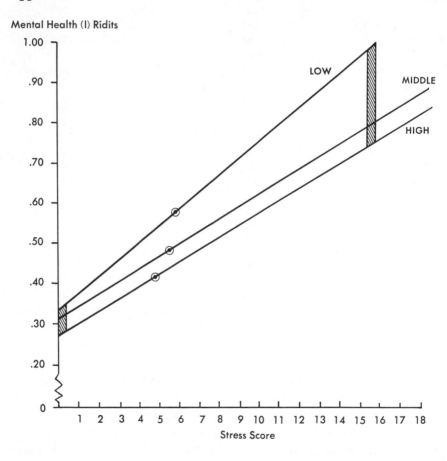

Figure 14-2. Average Mental Health (MH I) of Respondents, According to Childhood-Adult Combined Stress Score and Respondents' Socioeconomic Status

more than doubled (about .23). With increasing stress, the low SES group seems to fare progressively worse than the Highs.

## Some Explanatory Hypotheses Concerning SES Differences in Impairment Risk When Stress Is Held Constant

Several hypotheses can be invoked to explain why the low SES impairment risk is greater, even when the number of stresses is controlled. Put differently, why do low SES persons, on the average, seem to exhibit greater psychiatric impairment than high SES persons, when faced with what is apparently the same amount of environmental stress? These hypotheses, which will constitute the major focus of the remainder of this volume, can be given shorthand designations for purposes of clarity. In brief they are:

A. *Residual Stress.*    We have certainly not included in the questionnaire the total universe of stresses to which any individual might be exposed. (1) In addition, some stresses included in the questionnaire were not utilized in the Stress Score. (2) We have left out of the combined Stress Score several factors that become stresses for the high or low SES alone. The proportional distribution of potential stress items according to socioeconomic status will be discussed in some detail.

B. *Measurement of Stress.*    We have not been able to measure accurately the severity of these experiences. The measurement of a stress, as opposed to the subjective interpretation of that stress, is a major problem in itself. For example, what the low SES individual reports as good health the high SES person may report as poor health. The meaning of the stress factors, then, may vary between status levels. This problem has been discussed at length in Chapter 6.

C. *Resilience and Resistance.*    Another hypothesis to explain the SES differences is that the low SES individual is made of different material. His personality structure may not be as *resistant* to stress or as *resilient* in recovering from stress as that of the high SES individual.

D. *Cushioning.*    The stress on the Highs may be "cushioned" by wealth, education, and other favorable circumstances.

E. *Adaptive Devices.*    At a particular level of stress, the low SES group may exhibit psychological adaptive mechanisms or devices that are more impairing. There is evidence from the survey data that the Highs tend to exhibit neurotic devices, while the Lows show psychotic adaptations in their efforts to meet any given level of stress. The degree to which various "probable" diagnostic categories explain the residual impairment variation between SES groups will be discussed in Chapter 15.

## A. RESIDUAL STRESS

Do the individual stresses in the ten-factor Stress Score occur disproportionately among the Lows? Let us describe the three socioeconomic groups in terms of the Stress Scores. What proportion of each status group shares in each factor? Those born into low status families are much more likely to suffer economic deprivation in childhood and are somewhat more prone to experience early broken homes (see Table 14-5).

With the exception of economic deprivation, there is a striking similarity in the childhood experiences of the SES groups. This similarity is evidenced by Table 14-6, which examines the proportion of each socioeconomic group, giving the presumed stressful responses. The three status groups showed no differences in the proportion of parents in poor health, the number of mother's psychosomatic conditions, the proportion of worrying parents, and the physical health of respondents in childhood. There were no major SES differences in the proportion reporting that father spent too little time with them, that he or the mother wanted to run their lives, or that their mother didn't understand them, that parents weren't always proud of them, or didn't always practice what they preached. The frequency of parents' quarrels and the respondent's disagreements with his parents was rather similar in all three groups.

A larger proportion of those born into low status families said their parents had unemployment and financial problems, and had a hard time making ends meet. (These items make up the Economic Deprivation factor.) Almost twice as many had mothers who worked outside the home. As mentioned before, the Lows were slightly more prone to lose a parent before the age of six. The Highs reported more psychosomatic diseases of their fathers, and showed some tendency to have more colds and to disagree more frequently with their parents.

Some items of information were closely related to the Mental Health Ratings, but they could not be included in the factors. These are listed in Table 14-7, which indicates that the Lows were less likely to get along well with substitute parents, were more likely to feel that "home is a place where people get in each other's way," and more frequently followed the traditional practices of their national background during their childhood. These responses are all associated with greater mental health risk.

## TABLE 14-5

## PROPORTIONS OF RESPONDENTS ACCORDING TO
## TRICHOTOMIZED CHILDHOOD FACTORS AND
## FATHERS' SOCIOECONOMIC STATUS

| Childhood Factors | Trichotomy | Fathers' Socioeconomic Status | | |
|---|---|---|---|---|
| | | LOW Per Cent | MIDDLE Per Cent | HIGH Per Cent |
| Parents' Poor | + | 33.2 | 27.9 | 33.1 |
| Physical Health[a] | - | 66.8 | 72.1 | 66.9 |
| Parents' Poor | + | 3.9 | 6.7 | 6.5 |
| Mental Health | 0 | 18.5 | 17.7 | 20.1 |
| | - | 78.6 | 75.6 | 73.4 |
| Childhood Economic | + | 18.5 | 14.0 | 4.1 |
| Deprivation | 0 | 30.1 | 25.9 | 14.6 |
| | - | 51.4 | 60.1 | 81.3 |
| Childhood Poor | + | 15.1 | 13.7 | 16.2 |
| Physical Health | 0 | 22.2 | 22.5 | 23.5 |
| | - | 62.7 | 63.8 | 60.3 |
| Childhood Broken | + | 19.7 | 13.9 | 13.8 |
| Homes | 0 | 19.3 | 19.4 | 20.5 |
| | - | 61.0 | 66.8 | 65.7 |
| Parents' Character | + | 13.7 | 10.9 | 11.1 |
| Negatively | 0 | 21.2 | 23.8 | 21.0 |
| Perceived | - | 65.1 | 65.3 | 67.9 |
| Parents' Quarrels | + | 14.3 | 16.1 | 14.8 |
| | 0 | 29.3 | 28.9 | 23.1 |
| | - | 56.4 | 55.0 | 62.1 |
| Respondents' | + | 10.2 | 12.7 | 14.8 |
| Disagreements | 0 | 30.3 | 28.0 | 34.3 |
| with Parents | - | 59.5 | 59.3 | 50.9 |
| Total Number of Cases (N=100 per cent) | | 482 | 671 | 507 1660 |

[a] This factor was dichotomized because there were too few cases in the trichotomized "plus" group.

## TABLE 14-6
## PROPORTIONS OF RESPONDENTS REPORTING ITEMS IN CHILDHOOD FACTORS ACCORDING TO FATHERS' SOCIOECONOMIC STATUS

| Childhood Factor Items | | Fathers' Socioeconomic Status | | |
|---|---|---|---|---|
| | | LOW Per Cent | MIDDLE Per Cent | HIGH Per Cent |
| Either Parent in Poor Health | Yes | 33.2 | 27.9 | 33.1 |
| Fathers' Psychosomatic Score | 2 or more | 8.5 | 12.8 | 15.6 |
| Mothers' Psychosomatic Score | 2 or more | 17.0 | 17.8 | 21.9 |
| Parents the Worrying Type | Yes | 52.0 | 54.9 | 51.0 |
| Parents' Chief Problems | Unemployment | 7.9 | 3.4 | 1.0 |
| | Financial | 66.0 | 58.4 | 42.0 |
| Parents' Hard Time Making Ends Meet | Often | 38.0 | 29.7 | 15.0 |
| Mother Worked Outside Home | Yes | 38.4 | 34.4 | 20.1 |
| Early Childhood Physical Health | Poor | 10.0 | 9.2 | 8.9 |
| Caught Colds in Childhood | Often | 23.9 | 21.3 | 28.2 |
| Lived with Real Parents Through Age Six | No | 19.7 | 13.9 | 13.8 |
| Father Spent Too Little Time with Respondent | Yes | 24.9 | 27.0 | 24.2 |
| Father Wanted to Run Children's Lives | Yes | 21.4 | 19.4 | 16.8 |
| Mother Wanted to Run Children's Lives | Yes | 27.5 | 27.7 | 29.6 |
| Mother Didn't Understand Respondent | Yes | 27.6 | 28.6 | 33.1 |
| Respondents' Parents Always Proud of Children | No | 14.5 | 12.7 | 17.9 |
| Parents Didn't Practice What They Preached | Yes | 22.4 | 20.6 | 15.2 |
| Parents' Quarrels | Often | 14.3 | 16.1 | 14.8 |
| Respondents' Disagreements with Parents | Often | 10.2 | 12.2 | 14.8 |
| Total Number of Cases (N=100 per cent)[a] | | 482 | 671 | 507 |
| | | | | 1660 |

[a] Percentages are only of those giving the particular response indicated.

# TABLE 14-7

## PROPORTIONS OF RESPONDENTS REPORTING ITEMS RELATED TO MENTAL HEALTH (RANK 1) NOT INCORPORATED IN FACTORS, ACCORDING TO FATHERS' OR RESPONDENTS' SOCIOECONOMIC STATUS

| Nonfactor Items[a] | | *Fathers' Socioeconomic Status* | | |
| --- | --- | --- | --- | --- |
| | | *LOW* Per Cent | *MIDDLE* Per Cent | *HIGH* Per Cent |
| *Childhood Items* | | | | |
| How many of the traditional ways of nationality of descent did your family practice? | Many and some | 57.0 | 47.4 | 31.6 |
| "Home is a place where people get in each other's way." | Yes | 19.9 | 16.4 | 11.4 |
| Did your Mother (Father) remarry? | Yes | 36.6 | 43.5 | 40.1 |
| How well did you get along with your parent substitute? | Not so well and not at all | 37.2 | 26.8 | 24.2 |
| Total Number of Cases (N = 100 per cent) | | 482 | 671 | 507 |
| *Adult Items* | | *Respondents' Socioeconomic Status* | | |
| Compared to four or five years ago, would you say your health now is same, better, or not as good? | Not as good | 20.2 | 14.6 | 12.5 |
| Is health something that worries you? | Often | 13.6 | 7.9 | 3.9 |
| Did you ever have to stop working for any long periods because of health reasons? | Yes | 31.7 | 22.7 | 18.7 |
| Has your work ever affected your health? Yes (men only). Why? | Physical conditions | 5.3 | 3.2 | 1.3 |
| | Heavy responsibility | 2.2 | 6.7 | 13.9 |

## TABLE 14-7 (Continued)

### PROPORTIONS OF RESPONDENTS REPORTING ITEMS RELATED TO MENTAL HEALTH (RANK 1) NOT INCORPORATED IN FACTORS, ACCORDING TO FATHERS' OR RESPONDENTS' SOCIOECONOMIC STATUS

| Nonfactor Items[a] | | Respondents' Socioeconomic Status | | |
|---|---|---|---|---|
| | | LOW | MIDDLE | HIGH |
| Adult Items | | Per Cent | Per Cent | Per Cent |
| Has your work ever affected your health? (married women only) | Yes | 20.0 | 28.6 | 35.1 |
| Job Status (men and never-married women) | Unemployed Men | 9.7 | 6.5 | 0.9 |
| | Unemployed Women | 10.7 | 7.6 | 4.2 |
| How much do you like the work you are doing? | Not at all | 15.5 | 14.5 | 6.1 |
| Anomie Scale. | (Agree with three or more statements) | 52.9 | 34.0 | 19.8 |
| Do you feel you have as many friends as you want, or would you like to have more friends? | Would like to have more | 25.0 | 36.0 | 45.2 |
| Is loneliness something that worries you? | Often | 11.6 | 5.8 | 4.3 |
| Occupational homogeneity–heterogeneity (married, both spouses working) | Respondent is husband. Occupation lower than wife. | 33.9 | 32.8 | 15.7 |
| | Respondent is wife. Occupation higher than husband. | 27.3 | 36.6 | 18.1 |
| Most people think a great deal about sex matters. | Yes – men | 53.5 | 62.1 | 76.2 |
| | Yes – women | 43.0 | 42.0 | 48.1 |

## TABLE 14-7 (Continued)

### PROPORTIONS OF RESPONDENTS REPORTING ITEMS RELATED TO MENTAL HEALTH (RANK 1) NOT INCORPORATED IN FACTORS, ACCORDING TO FATHERS' OR RESPONDENTS' SOCIOECONOMIC STATUS

| Nonfactor Items[a] | | Respondents' Socioeconomic Status | | |
| --- | --- | --- | --- | --- |
| | | LOW | MIDDLE | HIGH |
| Adult Items | | Per Cent | Per Cent | Per Cent |
| A person does better for himself by keeping away from his family (close relatives). | Agree | 23.5 | 20.1 | 18.0 |
| Is "Old Age" something that worries you? | Often | 5.9 | 4.0 | 4.3 |
| Is "the Atom Bomb" something that worries you? | Often | 6.1 | 4.9 | 3.9 |
| Do you ever feel you would like to make a change in residence? | Yes | 68.8 | 74.8 | 56.6 |
| Total Number of Cases (N = 100 per cent) | | 544 | 556 | 560 |
| | | | | 1660 |

[a]This table includes only the Rank 1 nonfactor items. These were not included in the final composition of the factors, usually because they did not increase the mental health risk (or were actually considered symptoms of mental disturbance, rather than factors associated with mental disturbance). Rank 1 items had to show a relation to mental health risk at the 5 per cent level of confidence in all three socioeconomic groups.

As adults, the Lows are in poorer Physical Health and are more likely to have Poor Interpersonal Affiliations and Parental Worries (see Table 14-8). They are less apt to be hospitalized, even though their health is reportedly worse. They are more friendless, less active in organizations, more lonely, and more apt to dislike their present work. More of them report problems with their children, and the Lows tend to think that children give them more trouble than pleasure (see Table 14-9).

For various reasons, some adult items correlated with mental health could not be included among the factors (see Table 14-7). Several of these were found to be more typical of the Lows. The Lows had much higher "anomie" scores, indicating feelings of futility and alienation. They were more worried about loneliness and health. More Lows thought their health was not as good as it had been five years ago. Low status males reported that physical conditions of work had affected their health, while high status males blamed the heavy responsibility of their work. More Lows had to stop working because of their health, more were unemployed at the time of the interview, and more who were working didn't like their work at all. Much more frequently among the Lows, the wife was in a higher occupation than the husband. This condition was associated with poorer mental health for both husband and wife. More Lows wanted to make a change in residence, although almost two-thirds of the population had the same desire.

Although the Lows are "lonelier," a larger proportion of Highs would like to have more friends. Working wives of high status are more likely to report that their work has affected their health, although fewer high status wives work. It should be noted that working full time involves a much greater mental health risk for high than for low status wives. This seems plausible, since, in Midtown, working for money is less common and perhaps less socially acceptable for wives of high status. Their work may also involve heavy responsibility, for many of these women are in professional and semiprofessional occupations. As mentioned before, high status males claim that responsibility affects their work, and this may also be true of their working wives (see Table 14-7).

We considered the average Stress Scores of the three SES groups, and found differences, but these alone were not great enough to account for the differences in impairment risk among the status groups. Even when items of information not included in the final stress factors are considered, there is little difference in the reported stresses during childhood among the three SES levels (with the exception of Economic Deprivation, which

TABLE 14-8

## PROPORTIONS OF RESPONDENTS ACCORDING TO
## TRICHOTOMIZED ADULT FACTORS AND RESPONDENTS'
## SOCIOECONOMIC STATUS

| Adult Factors | Trichotomy | Respondents' Socioeconomic Status | | |
| | | LOW | MIDDLE | HIGH |
| | | Per Cent | Per Cent | Per Cent |
|---|---|---|---|---|
| Adult Poor | + | 28.7 | 17.3 | 10.4 |
| Physical Health | 0 | 50.7 | 50.9 | 38.0 |
| | – | 20.6 | 31.8 | 51.6 |
| Work Worries | + | 11.6 | 13.7 | 15.4 |
| | 0 | 16.2 | 14.8 | 18.6 |
| | – | 72.2 | 71.6 | 66.0 |
| Socioeconomic | + | 12.3 | 13.3 | 10.5 |
| Status Worries | 0 | 20.8 | 14.0 | 14.8 |
| | – | 66.9 | 72.7 | 74.7 |
| Poor Interpersonal | + | 18.4 | 14.4 | 5.2 |
| Affiliations | 0 | 41.0 | 37.9 | 29.1 |
| | – | 40.6 | 47.7 | 65.7 |
| Contingent Factors[a] | | | | |
| Marital Worries[b] | + | 15.1 | 13.9 | 23.4 |
| | – | 84.9 | 86.1 | 76.6 |
| Parental Worries | + | 21.3 | 10.7 | 3.6 |
| | 0 | 34.5 | 40.8 | 53.4 |
| | – | 44.2 | 48.5 | 43.0 |
| Total Number of Cases (N=100 per cent) | | 544 | 556 | 560 |
| | | | | 1660 |

[a] The proportions for Marital Worries are based on the 987 cases of married respondents, and for Parental Worries on the 837 cases of respondents who were parents.

[b] This factor was dichotomized because there were too few cases in the trichotomized "plus" group.

## TABLE 14-9

## PROPORTIONS OF RESPONDENTS REPORTING ITEMS IN ADULT FACTORS ACCORDING TO RESPONDENTS' SOCIOECONOMIC STATUS

| | | Respondents' Socioeconomic Status | | |
| --- | --- | --- | --- | --- |
| | | *LOW* | *MIDDLE* | *HIGH* |
| *Adult Factor Items* | | Per Cent | Per Cent | Per Cent |
| Hospitalizations | 3 or more | 18.4 | 20.9 | 35.9 |
| Respondents' Present Health | Poor or Fair | 34.4 | 21.6 | 11.1 |
| Worrying about Work | Often or Sometimes | 34.4 | 38.5 | 52.1 |
| Worrying about Overwork | Often or Sometimes | 22.8 | 22.8 | 27.0 |
| Worrying about Getting Ahead | Often | 14.3 | 15.1 | 11.4 |
| Worrying about Cost of Living | Often | 26.8 | 19.1 | 20.0 |
| Neighbors Known Well | None | 31.8 | 32.7 | 33.4 |
| Close Friends | None | 12.7 | 5.9 | 1.8 |
| Organizations in Which Active | None | 63.6 | 57.9 | 43.6 |
| Marital Status | Divorced or Separated | 9.5 | 8.3 | 7.9 |
| | Widowed | 8.5 | 5.6 | 2.9 |
| | Never-Married | 21.3 | 30.2 | 27.5 |
| (Married Only)[a] Worrying about Marriage | Often or Sometimes | 15.1 | 13.9 | 23.4 |
| (Parents Only)[b] Worrying about Children | Often | 17.1 | 14.2 | 13.4 |
| Problems with Children | Yes | 77.6 | 49.3 | 59.5 |
| Children More Trouble than Pleasure | Agree | 21.3 | 10.7 | 3.6 |
| Total Number of Cases (N = 100 per cent)[c] | | 544 | 556 | 560 1660 |

[a]Based on 987 cases of married respondents.
[b]Based on 837 cases of respondent parents.
[c]Percentages are only of those giving response indicated.

is a somewhat redundant finding). The low SES definitely has more than its share of adult stress items not included in the final Stress Score.

Two facts seem to argue against these "residual stresses" as the primary source of the remaining SES variation in impairment risk. First, with ten factors included in the Stress Score, a score of zero exhibits almost no SES differences in mental health risk. Persons without these ten sources of stress are so similar that their impairment is no longer typical of their status group. These ten stresses, then, must be related to, be correlated with, or cover a large number of the "residual stresses" that we are discussing. They are pulling more than their weight in the boat, as it were, by being related to other stresses not included in the Stress Score. Second, this interpretation is strengthened by the fact that the addition of a larger number of stresses does not seem to improve the prediction of impairment. The impairment disparity between each of the three SES levels is just as evident in Stress Scores of five childhood factors or four adult factors as it is in a combined Score of ten factors. The inclusion of a large number of "residual stresses" we have left out of the final Stress Score would probably not make for any great change in disparity of impairment risk between the SES groups at any given level of stress.

### B.   MEASUREMENT OF STRESS

This problem has been discussed in Chapter 6. The possibility that the same question may mean different things to a low or high status person is pointed out in several examples.

### C.   RESILIENCE AND RESISTANCE

Perhaps another reason why the low SES exhibits more impairment—regardless of the amount of stress experienced—is that the Lows may have a less resilient and less resistant personality. The resistant personality would not yield to the initial stresses. The resilient personality would be capable of recovering from strain or deformation due to stress.

The inclusion of resilient or resistant personality structures as hypothetical explanations brings us back to the original conceptual framework of stress and strain. Personality is assumed to mediate between stress and strain. It determines, to some extent, how much strain or disorder will be associated with a fixed amount of stress. The strain, or disordering, is a disarrangement of the component parts or processes of the organism, or of the parts of an inanimate object.

Let us draw some analogies to make the role of personality in the stress-strain model more concrete. Suppose we consider the stress factors as "hammer blows" acting on people who are bars of metal. The first hypothesis would assume that the low SES bar gets beaten down more (has more impairment or distortion) due to the same hammer blow because it is made of a softer metal—let us say copper—while the high SES bar is made of steel. The low SES may have poor initial resistance to the stress of the blow, less strength in compression. A corollary hypothesis is that the high SES has a more resilient personality, analogous to a bar of flexible material, such as rubber. This would enable the Highs to bounce back after stress. Their deformation would be more temporary than the Lows.

### D.  CUSHIONING

Even beyond resilience lies another possibility: that the blow on the high SES, although of equal force originally, is "cushioned" by advantages that accrue to this stratum. In the high SES, the widowed mother at least has money in the bank. Children of low intelligence or diligence can be expelled from a school or college, yet parents with financial means can assure their placement in another institution of learning. Physical or mental ailments are less likely to impair the child's general functioning. These conditions are not only more easily recognized by parents who have a better education, but there is a positive attitude toward medical services, more money to pay for the best of such services, and more time available to see that the children get such services when the mother does not work. The high SES person has more freedom to move from jobs which are unsatisfying. Thus, the "hammer blows" that might originally be as damaging to mental health as they seem to be in the low SES could be cushioned by the generally favorable circumstances in which the high SES people find themselves.

To the best of our knowledge, the hammer blows, as reported by the respondents, are approximately equal. The risks of the factors and their distribution do not show great SES variation. However, the material being hammered—the personality makeup—is probably of quite different strength and consistency in the various socioeconomic levels. This is indicated later, when we attempt to delineate the basic personality types associated with each SES level and with upward and downward mobility. The rigidity of the low SES (as opposed to the nonrigid anxiety of the high SES) suggests that the low SES personality, with its defense mechanisms, is in some ways more like a well-structured but breakable wooden bar and the high SES is more like resilient rubber.

An hypothesis has been suggested that attempts to find the origins of the poor resistance and weak ego strength of the low SES in their low position in the society. The hypothesis says, in short, that our self-image is determined by what others (the larger society) think of us. If they think we are inferior, we also consider ourselves inferior.

If persons born into the low SES develop poor self-esteem and hence poor ego strength, then it is entirely possible that the identical "hammer blow" may flatten them more than it would the self-confident, self-accepting person of high SES. This does not deny that there are people with poor self-esteem at all SES levels, but it does suggest that they may predominate in the low SES.

The hypotheses of differential SES resistance, resilience, cushioning and adaptive devices seem compatible with the finding that SES differences disappear at a Stress Score of zero. If we inspect the 42 persons exposed to none of the six childhood and four adult factors, we find that their MHR I (assigned without knowledge of the stresses) is virtually identical, regardless of their SES. As mentioned before, among persons with a Stress Score of zero, those of low, middle, and high SES have adult mental health risks of .26, .25, and .24, respectively. Perhaps these people have similar mental health because none of them have very much to be cushioned against, or any hammer blow to which they need to be resistant or resilient, nor any need for invoking an adaptive device in the face of stress. *When there is little or no stress, the three SES groups show an almost identical lack of strain (mental health risk). Put them under the stress of the experiential factors (the hammer), and the low SES quickly shows a more rapid increase in strain (deformation, distortion, disturbance).*

This differential increase in strain as stress increases is indicated by the slope or pitch of the low and high SES ridit distributions shown in Figure 14-2. The slope of the low SES is steeper, indicating a more rapid increase (less resistance, resilience, or cushioning) in the ridits as the Stress Score increases.

### E. ADAPTIVE DEVICES

The hypothesis that socioeconomic differences in impairment under similar stress (within the limits of the measurement techniques employed) are due to the use of different adaptive reactions to stress is explored in Chapter 15. Some statistical evidence is given there which tends to support the idea that the high SES group typically employs less impairing adaptive reactions, while the low SES group generally employs more impairing adaptive devices for dealing with environmental stress.

## Summary

When a Stress Score composed of six childhood and four adult factors showed a linear relationship to the Mental Health Rating ridit, the associations expressed in the stress-strain model had been given some support. When the stress-strain relationship was examined within each of the three SES groups, it was shown to be stronger (or, graphically, to have a steeper slope) among the Lows. The fact that the Lows exhibit more strain (impairment) per unit of stress had to be explained. Had this been true at all stress levels (in which case the lines would have been parallel), our task would have been easier. Instead, the Lows showed increasingly greater strain than the Highs as the Stress Score increased, shown by the fanning out of the three lines.

Five hypotheses were suggested which might partially explain the results: A. *Residual Stress*. All possible stresses were not included in the questionnaire. In addition, not all stresses included in the questionnaire were utilized in construction of the Stress Scores. B. *Measurement*. Stress is difficult to measure. What the Lows report as good health, for example, may be reported as poor health by the Highs. C. *Resistance and Resilience*. The Lows might have a less resistant personality, unable to withstand the initial onslaught of stress. They might also have a less resilient personality, less able to recover from stress. D. *Cushioning*. The stress on the Highs may be cushioned by wealth, education, and other favorable circumstances associated with high socioeconomic status. E. *Adaptive Devices*. The Lows may employ more impairing adaptive devices in the face of stress. Perhaps the Highs exhibit neurotic adaptations, while the Lows show a greater rate of psychotic adaptations.

Any or all of these hypotheses are plausible, but the last may be tested with data available from the Midtown survey. The task of the following chapter is to establish the average impairment associated with various adaptive devices, to show that these devices are distributed differentially between the SES groups, and to demonstrate that these adaptive devices (modes of reaction, styles of coping) are increasingly prevalent as the Stress Score increases.

*Notes*

1. The four noncontingent factors (those applying to the whole sample) were used. They were Adult Poor Physical Health, Poor Interpersonal Affiliations, Work Worries, and Socioeconomic Status Worries.

2. Thomas S. Langner, "Psychophysiological Symptoms and Women's Status in Two Mexican Communities," in J. M. Murphy and A. H. Leighton (eds.), *Approaches to Cross-Cultural Psychiatry* (in preparation). Also Thomas S. Langner, "A Twenty-Two Item Screening Score of Psychiatric Symptoms Indicating Impairment," *Journal of Health and Human Behavior*, Vol. 3, Winter 1962, pp. 269–276.

3. The slope of the Lows is .043, of the Middles .031, and of the Highs .036. For a unit increase in the Stress Score (the $x$ axis) the Lows, for example, will show an increase of .043 ridits. The slope of the Middles and Highs is less steep. The points, based on the averages, are located at .59, .50, and .41 on the $y$ axis (MHR I) and at 5.7, 5.3, and 4.7 on the $x$ axis (the Stress Score) for the Lows, Middles, and Highs respectively. By means of the "point" and "slope" the lines are constructed.

# Adaptation to Stress: Regulatory Devices and Socioeconomic Status

T H O M A S   S .   L A N G N E R

## Regulatory Devices

Residual differences in impairment were found between socioeconomic groups even when the exposure to stress was similar. This can in part be explained by the manner in which the SES groups typically adapt to stress (see Chapter 14, p. 383). Many, though not all, of the common psychiatric diagnostic entities can be considered as modes of adaptation to the environment.

Our interest centers, more specifically, on psychological adaptations to the sociocultural environment. This means that we have made the assumption that psychological adaptations do exist and that they are, if not causally related, at least closely correlated or associated with characteristics of the sociocultural environment. This is not meant to imply that every syndrome is necessarily a psychological adaptation to the sociocultural environment, or even a psychological adaptation at all. A psychosis due to organic brain disease caused by syphilis or arteriosclerosis would not be a psychological adaptation, nor would it be attributable primarily to factors in the sociocultural environment. It is difficult to find a term equivalent to "behavior pattern," which also links behavior to the sociocultural environmental stresses. The term reaction implies a response *to* something, which we often cannot identify. (The Diagnostic Manual of the American Psychiatric Association[1] uses the word "reaction" to describe each syndrome, but the term is meant only in the broadest sense, as in a "pattern of behavior.")

398

A psychological reaction does not imply as much permanent change in the personality as does the term "adaptation." The term "defense" is too limiting, since it defines the direction of adaptation. For example, one form of adaptation is not defense, but direct "offense" or attack. The use of "adjustment" also implies direction, and is therefore objectionable. "Mode of coping" suggests a strong conscious motivation on the part of the organism or individual. The use of the word "mechanism" seems ill-advised, mainly because of the narrow connotations of the phrase "defense mechanism." Because of these objections we have fallen back on the more general terms adaptation and adaptive or regulatory device.

Two classifications were made which described the *type* of behavior (rather than the amount of impairment associated with that behavior, which was measured by the Mental Health Ratings). These two classifications, assigned by psychiatrists, were called the Gross Typology and the Symptom Groups. Our concern will be mainly with the Gross Types. They are, briefly, the Probable Organic, Psychotic, Neurotic, Psychosomatic, Personality Trait, and Well types.

Although we originally used the phrase "reaction type" after each diagnostic category, it would seem less confusing to drop the word "reaction" completely and employ the term *adaptation* in our discussion.

The Gross Types and Symptom Groups are defined in detail in Chapter 3. Since the Gross Types will concern us primarily, a brief review may be helpful. The Probable Psychotics were recognized chiefly by bizarre verbal productions, affective disturbances, and delusion formation. The Probable Neurotics were persons with anxiety, but no major character disorders or psychosomatic problems. The Probable Organics suffered from chronic brain disorders. The Probable Psychosomatic Types reported disorders such as colitis or peptic ulcer, without much evidence of anxiety in their responses. The Probable Personality Trait Types showed character disorders: they were primarily rigid, suspicious, or passive-dependent. The Wells were essentially symptom free. The conceptual framework within which these quasi-diagnostic[2] categories are examined is crucial to an understanding of socioeconomic differences in impairment. If we view the majority of these "diagnoses" as psychological adaptations to stress, as regulatory or homeostatic devices, we can attempt one explanation (among many possible explanations) of the persistent socioeconomic differences in impairment.

It must be granted, first of all, that the degree of impairment and the type of disturbance (or, as we are now viewing it, the type of psychological adaptation or maladaptation, hence disturbance) are two relatively independent entities. There is no reason to say, *a priori,* that *any* Probable Psychotic will exhibit more impairment than *any* Probable Neurotic. There are, of course, many Probable Neurotics who are almost totally impaired, while many a Probable Psychotic is functioning with only slight impairment. It is nevertheless possible to consider most of the diagnostic categories as a series of psychological regulatory (or adaptive) devices involving increasing urgency, disorganization, and impairment of the organism's total functioning.

We have attempted to show that as environmental stress increases, the adaptation to that stress (which is often impairing) increases. This psychological adaptation or maladaptation, which we have called strain, is evidenced by the development of various symptoms. It is clusters of these symptoms, found in rather enduring adaptational syndromes, that Menninger views as a hierarchy of regulatory devices.[3] "First come those mild symptoms called by the layman 'nervousness'; a second order of devices would include neurotic phenomena; the third order embraces episodic and explosive discharges, and the fourth order various syndromes of more persistent and severe disorganization."[4]

Menninger's detailed description of these levels can be paraphrased briefly, with some examples of symptoms covered by the Midtown questionnaire. On the first level of psychological adaptation there is an increase in awareness of discomfort, difficulty of concentration or self-control, leading to some restriction and inhibition in behavior. There is more rigidity in an attempt to control impulses. There is increased tenseness and nervousness, and an increase in psychophysiological symptoms, such as flushing, cold sweats, sleeping problems, dizziness, loss of appetite, tachycardia ("my heart beats hard often"), tremor, enuresis, and diarrhea. There may also be excesses of emotion, such as fear or depression, together with worrying or obsessional thinking.

The second level of adaptation involves partial withdrawal or detachment from the threatening reality, the stress situation. Such symptoms as fainting or amnesic periods (as well as alcoholism and drug addiction) are considered evidence of withdrawal by dissociation. Related symptoms noted in this study were feelings of unreality or depersonalization ("I am a stranger to myself") and social shyness and avoidance ("I prefer to go out alone"). Displacement of aggression (as in phobias and obsessions), substitution of compulsions and rituals for aggressive action, and focusing of aggression on self (as in somatic preoccupation and production of psychosomatic disorders) are other symptoms on the second level.

The third level of adaptation to stress involves assaultive violence and schizoid attacks, convulsions, panic attacks, and catastrophic demoralization. Evidence from court records of violence and "acting out" was attached to the questionnaire in some cases.

The fourth level includes disorganized excitement (manic, catatonic), melancholy, incoherent speech and behavior (hebephrenic), apathetic inertia, delusional preoccupation (paranoid), and confusion. The interviewer's description, case records, and a few responses such as "My memory is not all right" provided some evidence for this level of adaptation. "I often worry about personal enemies" and similar statements were sometimes clues to paranoid tendencies.

The fifth level, not seen in the community sample, would include complete disorganization, continuous mania ending in exhaustion or death.

These five levels of strain, which we choose to consider as only partially successful adaptive devices, lie on a general continuum of progressive deterioration. It is possible that as each device fails to alleviate the stresses, more drastic devices are utilized. It is also possible that these devices or adaptations are learned and that a specific stratum of the population may exhibit primarily a particular level or type of adaptation. New stresses may disturb a previous balance achieved by one of the minor devices. On the other hand, the alleviation of some stresses (such as the death of a dominating parent, a good marriage, a bettering of one's economic situation) may allow the individual to drop some of the adaptations he has previously used.

This suggested continuum of impairment exhibited by various "diagnostic" types was not part of the original explicit Midtown psychiatric conceptualization. While it was agreed that all patients or respondents could be rated on a rough continuum of impairment and symptom severity, there was at no time the suggestion that the "diagnostic" groups themselves lay on a continuum of severity or impairment. The example of the severely impaired neurotic and the moderately well-functioning psychotic is a case in point.

When comparing "diagnostic" categories, we can never say that all

# TABLE 15-1

## PROPORTIONS AND AVERAGE MENTAL HEALTH (MH I) OF RESPONDENTS ACCORDING TO GROSS TYPOLOGY AND RESPONDENTS' SOCIOECONOMIC STATUS

| Gross Types | | Respondents' Socioeconomic Status | | | | | | | |
|---|---|---|---|---|---|---|---|---|---|
| | | LOW Per Cent | MIDDLE Per Cent | HIGH Per Cent | TOTAL Per Cent | LOW $\bar{R}$ | MIDDLE $\bar{R}$ | HIGH $\bar{R}$ | TOTAL $\bar{R}$ |
| Probable Organic Type | L | 4.4 | .9 | 0.0 | 1.7 | .86 | (.79) | — | .85 |
| Probable Psychotic Type | L | 13.1 | 8.3 | 3.6 | 8.3 | .83 | .81 | .81 | .82 |
| Probable Neurotic Type[a] | H | 24.5 | 35.5 | 42.5 | 34.3 | .63 | .58 | .52 | .57 |
| Probable Psychosomatic Type | NS | 8.1 | 5.2 | 5.4 | 6.2 | .59 | .53 | .53 | .55 |
| Probable Personality Trait Type | L | 14.9 | 10.1 | 4.5 | 9.8 | .51 | .49 | .46 | .50 |
| Probable Neurotic Psychosomatic Type | NS | 5.5 | 4.7 | 6.8 | 5.7 | .63 | .64 | .52 | .59 |
| Probable Neurotic-Trait Type | L | 19.7 | 17.1 | 11.3 | 16.0 | .60 | .50 | .49 | .54 |
| Well | H | 9.8 | 18.0 | 25.9 | 17.9 | .12 | .11 | .10 | .11 |
| Total Number of Cases (N = 100 per cent) | | 544 | 556 | 560 | 1660 | | | | |

[a] One case classified as Probable Transient Situational Personality Reaction Type was included.

Parentheses ( ) enclose Ridit based on less than ten cases.

L — The proportion of low SES is significantly larger at the .001 level.

H — The proportion of high SES is significantly larger at the .001 level.

NS — The difference between the proportions of high and low SES groups is not significant.

Probable Psychotics are bound to be more impaired than all Probable Neurotics. However, we can compare the average impairment of "diagnostic" groups. Since both a psychiatric impairment rating (Mental Health Rating) and a "diagnostic" classification (Gross Typology) were made, we are able to examine them simultaneously.

## The Gross Typology and Impairment

Despite the lack of any explicit procedures or definitions governing the minimum or maximum impairment rating allowed for a Probable Psychotic or Probable Neurotic, distinct average impairments appear for various "diagnostic" groups (see Table 15-1).

The Probable Psychotic Types have a risk of .82. They are statistically quite distinct (at the one per cent level) from the various Neurotic Types (.57, .59, and .54) and the Psychosomatic Types (.55). The Personality Trait Types (character disorders) have the same risk as the whole sample (.50), and are statistically distinct from the Probable Neurotic Type (.57). Those classified as Well have a risk of only .11, which again is distinct from both the Neurotic and Psychotic risks. (The Probable Organic Type, unlikely to be a psychological adaptive type, will not be discussed further.)

It must again be asserted that these are averages, and many individual cases labeled "Neurotic" actually received Mental Health Ratings which indicated impairment greater than that of some of the "Psychotics."

By and large, however, it can be clearly seen that the Psychotic Type forms a statistically distinct severe impairment group, the Neurotic Type a distinct moderate impairment group, the Personality Trait Type a distinctly milder impairment group, and the Wells a distinct and virtually unimpaired group. (It was part of the explicit procedure that cases having a MHR II of 0 should be classified as Well. The low impairment risk of the Wells, then, is not surprising. No such rules were made concerning other Gross Types, however.)

These data seem to lend support to the general thesis that modes of psychological adaptation to stress lie on a continuum of impairment severity. The Gross Typology, ranked according to average impairment, and the Menninger levels of regulatory devices are roughly parallel, and could be graphically represented as follows:

| LEVELS OF REGULATORY DEVICES (MENNINGER) | GROSS TYPOLOGY RANKED BY IMPAIRMENT | RIDIT |
|---|---|---|
| A (Menninger does not describe the regulatory devices of well persons) | Well | .11 |
| B "Nervousness" | Probable Personality Trait Types | .50 |
| C Neurotic Phenomena | Probable Neurotic Type | .57 |
| D Episodic and Explosive Discharges (Assaultive violence, schizoid attacks, convulsions, panic attacks, catastrophic demoralization) | Probable Psychotic Type | .82 |
| E Persistent and severe disorganization (Manic, catatonic, hebephrenic, paranoid)<br><br><br>F Complete disorganization, continuous mania ending in exhaustion or death | (Most of these persons would be in hospitals or prisons and would be infrequently found in the community sample. Obviously, few such respondents were found in the community sample. They would be a minute fraction of the total. Only 0.5 per cent of the population are now in mental hospitals and only a small number of these exhibit level F) | |

If these Gross Types do show distinct levels of impairment, perhaps this can explain some of the SES differences in impairment. If we can demonstrate that the low SES typically exhibits psychological adaptations involving great average impairment, and the high SES typically shows adaptations which involve less average impairment, then the proportional distribution of adaptive types may be partly responsible for the Low's greater impairment, regardless of stress.

## Distribution of the Gross Typology in the Whole Sample

What are the proportional distributions of adaptive types *without* regard to socioeconomic status? The distribution of Gross Types in the sample as a whole (see Table 15-1) shows that 8.3 per cent are classified as Probable Psychotic Types. While a figure this high may seem incredible for a community population, it should be noted that previous hospitalizations, court records, and similar data were heavily used in classifying these types. Moreover, the community demands for functioning may actually be quite minimal, particularly among the older unmarried or widowed persons. This allows them to remain in Midtown, their symptoms unnoticed. It is also pertinent that in the Patient Census almost half of the Midtown patients diagnosed as psychotic were being treated on an ambulatory basis by private therapists or in clinics rather than as in-patients. This is another reminder that some preconceptions about the psychotic as a totally disabled person should be dispelled.

The large proportion of Neurotic Types (34.3 per cent), together with those Neurotics also showing psychosomatic symptoms (5.7 per cent) or personality trait disorders (16.0 per cent), comprised a majority of the sample (56.0 per cent). Again, this may seem like a paradox, since slightly over half of the population is classified as Probably Neurotic in combination with other symptoms. This does not seem illogical, however, if we say that about half of the Midtowners told us they are anxious, worried, "nervous," restless, and often have stomach upsets and trouble sleeping. The "average man" in Midtown is functioning with little or no difficulty, but he has mild symptoms. By his responses he has partially documented the fact that there is a "neurotic personality of our time."

A smaller proportion of Psychosomatic Types (6.2 per cent) was noted. These were individuals who reported psychophysiological disorders (asthma, hay fever, colitis, hypertension, and the like) but did not necessarily evidence much anxiety. Only 9.8 per cent were classified as Personality Trait Types (immature, rigid, suspicious, passive-dependent).

In the entire sample, only 17.9 per cent were classified as Well. These persons were usually symptom free, seldom worried, and were apparently functioning well on the job, in marriage, and as parents.

## Distribution of the Gross Typology According to SES

Many comments and interpretations could be made concerning the proportions of these types found in a community sample as a whole, but our primary purpose in presenting this material has been to interpret socioeconomic differences in impairment. With this in view, let us look at the proportional distributions of Gross Types according to the respondents' SES (see Table 15-1). It is clear that significantly larger proportions of the Lows were Organic Types (4.4 per cent of the Lows, 0.9 per cent of the Middles, and none of the Highs). Similarly, over three times as many Lows (13.1 per cent) as Highs (3.6 per cent) were classified Probable Psychotic Types. The Lows also tended to be Personality Trait Types or Neurotic Trait Types. (Proponents of the "drift theory" might claim that persons who were psychotic would end up in the low SES group principally because of downward mobility. Our data do not support this contention. Persons whose fathers were of low SES were twice as likely to be classified Probable Psychotic as those from high SES families.[5])

On the other hand, significantly more Highs than Lows were Neurotic Types. As SES increased, the proportion of Neurotic Types also increased. This is the rare instance in which the high SES is more prone to a type of disturbance than the low SES. The Neurotic reaction, however, involves a risk of only .57, as opposed to the Psychotic risk of .82. It seems clear that the Highs have more of something less impairing, while the Lows have more of something more impairing. If this can later be shown to be true regardless of the number of stresses reported, it may help to explain the SES disparity in impairment.

## The Symptom Groups in the Whole Sample

Certain clusters of symptoms which seemed applicable to each respondent were checked during the psychiatric rating process. All the major symptom areas which applied were checked off, since more than one symptom area might apply to an individual. If both psychiatrists assigned different symptoms to an individual, all symptoms were considered to be valid. For instance, an alcoholic might be assigned to "Alcoholic" and "Schizophrenic" by one psychiatrist, and to "Alcoholic" and "Brain Disease" by the other. The individual was finally considered to show evidence of all three "symptom groups." The process of assigning Symptom Groups and the definitions of the groups are described in Chapter 3.

Table 15-2 shows the proportional distribution of the Symptom Groups according to the respondents' socioeconomic status[6] and in the sample as a whole. The fact that 70.8 per cent evidence Mixed Anxiety, or that 51.7 per cent report some Psychosomatic Symptoms should not be cause for alarm. The major portion of persons with these symptoms is not significantly impaired by them. This is not true, however, for such Symptom Groups as Schizophrenic, Epileptic, Cycloid-Affective Psychosis, and Brain Disease. (The impairment risks of the Symptom Groups are not presented in this volume.)

## Distribution of the Symptom Groups According to SES

The majority of the Symptom Groups are more prone to occur in the low rather than in the high SES (differences were noted at the .001 con-

## TABLE 15-2

## PROPORTIONS OF RESPONDENTS ACCORDING TO PSYCHIATRIC SYMPTOM GROUPS AND RESPONDENTS' SOCIOECONOMIC STATUS

|  | | Respondents' Socioeconomic Status | | | |
|---|---|---|---|---|---|
|  | | LOW | MIDDLE | HIGH | TOTAL |
| Psychiatric Symptom Groups | | Per Cent | Per Cent | Per Cent | Per Cent |
| Epileptic | NS | 0.7 | 0.5 | 0.0 | 0.4 |
| Retarded | L | 6.4 | 1.1 | 0.0 | 2.5 |
| Alcoholic | L | 6.6 | 4.5 | 2.7 | 4.6 |
| Brain Disease and/or Senility | L | 2.8 | 0.5 | 0.4 | 1.2 |
| Sex Deviant | NS | 0.4 | 1.1 | 1.4 | 1.0 |
| Dyssocial | L | 3.1 | 2.5 | 0.2 | 1.9 |
| Mixed Anxiety | NS | 73.0 | 69.8 | 69.6 | 70.8 |
| Free-floating Anxiety | NS | 13.1 | 13.1 | 19.1 | 15.1 |
| Phobias | NS | 26.5 | 28.2 | 23.6 | 26.1 |
| Obsessive—Compulsive | NS | 8.6 | 9.2 | 6.6 | 8.1 |
| Psychosomatic | L | 60.3 | 49.1 | 45.9 | 51.7 |
| Hypochondriacal | L | 31.2 | 23.9 | 20.4 | 25.1 |
| Neurasthenia | NS | 20.4 | 19.4 | 15.2 | 18.3 |
| Passive—Dependent | L | 36.0 | 28.8 | 17.1 | 27.2 |
| Depressed | L | 36.2 | 23.9 | 11.1 | 23.6 |
| Rigid | L | 52.0 | 34.5 | 16.4 | 34.2 |
| Schizoid | L | 19.5 | 18.5 | 7.9 | 15.2 |
| Aggressive | H | 2.2 | 5.8 | 11.1 | 6.4 |
| Suspicious | L | 40.3 | 29.0 | 16.4 | 28.4 |
| Schizophrenic | L | 7.2 | 5.8 | 1.8 | 4.9 |
| Cycloid—Affective Psychosis | NS | 0.4 | 0.0 | 0.5 | 0.3 |
| None of the above symptoms | H | 3.3 | 6.1 | 11.1 | 6.9 |
| Total Number of Cases (N=100 per cent)[a] | | 544 | 556 | 560 | 1660 |

[a] Percentages total more than 100 per cent because of multiple classifications.
L — The proportion of low SES is significantly larger at the .001 level.
H — The proportion of high SES is significantly larger at the .001 level.
NS — The difference between proportions of high and low SES is not significant.

fidence level). Most notable is the predominance of the Rigid, Depressed, Suspicious, and Passive-Dependent Symptom Groups among the Lows. Only two Symptom Groups were more populous in the high SES, the Aggressive and those who were asymptomatic (the Wells).

The Lows also had more than their share of the Schizoid, Schizo-

## TABLE 15-3

### DISTRIBUTION AND AVERAGE SYMPTOM SCORES

*Symptom Scores (in per cent)*

| Numerical Scores | Immaturity | Rigidity | Suspiciousness | Withdrawal | Frustration-Depression | Neurasthenia | Gastrointestinal Symptoms |
|---|---|---|---|---|---|---|---|
| 0 | 20.3 | 28.9 | 40.5 | 29.0 | 56.2 | 65.4 | 85.2 |
| 1 | 26.6 | 23.3 | 31.3 | 39.4 | 25.7 | 22.7 | 12.5 |
| 2 | 23.5 | 16.8 | 18.0 | 20.8 | 10.4 | 9.0 | 1.8 |
| 3 | 14.6 | 12.8 | 9.3 | 8.8 | 3.9 | 2.7 | 0.3 |
| 4 | 8.7 | 9.6 | 0.5 | 1.5 | 2.6 | + | + |
| 5 | 3.5 | 5.5 | + | + | 0.8 | | |
| 6 | 1.4 | 2.7 | | | + | | |
| 7 | 0.5 | + | | | | | |
| 8 | 0.5 | | | | | | |
| Unscored | 0.4 | 0.4 | 0.4 | 0.5 | 0.4 | 0.2 | 0.2 |
| Average Score | 1.9 | 1.8 | 1.0 | 1.1 | 0.7 | 0.5 | 0.2 |
| Total Number of Cases (N=100 per cent)[a] | | | | | | | 1660[a] |

+ End of score range for this Symptom Score.
[a] Each column is percentaged on 1660 cases.

phrenic, Psychosomatic, Hypochondriacal, Dyssocial, Alcoholic, and Structural Brain Disease groups.

## Symptom Scores: Their Construction

A series of psychometric scores were used for comparison with some of the psychiatric judgments. These scores were not tested for uni-dimensionality, but were compiled simply on the basis of the manifest content. A cluster analysis of all symptoms was initiated but could not be completed because of lack of funds. However, small test matrices showed a high degree of internal consistency for some of these scores.

After the items had been grouped according to content, a weight of 1 was assigned to each extreme answer category. The content of the scores, the extreme category associated with greater impairment risk, and the proportion giving that response are shown in Table 2-1. (These symptom items are discussed as part of the questionnaire content in Chapter 2.) The distributions of the scores are shown in Table 15-3, with the average score for all 1660 respondents. It is these averages that will be compared across the socioeconomic groups.

The average Symptom Scores generally decrease as the respondents' socioeconomic status increases.[7] (See Table 15-4.) For example, the average Low agreed with 2.5 Immaturity items, while the average High agreed with only 1.4 items. In other words, the Lows, on the average, reported one more symptom of Immaturity than the Highs. (Immaturity was generally signified by poor impulse control, i.e., "When I want something I want it right away.") The Symptom Scores circumvent the psychiatric judgment process. They corroborate the findings, based on those judgments, that the Lows are more prone to the character disorders. The scores associated with Rigidity, Immaturity, and Suspiciousness confirm our slowly developing picture of the low socioeconomic group.

The Frustration-Depression score illustrates the concordance of the

## TABLE 15-4

### AVERAGE (MEAN) SYMPTOM SCORES OF RESPONDENTS ACCORDING TO RESPONDENTS' SOCIOECONOMIC STATUS

| | Respondents' Socioeconomic Status | | | |
| Symptom Scores | LOW Mean | MIDDLE Mean | HIGH Mean | TOTAL Mean |
|---|---|---|---|---|
| Immaturity | 2.5 | 1.8 | 1.4 | 1.9 |
| Rigidity | 2.8 | 1.8 | 0.8 | 1.8 |
| Suspiciousness | 1.5 | 0.9 | 0.6 | 1.0 |
| Withdrawal | 1.4 | 1.1 | 0.9 | 1.1 |
| Frustration-Depression | 1.1 | 0.7 | 0.4 | 0.7 |
| Neurasthenia | 0.7 | 0.4 | 0.4 | 0.5 |
| Gastrointestinal Symptoms | 0.2 | 0.2 | 0.1 | 0.2 |
| Total Number of Cases (N=100 per cent) | 544 | 556 | 560 | 1660 |

psychometric measures and the classifications made by the psychiatrists. The Frustration-Depression score is based purely on responses to specific questionnaire items; the Depressed Symptom Group was assigned to various respondents on the basis of a total impression of the pattern of their responses to more than 400 questions. The fact that the average Frustration-Depression score is greater among those of low SES corroborates the heavier assignment of the Depressed Symptom Group classification to persons of low status.

The fact that there are more Probable Neurotics in the high SES has not been evaluated by the Symptom Scores. Perhaps this is because no score was ever devised to measure the characteristic. Such a score might have been constructed out of items dealing with anxiety, "worries," awareness of mild tension, and other response patterns simultaneously exhibiting a lack of somatization or character trait formation. However, the construction of a psychometric index which could parallel a psychiatric judgment as complex as Probable Neurotic is an extremely difficult task. The only use to which we have put these psychometric measures is to reinforce the complex clinical judgments in their relationship to SES.

In addition to the Gross Typology, Symptom Groups, and Symptom Scores, some scales of social attitudes, such as the Anomie Scale and the Authoritarian or "F Scale" will be discussed in relation to SES. These social attitudes are more widespread in the low SES and will be introduced as part of a general description of the personality patterns of the socioeconomic groups in Chapter 16.

## The Gross Typology, the Stress Score, and SES

It is not possible to examine all of the nosological classifications and scores in relation to the Stress Score. Most of our attention will center on the differing proportions of Probable Psychotics and Neurotics within each SES and stress level and the impairment associated with those proportions.

If the Gross Typology is examined according to the respondents' SES and the various Stress Score levels (see Table 15-5), it is apparent that the proportion of each type increases as stress increases, with the notable exception of the Personality Trait Type and, of course, the Wells.[8]

Since our main concern is with the Gross Types which show sharp SES differences, let us look at the proportions of Probable Psychotics and

### Table 15-5
### Proportions of Gross Typology According to
### Stress Score and Respondents' SES

| | | STRESS SCORE (IN PER CENT) | | | | | |
|---|---|---|---|---|---|---|---|
| | SES | 0–2 | 3–4 | 5–6 | 7–8 | 9–10 | 11–18 |
| Probable Organic Type | Low | 2.6 | 2.1 | 4.6 | 7.2 | 3.6 | 9.8 |
| | High | 0.0 | 0.0 | 0.0 | 0.0 | 0.0 | 0.0 |
| Probable Psychotic Type | Low | 3.8 | 7.8 | 12.2 | 17.5 | 23.2 | 26.8 |
| | High | 1.4 | 3.8 | 3.9 | 4.8 | 6.4 | 4.3 |
| Probable Neurotic Type | Low | 11.5 | 20.6 | 29.8 | 26.8 | 32.1 | 31.7 |
| | High | 29.5 | 41.5 | 42.6 | 60.3 | 61.7 | 43.5 |
| Probable Psychosomatic Type | Low | 9.0 | 9.2 | 6.9 | 10.3 | 5.4 | 4.9 |
| | High | 2.9 | 5.0 | 9.3 | 3.2 | 4.3 | 8.7 |
| Probable Personality Trait Type | Low | 29.5 | 17.7 | 16.0 | 7.2 | 7.1 | 2.4 |
| | High | 6.5 | 3.8 | 3.9 | 3.2 | 0.0 | 13.0 |
| Probable Neurotic-Psychosomatic | Low | 3.8 | 5.0 | 5.3 | 7.2 | 7.1 | 4.9 |
| Type | High | 4.3 | 7.5 | 7.0 | 7.9 | 8.5 | 8.7 |
| Probable Neurotic-Trait Type | Low | 12.8 | 23.4 | 17.6 | 22.7 | 19.6 | 19.5 |
| | High | 10.1 | 11.3 | 10.9 | 11.1 | 10.6 | 21.7 |
| Probable Well | Low | 20.5 | 12.8 | 9.9 | 1.0 | 1.8 | 0.0 |
| | High | 38.1 | 19.5 | 20.2 | 6.3 | 6.4 | 0.0 |
| Probable Well* | Low | 6.4 | 1.4 | 0.0 | 0.0 | 0.0 | 0.0 |
| | High | 7.2 | 8.2 | 2.3 | 3.2 | 2.1 | 0.0 |
| Probable Well and Well* | Low | 26.9 | 14.2 | 9.9 | 1.0 | 1.8 | 0.0 |
| (Total) | High | 45.3 | 27.7 | 22.5 | 9.5 | 8.5 | 0.0 |
| Total Number of Cases | Low | 78 | 141 | 131 | 97 | 56 | 41 |
| | High | 139 | 159 | 129 | 63 | 47 | 23 |

Well* means especially well.

Probable Neurotics, and compare only the low and high socioeconomic thirds of the sample.

The proportion of Probable Psychotics increases uniformly as the Stress Score increases in the low SES (3.8, 7.8, 12.2, 17.5, 23.2, and 26.8 per cent). There is a very slight tendency for the proportions to taper off at the higher stress levels (see Figure 15-1). In the high SES, however, the proportions do not vary greatly as the Stress Score increases. At a score of 3 to 4 the proportion of Probable Psychotics reaches a virtual plateau among Highs (1.4, 3.8, 3.9, 4.8, 6.4, and 4.3 per cent). Thus, two major SES differences appear.

First, the proportions of Probable Psychotics at any Stress Score level are much larger among the Lows than among the Highs. Second, the rate of increase in the proportion of Probable Psychotics as stress increases is

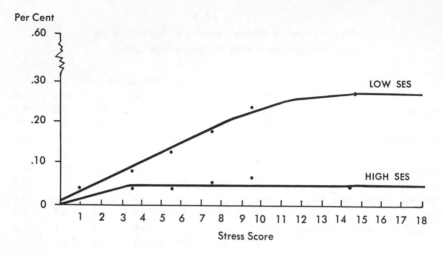

Figure 15-1. Proportion of Probable Psychotics, According to Stress Score and Respondents' Socioeconomic Status

very great among the Lows, and almost nil among the Highs. This is illustrated in Figure 15-1. The Lows show a line with a sharp upward slope, while the Highs' graph is closer to horizontal.

The proportion of Probable Neurotics also increases with stress (see Table 15-5 and Figure 15-2). Among the Lows, the proportions rapidly reach a plateau (11.5, 20.6, 29.8, 26.8, 32.1, 31.7 per cent). Among the Highs, however, the Probable Neurotic Type becomes increasingly more common as stress increases (29.5, 41.5, 42.6, 60.3, 61.7, 43.5, per cent; see Figure 15-2). There is again a tendency for the proportion to taper off a bit in the extreme stress group.

Let us compare the proportions of Probable Psychotics and Probable Neurotics in the high and low SES as stress increases. The figures (excerpted from Table 15-5) are as follows:

|  |  | STRESS SCORE (IN PER CENT) | | | | | |
|---|---|---|---|---|---|---|---|
|  |  | 0–2 | 3–4 | 5–6 | 7–8 | 9–10 | 11–18 |
| Probable Psychotics | Low | 3.8 | 7.8 | 12.2 | 17.5 | 23.2 | 26.8 |
|  | High | 1.4 | 3.8 | 3.9 | 4.8 | 6.4 | 4.3 |
| Probable Neurotics | Low | 11.5 | 20.6 | 29.8 | 26.8 | 32.1 | 31.7 |
|  | High | 29.5 | 41.5 | 42.6 | 60.3 | 61.7 | 43.5 |
| Total Number of Cases | Low | 78 | 141 | 131 | 97 | 56 | 41 |
| (N = 100 per cent) | High | 139 | 159 | 129 | 63 | 47 | 23 |

As noted before, the Lows exhibit a greater proportion of Probable Psychotics, regardless of the stress level. Moreover, as stress increases,

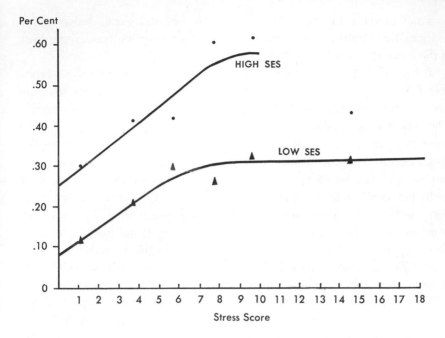

Figure 15-2. Proportion of Probable Neurotics, According to Stress Score and Respondents' Socioeconomic Status

the ratio of low to high SES Psychotics increases sharply. At lower stress levels there are proportionally 2 to 3 times more Low than High Psychotics. At greater stress levels there are 4 to 6 times more Low Psychotics than High Psychotics. The Highs seem to show a fixed proportion of Probable Psychotics (somewhere between 4 per cent and 6 per cent) no matter what the stress level.

Clearly, then, the Probable Psychotic Type is more typical of the Lows. As stress increases, they are increasingly prone to exhibit this mode of adaptation. In the extreme stress group, over one-fourth of the Lows and only one twenty-fifth of the Highs evidence this group of regulatory devices.

The picture is just as interesting, in reverse, for the Probable Neurotic Type. Within any stress level, the Highs consistently show a greater proportion of Neurotics. The Lows show a tendency to a fixed proportion of Probable Neurotics regardless of stress level. (This tendency is somewhat weaker than the Highs' tendency to exhibit a fixed proportion of Probable Psychotics regardless of stress level.) The ratio of High to Low Neurotics does not increase rapidly with stress, however, and varies between 1.4 and 2.6. The Highs more typically employ this adaptive type, regardless of the amount of stress they report.

It is clear that the high SES Probable Neurotics and the low SES Probable Psychotics show a tendency to taper off in numbers in the extreme stress group. This might possibly be a result of the small number of people who reported such extremely stressful lives. The data, however, seem to point to at least one alternative explanation. The sharp increase in the proportion of Probable Personality Trait Types among the Highs in the extreme (11-18) Stress Score category, jumping from around 4 per cent to 13 per cent, indicates that the high SES persons were classified as Personality Trait Types more frequently only when they reported very stressful lives (see Table 15-5). That this tendency is not just due to pure chance is indicated by a similar sharp increase in the Probable Neurotic Trait Type category among high SES reporting extremely stressful lives (rising sharply from around 10 per cent at the first five stress levels to 21.7 per cent; see Table 15-5). This can be viewed as an aspect of the quasi-diagnostic process, or as a "bias" on the part of the clinicians. The reader has been amply warned, however, that the Gross Typology and the Symptom Group classifications, unlike MHR I, are open to this type of methodological circularity. Since all diagnoses made in clinical practice include a knowledge of the patient's social background, the Gross Type classifications are at least no more biased than those made every day in psychiatric practice.

The impression that the Highs avoid the Probable Psychotic adaptation to stress (or avoid classification as Probable Psychotics) is supported by other comparisons. For example, even at the most extreme stress level, the Highs show only 4.3 per cent Probable Psychotic, opposed to 43.5 per cent Probable Neurotic. The comparable group of Lows are classified 26.8 per cent Probable Psychotic and 31.7 per cent Probable Neurotic. Among the Lows under extreme stress, the proportion of Psychotics almost equals that of the Neurotics. Clearly, then, the Highs seem to avoid the psychotic adaptation, no matter how stressful their lives. Contrarily, they are about twice as prone to the neurotic adaptation as the Lows. (As mentioned before, the Highs tend to be classified in categories other than Probable Psychotic in the extreme stress group. However, their tendency to be placed in the Personality Trait Type category in the extreme stress group does not explain their "avoidance" of the Psychotic classification at lower stress levels.)

The tendency for clinicians to diagnose individuals in terms of their treatability and socioeconomic status, suggested by early studies and confirmed most recently by the New Haven Study of Hollingshead and Redlich,[9] is a problem that has been partially circumvented in the Midtown Gross Typology. The psychiatric rater, working with an abstract of an individual's responses to a questionnaire survey, has nothing to gain by assigning to him a diagnosis which will mean long or short-term treatment. The respondent is not in treatment. No matter what his ability to pay for therapy, he will not become a patient of the doctor doing the rating. Since no therapy is involved, there is much less motivation to diagnose the high SES individuals as neurotic, which would then suggest treatment by psychotherapy or psychoanalysis. There is also no motivation to assign the psychoses predominantly to persons of low SES, which (as the New Haven researchers point out) usually means assignment to a state hospital and more often involves psychosurgery.

This disclaimer does not mean that in assigning the Gross Types the Midtown research-oriented psychiatrists were entirely uninfluenced by their previous experience in psychiatric hospitals or by the knowledge that they could not maintain their private practices with patients who were unable to pay. It simply suggests that making quasi-diagnoses and estimates of impairment from abstracts of questionnaire interviews was a new and different experience from usual clinical practice. Quite possibly, then, there were concomitant changes in the cues used for making these new quasi-diagnoses.

Despite the partial circularity of the Gross Typology, we feel confident that these proportions and graphs support the contention that the Highs tend to exhibit an adaptation to stress which, on the average, is *less* impairing (the Probable Neurotic Type, with a risk of .57). The Lows, on the other hand, clearly demonstrate an increasing prevalence of an adaptive type as stress increases which, on the average, is *more* impairing (the Probable Psychotic Type, with a risk of .82).

Even though the distribution of Psychotic and Neurotic adaptations does help to explain some of the increased impairment risk in the low SES, it should not be given more weight than the other hypothetical factors presented in Chapter 14. While the Psychotic risk of .82 and the Neurotic risk of .57 apply to the sample as a whole, the low SES Neurotic *still* exhibits more impairment than the high SES Neurotic.

The risk of the Low Neurotic is .63 (see Table 15-1), while that of the High Neurotic is only .52. Despite the adaptive type, there is much variation in impairment among the SES groups.

The higher the SES, then, the less impaired the neurotic is likely to be. (This sheds more light on the finding reported in Volume I that the high SES is getting proportionally more treatment for proportionally less impairment.)

The SES variation in impairment risk between Probable Psychotics, however, is not statistically significant. The low SES Psychotics have a risk of .83, similar to the high SES Psychotics' risk of .81. (The impairment associated with the neurotic but not the psychotic adaptation varies between SES levels.)

Some portion of the low SES group's greater degree of impairment at comparable stress levels can be explained by hypothesizing a tendency of the Lows to utilize or employ the psychotic adaptation to stress. Unfortunately, we are unable to demonstrate that there is a choice of adaptive devices or that in any individual case a specific mode of adaptation was consistently employed, consciously or unconsciously, to reduce impairment. We have demonstrated an association between variables which strongly suggests a dynamic connection as well as a statistical association. The psychotic adaptation involves great impairment risk, regardless of socioeconomic status. The influence of the proportional distribution of the neurotic adaptation in reducing the over-all high SES risk is less clear, because of the wide range of neurotic impairment.

## Impairment of Probable Neurotics and Probable Psychotics Within Stress and SES Levels

The neurotic reaction of the Highs seems on the average to be less impairing than the more typically psychotic reaction of the Lows. Is this actually true at all stress levels? If low SES Probable Psychotics showed a decrease in impairment at higher stress levels, the adaptive types would not help us to explain the SES differences in impairment as stress increased. Figure 15-3 shows the average impairment (MHI) for Probable Neurotics and Probable Psychotics of high SES.

It can be clearly seen that at each stress level the average impairment of the High Psychotics is greater than that of the High Neurotics. Thus we can say that the Highs actually have more of something less impairing (probable neurosis), regardless of stress.

It is also of interest that while the average impairment of the high

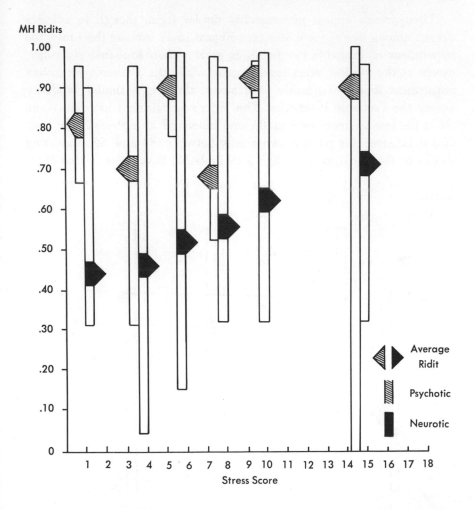

Figure 15-3. Average Impairment (MH I) and Range of Impairment, According to Psychotic and Neurotic Types for High SES Respondents

SES Probable Psychotics tends to fluctuate between .68 and .93 at different stress levels, there is no apparent pattern to this fluctuation. In general, there seems to be random fluctuation around the over-all average of .81 for high SES Probable Psychotics. The high SES Probable Neurotics, however, show a steady increase in impairment as stress increases (.44, .46, .52, .55, .62, and .71). A secondary finding, then, is that among those of high SES the impairment of Probable Neurotics increases with stress, while the impairment of Probable Psychotics remains, more or less constantly, at a greater level.

These trends appear in somewhat similar form, though to a lesser degree, among those of low SES (see Figure 15-4). Among the Lows, the impairment of Probable Psychotics is greater than Probable Neurotics, except at the mildest stress level. Again, while the Probable Neurotics' impairment increases steadily with stress, there is a similar tendency among the Probable Psychotics. The latter's impairment increases from .44 at the lowest stress level to .69, and tapers off at a Stress Score level of 5 to 6. After this point it varies only between .84 and .92, appearing similar to the impairment of high SES Probable Psychotics in that there

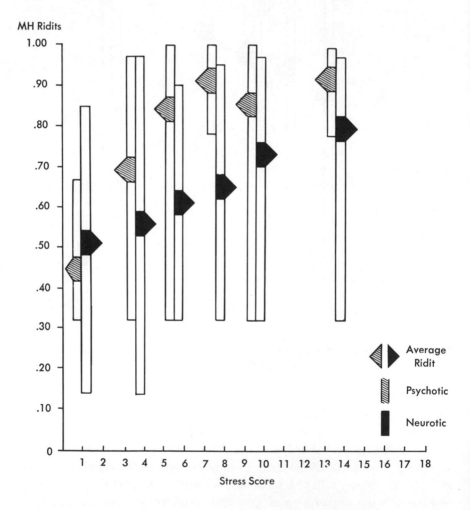

Figure 15-4. Average Impairment (MH I) and Range of Impairment, According to Psychotic and Neurotic Types for Low SES Respondents

is evidence of a plateau with only minor fluctuations. (The average impairment of the low and high SES Probable Neurotics and Probable Psychotics within each stress group is given in Appendix D.)

Figures 15-3 and 15-4 indicate that in general the impairment of Probable Psychotics greatly exceeds the impairment of Probable Neurotics in both the high and low SES regardless of the stress level. This lends more strength to our hypothesis that socioeconomic variation in adaptive types may be one of the forces making for differential impairment in the low and high SES groups at the same level of stress.

Perhaps the role of adaptive types in determining impairment is placed in proper perspective by examining the impairment of the Wells. The Wells have no impairment to speak of, their average risk being .11 (see Table 15-1). They constitute 25.9 per cent of the Highs and only 9.8 per cent of the Lows. This group can be considered as having a "Well" or effective adaptation to stress. (It should be noted that even persons with a Stress Score of 0 have doubtless been exposed to some stress during their lives.) We assume that the Wells have not had to employ impairing devices to keep their balance. The fact that most of these Wells are in the high SES accounts by itself for some of the reduction in risk of the Highs, and a consequent increase among the Lows.

The decrease in the proportion of Wells is clear as stress increases (see Table 15-5). The Highs start with 45.3 per cent Well, about twice that of the Lows (26.9 per cent). Clearly, more Highs than Lows can remain symptom free and unimpaired as stress increases. This fact supports the *resistance* and *resiliency* hypotheses rather than the *adaptive device* hypothesis.

With the exception of the Probable Psychotics and the Wells, the Lows seem to have more impairment regardless of adaptive type. This SES variation in impairment, within each adaptive type, supports the hypothesis that the Highs are more resilient. The tendency for the low SES group to exhibit a greater proportion of Probable Psychotics as stress increases seems to give credence to the *adaptive type* hypothesis.

## Specific Stresses and Adaptive Devices

While demonstrating that the risk of impairment becomes greater as the sheer number of stress factors increases, we may have given the impression that the individual stresses do not matter. Our data suggest that the sequence and content of the stresses may have only an indirect bearing on the degree of impairment.

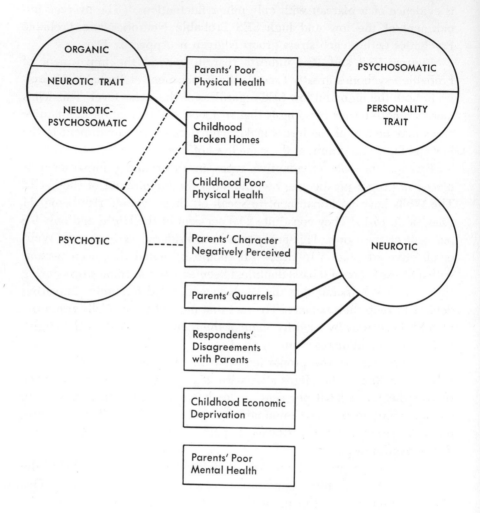

**Figure 15-5. Association of Adult Reaction Types with Childhood Stress Factors (Chi Square at or better than .05 level)**

The individual stresses, however, do exhibit quite specific relationships to the adaptive devices exhibited. The way people grapple with stress appears to be partly a function of the stresses to which they have been exposed.

For example, there are two types of adult adaptation significantly associated with only one childhood stress, Parents' Poor Physical Health. One is the Probable Personality Trait Type, who exhibits character disorders such as rigidity, suspiciousness, or dependency. Poor parental health by itself is also typical of those who manifest Probable Psychosomatic symptoms as their primary mode of adaptation (see Figure 15-5).

The Personality Trait and Psychosomatic Types are significantly associated with only one stress. However, three adaptive types (Probable Organic, Probable Neurotic with Personality Traits, and Probable Neurotic with psychosomatic features) are linked to a background of two stresses; namely, Parents' Poor Physical Health and Childhood Broken Homes. Since about three-fifths of the Childhood Broken Homes were due to the death of one or both parents before the child was sixteen, this pattern seems to be a stronger statement of Parents' Poor Physical Health. This was poor health which often ended in the parents' death.

The Probable Psychotics' typical stress experience was also Poor Parental Physical Health and a Broken Home. Added to this, however, was a negative perception of parents' character. Thus a report of domineering or rejecting parents adds an important new dimension to a family history of poor health.

Finally, the Probable Neurotics shared in the widest variety of early stresses. Their own poor health in childhood was added to their Parents' Poor Physical Health as a possible factor. Again they perceived their parents negatively. In addition, Probable Neurotics tend to have parents who quarreled frequently. As a group they might also have disagreed more frequently with their parents during adolescence. The new stress dimension among Probable Neurotics (as opposed to other types) is their quarrelsome preadult family life.

Viewed from another angle, each stress or combination of stresses seems to favor particular adaptive devices. The most striking of these associations is that *quarrelsome homes may be related to neurosis, the early death of parents possibly linked to psychosis, and a very negative perception of one's parents associated with both neurosis and psychosis.* Parental health plays some part in all types of adaptation; it is therefore not prognostic of any particular adaptation, except when it is the only factor involved.

These data suggest that the particular stresses to which people have been exposed seem to be connected with the way they react to subsequent stress. Our findings now suggest a revised theoretical model in which different types of early environmental stress (together with positive aspects of the environment) interact with genetic endowment. Typical and enduring ways of reacting or adapting are formed as the resultant of these stresses having different direction and strength. In this fashion the child comes to develop what we call his "personality." The personality interacts with the environmental stresses, producing various degrees of impairment depending on resistance, resilience, cushioning, and other factors. The personality may also change the environment in the process of interaction.

The strain or impairment he exhibits at any point in time is a product of the interaction of his endowment, the past and present stresses and supports in the environment, and his personality which interprets the environment and fixes his modes of adaptation. This research, as well as common sense, suggest that low socioeconomic status may be a potential source of environmental stress, particularly in adult life. More important is the possibility that various socioeconomic groups have different modes of reacting to a given stress. SES may therefore turn out to be a major factor in determining how much impairment is associated with other *non*socioeconomic stresses.

## Summary

The *differential prevalence of adaptive devices* helps to account for the socioeconomic differences in impairment. In the hierarchy of devices, the low SES individual is more likely to choose the "acting out" and psychotic devices of the third and fourth levels. The high SES person is more prone to choose mild neurotic first-level devices. He shows more tenseness and nervousness and obsessional symptoms (worrying), yet he worries more about his work, so that the focus of his obsession is different from that of the low SES individual. His adaptive worrying helps him maintain his position in the higher income brackets.

To suggest that members of the low SES group merely tend to have less "ego strength" or a "weaker personality structure" is somewhat over-simplified and perhaps misleading. This was, in fact, a first impression. drawn from the relationship of stress factors to the impairment ratings (Mental Health Ratings). An examination of the type of disturbance (rather than the level of impairment) shows a very different distribution of adaptive devices at different social levels.

There also appear to be specific relationships between certain groups of stress factors and particular adaptive devices. The sheer number of factors is no longer as meaningful as the pattern of factors when examining types of adaptation. This is expectable, for when we ask what types of adaptation are exhibited by various social groups, we must know to what they were adapting, to what they were adjusting. Then the differential life experience of the three SES groups becomes crucial for understanding these different adaptive types.

Further questions are raised by our findings. How do the different SES groups develop different modes of adaptation? Do people with certain adaptive styles or personality types actually move into the low or high SES strata? Does personality structure play a role in maintaining social stratification? These questions are the focus of Chapter 16.

## Notes

1. *Mental Disorders*. Diagnostic and Statistical Manual, American Psychiatric Association Committee of Nomenclature and Statistics, 1960.

2. Since no direct contact existed between psychiatrist and respondent, and because of the absence of much detailed history, the term "diagnosis" is not really applicable.

3. See *A Psychiatrist's World*, The Selected Papers of Karl Menninger, M.D., Bernard H. Hall (ed.), The Viking Press, New York, 1959, pp. 497–515.

4. *Ibid.*, p. 527.

5. Similar trends were observed in the distributions of the Gross Typology according to the fathers' SES. The percentages of low, middle, and high fathers' SES respectively for the various Gross Types are as follows: Organic Type: 2.5, 2.5, 0.0; Psychotic Type: 10.2, 9.2, 5.2; Neurotic Type (including one case, 0.2, of Probable Transient Situational Personality Reaction Type): 29.9, 32.0, 41.8; Psychosomatic Type: 7.7, 6.0, 5.2; Personality Trait Type: 13.9, 9.7, 5.9; Neurotic-Psychosomatic Type: 4.6, 5.7, 6.7; Neurotic-Trait Type: 19.7, 16.1, 12.2; Well: 11.5, 18.6, 23.0; Total Number of Cases: 482, 671, 507.

6. The distributions according to fathers' SES are quite similar. They again indicate that one's status may be an etiological factor as well as a result of mental disturbance. The percentages of low, middle, and high fathers' SES respectively for the various Symptom Groups are as follows: Epileptic: 0.6, 0.6, 0.0; Retarded: 3.7, 3.0, 0.6; Alcoholic: 5.6, 4.0, 4.3; Brain Disease and/or Senility: 1.7, 1.6, 0.2; Sexual Deviant: 1.0, 0.6, 1.4; Dyssocial: 1.9, 2.4, 1.4; Mixed Anxiety: 72.4, 68.6, 72.4; Free-Floating Anxiety: 11.8, 16.4, 16.6; Phobias: 27.2, 26.5, 24.5; Obsessive-Compulsive: 10.2, 8.6, 5.5; Psychosomatic: 55.0, 53.2, 46.5; Hypochondriacal: 28.4, 25.3, 21.7; Neurasthenic: 19.5, 18.5, 17.0; Passive-Dependent: 37.8, 26.5, 18.1; Depressed: 30.5, 25.3, 14.8; Rigid: 48.3, 33.5, 21.5; Schizoid: 20.1, 15.5, 10.3; Aggressive: 4.4, 5.2, 9.9; Suspicious: 34.0, 30.0, 21.1; Schizophrenic: 6.2, 4.5, 4.1; Cycloid-Affective Psychosis: 0.2, 0.3, 0.4; None of Above: 5.0, 6.3, 9.5; Total Number of Cases: 482, 671, 507. Percentages total more than 100 per cent because of multiple classifications.

7. Similar trends are found according to fathers' SES.

8. That the proportion of Personality Trait Types decreases as stress increases seems paradoxical. It may be, however, that suspicious and rigid types tend to become adjudged in the Probable Psychotic group as stress and impairment increase.

9. A. B. Hollingshead and F. C. Redlich, *Social Class and Mental Illness: A Community Study*, Wiley, New York, 1958.

# Social Mobility, Socioeconomic Status, and Types of Mental Disturbance

T H O M A S   S .   L A N G N E R

The adaptive styles of the socioeconomic groups help to explain the discrepancy in impairment between the groups at similar stress levels. Moreover, the specific early stresses seem related to particular adaptive styles (or diagnostic types) among Midtown adults. The importance of the *type* as well as the degree of disorder in understanding the structure of our society becomes increasingly apparent. This final chapter is an attempt to synthesize what is known about the basic personality, adaptive style, and diagnostic types in the socioeconomic strata of Midtown and the social classes of the United States. First, we ask whether certain adaptive types move into the low or high SES. Does selective vertical social mobility help to account for the present diagnostic composition of the various social strata? Who moves up and who moves down in the system? Second, we want to examine the experiences, values, and attitudes of the status groups for clues about the development of different adaptive types. What can account for the Lows' tendency to psychosis and character disorders? To state it more accurately, why do more of the Lows exhibit delusions, withdrawal, dissociation and rigidity, suspiciousness and dependency? Why are the Highs more given to neurosis; that is, anxious, worrisome states, hypochondriasis, self-dissatisfaction, certain signs of tension, and other neurotic symptoms? Aside from any hereditary tendencies which might be involved, how could such behavior be taught or encouraged? What in the low and high status environments abets the development of psychosis and character disorders, as opposed to neurotic behavior?

## Social Mobility and Type of Mental Disturbance

Social mobility is the dynamic aspect of social stratification; through it we can obtain a better understanding of how social classes are formed and how they came to their present diagnostic composition. We can get clues to such problems as "How is mental health related to the development of social classes?" "What is the recruitment pattern of persons in these classes?" "Are people more similar in personality to the class in which they were born or to the class toward which they are moving?"

### A.   THE INDEX OF SOCIAL MOBILITY

Before we consider these problems, our index of social mobility must be specified and its relation to the degree of impairment (Mental Health Rating) examined. Then we can discuss the types of mental disturbance most common to upward and downward mobile persons and to the various SES groups. In this volume social mobility was measured by comparing the socioeconomic status of the respondent with that of his father. The SES of the father (based on the father's highest educational level and his occupation when the respondent was 8) was divided into three groups as close to equal size as possible (482, 671, and 507 cases in the low, middle, and high SES respectively). The SES of employed male respondents was determined by present occupation, education, rent, and family income; for currently married women the SES was based on husband's occupation, rent, family income, and own education; for unmarried women and a small group of students, by father's occupation, rent, income, and respondent education. The respondents' SES was also divided into three approximately equal segments to give groups of 544, 556, and 560 in the low, middle, and high respondents' SES respectively.[1]

The cross-tabulation of fathers' and respondents' SES yielded nine groups (see Table 16-1): those born in the low SES who remained there, or who moved up to the middle or high third; those born in the middle who moved down to the lowest third, rose to the upper third, or stayed in the middle; and those born into the upper stratum who remained there, or went down to the middle or lowest third.

If we combine the cells, we find that, relative to the SES distribution of their own generation, 375 persons moved down, 371 moved up, and 914

## TABLE 16-1

### AVERAGE MENTAL HEALTH (MH I) OF RESPONDENTS ACCORDING TO RESPONDENTS' AND FATHERS' SOCIOECONOMIC STATUS

| Respondents' Socioeconomic Status | Fathers' Socioeconomic Status | | | | | |
|---|---|---|---|---|---|---|
| | LOW | | MIDDLE | | HIGH | |
| | No. of Cases | $\bar{R}$ | No. of Cases | $\bar{R}$ | No. of Cases | $\bar{R}$ |
| Low | 278 | .61 | 225 | .57 | 41 | .57 |
| Middle | 168 | .50 | 279 | .49 | 109 | .51 |
| High | 36 | .41 | 167 | .41 | 357 | .42 |
| Total Number of Cases (N=100 per cent) | 482 | | 671 | | 507 | 1660 |

| | Summary of Social Mobility | | |
|---|---|---|---|
| | DOWNWARD[a] | NONMOBILE[b] | UPWARD[c] |
| | $\bar{R}$ | $\bar{R}$ | $\bar{R}$ |
| Respondents' Adult Mental Health | .55 | .50 | .45 |
| Total Number of Cases (N=100 per cent) | 375 | 914 | 371 |
| | | | 1660 |

[a] Fathers' SES High, Respondents' SES Middle or Low; Fathers' SES Middle, Respondents' SES Low.

[b] Fathers' and Respondents' SES the same.

[c] Fathers' SES Low, Respondents' SES Middle or High; Fathers' SES Middle, Respondents' SES High.

stayed the same as their fathers. It is interesting that equal numbers moved up and down, and that a majority (55 per cent) "stayed the same" (that is, while the country as a whole increased in educational and occupational level from the fathers' level, these persons remained in the same third of the status hierarchy).

First, what is the mental health of the various mobility groups, according to their average Mental Health Rating (I)? As is quickly observable, virtually all the mental health variation is due to the respondent's present status, not that of his father.[2]

What of the relative importance of mobility and present SES? The average risks of the mobility groups range from the extreme upwardly mobile (.41) to extreme downwardly mobile (.57). The range or over-all statistical effect of mobility, then, is .16 ridits. The range of the nonmobile or static cells is from .42 in the high SES to .61 in the low SES, or an effect of .19. If mobility tells us nothing more than nonmobility does about the risk of impairment, we would gain little by including it in a prediction scheme over and above the respondents' SES.

Our primary purpose in including the impairment ridits in relation to mobility is to show again that the global impairment rating serves entirely different functions from the symptom classifications and quasi-diagnostic judgments made by the team psychiatrists. The impairment rating is most useful for answering "Who?" and "How much?" The type of disturbance, its demographic location, and its relation to the average life experience of persons in these demographic strata or groups are more likely to give us further leads to the genesis of these diseases. This further investigation, then, can teach us about the social structure, institutions, and value-attitude systems which promote or inhibit the development of particular disease entities. In this way, we simultaneously learn more about both mental disease and social structure.

Social mobility bears a definite relationship to certain *types* of mental disturbance. There are indications that downward mobility is associated with the character disorders, or personality trait disturbances. Those who were born into a high SES family but are now in the low SES (extreme downward mobility) are somewhat more likely to be classified as Probable Personality Trait Types (19.5 per cent) than persons who were born into the low SES and stayed there (15.8 per cent; see Table 16-2). This can mean that people with character disorders tend to become downwardly mobile as these traits interfere with their occupational functioning, or that downwardly mobile people develop these particular character traits as an adaptive system which fails and only speeds them further along the downward path.

The Symptom Group classifications give us some notion of what types of character disorders are involved in downward mobility. The downwardly mobile, or "Downs," are more prone to be Alcoholic (9.8 per cent) than the static low SES who were born into the low SES and stayed there (6.8 per cent; see Table 16-3). The Downs are also slightly more apt to be Passive-Dependent than the static Lows. They are also more neurasthenic.

**TABLE 16-2**

## PROPORTIONS OF RESPONDENTS ACCORDING TO GROSS TYPOLOGY, RESPONDENTS' AND FATHERS' SOCIOECONOMIC STATUS

*Fathers' Socioeconomic Status*

| Gross Types | LOW | | | MIDDLE | | | HIGH | | |
|---|---|---|---|---|---|---|---|---|---|
| | Respondents' Socioeconomic Status | | | | | | | | |
| | *Per Cent* LOW | MIDDLE | HIGH | *Per Cent* LOW | MIDDLE | HIGH | *Per Cent* LOW | MIDDLE | HIGH |
| Probable Organic | 3.2 | 1.8 | 0.0 | 6.7 | .7 | 0.0 | 0.0 | 0.0 | 0.0 |
| Probable Psychotic | 12.2 | 7.7 | 5.6 | 14.7 | 7.9 | 4.2 | 9.8 | 10.1 | 3.1 |
| Probable Neurotic[a] | 27.2 | 35.6 | 24.9 | 20.8 | 35.4 | 41.2 | 29.2 | 35.7 | 45.1 |
| Probable Psychosomatic | 8.6 | 5.4 | 11.1 | 8.0 | 5.7 | 3.6 | 4.9 | 3.7 | 5.6 |
| Probable Personality Trait | 15.8 | 10.7 | 13.9 | 12.9 | 9.7 | 5.4 | 19.5 | 10.1 | 3.1 |
| Probable Neurotic-Psychosomatic | 4.3 | 4.8 | 5.6 | 7.1 | 3.6 | 7.2 | 4.9 | 7.3 | 6.7 |
| Probable Neurotic-Trait | 21.2 | 17.3 | 19.4 | 17.8 | 17.9 | 10.8 | 19.5 | 14.7 | 10.6 |
| Well | 7.5 | 16.7 | 19.5 | 12.0 | 18.7 | 27.6 | 12.2 | 18.4 | 25.8 |
| Total Number of Cases (N=100 per cent) | 278 | 168 | 36 | 225 | 279 | 167 | 41 | 109 | 357 |
| | | | | | | | | | 1660 |

[a] Including one case, .1 per cent, classified as Probable Transient Situational Personality Reaction Type.

## TABLE 16-3
## PROPORTIONS OF RESPONDENTS ACCORDING TO PSYCHIATRIC SYMPTOM GROUPS, RESPONDENTS' AND FATHERS' SOCIOECONOMIC STATUS

Fathers' Socioeconomic Status

| Psychiatric Symptom Groups | LOW | | | MIDDLE | | | HIGH | | |
|---|---|---|---|---|---|---|---|---|---|
| | Respondents' Socioeconomic Status | | | | | | | | |
| | LOW | MIDDLE | HIGH | LOW | MIDDLE | HIGH | LOW | MIDDLE | HIGH |
| | Per Cent | | | Per Cent | | | Per Cent | | |
| Epileptic | 0.7 | 0.6 | 0.0 | 0.9 | 0.7 | 0.0 | 0.0 | 0.0 | 0.0 |
| Retarded | 6.5 | 0.0 | 0.0 | 6.7 | 1.8 | 0.0 | 4.9 | 0.9 | 0.0 |
| Alcoholic | 6.8 | 0.0 | 0.0 | 5.8 | 3.6 | 2.4 | 9.8 | 6.4 | 3.1 |
| Brain Disease and/or Senility | 2.2 | 0.6 | 2.8 | 4.0 | 0.7 | 0.0 | 0.0 | 0.0 | 0.3 |
| Sexual Deviant | 0.4 | 2.4 | 0.0 | 0.0 | 0.4 | 1.8 | 2.4 | 0.0 | 1.4 |
| Dyssocial | 2.5 | 1.2 | 0.0 | 4.0 | 2.2 | 0.6 | 2.4 | 5.5 | 0.0 |
| Mixed Anxiety | 73.7 | 70.8 | 69.4 | 70.2 | 69.2 | 65.3 | 82.9 | 70.6 | 71.7 |
| Free-Floating Anxiety | 12.2 | 12.5 | 5.6 | 13.7 | 15.8 | 21.0 | 14.6 | 7.3 | 19.6 |
| Phobias | 25.9 | 29.2 | 27.8 | 27.1 | 27.2 | 24.6 | 26.8 | 29.4 | 22.7 |
| Obsessive-Compulsive | 9.0 | 11.3 | 13.9 | 8.4 | 9.3 | 7.8 | 7.3 | 5.5 | 5.3 |
| Psychosomatic | 59.0 | 51.2 | 41.7 | 62.2 | 47.0 | 51.5 | 58.3 | 51.4 | 43.7 |
| Hypochondriacal | 31.7 | 25.0 | 19.4 | 30.2 | 23.3 | 22.2 | 34.2 | 23.9 | 19.6 |
| Neurasthenic | 19.8 | 17.9 | 25.0 | 18.7 | 21.9 | 12.6 | 34.2 | 15.6 | 15.4 |
| Passive-Dependent | 40.3 | 31.6 | 47.0 | 29.3 | 29.4 | 18.0 | 43.9 | 22.9 | 13.7 |
| Depressed | 38.1 | 22.0 | 11.1 | 36.4 | 24.0 | 12.6 | 22.0 | 26.6 | 10.4 |
| Rigid | 56.8 | 39.3 | 25.0 | 48.0 | 31.2 | 18.0 | 41.5 | 35.8 | 14.9 |
| Schizoid | 19.1 | 20.8 | 25.0 | 20.0 | 16.5 | 7.8 | 19.5 | 20.2 | 6.2 |
| Aggressive | 2.9 | 6.0 | 8.3 | 0.9 | 6.1 | 9.6 | 4.9 | 4.6 | 12.1 |
| Suspicious | 39.2 | 29.8 | 13.9 | 42.7 | 26.9 | 18.0 | 34.2 | 33.0 | 16.0 |
| Schizophrenic | 6.8 | 6.5 | 0.0 | 8.4 | 3.6 | 0.6 | 2.4 | 10.1 | 2.5 |
| Cycloid-Affective Psychosis | 0.4 | 0.0 | 0.0 | 0.4 | 0.0 | 0.6 | 0.0 | 0.0 | 0.6 |
| None of Above | 2.9 | 7.7 | 8.3 | 4.4 | 4.7 | 11.4 | 0.0 | 7.3 | 11.2 |
| Total Number of Cases (N = 100 per cent)[a] | 278 | 168 | 36 | 225 | 279 | 167 | 41 | 109 | 357 |

[a]Percentages total more than 100 per cent because of multiple classifications.

The upwardly mobile, on the other hand, are more likely to be Obsessive-Compulsive than the static Highs (13.9 per cent versus 5.3 per cent, see Table 16-3). They are more apt to be Schizoid (25.0 per cent) than persons whose past and present status is high (6.2 per cent). They are less Suspicious, Rigid, or Depressive than the stratum into which they were born, but they are even more Passive-Dependent. Since both downward (43.9 per cent) and upward mobility (47.0 per cent) show an increase in the proportion of Passive-Dependents, some sort of contradiction is involved. Perhaps upwardly mobile Passive-Dependents tend to comply with and be submissive to their parents' wishes for their success, while they may be more aggressive with an interviewer or appear aggressive in their pusuit of a career. Downwardly mobile passive persons seem to fall into a more logical category, because we expect them to be less aggressive and perhaps to have developed dependency through the overprotection of their high SES parents.

A less critical test of the relationship of mobility and type of disturbance is afforded by performing a test of significance of the difference between the proportions (or averages, in the case of scores) of the upwardly and downwardly mobile groups showing any particular type of disturbance. An examination of the data (Tables 16-4, 16-5, and 16-6) shows that the downwardly mobile were significantly (at the 5 per cent level) more prone than the upwardly mobile to be Probable Organics, Probable Psychotics, Intellectually Retarded, Alcoholics, Senile or showing Structural Brain Disease, Dyssocial, Depressed, Rigid, Suspicious, Schizophrenic, and to have higher Immaturity, Rigidity, Suspiciousness, and Frustration-Depression Scores.

The upwardly mobile were significantly more prone than the downwardly mobile to be classified Probable Neurotic Types, Wells, and Aggressive. There are slight, but not significantly, higher proportions of the upwardly mobile who have Free-Floating Anxiety, or are classified as Obsessive-Compulsive or Sex Deviants. These findings, however, illustrate the importance of the respondents' present socioeconomic status, rather than the importance of social mobility in relation to type of mental disturbance. It is only by specifying the class into which the individual is born and the class in which he now finds himself that we can really convey the degree as well as the direction of mobility. This detailed type of analysis, discussed previously, suggests only two findings; namely, that Downs are prone to Character Disorders and Alcoholism while Ups are likely to be Obsessive-Compulsive.

## TABLE 16-4
## PROPORTIONS OF RESPONDENTS ACCORDING TO GROSS TYPOLOGY AND SOCIAL MOBILITY

| Gross Types | | Social Mobility | | |
|---|---|---|---|---|
| | | DOWNWARD[a] | NONMOBILE[b] | UPWARD[c] |
| | | Per Cent | Per Cent | Per Cent |
| Probable Organic | D | 4.0 | 1.2 | .8 |
| Probable Psychotic | D | 12.8 | 7.3 | 5.9 |
| Probable Neurotic | U | 26.1 | 36.6 | 37.3 |
| Probable Psychosomatic | NS | 6.4 | 6.6 | 5.1 |
| Probable Personality Trait | NS | 12.8 | 9.0 | 8.6 |
| Probable Neurotic-Psychosomatic | NS | 6.9 | 5.0 | 5.9 |
| Probable Neurotic-Trait | NS | 17.1 | 16.1 | 14.6 |
| Well | U | 13.9 | 18.1 | 21.8 |
| Total Number of Cases (N = 100 per cent) | | 375 | 914[d] | 371 |
| | | | | 1660 |

[a]Fathers' SES High, Respondents' SES Middle or Low; Fathers' SES Middle, Respondents' SES Low.

[b]Fathers' and Respondents' SES the same.

[c]Fathers' SES Low, Respondents' SES Middle or High; Fathers' SES Middle, Respondents' SES High.

[d]Including one case, .1 per cent, classified as Transient Situational Personality Reaction Type.

D – indicates proportions of Downwardly Mobile significantly larger than proportions of Upwardly Mobile at the 5 per cent level of confidence.

U – indicates proportion of Upwardly Mobile significantly larger than proportions of Downwardly Mobile at the 5 per cent level of confidence.

NS – indicates no significant difference at the 5 per cent level of confidence in the proportions of Upwardly and Downwardly Mobile.

*B.*   THE LITERATURE ON SOCIAL MOBILITY
AND TYPE OF MENTAL DISTURBANCE

These data seem to corroborate some of the hypotheses put forth in the literature concerning mental disturbance and social mobility. While most of the hypotheses are based upon pure conjecture, some—such as those of Ruesch or Hollingshead and Redlich—are based upon observation of patients in the clinic and examination of patient records. There are con-

## TABLE 16-5

### PROPORTIONS OF RESPONDENTS ACCORDING TO SYMPTOM GROUPS AND SOCIAL MOBILITY

| Symptom Groups | | Social Mobility | | |
| | | DOWNWARD[a] | NONMOBILE[b] | UPWARD[c] |
| --- | --- | --- | --- | --- |
| | | Per Cent | Per Cent | Per Cent |
| Epileptic | NS | 0.5 | 0.4 | 0.3 |
| Retarded | D | 4.8 | 2.5 | 0.0 |
| Alcoholic | D | 6.4 | 4.4 | 3.2 |
| Brain Disease and/or Senility | D | 2.4 | 1.0 | 0.5 |
| Sex Deviant | NS | 0.5 | 0.8 | 1.9 |
| Dyssocial | D | 4.3 | 1.4 | 0.8 |
| Mixed Anxiety | NS | 71.7 | 71.6 | 68.2 |
| Free-Floating Anxiety | NS | 12.0 | 16.2 | 15.6 |
| Phobias | NS | 27.7 | 25.1 | 27.0 |
| Obsessive-Compulsive | NS | 7.5 | 7.7 | 10.0 |
| Psychosomatic | NS | 58.7 | 49.3 | 50.4 |
| Hypochondriacal | NS | 28.8 | 24.4 | 23.2 |
| Neurasthenic | NS | 19.5 | 18.7 | 16.2 |
| Passive-Dependent | NS | 29.1 | 26.6 | 27.0 |
| Depressed | D | 32.0 | 23.0 | 16.7 |
| Rigid | D | 43.7 | 32.6 | 28.3 |
| Schizoid | NS | 20.0 | 13.2 | 15.4 |
| Aggressive | U | 2.4 | 7.4 | 7.8 |
| Suspicious | D | 38.9 | 26.4 | 22.9 |
| Schizophrenic | D | 8.3 | 4.2 | 3.2 |
| Cycloid-Affective Psychosis | NS | 0.3 | 0.3 | 0.3 |
| None of Above | U | 4.8 | 6.7 | 9.4 |
| Total Number of Cases (N = 100 per cent) | | 375 | 914 | 371 / 1660 |

D — indicates proportion of Downwardly Mobile significantly larger than proportion of Upwardly Mobile at the 5 per cent level of confidence.

U — indicates proportion of Upwardly Mobile significantly larger than proportion of Downwardly Mobile at the 5 per cent level of confidence.

NS — indicates no significant difference at the 5 per cent level of confidence in the proportions of Upwardly and Downwardly Mobile.

[a] Fathers' SES High, Respondents' SES Middle or Low; Fathers' SES Middle, Respondents' SES Low.

[b] Fathers' and Respondents' SES the same.

[c] Fathers' SES Low, Respondents' SES Middle or High; Fathers' SES Middle, Respondents' SES High.

## TABLE 16-6

### AVERAGE SYMPTOM SCORES OF RESPONDENTS ACCORDING TO SYMPTOMS AND SOCIAL MOBILITY

| | *Social Mobility* | | |
| | DOWNWARD[a] | NONMOBILE[b] | UPWARD[c] |
| Symptom Scores | Mean | Mean | Mean |
|---|---|---|---|
| Immaturity | 2.3 | 1.8 | 1.5 |
| Rigidity | 2.4 | 1.7 | 1.3 |
| Suspiciousness | 1.3 | 0.9 | 0.8 |
| Withdrawal | 1.3 | 1.1 | 1.0 |
| Frustration-Depression | 1.0 | 0.7 | 0.5 |
| Neurasthenia | 0.5 | 0.5 | 0.4 |
| Gastrointestinal Symptoms | 0.2 | 0.2 | 0.2 |
| Total Number of Cases (N = 100 per cent) | 375 | 914 | 371 1660 |

[a]Fathers' SES High, Respondents' SES Middle or Low; Fathers' SES Middle, Respondents' SES Low.

[b]Fathers' and Respondents' SES the same.

[c]Fathers' SES Low, Respondents' SES Middle or High; Fathers' SES Middle, Respondents' SES High.

gruences and disagreements between these observations and our findings.

Hollingshead and Redlich describe the downward mobile patient in terms that we find equally applicable to downward mobile nonpatients in the community.

These patients (downward mobile) present the psychiatrist with severe problems, such as *alcohol* or drug addiction, crime and, most of all, with serious *character disorders*. They are labeled clinically as *sado-masochistic* characters or as destructive and self-destructive personalities. Some of their disorders present the syndrome of a "fate" neurosis. The spell of gloom, failure, and disaster which these patients exude, even when they are not depressed, makes them rather unapproachable and dreaded by therapists. (Italics ours.)[3]

The Midtown downward mobile are similarly more Alcoholic and have more of the character traits of Depression, Rigidity, and Suspiciousness.

These same authors point out that mobility is a good predictor of the outcome of therapy.

Lower class patients in this study who had a good relationship in dynamic psychotherapy with their psychiatrists were invariably upward mobile. The downward mobile patient, in whom the lack of a capacity to sublimate, unwillingness to achieve, often an extraordinary dependency, a tendency to regress and to destroy himself and others, makes insight therapy particularly difficult.[4]

The "lack of a capacity to sublimate" in the downward mobile is suggested by the nonpatient data of Midtown. The high average Immaturity Score of the downward mobile (see Table 16-6) indicates a lack of impulse control, which may indicate poor ability to "sublimate." This is suggested by some of the Immaturity Score items, such as "When I want something I want it right away," or "I'm a gambler at heart." The dependency observed in downward mobile New Haven patients is paralleled by the Midtown nonpatients. However both upward and downward mobile in Midtown were somewhat more Passive-Dependent than the nonmobile (see Table 16-3).

Ruesch[5] found that social decliners frequently did not have psychosomatic conditions but were prone to alcoholism. He felt that this decline brings about isolation and a change of social techniques. Even though we found more alcoholics among the downward mobile Midtown nonpatients, the proportion of psychosomatic types and those with psychosomatic symptoms was as large (or larger) in the downward mobile groups as in the static and upward mobile groups. There is no evidence in our data that the psychosomatic types are predominantly upward mobile, as Ruesch has found, ". . . among the bearers of psychosomatic conditions there is an unusually large number of people with strivings to increase their status."[6]

If we eliminate the word "unusually," the Midtown nonpatient data would agree with Ruesch's impressions of patients in the Langley Porter Clinic of the University of California Medical School; for just about half the Midtown population reported one or more presumably psychosomatic conditions, *regardless* of their social mobility.

The New Haven Research on patients indicated that the upward mobile have

a certain proneness for neurotic disorder and are apt to cause social troubles. They need not be highly unconventional or flout accepted values—actually, many highly mobile persons are quite conventional—but they are uncertain about their values and some of them can be, at times, obnoxious and hard on others as well as themselves in their attempt to reach their goals. Psychiatrists encounter many mobile persons with such unpleasant character traits that, behind external conformity, they cannot get along with anybody and do not care for anyone but themselves and their goals.[7]

These clinical impressions of the upward mobile jibe more with our data than does Ruesch's impression of high rates of psychosomatic disturbances. Midtown social climbers are more likely to be compulsive, which indicates an overdetermined and superficial conformity to social norms. The fact that they are as aggressive as people who have already "made the grade" may be disturbing to middle- and upper-class clinicians.

No doubt the tremendous drive for achievement, while socially approved, does not appeal to the middle- or upper-class person if it is not accompanied by a deeply internalized set of "rules of the game" about how to achieve these goals. Thus, Merton suggests that "innovation" as a mode of adaptation is most prevalent in the lowest social stratum.

This response (innovation) occurs when the individual has assimilated the cultural emphasis upon the goal without equally internalizing the institutional norms governing ways and means for its attainment.[8]

Goals are held to transcend class lines, not to be bounded by them, yet the actual social organization is such that there exist class differentials in accessibility of the goals. In this setting, a cardinal American virtue, "ambition," promotes a cardinal American vice, "deviant behavior."[9]

The clinician, of course, sees the "strainer" as only externally conformist, for the strainer internalizes only the goal, not the means to that goal. It is possible, however, that his type of mental disturbance, his compulsivity, indeed, the success striving itself, is a form of ego-defense which utilizes a socially approved expression of hostility he would actually like to direct toward: his demanding parents whose own ambitions are so much higher for their children than their own achievements, who "live through" their children; the society which makes it so difficult for him to rise; the hostility engendered by his having to give up some of the precocious sexual activity of the nonmobile low SES,[10] and some of their direct physical expression of aggression.

We have made some suggestions about the types of disturbances associated with upward and downward mobility. Mobility may be one of the causes of some types of mental disturbance, while mental disturbance and certain personality characteristics may, in turn, cause a person to rise or fall in status. Much research into the connections between mobility and mental disorder is needed, and our findings should provide some rough indication of the most fruitful areas for investigation.

## Socioeconomic Status and Type of Mental Disturbance

### A.   A PICTURE OF CLASS AND PERSONALITY

Our methods cannot yield conclusive data, but we can sketch the outlines of the social character of the various social classes. Most important, we can develop hypotheses about the class differences in experience which may possibly be sources of particular types of mental disorder. But first a review of our findings and mention of some other studies which have been able to say something about class differences in type of mental disturbance, personality structure, social character, and the like.

Much of the literature utilizes the term "social class" and divides it into upper, middle, and lower. Therefore, we must relate the Midtown SES categories to the class terminology. This will enable us to compare our data with such findings as those of Ruesch ". . . the lower class culture . . ." (see page 437) and Hollingshead and Redlich ". . . dominance . . . in middle class families . . ." (see page 446).

The Midtown low SES is roughly equivalent to the "lower class" in most references and to classes IV and V in the Hollingshead and Redlich studies. The Midtown middle and most of the high SES are equivalent to the "middle class" in much of the literature on stratification and to Hollingshead and Redlich's classes II and III. There are very few people in Midtown who could be considered strictly "upper class" in its original sense of landed gentry or nobility. However, according to the current American sociological usage of this term, "old families" and those of extremely high SES should be included.

According to our data, persons of low SES are more prone to have organic brain damage, psychoses and character disorders, and are less likely to have neuroses. In particular, they are more rigid, suspicious, and have a fatalistic outlook on life. They do not plan ahead, a characteristic associated with their fatalism. They are prone to depression, have feelings of futility, lack of belongingness, friendlessness, and lack of trust in others. They are more authoritarian in their attitudes, stressing obedience, power, and hierarchical relations.

The tendency to "act out" problems in the lower class has been often noted, as well as the preponderance of lower-class psychotics and upper-class neurotics. Although he disagrees with our findings about psychosomatic reactions and omits the preponderance of lower-class schizophrenia, Ruesch is in essential agreement with our data.

the lower class culture favors conduct disorders and rebellion, the middle class culture physical symptom formations and psychosomatic reactions, and the upper class culture psychoneurosis and psychosis of the manic depressive type.[11]

Although the psychiatrist (who bases his observations chiefly upon the preselected types of patients he sees in his clinic) is at the mercy of the biases of self-selection in the upper class and police selection in the lower class, his views are nevertheless corroborative of and tend to illuminate our nonpatient findings.

We may indulge in the following generalizations as viewed by the psychiatrist: the class V neurotic behaves badly, the class IV neurotic aches physically, the class III patient defends fearfully and the class I-II patient is dissatisfied with himself.[12]

Of course, it is possible that lower-class patients who do not act out their problems and are merely dissatisfied with themselves neither seek treatment nor are referred by the police, since they are not in "trouble." This criticism does not seem to hold, for our nonpatient study shows a much greater proportion of the acting out Personality Trait Type in the low SES. In this respect at least, the tiny patient population resembles the "parent" nonpatient population.

Only a few observational studies have compared the personality structure of the different social classes. This is quite unbelievable, particularly in view of the hundreds of detailed clinically oriented anthropological studies of cultures other than ours. One study which, although small in scale, actually tries to pin down personality dynamics of lower and upper class was conducted in England by B. M. Spinley, a clinical psychologist. Participant observation, structured interviews with selected informants, life histories, and Rorschach Tests were used to compare slum dwellers with public or boarding school level (high SES) individuals. The findings are so crucial to further work in the field of social psychiatry that it would seem best to quote them at length.

The (slum) individual shows a marked absence of a strict and efficient conscience, an unwillingness and inability to deal with disturbing or unpleasant situations, and a flight from these. He is unable to postpone satisfactions. He is seriously disturbed in the sexual areas of his development with predominantly feminine identifications which interfere with his adoption of the masculine sexual role. He has narcissistic trends. (The girl is also disturbed in spite of her feminine identifications, since she feels uneasiness in, or fear of, her feminine sexual role.) Relations with other people are coloured by negativism, distrust, suspicion and excessive fear of ridicule, this last so strong that feelings of inferiority are indicated. He has marked aggressiveness, which is permitted violent expression, and his attitude towards authority is one of hostility and rebellion. Emotional response and fantasy production are constricted and intellectual discrimination poor. His response to failure, frustration, or mishap of any kind is extrapunitive.

The (public school) individual has a strict, effective conscience; he faces disturbing situations and attempts to deal adequately with them. Present satisfactions are postponed for the sake of greater ones in the future. He does not show any serious sexual disturbance. . . . Insecurity is present but few or no indications of inferiority feelings. Aggression is inhibited or even at a deeper level, repressed, and his response to frustration tends to be intropunitive. He is characterized by an internalization of the standards of his own group. . . . In most situations he accepts authority, but may discard rules and commands if they conflict with the standards of his own social group (his own conscience). . . . He has a spontaneous, rich and creative fantasy and good powers of intellectual discrimination. He is more mature than a number of the slum group of corresponding age.[13]

The major points of congruence between these findings and those of other authors are that the low SES has (1) a weak super-ego, (2) a weak ego, with lack of control or frustration tolerance, (3) a negative, distrustful, suspicious character with poor interpersonal relations, (4) strong feelings of inferiority, low self-esteem, fear of ridicule, and (5) a tendency to act out problems, with violent expression of hostility and extrapunitive tendencies.

With some important omissions, such as the predominance of depressive and passive-dependent tendencies in the lower class, these findings agree with the Midtown data. They leave no doubt that social class levels have specific psychological characteristics or basic personality types of their own, even though there is a good deal of overlapping between classes. This character structure is closely related to the types of mental disturbance that we find most prevalent at each level.

### B. LIFE EXPERIENCES OF THE CLASSES

Now that we have reviewed the social character of the lower and upper classes, we can look at what we and others have learned about the difference in the life experiences of the classes. We know that mental disturbance varies in degree of impairment and type with social class and social mobility. It is only reasonable to assume that, over and above hereditary influences, there may be some sources of particular types of illness in the differential class environment. The detailed specification of the class environments and their relation to mental disorder is a task we must initiate at this time, if only in scant detail, and with little actual research data to test our hypotheses. Our goal is to find out how social class might be conducive to differential rates of impairment and different types of disturbances. What aspects of the classes can we consider as potential sources of class differences in personality and mental disorder?

## C.   CHILD-REARING

*Permissiveness; the Channeling of Drives and Needs.*    One very likely source is the class differences in child-rearing practices and child-rearing atmosphere. For instance, Hollingshead and Redlich feel that the lower-class infant is less apt to receive affection.[14]

There are experts who feel that the middle-class child is more apt to be rejected, and they point to the lax toilet training and lengthier breast feeding which has been reported in the lower class. In England Spinley found the lower-class first year one of indulgence, ending abruptly with the birth of the next child, particularly with working mothers who probably could afford only brief breast feeding.[15] Bronfenbrenner,[16] however, has shown rather conclusively that while the middle class in the United States was more severe in its socialization and infant care from 1930 to just after World War II, it has become progressively milder in its practices, so that it is now more "permissive" than the lower class. During the last quarter century the middle and lower classes have traded places, so to speak. Middle-class mothers are more apt to feed their children on demand and to wean late, even though they still are less likely to breast feed. They are also more permissive in other areas of oral behavior, toilet accidents, dependency, some types of sexual expression, aggressiveness (in young but not preadolescent children), and freedom of movement outside the home. The middle-class child, however, is given responsibility (even for household chores) earlier, and more demands are made on him, particularly in relation to success in school.

These rather sweeping generalizations tend to conceal a multitude of apparently major disagreements in data and their interpretation by various investigators. To label one social stratum as more permissive than another does a great injustice to the actual findings, for permissiveness is a sponge term. One author may use it to describe late, as opposed to early, toilet training or weaning. The age at which potentially frustrating training practices are initiated or completed is assumed to indicate mildness or permissiveness. The term is also used to describe the degree of freedom allowed by the parents. The direction the behavior takes, the type of behavior, its intensity, and the objects of that behavior may be so important that they should be specified in each study. This is a necessary step before over-all estimates of differential permissiveness according to social class are possible.

An interesting example is that of aggression. Maccoby and Gibbs,[17] after interviewing 198 white upper-middle and 178 upper-lower-class mothers of kindergarten children, concluded that the higher SES parents allowed more expression of aggression toward other children and toward themselves. Davis[18] found that middle-class parents were *less* tolerant of aggression. Even though Davis studied older preadolescent children rather than those in kindergarten, the disagreement can be explained in terms of the *target* of the aggression. Midtown data show that few low SES children disagreed or argued with their parents, compared to the Middles and Highs. If we say that aggression against parents is more often permitted at higher social levels, and aggression against nonfamily members is condoned or even encouraged at lower levels, the contradiction is partially solved. In fact, the stern *paterfamilias* of the immigrant low status household, by discouraging any verbal or physical expression against himself, is all the more likely to create a need for substitute targets for hostility outside the home. The apparent permissiveness of the higher strata with regard to aggression does not extend to groups outside the family. The Highs probably encourage verbal rather than physical expression, and probably dampen physical expression in both sexes against the parents and siblings at an earlier age, though they are more permissive with the preschool and kindergarten child.

Indeed, which is more permissive: demand bottle feeding with late weaning among the upper strata, or the recently shorter breast feeding of the lower stratum? Some authors are impressed by the harsh physical punishment of the lower class; others bemoan the quashing of instinctual drives and the strict and early demands made on the middle- and upper-class child. Which is more harsh, which more permissive? If our concern is, instead, with the psychodynamic consequences of physical punishment, on one hand, and control through the threat of withdrawal of love on the other, no such problem of defining harshness or permissiveness need arise. Ideally we might measure the consequences of such methods with detailed scales of social and psychological impairment, but little research has been done along such lines. While we cannot cite research on the results of these methods of control in terms of impairment or type of disorder, we can make careful guesses based on the child development literature and our knowledge of Midtown's SES distribution of diagnostic entities.

Despite the problems of definition, let us assume that Bronfenbrenner is justified in using the blanket term "permissiveness," especially since he goes into great detail about the individual items or indices of permissiveness. Since the Midtown respondents were at least twenty years old in 1953, they were all children well before the end of World War II; in other words, they were children when the lower-class child-training practices were more permissive than those of the middle class. One-third of the sample, the immigrants, were European-born, and these class characterizations of child-training practices may not apply equally well to them. By and large, however, the middle-class respondents (who are now adults) should have been raised somewhat more "strictly" than the lower-class respondents. Although we tend to think of strict rather than permissive upbringing as damaging to mental health, it is probably more accurate to say that both extremes are damaging and produce different types of disorder.

*Inconsistency.* Furthermore, it was pointed out some years ago that demands on the adult which are inconsistent with childhood training may be quite damaging to the adult personality.[19] Another aspect of inconsistency is the conflicting methods of child-rearing to which the lower-class child is exposed, since the values and methods of his middle-class schoolteachers are bound to differ from those of his parents. Inconsistency is found not only in the demands made by one parent, or the differing values of the father and mother, but also in the parents' or peer-group values as against those of the schoolteacher, clergyman, judge, social worker, and court psychiatrist. There is much less of this latter type of value conflict in the life of the middle-class individual, for parental and larger societal values are more likely to be in accord.

The middle-class respondents, who are roughly equivalent to the middle and high SES groups, show considerably better mental health than the lower-class respondents, despite their (presumed) stricter upbringing in the 1930s. However, it is doubtful that child-training practices *alone* could produce impairment in adult functioning, and evidence in this volume points to the importance of many factors outside of childhood entirely.

*Civilizing, Taming, and Redirection Related to Type of Disorder.* A more profitable question is, "What types of mental disturbances are engendered by class differences in child-training?" Having no observational data on the child-training to which our respondents were exposed, we can only make guesses about the association of training and disturbance. We also cannot assume that a particular type of child-training causes the development of a particular type of mental disturbance.

Our data show that the middle and upper SES groups are more prone to neurosis (that is, symptoms of anxiety without concomitant psychosomatic manifestations), while the low SES (or lower class, roughly speaking) is more likely to exhibit psychosis or character disorders (suspiciousness, rigidity, dependency). Our tentative hypothesis is that the anxiety found in the middle and upper levels may be due to the relatively severe suppression and accompanying repression and redirection of sexual and aggressive instincts; a sort of "oversocialization." On the other hand, the lower class may be "undersocialized" in certain areas, resulting in an acting-out of problems which we label "character disorders." Hollingshead and Redlich suggest:

Most young people in classes IV and V pass directly from childhood to the occupational, social and marital responsibilities of adulthood. In doing so, they miss, in varying degrees, what we have come to refer to as sublimation. Their sexual, aggressive, and dependent impulses remain much more pronounced and more primitive than those of classes I and II.[20]

It doesn't really matter whether we use the term sublimation, socialization, or repression as long as we recognize that this is one element which is sometimes missing, in less abundance, or somehow different in the lower class. It is not the age at which the child of each social class identifies with and enters into the adult role, nor is it the lack of an interim period such as our "adolescence" which is crucial for the development of adult personality. It is, rather, the type of adult role he has internalized and the degree (and areas) of repression it involves which determine the kind of adaptation or disturbance he will manifest. That the age of socialization is not crucial to personality development was neatly pointed out by Baldwin.

you find so many so-called primitive societies in which presumably you have so many different cultural patterns and different personalities, but all of the children in all of these societies are identified with adult roles very early.[21]

The adult role at which the middle-class child-training has been aimed can be summed up by the phrase "The Protestant Work Ethic." This ethic with its emphasis on tangible success and initiative is being slowly eroded by a new emphasis on "inner success," on "psychological income," and social rather than occupational skills, which the author hopes to analyze in a future volume. For the present, a description of middle-class norms given by Cohen[22] is adequate for our purposes, even though strong counternorms have been growing in both the middle and lower class independently. Cohen's list has been summarized by Simpson[23] and shortened by us, as follows: (1) Ambition, (2) Individual responsibility, (3) Skills and achievements, (4) Worldly asceticism (postponing immediate satisfaction for long-term goals), (5) Rationality, (6) Getting along with people (manners, courtesy, personability), (7) Control of physical aggression, (8) Constructive leisure, (9) Respect for property; one "is" what one has; don't take other's property. This list of norms, values, and goals of the middle class is not merely an impression; it has been documented by previous studies. Davis and Havighurst, for example, on the basis of interviews with 200 white and Negro lower-class and middle-class mothers, stated that "middle class children are subjected earlier and more consistently to the influences which make a child an orderly, conscientious, responsible, and tame person."[24]

The "taming" of the socioeconomic strata may be different in degree, the middle stratum possibly being more tamed. However, the taming is different *in kind* as well as in degree. We have talked about training for aggression within the family and to outsiders. While the middle- and upper-class child is surely weaned away from physical expression of aggression, he is encouraged to develop his capacity for oral combat. Verbal skills may win many more battles in our legalistic society and are rewarded more on the job and at the conference table than a ready fist. People can be destroyed by a quick tongue, a slander campaign, and by legal maneuvers. Thus the child of the higher strata learns other techniques for gaining power, legitimate types of violence, and one could hardly call him completely tamed. As we shall note, pre-marital sexuality is not exactly "tamed" in the middle class, but is redirected more into masturbation and petting rather than coitus. When we talk of under- or oversocialization, then, we are taking as our standard of socialization the middle-class norms, which is a convenient but hardly objective or scientific basis for our terminology. These prefixes tend to ignore the specific content of socialization at different status levels, which we shall emphasize.

What clues do we have so far about child-training practices conducive to the development of class differences in psychosis and character disorders as opposed to neurosis? Widespread training for orderliness suggests obsessional behavior and repetition compulsion amounting to a socially patterned defect in the middle class. Here, perhaps, is a potential pool of middle-class neurotics, which may help to account for our increasing rates in the higher SES groups. Moreover, taming, even when it involves not total blocking but merely rechanneling of sexual or aggressive behavior, is likely to result in anxiety and guilt. This is typical of neurosis, and the mechanisms are discussed below in terms of the rechanneling of middle-class premarital sexual expression into noncoital forms in favor of prolonged education.

The equating of psychoses and character disorders with the "untamed" nature of the lower class is an attractive but highly oversimplified explanation of the greater rates of such disturbances at lower status levels. Aside from hereditary tendencies to schizophrenia, which may play some part in this phenomenon, there are numerous aspects of family structure and interaction which might promote the development of the psychoses and character disorders. Some of these are the differential development of the superego and ego, middle-class training for a sense of identity and individuality, middle-class emphasis on expression and communication within the family, and the often severe adult life conditions of the lower class.

*Training for a Sense of Identity.*   While it represses and redirects the sexual and aggressive behavior of its children, the middle class also attempts to inculcate a sense of individuality and identity which often seems lacking at lower social levels. This sense of identity we choose to treat separately from the problem of the negative self-image in the lower class. The identity of the middle-class child is enhanced and established in many ways. Not the least of these may be the lower birth rate of the middle class. The only child, or the child with few siblings, may well tend to feel more of an individual. He does not need to share his toys or wear hand-me-down clothing. His parents are less apt to relate to "the children" as a group. The expression "two's company, three's a crowd" might apply to children as well. A certain impersonality almost inevitably develops when there is a large group involved, be it guests or family members. The equanimity of the group, and not its individual members, becomes paramount. The lower the status, the greater the family size in Midtown, as might be expected. Individual identity, therefore, may be enhanced by smaller families typical of the higher strata.

A study of underprivileged children in New York City[25] uncovered an illuminating fact: some of these third to sixth grade children had never been to a birthday party, and very few of them knew their own birth dates. Perhaps no single act of the parents symbolizes the identity of the child more clearly than the celebration of his birthday. This is a formal recognition of his growth and development, and a reaffirmation of his membership and acceptance in the family as an individual.

Other middle-class practices seem to have a latent function of feeding the child back his own image and developing in him a sense of growth and accomplishment. The individual scrapbook, the baby book, and the family photo album all help develop the child's sense of identity. Again, individual clothing is emphasized in the upper strata. A girl must not be "caught dead" in the same party dress as her sister or friend. The idea of a uniform style of dress, or working uniform, so common among poorer and especially peasant peoples of the world is repugnant, excepting the higher-status "gray flannel suit." The strength of the repugnance, it is suggested, may stem from its discouragement of individuality. The romantic-love complex, limited mostly to the upper classes of the middle ages, and later to the middle and upper classes stemming from Western Europe, stresses the "one and only love of a lifetime." Among other things, this represents a highly individual approach to marriage, with the choice of partner taken away from the family group. The idea of indispensability is fostered in many ways for the high status person, and the low status person is constantly reminded of his replaceability, whether in the family or the factory. In the higher strata the smaller classes in private schools and individual tutoring of lessons (an upper-class phenomenon rapidly dying out) make for a greater sense of identity and perhaps concern with self. The somewhat surprising finding that middle-class parents make demands for individual responsibility earlier than lower-class parents is further evidence of this subtle training. The busy lower-class mother does not have time to train children to set the table, feed the dog, or make the beds when they are not really old enough to help.

Perhaps a sense of identity, although a false sense, so to speak, comes from the possession of material objects in the middle and upper classes. A widely accepted tenet of the Protestant Ethic is "One is what one has." Originally, a person might point to his possessions as evidence that he had worked hard in the occupation to which God had "called" him. Tangible evidence (material possessions) of hard work made one at least an eligible candidate for a state of grace. If we still believe, by and large, that one is what one has, then the "have-not" individual "is not."

The expression "He's a nobody" does not refer to a disembodied spirit, but rather to a dispirited person of low status. The middle-class child is trained to want to be "somebody." In a very basic sense, then, one does not *gain* identity unless one has possessions. Conversely, if one loses possessions, one loses identity. This equation is certainly limited to particular segments of particular cultures, and runs almost counter to much Oriental philosophy, which maintains that until one is stripped of earthly possessions one cannot find oneself.

Identity based upon possessions is certainly unstable and impermanent. The fear of losing possessions, then prestige, and finally identity may very well enter into the formation of neurotic anxiety. Nevertheless, possessions may help to foster a sense of identity in a middle-class environment, and as long as this identity is not based *solely* on possessions, it will be relatively stable. Thus the struggle for possessions may encourage neurosis and the lack of possessions encourage loss of identity and perhaps psychosis, especially in the pervasive middle-class atmosphere of pecuniary emulation found in the metropolis. In all probability, the rate of neurosis increases as the rate of individualism increases; perhaps a worthwhile compromise.

The relation of neurosis to identity is certainly not clear. Hollingshead and Redlich feel that identity based on sex and dominance is better developed in the middle class. "We also think that the identity formation covering sex, and possibly also dominance, emerges more clearly defined in the middle class families where the dissolution of the oedipal conflict is more apt to take its classical course than in lower class families."[26]

Ivy Bennett[27] (see page 449), comparing delinquent and neurotic children, comes to somewhat different conclusions. The delinquents are predominantly lower class, the neurotics, half lower and half middle class. The sexual identification of the neurotics was often confused; this was not evident among the delinquents. While this finding is based on patient data, so is the New Haven Study. Our own feeling is that the oedipal resolution of middle-class *girls* is relatively poor. Moreover, the middle-class resolution of dominance seems to be more complete, since in Midtown there are fewer passive, dependent, and submissive persons in this social group and a greater proportion of aggressive ones. Interestingly enough, Midtown women who say they "take after father" are predominantly of higher status, and have a substantially reduced mental health risk. Perhaps some masculine identification is an asset among these younger unmarried women who are often holding more prestigeful jobs than their fathers.

The pathology of excessive concern with identity (as opposed to loss or lack of identity) is given detailed treatment by Hans Syz. What he describes is the neurotic self-destructiveness involved in continual concern with the self-image, a problem more typical of the higher status individual.

I use the term autistic image dependence to characterize the dynamic trend in self-structure as well as in social interaction that is intensively preoccupied with and dependent upon the defense of the self-image, experienced as a detached entity which is potentially opposed or hostile to other humans and the outside world.[28]

The dynamics of autistic image-bondage are expressed in the prevailing forms of education and social conditioning in which each child is trained to respond to right-wrong signals which are used for parental convenience, as a promise of love and protection, and as mutual defense of personal advantage and distinction. These educational techniques tend to perpetuate a dynamic structure in individual and society through which the *appearance* of social interest is employed for unacknowledged competitive interests and self-centered defenses.[29]

Identity, whether absent, blurred, or excessive, creates a problem for all the social strata. The Lows, however, may have too little identity and the Highs too much, so to speak.

*Training for Communication.* The establishment of channels for communicating emotions and expressing feelings might be considered one of the primary eugenic functions of the family. Where such communication is blocked, the feelings, whether of love or of hate, must be focused outside the family or released in fantasy. Strong peer-group formation and high rates of juvenile delinquency suggest that low SES children must focus love and hate to a great degree outside the family. Again, the high rates of psychosis and schizoid symptoms among the Lows might support the hypothesis that withdrawal and fantasy are important alternative modes of adaptation to this stress, blocked communication.

What evidence have we that there are class differentials in communication? On the most general level, middle-class children show much earlier language development, which in itself enables them to tell others how they feel and to understand how their parents feel. Infants under a year old who come from professional and business families vocalize more and employ more different sounds than children from lower-class homes.[30]

Another study showed that children with delayed speech came more from lower status homes than those who spoke at a normal age.[31] Twins of the upper three occupational classes were found superior in language development to twins of the lower three occupational classes.[32] Ella Day, in summarizing previous work, tells us that Descoeudres,[33] Drever,[34] Gesell and Lord,[35] Hetzer and Reindorf,[36] Smith,[37] and McCarthy[38] have all found a positive relationship between socioeconomic status and language development.[39]

The higher status child not only is better equipped to say how he feels but also is allowed to express those feelings more frequently to his parents than the low status child.

Evidence is given in Chapter 10 which substantiates this SES difference. For example, 36.9 per cent of the Lows compared with 23.5 per cent of the Highs said they did not have teenage disagreements with their parents (see Table 10-19). More high status men disagreed with their fathers, and more high status women disagreed with their mothers, when compared to the low status half of the sample (see Table 10-20, based on dichotomized high and low SES groups which include the middle SES). The Highs consistently showed a larger proportion disagreeing, as in Table 10-19, where only 7.7 per cent of the Lows, compared with about twice the percentage of Highs (13.8 per cent) said they disagreed with both parents.

These data are in apparent contradiction to some of Davis' generalizations concerning lower-class aggression. The lower-class "girls and boys at adolescence may curse their father to his face or even attack him with fists, sticks or axes in free-for-all family encounters."[40]

The direction of verbal or physical aggression toward the parents, particularly the father, in the lower-class home is perhaps less frequent than we have been led to believe. That there is more aggressive expression outside the low SES home can be accepted as fact. However, other research seems to corroborate the Midtown data just mentiond. For example, Maccoby and Gibbs[41] found that high SES parents gave their children greater freedom to be aggressive toward them. Perhaps these findings are not truly contradictory, for long-suppressed anger which has been given no vent by very strict low SES parents may burst the dam with greater frequency than in higher SES families, which have a type of safety valve in more frequent verbal battles.

We can only suggest that this lack of emotional communication makes the low SES family a breeding ground for delinquency, when hostile feelings are acted out chiefly beyond the confines of the home, and for withdrawal into fantasy when extrafamilial expression is also forbidden. Perhaps the low communication also fosters the development of character disorders and the personality traits of suspiciousness and rigidity. Suspicion is bred when conflicts are not aired, rigidity is encouraged as a defense against unexpressed hostile feelings (as well as sexual feelings which are more directly expressed at the lower SES levels). The Lows greater rate of sociopathy, of psychosis (particularly paranoid schizophrenia, which involves the projection of hostile and often homosexual feelings onto others), and character disorders may all be partly related to poor emotional communication in the lower-class family.

Communication is a double-edged sword, however. The improved communication in the higher SES family may also communicate the status anxiety, the competitiveness, the obsession with self which seem more typical of the neurotic. While reducing overt aggression to acceptable levels, the middle-class family's communicative and rechanneling efforts may be less effective in the sexual area. Some data might be construed as casting doubt on the sexual identification of higher SES Midtowners. As we move from the immigrant to the fourth generation (which is almost 100 per cent high SES), there is a steady increase in the number of boys who "take after" their mothers, and girls who "take after" their fathers in "character, personality, and temperament." Bennett[42] found evidence of confused sexual identification in neurotic children, who came half from middle-class and half from lower-class homes. She did not find such evidence of inversion among delinquents, two-thirds of whom came from lower-class homes.

We found in many of the neurotic children trends in their behavior, interests and activities contrary to their biological role and sexual disposition, and indicative of confused identification patterns within their characters. This finding offers indirect support for Freud's theory of the sexual aetiology of the neuroses and of the tendency towards inversion that lies behind many adult neuroses.[43]

The association of both higher rates of neurosis and evidence of a greater proportion of cross-sex identification with higher SES in Midtown seems to have a curious consonance with Bennett's findings. At all times it is important to remember that while the Highs suffer less impairment, persons at both ends of the socioeconomic scale exhibit maladaptive behavior, and that for every sociopath or psychotic among the Lows there is probably a neurotic among the Highs.

## D. SEX AND EDUCATION

Closely related to the problem of child-rearing is the area of sex and education, in which the greater contrast between the behavior of the social classes occurs. The sexual training of the child seems selected to produce the correct social type desired in each class. For instance, we find masturbation still frowned upon in the lower class, whereas early intercourse is condoned, if not encouraged. To reiterate, Kinsey found that males who had not had sexual intercourse by age seventeen were either mentally deficient or on their way to college. The nonacceptance of masturbation and the condoning of early intercourse tends to channel the lower-class adolescent into early marriage. By age fifteen, almost 50 per cent of lower-class males and only 10 per cent of higher SES males have had sexual intercourse.[44] The parents of the middle-class child certainly condone and may even encourage masturbation, but they frown on early intercourse. The chance of a pregnancy may mean an early marriage, thus interfering with college education. This education will provide the technical and social skills which will allow the young person to maintain a status equal to or better than that of their parents. Masturbation and petting are thus socially sanctioned premarital sexual outlets for the middle class.

The girlhood of Herman Wouk's Marjorie Morningstar, is a good example of the redirection of middle-class premarital sexual expression away from intercourse. After almost 200 pages of constant dating, her boyfriend, Noel, complains,

"Look—I'm not a college boy. Necking disgusts me. I can have all the sex I want, when I want it, with the pleasantest of partners—"
"Not with me you can't," she broke in without thinking.[45]

Three hundred and fifty pages later she is still weighing the question of virginity.

Twentieth century or not, good Jewish girls were supposed to be virgins when they married. . . . For that matter good Christian girls are supposed to be virgins too; that was why brides wore white.[46]

It is the middle-class adolescent to whom the terms "stretched puberty" and "psychosexual moratorium" apply, for they are forced to delay or rechannel their sexual gratifications. The relationship between higher education (part of the index of socioeconomic status) and neurosis, so obvious in our data, was foreshadowed by Freud, who felt that neurosis is the price we pay for civilization.

If the evolution of civilization has such a far-reaching similarity with the development of an individual, and if the same methods are employed in both, would not the diagnosis be justified that many systems of civilization—or epochs of it—possibly even the whole of humanity—have become "neurotic" under the pressure of civilizing trends?[47]

. . . the price of progress in civilization is paid in forfeiting happiness through the heightening of the sense of guilt.[48]

Neurosis is inevitably bound up with the general asceticism necessary to complete a course of higher education. Our educational system is, indeed, the transmitter of our culture and civilization and the source of our growing knowledge and skills. It is the civilizing of sexual and aggressive impulses that enables us to have "civilization," but at the price of neurotic anxiety. Hollingshead and Redlich feel that "It is also possible that more intensive sexualization plays a role in the class V child's inhibition to learn in school."[49] This seems to be putting things backwards, for it is more likely that the *de*sexualization of the middle-class child enables him to continue on the rigorous program of prolonged schooling (or more properly, the channeling of the sexual drives into masturbation, petting, and necking rather than intercourse). These authors also point out that identification with role models (people with higher education and "good manners," or people with lower education given to physical as well as verbal expression of their feelings) has a major part in determining the development and career of the child.

The importance of the channeling of the sexual drive in creating class differences in personality must not be underemphasized. Kinsey[50] found that the sexual history invariably predicts where the individual will end up in the status system. Boys destined for a higher education have later and less frequent intercourse, are more prone to masturbate, neck or pet, will have less frequent intercourse during their lives, and will cease having intercourse earlier. These patterns are already laid down early in life, therefore preceding the social mobility of the individual. There is good reason to believe that they may be causally related to the mobility patterns that follow. This is all the more true at this stage in our country's development where education is the primary means of achieving upward social mobility. Formerly, fortunes were made quickly in exploiting the raw materials of an expanding frontier, but many of these sources have been exploited, and the man with technical and professional skills is now most likely to "make good." Thus, the parents who can train their children to develop the frustration tolerance necessary to put off such major pleasures as sexual intercourse, marriage, and having children until one is "earning a good living" (i.e., $10,000 to $15,000 a year) will not have downwardly mobile children.

We have found that the Obsessive-Compulsives are more numerous among the middle and high SES strata and particularly among the upwardly mobile. (The rigid types, associated with the rigid-hostile-suspicious syndrome, are more common in the low SES, however.) The obsessives are more punctual, orderly, and perfectionistic. These characteristics enable them to climb in the social system, for it is this type of organization and punctuality that is necessary for most white collar and many managerial jobs. This type of personality and the obsessional neurosis are usually assumed to be linked to fairly severe toilet training and anal fixation. Certainly our middle class used to have more severe toilet training than did the lower class. This may be causally related to obsessive-compulsive characteristics, or it may be due merely to the fact that parents who want their children to "do better" also tend to be fairly strict in their toilet training, since they want them to do better in that area also. The desire for early speech, early weaning, early toilet training, and rapid advancement in school may well be part of a general desire to achieve and/or maintain status through the child. This desire for early development is coupled, of course, with an apparently inconsistent desire for *late* development in sexual activity. The early or severe toilet training in itself may not be significant, although it may be an index of a parent's general desire for the child to mature rapidly and excel others. It is also not unbelievable that the frustration of sexual and eliminatory pleasures builds up a frustration tolerance which makes its possible for the middle-class child to hold back from forbidden heterosexual activities and develop a general retentiveness which will aid the educational and, later, the financial processes.

Of course, the development of obsessive-compulsive characteristics may eventually interfere with functioning and with advancement, even in a bureaucratic setting. Such writers as Merton[51] and Burke[52] have shown how the bureaucratic personality may eventually interfere with the functions of the individual and the organization. At higher levels, where decision-making and a certain ability to break the rules are necessary, the obsessive bureaucrat is "fit in an unfit fitness." He has become unfitted for advancement, just by fitting so well into his punctual, perfectionist, and rule-abiding role at the lower positions he has held.

The large number of factors—as indicated by the low SES' elevated average Stress Score—shows us that persons of low status get more hard knocks in adulthood, but about the same number as the middle class in childhood. It should be remembered, however, that our low SES is chiefly an older and immigrant group. They are no more likely to report broken homes or parental rejection than the middle class (middle and high SES), and only in the sphere of economic deprivation does their childhood seem more severe than that of the middle class. In New Haven, the impression of the research team is that the lower class has a worse time emotionally as well as financially.

Lifelong dependency and characterological states of dejection, apathy, and lack of trust in others may be related to damage in this phase of the life cycle (early infancy). We postulate that the presence or absence of these characteristics is related to the child-rearing practices associated with families in the different social classes. For instance, a loveless infancy is more likely in a class V family than in a class II family.[53]

While depression and suspiciousness are certainly more numerous in our lower class (of nonpatients), the respondents' reports of rejecting or domineering parents (Parents' Character Negatively Perceived) do not vary proportionally between the classes. It may be that the dejection, apathy, and suspicion which is part of every infancy is more strongly fostered by childhood, adolescent, and adult experiences of the lower-class individual who finds himself rejected by society, so to speak. Thus, any lower-class parental rejection will be reinforced by societal rejection in adult life, while the compensations of status, power, and other gratifications may be accorded the wealthier individual, thereby counteracting his earlier rejection.

### E.  ADULT LIFE EXPERIENCES

The low SES has more than its share of adult factors. A much larger proportion of the Lows than of the Middle or Highs report Adult Poor Physical Health, Poor Interpersonal Affiliations, and Parental Worries. The physical health factor, it will be remembered, was twice as powerful as any other factor because it was always associated with greater impairment. The high SES is more given to Work Worries (associated with less impairment) and Marital Worries. We already know that a larger proportion of the low than the high SES worry about the cost of living, feel that life is futile (according to the Anomie Scale), are friendless, and worry about loneliness (see Table 16-7). They also tend to dislike their jobs. They are worse off in terms of physical health, interpersonal relations, and work. The high SES, however, are more apt to worry about a variety of problems that are actually more prevalent at lower SES levels. The most important difference between the classes is that the Lows have, on the average, a greater number of adult stresses than the Highs. Add to this the fact that the low SES stresses seem to involve more mental health risk than the typically high SES stresses, and you have some substantiation of the hypothesis suggested by the New Haven research team:

Lower class living appears to stimulate the development of psychotic disorders. We infer that the excess of psychoses from the poorer area is a product of the life conditions entailed in the lower socioeconomic strata of the society.[54]

We can even go further, and suggest that it is the adult life conditions in particular that stimulate the development of high rates of psychosis in the lower class; for the childhood conditions, at least as reported by our respondents, do not vary substantially between the classes.

## F.   SELF-ESTEEM AND EGO-STRENGTH

This brings us to another possible source of class differences in type of mental disturbance: the self-image, self-esteem, and ego-strength. In our country there is a general stigmatization of manual labor. The laborer is looked down upon, and successive waves of immigrants have provided the unskilled labor necessary. Manual labor has not lost its stigma as immigration decreased.

The doctrine of luck is used to preserve the self-esteem of the lower class. Luck, fate, and God's will are often invoked to explain one's poverty and poor health, when these ills may be the result of technological unemployment, poor education, or bad diet. Or, the system may be blamed, so that such expressions as, "It's not what you know, but whom you know" are also more accepted at lower-class levels.[55] The Midtown questionnaire statement, "There are no right and wrong ways, only easy and hard ways to make money," and similar items are invariably agreed with more in the low stratum than among the Middles or Highs. The phrase, "It's all a racket," is the lower-class way of looking at the chancy American Dream, the success pattern which depends not on your skill and stick-to-itiveness but rather on some freak and irrational accident. Life is just a series of hardships or "breaks."[56]

Typically, the lower-class person reduces his status anxiety by lowering his sights, by "dreaming in second gear," as Russell Lynes[57] put it. Surveys have shown that the lower class wants safe jobs in preference to jobs with a chance of advancement. Security quite naturally comes first in the value system of the have-not. "A bird in the hand is worth two in the bush." The lower-class individual doesn't stick his neck out, because he knows the odds are that he'll get it cut off. The middle- and upper-class individual, whose life has been easier, is willing to take a chance, and he has some capital or cushioning behind him in case of failure.

The reduction of aspiration level is seen vividly in studies of high school seniors. Those from lower-class backgrounds reduce their aspirations in their senior year, as they get nearer to graduation and to the reality of their social class position.

The self-esteem of a child is based, to a large degree, on the status of the parents, and the parents' self-esteem. The son of a laborer is more likely to internalize a self-rejecting father, a father who judges himself in the same way society judges him. This lowers the self-esteem of the son. Perhaps he is also a member of a minority or immigrant group. This, in turn, lowers his liking of himself and he is apt to develop a negative self-image. A good example of how society produces poor self-esteem is this complaint by the son of an Italian immigrant.

You don't know how it feels to grow up in a district like this. You go to the first grade—Miss O'Rouke. Second grade—Miss Casey. Third grade—Miss Chalmers. Fourth grade—Miss Mooney. And so on. At the fire station it is the same. None of them are Italians. The police lieutenant is an Italian, and there are a couple of Italian sergeants, but they have never made an Italian captain in Cornerville. In the settlement houses, none of the people with authority are Italians.

Now you must know that the old-timers here have a great respect for schoolteachers and anybody like that. When an Italian boy sees that none of his own people have the good jobs, why should he think he is as good as the Irish or the Yankees? It makes him feel inferior.[58]

There is a somewhat academic yet interesting distinction between the dynamics of the first- and second-generation identification. The child of the immigrant identifies with a parent who still thinks highly of the ways and values of the "old country," and of himself since he behaves in accordance with those values. The grandchild of the immigrant identifies with a parent who has become partially acculturated, and perhaps thinks less of himself because he is not totally acculturated. Thus the grandchild of the immigrant internalizes a parent with a negative self-image. The child of the immigrant internalizes a parent whose ways are more openly at odds with the new culture and whose self-image may be more positive. These differences, even if valid, do not seem to be associated with broad generation differences in psychiatric impairment, as noted before. Immigrants of low SES exhibit more impairment than immigrants of high SES, and the same is true for their children. What really hurts, as the street-corner boy tells us, is that not one of the Italians has the good job, the job with authority.

The fact that one's parents (particularly one's father) hold an inferior position may do more than create feelings of inferiority or shame. It may lead to social isolation from peer-groups. The feelings of shame may cause the child to withdraw for fear of ridicule, or rejection by children of higher status may produce the same result. Another possible result is the intensification of the normal conflict with the like-sex parent. The son may focus his hostility to his father on the father's menial occupation. He will find that the neighbors or his teacher support his negative perception of his father, which only adds fuel to the fire. The acceptance of the denigration of their fathers is seen in these cases quoted by Simpson:

When I was in the sixth grade a neighboring woman told me that she considered my father's occupation rather scummy and that she did not want her children contaminated by association with me. It dawned on me that not everybody regarded my father like I did when I was a child, *so that I came not to tell what my father did.* . . .

I seem to have gotten an increasing awareness of the lack of prestige that was associated with my father's occupation. It came to a point where, if I could avoid it, *I never mentioned him.*

I came to feel a sense of *shame* and *embarrassment* about my father's job, not because of the lack of money, but because of the lack of status. I recall being very impressed with the status of occupations of other parents and *secretly wishing that my father could achieve that status* so that I could impress other boys and girls. (Italics Ours.) [59]

Ego-strength and the self-image arise primarily from the strength of the ego-ideal, the internalized parents (in their positive, rather than restrictive, aspects). Recently, several investigators have noted that the lower class suffers from poor ego-strength.

Such future work might explore systematically our impression that members of the lower classes, particularly of class V, have a weaker ego than members of the higher classes. Many of them seem to be less able to check their own impulses, and they are more passive in their attempts to master the harsh reality aspects of their lives.[60]

Other authors consider ego-strength and self-esteem part of the same system. They feel that the individual's self-image is to a large extent an incorporation or introjection of what others think of him. Public definitions of the self tend to be accepted as correct.

Our theory is that the whole network of prerogatives, attitudes, and expectations surrounding any class position has important consequences for the individual ego-structure which, in turn, is an important factor in determining resistance to mental illness. By ego-structure is meant the complex of factors concerning the ego—the self picture, self-esteem, feelings of adequacy, and most important of all, the ego-strength which prescribes, on one hand, the amount of impulse control and, on the other hand, the degree of successful management of the environment.[61]

As kind, generous, and loving as a lower-class father may be, he still does not make a good role model or identification figure as long as he, like the majority of his class, accepts what society thinks of him. Economic achievement, in our culture, is considered to be ultimate proof of individual superiority. The roots of this belief have been traced from the "state of grace" which hard work in a "calling" gave to the Protestant individual after the Reformation. The Protestant Ethic was important in laying the groundwork for the pecuniary emulation and invidious comparisons based on money, leisure, and consumption described by Thorstein Veblen. The American male who is not earning a good living is not considered to be "a man," and his morality, as well as his virility and mental health, is open to question.

Since "worldly asceticism" (the denial of instinctual drives in favor of long-term occupational goals) is assumed to be a social value, and vertical mobility and advancement are only "natural," it follows that everyone must have a function, i.e., the performance of useful work, in order to maintain his mental health. By the same token, those who are not working or are having difficulty in their work are "mentally disturbed."

The psychiatrist, in accord with the conventions of his culture, which sanction work and condemn idleness, assumes as a rule, that the person who does not work is ill and that the ability to work once more is evidence of the recovery of mental health.[62]

Not only is unemployment or work difficulty considered to be a *result* of mental disturbance, but sometimes the striving for economic security is written off as a mere displacement, as just a symbol of a "deeper" emotional insecurity. While this may in part be true of the wealthier neurotic (who is more likely to be analyzed in these terms), the emotional insecurity of the lower-class individual may very well arise from an even more basic economic insecurity, perhaps starting with food deprivation in infancy or childhood.

Suffice it to say that work as a value pervades our culture and hence our clinics. Although economic striving dominates our lives, as Davis points out, case histories seldom give the full details of the effects of our system of striving and stratification.

Much attention has perforce been devoted to guilt feelings, inferiority complexes, anxiety states, and emotional conflicts. Yet, though these clearly reflect the power of invidious comparison, they are hardly seen to be social at all.[63]

Certainly future research should not neglect the investigation of the exact mechanisms by which status differentials, "relative deprivation," class reference and class membership, and particularly status disequilibration aid in the production of mental disturbance. How often has the individual (or patient) been compared to or compared himself to a superior individual or group? Have emotionally significant people made these comparisons? Have parents denigrated their own economic achievements, lack of education, or taste? Have teachers held the parents' ideals up to ridicule? Have the parents come from different social classes, or different generations with respect to immigration? How meaningful is achievement for a particular lower-class individual? How does he define achievement, and in these terms, has he "achieved," is he "successful?" (Dr. Abraham Kardiner, the psychoanalyst, once told of a patient who was a trigger man and whose trigger finger was paralyzed. He didn't want to be analyzed out of killing, he just wanted to continue to be a success in what he considered a promising career.)

The internalization of socially-disapproved low status parents, or inability to identify with them, the recurring rejections suffered outside the family by the minority group member and the lower-class individual, the constant reminders of status differentials carried by the mass media, particularly television, all make for reinforcement of a negative self-image. The ability to meet stress and the normal disaster, to fight back and to master life comes, in large part, from self-confidence. This self-confidence, in turn, comes largely from experiencing the love of parents who love and accept themselves.

## G. THE SUPEREGO AND RELATED ATTITUDES

Directly related to ego-strength is impulse control, for the ego and the superego both take a part. The lower-class person is more likely to have a poorly internalized superego. This may be, in part, because the physical punishment to which he is subjected by parents is more direct and external. Principally, however, the development of a superego is contingent on a strong bond of love between parent and child. The child who is physically punished without the threat of loss of love will play according to the rules only as long as the policeman is watching. The middle-class child, on the contrary, has internalized the policeman, and will stick to the rules even if nobody is looking. This quality in itself is necessary for success, as defined by the middle class in our culture. The development of guilt, the anxiety over loss of love necessary to make an individual sacrifice or redirect both sexual and aggressive activities— these are the mechanisms by which children are prepared to maintain or achieve high social status.

The love bond between parent and child is a key to why the process of civilization or taming results primarily in neurosis rather than in any other variety of mental disorder. First, the middle and upper classes, inasmuch as they bring about greater repression and redirection of the sexual instincts, are more "civilizing." Now if the upper class simply suppressed sexual activity, their children would be covertly rebellious and would engage in coitus whenever they were not being watched. Through the medium of love and the close emotional attachments of parent and child in the middle and upper classes, the sexual prohibitions are deeply internalized by the child. The unconscious desire to circumvent these internalized rules and the hostility aroused against the parent for curtailing sexual activities (as well as aggressive behavior) lead to severe guilt feelings. No guilt is associated with suppression alone. The class differences, then, may find some origins in the strong and demanding child-parent bond in the middle and upper classes. This bond produces a deeply internalized superego and anxiety over possibly losing the parents' love. The low SES child may tend more toward a fear of physical punishment and, due to a less intense relationship with the parents, will probably develop less guilt. As Freud pointed out, the severity of the child's superego does not correspond to the severity of the treatment it has received.[64]

One reason for this is that the kind, loving, intense relationship between parent and child appears to be mild rather than severe treatment. But it is this very "mild" treatment which results (because of the strength of the love bond) in the more "severe" superego formation. The "severe" treatment of the lower-class child by violent and sporadic outbursts of temper and physical punishment punctuating long periods of almost no parental supervision whatsoever results in a "mild" superego. If, from another viewpoint, we examine the mildness or severity of instinctual repression and of emotional and behavioral demands made on the child, then the upper classes are more "severe," and this severity coincides with the severity of the child's superego formation.

The very fact that there is such a strong love bond in the higher stratum makes us feel that there will be closer identification of child with parent. We previously suggested that identification with the low status father or mother is difficult for the lower-class child surrounded by higher status models (teachers), and this status problem further weakens their superego formation. If the parent is not in authority by virtue of his skill and knowledge ("rational authority")[65] he must rely on the use of "irrational authority," that is, "Obey me simply because I am your parent." This is more typical of the lower-class parent, who has little "rational authority" because of his low status in the community at large.

Of course, we may be misled through case histories reported by high status clinicians into believing that only a weak or superficial superego is developed in the low SES. Certainly the lower class has deeply internalized the success goals of the American Dream. They want to get ahead as badly as anybody else. In fact, they want to get ahead so badly that they will use means which are not acceptable to the middle class in order to attain success. As Merton has pointed out, they have internalized the goals, but not the means to those goals.[66] Thus, we find many lower-class persons with a strongly internalized success drive becoming gangsters or going into ward politics. These channels to success are not socially acceptable to the middle class. It is perhaps not the degree of internalization as much as the integration of the superego that the lower classes lack. Integration involves the incorporation of the "thou shalt nots" as well as the "thou shalts," the acceptance of the middle-class rules of the game as well as the goal of winning.

## *H.* EGO-IDEAL AND PLANNING

We can differentiate between the internalized restrictions, or super-ego, and the internalized positive goals, which we shall call the ego-ideal. The lower class is found to be lacking only in the area of restrictions. They possess a more primitive superego, not the internalized mature conscience we expect in the middle class. They internalize less of the social inhibitions but, on the other hand, they seem perfectly capable of internalizing most of the social goals, such as success. It therefore seems plausible that their ego-ideal is not so impaired as we have been led to believe. Such phenomena as psychopathy, "acting out," dyssocial be-havior, and delinquency do not stem perhaps so much from poor inter-nalization of goals as from poor internalization of socially accepted means to those goals. One questionnaire item attempted to assess this very same emphasis on the goals without a corresponding emphasis on the appropri-ate means to those goals. A much larger proportion of Lows than Highs agreed that, "To make money there are no right and wrong ways any more, only easy ways and hard ways" (see Table 16-7). This weakness of the inhibitory functions, coupled with what appears to be strong goal striving, makes for an increase of antisocial behavior in the lower class.[67]

It would be logical to expect that along with a disregard for the legitimate means to achieving goals, the immature superego of the lower class would create infantile demands for immediate goal fulfillment. On the contrary, the low SES did not agree more than the middle or upper SES with the statement "When I want something very much, I want it right away" (Lows 28.5 per cent, Middles 22.1 per cent, Highs 34.8 per cent). While these results do not seem to corroborate the hypoth-esis that the Lows have an immature superego, the following points should be noted.

Approximately one-fourth of the low SES agreed there were only "easy and hard ways to make money" and that they want things "right away." Further analysis may indicate that these are the same individuals, which would tend to corroborate the hypothesis. A type of adaptation which may be reducing the prevalence of immature acting-out types in the low SES is a widespread lowering of aspiration level. The lowering of ambition and the curtailing of the fantasy life of children found among Lows is better calculated to produce agreement with an imaginary state-ment such as "When I want something very much, I just try to forget about it." The lower-class individual is less likely to plan ahead for something he wants very much. A somewhat larger proportion of the Lows agreed that "Nowadays, a person has to live pretty much for today and let tomorrow take care of itself" (see Table 16-7). A larger proportion of the Lows, then, may exhibit a short-term approach to their lives, and avoidance of planning. The abandonment of goals is more typical of persons of low frustration tolerance, while the long-range planner chooses the calculated risk of long-term frustration in order to achieve his goals. At the risk of oversimplifying, it still seems probable that the constant postponement of eliminatory drives until it is "time to sit on the potty," the postponement of hunger until it is "mealtime," and of heterosexual relations until one is "ready to support a family" trains the middle- and upper-class individual to wait for the things he wants. The knowledge that he will probably get what he wants aids him during the waiting period. The knowledge, based on past experience, that he often doesn't get what he wants leads the lower-class person to "eat, drink, and be merry" while he can.

The depressive quality of the lower SES outlook has been established in previous chapters by their high Frustration-Depression Score and by their predominance in the psychiatrists' category of "depressed" (Lows 36.2 per cent, Middles 23.9 per cent, Highs 11.1 per cent). This category is typified by the item, "I am in low, or very low, spirits most of the time." Along with depression, the Lows exhibit pervasive feelings of futility as indicated by the "anomie" items.[68] (See Table 16-7.) More Lows felt that "It's hardly fair to bring a child into the world with the way things look for the future." They also agreed that "In spite of what some people say, the lot (situation, condition) of the average man is getting worse, not better." Their alienation from others and political apathy are reflected in their strong agreement with such statements as "These days a person doesn't really know whom he can count on" and "Most public officials are not really interested in the problems of the average man." Another item indicating their feelings of futility and social isolation is "Most people don't really care what happens to the next fellow." Thus, the complex of depression and futility, political apathy and lack of trust in others and oneself is more typical of the lower class. When Fromm labeled the German lower middle class "sadomasochistic,"[69] he might just as well have been describing the low SES in our metropolitan setting.

It seems that Erich Fromm's use of the term lower middle class is more equivalent to the Midtown Lows than to the Midtown Middles. The German *Kleinbeamte*, or small official, such as streetcar conductors

TABLE 16-7
## PROPORTION OF RESPONDENTS AGREEING WITH "ANOMIE" STATEMENTS ACCORDING TO RESPONDENTS' SOCIOECONOMIC STATUS

| | Respondents' Socioeconomic Status | | |
|---|---|---|---|
| | LOW | MIDDLE | HIGH |
| "Anomie" Statements | Per Cent | Per Cent | Per Cent |
| It's hardly fair to bring a child into the world with the way things look for the future. | 32.0 | 17.8 | 5.9 |
| In spite of what some people say, the lot (situation, condition) of the average man is getting worse, not better. | 48.0 | 28.6 | 11.6 |
| These days a person doesn't really know whom he can count on, | 64.5 | 52.0 | 26.4 |
| Most public officials (people in public office) are not really interested in the problems of the average man. | 60.8 | 54.3 | 40.9 |
| Most people don't really care what happens to the next fellow. | 53.5 | 40.1 | 23.4 |
| To make money there are no right or wrong ways any more, only easy and hard ways. | 24.1 | 14.0 | 4.3 |
| Nowadays a person has to live pretty much for today and let tomorrow take care of itself. | 50.7 | 36.7 | 29.6 |
| Total Number of Cases (N≐100 per cent) | 544 | 556 | 560 |

or post-office personnel derived some prestige from the fact that they were appointed officials. Such occupations can be classified as either Low, if manual, or Middle, if clerical, in the Midtown job hierarchy which is based on American prestige rankings. Since the *Kleinbeamte* made up a large part of the lower middle class in Germany, Fromm's "lower middles" fall mostly in the low and to some extent in the middle SES groups in Midtown.

The feeling of impending doom and disaster, the fatalism and resignation, seem similar to Hollingshead and Redlich's picture of the downwardly mobile individual. The Lows and the downward mobile are both given to alcoholism and character disorders. Whether the crime and drug addiction rates are greater in the Midtown low SES cannot be said, but it is quite likely.

Indeed, even authoritarianism is prevalent in the low SES (see Table 16-8), again pointing to an association with sadomasochism. Such items as "Prison is too good for sex criminals: they should be publicly whipped, or worse," indicate the sadistic component of authoritarianism. The projection of hostile and sexual impulses onto others and the punishment of others for one's own real or imagined misdeeds is typical of persons with an externalized superego. The middle-class person feels guilt, and often punishes himself. The lower-class person is more apt to punish others and to project his motives onto others, such as minority groups, hidden Communists, and Martians, thus avoiding guilt feelings. The interdependence of sadism and masochism is seen in the other four authoritarian items. The Lows agree overwhelmingly with each of these items, "There are two kinds of people in this world: the weak and the strong." "Any good leader should be strict with people under him in order to gain their respect," "The most important thing to teach children is absolute obedience to their parents," and "What young people need most of all is strict discipline." It is unlikely that the large SES differences in agreeing with these questions are due entirely to response biases, such as acquiescence. The latter characteristic is in itself part of the masochistic component of the authoritarian complex, and doubtless is more typical of the low SES.

The authoritarian statements reflect the hypothesized relationship between the lower-class parent and child. The parent is strong, the child weak. When the child becomes strong, he can get away with behavior which was formerly avoided because of fear of physical punishment by the parents. By the same reasoning, a good leader (or parent) should be strict in order to gain respect. The respect for authority is irrational, in the sense that it is based upon strictness and punishment. The upper status parent, on the contrary, does not demand automatic "respect for elders," but gains such respect, for example, through the occupational sphere, through signs of deference given by subordinates (such as doormen and other servants), and through the threat of withdrawal of love.

The emphasis on discipline and obedience in the lower class seems paramilitary. This is not just a superficial resemblance. The army drains off hostility through war and hatred of the common enemy. The lower

## TABLE 16-8

### PROPORTION OF RESPONDENTS AGREEING WITH "AUTHORITARIAN" STATEMENTS ACCORDING TO THE RESPONDENTS' SOCIOECONOMIC STATUS

| | Respondents' Socioeconomic Status | | |
| --- | --- | --- | --- |
| | LOW | MIDDLE | HIGH |
| "Authoritarian" Statements | Per Cent | Per Cent | Per Cent |
| Prison is too good for sex criminals: they should be publicly whipped, or worse. | 46.3 | 36.5 | 8.0 |
| There are two kinds of people in this world: the weak and the strong. | 72.4 | 50.4 | 30.9 |
| Any good leader should be strict with people under him in order to gain their respect. | 64.9 | 46.6 | 27.7 |
| The most important thing to teach children is absolute obedience to their parents. | 74.8 | 52.3 | 14.5 |
| What young people need most of all is strict discipline. | 63.6 | 49.1 | 24.8 |
| Total Number of Cases (N=100 per cent) | 544 | 556 | 560 |

class expresses similar hostility in delinquency, crime, alcoholism, and outbreaks of physical violence. This is the essence of the externalized superego, or immature conscience. Strangely, it is the inability to externalize, to stop feeling guilty, to stop punishing themselves, that leads many upper status neurotics to the psychoanalyst's couch. The acting-out disorder of the lower class is often a major therapeutic goal for the upper status patient.

While the lower-class parental and societal authority is not supposed to be questioned, it is something that can be "gotten around" when nobody is watching. Authoritarianism indicates an underlying disrespect for all constituted authority, and only a thin shell of superficial conformity hides the violent impulses which sporadically break through.

The complex of rigidity, suspicion, and depression best characterizes the low SES. Tied to this complex is authoritarianism, sadomasochism, anomie, and futility, and social and emotional isolation stemming from distrust and hostility. A poor self-image and weak ego-strength abet this picture. This, together with a poorly internalized superego, results in inability to meet crises, to rise in the status system, and to inhibit socially unacceptable impulses in favor of striving toward approved long-term middle-class goals. A fear of failure in the pursuit of these approved goals, a realistic fear based on past rebuffs, eventually results in a lowering of the aspiration level or a shift in the means used to attain those goals.

The above data and hypotheses enable us to formulate further guesses about the nature and formation of the social classes. We should not view class as a static phenomenon, but see that certain passive-dependents, alcoholics, and rigid or suspicious people are always filtering from the upper down to the lower levels. Similarly, rather anxious and obsessive-compulsive types are climbing up the social ladder. Thus, the social class into which we are born does not completely determine where we are going to end up. Social mobility allows the classes to select certain types which are best suited to rise or fall in the system. People tend to migrate toward the social level that best fits their personality structure. While the middle and upper class generally try to imprint the repressed or "civilized" character on their children, and while the lower class seems to imprint the acting-out character on its children, there are many "misses," and a wide range of types develops in each class. This makes for a rotation of types, a circulation of emotional elites and non-elites which tends to keep the class system somewhat open. We can only hope that intensive studies will soon be available to spell out the methods by which the children of the various classes are imprinted with the social character of their class. These studies will perhaps also tell us how the class deviants develop; how the repressed "college boy" evolves in a slum environment of "corner boys." Perhaps future research will also indicate ways of preparing the low SES individual to meet the stress of his environment with less impairing adaptive devices, and perhaps of alleviating the very conditions which seem to plague his adult life.

## Summary

The differences between the socioeconomic strata can be summarized in tabular form ( see Table 16-9 ). Those differences based upon data from the Midtown sample appear in roman type. Hypotheses based upon other research or impressions based upon the literature appear in italic type. Al-

*Table 16-9*
## Comparison of Experience and Behavior of Lower and Higher Status Groups: Findings and Hypotheses

| | Lower Status | Higher Status |
|---|---|---|
| **CHILDHOOD STRESSES** | Slightly more broken homes before age seven.<br>Greater proportion reporting economic deprivation in childhood. | Disagreed with parents more frequently. |
| **ADULT STRESSES** | Report worse adult physical health.<br>More persons with poor interpersonal affiliation—especially lack of friends.<br>Tend to feel children are more trouble than they are worth, to worry about them, and to have problems with them. | More likely to worry about work.<br>More likely to worry about marriage. |
| **STRESS AND IMPAIRMENT** | More adult stress.<br>Greater impairment per stress unit.<br>*No financial or other reserves.*<br>*Less resilience, less resistance.* | Less adult stress.<br>Less impairment per stress unit.<br>*Financial reserves, cushioning.*<br>*Greater resilence and resistance.* |
| **TYPE OF ADAPTATION TO STRESS** | Exhibit increasingly greater proportion of psychotics with increasing stress.<br>Show moderate increase In proportion of neurotics with increase of stress, ending in a plateau.<br><br>Greater proportion of following gross types:<br>1. Probable psychotic type<br>2. Probable organic type<br>3. Probable personality trait type (character disorder).<br><br>Greater proportion of following symptom groups and diagnostic types:<br>Alcoholic, brain disease, dyssocial, psychosomatic, hypochondriacal, passive-dependent, depressed, rigid, schizoid suspicious, schizophrenic. | Exhibit a constant low proportion of psychotics, regardless of stress.<br>Show sharp increase in proportion of neurotics with increase of stress.<br><br>Greater proportion of following gross types:<br>1. Probable wells<br>2. Probable neurotic type.<br><br>Greater proportion of following symptom group:<br><br>Aggressive (in interview situation, primarily). |
| **MOBILITY** | Passive-dependent, rigid, and suspicious individuals as well as alcoholics are moving downward from the high into the low stratum. | Anxious and obsessive-compulsive persons are moving upward from the low into the high stratum. |

## Table 16-9 (cont.)

| | Lower Status | Higher Status |
|---|---|---|
| **ANOMIE** | Greater proportion agree with "anomie" items, suggesting feelings of futility, alienation from group and society, depression, resignation, social isolation, and concomitant distrust of others. | Greater proportion disagree with "anomie" items, suggesting that effort will be rewarded, integration with the group and society, absence of depression, determination, social integration, and confidence that others can be counted on. |
| **AUTHORITARIANISM** | Greater proportion agree with authoritarian items, suggesting strong authoritarian attitudes. | Greater proportion disagree with authoritarian items, suggesting moderate or anti-authoritarian attitudes. |
| | Sadistic or punitive attitudes toward the weak.<br>Masochistic or submissive attitudes toward the strong. | Less sadomasochism, possibly more egalitarian. |
| | Belief in strict discipline.<br>Stronger moralistic trend. | Belief in rewards and conditional love for child training. |
| | Greater projection of hostile and societally disapproved sexual impulses onto others. | Less projection, possibly more intropunitive.<br>More guilt and self-blame. |
| **SUPEREGO** | Tendency to externalized, superficial, or "immature" superego. | Internalized strict conscience. |
| | Social control is by shame, ridicule, or threat of punishment. | Social control primarily by creation of guilt; less shaming or disparagement, less physical punishment. |
| | Underlying disrespect for, but inability to question established authority, combined with superficial and sporadic conformity to middle-class norms (corresponding more to Piaget's state of "moral realism"). | Some ability to question established authority if necessary, with generally internalized and consistent conformity to middle-class norms (corresponding more to Piaget's state of "moral relevance"). |
| | Rigid adherence to the rules in judging morality, with emphasis on "natural" (hence external) law. | Emphasis on individual judgment, taking account of extenuating circumstances, motivation and intention of the individual |
| | Authoritarian quality of control system also suggested by high agreement with Authoritarian Scale statements. | |
| | Authority is not to be questioned but can be circumvented. Acting on impulse, or the "spur of the moment" legitimates the circumvention. | Repression of impulses and redirection ("sublimation"). |

## Table 16-9 (cont.)

| Lower Status | Higher Status |
|---|---|
| *May encourage:* | *May encourage:* |
| *Inability to postpone gratification; more irritability and explosiveness in the face of frustration, less apparent self-control* | *Inhibition of socially unacceptable impulses in favor of striving toward long-term goals, greater frustration tolerance; tendency to extreme self-control* |
| *Possibly predisposes to:* | *Possibly predisposes to:* |
| *Psychopathy (lack of conscience and improper internalization of norms).* | *Neurosis—establishment of internal conflict, signified by guilt, compulsions.* |
| *Sociopathy (internalization of middle-class goals, but use of disapproved means to achieve those goals.* | |

**GENERAL CHILD TRAINING**

| | |
|---|---|
| *Irrational authority exerted by parents; "Respect for elders," "Do as I say, not as I do."* | *Rational authority.* *Parents must earn the child's respect through their behavior and occupational achievements; teaching by example.* |
| *Methods of social control (see above).* | *Methods of social control (see above).* |
| *The authority and control methods may lead to:* *an externalized superego.* | *The authority and control methods may lead to:* *an internalized superego.* |
| *Later abrupt responsibility is thrust on the child.* | *Early individual responsibility training in household chores and school work.* |
| *Current mothers more likely to breast feed, but with abrupt weaning, especially full-time working mothers.* | *Current mothers feed on demand, wean later, toilet train later, allow more freedom of movement outside home.* *Formerly (1930s) were less "permissive" in these areas.* |
| *Less consistent, more sporadic training.* | *More consistent training, less a function of parental mood.* |
| *Discourage expression of hostility against parents. Encourage or accept hostile expression or behavior outside the family and toward siblings.* | *Accept expression of hostility, particularly in younger male child, toward parents and siblings, but not outside the family.* |
| *Training by teachers and others conflicts with parents' values.* | *Teachers' values coincide with parents' values.* |

**IDENTITY TRAINING**

| | |
|---|---|
| *Less identity training.* | *Identity training through scrapbooks, baby books, family albums, birthday parties.* |

## Table 16-9 (cont.)

| Lower Status | Higher Status |
|---|---|
| Interchangeability of function emphasized, clothes and toys (if any) handed down, large school classes. Expendability of individual reinforced by job experience of parents. | Individuality emphasized—in clothing, love, school work, possession of own toys rather than sharing. |
| Identity formation concerning dominance may be poor, reflecting low status of parents. Parental sex roles, however, are distinct. A man does not do a woman's job in the house. However, more women work full time outside the home. | Sexual identity may be more confused, one possible basis for increased rates of neurosis. Parental sex roles are less distinct and may promote diffuse or cross-sex identification. |
| Inadequate concern with identity may result. | Excessive concern with identity or self-image may be promoted. |
| Internalization of middle-class norm, "One is what one has," may result in the feeling that one is "nobody." Lack of possessions may promote lack of identity. | Possessions and property promote the feeling that one is "somebody," or will "grow up to be somebody." |

**COMMUNICATION TRAINING**

| Lower Status | Higher Status |
|---|---|
| Slower development of verbal communication. | Rapid development of verbal skills. |
| Less room for expression of disagreements with parents; "Children should be seen but not heard." | Greater permission to argue or disagree with parents. |
| Either no expression of hostility to parents, or sporadic physical violence toward parents—an "all or none" expression. | Verbal expression of hostility to parents, providing a "safety valve." |

**SEX AND EDUCATIONAL TRAINING**

| Lower Status | Higher Status |
|---|---|
| Masturbation, petting tabooed. Early intercourse condoned, especially for boys. | Masturbation, petting condoned. Early intercourse tabooed. |
| Shorter adolescence. | "Stretched puberty." Sexual union and marriage deferred in favor of higher education, attainment of occupational and social skills. |
|  | Development of sexual "frustration tolerance," or a rechanneling of sexual behavior away from coitus. |

## Table 16-9 (cont.)

| | Lower Status | Higher Status |
|---|---|---|
| **TRAINING FOR GRATIFICATION AND PLANNING** | Little training for retentiveness or compulsive trends. | "Holding back" and other training in sex, eating (at meals only), and elimination may promote educational and financial retentiveness. Ability to memorize, to save money, to be punctual, excessive concern with personal cleanliness, and a bureaucratic personality may all stem in part from this type of training. |
| | Less planning and a present orientation—"Live for today and let tomorrow take care of itself." | Emphasis on planning is related to "holding back," and to a future orientation. |
| **POVERTY AND PLANNING** | Poverty reduces planning, promotes the immediate gratification pattern. Poverty in childhood seems associated with depression or apathy in adults. Being poor may also have effects through inadequate diet or malnutrition, for example, which might promote depression, apathy, and lack of trust in others. Poverty, or its lack, is part of the child-training complex. | Plenty creates an atmosphere more conducive to planning—one has time to consider the future, one has been rewarded, and plans toward the next reward. |
| **SELF-ESTEEM AND EGO-STRENGTH** | Parents' occupation despised or causes shame and embarrassment leading to disidentification. | Parents' occupation respected, leading to strong identification. |
| | Negative self-image due to acceptance of negative stereotypes of the low status person or to internalization of low status parent. | Generally a more positive self-image.<br>Those in prestigeful occupations or families are in a "state of grace." Emphasis on maintaining the self-image may be conducive to neurosis: "I'm not living up to myself—to my family name." |
| | Pecuniary emulation results in relative deprivation, shame, and hostility which is often expressed physically, resulting in lowered status. | Pecuniary emulation may produce some anxiety, but this often maintains the status, if it is channeled into work anxiety and competition. |
| **NORMS** | Limited ambition. | Greater ambition—high aspiration. (Recently the middle-class college student has started "dreaming in second gear," showing lower aspiration levels.) |

### Table 16-9 (cont.)

| Lower Status | Higher Status |
|---|---|
| Group responsibility. | Individual responsibility. |
| Less emphasis on technical skills. School of "hard knocks" is the best teacher; "It's not what you know, it's whom you know. | Development of skills and achievements—through education. |
| Less postponement of satisfaction; experience teaches that postponement of gratification seldom brings rewards; Doctrine of luck replaces doctrine of hard work. | Worldly asceticism; work hard, postponing pleasures for future goals. Planning pays off. |
| Emotional expression. | Rationality. |
| Individual expression—content of relationship with others rather than form. | Getting along with people—manners, courtesy. |
| Expression through physical aggression when called for. | Control of physical aggression. Use of verbal or legal aggression ("White Collar Crime"). |
| Enjoyment of leisure. | Constructive leisure, ·self-improvement, develop a hobby outside your work. |
| Less emphasis on property values and/or individual ownership. | Respect for property; One is what one has. |

though this table does not summarize the complete findings of this volume, it can act as a guide to the major socioeconomic differences in experience and adaptive behavior. More detailed information on stresses or diagnostic categories which did *not* exhibit socioeconomic variation can be rapidly gleaned from the individual chapter summaries.

## Notes

1. It may be argued that rather than divide the population of present respondents into three equal SES groups, they should be judged not in relative terms but in terms bearing an absolute relationship to the father's SES. Thus, only the variables of occupation and education would have been used, and these would have been calibrated on the same scale for father and child. However, there are several arguments against this seemingly more objective method of measuring mobility from the parents' position. First of all, the relative importance of a high school education has decreased tremendously in the last thirty years. A college degree is virtually the equivalent of

the high school diploma of a few decades ago. A father with a high school diploma might be considered high status, but a respondent with a high school diploma is just average or middle SES. A second problem is the shift in the occupational structure of the United States, the growth of unions, and the subsequent rise in the income (and therefore prestige) of the skilled and semiskilled laborer. The status of the white collar clerical groups has been declining because their income has stood still while that of labor has increased. Their claim to being an elite group by virtue of their educational skills (reading and writing) is no longer legitimate, because of the widespread literacy in our country. The attempt to reclassify occupations in terms of the shifts in accorded prestige from 1910 to 1953, the date of the interviewing, would call for a research project in itself. Thus, the relativistic division of the parent generation and the respondent generation into three approximately equal socioeconomic groups seemed a practical and not theoretically untenable solution.

2. In Table 16-1 the rows indicate the small effect of fathers' SES on the ridits (the "Low row" .61, .57, .57; the "Middle row" .50, .49, .51; and the "High row" .41, .41, and .42). The columns indicate the effect of the respondents' SES on the ridits (the "Low column" .41, .50, .61; the "Middle column" .41, .49, .57; and the "High column" .42, .51, and .57). The average "effect" of the respondents' SES with the fathers' SES controlled is .17. So much for the relative importance of the fathers' and respondents' status from the standpoint of pure prediction of mental health risk.

3. August B. Hollingshead and Fredrick C. Redlich, *Social Class and Mental Illness*, Wiley, New York, 1958, p. 369.

4. *Ibid.*, p. 370.

5. Jurgen Ruesch, "Social Technique, Social Status and Social Change in Illness," in Clyde Kluckhohn and Henry A. Murray (eds.), *Personality in Nature, Society and Culture*, Knopf, New York, 1949, pp. 117–130.

6. *Ibid.*, p. 125.

7. A. B. Hollingshead and F. C. Redlich, *op. cit.*, pp. 368–369.

8. Robert K. Merton, "Social Structure and Anomie," in Robert K. Merton (ed), *Social Theory and Social Structure*, The Free Press of Glencoe, New York, 1949, p. 134.

9. *Ibid.*, p. 137.

10. Alfred Kinsey mentions the sexual precocity of the lower-class male when compared with the middle-class male. The upwardly mobile boy who is going on to college does not show this same sexual precocity, Kinsey says that

So nearly universal is premarital intercourse among grade school groups that in two or three lower level communities in which we have worked we have been unable to find a solitary male who has not had sexual relations with girls by the time he was 16 or 17 years of age. In such a community, the occasional boy who has not had intercourse by that age is either physically incapacitated, mentally deficient, homosexual, or ear-marked for moving out of his community and going to college.

See: A. C. Kinsey, W. B. Pomeroy, and C. E. Martin, *Sexual Behavior in the Human Male*, W. B. Saunders Co., Philadelphia and London, 1948, p. 381.

11. Jurgen Ruesch, *op. cit.*, p. 125.

12. A. B. Hollingshead and F. C. Redlich, *op. cit.*, p. 240.

13. B. M. Spinley, *The Deprived and the Privileged, Personality Development in English Society*, Routledge and Kegan Paul, London, 1953, pp. 129–130.

14. A. B. Hollingshead and F. C. Redlich, *op. cit.*, p. 361.

15. B. M. Spinley, *op. cit.*, p. 131.

16. Urie Bronfenbrenner, "Socialization and Social Class Through Time and Space," in Eleanor E. Maccoby, T. M. Newcomb, and E. L. Hartley, *Readings in Social Psychology*, Holt, New York, 1958, pp. 400–425.

17. E. E. Maccoby, P. K. Gibbs, and the Staff of the Laboratory of Human Development, Harvard University, "Methods of Child Rearing in Two Social Classes,"

in W. E. Martin and C. B. Stendler (eds.), *Readings in Child Development*, Harcourt, Brace, New York, 1954, pp. 380–396.

18. Allison Davis, "American Status Systems and the Socialization of the Child," *American Sociological Review*, Vol. 6, No. 3, 1941, pp. 345–354.

ᐧ 19. Ruth Benedict, "Continuities and Discontinuities in Cultural Conditioning," *Psychiatry*, Vol. I, No. 2, 1938, 161–167, reprinted in C. Kluckhohn and H. Murray, *op. cit.*, pp. 414–423.

20. A. B. Hollingshead and F. C. Redlich, *op. cit.*, p. 364.

21. See Alfred L. Baldwin's discussion of M. Kuhn, "Family Impact on Personality," in J. E. Hulett, Jr., and Ross Stagner (eds.), *Problems in Social Psychology*, Papers and Proceedings of the Allerton Conference on Social Psychology, Monticello, Illinois, December 1950, University of Illinois, Urbana, Illinois, 1952, p. 54.

22. Albert K. Cohen, *Delinquent Boys*, The Free Press of Glencoe, New York, 1955, pp. 88–93.

23. George Simpson, *People in Families*, Crowell, New York, 1960, pp. 291–292.

24. Allison Davis and Robert J. Havighurst, "Social Class and Color Differences in Child Rearing." *American Sociological Review*, Vol. 11, No. 6, 1946, pp. 698–710.

25. Judith I. ,Krugman, "Cultural Deprivation and Child Development," *Strengthening Democracy*, Vol. 9, No. 5, May 1957, Board of Education of the City of New York, Brooklyn, New York.

26. A. B. Hollingshead and F. C. Redlich, *op. cit.*, p. 362.

27. Ivy Bennett, *Delinquent and Neurotic Children*, Basic Books, New York, 1960.

28. Hans Syz, "Problems of Perspective Against the Background of Trigant Burrow's Group-Analytic Researches," *International Journal of Group Psychotherapy*, Vol. XI, No. 2, April 1961, p. 151.

29. *Ibid.*, pp. 151–152.

30. O. C. Irwin, "Infant Speech: The Effect of Family Occupational Status and Age on Use of Sound Types," *Journal of Speech Hearing Disorders*, Vol. 13, No. 3, 1948, pp. 224–226.

31. R. E. Beckey, "A Study of Certain Factors Related to Retardation of Speech," *Journal of Speech Disorders*, Vol. 7, No. 3, 1942, pp. 223–249.

32. Ella J. Day, "Language Development in Twins," in Wayne Dennis (ed.), *Readings in Child Psychology*, Prentice-Hall, Englewood Cliffs, New Jersey, 1958.

33. A. Descoeudres, *Le Développement de L'Enfant de Deux à Sept Ans*, Delachaux et Niestle, Neuchâtel and Paris, 1921.

34. J. Drever, "The Vocabulary of a Free Kindergarten Child," *Journal of Experimental Pedagogy*, Vol. 5, No. 1, 1919, pp. 28–37.

35. A. Gesell and E. Lord, "A Psychological Comparison of Nursery-School Children, from Homes of Low and High Economic Status," *Pedagogical Seminary*, Vol. 34, No. 3, Sept. 1927, pp. 339–356.

36. H. Hetzer and B. Reindorf, "Sprachentwicklung und Soziales Milieu," *Zeitschrift für Angewandte Psychologie*, Vol. 29, 1928, pp. 449–462.

37. M. E. Smith, "An Investigation of the Development of the Sentence and the Extent of Vocabulary in Young Children," *University of Iowa Studies in Child Welfare*, Vol. 3, No. 5, 1926.

38. D. A. McCarthy, *The Language Development of the Preschool Child*, Institute of Child Welfare Monograph Series No. 4, University of Minnesota Press, Minneapolis, 1930.

39. E. J. Day, *op. cit.*, p. 300.

40. Allison Davis, "Child Rearing in the Class Structure of American Society," in Community Service Society of New York, *The Family in Democratic Society*, Columbia University Press, New York, 1949, pp. 49–69.

41. E. E. Maccoby and P. K. Gibbs, *op. cit.*

42. I. Bennett, *op. cit.*

43. *Ibid.*, pp. 216–217.

44. A. C. Kinsey, W. B. Pomeroy, and C. E. Martin, *op. cit.*

45. Herman Wouk, *Marjorie Morningstar*, Doubleday, New York, 1955, p. 170.

46. *Ibid.*, p. 552.

47. Sigmund Freud, *Civilization and Its Discontents*, translated by Joan Riviere, Fourth impression, The Hogarth Press, London, 1949, p. 141.

48. *Ibid.*, p. 123.

49. A. B. Hollingshead and F. C. Redlich, *op. cit.*, p. 363.

50. A. C. Kinsey, W. B. Pomeroy, and C. E. Martin, *op. cit.*, p. 419.

51. R. K. Merton, *op. cit.*

52. Kenneth Burke, *Permanence and Change*, New Republic, New York, 1935.

53. A. B. Hollingshead and F. C. Redlich, *op. cit.*, p. 361.

54. *Ibid.*, p. 242.

55. R. K. Merton, *op. cit.*, pp. 136–140.

56. Leo Lowenthal, "Biographies in Popular Magazines," in Paul F. Lazarsfeld and Frank Stanton (eds.), *Radio Research, 1942–3*, Duell, Sloan & Pearce, New York, 1944, pp. 507–549.

57. Russell Lynes, *A Surfeit of Honey*, Harper, New York, 1953.

58. William Foote Whyte, *Street Corner Society*, University of Chicago Press, Chicago, Illinois, 1943, p. 276.

59. George Simpson, *op. cit.*, pp. 304–305.

60. A. B. Hollingshead and F. C. Redlich, *op. cit.*, p. 366.

61. Bert Kaplan, Robert B. Reed, and Wyman Richardson, "Comparison of the Incidence of Hospitalized and Non-Hospitalized Cases of Psychosis in Two Communities," *American Sociological Review*, Vol. 21, No. 4, August 1956, p. 479.

62. Stanley A. Leavy and Lawrence Z. Freedman, "Psychoneurosis and Economic Life," *Social Problems*, Vol. 4, No. 1, July, 1956, p. 59.

63. Kingsley Davis, "Mental Hygiene and the Class Structure," in Arnold M. Rose (ed.), *Mental Health and Mental Disorder*, Norton, New York, 1955, pp. 590–591.

64. S. Freud, *op. cit.*, p. 116.

65. Erich Fromm, "Individual and Social Origins of Neurosis," *American Sociological Review*, Vol. 9, No. 3, 1944, pp. 380–384.

66. R. K. Merton, *op. cit.*, p. 146.

67. It was suspected that the emphasis on luck and fate in the lower class is bound up with the spirit of gambling (not that the Middles and Highs don't gamble on horses and the stock market). The data make this assumption questionable, since about 22 per cent of all three SES levels said, "I suppose I'm a gambler at heart."

68. Leo Srole, "Social Integration and Certain Corollaries, An Exploratory Study," *American Sociological Review*, Vol. 21, No. 6, 1956, p. 709.

69. Erich Fromm, *Escape from Freedom*, Farrar and Rinehart, New York, 1941.

# Prognosis

THOMAS S. LANGNER

During the ten years it took to bring this research to fruition there have been few major changes in family life, socioeconomic stratification, or the stresses of normal living in this world. Two major worldwide changes have occurred, however: a recognition of the sharp increase in the world's population, and the rapid deterioration of relations between the Soviet Union and the United States. While the first change promises only slow starvation for the world's future millions, the second change, with its threat of full scale nuclear war, could lead to a rapid end of most life on earth. Is there anything in our data which could help us to avoid the war guaranteed to end all wars and to end everything? Here is the final test of the clinical severity of a symptom: Does it threaten to wipe out the individual—and the human race? It is necessary, of course, to take the teleological viewpoint that life is an end in itself. Once this is assumed, we should use every bit of information we can muster to promote life.

The drift toward war has become a human habit. The only difference between past wars and future ones lies in the fact that the next conflagration promises to be almost total in its destruction. Perhaps there are characteristics of leaders and followers who join forces to make war which can be clarified by our findings. War may be fed by the release of hostile impulses in two communities. However we have found that there is not just one morbid fraction in a community, but morbid fractions, each with its special varieties of psychopathology and personality structure.

Despite the risk of drawing analogies between individuals in psychiatric treatment and groups exhibiting subclinical disorders, we could say that the higher and lower socioeconomic groups, not only in Midtown but in other parts of the nation and the world, are involved in a *folie à deux*. The typical *folie à deux* involves a dominant and a submissive partner, such as husband and wife or mother and child. The submissive partner eventually comes to share in the psychotic symptoms of the more dominant partner. The term has also been applied to mass hysteria and other group phenomena. Whether the *folie à deux* involves psychosis or neurosis or both, or if the term applies strictly to a leader and his group of followers, need not concern us now. The term is used here merely to suggest the interaction of two different types of disorder found at different social levels.

The excessive concern of a fraction of the higher status group with prestige, possession, and finally power may preselect a certain proportion of neurotics for leadership. We have seen that holding office in an organization is almost exclusively a high status prerogative in Midtown. Leadership certainly aids the community. At the same time some leadership serves to enhance the self-image of the leader. If the enhancement of his self-image becomes the *exclusive* goal of the leader, the community soon suffers. Too many despots have flowered in recent years for us to ignore grandiose preoccupation with self.

On the other hand, a segment of the lower status group in many countries has been exposed to extreme poverty, negative childhood experiences, and repeated adult stresses and frustrations. Through this, perhaps, they may have developed a tendency toward a depressed, suspicious, and passive-aggressive authoritarian character which seeks strict leaders to control unmanageable impulses. These class differences may be even more exaggerated outside of Midtown and the United States, which has a large middle class and therefore a smaller range of stratification, and some freedom of mobility across class lines. Status differences in social character may be even more pronounced in countries exhibiting only the extremes of wealth and poverty.

As in the *folie à deux*, the symptoms are transmitted from a dominant to a dependent person. (Here the parallel is far from accurate, since, according to our data, the dominant higher status leaders are unlikely to be psychotic and only a small proportion of the lower status followers could be so classified.) The delusion, so to speak, is that war is inevitable, that the enemy is planning to attack, that discussion is only a ruse for gaining time, that inspection is spying, and that disarmament is a plot to weaken one's defenses. Both the leader and the follower enter into this delusion. The acceptance and perpetuation of this delusion enhances the power and therefore the self-image of the leader. How does it relate to the needs of the lower status followers? They have sought external authority and found it in a strong or even dictatorial leader. A leader, unfortunately, must always lead somewhere; he may direct the energies of his nation toward building for the future (since, by background, he is a planner) constructively through education and science, or destructively through war and aggrandizement. His followers have not only a passive but also an aggressive side to their natures, and this can be used in building or destroying. (How close these activities are, for we often hear the term "building an empire.") Having handed over responsibility for control to their leader, they may press him for new socially-sanctioned targets for their precariously controlled aggression. "Show us the challenge or show us the enemy!" Hopefully, the leader directs his people's energies toward the constructive challenge. If this fails, for any number of reasons (including the enemy's actions), he may be forced to divert all activity toward war.

Thus war and other destructive group action is one possible outcome of the interplay of class differences in psychopathology. Without pathological concern with the self-image, a disorder which seems more prevalent in the higher strata, we might be faced merely with the problems of crime and delinquency. With the development of excessive self-concern in higher strata, or through emulation of these strata by upwardly mobile individuals born in lower strata, a foundation may be laid for neurotic leadership. Under healthy leadership the mass resentment and bitterness of the thwarted can be channeled creatively. Under neurotic leadership there is more likelihood that the charismatic qualities and crystallizing skills will be used to galvanize people into destructive action and into joining movements espousing political extremes of right or left.

Surely another war would be *folie* in its deepest sense, madness. And is international madness "subclinical"? In our present world it could well be considered of the same clinical severity as suicide. The Midtowners do not want war, nobody wants war. Yet it is probable that all peoples—like those in Manhattan—harbor enough anxiety, hostility, suspicion, and loneliness to make the concreteness, the grand simplicity, the expressiveness, and even the "togetherness" of war sound attractive. Symptoms abound in the population; yet the majority continue to live without major impairment. They are still able to weather their disorders and even manage to enjoy life. What a tragedy if the common man, hoping to solve his problems, replaced the more moderate leaders of today. He would actually be choosing that final and most maladaptive device, the most unprofitable defense mechanism, the hydrogen bomb. Then it would truly be the hour described in *Peer Gynt:* the triumph of self and the downfall of reason. As the scene opens, Dr. Begriffenfeldt, director of a mental hospital in Cairo, is showing Peer Gynt the patients:

*Begriffenfeldt.* Yes, here you'll find them, bag and baggage—the coterie of seventy professors of Exegesis. Lately a hundred and three new ones joined them.—(Calls to the Keepers.) Mikkel, Schlingelberg, Schafmann, Fuchs—into the cages with you! Quick!

*The Keepers.* We!

*Begriffenfeldt.* Yes—who else? Get on! get on! As the world's topsy-turvy, we must follow suit! (Shuts them up in the cage.) The mighty Peer has come to us to-day; so you can join the others.—I will say no more.

[Locks the cage and throws the key into a well.]

*Peer Gynt.* But why—my dear Director—?

*Begriffenfeldt.* Don't call me that! I *was* Director until— Sir, can you keep a secret? I must unburden myself—

*Peer Gynt.* What is it?

*Begriffenfeldt.* Promise me that you will not tremble.

*Peer Gynt.* I will try not to.

*Begriffenfeldt* (takes him into a corner and whispers). Absolute reason expired at eleven o'clock last night!

*Peer Gynt.* God help us—!

*Begriffenfeldt.* Yes, it's a great disaster. In *my* position, too, you see, it's doubly disagreeable; because this place, until it happened, was known as a lunatic asylum. . . . All persons who up to that time were known as mad at eleven o'clock last night became normal; this, in conformity with Reason in its newest phase. And, if you consider the matter farther, it's clear that from the selfsame hour our socalled wise men all went mad. . . . [The mad folk come one after another into the courtyard.]

*Begriffenfeldt.* Good morning to you! Come out and greet the dawn of freedom! Your Emperor's here!

*Peer Gynt.* Their Emperor? . . .

*Begriffenfeldt.* The man who guessed the Sphinx's riddle! Who is himself!

*Peer Gynt.* That's just my trouble. I am myself in every way! but here, so far as I can see, everyone gets outside themselves.

*Begriffenfeldt.* Outside themselves? Oh, no, you're wrong. It's here that men are most themselves—themselves and nothing but themselves—sailing with outspread sails of self. Each shuts himself in a cask of self, the cask stopped with a bung of self and seasoned in a well of self. None has a tear for others' woes or cares what any other thinks. We are ourselves in thought and voice—ourselves up to the very limit; and, consequently, if we want an Emperor, it's very clear that you're the man.[1]

*Note*

1. *Peer Gynt* in *Eleven Plays of Henrik Ibsen*, Random House, New York (n.d.), pp. 1136–1138.

# APPENDICES

# Additional Comments
# by the Psychiatrist

S T A N L E Y  T .  M I C H A E L

The Midtown Study was designed on a broad scale to disclose mental health or disorder, past experience and present living, social integration, enjoyment of life or tragedy, physical health, emotional needs, and community attitudes of an urban population. So extensive were the data gathered by the field operations that the possible combinations of the questionnaire responses seemed infinite. As a consequence a system of analysis and a design of reporting had to be devised to sort out a reasonably comprehensible compilation from the otherwise unmanageably voluminous information.

## Emphasis on Etiology

The two central themes of the investigation were an estimate of the prevalence and severity of mental symptomatology and an appraisal of personal and social functioning in relation to mental health. In this respect the study was firmly anchored in the realm of the medical specialty of psychiatry. In conformity with the emphasis on etiology—the science of discerning causes of malfunction, important to both clinician and theoretical specialist—the framework for this volume was designed to reveal relationships between mental health and social experience that might be interpreted as containing a sociogenic etiology of mental disturbance.

This does not mean that we included all the information of etiological significance. Nor do we mean to imply that the etiological relationships are the only interpretation of the correlations. Rather, the sociogenic etiology is to be considered as a focal concept that we have subjected to exploration.

The study produced data significant to the clinician. It also provided a framework for testing psychological hypotheses. The interviews with the respondents, controlled and structured by the questionnaire, yielded data classifiable by statistical methods. The loss to the clinician of the flavor of the individual case consequent on the statistical elaboration is redeemed by the

483

confidence in the universal applicability of the findings. The basic criterion for the validity of an etiological factor is the relative certainty that the causative agent will be followed by the disorder, that the two will be invariably correlated under equivalent conditions. The statistical method assures us of a predictable association of the presumed cause and effect.

A principal finding relates certain untoward experiences to poor mental health. An observation is made that as the number of unfavorable experiences increases, mental health becomes worse. Not any one critical experience, nor any specific combination of experiences, but rather the progressive accumulation of numbers of adverse experiences is linked to increasingly poor mental health. The association of a numerical summing up of experience with mental disorder tends to evoke resistance in the clinical psychiatrist who, in his patients, is impressed by the impact of events significant to each individual. The importance of these events in psychotherapy is not in their universal applicability as noxious agents, but rather in their significance in the succession of private experiences in each individual patient.

Nevertheless, even within the context of the personal reaction of the patient to an incident, there are certain crises, such as death of a parent or spouse, serious illness, loss of employment or business, social ostracism, rejection by family, or low socioeconomic status which are presumed to have a deleterious effect on mental health. Information about these social experiences was obtained through our questionnaire and tested for significance against the Mental Health Rating. The parallel increase in the number of social crises with increasingly poor mental health seems to indicate that experiences which are traumatic to psychiatric patients are also important to the lives of people who are not in treatment.

## Three Interpretations of Correlation Between Mental Health and Social Experience Factors

The stress factors referred to in this volume were derived from experiences reported by the respondents. These data on social functioning were contained in Part II of the Psychiatrist's Summary of the questionnaire. They were not known to the psychiatrist when he made his rating based on the symptomatic part of the questionnaire. The high statistical correlation of these particular experiences with MHR I is not therefore attributable to methodological circularity in the rating process. Considering the correlation from the clinical point of view, we are struck by the possibility of at least three interpretations of the relationship.

### MENTAL HEALTH IS CONSEQUENCE OF SOCIAL EXPERIENCE

Foremost is the etiological interpretation. The difficult life experiences were stressful and therefore led to the breakdown of mental health. This interpretation is consistent with the psychogenic interpretations of mental symptoms advanced by the dynamic schools of psychiatry. It has been frequently discussed throughout this volume and will not be further elaborated here.

## CORRELATION DUE TO CONSISTENTLY MORBID REPORTING BY RESPONDENTS

Two other possible interpretations of the statistical correlations, however, seem to be worthy of comment. One has to do with the problem of reporting by the respondent, which was extensively discussed in Chapter 6. A respondent who is ill perceives himself as suffering and reports his symptoms and pains, his dissatisfactions, anxieties, despondencies or negative and distrustful attitudes. These were contained in Part I of the Psychiatrist's Summary and a MHR I was assigned on the basis of these reports. It would be inconsistent for this same respondent to assume an optimistic point of view in the items of Part II of the Psychiatrist's Summary. Rather, he will also report his life experiences as unsatisfactory or unhappy. He may have always perceived life this way and remembers his past experiences as disillusioning and reports them thus. The consistency of reporting in both parts of the Psychiatrist's Summary would lead to a correlation of the unhappy experiences reported in Part II with a poor Mental Health Rating derived from Part I. The correlation between the social experience factors and poor mental health may thus be a result of the uniformly morbid, pessimistic perception and reporting by the respondent of both the symptoms and attitudes contained in Part I of the Psychiatrist's Summary and the life experiences summarized in Part II.

## STRESSFUL EXPERIENCES RESULT FROM PSYCHOPATHOLOGY OF RESPONDENT

A third interpretation of the statistical correlation of poor mental health with accumulation of unfortunate life experiences might be based on the hypothesis that morbid personalities are likely to experience morbid lives. The psychic distress, the psychosomatic symptoms, the depressed and distrusting attitudes reported in Part I of the Psychiatrist's Summary may be interpreted as evidence of disorganization of psychophysiological homeostasis, of reasoning, and social adaptability. Respondents with disturbed personalities tend to become involved in conflicts, generate interpersonal distress, or create socially destructive situations. They may perceive normal social situations as unfavorable or hostile, insurmountable, or damaging. Their personality structure may have always been disorganized with the result that many of the experiences reported in Part II of the Psychiatrist's Summary Form were either precipitated or not precluded as might have been the case in respondents possessed of better emotional adaptability or more effective control of the environment. In this interpretation the poor mental health is the source of the difficult experience rather than its consequence.

## Corollaries in Clinical Psychiatry

The three separate interpretations of the correlation between the experience factors and mental health have corollaries in clinical psychiatry. The sociogenic, etiological interpretation is consistent with the dynamic theories of psychiatry, particularly as they relate the genesis of psychopathology to previous traumatic experience. The second interpretation which ascribes the correlation to a consistently biased attitude in answers to both the symptomatic and experiential items of the questionnaire is analogous to endogenous depression in which the patient with a characteristic, monotonous attitude of despondency, pessimism, and helplessness interprets the world and himself as doomed to failure. Also the consistently hostile, suspicious, projective approach to life of the paranoiac fits this category. The third interpretation of the correlation based on poor adaptability of the respondent finds its counterpart in the accident prone individual, in the self-destructive, masochistically compulsive neurotic, also in the personality disorders, particularly the sociopathic types.

The formulation of three distinct interpretations of the correlation between the life experience factors and mental health is not intended to convey that each one of these by itself explains fully the described relationship. It is more likely that all three are applicable even in a single individual. We can conceive of a respondent with a basically inadequate personality who encounters difficult life experiences and reacts to them by the development of patterns of symptoms which are maladaptive. He would be likely to perceive his life and the world as unfavorable and report them thus.

We can conclude only that interaction between personality structure, experience, and perception is complex. We hope that the formulations which have evolved from this investigation may contribute to the unraveling of the unresolved disputes concerning etiology of psychiatric symptoms and social pathology, both of which appear to be bound to each other in a reciprocal relationship.

## Social Psychiatry and the Community

Social psychiatry is concerned with people in numbers.[1] Unlike clinical psychiatry, which deals with the individual patient, social psychiatry studies psychopathology as it affects individuals in social relationships. In the Midtown investigation the integration of the community and its people may be described at four distinct conceptual levels.

At one level we have learned about the people as individual respondents. From the statistical average of all respondents we can extrapolate and project back onto the individual. We can formulate the characteristics of the typical respondent. From the psychiatric viewpoint we find that the average respondent has mild or moderate symptoms which do not particularly interfere in his life adjustment. The symptoms are most frequently of a neurotic type.

When questioned about it, the average individual recognizes in himself significant worries, tension, and nervousness.

At another level of perception we have learned how these individuals make up the community. We know the age and sex distribution of the respondents, how many are of American, English, Irish, or German derivation; how many are Catholic, Protestant, or Jewish. We know their educational level. We have determined how many are mentally well; how many have poor mental health. We have estimated the proportional distribution of these individuals according to the predominant characteristics of their symptoms into neurotic, psychotic, organic, psychosomatic, or personality trait types. We have estimated the prevalence of certain psychiatric symptoms and symptom complexes, and we know how many respondents have seen a psychiatrist.

At a third, more abstract level, we were able to test certain hypotheses about psychopathology. Incorporated in the design of the questionnaire were categories of life experience which had previously been presumed to influence mental disorder. On this level we found strong associations between psychopathology and such factors as age, physical health, and socioeconomic status. We noted that persons who considered their relationship to their parents unsatisfying carried a heavier load of psychiatric symptoms. We found further that disruption of home by death or separation of the parents is not necessarily associated with poor mental health in the offspring. There are exceptions to this rule and we can predict on the basis of our data when these exceptions apply.

## Personality Structure Determines Function in Society

Finally, at a sociological level implicating the life of the community, we were able to observe the effect of mental health and personality structure on the integration of people in a social organization. We are convinced that this aspect of the study revealed particularly unexpected insights, germane to social psychiatry. Here actions of the people and the life of the community may be interpreted as resulting from the psychiatric makeup of the component individuals of the group. This area of social psychiatry offers singular promise of improved comprehension of community organization and function.

The Midtown Study was not originally designed to test community functioning. Rather, it was a morbidity prevalence study with emphasis on the effect of sociogenic factors on psychopathology. Appropriate to its purpose, a representative probability sample was selected as the base for the investigation. As the analysis of the sample evolved, it became evident that groups of individuals could be separated from the sample, on the basis of certain common denominators. Some of these were demographic, others derived from answers to items of the questionnaire or from psychiatric ratings. Thus subcategories with common characteristics were separated from the total sample. In turn, these subdivisions could be correlated to particular qualities or functions. It is important to recognize that when we refer to attitudes or actions of the people who make up these subcategories, we do not mean the type of group action and communication which might be characteristic of a church meeting or a political rally. Rather, our reference is to a common way of thinking and acting of separate individuals who are not necessarily in communication, but who have in common a certain way of life.

## Socioeconomic Subdivisions and Characteristic Psychopathology

An example of subcategories derived from the sample population are the three subdivisions of the total sample according to the socioeconomic indices of the individual respondents. In terms of characteristic psychiatric symptoms, these three subdivisions differ substantially from one another. The difference is particularly noticeable when the two extremes—the low socioeconomic third and the upper third—are compared. The low socioeconomic third is characterized to a significantly greater extent by organic, psychotic, psychosomatic, and character trait types of personalities and by alcoholic, asocial, depressed, hostile, schizoid, and schizophrenic symptoms (see Tables 15-1 and 15-2). On the other hand, the upper socioeconomic third tends to be composed of individuals without psychopathology, of psychoneurotic types, and of persons with social initiative and aggressiveness. These three divisions of our sample are not identical with social class; nevertheless, extrapolations may be made from our three socioeconomic groups to the qualities and tendencies of the various social classes.

If these socioeconomic subdivisions are conceived as social forces which determine organization and action in the community, it is possible to predict that the attitudes, demands, and actions of component sections of the community may be decided by the personality characteristics, even psychopathological elements, of its component individuals. Support for such a hypothesis can be found in the answers of our respondents to the Srole Anomie Scale and the California Authoritarian Scale.

## An Interpretation of the Anomie and Authoritarian Scales

Anomie is a sociological descriptive term that indicates a lack of consonance of interests between the community and a portion of its people. There is a feeling of distrust, nonacceptance, and a tendency to isolation and social withdrawal. Anomie is associated with low socioeconomic class.

Authoritarianism is a psychological attitude, perhaps a philosophy of life, which endorses strong, forceful methods of control in social relationships. Authoritarian attitudes too are associated with low socioeconomic class.

The anomie and authoritarian attitudes were tested in our sample by inclusion of the Srole Anomie Scale[2] and the California Authoritarian Scale[3] as questionnaire items. As anticipated, the low index socioeconomic third of our sample agreed significantly with the items of these two scales. In contrast, the high socioeconomic third tended to disagree with these statements. The answers of the low socioeconomic third pose a paradox. The same group which despairs of its neighbors and public officials in the Anomie Scale strongly endorses strict community organization in the Authoritarian Scale. The seeming discrepancy in these attitudes to social organization may be reconciled if they are interpreted on the basis of the personality structure of the component members of the group. Characteristically, the members of our low socioeconomic group were passive, depressed, distrusting, and withdrawn. They lacked the personality qualities that would allow them to take advantage of unstructured social situations. The agreement with such statements as "These days a person doesn't really know whom he can count on," "Public officials are not really interested in the problems of the average man," or "Most people don't really care what happens to the next fellow" may indicate not an accusation but rather a complaint that nobody is willing to help.

It is recognized[4] (see Chapter 16) that members of the low socioeconomic class tend to act out their impulses, to be outspoken and easily swayed to antisocial and immoral acts. Yet in the agreement with the California Authoritarian Scale they condemn immorality and voice agreement with imposition of strict discipline. The inconsistency between the facts and the expressed opinions may be reconciled if the agreement with the California Scale is interpreted as involving a mental mechanism of projection. Individuals of the low SES group lack confidence in their ability to control their impulses and to organize their lives. Yet they recognize the need for social integration and project their wish for better control on the authorities. They want an outside agent to provide for them the order, organized initiative, and leadership to compensate for the psychopathology which tends to precipitate them into social conflicts and disorganization[5] The authority, the community administration, is expected to impose restraints on impulses and by decisive command give clear directions for action, thus eliminating conflicts, confusion, and distress.

The high SES group, by contrast, agrees with the Authoritarian Scale less often than the low index group. The Anomie Scale is favored even less than the California Scale (see Table 16-7, items 1 to 5, and Table 16-8). The high SES third is composed of substantial numbers of individuals whose symptoms are of a neurotic type, or who are relatively free of symptoms.

The basically neurotic personalities of the upper SES reject blind obedience. They prefer to give free play to the mechanisms involved in conducting their own affairs; to choose from right or wrong, or to remain suspended in middirection; to select from white or black, or the many shades in between; or just to reserve the privilege of choice. When they decide, their moves will not be impulsive or extreme. They will be conservative, not extravagant, as deliberation was also given to the advantages of nonaction. The high SES group disagrees with the Anomie Scale. They have created the social order for the conservation of their moral values (the product of their reasoning) and for the protection of their property (the product of their cautious actions).

Agreement or disagreement with the Anomie and Authoritarian Scales by the upper and lower socioeconomic index thirds of our sample population are consistent with the basic personality structures of these two groups. This applies also to the middle third of the sample which in its scores on the Anomie and Authoritarian Scales and in personality structure lies between the two extremes.

Our data allow us to surmise on the probable validity of the tentative hypothesis that the symptoms and personality structures found in the various socioeconomic divisions of our sample population are consistent with the attitudes expressed by their scores on the Anomie and Authoritarian Scales.

Accepting the assumption that the answers to the Anomie and Authoritarian Scales are influenced by the personality structure of the respondents, we may proceed further with the evaluation of the significance of the nonclinical symptoms of our "normal" population. Is there any evidence that these symptoms are the source of unhealthy patterns of living? Do these symptoms lead to actions which are detrimental to the respondent or to society? These questions are not so easily answered as might be desired. The assumption might be made, for instance, that the symptoms we have found in our low SES individuals are so malfunctional that they interfered with the respondents' social adaptation and thus caused them to appear in the low SES group. However, it may be claimed with equal validity that the respondents' low SES and that of their parents were the cause of the development of the malfunctional symptoms.

Some evidence in answer to this dilemma may be found in our data on social mobility. In our investigation a respondent is considered to be socially mobile if he is now located in a SES division different from that of his father (see Chapter 16, pp. 425–426). Downward mobility, thus defined, is significantly associated with personality pattern disturbances and alcoholism, upward mobility with neurotic trends. The quality of these symptoms favor the hypothesis that the symptoms preceded or caused the mobility. It is highly unlikely that a personality pattern deviation was caused by the downward mobility, since such deviations are presumed to have been established in early childhood. Similarly, the neurotic trends found in the upward-mobile are also theoretically established during the Freudian psychosexual stages of development in infancy. The change in social status of our respondents, for better or worse, occurred, by definition, after the respondent's eighth year, in many instances after separation from the family. The developmental patterns of the character disorders and the neurotic personalities favor the conclusion that the foundations for these symptoms were present before the change in socioeconomic status. Considering the nature of these symptoms, they most likely contributed to the causes of the social mobility. We then have evidence in our data on social mobility that the nonclinical symptoms may have a decided influence on the way of life of the respondents.

Assuming the importance of these psychiatric symptoms in the community, we are faced with the problem of corrective action. Can these symptoms be changed? Can their impact be minimized? What measures are to be taken for their prevention? We are obviously confronted here with the limitations of our present method of psychiatric therapy. In medicine in general, therapy is limited to the treatment of seriously incapacitating illness. For manifest reasons the individual approach would not be practical for the treatment of the subclinical psychopathology found in the community which has more of the quality of a public health problem. Even in public health medicine, problems of epidemic proportions are dealt with by preventive actions aimed at each individual as in the case of mass immunizations. However, the more substantial and continuous public health measures deal with organization of daily living, exemplified by the prevention of infectious illnesses, maintenance of sanitary standards of dwellings, of purity of drinking water and food supply, removal of refuse, control of air pollution, and prevention of accidents. These problems were apparent and occasionally dealt with at the community level long before the establishment of organized public health. Some have become religious and cultural rituals.

Public Health measures have permeated the organization of our communities to such an extent that we are barely aware of their influence on our daily living. It seems that the role of social psychiatry will be no less penetrating. In the past we were aware of the more obvious psychopathology smouldering in our communities: the psychotic individuals, the criminals, the delinquents. More recently we have recognized that truancy, inability to learn in school, marginal or irregular employability, excessive consumption of alcohol, and marital distress are also attributable to psychopathology. We are still closing our eyes to the probability that the periodic, cataclysmic, fratricidal rages of societies called war are essentially a pathological symptom, an epidemic release of endemic, hostile impulses of a morbid fraction of the community. We may also need to investigate scientifically the motives and potential psychopathology involved in political and economic strife.

The preventive task of social psychiatry seems then to have several ramifications. On the one hand there is the problem of preventing the development of fully evolved clinical psychopathology as exemplified by treatment or hospitalization of psychiatric patients, by the segregation and rehabilitation of sociopathic, disruptive individuals. The problems in this area have been recognized and dealt with by appropriate corrective measures. At another level is the marginal psychopathology in the community and the question of pathological conduct of societal organizations. These areas are still in great need of exploration. From our data it would seem that the solution goes beyond the private dispensing of psychiatric treatment to individuals. Instead we foresee the necessity for intensified investigation of the problems of social integration, of leadership and identification with societal organization. The goal of such studies should be a more rational structure of administration of human affairs.

Our data indicate that we must begin to recognize that the community is composed of individuals who may be subject to morbid impulses. The operation of the community may depend on the personality structures of the component individuals, and on actions and attitudes derived from psychopathology. The differentiation of the three socioeconomic strata of our community sample in terms of the psychopathological composition of their respondents, and particularly in the manner in which their psychopathology correlates with the attitudes derived from the answers to the Anomie and Authoritarian Scales, are a good example of the potential contributions of social psychiatry. The observation is even more significant since it evolved from the data rather than from a presumed hypothesis. Hopefully, future investigations will be more intentionally designed to uncover not only the psychopathological composition but also the associated attitudes and actions of people and the factors involved in the determination of social and political integration.

## Notes

1. Alexander H. Leighton, *An Introduction to Social Psychiatry*, Charles C Thomas, Springfield, Illinois, 1960.

2. Leo Srole, "Social Integration and Certain Corollaries, An Exploratory Study," *American Sociological Review*, Vol. 21, 1956, p. 709.

3. T. W. Adorno, E. Frenkel-Brunswik, D. J. Levinson, and R. N. Sanford, *The Authoritarian Personality*, Harper and Brothers, New York, 1950.

4. See August B. Hollingshead and Fredrick C. Redlich, *Social Class and Mental Illness*, Wiley, New York, 1958.

5. Stanley T. Michael, "Social Attitudes, Socio-Economic Status and Psychiatric Symptoms," *Acta Psychiatrica et Neurologica Scandinavica*, Vol. 35, Fasc. 4, 1960, pp. 509–517.

# Further Data from Chapter 5

## I. Calculation of Odds from the Ridits

Bross gives us a rule of thumb for calculating the odds when comparing two classes of people, neither of which is the reference class (neither of which is the total sample of 1660 persons). This is the typical comparison made in our data between classes, for example, parents quarreled often, occasionally or rarely. We quote directly from Irwin D. J. Bross and Rivkah Feldman, *Ridit Analysis of Automotive Crash Injuries,* published by the Division of Automotive Crash Injury Research, Department of Public Health and Preventive Medicine, Cornell University Medical College, October 15, 1956:

"Suppose that we have two classes (neither of which is a reference class) and we wish to compare the average ridits. For example, suppose that we wish to compare center and right front seat occupants in 'moderately severe' accidents who are ejected with the corresponding individuals who are not ejected. The respective average ridits are 0.54 and 0.38 and the difference is 0.16. What can we say about the situation in these two classes with respect to *each other* (i.e., without involving the reference class)? An estimate of the corresponding relative probabilities for the two classes can be obtained very simply by adding 0.50 to the numerical difference. Here if we add 0.50 to 0.16, we obtain 0.66. In terms of odds this would mean that the chances are about 2 to 1 that the ejected occupant will sustain a worse injury than the corresponding non-ejected occupant. The rule here given is an approximate one which eventually breaks down if the differences are close to 0.50 (or larger than 0.50). However, if in a particular instance a better estimate is required, this estimate can be obtained by setting up a new system of ridits using one of the classes to be compared (ordinarily the class with the larger number of individuals) as the new reference class."

## II. Calculation of Confidence Limits for Significant Differences at the 5 Per Cent Level of Confidence Between Average Ridits

Since ridits are percentile scores, the average ridit of a part of the sample is an average of its individual percentile score. Furthermore, the standard error of the ridit can be computed in the same way as the standard error of the mean. The formula is:

$$6\bar{R} = \sqrt{\frac{\Sigma(.500 - Ri)^2}{(N-1)^2}}$$

where N = Number of cases, and Ri = each individual ridit, and $\Sigma(.500 - Ri)^2$ = the sum of the squared differences between the mean ridit of the entire sample (always .500) and each individual ridit, that is to say, the total variance.

This method is rather lengthy when numerous confidence limits have to be computed. Dr. Irwin D. J. Bross, who developed the *ridit* system, has devised a formula that provides a rough approximation to the 5 per cent confidence interval, providing that the ridit in question does not deviate too far from .500 (that is, not more than about .650 nor less than .350). This formula is

$$2.00\ 6\bar{R} = \frac{1}{\sqrt{3N}}.$$

To be precise, under the normal distribution curve, 95 per cent of all individuals will fall between 1.96± standard deviations of the mean, 99 per cent of all individuals will fall between 2.58± standard deviations of the mean. The difference between 2.00 6$\bar{R}$ and 1.96 6$\bar{R}$ does not warrant multiplying each confidence interval $\left(\dfrac{1}{\sqrt{3N}}\right)$ by .98, that is by $\dfrac{1.96}{2.00}$ , especially since the slight error tends to make the 5 per cent level of confidence even more conservative than it actually is. Therefore, the formula used to compute the confidence limits is as follows:

$$5\text{ per cent confidence limits} = \bar{R} \pm \frac{1}{\sqrt{3N}}.$$

For instance, if a group of 81 cases has an average ridit of .560, the 5 per cent confidence limits are computed as follows:

$$.560 \pm \frac{1}{\sqrt{3N}} = .560 \pm \frac{1}{\sqrt{81}} = .560 \pm \frac{1}{9} = .560 \pm .11 \text{ or } .670 \text{ to } .450.$$

## III. Additive Versus Interactive Ridits

A distinction must be made between additive and interactive pairs of items (variables, factors). Two items are additive if a "Yes" to both items is equal to the sum of the increments over .50 of the "Yes" answers to each item alone. Typical non-additive ridits would be No-No, .43; No-Yes and Yes-No, .55; Yes-Yes, .55. (See cross-tabulation of items A and B below.)

|  |  | Item A | |
|---|---|---|---|
|  |  | Yes | No |
| Item B | Yes | .55 | .55 |
|  | No | .55 | .43 |

As for additivity, typical additive ridits would be No-No, .43; No-Yes and Yes-No, .55 and Yes-Yes, .60. (See items C and D below.)

Item C

| | | Yes | No |
|---|---|---|---|
| | Yes | .60 | .55 |
| Item D | No | .55 | .43 |

On the other hand, interaction over and above additivity may take place between items. Although we rarely found any interaction between paired items, an interacting pair would look like this: No-No, .43; No-Yes and Yes-No, .55 and Yes-Yes, .85. (See items E and F below.)

Item E

| | | Yes | No |
|---|---|---|---|
| | Yes | .85 | .55 |
| Item F | No | .55 | .43 |

This shows that saying "Yes" to both items makes one "worse off" than would be expected if the effect of items E and F were simply added together. Saying "Yes" to *both* E and F triggers off something—that is, E and F "interact"; there is a synergistic effect. The whole, E plus F, is greater (or less) than the sum of its parts.

At our request Dr. Bross suggested a simple method of calculating the expected additive ridit (or theoretical ridit) in the Yes-Yes cell. The following scheme (Table B-1) explains how this method works.

### Table B-1

**MOTHER DOESN'T UNDERSTAND ME**

| | | Yes | No | Total Average Ridit |
|---|---|---|---|---|
| (FATHER SPENDS TOO LITTLE TIME WITH ME) | Yes | $.55 - .50 = +.05$<br>$.56 - .50 = +.06$<br>Theoretical Ridit $= .50 \quad +.11 = .61$ | $.48 - .50 = -.02$<br>$.56 - .50 = +.06$<br>Theoretical Ridit $= .50 \quad +.04 = .54$ | .56 |
| | No | $.55 - .50 = +.05$<br>$.47 - .50 = -.03$<br>Theoretical Ridit $= .50 \quad +.02 = .52$ | $.48 - .50 = -.02$<br>$.47 - .50 = -.03$<br>Theoretical Ridit $= .50 \quad -.05 = .45$ | .47 |
| | Total Average Ridit | .55 | .48 | .50 |

Taking the Yes-Yes cell as an example, we obtain the theoretical ridits in the following way. First we calculate the ridits for the total "Yes" group on

"Mother Doesn't Understand Me" (.55) and the total "Yes" group on "Father Spends Too Little Time With Me" (.56). Second, we derive the respective differences between these two subtotal ridits and the ridit for the whole sample (.50). These are: .55 − .50 = .05, and .56 − .50 = .06. Then we add the two differences (.05 + .06 = .11). Finally, we add the total of the two differences to .50 (.50 + .11 = .61). The theoretical ridits for the other three cells are computed in the same manner.

## IV. Pyramiding of the Factor "Parents' Character Negatively Perceived"

Step 1: The cross-tabulation of mother-mother and father-father items has been explained in some detail in the text of Chapter 5, and is illustrated in Table B-2.

### Table B-2
### The Pyramiding of Parents' Character Negatively Perceived (Mother)

| Mother Alienating | | | Mother Dominating (Mother Wants to Run Children's Lives) | |
|---|---|---|---|---|
| | | | Yes | No |
| | Yes | W | 1 | 1 |
| (MOTHER DOES NOT UNDER- STAND ME) | | $\bar{R}$ | .56 | .54 |
| | | N | 300 | 231 |
| | No | W | 1 | 0 |
| | | $\bar{R}$ | .52 | .47 |
| | | N | 211 | 918 |

Total N        1660

W—the weight assigned each cell.
$\bar{R}$—the average ridit of the cases in each cell.
N—the number of cases in each cell.

*Step 2:* We now cross-tabulated one father item against one mother item.

### Table B-3
### The Pyramiding of Parents' Character Negatively Perceived
### (Mother and Father)

| Mother Alienating | | | Father Alienating (Father Spends Too Little Time With Me) | |
|---|---|---|---|---|
| | | | Yes | No |
| | Yes | W | 2 | 1 |
| (MOTHER DOES NOT UNDER-STAND ME) | | R̄ | .61 | .52 |
| | | N | 157 | 336 |
| | No | W | 1 | 0 |
| | | R̄ | .52 | .47 |
| | | N | 261 | 906 |
| | Total N | | | 1660 |

W—the weight assigned each cell.
R̄—the average ridit of the cases in each cell.
N—the number of cases in each cell.

*Steps 3, 4, and 5:* Two trichotomies weighted 0, 1, 2 were established: one based on four "mother-father" items; the other based on two "parent" items. Table B-4, the final pyramid, shows how these two trichotomies were combined.

## Table B-4
### The Pyramiding of Parents' Character Negatively Perceived
### (Both Parents Combined)

FATHER AND/OR MOTHER ALIENATING AND/OR DOMINATING

PARENTS INADEQUATE
(My Parents Are Not Always Proud of Their Children[a] and/or My Parents Don't Practice What They Preach)

| | | | Yes to Both Items (2)[b] | Yes to Either Item (1) | No to Both Items (0) |
|---|---|---|---|---|---|
| (FATHER SPENDS TOO LITTLE TIME WITH ME AND/OR FATHER WANTS TO RUN CHILDREN'S LIVES; AND/OR MOTHER DOESN'T UNDERSTAND ME AND/OR MOTHER WANTS TO RUN CHILDREN'S LIVES) | Yes for Both Parents (2) | W | 4 | 3 | 2 |
| | | R̄ | .67 | .64 | .56 |
| | | N | 29 | 132 | 155 |
| | Yes for One Parent (1) | W | 3 | 2 | 1 |
| | | R̄ | .59 | .55 | .46 |
| | | N | 34 | 207 | 438 |
| | No for Both Parents (0) | W | 2 | 1 | 0 |
| | | R̄ | .61 | .51 | .45 |
| | | N | 6 | 90 | 569 |
| | Total N | | | | 1660 |

[a] The wording of this item has been changed from positive to negative in order to facilitate clear presentation of the two combined items.
[b] The numbers in parentheses are the weights allotted in the previous steps of the pyramiding.
W—the weight assigned each cell.
R̄—the average ridit of the cases in each cell.
N—the number of cases in each cell.

The weights found in Step 4 are given in parentheses. They do not form the basis for assigning weights for this next step, however. The weights in Table B-4 for Step 5 (which run from 0 through 4) were assigned on the basis of the average ridits *within the cells*. If we draw diagonal lines through the table running from upper right to lower left, separating the "0's" from the "1's," the "1's" from the "2's," and so forth, the ridits seem to fall into fairly distinct groupings. Reading from lower right to upper left, the ridits grouped by weight are as follows:

| Weight | Average Ridit of Cells | Average Ridit for Each Weight |
|---|---|---|
| 0 | .45 | .45 |
| 1 | .46, .51 | .47 |
| 2 | .56, .55, .61 | .56 |
| 3 | .64, .59 | .63 |
| 4 | .67 | .67 |

The "smoothness" with which the ridits follow the weighting system is one index of how successful the pyramiding has been.

# Further Data from Chapter 6

## I. The Childhood Mental Health Index

The Childhood Mental Health Index was made up of the following four subscores, combined to give each score approximately equal weight in the final index.

### Table C-1

#### CHILDHOOD NEUROTIC SCORE

|  |  | f[a] | Per Cent |
|---|---|---|---|
| "As a child, did you fairly often have trouble falling asleep?" | "Yes" | 79 | 4.8 |
| "As a child, did you ever have trouble with stuttering or stammering in your speech?" | "Yes" | 94 | 5.7 |
| "As a child, did you fairly often have an upset stomach?" | "Yes" | 187 | 11.3 |
| Total Number of Cases (N = 100 per cent) |  | 1660 |  |

[a] f represents the frequencies of the particular response. The total number of cases in the sample is 1660.

#### CHILDHOOD PSYCHOSOMATIC SCORE

|  | f | Per Cent |
|---|---|---|
| Arthritis or Rheumatism (stiff or painful joints) | 68 | 4.1 |
| Asthma (noisy and difficult breathing) | 28 | 1.7 |
| Bladder trouble | 33 | 2.0 |
| Colitis (diarrhea with blood) | 14 | .8 |
| Hay fever (running nose, watery eyes, not due to a cold) | 59 | 3.6 |
| High blood pressure | 12 | .7 |
| Neuralgia or Sciatica (pains in the muscles or nerves not due to injury) | 39 | 2.3 |
| Stomach Ulcer (stomach pains after meals, relieved by eating) | 7 | .4 |
| Skin Condition (hives, rashes) | 150 | 9.0 |
| Nervous Breakdown (nervous upset preventing usual work or activities) | 16 | 1.0 |
| Total Number of Cases (N = 100 per cent) | 1660 |  |

### CHILDHOOD FUNCTIONING SCORE

|  |  | f | Per Cent |
|---|---|---|---|
| "I am happy only when I am at home. When you were growing up, did you ever feel that way too?" | "Yes" | 309 | 18.6 |
| "Now as to when you were a teenager, say thirteen to eighteen years old. In those years, did you usually have dates with girls (boys) more often or less often than most other boys (girls) of your age?" | "Less often" | 785 | 47.3 |
| "Some children like school, others don't. As a child, how did you feel about going to school? Would you say you liked school very much, liked it all right, disliked it, or hated it?" | "Disliked or hated it" | 317 | 19.1 |
| Total Number of Cases (N=100 per cent) |  | 1660 | |

### CHILDHOOD FEAR SCORE

|  | Not At All | A Little | Much | Other, Don't Know or No Answer |
|---|---|---|---|---|
|  | | (in per cent) | | |
| "As a child how much were you afraid of strangers?" | 68.1 | 24.1 | 5.8 | 2.0 |
| "As a child, how much were you afraid of thunderstorms?" | 62.8 | 21.1 | 15.2 | .9 |
| "As a child, how much were you afraid of being left alone?" | 67.1 | 18.6 | 12.3 | 2.0 |
| "As a child, how much were you afraid of being on high places?" | 68.2 | 15.1 | 14.3 | 2.4 |
| "As a child, how much were you afraid of large animals?" | 73.5 | 17.3 | 7.2 | 2.0 |
| "As a child, how much were you afraid of being laughed at by other children?" | 54.1 | 25.9 | 16.9 | 3.1 |
| "As a child, how much were you afraid of family quarrels?" | 58.3 | 19.8 | 19.2 | 2.7 |
| "As a child, how much were you afraid of getting bawled out?" | 33.7 | 34.1 | 29.9 | 2.3 |
| Total Number of Cases (N=100 per cent) | | | 1660 | |

## II. *Construction of Indices of Socioeconomic Status*

Several indices of SES were constructed for use in the Midtown Volumes. For purposes of comparison with hospital records, a special index was constructed and used throughout Volume I. It was based upon the respondent's occupation and education. In this volume, a more detailed index was permissible, since no comparison with hospital records (which lack data on income and rent) was necessary.

The respondent's SES was based upon four variables—occupation, education, income, and rent—given approximately equal weight. Each variable was divided into six categories, making for fairly even distribution of the population whenever possible, (as in the case of income and rent) and following absolute categories of occupation and education. The low categories—unskilled labor, no schooling, low income and low rent—were assigned a score of 1. The highest categories were assigned a score of 6. The score values, categories, and frequency distributions are shown in Table C-2.

## Table C-2
### Construction of Respondents' SES Index

| Score | Occupation | N | Education | N | Weekly Income | N | Monthly Rent | N |
|---|---|---|---|---|---|---|---|---|
| 1 | Blue Collar Low | 253 | No schooling | 6 | Under $49 | 194 | Under $30 | 322 |
| 2 | Blue Collar Middle | 198 | Some Grammar School | 206 | $50– 74 | 438 | $30– 39 | 313 |
| 3 | Blue Collar High | 208 | Grammar School Graduate | 289 | $75– 99 | 372 | $40– 49 | 267 |
| 4 | White Collar Low | 247 | Some High School | 280 | $100–149 | 245 | $50– 79 | 283 |
| 5 | White Collar Middle | 447 | High School Graduate | 377 | $150–299 | 180 | $80–199 | 284 |
| 6 | White Collar High | 305 | Some College | 198 | $300 and over | 164 | $200 and over | 188 |
|  | Unknown | 2 | College Graduate + | 303 |  | 67 |  | 3 |
|  |  |  |  | 1 |  |  |  |  |
| Total |  | 1660 |  | 1660 |  | 1660 |  | 1660 |

These scores, when combined, yielded a score range of 4 to 24. Each individual received an SES score. Scores 4 to 10 were called *low SES* (543 cases); scores 11 to 16 were called *middle* SES (557 cases); scores 17 to 24 were called *high* SES (560 cases). On this basis, we were able to divide the sample into three almost equally populated SES groups.

Some details of the occupational classification are necessary. The following list describes the various occupation included under High, Middle, and Low, White Collar and Blue Collar.

## FATHER'S SES AND OCCUPATION

| SES | OCCUPATION |
|---|---|
| White Collar High | Owner high<br>Manager and official high<br>Professional self-employed<br>Artist self-employed<br>Professional employed by others |
| White Collar Middle | Owner-proprietor middle<br>Farmer high and middle (owner)<br>Manager and official middle<br>Artist employed by others<br>Semiprofessional<br>Sales high |
| White Collar Low | Owner-proprietor low<br>Manager and official low<br>Sales and clerical low |
| Blue Collar High | Service high<br>Skilled manual self-employed<br>Farmer low<br>Skilled manual employed by others |
| Blue Collar Middle | Semiskilled<br>Self-employed and employed by others |
| Blue Collar Low | Farmer low (tenant)<br>Service low<br>Unskilled labor |

The occupation of the respondent was actually an occupational index. This was composed of the respondent's actual occupation for men and never-married women who were working. For unmarried women not working and students living with their families, their father's occupation was used. For married women, whether working or not, the husband's occupation was used.

The Index of Father's SES utilized only two variables: his education and occupation. His rent and income would have been unknown to the respondent as a child and seemed little related to rentals and incomes in the present-day United States. Even the occupation and education distributions have changed dramatically in the last fifty years, as can be seen from the frequencies in the father's and respondent's tables.

The procedure for the construction of the Father's SES was to sort into six levels the father's occupation at the time the respondent was aged eight to nine. This classified 1545 of the fathers, leaving 115. Another 53 were grouped according to father's occupation when respondent was aged eighteen to nineteen. In the remaining 62 cases, an estimate of father's occupation was used. This estimate was made only in cases where we also knew the father's education. We made our estimate on the basis of the father's education, nationality background, and generation with respect to immigration.

The distribution of the father's occupational levels is shown in Table C-3. Each of these six groups was then combined with six levels of father's education. Table C-3 shows that in 268 cases father's education was unknown, mostly as a result of his early death. In these cases we simply doubled the occupational ranks.

### Table C-3
### Construction of Father's SES Index

| Score | Occupation | N | Education | N |
|---|---|---|---|---|
| 1 | Blue Collar Low | 206 | No Schooling Some Grammar School | 100 |
| 2 | Blue Collar Middle | 310 | Grammar School Graduate | 677 |
| 3 | Blue Collar High | 292 | Some High School | 107 |
| 4 | White Collar Low | 165 | High School Graduate | 165 |
| 5 | White Collar Middle | 454 | Some College | 98 |
| 6 | White Collar High | 233 | College Graduate + | 245 |
| | | | Don't Know, or Education Unclassifiable | 268 |
| Total | | 1660 | | 1660 |

By adding the score values from 1 to 6 for the two variables we obtained a total score range of 2 to 12 for the father's SES index. We were able to divide the sample into three groups, though not nearly as equal in size as in the case of the respondent's SES index. Father's scores of 2–4 were called *low father's SES* (482 cases); scores of 5–8 were called *middle father's SES* (671 cases); scores of 9–12 were called *high father's SES* (507 cases).

It should be noted that the occupational categories are identical for father and respondent. However, there were so many fathers (100 cases) with no education that this was kept as a separate category. It was not necessary to match categories for father and respondent in SES indices. When constructing indices of educational and occupational mobility, however, great care was exercised in matching the categories exactly. An index of SES mobility, used in this volume, is based upon both occupation and education of father and respondent. In this instance the respondent was judged upwardly mobile, for example, if he moved from the lowest third of his father's SES upward to the middle or top third of the respondent's SES index. These mobility categories are therefore relative to the SES distribution of the father's and respondent's generations.

Further details of the rationale behind the SES indices are found in Volume I, Chapter 11.

# Further Data from Chapter 15

### Table D-1
### Average Impairment (MH I Ridits) According to Psychotic and Neurotic Types for High and Low SES Respondents

|  |  | STRESS SCORE | | | | | |
|---|---|---|---|---|---|---|---|
|  |  | 0–2 | 3–4 | 5–6 | 7–8 | 9–10 | 11–18 |
| High SES | Psychotic $\bar{R}$ | (.81) | (.70) | (.90) | (.68) | (.93) | (.90) |
|  | Neurotic $\bar{R}$ | .44 | .46 | .52 | .55 | .62 | .71 |
| Total Number of Cases |  |  |  |  |  |  |  |
|  | Psychotic | 2 | 5 | 5 | 3 | 3 | 1 |
|  | Neurotic | 41 | 66 | 55 | 38 | 29 | 10 |
| Low SES | Psychotic $\bar{R}$ | (.44) | .69 | .84 | .92 | .85 | .92 |
|  | Neurotic $\bar{R}$ | (.51) | .56 | .61 | .65 | .73 | .79 |
| Total Number of Cases |  |  |  |  |  |  |  |
|  | Psychotic | 3 | 11 | 16 | 17 | 13 | 11 |
|  | Neurotic | 9 | 29 | 39 | 26 | 18 | 13 |

Parentheses ( ) enclose Ridit based on less than ten cases.

# Subject Index

# Name Index

Adorno, T. W., 492 *n*
Ansley, Clarke F., 29 *n*
Applebaum, Stella B., 190 *n*, 265 *n*
Arensberg, C. M., 30 *n*

Bailey, Margaret, 33
Baldwin, Alfred L., 442, 474 *n*
Beam, Lura, 176, 189 *n*
Beckey, R. E., 474 *n*
Benedict, Ruth, 474 *n*
Bennett, Ivy, 449, 474 *n*
Bloch, Maurice, 84 *n*
Bronfenbrenner, Urie, 145 *n*, 439, 441, 473 *n*
Bross, Irwin D. J., 95, 97, 114 *n*, 115 *n*
Bruch, Hilde, 190 *n*, 224 *n*
Burke, Kenneth, 452, 475 *n*
Burlingham, D. T., 158, 188 *n*

Christie, R., 146 *n*
Clausen, John, 127, 146 *n*
Cohen, Albert K., 443, 474 *n*
Cook, Stuart W., 114 *n*

Davis, Allison, 440, 443, 448, 474 *n*
Davis, Kingsley, 458, 475 *n*
Day, Ella, 448, 474 *n*
Descoeudres, A., 448, 474 *n*
DeSola, Alis, 265 *n*
Deutsch, Morton, 114 *n*
Dickinson, Robert Latou, 176, 189 *n*
Drever, J., 448, 474 *n*
Dunham, H. W., 146 *n*

Engel, George L., 9, 30 *n*

Fanshel, David, 189 *n*
Faris, R., 146 *n*
Feldman, Rivkah, 114 *n*, 115 *n*
Fisk, Fern, 160, 189 *n*
Franzblau, Abraham N., 146 *n*
Freedman, Lawrence Z., 475 *n*
Freeman, Lucy, 145 *n*
Frenkel-Brunswik, E., 492 *n*

Freud, A., 158, 188 *n*
Freud, Sigmund, 15, 459, 475 *n*
Friedman, Paul, 158, 188 *n*
Friedman, Stanley, 146 *n*
Fromm, Erich, 189 *n*, 462–3, 475 *n*

Gesell, A., 448, 474 *n*
Gibbs, P. K., 440, 448, 473 *n*, 474 *n*
Green, Arnold W., 168, 189 *n*
Grinker, Roy R., 30 *n*

Hall, Bernard H., 423 *n*
Harding, John S., 48 *n*
Hargreaves, G. Ronald, 29 *n*
Hartley, E. L., 146 *n*, 473 *n*
Havighurst, Robert J., 443, 474 *n*
Hetzer, H., 448, 474 *n*
Hilgard, Josephine, 160, 189 *n*
Hinkle, Lawrence E., Jr., 244 *n*
Hoffer, Charles R., 146 *n*
Hollingshead, A. B., 415, 423 *n*, 431–4, 436, 439, 442, 446, 451, 463–4, 473 *n*, 474 *n*, 475 *n*, 492 *n*
Hughes, Charles C., 48 *n*
Hulett, J. E., Jr., 474 *n*
Hyman, Herbert, 146 *n*

Irwin, O. C., 474 *n*

Jahoda, Marie, 114 *n*, 146 *n*
Jezer, Ann, 84 *n*

Kaplan, Bert, 475 *n*
Kardiner, Abram, 331, 344 *n*, 458
Kaufman, M. Ralph, 146 *n*
Kimball, S. T., 30 *n*
Kinsey, Alfred, 450–1, 473 *n*, 475 *n*
Kirkpatrick, P., 47 *n*, 76, 81
Kitt, Alice, 344 *n*
Kluckhohn, Clyde, 473 *n*, 474 *n*
Kohn, Melvin, 146 *n*
Komarovsky, Mirra, 331, 344 *n*
Krugman, Judith I., 474 *n*
Kuhn, M., 474 *n*
Kutner, Bernard, 189 *n*